THE
Fellow-Travellers

A Postscript to the Enlightenment

DAVID CAUTE

THE MACMILLAN COMPANY

NEW YORK, NEW YORK

Contents

I'm always thinking of Russia,
I can't keep her out of my head,
I don't give a damn for Uncle Sham,
I am a left-wing radical Red.

H. H. LEWIS *Thinking of Russia*, 1932

Introduction:
The Future is There

An anecdote concerning the Anglican Dean of Canterbury, the Right Reverend Hewlett Johnson, carries the force of a minor allegory. The Dean had been attending in 1950 a meeting of the World Peace Council in Rome. Delighted but a little overwhelmed by the enthusiasm of a peace-loving crowd ("an honest priest, he should be our Pope," they cried), he and his wife escaped to the Italian countryside where, finding a local bus meandering towards an unknowable destination, they gaily climbed aboard. Said Hewlett Johnson to the driver: "Tickets to the end of the route, please." The impulse was entirely appropriate, for this saintly-looking cleric was one of the most perseverant fellow-travellers of his time.

But what is a fellow-traveller? A century ago Alexander Herzen employed the term in a political context which today must seem paradoxical. "In her future," wrote Herzen, "Russia has only one comrade, one fellow-traveller – the United States of America."[1] In 1918 Leon Trotsky, as Commissar for Foreign Affairs in the new bolshevik government, reverted to the same theme, though in a more guarded fashion: "America and Russia may have different aims, but if we have common stations on the same route, I can see no reason why we cannot travel together in the same car, each having the right to alight when so desired."[2] But the "right to alight" was not one which in later years the Soviet regime readily accorded to its non-communist sympathizers, particularly if they were Russians. When Trotsky, in his *Literature and Revolution* (1923), attached the label "fellow-travellers" or *paputchiki* to the hesitant, doubt-ridden supporters of Marxian communism, his general spirit of tolerance was offset by a sharp note of complaint. "They do not grasp the Revolution as a whole and the communist ideal is foreign to them," explained Trotsky. "They are all more or less inclined to look hopefully at the peasant over the head of the worker. They are not the artists of the proletarian revolution, but her artist 'fellow-travellers'. . . . As regards a 'fellow-traveller', the question always comes up – how far will he go?"[3] Trotsky illustrated his point. The Imagist poet

1

Sergei Yessenin, for example, continued to infuse his poetry with the personality and imaginative universe of the *muzhik*. And Boris Pilnyak, although not opposed to the Revolution, remained a primitivist at heart, harbouring his own vision of a peculiarly Russian and partly Asiatic bolshevism, while rejecting the modern, urban, proletarian dimension of Marxism. Trotsky also described Alexander Blok as a fellow-traveller, and his poem, "The Twelve", as the "swan song of the individualist art which sought to join the Revolution".[4]

The concept was soon absorbed into the official Soviet literary vocabulary. Ilya Ehrenburg recalls discovering a bookshop window where a "tree of Soviet literature" was depicted, its branches labelled (from left to right) "proletarians", "LEF",[*] "peasant poets", "left-wing fellow-travellers", "centrist fellow-travellers", "right-wing fellow-travellers", and, finally, "neo-bourgeois". This relatively relaxed state of affairs was not allowed to endure for long. Addressing the first Congress of Soviet Writers in 1934, Karl Radek congratulated the regime on having protected the "fellow-travellers of the Revolution", but he neglected to add that after Trotsky's fall the fellow-travelling sheep had been mauled by the "proletarian" wolves of RAPP,[†] and that after "socialist realism" became official dogma in 1932 there were no more Russian fellow-travellers – only "non-Party Bolsheviks".

But Western sympathizers were a different matter. They demanded and had to be accorded a greater indulgence: if not exactly "the right to alight", at least the privilege of keeping one leg dangling from the car. In point of fact the *paputchik* concept was not immediately adopted in the West: not until the early 1930s did fellow-travelling become a common political notion in Europe and America, with appropriate national translations: *compagnon de route, sympathisant* or, more polite, *progressiste* in France; *Sympathisierender auf den Weg* or, less respectful, *Mitläufer* in Germany; *compagno di viaggio* or *di strada* in Italy.[‡] Unfortunately the term has acquired an increasingly pejorative connotation, a label of abuse or accusation, so that one finds, for example, Konni Zilliacus, at one time Labour MP for Gateshead and an outstanding fellow-traveller of the Left, referring disparagingly to "latter-day Tories and their intellectual bondsmen and fellow-travellers within the Labour Party. . . ."[5] The structural meaning is here the same, but the political orientation is reversed. So indiscriminately and aggressively was

* Left Front in Art.
† Russian Association of Proletarian Writers.
‡ The Western fellow-travellers discussed in this book are mainly American, British, French and German. It did not prove possible, within the limits of this study, to accord the Italian scene the attention it deserves. I therefore decided to omit the Italians entirely.

the term bandied about during the post-war American witch-hunts that it came to signify anyone who received *Pravda* through the post, anyone who took the First or Fifth Amendments, anyone who defended the constitutional rights of those who did, anyone who had doubts about the guilt of Alger Hiss, or anyone who dared to contend that Russia had made a major contribution to winning the war. At that stage all rational dialogue broke down; one hopes that it is now possible to re-examine the fellow-travellers in their real historical and ideological context.

What, then, were the main characteristics of the Western fellow-travellers? Apart from a certain reticence in their commitment, they shared few qualities in common with the Russian *paputchiki*. Far from being anti-rationalist, anti-urban, anti-modern, anti-Western and in love with the peasantry, they were on the contrary true sons and daughters of the Enlightenment, of the doctrine of Progress.* They heartily welcomed the torments and upheavals inflicted on the Russian peasantry during collectivization, arguing that only by such drastic social engineering could these backward illiterates be herded, feet first, into the modern world. Admittedly the primitive aspects of Russia, and later China, captivated the imaginations of such intellectuals, but only in so far as dramatic underdevelopment provided a *tabula rasa* for planned construction and rational experimentation.

Such attitudes were also common among Western communists, but the fellow-travellers were not communists: they were, to adapt Lenin's phrase, "me-too communists". In 1938 the exiled Trotsky accurately explained what separated the fellow-travellers from genuine revolutionaries: "A whole generation of the 'left' intelligentsia has ... turned its eyes eastwards and has tied ... its fate not so much to the revolutionary working class as to a victorious revolution, which is not the same."[6] This was correct, except that the fellow-traveller did not "tie his fate" to the USSR unless in the somewhat naïve and sentimental form expressed by the American artist Rockwell Kent: "Is Stalin backing us? God bless you, Stalin! – as once our fathers prayed that God should bless the King of France. God bless our fellow-travellers."[7] Basically, fellow-travelling involves commitment *at a distance* which is not only geographical but also emotional and intellectual. It is remote-control radicalism, as was vividly expressed by Lincoln Steffens, writing in 1926 from the comforts of the Italian Riviera: "I am for them to the last drop, I am a patriot for Russia; the future is there. . . . But I don't want to live there. It is too much like serving in an army at war with no mercy for the weak . . . . My service to it has to be outside, here." And he went on to lament

* For a discussion of the Enlightenment legacy, see Chapter Seven.

3

that the bolsheviks just could not comprehend how "a man can state the whole case of Soviet Russia aright and not be a communist".[8] His wife Ella Winter later described in a more feminine idiom one aspect of the gulf separating the Soviet people from their Western champions. Soviet girls, she reported, "feel feverishly my foreign clothes ... sample the material, stroke the silk, almost pull my underwear from under my blouse in their frenzied hunger".[9] But if Steffens was expressing one type of schizophrenia common among fellow-travellers, the journalist Anna Louise Strong represented, on her own confession, a rarer and more remarkable variety. She, far from taking refuge in silk garments and Mediterranean villas, thrived like a cactus in the desert, devoting her whole life to Russia and China during the most punishing phases of social-ist construction. Yet she too believed in the special mission of Russia, of the East: "The Russian Party," she wrote, "one could adore for its tremendous achievements: but the American Party – no! If I must have a lifelong boss, let it be a big one. Like ancient Jewish tribes wanting their Jehovah to be all-powerful, like a woman wanting an important husband."[10]

Anna Louise Strong was unusual in her willingness to submit her body and energies, as well as her mind, to this boss-husband. On the other hand she was quite typical among fellow-travellers in her contempt for the Communist Party of her own country. The fellow-traveller does not recommend world revolution: he prefers "socialism in one country" – but not his own. He is sometimes not ashamed to say that whereas the Russians (or Chinese, or Bulgarians) were giving up nothing in adopting one-party government, we, the British, the French, the Americans, the Germans, we are wedded in our greater maturity to ancient and unalien-able liberties. The point was well put by the distinguished, progressive headmaster A. S. Neill who, although not properly speaking a fellow-traveller, perhaps figured among those whom George Orwell once described as "the fellow-travellers of the fellow-travellers". Neill commen-ted in 1940 that "pinks" like himself did not "go the whole hog" because, while they regarded Russia as the only "hope of the future", they didn't welcome the prospect of interfering commissars telling them how to run *their* schools. In short we are different here.

When J. Robert Oppenheimer admitted to a security officer in 1943 that he had until recently been a fellow-traveller, he offered a definition of his own: "someone who accepted part of the public programme of the Communist Party, but who was not a member".[11] It is certainly the case that the overwhelming majority of fellow-travellers were not members of the Party, but we must guard against making this too rigid a point of definition. A dedicated Leninist may for tactical reasons eschew formal membership: to remember that Kim Philby was never a member of the British CP is to recall the most dramatic among such reasons. It is also not unknown for a fellow-traveller (as defined by other criteria) to drift into the ranks of the Party, particularly at times of high national temperature such as occurred in France under the German occupation. The poets Cecil Day Lewis and Stephen Spender joined the British Party, the one for three years and the other for three weeks, yet both remained in essence fellow-travellers; whereas John Strachey apparently never joined the Party although he remained throughout the thirties a most effective spokesman for the Marx-Lenin-Stalin praxis in all spheres, domestic as well as foreign, theoretical as well as practical. Outside the Party, Strachey was nevertheless a communist. On the other hand Pablo Picasso turned up at the Paris headquarters of the French Party after the Liberation, to receive his membership card amid general celebration, but he remained in outlook only a well disposed fellow-traveller who confessed honestly in 1956 : "I am unfit for politics."

Why do fellow-travellers decline to join their local Party in nine cases out of ten? Is it because – as a widespread misconception would have it – they are inherently anaemic and lacking the courage of their convictions? To put it this way is completely to misunderstand the climate of opinion which revolved round such organs as *The Nation*, the *New Republic* and *PM* in America, the *New Statesman, Tribune* and *Peace News* in Britain, *Les Temps Modernes* and *Europe* in France, or *Die Weltbühne* in Germany. (Not that these papers by any means represent identical philosophies.) The truth is that the fellow-traveller's commitment takes a different form from that of a communist because his disillusionment with Western society is less radical, less total, less uncompromising. The fellow-traveller retains a partial faith in the possibilities of progress under the parliamentary system: he appreciates that the prevailing liberties, however imperfect and however distorted, are nevertheless valuable. The fellow-travellers (or, to be more accurate, potential fellow-travellers) took note of the bloody civil war, terror, executions and famines which swept Russia from 1917 until 1922, and they recoiled in horror. Even in later years their actions often belied their words: the German novelist Lion Feuchtwanger announced in 1937 that he had discovered "genuine" freedom in Russia, as compared with the "bogus" freedoms of the West, but after two weeks he returned to France and never set foot in Russia again.

Nevertheless we can understand fellow-travelling only in terms of a disillusionment. The societies which nailed "Liberty, Equality, Fraternity" to their mastheads failed to live up to these ideals: the once-progressive doctrine of *laissez-faire* and enlightened self-interest resulted in poverty, unemployment and inexcusable inequalities of wealth and opportunity. Freedom came to mean exploitation, treating the worker as a wealth-producing object. Nations which valued liberty at home trampled colonial peoples underfoot. Capitalists and the politicians who served their interests did not scruple to embark on vast, decimating wars. Education, knowledge and culture remained minority privileges while art, appalled by its environment, turned its back on life. In short, the great promises of the eighteenth-century Enlightenment were not realized. By the time the swastika rose over Germany, the theory of progress-by-evolution was already in ruins.

Hence the desperate search for an alternative solution to the problem of ends and means. Marx had accepted the optimistic assumptions of the Enlightenment and of the Utopian Socialists, but he offered little comfort to the proponents of peaceful change. Force, he said, is the midwife of history: within a given socio-economic structure contradictions accumulate until a violent convulsion introduces the next historical formation. As for that "universal reason" in which the *philosophes* had invested their faith, it would not, Marx insisted, persuade a bourgeoisie whose favoured position was inherently irrational. Only proletarian reason coincided with, or was a prelude to, the ultimate, universal reason. Hence the necessity and inevitability of a proletarian revolution followed by a transitional dictatorship. This is what Lenin and Trotsky believed, and they acted on their beliefs.* But to remain true to such an outlook requires either desperate personal circumstances or an abstract logic verging on fanaticism. The fellow-travellers were neither desperate nor fanatical. They realized that the socialist vision had been betrayed time and again by the compromises of the reformist parties, and they looked hopefully to the bolsheviks if only because Lenin and his followers had been as good as their word. "As far as I can tell," said Bernard Shaw approvingly in 1920, "a bolshevik is someone who does something about it." Yet they hesitated. Tales of anarchy and barbarism poured out of Russia. Some, like Bertrand Russell, quickly concluded that the light was not worth the candle. And then, after 1928, the whole image of Soviet Russia changed. At last the USSR entered the great phase of construction: planned, "scientific" social engineering replaced the image of violent insurrection and the compromises of the New Economic Policy. Immediately a tide of pent-up goodwill, optimism and moral idealism flooded from the West into Russia. Trotsky was gone, and with him the forbidding spectre of permanent revolution. The fellow-travellers cultivated a convenient schizophrenia: they scorned democracy – at a distance; they invested

* It should be noted that during the 1960s the Western CPs all more or less committed themselves to peaceful or constitutional change.

their dreams of positivistic experimentation and moral regeneration – at a distance.

Neither were they obliged to abandon their own national traditions, their own perch on the family tree of the Enlightenment. Among the British, there were Benthamite or Fabian or Protestant fellow-travellers; among the French, disciples of Descartes or Jaurès; there were Americans who saw in the figure of Stalin a reincarnation of the spirit of Paine and Jefferson and there were Germans who at last found cause to celebrate the long awaited marriage of spirit (*Geist*) and power (*Macht*), of reason (*Vernunft*) and society (*Gesellschaft*). In praising Soviet achievements the fellow-travellers by no means felt obliged to adopt the alien Hegelian-Marxist dialectical vocabulary: on the contrary, the Russians and the local communists seemed delighted to emphasize that their appreciation was entirely unprejudiced! And since they belonged to no party, or at least not to the CP, their intellectual independence appeared unimpeachable.

The outlines, at least, of the fellow-travelling physiognomy should now be visible. Raymond Aron has written: "The communist, whether Stalinist or Malenkovist or Khrushchevist, is above all a man who makes no distinction between the cause of the Soviet Union and the cause of the Revolution."[12] Leaving aside the new problems posed by the Sino-Soviet dispute, the description is just. To discover a Trotskyist, anarchist or adherent of the New Left, one need merely make a substitution for the words "the Soviet Union"; but to locate the typical fellow-traveller one deletes instead the word "Revolution", substituting for it a family of related notions such as progress, social justice, scientific rationality, peace, equality, the workers' state.

There are ways in which a communist intellectual can serve the cause but which are beyond the reach of most fellow-travellers. The fellow-travelling philosopher is normally not an orthodox Marxist, and the fellow-travelling novelist or playwright is never an orthodox socialist realist: consequently they are not expected to make serious contributions to the *ideological* education of the masses. They are confined, in fact, to three main avenues of useful activity: political journalism, membership of communist front organizations, and, where appropriate, the loan of their prestige, their lustre, the respect in which they are widely held.

In one important respect the fellow-traveller with a glittering international reputation stands apart from his colleagues and is a law unto himself. To understand this one must appreciate that the general attitude of the international communist movement towards fellow-travellers (as indeed towards communist intellectuals) has not been uniformly warm, but has fluctuated in relation to Comintern policy, Soviety strategy and international tensions. Yet the famous fellow-traveller has always been treated with a special indulgence and has almost always been a welcome guest in Moscow.

Let us first glance at the ebb and flow of communist policy towards sympathetic intellectuals in general. Broadly speaking the *main* has been *tendue* whenever the communist movement in the West has embarked on a broad-based alliance with socialists, radicals and liberals in defence of democracy or national independence. At such times fellow-travellers have been courted assiduously. This policy was most clearly operative during the popular front era, from 1935 to 1939, but it was also energetically revived after 1941, when Hitler invaded the USSR and Western communists everywhere took the lead in forming broad-based war coalitions and Resistance movements. On the other hand the *poing* has been *brandi*, and mere sympathizers treated with a suspicion verging on contempt, during periods of revolutionary sectarianism or of Soviet diplomatic isolation. This state of affairs prevailed from 1928 to 1935, between the fifth and sixth congresses of the Comintern, and there were signs of it again during the coldest years of the Cold War, from 1948–9 until the mid-fifties. The reason for this is not obscure: when the shock troops find themselves besieged in their fortress, then hangers-on infiltrating the gates are liable to sow dissensions and weaken morale.

During the early years of the revolution every effort was made to woo hesitant foreign sympathizers, the task being mainly entrusted to the capable and sincere Commissar for Public Instruction, Anatole Lunacharsky. In articles widely reprinted in the Western communist press, he strenuously repudiated on behalf of his government any manichean, "for us or against us" attitude. Those who are against capitalism, he insisted, are for us. While admitting that the greater part of the Russian intelligentsia had turned its back on the Revolution, thrown in its lot with the Whites, or retired into exile, he was desperately anxious to dispel the impression that the Soviet State was directed by, or at the mercy of, barbarian anarchists levelling with iconoclastic fury every institution of learning and culture to the ground. He wished, in effect, to reassure the "Dr Zhivagos" of the West, and so great was his belief in the influence wielded by famous names that he insisted that if a Gorky or an Einstein publicized merely their lack of hostility towards the Soviet power, then Western students would rapidly shed their anti-communist prejudices. The French Communist Party (PCF) adopted this approach with alacrity. In March 1921, *l'Humanité*, the Party's daily paper, accorded headline prominence to denunciations by Anatole France, Romain Rolland and other prominent intellectuals of legal sentences against leading French communists. Anatole France's salute to the fifth anniversary of the Bolshevik Revolution was printed in banner headlines. Readers of the paper were frequently assured that "the world of intellectuals responds to our appeal", or, to quote again, "the intellectual élite is with us, for an amnesty and the liberation of André Marty". When after a period of disaffection Romain Rolland re-embraced the Soviet Union, describing it as "the hope, the last hope for the future of mankind", Lunacharsky immediately responded warmly, brushing aside years of mutual abuse and promising Rolland complete freedom from censorship if he would only write for the Soviet press.

But whereas a hand held out by a Romain Rolland would be readily grasped at any time or period, the majority of sympathetic intellectuals began to notice a distinct cooling of the atmosphere after the death of Lenin in 1924. Trotsky's active supporters in the West were mainly intellectuals; consequently the "Bolshevization" or "Stalinization" of the Western Parties assumed a distinctly anti-intellectual colour. This frosty mood was both intensified and given ideological precision after 1928, when the Comintern branded all social-democrats, hesitant sympathizers and waverers as "social-fascists" – a discouraging label. The trials of the menshevik engineers and foreign specialists which ensued in Russia pointed more than ever to the ineradicable original sin of the intelligentsia. On the other hand, as the menace of fascism increased, the more intelligent members of the communist hierarchy realized that this policy was counter-productive. Unable to renounce formally the official Comintern line, local CPs learned to keep their right hand in ignorance of what their left hand was doing. Thus the whole scheme of front-organizations master-minded by the German communist Willi Münzenberg was designed to enlist and harness fellow-travelling support by disguised means. Similarly, at the height of the freeze in the early thirties, Maurice Thorez, the leader of the PCF, was quietly but doggedly cultivating the friendship of distinguished non-communist intellectuals: he called Rolland "the greatest French writer of our epoch" while contriving to assure André Gide that he was no less great.

By 1936 the popular front policy was in full swing and henceforward the names of notable fellow-travellers cascaded from the mouth of Party spokesmen during what might be called "the years of tribute". In France, the Party's spokesman on cultural affairs, Paul Vaillant-Couturier, announced a bumper harvest: eminent scientists like Paul Langevin and Jean Perrin, architects such as Le Corbusier and Francis Jourdain, the painter Fernand Léger, and the writers Rolland, Gide, Julien Benda, Luc Durtain and Jean-Richard Bloch – all were now travelling within the Party's wider orbit, all were devoted friends of the Soviet Union. (This

9

was in October 1936: a few months later Gide was consigned to the ranks of the Gestapo on account of his critical report of the USSR.) Meanwhile the exiled Kommunistische Partei Deutschlands busily harnessed the support not only of the fellow-travellers but also of the plain liberals among the eminent émigrés. When Sidney and Beatrice Webb published their highly favourable account of the Soviet system, *Soviet Communism: a new Civilisation?*, the British Party's leading ideologue, R. Palme Dutt, declared candidly: "Their concrete picture will win conviction in many quarters where the current generalizations fail to reach!"[13] He meant that an illustrious pair of Fabian voices was worth at that time any number of Marxist ones.

But it was the deluge of praise emanating from Moscow, from the capital of the brave new world itself, which did most to confirm the fellow-travellers' sense of the relevance of their commitment. Just as Russian peasants had once distrusted or detested the local agents of royal power, while remaining loyal to the "little Tsar" in St Petersburg, so the fellow-travellers easily convinced themselves that the wise Stalin was not responsible for the follies and intolerant excesses of his foreign underlings. Stalin himself encouraged this attitude, hinting to Western visitors that his boys in the West, though honest and industrious types, lacked subtlety and sophistication. And although the Comintern apparatus was rigorously controlled by Moscow, Soviet government agencies increasingly pleaded that they could not be held responsible for the subversive propaganda of an international movement. Meanwhile accolades were distributed unsparingly. When Karl Radek addressed the first Congress of Soviet Writers, in 1934, he heaped praise on the heads of Shaw, Rolland, Bloch and Gide, announced that Theodore Dreiser had "openly joined the side of the proletariat", and congratulated John Dos Passos on effectively depicting the collapse of American capitalism and the growth of revolutionary consciousness among the petty-bourgeoise. Upton Sinclair had recently declared, "Soviet Russia is coming up, the capitalist nations are going down" – Radek held his message to be worth repeating. Naturally he acknowledged the immense value of the anti-fascist stand adopted by Heinrich Mann and Feuchtwanger, and then, summing up the role of the fellow-travellers, he said: "Their actions are of enormous political significance, and not only as a symptom of the state of feeling among the 'intermediate strata' in the capitalist countries . . . they are hindering world imperialism in its effort to engineer a new and supreme crime – namely, an attack upon the USSR."[14]

When Radek spoke the Soviet Union was about to meet the fascist menace by embarking on the dual alignment of popular fronts in domestic politics and collective security in the international field; accordingly every sincere ally was welcomed. But if we revert to our earlier emphasis on eminence, fame and prestige, we discover that year after year the Hotel Metropole in Moscow was given over to lavish hospitality in honour of foreign notables, many of them fellow-travellers, either potential or confirmed. When the celebrated young German playwright Ernst Toller arrived in Moscow in 1924 he was greeted by separate delegations from the Academy of Art, the Society for Cultural Relations with Foreign Countries (VOKS – a key organization in this respect) as well as by journalists, photographers and comrade writers. By the kind of coincidence which became a habit, Toller's play, *Hinkemann,* happened to be in performance in Leningrad during his visit. Invited to attend, he was warmly applauded by both cast and audience. Even more glittering was the reception accorded to a more renowned playwright, Bernard Shaw. Travelling from Victoria Station, London, to Moscow's White Russia Station in July 1931, the seventy-four year old writer found thousands on hand to greet him, plus a brass band. When he arrived at the Kamerny Theatre to see Tairov's production of *The Beggar's Opera,* the entire company paraded on stage with a banner: "To the brilliant master Bernard Shaw – a warm welcome to Soviet soil." (The Kamerny had already staged *Saint Joan.*) Shaw's interview with Stalin lasted two hours.

Five years later another eminent veteran who, like Shaw, was a heavyweight in moral if not in physical stature, arrived from France. André Gide was lavishly received, accommodated in the grand style, covered with flattery and never permitted by the workers' state, despite his considerable private fortune, to put his hand in his pocket. But on this occasion the comforts yielded poor dividends: on his return to France Gide complained that he had travelled to Russia in search of a new world only to be offered the privileges he abominated in the old. Had he ever attempted to renounce in the old world the privileges he so abominated, the reaction might have seemed less perverse. As a result of this débâcle considerable significance was attached to the subsequent visit of the novelist Lion Feuchtwanger, then exiled from his native Germany. His portrait was everywhere to be found on display in bookshop windows and his visits to the theatre, like Shaw's, provoked speeches and applause. "The honours with which I was received in Moscow," he wrote, "served to increase my uncertainty. Good friends of mine, and, moreover, quite intelligent individuals, had had their judgment clouded by the effusiveness of the German fascists."[15] Feuchtwanger was nevertheless wooed and won: whereas Shaw had swallowed a lot but kept his tongue in his cheek, and Gide had coughed it all up, Feuchtwanger virtually swallowed his tongue. His *Moscow 1937* became one of the most exploitable fellow-travelling eulogies of the entire Stalin era.

The red carpets continued to unfold. In 1952 Feuchtwanger's friend Arnold Zweig, a fellow-traveller of the same stripe and by then an honoured citizen of the German Democratic Republic, visited Moscow for the Gogol festivities. In the invariable Hotel Metropole he and his wife were provided with a small apartment, expert medical attention for his sore throat, and tickets to every possible entertainment, not to mention three hundred rubles pocket money provided by the Writers' Association. Sometimes hospitality went so far as to endanger health: when Jean-Paul Sartre first visited the USSR in 1954 his legs gave way after a four-hour banquet at the dacha of the writer Simonov, and following a similar feast in Moscow the stunned visitor tried to walk off the effects by the Moskova River, but his heart beat so loudly that he withdrew to hospital.

Zweig received an allocation of pocket money, but more than pocket money was involved. Zweig himself was promised a new edition of sixty thousand copies of a Russian translation of his novel, *Erziehung von Verdun*, but by Soviet standards such a printing was negligible. Feuchtwanger's arrival in 1936 had been preceded by the publication in Russian of nine of his books, with a total printing of two hundred and sixty thousand copies. His anti-nazi novels, *Erfolg* and *Die Geschwister Oppermann*, were scheduled for filming, and his itinerary in Moscow was crowded by meetings with translators, producers and publishers. His friend Heinrich Mann, the most prestigious German fellow-traveller during the Popular Front era, was published in Russia to the tune of two million copies. In 1943 he wrote: "I love the Soviet Union completely at the present. She is near me – and I her. She reads me massively, gives me life, and I gaze at her as if she were already the posterity which will know me."[16] As for Romain Rolland, one million seven hundred thousand copies of his works were sold in the Soviet Union. Upton Sinclair claimed in the mid-1930s that three million copies of his books had reached Soviet readers. Before 1928, that is to say until he visited the USSR and began to manifest sympathy for it, Theodore Dreiser's books were published in Russia without permission or payment. After 1928 he began to receive a ten per cent royalty. This aspect of life obviously was of prime importance to Dreiser: he demanded to see royalty statements, and in 1934 he wrote rather petulantly to an official of VOKS in Moscow, complaining that his film scenario, *Tobacco*, had cost him two thousand dollars to prepare: if the Russians wanted to film it, fine – but they must pay! "I have been called upon by the militant communists of this country to perform every known service from writing and speaking to entering dangerous areas ... and always at my expense."[17]

Such men could not, of course, be "bought". What these figures represent is not so much money as recognition; and the writer's life, after all, is a constant striving after recognition not only for himself but also for what he takes his work to represent. The same pleasure in being recognized must also have affected the many Western scientists who were invited on elaborate conducted tours of Soviet laboratories. Not a few of them returned home confirmed fellow-travellers.

But one sad thing is clear, if only in retrospect. Both the Western communists and the fellow-travelling intellectuals deepened the despair of the non-official Soviet intelligentsia during the years of persecution and terror. In their darkest hours they heard themselves condemned by their own kind, by foreigners who shared their own idealistic traditions and whose immunity from imprisonment or death was due solely to the accident of nationality. Under the Tsars exiled radicals had enjoyed the moral support of the democratic intelligentsia both within Russia and without. Even in Siberia a prisoner's morale and self-esteem can mitigate the effects of hunger or frostbite. But the Stalinist terror was totalitarian to an extent unknown in pre-revolutionary Russia and it inexorably intimidated a population, which would once have considered it a moral duty to take pity on political convicts, into treating them as pariahs. The victim found himself totally isolated in a wilderness of arbitrary violence and pervasive fears. Meanwhile the "engineers of souls" in the West lauded his tormentors and spat on his grave – then denied his death. One who lived through it all and lost her husband in the purges, Nadezhda Mandelstam, writes: "When I see books by the Aragons* of this world, who are so keen to induce their fellow countrymen to live as we do, I feel I have a duty to tell about my own experience."[18] She has, one feels, not only a duty but a right.

During the years 1928–56 some of the most distinguished writers, philosophers, critics, scientists and publicists of the West became communists or fellow-travellers. But this state of affairs no longer prevails. We shall attempt to discover why. The fact is that fellow-travelling *vis-à-vis* the Soviet Union (if not to the same extent China) can now be studied as a historical phenomenon with a defined time-span. The aims, ideology and life style of the New Left have practically nothing in common with those of yesterday's fellow-travellers: *they* belonged squarely to the Old Left. Those militants of the New Left who ardently

---

* Louis Aragon, leading French communist poet and novelist.

admire Mao's China or Castro's Cuba adopt those regimes as models for their own revolutionary activities. They are Leninists with a new, half-anarchist, face. This is only one reason why it is not sensible to encompass the opposition to the Vietnam war in the present study. Admittedly some journeys to Hanoi have resulted in reports similar in mood and style to those that followed journeys to Moscow. But the war, in its terrible protraction, has dissolved old ideological frontiers, propelling hardened Cold Warriors into a dissenting posture which owes more to disgust and guilt than to naïve acceptance of all claims made by Hanoi and the National Liberation Front. As in the case of Spain thirty years earlier, cumulative outrage has seized men of conscience who could not be described as fellow-travellers, let alone communists.

Part One: Hopes

I

Thinking of Russia

The fellow-travellers of the later Stalin era were drawn to the Soviet Union as pilgrims, as converts; their journeys were the consequence rather than the cause of their commitment. Transported by aeroplane and greeted by flower-laden reception committees, they conducted their benign odysseys in an atmosphere of physical and spiritual comfort. But during the early years of the Bolshevik Revolution the pattern had been very different. Little was known about a land ravaged by civil war, famine and bloody anarchy, and the foreign investigator had to contend with hunger, frostbite and the possibility of an unceremonious death. At a time when the British, French and American Governments were lending active military and logistical support to the White armies, his very presence in the bolshevik-occupied areas deprived him of diplomatic or consular protection.

In the years of civil war and blockade, the most accessible gateway to Russia was the Finland Station, Petrograd. It was here that Lenin himself arrived back from exile on 4 April 1917. At about the same time Trotsky, having harangued the crowd on the pier, set sail from New York. He was subsequently removed from the ship and interned by the British authorities at Halifax but, although the Russian Provisional Government was at heart no more anxious than the British to set this subversive at large, considerations of diplomatic prestige and domestic agitation prevailed, and Trotsky finally reached the Finland Station only a month after Lenin.

Into a world of warring "Swallows and Amazons" stepped the author of so many delightful adventure stories for children, Arthur Ransome. A prolific writer (between 1904 and 1915 he published twelve books), he knew both Russia and Russian well. A correspondent for the *Manchester Guardian*, he was one of only two British eyewitnesses of the October Revolution.* He also gained the confidence of a number

---

* A number of foreigners who witnessed the Revolution or its aftermath became dedicated communists. This happened to a group of French writers, journalists and military attachés whose previous outlook was "bourgeois" and pro-war: Jacques Sadoul, Pierre Pascal and

of leading bolsheviks. Admittedly Zinoviev, who distrusted all Englishmen, treated him with suspicion but Bukharin, Kamenev, Chicherin and the garrulous Radek all took him into their confidence. Physically tough and professionally dedicated, he endured the appalling hunger and cold of Moscow and Petrograd in order to write dispatches designed to dispel the prevalent English image of the bolshevik as a devil with horns. After an interval abroad, he returned to Russia in 1919 braving all hazards. "We crossed by boat to Abo, grinding our way through the ice, and then travelled by rail to the Russian frontier . . . We were told that the Russian White Guards had planned an attack on the train." Then "the Finns lifted their toll bar. . . . Crossing that bridge we passed from one philosophy to another . . . from the dictatorship of the bourgeoisie to the dictatorship of the proletariat. . . ."[1] The Russian train turned out to be unheated but he kept himself in good spirits by chatting to Maxim Litvinov and dancing to the mandoline. "It was dusk when we reached Petrograd. The Finland Station, of course, was nearly deserted . . ." Although British military censorship interrupted the free flow of his reports to the *Manchester Guardian*, his simple, direct accounts of what was happening in Russia were prized in America, where Max Eastman's *Liberator* published his "Conversations with Lenin". Ransome summed up the virtues of the new order with the remark that it would be at least a hundred years before any Russian could again be unhappy in the way depicted by Chekhov in *Uncle Vanya*. True, perhaps: but the intellectuals of Nadezhda Mandelstam's generation might have envied Vanya his unhappiness, not to say his Chekhov.

The other British eyewitness of the Revolution was M. Philips Price, a well-to-do Gloucestershire squire, a cousin of the Trevelyans, an ex-Harrovian, a graduate of Trinity College, Cambridge, and a founder member of the Union of Democratic Control – a left-liberal, quasi-pacifist group which included the Trevelyans, Bertrand Russell, Lowes Dickinson and E. D. Morel, none of whom in the event found bolshevism more than transitorily appealing. Having taken part in a prolonged botanical and geological expedition to Central Siberia from 1910 to 1914, Price returned to Russia during the war to work, like Ransome, for the admirable *Manchester Guardian*. Like his colleague also, Price was

---

René Marchand. Henri Guilbeaux and Raymond Léfèbvre had already adopted a pacifist, anti-war posture before the Revolution. Like the American communist John Reed, Léfèbvre lost his life in the course of the civil war. Both were ardent and courageous young idealists who fully accepted Marxism-Leninism. Reed, who took over Jack London's mantle as the leading American revolutionary adventurer, must be the only communist to be honoured with an imposing statue in a Harvard House: no doubt a runaway wedding cut short by death can be posthumously dissolved and forgiven.

shocked and disgusted when Western military intervention in Russia exceeded its proclaimed purpose of strengthening the Eastern front against Germany and became blatantly committed to the overthrow of bolshevism. His later dispatches were stopped by the British censor and those that did reach C. P. Scott in Manchester were generally not published as a result of official pressure. Consequently Price's radicalism deepened; as he recently recalled, "I had, in fact, become a 'fellow-traveller'."[2] At the end of 1918 he moved to Germany in time to witness the abortion of the revolution there. He met Rosa Luxemburg and Karl Liebknecht shortly before their assassinations and became one of the many who called on Karl Radek in Moabit prison. Scornful of both the reactionary Majority Socialists and the "flabby pacifism" of the Independent Socialists, Price adopted the communist viewpoint and referred, in a style untypical of fellow-travellers, to the "hard facts of the class war".[3] Accepting the Leninist view of the white proletarian aristocracy as the social basis for reformist imperialism, he had nothing but contempt for the complaints voiced by Abramovitch and the Russian mensheviks in exile. But by the time he left Germany in 1923 he had come to the sad conclusion that the German working class was not worth a revolution. His enthusiasm for bolshevik Russia remained undiminished.

During 1919, H. G. Wells and Bertrand Russell visited Russia. Although their ideological background was not dissimilar to Price's, their verdicts were very different. In the course of an interview with Lenin, Wells spoke up for gradualism, expressed doubts about Russia's future and poured ridicule on such Marxist clap-trap as "proletarian science". On his return to England he wrote *Russia in the Shadows.* Russell concluded that the bolsheviks were altogether too impatient in their zeal to create a new world without pausing for the necessary preparatory work of mental and emotional acclimatization. And he predicted for Russia not a genuine democracy but a form of Napoleonic tyranny (*The Practice and Theory of Bolshevism*).

With H. N. Brailsford the bolsheviks had more luck. Formerly a foreign legionnaire for Greece in the Turco-Greek war of 1897, then an assistant professor of logic at Glasgow University, Brailsford's true *métier* was that of editor, journalist and publicist. (From 1922 to 1926 he edited the socialist *New Leader*.) Reaching Russia in the autumn of 1920 for a two month inspection tour, he made short shrift of those who bewailed the extinction of Russian democracy. What democracy? The Constituent Assembly which the bolsheviks had suppressed in December 1918? No, he said, there were too many factions to make it a practical proposition. (The French parliament was also notoriously divided into competing factions, but very few fellow-travellers would have contemplated its suppression on such grounds: already we see the beginning of East–West schizophrenia.) Furthermore, said Brailsford, genuine Russian democracy would serve the will and the way of the vast peasantry – a disaster. Acute enough to notice that the soviets were no longer a form of genuinely representative government, he recommended that they be accepted as fighting units of the necessary communist dictatorship.[4] But he was not attracted by a communist solution for Britain.

Many of the Americans whom Herzen and even Trotsky had envisaged as fellow-travellers of Russia hurried to the scene to find out whether they were. The "revolution" which drew Samuel Harper was not the Bolshevik Revolution of October, but its bourgeois-democratic predecessor of February, which had overthrown the Tsar and brought the moderates Miliukov and Kerensky to the helm. The eldest son of the President of Chicago University, a budding Russian scholar and himself a witness of the Bloody Sunday massacre of 1905, Harper "rushed through Norway and Sweden and down through Finland as quickly as possible, in order to get to the centre of revolution without delay".[5] This was in midsummer 1917. But when the tottering democracy fell to the bolshevik onslaught, resulting in the liquidation or exile of his many Russian liberal friends, Harper was appalled; it was to be almost twenty years before he recovered sufficiently to reconcile himself fully to Stalinism. Another American cast in a different mould, Colonel Raymond Robins of the Red Cross, soon became one of bolshevism's most influential apologists. A liberal rather than a socialist (he had joined the Progressive Party in 1912), Robins like so many other future converts did not at first take bolshevik anti-war propaganda seriously. Would the bolsheviks really acquiesce in the dismemberment of their country by German imperialism? Surely not. In any case if they succeeded in turning German front line soldiers into rebels, this would serve America's war interests more effectively than Russia's disastrous record of military defeats. It is interesting to note that neither Price nor Ransome had at first recognized any basic contradiction between Allied and bolshevik war aims, and the same was true of Arno Dosch-Fleurot, correspondent of the New York *World,* Louis Edgar Browne and Isaac Don Levine of the Chicago *Daily News.* When Trotsky shattered the illusion and stepped right out of the war at Brest-Litovsk in March 1918, both Dosch-Fleurot and Browne expressed indignation at the "betrayal". Levine later became a leading anti-communist militant.

But Robins refused to be discouraged or "betrayed". When he spoke to Trotsky in March he concluded that the bolsheviks would continue the war if sufficient economic and military assistance were provided by

Washington. In fact Trotsky, who had learned the diplomatist's art of innuendo, had avoided any such firm commitment; he had used Robins to sound out US Ambassador David R. Francis on what American reactions would be if the Congress of Soviets should "decide" to disavow the Treaty of Brest-Litovsk. Francis transmitted the inquiry to Washington: in August President Wilson dispatched troops to Vladivostock in an interventionist operation disguised as war aid. It was this kind of manoeuvre which really welded hesitant sympathizers to the bolshevik regime. Returning to the US in June, Robins energetically canvassed his many highly-placed friends: Theodore Roosevelt, Herbert Hoover, La Follette, William C. Bullitt and Secretary of State Lansing. In March 1919 he testified to the Senate's Overman Committee, but all to no avail.

Lenin once asked Arthur Ransome whether Colonel Robins was really as friendly as he made out. "Yes," replied the Englishman, "if only as a sportsman admiring [Russia's] pluck and courage in difficulties." Robins had told Ransome: 'I can't go against a baby I have sat up with for six months.'[6] Later Ransome provided an excellent if unwitting portrait of the fellow-travelling impulse. "I should have liked to explain what was the appeal of the Revolution to men like Colonel Robins and myself, both of us men far removed in origins and upbringing from the revolutionary and socialist movements in our own countries. ... There was the feeling, from which we could never escape, of the creative effect of the Revolution ... the living, vivifying expression of something hitherto hidden in the consciousness of humanity."[7] In May 1919 Robins himself observed with a certain *Schadenfreude* that the foolish Allied policy of anti-bolshevik intervention would drive Germany into Russia's arms, and the Russian Revolution thereby "end in the emancipation of half the world". But it's perfectly clear that he envisaged this emancipation stopping short of the USA: he was no communist.

Back in America, Robins exploited his powerful oratorical gift to extol the soviets as genuinely democratic organs of government. Indeed the myth that the soviets themselves remained representative of a popular democracy was naïvely accepted by many of bolshevik Russia's early sympathizers. Writing in *The Nation* in March 1919, Evans Clark described the soviets as "controlled by the masses at every point", whereas American political institutions were designed to check and balance the popular will.[8] Apparently the bolshevik Government enjoyed executive power purely on sufferance: the soviets, which were assumed to be indigenous Russian institutions rooted in the old rural *mir*, could throw it out at any time. This was the kind of language spoken by Robins, by Oswald Garrison Villard, who took control of *The Nation* in July 1918 and soon committed it to the bolshevik cause, and by Robert Morss

Lovett whose *Dial* castigated American intervention. *Dial* published the first Soviet Constitution and pressed for the recognition of the bolshevik Peter Martens as Soviet ambassador. Each of these early fellow-travellers privately re-created bolshevism in conformity with his own ethical code: "From the outset," wrote Lovett, "I was in favour of the Russian Revolution, which Miss [Jane] Addams called the greatest social experiment in history . . . I quoted the cautious advice of Gamaliel to the Jews in regard to their treatment of the early Christians. . . ."[9] This was not the language of John Reed and Albert Rhys Williams, who promised the Russians that the American proletariat would follow the same model of violent and dictatorial struggle: the language, in short, of communists. And it was this latter idiom which was increasingly adopted by *Liberator*, the magazine associated with Reed, Floyd Dell and Max Eastman, and then in the early 1920s with the American communist leaders William Z. Foster, C. E. Ruthenberg and Jay Lovestone. In 1922 *Liberator* was actually turned over to the CP and in 1924 it was merged with two other communist journals.

Born in 1883, Max Eastman had been a pupil of John Dewey, a philosophy instructor at Columbia and, since 1912, editor of *The Masses*. Soon one of the best-known literary radicals in America, in 1918 he published Lenin's "Letter to American Workingmen" and praised the bolshevik Government as both "humane and democratic". Apparently bolsheviks like Lunacharsky reminded him of Plato's Philosopher Kings. There is no doubt that the *Liberator*, whose circulation he brought up to sixty thousand, exercised an immense influence on young intellectuals disillusioned by the lies and broken pledges of the Wilson era. In 1923 Eastman embarked on a long stay of twenty-one months in Russia, during which time he involved himself in leadership disputes, reinforced his knowledge of Marxism, and learned Russian with the help, he liked to recall, of various females of the species. He travelled for some time in the company of Albert Rhys Williams for whom, as he put it, the October Revolution "had taken the place of Christ's Second Coming". He then persuaded Trotsky to let him write his biography (a scoop which Anna Louise Strong also attempted but failed to achieve). Eastman had now become a communist. But with Stalin's rise to power he adopted Trotsky's cause and case, and was therefore ousted from the American Party. For some years thereafter he continued to regard himself as pro-Soviet, but the publication in 1934 of his *Artists in Uniform* heralded a definitive break with all things Stalinist. Six years later he renounced the socialist vision in its entirety with the all too common fanaticism of one who insists that his own disillusionment should automatically entail everyone else's.

As a young man the playwright Elmer Rice heard two powerful appeals on behalf of bolshevik Russia, one delivered by Colonel Robins and the other by Lincoln Steffens, already famous as the muckraking author of *The Shame of the Cities*. An effective, dramatic orator who enjoyed a captive audience as much as he enjoyed his own captivation of it, Steffens had hurried to the theatre of revolution in the early spring of 1917: ". . . we travelled by train up the east coast of Sweden . . . all night to the Russian frontier, sledded across it, surviving examinations, and so dropped down over some Finnish territory to Petrograd . . . where we arrived at night in a wintry, cold, deserted station and were driven out over vacant, bumpy streets that felt like a battlefield . . . Lenin had but just arrived."[10] Of local conditions he came almost entirely ignorant: ". . . Crane says Miliukov has economic ideas," he had written on 22 March. Five days later: "I have seen the Mexican Revolution. I want to understand revolutions. There are not many."[11] He believed not only that Kerensky represented the fears, faith and hope of the Russian people but also that he, Steffens, the scourge of American municipal corruption, had an ear for the popular will. "You can interview a mob; it's a solid mass all of one mind, one mood, concentrated . . ."[12] He met Hugh Walpole and several other English gentlemen who were endeavouring to keep Russia at war with Germany. He did not disagree with this aim, but the encounter brought out in him a strain of anglophobia common among American populists. "Looking at him and looking at the stinking, earnest, high-aspiring Russian mob, it seemed to me that the mob was the gentleman, not the British novelist-lobbyist."[13] Steffens did hear Lenin speak but the events made little impression on him and he left Russia before the October Revolution, carrying a message from Kerensky to Wilson asking for an abrogation of the secret treaties which put the Anglo-French-Russian wartime alliance in so unfavourably imperialist a light. So he departed on what he justly later called a "bourgeois-democratic" mission, thereby incurring the penalty of rifle fire from a passing bolshevik troop train. However it was gratifying to be received by Wilson himself even if events had meanwhile removed Kerensky from the scene. Would Steffens now travel the road of October? Hesitantly he would. By January 1918 he was insisting that Lenin and Trotsky were not pro-German, not crooks and not crazy: they were merely misunderstood. But a month later he wrote to Colonel House saying that Trotsky was making a serious blunder in doubting the sincerity of Wilson's anti-imperialist passion . . . an issue about which Trotsky was obviously better informed than Steffens. Completely untutored in bolshevik ideology, ignorant even of Lenin's wartime manifestos, he was slow to recognize that the bolsheviks were not simply more resolute variations of Kerensky. And when he did fasten on to the truth, he thrashed around in the typical fellow-traveller's predicament. "I am a pacifist against the class war," he wrote to Dr Suggett. "It is too fierce, too expensive, too atrocious. It is not scientific ... evolution *is possible*. Only, doggone it, the evolutionists won't evolve – not while they have their precious privileges to protect."[14]

When Colonel House sent William Bullitt on a mission from Paris to Moscow to negotiate with the bolsheviks, Steffens tagged along. He now saw, or believed he saw, a revolutionary regime possessing an evolutionary plan to remove the causes of poverty, graft, tyranny and war. A small minority was temporarily wielding dictatorial power in order to lay scientifically the foundations of a genuine economic democracy, the essential prerequisite of political democracy. On meeting Lenin, he asked him for definite assurances which he could convey to Wilson that the Red Terror would soon abate. Lenin gave him a sharp left-hander. Had these humanitarian gentlemen gathered in Paris shrunk from the bloody slaughter of war? Steffens had a genuinely big and generous nature; castigation of this kind from a leader of Lenin's calibre impressed rather than offended him. Back in Paris he declared in words which were to become famous: "I have been over into the future, and it works." A fully-fledged fellow-traveller now, he set about convincing audiences that the bolshevik leaders sincerely did *not want* to be dictators and would happily abandon that painful role as soon as the economic revolution was secure. Like Robins, Steffens had influential friends and channels of influence open to him. In November 1919 he addressed the independent liberals at a House of Commons luncheon, and advised them to accept the bolsheviks for what they were. The anti-bolshevism of Ramsay MacDonald and other social democratic leaders now irritated him: "The most reasonable, the soberest and most practical minds in the Socialist movement are the statesmen round Lenin."[15] Even so, it wasn't the kind of sober political rationality he could recommend for the West where, he hastened to affirm, "there must be liberalism. The English have it in its finest form."

An Irishman who would rather have endured the rack and gallows than admit as much was Sean O'Casey. Whereas Steffen's mild anglophobia had its limits, the only concession O'Casey ever made to England was to live there. It was indeed out of the Irish troubles that the playwright's russophilia sprang; one might call it a transference of the extreme radicalism that he could not sustain at home in Ireland. Early in the 1920s a Russian friend sent him some snapshots: "In the spirit, Sean stood there with these children, with these workers, with these Red Army men, pasting away the ruin they were rising from ... adding his cheers to the cheers of the Soviet people."[16] In the spirit this third-person Sean was to prove a faithful fellow-traveller, though never in the flesh, even though this Sean, so he thinks, so he says, possessed the first Irish ears to hear the silver trumpets from civil-war Russia ... We shall come across him again, in 1956, cheering the Red Army into Budapest, in the spirit. ...

In France also, distinguished voices were raised in protest against the policy of armed intervention initiated by Clemenceau in league with Lloyd George. Old Anatole France called on French workers to rally and demonstrate in favour of their Russian brothers: they did. The noted physicist Paul Langevin who, like Anatole France, belonged to a generation whose formative political experience had been the Dreyfus affair, boldly spoke up in favour of both the Russian and German Revolutions. When in 1920 the Paris Government recognized General Wrangel as the legitimate ruler of Russia, his indignation was keen. Speaking at the Salle Wagram in 1921 he described Soviet Russia as "this first realization of hopes of universal liberation ... this first collapse of political despotism".[17] Though by no means a communist, he even predicted the spread of the Revolution along the lines foreseen by Marx. He threw his weight behind the campaign for the reprieve of André Marty, the leader of the anti-interventionist mutiny which had broken out in the French Black Sea Fleet. Marty had been condemned to twenty years' hard labour, but this sailor had, in Langevin's opinion, "an elevated conception of his civic duty". The scrupulous care with which he examined the smallest details of Marty's life and career to prove his essential worthiness foreshadowed Sartre's impassioned defence thirty years later of another condemned left-wing sailor, Henri Martin. Anatole France also praised Marty for having disobeyed "criminal orders". (Neither could foresee Marty's future career as a leading communist politician and as the jealous, domineering political commissar so tellingly depicted in Hemingway's novel of the Spanish Civil War, *For Whom the Bell Tolls*.) Every radical gesture or utterance offered by France or Langevin was enthusiastically reported in *l'Humanité*; not even Henri Barbusse, a Party member, was held in higher esteem. And France's role as the most prestigious literary fellow-traveller was all the more treasured in that Romain Rolland, overwhelmed by the universal wickedness of a world which refused to fulfil the demands of a pure, sublime *esprit*, had turned his back sadly on the Revolution.

In 1921 Anatole France was awarded the Nobel Prize; he brought to the bolshevik cause all the prestige of the grand old man of French literature. Yet he had been in his time both an ivory tower aesthete and a political conservative; the Paris Commune of 1871 provoked in him, as in Flaubert and the Goncourts, a reaction of repugnance, of disgust. In his *Les Désirs de Jean Servien* he depicted the Communard leaders as both mad and criminal. Then in the late 1880s he made the mistake of cultivating the friendship of General Boulanger, a would-be dictator whose Bonapartist ambitions fortunately evaporated in, or over, the body of a woman. It appears, however, that it was not this scandal so much as the Panama Canal affair of 1893, with its revelations of graft and nepotism in high places, which provoked the hiatus in Anatole France's ideological development. Ceasing to be an ambitious careerist of the fashionable salons, a patriotic novelist whose exquisitely refined style pleased the more ornamental segments of society, he became a socialist whose elegant wit now reached an increasingly wide public. George Orwell remarked that France remained by temperament a radical rather than a socialist: this was true; but he took socialism no less seriously than Shaw did and, like Shaw, he possessed a fiercely logical mind whose cutting edge put opponents to rout by means of *reductio ad absurdum*. (It was France who remarked that bourgeois democracy accords the rich the same right to sleep under the bridges of the Seine as the poor.) Nor did the French version of political Radicalism, with a capital "R", impress him; he made mincemeat of the anti-clerical, bourgeois and Radical Republic of the post-Dreyfus years in his satirical novel, *Penguin Island*. Scarcely an institution or a myth held sacred escaped him. The Army: "all armies are the finest in the world"; the judiciary: "the judges were certain, for there was no evidence"; he tore the Church to shreds only to turn on its political enemies with equal scorn: "Paul Visire and his collaborators wanted reforms, and it was in order not to compromise these reforms that they refrained from imposing them...."

Like Heinrich Mann, he admired Zola. To trace the pattern of his deepest beliefs is difficult since he wrapped himself in paradox: he was an optimistic pessimist and an idealistic sceptic. His novel, *Les Dieux ont soif*, suggests that revolutions exact too high a price in blood, while *La Pierre Blanche* places gelignite under the walls of utopia. Yet he held himself to be a revolutionary with a faith in man's ultimate capacity to fashion a decent, harmonious society. In 1875 he had written: "There are as many human truths as there are men and moments in the life of each of these men."[18] He justified his corrosive intellect in terms of French cultural history: had not – he asked friends – the great masters, Rabelais, Montaigne, Molière, Voltaire and Renan all been "sceptics"? Had they not fought against ignorance, intolerance, cruelty and blind hatred? Were they not in reality passionate idealists whose scepticism was a means of measuring man's failure to live up to his own moral claims and code? France thought so.

A charter member of the Ligue des Droits de l'Homme he testified for the defence at the trial of Emile Zola, whose *J'accuse* led to his condemnation and brief exile. It was now, at the turn of the century, that France began to speak in draughty halls and to take seriously the socialist movement. He hailed the 1905 Revolution in Russia and he now spoke frequently of the world proletariat and its mission. But he was of two minds about the parliamentary road to socialism; much as he admired Jean Jaurès, the spectacle of socialist politicians like Millerand, Briand and Viviani selling their principles for a seat in the cabinet disgusted him, as well it might. Yet he recognized that the fact of violent revolution does not of itself provide a solution to human nature; in *La Révolte des Anges*, he stressed prophetically that a mere change of personnel in high office or even a re-casting of institutions would not guarantee the triumph of virtue.

He was never an orthodox Marxist. The Hegelian dialectic and all that remained foreign to him, as to Shaw, though both strove to do their homework. But he gave his time and energy to the Popular University, a working men's night school whose inspirational genius was Jaurès. Like Gide in the 1930s, he became anxious to atone for his own privileged position and to quell his innate, patrician mistrust of mob folly; like Shaw, he believed that this folly could be eradicated by means of education alone. Of all the follies he surveyed, war was the one he most abominated. Yet in 1914 he proved unable to resist the tide of national indignation, the belief in the superiority of French civilization, which swept all but a few singular spirits before it. In short, he became a fierce patriot. He called the Germans barbarians. He condemned Romain Rolland's isolated and lonely pacifist stand. This second hiatus in his career did not last long. By 1916 he was giving the whole international scene a searching reappraisal, the outcome being that he fell over himself to make amends and gallantly supported Rolland for the Nobel Prize. His old distrust of chauvinism flared up in magnified form and he took the opportunity of his own Nobel Prize speech to break the rules of good conduct and to damn the Treaty of Versailles as nothing less than a prolongation of the war by other means. Meanwhile he had responded warmly to news of the Russian Revolution; time and again he made up his mind to visit Russia but apparently his doctors dissuaded him. He now wrote a preface for the French edition of Jack London's *Iron Heel*, in which he contended that the ultimate victory of socialism was inevitable, whatever black and reactionary torments might provisionally intervene.

In his old age he was an impressive figure, widely revered and enjoying the special status in national life which France regularly accords her most distinguished writers. His appearance commanded attention, the long, rather Turkish nose bisecting large, dark eyes, with the Sultan-effect reinforced by the inevitable skull caps which he collected as Simenon collects pipes. He could not write a word bare-headed. His writing had brought him wealth: his Paris house was called the Villa Saïd but in his last years he preferred the seclusion of La Béchellerie near Tours, from which he periodically emerged, white-bearded, to climb into his shiny red automobile. To demonstrate his solidarity with the workers he joined the CGT and marched in the May Day parade shoulder to shoulder with the typographical workers. When Jaurès's assassin was finally acquitted he headed the protest demonstration, while the quasi-revolutionary character of the big strikes of 1920 excited rather than diminished his support for them. But all was not solemnity: whenever his anxious doctors permitted it, he went gallivanting on short trips in an aeroplane: he never tired of observing the world at his feet.

What was his relationship to the new Communist Party founded at Tours in December 1920? A commonly accepted belief is that he actually joined it. Thus one of his biographers, Jacob Axelrad, wrote: "France became a communist," adding later, "he decided to resign from the Communist Party."[19] In 1945 communist spokesmen engaged in retrospectively counting the Party's intellectual assets twice claimed him as one of the earliest great Party members.[20] The communist historian Jean Fréville, using a present-tense narrative, later claimed that soon after the foundation of the Party France "apporte son adhésion".[21] But if we examine the Party press of the period in question an altogether different version imposes itself. On 12 January 1921 l'Humanité announced that while Henri Barbusse had joined the new Party, Anatole France had on the previous day "affirmed his solidarity with it". Barbusse's biographer, Annette Vidal, records that Barbusse found the old writer sympathetic to his political blandishments yet cautious: "You're right," he told Barbusse, "but I'm too old, I haven't the strength to follow you, but I have confidence in you."[22] However, the decisive evidence that France never joined the Party is to be found in an article written in February 1922 by Amédée Dunois. The title – "Anatole France and Us" – is itself revealing. Dunois's principal point was that although France belonged to no political party, he nevertheless remained a loyal friend of the Revolution.[23] Since Dunois was a member of the Central Committee, he cannot have been ignorant of the facts.*

* This conclusion, proposed in my *Communism and the French Intellectuals*, London, 1964, was subsequently independently corroborated by Carter Jefferson, *Anatole France: The Politics of Skepticism*, Rutgers, 1965. "He was not a member of the Party at all, but only a fellow-traveller" (p. 219).

During these last years of his life he was often visited at La Béchellerie by Jaurès's communist disciple Charles Rappoport, who would talk enthusiastically about bolshevism until the old man grew sleepy or bored. He rarely departed empty-handed: France usually produced a donation for Party funds, and doubtless such encounters left him brooding in solitude on the necessity of social violence. "If I am told that a revolution would bring suffering, I would nevertheless accept it although I hate suffering. . . . But, more than that, I hate mediocrity, sterility. To suffer is to live . . . intensely . . . if one wishes to see an era of justice established, one must be resigned to what may come to pass in its accomplishment – of injustice, of cruelties, and of blood. . . ."[24] He was sincere, of course, but in thus forging a heart of avenging steel he was forgetting his own nature. Doubts, hesitations and scruples soon reasserted themselves. When the Comintern at Trotsky's instigation blacklisted the Ligue des Droits de l'Homme and declared membership of it to be incompatible with membership of the Party, France felt the stigma keenly: and he was not the man to be bullied. Then alongside Rolland he protested in 1922 against the bolsheviks' conduct of the trial of the Socialist Revolutionaries: "In the name of humanity . . . do not perpetrate acts which could be interpreted as vengeance against political opponents. You could thereby irreparably damage the great cause of the liberation of the world's workers."[25] At Gorky's instigation he sent the Russian writer a public letter agreeing that the condemnation of the Socialist Revolutionaries would weigh heavily on the Soviet Republic. The communists hit back, criticizing his "indulgent eclecticism" and his notorious friendship for Foreign Minister Barthou. He declined to change his friends.

This attack notwithstanding, he published in November 1922 a "Salute to the Soviets" which the editors of l'Humanité publicized and attributed to "our greatest writer" – an accolade confirmed, incidentally, by two public opinion polls conducted in 1923. He recalled how the Red Armies had crushed the "hordes of bandits" sent to destroy them, and he somewhat rhetorically declared that in Russia the world now saw for the first time government of the people by the people.

But when a purge struck the PCF in 1923, France's affection for it cooled and died. He now fell back on the clear-cut distinction of allegiance and priority so common among fellow-travellers: the Soviet Revolution was magnificent but France, after all, had long ago had her own. . . . Perhaps recognizing the onset of this schizophrenia, l'Humanité publicly asked him with more than a hint of sarcasm: "If something happened, you understand, something, well, you would be for us, wouldn't you?"[26] The something which did happen was nothing so dramatic as a revolution; it was merely the first parliamentary elections to be held since the founding of the PCF. Anatole France's answer was clear-cut: he supported not the communist candidates but the radical-socialist alliance, the Cartel des Gauches led by Edouard Herriot, whom he publicly praised as a fine and cultured man. *Le Quotidien*, for whom he had begun to write occasional articles, paid tribute to his *"civisme"*, a notion straight out of the bourgeois Enlightenment. To which Anatole France, of course, really belonged. He lauded the Cartel's success (the PCF was routed) as "this great victory", evoking loud complaints from *l'Humanité*. What really delighted the old man was the defeat of Poincaré's right-wing Bloc National, responsible the previous year for the military occupation of the Ruhr. Since the communists had no chance of winning the election, he was after all only being practical. But being practical, as he himself so cogently demonstrated in *Penguin Island*, is the first step to compromise, self-contradiction and, ultimately, capitulation. When he died in 1924 the young Turks of the communist intelligentsia declared themselves nauseated by the memory of this "social traitor", this despicable, mendacious, money-grubbing "chauvinist". That was no doubt unfair, but the lavish State Funeral accorded him by the establishment might have prompted the thought that men get the last rites they deserve.

The early German fellow-travellers were for the most part weak types: where the Communist Party is strong, articulate and violent, as in the Weimar Republic, the natural fellow-traveller is a sentimental radical incapable of firm commitment. In search of austerity and ascetic communist virtue Alfons Goldschmidt journeyed to the frontier. In Reval – the time was 1920 – he was tempted by everything an epicurean heart could desire: good food, smiling girls, *Kitschtheater*, an insanely favourable currency exchange rate and cheap animal skins. "One is poisoned whether one wants to be or not." And so, poisoned by cheap animal skins, he crossed into the pure nothingness of ravaged Russia. *"Petrograd! Wir landen auf dem baltischen Bahnhof."* At once his enchanted eye fell on a propaganda train decorated with the slogan: THE BOOK BELONGS TO THE PEOPLE. Goldschmidt then stepped expectantly into the city, "where the worker rules", this city purged of its despicable Eberts and Scheidemanns,* where the fallen Karl Liebknecht was revered as a kind of "Siegfried of the proletariat", and where justice and progress flourished in an atmosphere of intense rationality. Although not well informed (he predicted with certainty that Russia would win the war

* F. Ebert and P. Scheidemann, Majority Socialist leaders instrumental in crushing the Revolution of 1918–19.

with Poland by the autumn) his admiration for the new Russia remained unshakeable.*

Another early German pilgrim was Arthur Holitscher, like Goldschmidt a Jew, but at fifty-one ten years his senior. Both were minor men of letters overcome by a busy interest in a world they were incapable of influencing. Enabled by his father's wealth to give up his career in a bank, Holitscher had mingled with the glittering Munich intelligentsia of the pre-war years and offered occasional witty contributions to the satirical *Simplizissmus.* Having a penchant for travel and for writing rather flatly about what he believed he had seen, whether in America, Palestine, Asia or Soviet Russia, he was easily magnetized by such distant good causes as the Achdut Ha'avoda wing of Zionism and bolshevism. While still incarcerated in Moabit prison, Karl Radek had proposed that Holitscher participate in a "commission of inquiry" into Soviet economic conditions. Holitscher duly participated. "I sought a religion in Russia and found a party. But a party which strives with all means of political power and diplomatic cunning to achieve a great idea, perhaps the greatest which men have thought of."[27] He also discovered that the bolsheviks were neither devils nor angels, and returned to Russia in 1923 to confirm this. Zinoviev summoned him along with Max Eastman, the cartoonist George Grosz and others with a view to forming a propaganda cell; Holitscher was elected secretary for Germany because, in Grosz's words, "first . . . he was old and esteemed, second . . . he believed almost everything anybody told him".[28] When he and Grosz met again it was at a sumptuous Russian embassy party in Berlin. Holitscher was later to end his days in lonely and somewhat disillusioned exile in Switzerland.

Needless to emphasize, all the early fellow-travellers harboured the greatest admiration for Lenin. Lenin appealed to them as a Russian who was content (so they mistakenly believed) to cultivate the bolshevik garden *inside Russia.* For Anatole France, Lenin was the greatest Russian since Peter the Great. Arthur Ransome reflected: "Walking home from the Kremlin, I tried to think of any other man of his calibre who had a similar joyous temperament. . . . I think it must be because he is the first great leader who utterly discounts the value of his own personality. He is quite without personal ambition. His whole faith is in the elemental forces that move people."[29] M. Philips Price devoted many words to Lenin's genius while Alfons Goldschmidt came up with a touching tale about Lenin sweeping out a Kremlin yard on May Day; furthermore this

* Combining a career as a financial editor for bourgeois newspapers like the *Berliner Tageblatt* and the *B.Z. am Mittag*, he also taught economics at Leipzig University, worked for Münzenberg's Red Aid and then, exiled in the 1930s, collaborated closely with *Das Wort* and *Die Neue Weltbühne*, both vehicles for communist-controlled fellow-travelling.

prodigious exemplary toiler received a salary of only six thousand five hundred rubles a month, the same as the average Moscow worker. For Theodore Dreiser he was "the greatest of all modern leaders, I think". But when Ernst Toller arrived in Russia shortly after Lenin's death, he confessed to a certain unease about the ubiquitous portraits, the burgeoning cult: was socialism wise, he asked, to create a substitute for bourgeois hero-worship or religious saint-worship?

Anatole France's positive response to Gorky's appeal on behalf of the Socialist Revolutionaries in 1922 reminds us that the early Russian fellow-travellers confronted an altogether more agonizing and dangerous predicament than their colleagues in the West. Of these, the one who deserved to be called "Colonel Survivor" returned voluntarily to Russia in 1918 following a ten year exile in the West. "A middle-aged Menshevik lady wearing a pince-nez," wrote Ilya Ehrenburg, "met us at the Finland Station and invited me to follow. I replied that I was under guard. She started cursing the guard and the guard cursed back."[30] Three years later he departed again, in the wake of Alexei Tolstoy, Andrey Byely and Boris Pilnyak.* In Paris he came across Tolstoy who kept puffing gloomily at his pipe and saying: "It's all muck. Can't understand a thing. They're all off their heads."[31] He told Ehrenburg curtly that his head had been filled with bolshevik nonsense. Then abruptly he would change his tune and praise the bolsheviks as the unifiers of Russia. Finally he decided that emigration was death for a writer, packed his bag, returned home and made an uneasy but increasingly conformist peace with the regime. Meanwhile Boris Pilnyak, as if fulfilling Trotsky's definition of a Russian fellow-traveller, arrived in Berlin and announced that the Revolution was "national" and a *"muzhik"*. But his outward simplicity of manner masked a certain cunning.

For a few years the Russian fellow-travellers enjoyed the protection of both Trotsky and Bukharin against the fierce onslaught of the proponents of proletarian literature grouped in RAPP. A second line of attack came from the October Group who in February 1924 demanded a firm Party commitment to proletarian literature. But after a heated debate during a conference summoned by the press section of the Central Committee in May, it was decided that no single literary movement could claim to represent the Party line. Later that month the fellow-travellers gained a further reprieve when the Thirteenth Congress of the CPSU officially reserved its neutrality between the different "trends, schools and groups" of Soviet literature. The New Economic Policy still prevailed, the dogs

* For a discussion of Ehrenburg's career, see Chapter Eight.

of renewed class struggle had not been unleashed, and no single leader
was yet placed to impose his will. In June 1925 the Central Committee
confirmed this mood of compromise when it called for a tactful approach
to fellow-travellers and tolerance for "intermediate ideological forms".

But a poet could not live by Central Committee resolutions alone.
Sergei Yessenin – one of Trotsky's *paputchiki* – was torn: he railed at
the new epoch yet he loved it. Once he had read his poems to the Tsarina;
young, tender, ardent, drunk and lyrical, he wished also to read his poems
to the Revolution. But he was living in an epoch too public, epic and
catastrophic for his vulnerable sensibility. So he announced that he would
give everything to the Revolution except: "Only my loved lyre, I will
not give." But this was precisely what a poet was expected to give:
could a peasant declare, "I will give everything to the Revolution – except my land"? Furiously attacked in the press, Yessenin sought drunken,
moody refuge in the lower depths of the Moscow taverns. He wrote:

> By what odd chance did I go shouting in my song
> That I am a friend of the people?
> My poems are no longer needed here.
> And I too – by your leave – I am no longer needed.[32]

He married Isadora Duncan. Her dancing proved a sensation in Russia
and drove the Red Army men wild, which in turn provoked in her a
different type of wildness: "I am convinced," she wrote in *l'Humanité*
in 1921, "that here in Russia is the greatest miracle that has happened
to humanity for two thousand years."[33] Did she mean the Revolution –
or Yessenin? The poet she brought to America though the Revolution
had to stay at home. He hated America. The marriage broke up. Soon
afterwards he committed suicide. The Revolution cannot be held entirely
responsible.

In the late 1920s the RAPP attacks intensified and the fellow-travellers
found themselves bereft of protection in high places. Trotsky was exiled
and Bukharin disgraced. It was now a case of conform or go under.
Tolstoy conformed. But Pilnyak had not yet learned how to silence his
muse and so avoid trouble. He dared to write *Tale of an Unextinguished
Moon*, which relates how a Red Army commander is carried to an
operating table against his will – and dies. Since this story bears a close
analogy to the fate of Frunze, Trotsky's successor as War Commissar,
the author was sailing close to the wind. Then his *Mahogany* brought a
load of trouble on his head; he changed the title and recanted strenuously under the force of a huge literary campaign mounted against
him. Perhaps shielded by Gorky, he hastened to make amends, writing
dutifully about progress in Soviet Asia and then turning up in America

as a spokesman for communist Russia. He later fell in the Great Purge.

As did Isaac Babel. Like his mentor Gorky, Babel was naturally at ease among speculators, thieves, cabbies and the relics of the old intelligentsia in the beer houses. A magnificent writer, he was also no sloth. Finding himself on the Rumanian front, in the Cheka, in the northern army fighting Yudenich, in the First Cavalry, and in the Commissariat for Education, he fought bravely and served loyally. His stories, *Red Cavalry*, were attacked by General Budienny as a libellous distortion of Red Army life, which merely confirms that generals should not be taught to read. For this book did more for Soviet Russia's image and literary reputation abroad than any other. Not only was it hailed by Thomas Mann, Barbusse, Roger Martin du Gard, Rolland and Brecht, but it also sold in large quantities and reached a wide public. While the creative mood inflamed by the years of physical action away from the pen lasted, Babel turned out *Tales of Odessa*, *The Story of My Dovecote* and the play *Sunset*. Then nothing. In a brief and cryptic address to the first Congress of Soviet Writers in 1934, he announced that he had mastered a new genre: silence. The following year, along with Pasternak, he was rushed to the Paris Congress for the Defence of Culture at the behest of Russia's number one professional fellow-traveller, Ilya Ehrenburg. In thus exposing his chubby features and his great reputation to the foreign sympathizers, Babel was rendering the Revolution one last service. In the spring of 1939 he disappeared, having interrogated with lively curiosity the widows of earlier literary victims. He was officially rehabilitated in 1954.

The summons to Paris irritated Pasternak. He abhorred public performances and speeches. Loving Russia enough to live with her, his survival appears in retrospect almost miraculous. In 1934 Bukharin had described him as remote from the great issues of the day, a voice from the old intelligentsia who remained closed up in "the mother-of-pearl shell of individual experiences, delicate and subtle", a poet suffering the "frail trepidations of a wounded and easily vulnerable soul". Yet, said Bukharin, Pasternak was a poetic master, an original talent and profoundly sincere.[34] Ironically it was Pasternak, not Bukharin, who survived the purges. On one occasion he received a phone call from Stalin himself, an event which echoed in every nook and cranny of Moscow's terrified intelligentsia within hours. Possibly the dictator had some peculiar regard for what Pasternak represented to the outside world, but the attempt to draw logical lines of demarcation between those who fell and those who survived during the Stalin terror tends to be futile. Eventually Pasternak produced the novel he had long planned,

Dr Zhivago, and its publication in the West provoked a hullabaloo of international vituperation. It is, indeed, a very fine novel; judged from its political dimension alone, it appears to be the testimony of a *faute de mieux* fellow-traveller who had never believed the engine was worth the wood it consumed.

Far and away the most distinguished – and internationally respected – of the Russian fellow-travellers was Maxim Gorky.

Gorky's natural imaginative universe was not that of Marxism. His best work is populated not by militant proletarians but by broken-down, *lumpen* characters from the lower depths, by gentry in decay, by Russian dreamers, by yesterday's strong men caught and trapped in premature old age. His fictional world has strong affinities to that of Chekhov, whom he so admired. As for politics, his radical sympathies left him remarkably free from the spirit of sectarianism. Although he persuaded the millionaire Savra Morozov to contribute two thousand rubles a month for the publication of Lenin's *Iskra*, Gorky himself also gave money to the mensheviks, the Socialist Revolutionaries, the anarchists and even the liberals. The climate in which he wrote the strongly didactic novel *Mother*, later hailed as the foundation stone of socialist realism, was an exceptional one: the crushing of the 1905 Revolution and Stolypin's subsequent repressions persuaded him that he must serve a Party. Lenin hailed the novel, and in 1907 the two men met fraternally in London. But Gorky proved politically and philosophically undependable, and by 1909 Lenin was denouncing the neo-Marxist deviations of Bogdanov, Lunacharsky and the other "god-builders" who were flourishing under Gorky's patronage on the island of Capri. This sunny outpost of Italy was to remain for Gorky a haven, a refuge.

In 1910 Lenin visited Capri and patched up their quarrel. The bolshevik leader forced himself to recognize the artist as an inherently idiosyncratic creature. But only three years later the writer exasperated the politician into a new tirade when he declared innocently that god had not yet been created. *God?* Gorky explained: "God-construction is the progress of the further development and enlargement of . . . social feelings in the individual and in society . . ." Lenin was furious, calling it "reactionary . . . hocus-pocus . . . lulling the class struggle to sleep . . ."[35] The question at issue was the source of man's idealistic and altruistic impulses. According to Lenin such ethical values are implicit and immanent within the historical process of class conflict; they acquire their final, authentic form in the course of the struggle for socialism. Gorky appeared to have fallen into the idealist trap of searching for the ethical universe outside of man, but in fact he was merely insisting that a political cause, however noble, must always serve certain lasting values, and that history alone does not necessarily endow man with these values. At the core of the Marxian dialectic he perceived a gap: ethical man. Oddly enough we find indirect confirmation of Gorky's outlook not so much in the massive crimes against humanity perpetrated by revolutionary regimes as in the insistence of later socialist realist theorists that the writer's duty is to be an "engineer of souls", to educate the "socialist" masses in the spirit of socialism at the personal level by means of fictional anecdotes and cautionary tales. In other words a change of consciousness neither automatically precedes a change of institutions nor automatically follows it. Many years later the Chinese Cultural Revolution carried similar implications.

When war broke out in 1914, Gorky's initial reaction only confirmed Lenin's suspicions. He signed an appeal by Russian intellectuals castigating Germany for committing atrocities and for attempting to destroy European culture. He then moved to Finland and launched a pacifist, internationalist review, thus drawing closer to the position of Romain Rolland rather than of Lenin. Even though Gorky praised the anti-war stand taken by the Reichstag deputy Karl Liebknecht, Lenin found his position "timid and confused". Gorky hated the war, whereas Lenin regarded it as the inevitable instrument of historical providence. Gorky called it "the suicide of Europe", whereas Lenin believed it to be the midwife of a new Europe. Lenin attributed the blame squarely to international imperialism, whereas the self-searching, mandarin side of Gorky led him to lament: "We are all guilty of this crime, each and every one of us."[36] In other words the real criminals were stupidity, cruelty and the legacy of the past. Scenes of mob violence witnessed in Petrograd during the summer of 1917 disgusted him and renewed his quest for "god", for a force which would cleanse the Russian people of their inbred slavery. The only possible salvation, he concluded, rested with "the slow flame of culture".[37] But Lenin was in a hurry.

Gorky became the bitter and outspoken critic of the Bolshevik Revolution and its aftermath. "For seventeen years," he wrote in 1917, "I have considered myself a Social Democrat . . . but I have never denied my services to other parties. . . . In every party and group I regard myself as a heretic."[38] He was now editor of *Novaya Zhizn* (New Life), a magazine published by a group of mensheviks including N. Sukhanov, whose policy was to strengthen the democratic basis of the soviets, convene the Constituent Assembly, and put an end to minority dictatorship. *Novaya Zhizn* was forcibly closed in February 1918, again in June and finally in

July. Only Gorky's prestige kept it alive for so long.* Throughout these crucial months he and Lenin never met, and the writer relented only when the politician was wounded in the neck by Fanny Kaplan's bullet.

On 17 October 1917 Gorky called on the bolshevik Central Committee to deny rumours of forthcoming violence. On 10 November he protested against the arrest of people he termed innocent, such as the Cadet members of the old Provisional Government. Lenin's "pitiless experiment," he wrote, "will destroy the best forces of the workers and will arrest normal development of the Russian revolution for a long time to come."[39] Two days later he called the gagging of bourgeois newspapers disgracefully undemocratic. "I am especially suspicious, especially distrustful, of a Russian when he gets power into his hands."[40] Lenin and Trotsky had been poisoned by the "corruptive virus of power". Depicting Lenin as a cold-blooded trickster who spared neither the honour nor the lives of the proletariat, he relegated him to the Nechaev-Bakunin tradition of destructive anarchy. As for the expulsion of bourgeois "Cadets" from the Constituent Assembly, was not this a violation of the will of hundreds of thousands of voters? So great was Gorky's indignation that he even described the Cadets as the most cultured and skilful intellectual workers Russia possessed. (In fact only seventeen Cadets and rightists had been elected to the Assembly.) But the bolsheviks were determined to put an end to a parliament in which they had won only 168 out of 703 seats. Gorky's reaction was predictable: this Assembly was what the "best people of Russia" had dreamed of for almost a hundred years, a genuine, representative democracy, and now the so-called People's Commissars had turned it out on the points of bayonets.

In March news reached him that bolshevik soldiers had slaughtered several hundred educated people in Sebastopol and elsewhere in the Crimea – his great fear was that Russian culture would be totally extinguished. And when he received threats from the militants of the Cannon Section of the Putilov Works, he replied scornfully: he had not fought "against the autocracy of swindlers and scoundrels to have it replaced by an autocracy of political savages".[41] But at some stage he seems to have realized, or been persuaded, that anger had driven him too far in support of the politicians of the discredited and short-lived bourgeois Republic. He no longer praised the Cadets. "Democracy has two enemies," he wrote in April: "their 'communist' lordships who crushed

---

* In later years Gorky's polemics against the bolsheviks were excluded from official Soviet bibliographies of his writings, as well as from the thirty-volume edition of his complete works published between 1949 and 1955. But in 1965 they were for the first time mentioned, albeit selectively in A. Ovcharenko's *The Journalistic Writings of Gorky*.

it physically, and the Cadets who are already starting the work of killing its spirit."[42] When Zinoviev accused him of scratching the back of the bourgeoisie, Gorky called him a demagogue. For Gorky the decimation of the intelligentsia was unbearable; every death of every educated person represented to him a new wound in the side of a profusely bleeding Russia. He increasingly publicized harrowing cases of death by slow starvation, like that of the seventy-five year old physicist, Professor Gezenko.

In June he made a clear-cut distinction between two types of revolutionary, and he did so in terms which foreshadowed Albert Camus's celebrated dichotomy of rebel and revolutionary. The eternal revolutionary, wrote Gorky, was a Promethean, the spiritual heir to the whole history of ideas seeking the ultimate perfection of man's relationship to man. Wishing to spiritualize the minds of men, resorting to physical coercion only in the last resort, untouched by motives of petty vengeance and striving to achieve a single-family of owner-workers, this authentic revolutionary would be completely satisfied by no existing social system. The revolutionary *pro tem*, on the other hand, was a spiritual conservative thirsting for revenge who invariably resorted to the foul methods of the old regime and who succeeded only in distorting and discrediting the human content of revolutionary ideas. In one sense, therefore, Lenin had been right: Gorky's search for "god" was bound, when the crunch came, to have practical consequences.

On 16 July Lenin gave the order to close Gorky's magazine.

It was during the Civil War and Allied Intervention that Gorky was reconciled with the bolshevik leaders – a reconciliation whose loud acclamation in *Pravda* indicated not only the scale of his prestige but also, indirectly, the punishment he had been able to inflict from the pages of *Novaya Zhizn*. The Government now exploited his concern for the persecuted intelligentsia to use him as a rallying point for reconciling dissidents to the new order. Here was the first hesitant experiment with the fellow-travelling utility principle. When an H. G. Wells arrived, the famous Gorky was there to welcome him: when a world appeal for famine relief was urgently required, the famous Gorky launched it. Follow us to a new life, he appealed, help us destroy the old order. In a sense, the fact that he had until recently opposed the bolsheviks lent added credibility to his conversion – as if the true dimensions of the situation had finally imposed themselves on an honest but sceptical intelligence. (Perhaps this was the case – for a while.) His table was perpetually occupied by people needing food, clothes, protection and advice. Lenin apparently thought he was wasting his time, and advised him that politics was a dirty business and that he was expending his energies on trifles.

Gorky did what he could for intellectuals who had incurred official hostility.* But the effort was too much, the future perspectives too bleak, and in 1921 he left Russia to settle in Sorrento, carrying with him an unrivalled, first-hand knowledge of the true plight of the Russian intelligentsia. In June 1922 he wrote to Jane Addams, estimating that only nine thousand authentic members of the species were left in all of Russia: "Without them it is impossible to live, as it is impossible to live without a soul . . . The nine thousand most precious people are gradually dying out. . . ."[43] And in this context one gains further insight into his god-building, his basic non-acceptance of dialectical materialism. Like Rolland and like Heinrich Mann, he insisted that intellectual force is the most powerful and subversive of all : sometimes he spoke of "intellect", sometimes of "spirit", and sometimes of "soul", but the guiding concept was that science and art were productive, unifying factors whereas politics was inherently divisive. The proletariat, he would add, must take the lead. But what could this mean in terms of his stated priorities? How could the "slavish", past-anchored Russian mob achieve its own enlightenment? The few events in Russia which did arouse his enthusiasm had nothing to do with proletarian initiative: the creation, for example, of the free Association for the Development and Dissemination of Positive Sciences, and also of the League of Social Education. Like Shaw and Anatole France, he was devoted to the principle of popular education, but his incompatibility with Marxism was well expressed in the tribute he paid to Lenin's memory in 1924: "I have an organic distrust for politics and am a very dubious Marxist, for I find it hard to believe in the intelligence of the masses in general. . . ."[44]

During his years of self-exile in Sorrento his relations with the Soviet regime were not always friendly. In 1922 he launched and co-edited a Berlin magazine which included the work of both Soviet and émigré writers; but no copies were allowed to enter Russia. In November of the following year he was outraged to hear that Soviet libraries had been purged of the works of Plato, Kant, Schopenhauer, Taine, Ruskin, Nietzsche and even, in some cases, Leo Tolstoy. Nor was his public praise

---

* One report has it that Gorky secured a promise that the poet Gumilev would not be executed, and felt betrayed when he was nevertheless shot. But according to Nadezhda Mandelstam, Gorky though informed of the pending execution did not get round to doing anything about it (*Hope Against Hope*, London, 1971, p. 110). She recalls that when her husband Osip Mandelstam returned to Petrograd from Wrangel's Crimea, half dead and without warm clothes, Gorky, in charge of the issue of vouchers for writers, crossed out the word "trousers" on Mandelstam's voucher, leaving only "sweater". This she attributes to Gorky's hostility towards literary trends foreign to him. He admired, she says, only solid learning.

of Hoover Famine Relief in line with Soviet policy. On the other hand he was given credit for his own prodigious efforts on behalf of the famine-stricken areas, which included the donation of his literary profits for medical aid. The fact was that Gorky's international prestige* became a dubious asset when he chose to live abroad, thus implying that he personally found conditions under the communists no more tolerable than under the Tsar. Although he praised the bolsheviks for saving Russia from disintegration and decomposition, he continually insisted that "it is not man who is made for the revolution, but the revolution for man".[45] His agitation against the trial of the Socialist Revolutionaries provoked violent personal attacks in *Pravda, Izvestia, l'Humanité,* and *Rote Fahne,* although the final decision to commute the death sentences, on condition that the SRs henceforward refrained from all political opposition, no doubt owed something to the international campaign he inspired.

During the twenties he seemed disposed to renounce or disown even those aspects of his past work which recommended him to the bolsheviks. In 1927 he wrote to Gladkov: "*Mother* is a really bad book, written under the spell of bad temper and irritation after the events of 1906 ...."[46] So much for the foundation stone of socialist realism. Party dictation in the arts disgusted him. According to Victor Serge, he told Fedin: "The Party commissar is at one and the same time policeman, censor and archbishop: he grabs hold of you, blue-pencils your writings, and then wants to sink his claws into your soul."[47] He had no wish to write about socio-political categories, only about man – often Man with a capital "M". "The new rules of Russia," he told Galsworthy in a letter, "do not recognize any person not infected with politics from the cradle."[48]

If this portrait of Gorky seems surprising it is because the image bequeathed to posterity is mainly based on the firm commitment to the Soviet Union associated with the last eight years of his life. Just how abruptly he made his decision to return to Russia is hard to determine. As late as 1928 he was being harshly attacked by the militants of RAPP. Then suddenly *Pravda* became very friendly and in December 1929 the Central Committee intervened to silence his critics for good. Having returned for his sixtieth birthday celebrations, he was awarded the Order of Lenin, a luxurious Moscow mansion, a villa in the outskirts, motor cars, a domestic staff and private secretaries (all members of or controlled by the KGB). Almost like any distinguished foreign visitor, he was taken on a conducted tour of the country, and thereafter a

* Contributors to his journal *Beseda*, which was not allowed into Russia, included Croce, Upton Sinclair, Pavlov, Rolland, Anatole France, Thomas Mann, Bernhard Kellerman and Gerhard Hauptmann.

stream of advisory and admonitory articles flowed from his pen, urging young writers to celebrate the great feats of socialist construction he had seen. Though continuing privately to throw his weight against the dry, furious and vituperative style fashionable among opportunistic critics, he inspired and edited in the best Stalinist manner a collective work about the White Sea Canal, painting a glowing portrait of the rehabilitation of the convict labourers employed on its construction. (In fact only an exceptionally strong and stoical minority survived. For the many political prisoners who were sent to the Canal, it was virtually a death sentence.)

His power to intervene on behalf of persecuted individuals was in abeyance; indeed his article "When the Enemy Does not Surrender, One Must Destroy Him" was widely interpreted as an endorsement of repression. According to one biographer he was elected in 1928 a member of the Party's Central Committee, but according to another source he remained outside the Party.[49] If Trotsky was justified in retrospectively characterizing him as "a somewhat equivocal fellow-traveller", the fact is that during his last years the equivocal dimension was well hidden from public view. Not that he was any more capable than Anatole France, Shaw, Gide, Feuchtwanger or Heinrich Mann of adapting his own creative writing to the tenets of socialist realism, but he like they made amends by way of speeches, pronouncements, endorsements and exhortations. He had become very rapidly a totem-pole, a symbol, a show-piece, and it was in this capacity that he bewildered many foreign delegates by his presidential address to the first Congress of Soviet Writers. He waffled and spouted dogma by turns: "The iron will of Joseph Stalin, the helmsman of the Party, is splendidly coping with deviations from the proper course...."[50] Could it really be *Gorky* denouncing literary individualism or dismissing discussions of form and content with an abrupt brutality worthy of Zhdanov himself?* Could this be the Gorky who had all along called himself a "suspect Marxist" who was now recommending scientific socialism as the writer's only bridge from the realm of necessity to the realm of freedom? Was there someone back-stage jerking the strings? When Romain Rolland, with whom he had corresponded for two decades, finally visited him in Moscow in 1935, the French writer was shocked to find him no longer his own master but hemmed in and governed by secretaries who intercepted all his corres-

* During the period of Gorky's ascendancy Georg Lukács performed one of his dialectical conjuring acts, revealing by a process of "objectification" that Gorky's work showed an increasing gravitation towards the proletariat and an increasing alienation from the early anti-heroes of instinctive despair.[51]

pondence. Rolland found a man lonely though rarely allowed to be alone, and, he judged, a man deeply disappointed.

Gorky died in June 1936, apparently of pneumonia. Two years later Yagoda, who had been chief of the GPU at the time, was accused of murdering him and his son through their doctors – on the orders of Trotsky! It seems clear that Gorky had wanted very earnestly to reconcile Stalin to the opposition and the regime to the intelligentsia. Stalin's resentment at this *extra curriculum* role was reflected in the first highly critical attacks on Gorky to appear since his return to Russia, notably the one written by Pauferov in *Pravda* in January 1935. Gorky's reaction to the show-trials planned by Stalin was obviously an unpredictable factor: the old rebel of 1918 might re-emerge and such a voice from within the citadel could no longer be tolerated. It is not anti-Stalin demonology so much as the pattern of events, particularly the manipulation of Kirov's murder, which strongly suggests that Stalin ordered Gorky's death, only later to attribute it to the ubiquitous Trotsky.

So died one whom V. S. Pritchett has called "a powerful blind man being led by a voracious, all-seeing child".

In 1924 a young German writer of high character, great talent and considerable personal charm made his first visit to the Soviet Union. "All the nerves are taut with expectation. At last! What an experience! And at the same time the oppressive thought: what shall we find? One is immediately overwhelmed by the thought that one is actually in the first socialist country."[52] By now, with the civil war and famine things of the past, the trappings of civilization were once more in evidence. "At last in a Russian train. The cleanness and disciplined organization strike me. . . ." Finding two classes of compartment, "hard" and "soft", the writer opted for soft. Presently the sleeping-car conductor came by and chatted with him about revolutionary perspectives in Germany. The writer was pessimistic; the conductor shook his head chidingly and announced that where there is a will there is a way. "Then I drove through Moscow in a sledge. What a barbaric muddle of town and village. . . ." But having spent five years in a Bavarian prison under a harsh regime which included bouts of solitary confinement, he was not easily disconcerted by the aesthetic shortcomings of his environment. Besides, he had come in search of a brave new world and he meant to find it. "Gradually the very absence of style becomes a style . . . after a couple of days, one is content."

The writer was the celebrated playwright and poet, Ernst Toller. That he should have been lectured on the revolutionary will and way by the sleeping-car conductor was not without irony, for Toller was one of the very few foreign sympathizers who had shown the will, gun in hand, only to find that the way led to incarceration and very nearly to summary execution. To understand how Toller became a fellow-traveller, if that is in his case an accurate description, is to learn something of German history and the rapid recession of the revolutionary perspectives which had appeared so promising immediately after the armistice.

He was a Jew born in 1893. At the age of nineteen he was an ardent patriot hoping for war, the true son of a town councillor who revered the Empire and prospered in its service. Having volunteered for the army, he became an artillery corporal; after thirteen months at the front he had an immaculate record, but physical and mental illness led to his discharge. Now for the first time he was subjected to contradictory influences. At Munich University he studied literature and law, attended readings by Thomas Mann and heard Frank Wedekind singing his diabolical ballads. But what made the most lasting impression on the young Toller was a lecture by Max Weber puncturing hallowed German myths and calling for prompt parliamentary reform. Moving to Heidelberg, Toller now took up the cause of international reconciliation and the abolition of poverty. When the military authorities reached out to arrest him he escaped to Berlin, fell in with a new bohemia and came under the influence of Gustav Landauer's *Aufruf zum Sozialismus*. It was in Berlin that he met his ultimate hero, Kurt Eisner, of whom he later wrote: "In him was embodied all that is finest in Nordic austerity and Latin rationalism."[53] Forgetting Max Weber, the young man assimilated Eisner's scorn for ballot-box democracy and its lack of organic contact with the people. Yet Eisner was one of nature's democrats and was later to guard the freedom of the Bavarian bourgeois press he despised. This, too, appealed to Toller's tolerant and generous nature.

Having followed Eisner to Munich, he joined a strike committee and found himself very promptly incarcerated in a military prison. There he completed the play, *Die Wandlung*, wrote expressionist poems and buried himself in the Marxist classics. Until the summer of 1918 the authorities controlled his movements by keeping him on reserve military service.

With the collapse of the German Reich, revolution broke out in Bavaria; Eisner summoned him. Despite his youth and lack of political experience, Toller became president of the Central Council of Workers', Peasants' and Soldiers' Soviets. In February he travelled with Eisner to Berne to attend the first post-war Congress of the Second International. Soon after his return Eisner was assassinated by a right-wing aristocrat. A chaotic period ensued – two successive Bavarian socialist republics lasting less than a month between them. The first of these was run by a

43

coalition of social democrats, independent socialists and anarchists, and headed by Gustav Landauer, an anarchist whose talent as a critic and writer was more obvious than his capacity to guide a government (indeed anarchists were not supposed to believe in government). Toller gave this precarious experiment his loyal support and attempted to persuade the communists to join the coalition. But the communists were interested only in one-party take-over. Determined to frustrate this and now living face to face with death, he was at one moment seized by communist militants only to be set free by a rival detachment of armed workers. He found himself obliged to suspend his newly acquired pacifism in parenthesis: "If I stopped to think of the possible bloody consequences of everything I did I should have to refuse all office."[54] His military experience acquired in a less worthy cause carried him to the leadership not only of the Bavarian Independent Socialists (USPD) but also of the Red troops engaged in full-scale fighting against the oncoming Whites. Toller commanded the successful seizure of Dachau.

This proliferation of left-wing factions must seem confusing. The USPD, to which Toller belonged, had first broken away from the main Socialist Party (SPD) in 1916. The extent to which its leaders were revolutionary Marxists varied from region to region, but as soon as the Communist Party was founded on the last day of 1918 the USPD could be defined by its rejection of two tendencies: the compromising reformism of the SPD on the right, and the pro-bolshevik, dictatorial elitism of the Communist Party (KPD) on the extreme left. The Independents in Bavaria were genuine revolutionaries, prepared to use force if necessary, but they were also committed democrats. History indicates that this is both an ideal and an untenable position.* On 13 April the Munich garrison mutinied and the Government disintegrated, giving way to a communist caucus led by Eugene Leviné, the type of ends-justifying-means fanatic that Toller distrusted. But Leviné and his friends did not last long. Munich soon fell to the White Freikorps, to the counter-revolution. Toller became a hunted man with a price of ten thousand Mark on his head and a charming police description:*"spricht schrift-*

---

* Many intellectuals were involved in varying roles in the Bavarian Revolution. Not a few of them were "foreigners" to Bavaria, thereby reinforcing a notion popular in Germany since 1848, that the *Literat* is inherently rootless, crazy, obnoxious and dangerous. One of Toller's colleagues in the fray, Erich Mühsam, retained in later years his anarchist, anti-state outlook, his bohemian scepticism about organized parties, and his innate pacifism. Even though he collaborated with the Communist-controlled Red Aid, he was critical both of the KPD and Soviet Russia and cannot be described as a fellow-traveller. Other Munich intellectuals like Heinrich Mann and Lion Feuchtwanger stayed on the sidelines of the Bavarian struggle, polishing their scruples. It was this type of intellectual who made the most devoted type of pro-Soviet fellow-traveller in the 1930s.

deutsch" – speaks educated German. After a series of hair-raising escapes he was finally trapped and brought to "justice"; Romain Rolland interceded on his behalf and he was lucky, unlike Landauer, Leviné and many other revolutionaries, to escape with his life. For five years Toller was held in Niederschönenfeld prison, where he spent 149 days in solitary confinement, 243 days deprived of writing materials, and 24 days without food. Yet not only did he contrive to write plays like *Masse-Mensch* and *Die Maschinenstürmer* which were performed in Berlin and abroad while he was still in prison, but his work during this period of captivity carried a power and beauty sadly unmatched by anything he wrote later as a free man.

In *Masse-Mensch*, Toller sets out a simple socio-political diagram which faithfully records his alienation from both the reformist and communist outlooks. The heroine is a socialist opposed to war, her husband a bureaucrat serving the bourgeois state. The masses are in ferment. Enter now "the Nameless One", an apostle of violent revolution perhaps modelled on Leviné. The heroine recoils from what he proposes: "I will not have a fresh murder." The revolution takes power. The heroine's husband is captured and sentenced to death. She pleads for his life. Says the prison sentry: "Only the masses count." Replies the heroine: "Only Man counts." Civil War ensues. The Nameless One orders the most brutal reprisals; he thinks only of the future. The heroine cries out: "Does lust for power, caged for centuries, impel you?" Then the counter-revolution triumphs and the heroine is arrested. The Nameless One appears in her cell (rather miraculously, considering the circumstances!) and offers to free her. But to do this will entail murdering a warder. She says no. The Nameless One tells her: "As yet there are no men. On this side men of the masses. On that side men of the State." But she will have none of it: "Strangely," she says, "you lead us to the promised land – the ancient land of human slavery."[55]

Such a précis or abstract inevitably does no justice to a play remarkable for its clarity of emotion and simplicity of language. But, taking the heroine's position to represent Toller's own, one notices the striking analogies with Gorky's outlook, particularly the humanistic insistence that the revolution must serve Man, and not Man the revolution. (The dialectic set out in *Masse-Mensch* was later closely echoed in Camus's *Les Justes*.) It is of course the case that writers like Gorky, Toller and Camus, in their anxiety to crystallize opposing philosophies of action, tend to caricature the bolshevik point of view; yet action is the test and those who suppressed and slandered the Kronstadt rising in the Name of the Future cannot complain if others re-fashion their thoughts to fit their actions. There is in addition a further proof that the cap fits:

45

though Toller in this play does not attach party labels to the different points of view, *Masse-Mensch* was not performed in Soviet Russia.

When Toller came out of prison he faced an impasse. The USPD, to which he had belonged, had split and disintegrated, its left wing consumed by the communists, its right wing by the social democrats. And while his judgment of the communists had been a critical one, how much more bitterly did he regard the conservative reaction which had smashed socialist risings throughout Germany by force of arms. It was not so much a vacillating nature as a rigorous honesty which pushed him into an equivocal position. On the one hand, as he reflected in 1933, "no political revolution can do without force. But ... there are distinguishable emphases"; on the other hand the masses are innately fickle: "At one moment they will stand by their principles; an hour later they abandon them."[56] Caught in this dilemma yet unable to abandon hope, he became a candidate fellow-traveller, searching for and finding in the Soviet Union at least a partial and preliminary fulfilment of the socialist vision. He was one of those pro-Soviet sympathizers (Holitscher, Goldschmidt and Rudolf Olden were others) whose natural affinity and affection was not for the German communists but for the radical intellectuals of the democratic Left. Thus he joined Kurt Tucholsky, Carl von Ossietzky and Heinrich Mann in the Deutsche Liga für Menschenrechte, founded in 1922 as a counterpart to the French Ligue des Droits de l'Homme – promptly proscribed, it will be recalled, by Trotsky and the Comintern. Toller however never embraced reformism; he remained a revolutionary with a tender heart. But henceforward he was doomed to an ornamental role. As his creative powers sadly slackened, he became an international celebrity and an inveterate congress-attender. Handsome, sometimes gay, sometimes melancholy, a lover of fine clothes and pretty women, he was there in Brussels for the Anti-Militarist Congress of 1927 and he was there in Amsterdam for the Anti-War Congress of 1932 – both master-minded by the communist Willi Münzenberg. In Berlin, Paris, Moscow and London he ran into another perpetually intinerant fellow-traveller, Ilya Ehrenburg. Who recalls: "he argued, persuaded, cursed, believed, despaired, and at the same time he was a dreamer, a joker, even a sybarite."[57] Toller took up and abandoned projects in bewilderingly rapid succession. After Hitler seized power he felt more than ever that the Soviet Union was the only hope: when the Soviet writers met in congress in 1934 he was there, when Spain and the International Brigade beckoned he was there, and when the left-wing intellectuals of Europe gathered in Paris in 1938 to "defend culture" he was there with his Latin head and his outbursts of Savonarola-like passion, a beautiful, sad fire-brand. His work was translated by Auden and

Spender and no left-wing periodical was complete without a contribution from Ernst Toller.

Like other fellow-travellers, he preferred to love the Soviet Union at a distance while constantly fighting within himself the poet's natural detachment from crude political causes. "The young writer no longer wants to live in the ivory tower, which was the ideal of artists for decades. We became aware that necessity moved us more strongly than beauty. We understand that our task is to integrate this necessity in our own work (*diese Not in unseren Arbeiten zu formen*), in order to free reality from it."[58] Nevertheless beauty was also a necessity; in 1936 he moved to Hollywood with his new wife, the nineteen-year-old actress Christiane Granthoff. In America life was never easy for a German émigré; the quest for money was constant and even a paper like the *New York Times* could call him, much to his indignation, "a communist leader". The contours of impending tragedy were already visible. Spain, on whose behalf he appealed so strenuously and whose sufferings stirred him profoundly, fell. His bewitching young wife left him.

On 11 May 1939 he visited the White House in the company of Klaus Mann and other German writers, and was briefly received by the President. He was very tired. To Klaus Mann he said: "If only I could get some sleep tonight. *Es ist schlimm wenn man nicht schlafen kann. Es ist das schlimmste.*"[59] On the evening of 21 May, in Ludwig Marcuse's New York apartment, he argued against suicide – the final solution to which many German exiles were soon to be drawn.* But he couldn't work or write, and he felt tormented by the gap between his fame, his reputation, and his recent literary achievements. And he couldn't sleep. Klaus Mann imagined him lying awake, tossing in bed, battered by the slogans heard and uttered at so many hopeless meetings: "*Genossen! Kameraden! Der Fortschritt ... das Proletariat ... unbesiegbar ... Seid einig! Glaubt! Seid stark!*"[60]† But no sleep. The day after his conversation at Marcuse's apartment he spent part of the morning quibbling with his agent over a percentage. When his secretary returned to the Mayflower Hotel after a short midday break she found Toller in the bathroom, hanging by the neck from a blue dressing-gown cord. He had put it all to rest. He lay in state in his coffin, painted – Marcuse recalls – like a gigolo.

Bertolt Brecht was another radical playwright, and one of more resound-

* Including Tucholsky, Hasenclever, W. Benjamin, Stefan Zweig, Ernst Weiss and, later Klaus Mann himself.

† "Comrades! Comrades! Progress... the proletariat... invincible... be united! Believe! Be strong!"

ing talent than Toller, whose formative years were those of the Weimar Republic. Ruth Fischer claimed that Brecht joined the KPD in 1930, but this is generally thought to be a mistake. When hauled before the House Un-American Activities Committee in 1947, he denied ever having joined with a seven-vowelled negative: "No, no, no, no, no, never!"[61] He once told Henry Pachter that it was necessary to stay close to the Party: he wanted communists to read and produce his work. Was he therefore a fellow-traveller? We have already warned against the fetish of the Party card, but the purpose here of indicating very briefly why Brecht can more usefully be regarded as an independent or maverick communist is to throw further light on the qualities separating communists from fellow-travellers. Needless to say, the fact that Brecht's case is politically ambiguous makes it all the more relevant.

Both politically and artistically Brecht went through several phases, but the late 1920s provide a definite turning-point towards Marxism, didactic theatre and the communist movement. Here the paramount influence on him was the great director Erwin Piscator. "I took part in all his experiments," said Brecht, "and every one was aimed to increase the theatre's value as education."[62] Piscator himself, though a Party member dedicated to creating a radical theatre which was – as he put it – "political in the sense approved by the Communist Party", was himself often in trouble with the functionaries of the KPD. Though he was an ardent Marxist, a *"Kulturbolschewist"* according to the right-wing press, and widely hailed by the left-wing intelligentsia as the genius of communist theatre, he did in fact bequeath to Brecht a distinctly heterodox legacy. And it is here that the ambiguity of Brecht's own career lies. Piscator loved the theatre more than he loved the Party. The Proletarian Theatre, Berlin, with which he was associated in 1920-21, had representatives from two of the KPD's rivals, the USPD and the KAPD (Communist Workers' Party), but none from the KPD itself. In *Rote Fahne* the Party expressed hostility to the project, accusing it of disparaging art. By December 1924 Piscator was back in high favour with his *Revue Roter Rummel,* which was apparently seen by ten thousand workers in fourteen days. Using the Reichstag deputy Ernst Torgler as a go-between, the KPD asked Piscator to show the revue at the Berlin "Party days" – the use of a go-between perhaps emphasizing Piscator's tendency towards independence. Soon afterwards he was temporarily back in disgrace. His production of Leo Lania's play, *Konjunktur,* depicted the USSR competing in the world oil market against American and British firms. In one scene a single woman represented both a Soviet oil syndicate and the Comintern – precisely the kind of abrasive irony favoured by both Piscator and Brecht. When KPD representatives and members of the Soviet trade mission attended a dress rehearsal in April 1928, they were furious. So Brecht, calmly sucking his black cigar, took a hand in rewriting Lania's play overnight, while Otto Katz, Piscator's suave business manager and later Willi Münzenberg's chief aide, set about coaxing the leading actress, Frau Durieux, into undoing everything she had rehearsed. Here, obviously, Piscator and Brecht showed considerable devotion to the Party, if not necessarily respect for its judgments.

Piscator was both a communist and a revolutionary Marxist who believed that the only hope for the world was a proletarian revolution followed by a dictatorship on the Soviet model. Brecht adopted this point of view with a part of his mind, even if his heart proved recalcitrant, and this attitude carried him out of the fellow-travelling orbit. While he shared with the vast majority of fellow-travellers a distrust or contempt for socialist realism on the Soviet model, the agitprop plays he produced in the early thirties were Marxist, didactic and "revolutionary" in a style not associated with the literary work of fellow-travellers. Possibly the "Schweik" or "Galileo" element in his nature kept him out of the Party, but the crucial factor was the unacceptability to Moscow of an aesthetic style and philosophy he refused to abandon. Here again Piscator's influence was decisive, with its emphasis on alienation techniques, documentary theatre, miraculous stage machinery, film screens and gaunt steel structures. Piscator was hostile both to lyricism (Toller) and naturalism which, he believed, established a deceptive congruence between literature and prevailing social conditions. Yet naturalism was the basis not only of the Stanislavsky style of acting officially supported in Russia, but of the whole socialist realist mode. Consequently Brecht found it hard to please the Party. His coldly logical celebration of an austere and ruthless communist discipline, *The Measures Taken*, failed to please either *Linkskurve* or Moscow. Not till his adaptation of Gorky's *Mother* reached the stage in January 1932 did he draw words of praise and acceptance from the communist critics. But though he did his duty during the years of exile, acting as nominal co-editor of the Moscow journal *Das Wort* and attending international writers' conferences, his plays went largely unproduced in the USSR. In 1951 the *Great Soviet Encyclopaedia* – a keen index of relative favour – accorded him only thirty-three lines as compared with seventy-seven for Louis Aragon and 112 for Johannes Becher. He had, after all, travelled to Vladivostock – only to catch a boat to California.

Having faced the Un-American Activities Committee in Washington and completely foxed and baffled it with quintessentially "Brechtian" replies, he bolted to Switzerland and thence to East Germany. (Piscator, after an unhappy time in Moscow in the early 1930s, henceforward steered clear of all workers' states.) Here, in the DDR, Brecht once more came face to face with the commissars of culture. On the credit side his prestige was recognized and he was permitted to build up the Berliner Ensemble in his own style and image. On the debit side his own plays were rarely performed, he was attacked as a formalist by *Neues Deutschland* and other Party organs, and he was bullied into modifying such productions as *Lucullus*. Accused of sabotaging Germany's cultural heritage, he counter-attacked in August 1953, lashing out at the State Commission for the Arts: "... a great ideology was not put before the artists as a tempting offering, but forced on them like sour beer...."[63] It was only boots, he remarked elsewhere, that could be made to measure. Brecht's relationship to communism and Stalinism was a complicated one and has been hotly debated; in this very brief sketch full justice cannot be done to any aspect of his work. The point to be made is that his relationship to the DDR and its ruling Socialist Unity Party was unlike that of a genuine fellow-traveller such as Arnold Zweig. Neither was a Party member: but Brecht was intimately embroiled as a Marxist, as a revolutionary, in what for him was *essentially a family quarrel*. He was a maverick, a black sheep, a heretic, a saboteur, but at the core a communist.

As with France, England and the United States, the fellow-travelling harvest did not ripen in Germany in all its rich plenitude until the 1930s. The factors which delayed a large-scale crudescence of authentic fellow-travellers were complex. The very imperfections of the Republic, its failure to live up to its own ideals, inevitably involved that section of the intelligentsia from which fellow-travellers are drawn in a perpetual pursuit of democracy on the French or English model. The fact that the old, imperial Germany had quickly reasserted itself, preserving the substance if not the shadow of power, the fact that yesterday's bureaucrats and judges had reoccupied the seats of policy and judgment after the frightening hiatus of 1918–19, the fact that the Army leadership, having picked up the pieces and effectively blamed the politicians for Germany's defeat, was once more creating a state within the state – all this provided radical intellectuals with a sphere of reformist aspiration which fell short of Soviet-style socialism. They might despise the Majority Socialists who, nominal heirs to the legacy of Marx and Engels, had reacted with bourgeois panic and authoritarian fury to the popular risings of the post-war months, calling in the most reactionary military battalions to crush them; but these intellectuals also felt, many of them, that the insurrectionist path chosen by the communists was foredoomed to disaster.

And then, from 1924 until 1929 at least, there was much to be grateful for. It was not fashionable to express gratitude or even to register it, but the subconscious exerts power enough. These were years of apparent political stability, of economic expansion, of the good life. And German intellectuals, despite occasional harassments, now enjoyed more freedom than their country had ever known. Learning, the arts and culture flourished. Sociology and psychology galloped alongside architecture; this was the age of the Bauhaus, jazz, mass sport, radio, the cinema. The theatres and cabarets of Berlin, now the cultural capital of Germany, boomed. The writers busied themselves with new "scientific" solutions – *"die neue Sachlichkeit"* and the *"Tatsachenroman"*. Alfred Döblin, Joseph Roth, Erich Kästner, Heinrich Mann and Lion Feuchtwanger dreamed of friendship with France and England, they attacked the Junkers, the courts, the churches, the prevalent hypocrisy and injustice, but they attached themselves to no party. They were proud of their independence and secretly delighted to have so many evils to scourge with virtual impunity. They even guarded their isolation with pride. Döblin wrote: ". . . at elections I rejoiced over the increasing vote of the reds. But it was clear to me that I was swimming in the air, a hopeless stickler for principles. . . ."[64] He was proud to be "hopeless".

Marxism was taken seriously in new, quasi-academic institutes like the Institut für Sozialforschung founded in Frankfurt in 1923. But the kind of academic, investigatory Marxism developed by Max Horkheimer, Erich Fromm, Leo Loewenthal, Theodore Adorno, Herbert Marcuse and Walter Benjamin had little political potential or sting: such scholars, acutely aware of the divorce between Marxist theory and the Soviet reality, also followed their own independent path. The feeling was prevalent that "science" rather than utopia was the proper province of intellectual activity; it was to take the physical and psychological shock of 1933 to convince some of the intellectuals that in the Soviet Union the claims of science and utopia had at last been reconciled. Lower down the ranks, it is true, among what Tucholsky called "the fourthclass intellectuals", communism had its attractions; in such quarters the *"Proletsnob"* flourished, denouncing the very culture to which he owed his meagre knowledge and understanding.

Germany differed from France and the Anglo-Saxon countries in that its academic circles contained little fellow-travelling potential. As an employee of the State, the German academic or schoolmaster traditionally suffered from an overpowering sense of respectability. To locate the sources of potential intellectual radicalism one must look to the wilder shores of literature, journalism and the arts, to provinces long since distrusted by bourgeois society. Two journals of particular importance in this respect were *Das Tagebuch* and *Die Weltbühne*, both of which had circulations of between ten and twenty thousand. A successor to the pre-1918 *Schaubühne*, *Die Weltbühne* stood broadly for the radical-democratic tradition of the French Revolution. Its two leading editors and contributors, Kurt Tucholsky and Carl von Ossietzky, mercilessly flayed the Republic for its failure to live up to its own pretensions: for being, as the saying went, a Republic without Republicans. Heinrich Mann was a contributor, as were Mühsam, Toller and the philosopher-statistician Emil Gumbel. Their general ideal was a *Vergeistigung*, or intellectualization, of political life, rather than the politicization of intellectual life which the communists and orthodox Marxists demanded.

Die Weltbühne continued to indulge in searching criticisms of Soviet economic and cultural policy, and in the autumn of 1930 it published a formidable protest of intellectuals, headed by Einstein, Heinrich Mann and Arnold Zweig, against the trial of forty-eight specialists then under way in Russia. As for the German communists, their ideological gymnastics and slavish adherence to the Comintern line inspired contempt. Ossietzky remarked that if Stalin suddenly became a Catholic the communists would find good Marxian arguments to justify it. (He thought he was joking: if he had lived to watch the French Party's "holy family" operation after 1945, he would have had to think again.)

By 1930 the crisis was on. Unemployment was rising and so was Hitler's support. Chancellor Brüning's emergency press decrees indicated the shape of things to come, and as a result elements of all left-wing groups came together in the Kampfkomitee für die Freiheit des Schrifttums. When Ossietzky and Walter Kreiser were indicted for espionage and treason in 1931 (their crime had been to write and publish an article exposing the Government's military aviation policy), the intellectual Left further closed its ranks. The *Vergeistigung* of politics was now a dream to be abandoned in favour of a desperate, last-ditch collaboration with the KPD. "Fascism can be beaten only in the streets," wrote Ossietzky. "Against the Nationalist Socialist rabble we have only one logic: the heavy knout. . . ."[65] And that meant the KPD and its organized street fighters. As a consequence the *Weltbühne* circle was now open not only to communist sympathizers but also to Party intellectuals like Egon Erwin Kisch and Ludwig Renn who showed some independence from the KPD's sectarian line on "social-fascists". The pages of the journal now featured more favourable accounts of Soviet life written by enthusiasts such as Axel Eggebrecht, author of *Im Lande der roten Macht* (1929) and a collaborator of Red Aid. The fellow-travelling species was beginning to appear in this time of crisis, though the nature of the crisis dictated that such men had to travel with the Party as much as with the Soviet Union.* In the last months of the Republic you could find side by side in *Weltbühne* not only "moderates" like Döblin, Ludwig Marcuse, Willy Haas and Thomas Mann, emergent fellow-travellers like Heinrich Mann and Feuchtwanger, and fellow-travellers such as Toller and Ehrenburg, but also communists like Brecht, Otto Katz, F. C. Weiskopf, Ernst Bloch and Erich Weinert. They had made a single bed; but their union was not destined to be blessed.

In the era now drawing to a close, Soviet culture had been creating an increasingly favourable impression in the West. Although the scientists and social scientists as yet found little in Russia to reassure them, those who cared about feminine emancipation or erotic freedom could react enthusiastically to Anna Kollontai's popular book, *Love in the New Russia*, with its famous "like drinking a glass of water" metaphor. In the field of culture, the Russians conducted a vigorous export trade, despatching to the West distinguished actors, directors, dancers, musicians and writers. Berlin or Parisian audiences were bound to conclude from their performances that bolshevism was less hostile to civilization than they had been led to imagine. (Besides, at any fashionable Berlin première one might see Commissar Lunacharsky in a white tie and his wife in Parisian haute couture.) The great directors came West, Stanislavsky bringing productions of Tolstoy, Gogol, Gorky and Dostoyevsky, and the celebrated Tairov with his "Unchained Theatre". There was Meyerhold, the Yiddish Theatre and a cabaret called the "Blue Bird" which played in the German language to full houses. It looked like the beginning of a brilliant new era of artistic creativity: who was to know that it was the tail end of one? Russians and Germans now shared a passion and a high aptitude for experimental film-making, and the visits of Eisenstein and Pudovkin in the wake of their magnificent epics were eagerly awaited events.

Nor was this cultural campaign confined to Germany alone. Between 1928 and 1930, forty Soviet films were shown in the United States, and

* Notable examples were Bruno Frei and Rudolf Leonhard. Frei was a Viennese doctor of philosophy who had worked for the Vienna socialist paper *Abend*, written warmly of the USSR, and then from 1929 to 1933 become editor-in-chief of Münzenberg's paper *Berlin am Morgen*. In 1934 he joined the KPD in exile and edited *Der Gegenangriff* and *Nouvelles d'Allemagne*, the news bulletin of the Volksfront in Paris. Arrested in France in 1939, he escaped to Mexico and returned to Austria in 1947 to edit *Abend*, now a communist paper. Rudolf Leonhard had volunteered for military service in 1914 but he later became a pacifist who joined the Spartacists in 1918. A doctor of law at Berlin University, he worked as a publisher's reader, wrote minor poems and essays, busied himself in the margins of literature, got briefly caught up in Kurt Hiller's radical pacifist movement, and then travelled resolutely with the communists in the 1930s.

Simone de Beauvoir was taking her friend Paul Nizan to see *Storm over Asia, Mother, The End of St Petersburg, The General Line* and *Earth* on the Champs Elysées. To see such films again today is perhaps to miss something of their original impact, but not much; genius is durable. One appreciates how the cinematographic work of Vertov, for example, could pulverize Western audiences while leaving them miserably uncertain whether they themselves could ever sustain life at such white heat. It took less than three hours to create an audience of fellow-travellers mesmerized by pulsating energy symbols. A master of propaganda, Vertov made some of his epics specifically for domestic consumption and others for export. A film like *Enthusiasm*, which depicts the efforts of the Don coal miners to perform in four years their part in the Five Year Plan, was not intended for a Soviet public and least of all for the Don coal miners. The message – hectic industrialization backed by enthusiastic mass effort equals socialism – was conveyed by a dazzling succession of virtuoso feats, both technical and stylistic, by an overwhelming barrage of sound tracks, fleeting images, sensational camera shots and euphoric collective rhythms. Such a film hit progressive, middle-class Western audiences in two solar plexuses: their susceptibility to avant-garde stylistic innovation, and their guilt about not having calloused hands. For Vertov showed men at work! What Western film did the same? But of course it was not real work, not the steady, monotonous drudgery that Don miners or Welsh miners would have recognized from their own experience. Vertov offered the Western middle class romanticized work, work-as-dance, work-as-sport, work-as-prayer.*

The Soviet writers were also ambassadors. Mayakovsky appeared in translation and occasionally in person. Ehrenburg was everywhere, conveying the impression that the Soviet Union was a place where a man who appreciated Chagall could live – even if Chagall couldn't. Simone de Beauvoir was fascinated by the work of Babel and Pilnyak, and by Sholokhov too – his impact was enormous. Even so, the "girl meets tractor" themes in Soviet novels left her wavering between admiration and distrust; for the time being she was not ready to travel. And when she was, all these writers except Sholokhov and Ehrenburg had met violent deaths.

But to drum up middle-class support for the Soviet Union one could not rely on random visits to cinemas on the Champs Elysées. Already in the 1920s a strategy was being rehearsed and practised which was to reap

* When Vertov came to London in November 1931 for the screening of *Enthusiasm*, his first sound film, he insisted on controlling the sound projection, raised the volume to ear-splitting levels, and finished up fighting the cinema staff for possession of the control panel while the walls shook and the audience sat pulverized.

its full rewards in the 1930s. Here we must introduce the Communist Front organizations, referred to henceforward as front-organizations.

Clarté was the first front-organization, though its teleology was only vaguely premeditated. Founded in 1919 and centred on Paris, but with branches in a number of countries, its original appeal was to intellectuals disillusioned by the war and anxious to do something about it. The brain-child of a little-known Frenchmann, Victor Cyril, Clarté was given substance and vitality by Henri Barbusse, then famous for his novel, *Le Feu*. Vitality to what end? "To organize the struggle against ignorance and against those who direct it like an industry ... it is not born of any political or national influence."[66] The first Directing Committee included some of Europe's best progressive names.* But when Barbusse, an ardent convert to communism, hailed the foundation of the Third International (Comintern), and the French section of Clarté transformed itself into a pressure group agitating for a communist take-over of the Socialist Party, the foreign affiliates withdrew. The German-Austrian group led by René Schickele, and the English contingent led by Thomas Hardy and E. D. Morel, became disillusioned, with the result that the non-French sections dissolved themselves or withered away. The French Party's specialist at handling wavering sympathizers, Paul Vaillant-Couturier, tried to repair the damage in December 1921 when he gave an assurance that Clarté was simply "a tribune of education and free discussion", but it was too late. Even the great names slipped out of the bag: Gorky briefly lent his distant support and Anatole France showed a transitory interest, but Rolland refused to have anything to do with it. In future the Party would learn from this early mistake.

Meanwhile the initiative passed to Germany. Communism in France began on a strong note but soon declined and then dwindled to negligible proportions, whereas German communism remained a power to be reckoned with.† Even more crucial was the fact that Germany possessed in Willi Münzenberg a genius without rival in the creation and manipulation of front-organizations. Born in 1889, the son of a drunken and brutal innkeeper, Münzenberg was orphaned at the age of thirteen. He became a barber's assistant, worked in a shoe factory, and in 1910

---

* Including Barbusse, Georg Brandes, Georges Duhamel, Anatole France, Charles Gide, Thomas Hardy, Vincente Blasco Ibanez, Andreas Latzko, Laurent Tailhade, E. D. Morel, Edmond Picard, Jules Romains, René Schickele, Séverine, Upton Sinclair, P. Vaillant-Couturier, H. G. Wells, Israel Zangwill, Stefan Zweig and others.

† The PCF reached its nadir in the early thirties. In the 1932 elections only ten communist deputies, supported by 774,000 votes, were elected. Party membership was little more than 20,000. Yet by the same period, 1932, the KPD had a membership of about 300,000, electoral support of six million, and had become the third largest party in the Reichstag with about 100 deputies.

moved to Zurich as a chemist's assistant. Attracted by anarchism, self-taught and avid for knowledge, he devoured the works of Kropotkin, Bakunin, Ibsen and Strindberg, as well as Marx, Engels and Mehring. Finding himself in Germany at the outbreak of war, he advocated a general strike and then made good his escape to Switzerland, where he had the benefit of sharing his exile with Lenin's circle. He became a Leninist and the editor of *Jugend-Internationale*. In November 1918 the Swiss authorities deported him just in time to take part in the Spartacist rising led by Luxemburg and Liebknecht. But Münzenberg's theatre of action on that occasion was Stuttgart not Berlin. As a result of this escapade he was imprisoned for five months. No sooner had he emerged than he became chairman of the Württemberg KPD. Displaying his genius for organization, he convened an international youth congress in Berlin and helped to set up the Communist Youth International. In time he was to become a member of the Party's Central Committee and also a deputy in the Reichstag, where he studiously avoided the limelight. He preferred power to fame – but never power for its own sake.

The world movement he sincerely believed in. If he sometimes flattered to deceive it was in a good cause, the most important of all crusades. The number of successful front-organizations he launched in rapid succession was prodigious. To rival the Hoover Relief Administration, he set up the International Workers' Relief (IAH), known as Red Aid, with Albert Einstein and the artists Käthe Kollwitz and George Grosz as charter members. The successful novelist Leonhard Frank as well as the fellow-travellers Holitscher and Goldschmidt were roped in. Sponsors (vital on the notepaper) included Anatole France, Barbusse, Shaw and Martin Anderson-Nexö. Not bad for a start. Nor was Münzenberg a man to adhere obsessively to original aims. By 1931, when the Russian famine had long since been forgotten, Red Aid claimed one hundred and five thousand members in Germany, had supported strikes in Shanghai and Canton and given assistance to the British General Strike, besides drumming up support for Sacco and Vanzetti and arranging international appeals on behalf of the imprisoned Hungarian communist Rákosi. It also organized evenings of Soviet films, rallies and other public events which attracted a total audience of one million in the year 1930. There were IAH–sponsored poetry and cabaret evenings with personal appearances by the director Erwin Piscator and the writer Erich Weinert, as well as art exhibitions featuring the work of Kollwitz, Grosz and Otto Dix. Out of Willi's hat came "Kolonne Links" and other agitprop troupes modelled on the Soviet "Blue Blouses" whom Münzenberg, of course, had brought to Germany. He could quickly conjure a script from the pen of the communist Brecht or the democrat Tucholsky with equal felicity.

He ran a string of newspapers. The circulation of his *Welt am Abend* had reached two hundred and twenty-nine thousand by 1931. The Austrian fellow-traveller Bruno Frei edited his *Berlin am Morgen.* Another of his journals sponsored by International Workers' Relief, *Arbeiter Illustrierte Zeitung*, enjoyed a circulation of one million: nor was it filled with turgid propaganda and dry Party rhetoric. To marshal collaborators he excavated the breadth and depth of the German Left: communist writers of real talent like Friedrich Wolf, Kisch, Anna Seghers, Wieland Herzfelde, Ludwig Renn, Kurt Kersten and Johannes Becher; fellow-travellers such as Toller, Béla Baláczs, Holitscher and Heinz Pol; radical democrats like Tucholsky and Walter Hasenclever and the occasional odd-ball anarchist like Mühsam. They all trusted him, and they had no reason not to. They all needed to be taken out of themselves, to be reassured of their relevance to the workers and to be paraded on a wider stage. He taught them the facts of political life and they liked it. Sometimes they were a little baffled, for he had no peer in his grasp of the fellow-travelling utility principle. Thus Heinz Pol was somewhat surprised to be offered a job on one of Münzenberg's enterprises on condition that he did *not* succumb to his growing inclination to join the Party. Willi used kings as pawns and made pawns feel like kings.

He went into the film business in a big way. In this sphere, as in all others, he proved his financial genius. He demonstrated that if communism could not smash capitalism in an afternoon, it could at least make money while it was trying. His was the directing influence behind the Meschrabpon-Filmgesellschaft, which employed four hundred people in its main studios in Moscow and sponsored such classics as *The End of St Petersburg, Mother, The Road to Life* and *Storm over Asia.* For such films the Prometheus-Filmgesellschaft acted as sole distributing agent in Germany: director, Willi Münzenberg. It remained only to get people to see these films, and not merely in the art cinemas. Accordingly he launched the popular Volksverband für Filmkunst, enlisting as sponsors Heinrich Mann, Piscator, W. G. Pabst and Karl Freund.

Part of the secret was his amzing independence of local Party control. In the very years when the Party and its main literary organ, *Linkskurve,* were blasting away at the cohorts of "social-fascism", Münzenberg was simultaneously building bridges, coaxing, cajoling and generally making allies of the same "social-fascists". This the Party tacitly permitted. Besides, he had powerful patrons in Moscow. He wore two masks. In his rare appearances as a politician, he rigorously toed the Party line. Thus in February 1932 he wrote in *Rote Aufbau* that Trotsky's proposal for an alliance between the KPD and the SPD was nothing short of criminal. Yet at the same moment he was engineering an even broader alliance in the shape of the International League against War and Fascism. He was an alert, sympathetic and immensely likeable man, and even his more machiavellian exploits had a charm and audacity which inspired affection.*

Of Münzenberg, his further activities in exile and sad end we shall hear more later.

But all this gallant activity was to no avail. Hitler came to power and the whole German democratic movement was smashed. At the very least Germany neeeded a Popular Front, but the mutual enmity of socialists and communists prevented the formation of even a united front. *Rote Fahne* continued to denounce the nazis and the social democrats in the same breath. The Comintern on Stalin's instructions had embarked on its suicidal "revolutionary" policy, and there would be no turning back until the lesson had been learned in blood. In October 1932 the KPD Party Conference blamed the SPD for preparing the way for the neo-fascist dictatorship of von Papen and von Schleicher. Thälmann, the communist leader, appealed to socialist workers to join ranks with their communist comrades, while insisting that no common action was possible with SPD leaders like Severing, Hilferding, Wels and Zörgiebel. Nor was this enmity generated by the communists alone. A socialist police chief was widely held responsible for the deaths of thirty-three demonstrating workers in 1929. The SPD never really abandoned the violently anti-communist attitude adopted by Ebert, Scheidemann and Noske in 1918–19. These were men who preferred a steel baron to a bolshevik. A slogan existed: "no enemies on the Left"; it sometimes seemed that their only enemies were on the Left.

Hitler became Chancellor in January 1933. On the night of 27 February the Reichstag burned and within hours thousands of communist officials and Reichstag deputies had been arrested. On 3 March the Gestapo caught Thälmann. Despite the terror waged by the nazi SA and SS, the communists won 12.3 per cent of the votes in the March elections. But the newly elected Reichstag never met. All parties except the nazis (NSAPD) were banned.

---

* Thus he alerted the left intellectuals to the fact that two "Swiss pacifists" had been arrested in Shanghai by Chiang Kai Shek's Government. Distributing a petition of protest, he soon got the signatures of Ossietzsky, Feuchtwanger, the respected drama critic Alfred Kerr, the architects Walter Gropius and Mies van der Rohe, the publisher Ernst Rowohlt, and the artist Paul Klee, as well as Theodore Dreiser and other distinguished foreigners. The two "Swiss pacifists" were duly released, the only disappointment being that they turned out to be a Ukrainian communist and his wife who had been working as Soviet intelligence agents in China.

For the German intellectuals, the spectrum of available choices had thus changed dramatically. Arrested, persecuted and uprooted from country, home and livelihood, they were compelled to think again. The Soviet Union became inevitably the principal beneficiary. The heroic age of fellow-travelling was about to begin; indeed for many French, American and British intellectuals it had already begun.

2

Conducted Tours

Approaching the era of the Five Year Plans we find the foreign image of Soviet Russia changing. During the NEP period (1921–8) a sympathizer could regard the USSR as a "workers' state", but the retention of large-scale private ownership scarcely permitted him to treat it as a fully socialist one. It is not surprising that during the twenties admiration was focused on the fringe benefits of socialism, on those aspects of social emancipation held dear by progressives since the time of Rousseau, Robert Owen and the Saint-Simonians. The emancipation of women in the Soviet Union attracted a good deal of favourable Western comment. Alexander Wicksteed, who had first gone there with Quaker famine relief and then stayed on for ten years as a teacher, admired nothing in the new Russia so much as the determination to free women from domestic drudgery with the help of day nurseries, kindergartens and summer camps. Toller was impressed by the free abortions and the public propaganda in favour of contraception. Dreiser was intrigued by the ease with which a Soviet couple could obtain a divorce; American divorces, he commented bitterly, were a racket. In Russia he found "the only sane treatment of the sex questions I have ever encountered".[1] Maurice Hindus pointed out that the mothers of illegitimate children suffered no social condemnation or ostracism. The romantic Waldo Frank concluded that women in Russia were women indeed, marching unafraid into the turmoil of public life and working beside men in the factories, yet remaining feminine and healthily lustful (as he put it). "Here in the Soviet Union the Strindbergian warfare of the sexes seems to have no meaning."[2]

In a sense Western observers in the 1920s were still asking pre-socialist questions, examining those aspects of communist policy most closely joined to the ideals of the bourgeois Enlightenment. The typical traveller's report during this first decade had chapter headings like these: Family, Religion, Women, Prostitution, Education, Prisons.

Educational policy generated the greatest excitement. It is surely the case that all communist states, while admittedly "indoctrinating" their children, have also shown a splendid care, regard and even love for their younger generations. Similarly, if the eradication of mass literacy is all you care about, then bring in a communist regime. In the terrible conditions of 1919 Arthur Ransome found more than one hundred and fifty thousand Moscow children getting free meals in school; felt boots were also distributed free to the young, when available. Even during the Civil War, Ransome noted, the number of libraries in Petrograd had almost doubled and the number in Moscow trebled. In Moscow educational institutes, not including schools, had increased from 369 to 1,357. A year later Brailsford was so impressed by the Soviet emphasis on education that he predicted for Russia (if given peace) the happiest and most cultivated younger generation in Europe within ten years. Holitscher found the children of even the poorest parents to be serene and privileged; villas, castles and palaces of the old empire had rapidly been transformed into children's homes, sanatoria and *Fröbelgärten*. As for food, he reported that the children got the lion's share of the available calories. Education was now free, obligatory, universal and co-educational. The relationship between pupil and teacher was being transformed into one of comradely respect. At the same time the polytechnic principle was eroding the compartmentalization of studies and integrating the natural with the technological sciences. Lunacharsky's work as Commissar for Public Instruction was widely admired in the West, as were the new principles of pedagogy elaborated by Krupskaya, Blonsky and others. Wicksteed, who lived in a large block of workers' dwellings with two hundred rooms housing one thousand people, reported that the children roamed the corridors, relaxed, carefree and self-assured, bursting open his door whenever they felt like it. Luckily he didn't mind. Obviously a man of saintly temperament, he regarded these rude intrusions as evidence that all complexes and repressions had been swept away. Toller found Soviet child-care impressive. Dreiser concluded that the Soviet Government was the first one to show genuine enthusiasm for the human mind as a creative instrument. Helene Stöcker, militant feminist, pacifist, social reformer, and the first woman in Germany to be awarded a university doctorate, strongly recommended Soviet educational policy as she saw it in the late twenties. As for those who had not seen for themselves, the statistics told their own story (as indeed they were intended to!). A hundred million had been taught to read and write, declared Upton Sinclair in 1938. Tens of millions of children from the lower classes had been sent to high schools and colleges: could this, he asked, be repression? (The monist outlook, the refusal to wrestle with the paradoxes of the balance sheet.) Feuchtwanger found Soviet educational achievements "wonderful", while Charles Vildrac contrasted the reduction of illiteracy in the USSR to two per cent (a highly unrealistic figure in 1937) with the situation prevailing in the Basses-Pyrénées, where apparently 49.5 per cent of the population remained illiterate. And André Chamson discovered in Russia "an extraordinary movement of spirits towards culture".

Only Gide struck a dissenting note. In July 1932 he had recorded in his *Journal*: "I admire nothing so much in the USSR as the organization of leisure, of education, of culture."[3] On his return from Russia in 1936 he did not entirely renounce this view, but he pointed out that the Government order in February to liquidate illiteracy among four million workers would have seemed more admirable had the same order not been made in 1923, with a four-year deadline for its accomplishment. He thought that Soviet teachers were poorly paid and that the curriculum in schools was solely designed to glorify the Soviet system. About this he was both unperceptive and ungenerous.

Education brings culture and culture demands leisure. Inspecting the scene just before the first Five Year Plan, Dreiser was impressed by the recreational facilities provided for workers. Bernard Shaw equated leisure with "the only freedom that Nature allows us", and emphasized that the Russians now enjoyed not only full employment and social security, but also shorter working hours than those prevailing in the West, leaving the workers free to pursue creative activities. (Shaw was mistaken: the forty-hour week was a French not a Soviet innovation.) What particularly delighted Western visitors, but also partially misled them, was that new Soviet sportsgrounds, educational institutes, recreation rooms, libraries, kindergartens, crèches, and even some theatres and hospitals, were attached to factories and other productive units, thus offering the hope of a more organic, integrated life; a life less "alienated". They were misled because, finding these admirable facilities invariably full, they concluded that the ratio of free time to working time was superior in Russia to the West.

Friendly Western visitors discovered something of the mood celebrated in Vertov's film, *Enthusiasm*. When the capitalist states hit the great crash of 1929, leaving their working class standing in long, disconsolate dole queues or lingering on street corners, hands in pockets, in a trough of enforced idleness and despair, then the euphoria on the surface at least of Soviet life became all the more irresistible. On leaving the Hotel Metropole, Shaw wrote in the visitors' book: "Tomorrow I leave this land of hope and return to our Western countries of despair."[4] Dreiser had already noticed the absence of jobbery, corruption, sales deception and phoney lawyers. (No doubt he hadn't seen or read Mayakovsky's *Bedbug*.) "No summer sales of lots that in winter are under water!"[5] The old left-idealist impulse to change "human nature" by environmental engineering swelled and burst in the breasts of Rousseau's heirs. "Russia is beginning to live bravely and smile," wrote Lincoln Steffens. "Russia proves that you can change human nature sufficiently in one generation. . . . These kids despise a business man. . . . Service for profit is a sham. . . . I believe they will make a race, the meanest of which will be as noble as the best men of our day."[6]

The gentle, vital, penetrating Waldo Frank avoided hyperbole. He was an impressionist not an expressionist, and he had discovered beauty in bullfighting, he had loved Zion, he was catholic by temperament, and he came to Russia in 1932. Finding himself almost the only passenger on the Leningrad express, he took a stroll along the platform during a halt at Rayayoki: "I smile up at the engineer, the first lord I have seen of the new kingdom of labour."[7] An image as nice as the man. He wanted to find the poor inheriting the earth, their earth, and he did; gone were the smart, successful people and their servants of the old Petersburg and of modern Paris, Madrid and Berlin. "What a joy. . . ." He had known John Reed in 1917 and they had not seen eye to eye, even though Frank published in that year his poem, "Holy Russia". Then his trips to Spain and Latin America had convinced him that the US had squandered its spiritual substance, and he went in search of that substance in Russia and found there a "deep potential energy" and also a boat on the Volga named after John Reed and his heart was bound to melt. Finding himself in an organic and natural community, he decided that the workers here, the actual rulers, were creating a cultural movement more fundamental than any since Christianity began. Certainly he hadn't found the "joyless experiment in force and fear" which greeted E. E. Cummings the previous year, but Evelyn Waugh still had to wish Frank wouldn't consider himself God's spy armed "with the lazy eye of intuition", and indulge himself in so many "pseudo-intimate personal emotions".

Julian Huxley was a biologist and therefore generally immune to both God and intuition, but the scientific visitors proved no less susceptible to the atmosphere of energy and optimism than their literary brethren. His hosts took him to a Moscow bathing park where the bathers were stripped down to the nude. All of them, he noted, were deeply bronzed by the sun and of a very fine physique. Maurice Hindus also confirmed that Russia's sports-loving young were in superb physical shape. But moral health was the main thing, the "great cry" of spiritual leadership that Gide heard from the East, the "great free road on firm soil" along which Charles Vildrac discovered "a whole people audaciously advancing".[8] Luc Durtain summed it up: "Yes, the statistics are fine! The density of matter created is splendid. . . . But the most beautiful achievement of the USSR is still the quality of its new men."[9] Harold Laski was scarcely less guarded in his enthusiasm: "There has been more realization of personality under the Soviet regime," he told *The Nation* in July 1934, "than any comparable epoch of history." In Russia he found "a buoyant and optimistic faith I have never before encountered".[10] Given such idyllic conditions, even a little purge could have its charm. The Webbs published a cheerful account (on hearsay) of a "cleansing" operation in a Moscow factory, apparently quite similar to those of the recent Chinese Cultural Revolution. And Edmund Wilson reported that in the USSR one felt at the "moral top of the world where the light never really goes out".[11] Sean O'Casey expressed himself no less euphorically: "Red Mirror of Wisdom, turning the labour in factory, field and workshop into the dignity of a fine song. . . . Herald of a new life, of true endeavour, of common-sense, of a world's peace, of man's ascent, of things to do bettering all things done. . . ."[12]

We now come to the era of the Five Year Plans, the time when the Soviet Union acquired its "constructive, scientific" image and began to accumulate fellow-travelling support in major proportions. The transmission belt from enthusiasm to heroic construction was *work*; and for manual labour, regenerated from its distorted form as capitalist wage-slavery, the progressive middle classes with their white, uncalloused hands felt a profound respect verging on awe. The Soviet shock brigades were cheered as symbols of the proletarian vanguard embracing a new ethic of co-operative endeavour. Work, as Stalin had said, had become "a matter of honour". The names of Stakhanov, the exemplary Donetz miner, of the sisters Vinogradova, the exemplary textile workers, and of Marie Demtchenko, the exemplary kolkhoz farm worker, were widely celebrated. Shaw recalled meeting a Stakhanovite worker who was immensely popular with his comrades, whereas, said Shaw, in England he would have had a brick on his head. (But in fact many Stakhanovite workers did suffer "accidents" and on this issue the fellow-travellers were both gullible and unreflective.) Having decided that it was good for Russia if the workers performed overtime for free, they sensibly adjusted the outlook of the Soviet workers to conform with their own. The Reverend Harry F. Ward, a leading American fellow-traveller, explained that free overtime was inspired by idealism, the spirit of "socialist emulation", and also by the admirable Soviet practice of posting up on workshop walls the names of drunkards, shirkers and perennial absentees. This was a *planned* change of attitudes. Ward was one of those who fed ravenously on anecdotes; they lent the flow of production statistics a human touch. So he related how a Soviet team, given the task of assembling the parts of an American locomotive, were expected by their

American supervisor to take forty-eight hours to complete the job. Finally they did it in eighteen. Ward also carried back to his transatlantic readers lengthy quotations from the "Appeal of the Tala Plant No. 1 to All the Workers of the USSR, to all the Kolkhozes".[13] But a distinguished biologist was as easily taken in as a clergyman. "Late one evening," Julian Huxley remembered, "as we passed this corner, we saw a gang of people working at the lines by the light of flares. . . . They were a volunteer gang, a *Subotnik* . . . who, having been told of the urgent job that needed doing, had come down after their own day's work was over to get it done – and, of course, without extra pay." However, one need not conclude from this that the working class was being especially imposed upon: ". . . one is told that Stalin himself sometimes comes down to the Moscow goods sidings to help."[14] Like hell, he came.

A stream of statistics burst upon the Western public. Raymond Aron has written : "No one can observe any connection between economico-technical development and the system of ownership."[15] This is by no means universally true. Feudalism obviously retarded or bottled up certain forms of economic development, whereas capitalist ownership accelerated them. Different social priorities based on differing systems of ownership create different patterns of research, investment and development. But Aron's statement, exaggerated as it is, draws one's attention to the opposite myth: that rapid Russian industrialization (or the victory over Germany or putting the first man into space) was somehow not only a "victory" for socialism, which is arguable, but represented the very essence of socialism. "Socialism works." The Western intelligentsia easily lost their heads over this, although at a time of capitalist crisis and depression it was easy to do so. Ludwig Marcuse refused to inspect a Soviet car factory for the excellent reason that he had never inspected one in Paris, Berlin or London, that he had no knowledge of the manufacture of automobiles, and that he couldn't care less. But he was an exception. Freda Utley, who lived in Russia in the early 1930s, put it well : "Communists and fellow-travellers, many of whom had never seen the inside of a factory or power station, journalists and authors, school teachers and 'intellectuals' of all kinds, came on conducted tours of the Soviet Union and worshipped before the shrine of the machine."[16]

Statistics were the sacred digits of socialism. Maurice Hindus rolled off the statistics for cars, tractors, locomotives, shoes, soap, coal, oil, pig-iron, and rolled steel. The British scientist J. G. Crowther did the same. The Webbs had an unrivalled passion for facts and figures. Here they report on Soviet State Insurance: "horses, camels, asses, mules, hinnies and reindeer from one year up, and pedigreed stock from six months up, against death . . . hunting and fishing boats against elemental destruction...."[17] (They omitted to mention that life insurance was quite unobtainable for human beings at this time; it just didn't pay.) The Webbs and their kind were capable of celebrating the birth of the industrial revolution in urban Russia one hundred and fifty years late, or the arrival of the wheel in rural Russia millennia late, as if man under their very eyes was throwing off the ape. Finally tiring of enumerating blast furnaces measured in cubic feet, they warmly recommended to the alert reader the three hundred pages of statistics contained in *Summary of the Fulfilment of the First Five Year Plan,* published by Gosplan, in English. Factories, percentages, machinery, tractors poured from the pens of Louis Fischer, Anna Louise Strong, Walter Duranty, Sherwood Eddy, John Strachey, Ella Winter, Harry F. Ward and many others. And twenty years later, in the early fifties, Corliss Lamont was still rattling off schools, electric power kilowatts per year, acres under cultivation, trees planted, canals. "The fish catch increased by 27 per cent." Did it? How do you know? "Baby foods went up 5.7 times above the pre-war level and vitamins 10.4 times." Collective farms, cement, weapons of war; lists of plans and norms exceeded ahead of time. New film clubs, amateur theatres, choral groups, cross-country runners, laboratories...."[18]

So to the plans themselves. "The success of the Five Year Plan is the only hope of the world," said Bernard Shaw.[19] "But above all I should like to live long enough to see Russia's Plan succeed and the States of Europe obliged to accept what they insisted on ignoring.... My whole heart applauds that gigantic and yet entirely human undertaking," said André Gide.[20] The plans, said Julian Huxley, expressed "a new spirit, the spirit of science introduced into politics and industry", the spirit of a coherently planned society, unlike Topsy and the out-of-hand individualism of the West, which simply "jest growed" (sic). For Stephen Spender the plans were instruments for creating a new civilization. Louis Fischer recalled after his many years in Russia that with the onset of the plans, "the communists did not spare themselves any more than they spared others. They neglected their health and families. They behaved as they would at the front." Everyone in the Soviet Union had felt "inspired in the presence of this spectacle of creation and self-sacrifice. I too was swept away by it.... A whole nation marched behind a vision."[21]

It was irresistible, even for hardened sceptics like Shaw. Letting rip during a BBC broadcast in October 1931, he declared: "Russia flaunts her budget surplus of 750 millions, her people employed to the last man and woman, her scientific agriculture doubling and trebling her harvest, her roaring and multiplying factories, her efficient rulers, her atmosphere of such hope and security for the poorest as has never before been seen in a civilized country on earth."²² A favourable view, one might think. But the context was – it cannot be over-emphasized – the factor which turned vegetarians into meat-eaters. For the Great Depression merely brought to a climax years, decades of disillusionment and disgust. The Enlightenment, having been betrayed and deformed in its own Western cradle, was now reborn on virgin soil. "In the abominable distress of the present world," said Gide, "new Russia's Plans seem to me salvation . . . the miserable arguments of its enemies, far from convincing me, make my blood boil."²³ He wanted to "cry aloud my affection for Russia: and that my cry should be heard, should have some importance." (It was, and did.) He confessed himself to be bending over distant Russia with a passionate curiosity, driven by his craving for scientific truth. Alone in his study, cushioned by a life of wealth and ease, he permitted himself the wetter sort of dream: "And if my life was necessary to ensure the success of the USSR, I should give it, at once. . . ."²⁴ (After all, so many millions of Russians were doing no more than that.)

Confronted with a plan which was driving the bourgeoisie "to desperation", Professor Jean Guéhenno, whose self-confessed petit-bourgeois, "Girondin" scruples had held him back in the twenties, now took the leap. In a planned, secure society the hated acquisitive impulses would disappear; he permitted himself the thought that perhaps human nature *had not yet changed completely* in Russia. But it would. The fellow-travellers who needed and demanded materially comfortable lives in the West were sure that this cursed human nature would in Russia shed every reflex of greed and gain . . . on *their* behalf. They scarcely noticed that the principle of voluntary labour symbolized by the shock brigades and by Stalin's overtime in the railway yards, had been overshadowed by an enormous increase in wage differentials. One who did notice this, and was courageous enough to remark on it, was the French sociologist Georges Friedmann. He recalled the fatal journey of the young communist idealist Raymond Léfèbvre to Russia in 1920 as having represented "a pilgrimage" on behalf of a circle of friends. After that Friedmann had passed through a phase of "sentimental adherence" before arriving at "a more conscious, rational" and inquiring approach. Between 1932 and 1936 he visited Russia three times and found much to recommend itself. But he also noticed falling living standards, rising prices, depressed wages and a shortage of basic consumer goods. He discovered that wage differentials favoured specialists, technicians and intellectuals to such an extent that working-class resentment was now widespread. He made bold to suggest that the excessive material rewards enjoyed by successful Soviet writers, generally hailed by sympathizers as proof of the high premium put on culture in the USSR, were scarcely compatible with ridding human nature of its acquisitive impulse. Friedmann became unpopular; he had committed heresy; his communist friends ostracized him.

Could he be wrong? Could he be guilty of what Gide called the "abominable deceit" of those who spoke of failures and even mass deaths? Alexander Wicksteed who, unlike most fellow-travellers, was prepared to live in the country he most admired, was quite frank about living conditions. Town housing was appalling and possibly eighty per cent of Moscow people were seriously tuberculous, according to a Soviet doctor he knew. Clothing was shoddy and scarce, and rationing more severe than had been promised in 1928. He had shown some Russian teachers Fenner Brockway's *Hungry England*; they concluded that the starving English were well off. Possibly the plans had pushed things too fast. On the other hand circumstances were hostile; the USSR was hit by lower prices on the world market (a bad argument since imported plant and machines were also cheaper), and, besides, seeking the kingdom of God was not an easy business. The transfer of one million peasants a year to the towns seemed to him a miracle.

One of the most widely-read and influential of pro-Soviet writers, Maurice Hindus,* was also fairly candid about economic set-backs. Himself born in Russia, and one of many American first- or second-generation Jewish immigrants from Eastern Europe who championed the Soviet cause, he listed the following negative consequences of the plan: food shortages, livestock depletion, mounting police severity, the deportation of whole Cossack communities, the constant uprooting of families, and the introduction of workers' passports. The economic schedule had failed in many respects. Nevertheless he felt it was all worth it – in order to remould civilization and produce a classless society. But worth it, to paraphrase Lenin again, *for whom*? Ludwig Marcuse's answer was simple: "The successful history of the plans," he wrote, "represents the sad history of the planned."[25] And he concluded that Marx had been in error to assume that capitalism represented the last historical form of exploitation, an error in whose name millions had been sacrificed. (Whether it was Marx's influence which prompted the error is doubtful.) Marcuse was one of those travellers for whom the god failed very promptly on arrival. He set out for Russia in 1936 in the company of Lion Feuchtwanger, but before leaving he had been told by Joseph Roth in Vienna that he was about to travel with God into hell. Marcuse didn't understand; the only hell he recognized was the nazi one which had driven him from Germany. At the frontier their train was delayed

* His popular books included *Humanity Uprooted, Red Bread, Broken Earth*, and *The Great Offensive*. Hindus broke with the Soviet Union after 1939.

while an excited customs official examined, or attempted to, a thousand-page manuscript about Richard Wagner – written in German. "We were in intellectual quarantine." From then on it was all downhill for the biographer of Heine, Strindberg, Freud and Ignatius Loyola.

Such cases were rare. Sidney and Beatrice Webb were intoxicated by the plans, and where excuses had to be made they made them. "There are ends more important than additional food supplies for immediate consumption"[26] – a sentence worth re-reading. National defence, for example; a somewhat Churchillian perspective, and one never canvassed by the hungry. The Webbs were excellent examples of the type which prefers mankind to people; which originally intends to sacrifice a few to save everyone and ends by sacrificing everyone to save a few.

In 1931 F. C. Weiskopf and Ernst Glaeser* published a book of photographs entitled *Der Staat ohne Arbeitslose* (The State without Unemployment) whose illustrations recapture for the contemporary reader the image of the USSR projected abroad at that time; an image widely accepted of a world reborn, healthy, buoyant, efficient, busy, cohesive, manifold: a smiling, healthy peasant girl from White Russia wears a patterned kerchief and is clutching a sheaf of corn; a herdsman of the Altai mountains, old and wizened, but smiling too; new dams; the construction of the Dnieprostroi Power Plant; oil-boring derricks near Baku; a refining plant; blast furnaces; smiling coal miners; a hand-some metal worker, leader of a shock brigade (the photographer had obviously fallen on one if not both knees for the shot); tractors at work; road construction; a shipyard; a conveyor belt at the Stalingrad tractor works; a wall chart showing the spirit of socialist competition; a club house for Moscow rubber workers; the fight against illiteracy; young pioneers demonstrate; a girl swimmer (caption: communism is not a menace to beauty); a march through Red Square; workers waving from a departing train (caption: back to work!); old-style rural hovels con-trasted with the new dwellings on a collective farm; babies in a crèche, their mothers marching to the fields in the background; Red Army men, smiling; women squeezing breasts at a collective station for mothers' milk. . . .

It has been said that the fetishism of the plan now replaced the capital-ist fetishism of the commodity. One important thing to remember is that there was a genuinely stirring reality behind these photographs, that Russia under Stalin was indeed once again on the move, that the

* Weiskopf was a communist who settled in Moscow after Hitler came to power. Glaeser was a left-wing socialist and the author of the successful novel, *Jahrgang 1902* (1928). In 1933 the nazis burned his books but in 1939 he returned to Germany and became editor of an army newspaper.

economic foundations for a higher standard of living were being laid, and that the poorer classes, driven into the mud for centuries, were at last being offered the vista of a better deal. The welfare state in Russia was an emerging reality and the Soviet medical system, with its comprehensive social security, is one to be genuinely admired. If Clement Attlee and Hugh Dalton could admire Russia's productive vitality during the era of the plans, we certainly have no cause to sneer. The fellow-travellers were entitled to admire and praise these often heroic achievements. But there were other things they refused to see or, alternatively, insisted on blandly condoning. It happened to be the case that in 1928–9, after the defeat of Tomsky and the Right, the Soviet trade unions were stripped of all wage-bargaining powers. And to put a halt to labour instability caused by constant migration in search of better jobs or living conditions, a system of internal passports was established in 1932. "Deserters" were henceforward deprived of ration cards and the right to claim living quarters. Economic and social life was militarized. How, then, could General William N. Haskell announce in 1930 that the worker's voice was the controlling factor in Soviet industry and politics? How could Congressman Henry T. Rainey, of Illinois, insist the following year that the labour force in the USSR was freer than in any country in the world? How could Ella Winter argue in 1933 that the Soviet worker, fully conversant with the process of manufacture, participated fully in determining industrial policy? The answer lay partly in double-think; on the one hand, as Hewlett Johnson said, there was no anti-strike law on the statute books, so presumably the workers could strike with impunity; on the other hand, "there is no combatant to fight and no point in striking".[27]

Those celebrated historians of British trade unionism, Sidney and Beatrice Webb, were not the least perturbed by the eradication of the Soviet workers' already fragile bargaining rights. On the contrary, they expressed contempt for Soviet trade unionists who failed to grasp that with the end of the NEP and the launching of the plans unreasonable wage demands could only subvert economic expansion and the development of the social services: "it was not for such an anarchic scramble after wages that Lenin had restored trade union independence."[28] There really was, they claimed, much more collective bargaining in Russia than in the West – but no longer between hostile parties. Apparently the plan provided job opportunities but nothing and nobody dictated to Ivan or Nikolai the job he should take. Really? In the course of a comprehensive survey covering more than a thousand pages, the Webbs accorded the internal passport system a single footnote! They simply recorded in small print that the issue of these passports had been entrusted to the GPU and the militia. Orwell called this serfdom; the Webbs didn't call it anything. The point was, you understand, that in the USSR "the management has no pecuniary inducement to 'cut' the rates!"[29] (The exclamation mark is the Webbs' own.) While admitting that Soviet trade union meetings were now mainly taken up by exhortatory speeches by managers and party bosses, and that decisions were invariably unanimous, they concluded that this was no bad way of arousing that "consciousness of consent" so necessary to effective democracy. Having observed the reality, they then superimposed on it the blueprint theory, observing that in the unions "the stream of power may be said to pass from the 186,640 factory and local committees . . . right up to . . . the single central committee representing them all. . . ."[30] Thus: we workers authorize you to tell us what to do and to override all our objections which in any case we shall refrain from expressing. The Dictatorship of the Pedagogues.

What were the real short-term effects of enforced collectivization? The myth of voluntary collectivization can easily be exploded; only in certain areas of Spain, where the anarchist-communist tradition ran deep, did it occur. Lenin's original analysis had been that the first or bourgeois revolution, aimed at the great landowners, would soon be followed by an intensification of the class struggle between the wealthy "*kulak*" farmers on the one hand, and the small peasants and landless labourers on the other. These sharpening tensions would therefore lead to a natural, organic socialist revolution in the countryside. It is true that the *kulaks* were widely detested; but they were also envied; the historical ambition of the poor East European peasant was always to acquire more private property of his own. Collectivization was bound to appear to him as yet another episode in the endless curse of fraudulent robbery from above. "What little we have they want to take away." Consequently the decision to collectivize was followed of necessity by an immense enlargement of the role of the police and the GPU, by the seizure of livestock and by the deportation not only of *kulaks* but of whole peasant communities. The desperate, bewildered peasants responded with acts of sabotage, neglecting their land and slaughtering their livestock. The scale of the disaster was reflected in the fact that by 1938, 7 per cent of all cows, 66 per cent of pigs and about the same proportion of sheep had again been restored to private ownership.[31]

Anna Louise Strong reported from Russia that the *kulaks* had resisted and some of the "middle peasants" had wavered. Then, lured by the provision of state-supplied machinery and subsidies, the great mass of peasants had moved "like an avalanche" into the collective farms. She also propagated the myth that in launching the whole operation Stalin had simply responded to the will of the peasants. Wicksteed, too, had no patience with *kulaks*; the bolsheviks could either socialize agriculture or go under. (True: but the question at issue was the method and the pace.) As for the sufferings involved, Wicksteed was quick to remind his readers of the degradations inflicted on English agricultural workers in the era of enclosures and forced expropriations. For Maurice Hindus collectivization was a fine thing, eliminating waste in seed resources and labour and putting an end to the ruinous parcelling of the land into small strips. Scientific management would now increase fertility. Harry F. Ward concluded after a conducted tour that the whole enterprise had been precipitated by the poor peasants' drive for socialism. Surveying the scene from a distance, Lincoln Steffens announced in 1930 that successful collectivization proved that labour can and will work without a profit motive. André Gide, a hyper-individualist who refused to sign any manifesto he had not himself written, rejoiced that the bolsheviks were crushing that pernicious peasant individualism which was a caricature of genuine individuality, just as superstition was a caricature of authentic religious feeling. "I believe that the more particular the individual, the more gripping the delight he takes in being suddenly absorbed into the mass and losing his identity."[32] Coming from Gide, this was revolting hypocrisy: passages in his *Journal* suggest that the whole Soviet enterprise represented to him a transferred masochistic fantasy. He did hear that minor set-backs and dislocations had occurred, but a speech by Stalin in June 1931 was enough to set his mind at rest.

According to the scientist Joseph Needham, collectivization was inevitable if only because advanced life is essentially order and organization. G. D. H. Cole could think of no other way to socialize the minds of the peasants. John Lehmann wrote to *Left Review* from Tiflis in 1936 with the news that the plans had done the trick everywhere and that collectivization was an enormous success. In March of the same year Pearl Binder reported: "It is collectivization which has finally conquered the food problem; the bounteous results cram the foodshops of the entire Soviet Union – delegations of peasants from the Ukraine, Uzbekistan ... come to Moscow to tell how much better off they are than before...."[33] Feuchtwanger, carried from one paid-up feast to another, concluded: "It is the peasants who are most deeply conscious of the difference between the wretched past and the happy present.... They never tire of illustrating the contrast."[34] But those who happened to be ordinary Russian people, who hunted for food, who saw the chaos at provincial railway stations, had another story. "Collectivization," wrote Nadezhda Mandelstam, "had uprooted vast hordes of people and they were roaming the country, desperately searching for somewhere to live and still sighing for their boarded-up huts."[35]

Famine? Mass deportations? Killings? In her reports of 1932 and 1933 Anna Louise Strong obliterated these non-facts. But two years later, when the worst was over, her version was modified: it was now safe for the Western public to learn a little more of the truth. She had complained to Borodin that Russia was not telling the world about the great hunger (nor was she), but in any case she knew who was responsible: inefficient peasants, sabotaging *kulaks*, stupid officials – everyone except the Party leaders. Hindus was more frank. He admitted widespread distress in the Ukraine and reported interviewing farmers who regarded collectivization as a catastrophe. Short of fodder, they had seen their produce snatched from their hands. Hindus went so far as to call the liquidation of the *kulaks* a human tragedy: cast out of their homes and packed into freight cars bound for the north, he had heard their desperate cries. But he declined to speculate about their subsequent deaths. Spender speculated a bit, regretting that press censorship made it impossible to accept the official Soviet version unreservedly; in his view the fate of the *kulaks* was "shrouded in obscurity". The Webbs respected Hindus, as well they might. When *he* provided first-hand reports from disaster areas they could not be dismissed as capitalist lies. So Sidney and Beatrice wrestled with the problem. They admitted that sixty million animals had been slaughtered in 1929–30, a quarter of the total, and that in the years 1931–3 eighty million more had gone the same way. Yes, grain storage plans in the Ukraine had failed and whole tracts of land had remained unsown. So what was the scale of the disaster? One could not know. But one could know that the figures had been greatly exaggerated. Had not Sherwood Eddy's travels convinced him of this? (Eddy's frequent journeys did have that tendency.) Maybe, concluded the Webbs with laudable scientific caution, these *partial* crop failures had affected one tenth of the Ukraine. Even so, causes had to be sought and the blame attributed. Had not Ukrainian anti-Soviet nationalist exiles claimed credit for the sabotage? Well, one had to admit that some kind of general strike by the peasantry had indeed occurred, but, concluded the old Fabians, when a class of peasants sabotaged or resisted they had to be dealt with.

Dealt with? After all, commented Upton Sinclair in 1938, killing is a Russian tradition. As for the reported famine, facts reaching him in California indicated that five million deaths was too high an estimate; he would settle for a million. If that seemed a lot, well, the peasants over there were ignorant and brutalized, there was no other way to deal with them, particularly when you considered that there would never again be famine in Russia and that "hundreds of millions" of lives would be saved.

No doubt the *kulaks* were indeed avaricious, cunning, exploitative and ready to hold the market to ransom. But, unlike the earlier aristocratic landowners, they were the creatures of a system which they did not create and could not control. "Rich" they may have been by local standards, but scarcely so when compared to Gide, the Webbs or Upton Sinclair. Compounded with the socialist ardour of these fellow-travellers there was also disdain, snobbery and the abstract cruelty of architects of the future. Of the Webbs this might be expected, yet Sinclair was the author of a harrowing depiction of human misery in the Chicago meat-packing yards, *The Jungle*. But now, years later and at a great geographical distance, he could no longer visualize people, only statistics and sweeping perspectives. Anna Louise Strong was of a different breed. She eschewed comfort and she saw a lot; her warm breast was often troubled.

She was born in 1885 in Friend, Nebraska, the daughter of a congregationalist minister. Having graduated from Oberlin College in 1905, she became the first woman to receive a doctorate from the University of Chicago, on the strength of a thesis entitled "The Psychology of Prayer". A large, strong-framed, blue-eyed evangelist, she threw herself into the Seattle labour movement. Then in 1922 she travelled to Russia by way of Poland on behalf of Quaker famine relief – the great adventure of her life was dawning. With leaping heart she first saw the caps of railway workers bearing, appropriately, the crossed hammer and monkey wrench. But life was not easy. Nursing two wagons of food from Moscow to Samara, she endured interminable delays while the train waited for engine repairs, the cutting of wood fuel and the passage of refugee trains even more broken down than her own. In five days she covered one hundred miles. But she was undismayed, her religious impulse carried her through: "This power, I saw rather mystically, as a Common Consciousness coming into being to plan the future of mankind."[36]

Her energy was prodigious. Time and again she travelled from Russia to America to China and back again, meeting Borodin, the Comintern agent, in revolutionary China, drumming up interest about Russia among American businessmen, squeezing investment plans out of industrialists and bankers, hurrying from Dreiser to Steffens and then on to Sinclair Lewis with cheering reports and requests for articles. She edited *Moscow News*, an English-language paper aimed principally at American engineers, specialists and miners working in the USSR, and this involved her in a long struggle with the bureaucrats. But she was tenacious. In 1932 she married a Russian agronomist, Joel Shubin, but he died ten years later and they had no children. He once asked her if she was at last preparing to join the Party: "I nodded, but at once panic seized me, as it always did when I approached ultimate decision." She was in fact one of nature's fellow-travellers, a woman who had fallen in love with the biggest Sunday School of them all. Eugene Lyons, at one time a correspondent in Moscow but later a violent anti-communist, said of Anna Louise Strong: "I recall days when she sat in my office, on returning from a trip outside Moscow, in a condition of near spiritual collapse . . . the poor blundering revolution needed her mothering and understanding. . . . Her whole emotional life was invested in this Russia."[87]

Eventually, as the result of an unfortunate incident, these emotions had to be re-invested in communist China. In the winter of 1948-9 she applied rather too tenaciously for a journalist's pass into Manchuria, at that time a highly sensitive area. During the night of 4 February 1949 three GPU agents burst into her hotel room and carried her away to the Lubianka prison where she was interrogated for five days. She was petrified: when they examined her medically she imagined they were estimating how much she could take; evidently her subconscious had taken note of those tales of GPU terror and torture which her public conscious had derided. Then they carried her by plane, car and jeep to the Polish border and simply chucked her out at a broken-down bridge spanning a lonely river. She was promptly denounced by Soviet radio as a notorious spy. Fortunately she had retained her American passport – one never knows. She had also contrived over the years to write not only for the American labour and radical press but also, more profitably, for Hearst's International News Service and other capitalist concerns. So now she told all – this monstrous indignity – in the *New York Herald Tribune*. Comrade fellow-travellers in the United States like Corliss Lamont felt this was really going too far and wrote protesting to the Soviet Ambassador. They received no reply, but in 1955 the Soviet Government officially "exonerated" Miss Anna Louise Strong.

Fascist leadership, explained Joseph Needham, comes from above. Communist leadership comes from within. On 14 August 1939 some four hundred Americans* signed an Open Letter denouncing "the

---

* Signatories included the clergymen Harry F. Ward, the Rev. Otis G. Jackson, and the Rev. Thomas L. Harris; there was Colonel Raymond Robins; the scholars Max Lerner, F. O. Matthiessen, F. L. Schuman, Ernest J. Simmons, R. M. Lovett and Leo Hubermann; the writers and journalists Donald Ogden Stewart, Dashiell Hammett, Corliss Lamont, Carey McWilliams, Waldo Frank, and the artist-writers James Thurber and Rockwell Kent.

These were among the leading fellow-travellers of the day. The Open Letter was also signed by a number of communist intellectuals, including Clifford Odets, John Howard Lawson and Richard Wright.

fantastic falsehood that the USSR and the totalitarian states are basically alike" – an accusation made by John Dewey's new Committee for Cultural Freedom. (The falsehood was all the more odious in that the Nazi–Soviet Pact still lay a week into the future.)

The system of government, or democracy, prevailing in the Soviet Union and within its ruling Communist Party is known as democratic centralism or, sometimes, Leninist centralism. What did the fellow-travellers have to say on this important subject?

There were those who subscribed with Arcadian simplicity to the theory of a workers' and peasants' state. Wicksteed discounted all talk of minority rule; only with the broad support and active participation of the immense majority could the leaders stay in power. Anna Louise Strong explained that a workers' dictatorship was a place where *you* express *your* will and where the proletariat lays down the law to its elected representatives in the soviets. Harry Ward, a writer capable of staggering tediousness, saw it all quite simply as "government of the workers, by the workers and for the workers". Stalin and Molotov had said so; he quoted them copiously. Indeed his sense of inappropriate quotation led him to cite no less an authority than State Prosecutor Krylenko on the imminent (and immanent) withering away of the state! The idea that a new bureaucratic class of office-holders could develop and dominate the Soviet Union he found logically absurd: how could such a thing be tolerated in a socialist state? No less addicted to simple solutions was another divine, Hewlett Johnson: "Where formerly the minority held power, the majority hold it now." But did the Party tend to dominate things? Not really, said Johnson in 1942; that is to say, less and less so. You couldn't afford to forget that the executive was entirely subordinate to the highest legislative body, the Supreme Soviet, which controlled the budget in the best British parliamentary tradition. Heinrich Mann was not inclined to adopt a more complicated approach. Russia was now "*der Staat der Arbeiter und Bauern*", it belonged to its own people and it was the product of man's long struggle to throw off the chains of which Rousseau had spoken.

Others showed more respect for reality. In 1920 Alfons Goldschmidt had recognized that the CPSU, with its six hundred thousand members, ruled the 150 million inhabitants of Russia. Like the Jesuit order, the Party was dedicated, determined and dictatorial about fundamentals but not, he thought, about details. The Party had the necessary cohesion and discipline of a pioneer corps and it alone possessed the capacity and the will to unify Russia. Ernst Toller recognized that Party discipline sprang from the idealism of the rank and file; the communists were "state pedagogues" – a really penetrating observation – teaching by example.

Then there were those who deplored aspects of the Party's dictatorial rule, yet finally concluded that it was exercised in the popular interest. In 1927 Dreiser, not yet fully converted, called Russia "a dictatorship with very little if any privilege of self-expression on the part of the mass".[38] Nevertheless he could not escape the conclusion that it was all done to maintain working-class hegemony and to bring about a classless society where brotherhood would replace authority. In the meantime, however, he judged "the dictatorship of the proletariat" to be a misnomer. But by 1941 he had cast aside such reservations and was describing Russia as a "great democracy which is doing more right now for its progressive millions than ever this country had consciously done for its...."[39] Spender found it impossible to sweep under the carpet the obvious limitations on political freedom and the role of the secret police, but he was confident that the repressive superstructure would wither away of its own accord once genuine economic equality had been achieved. Corliss Lamont, one of the most devoted of American fellow-travellers, was prepared to level surprising strictures against Soviet authoritarianism. "I am repelled," he wrote in 1952, "by the dictatorial and repressive aspects of the Soviet regime...." In terms of civil liberties he regretted that the Soviet Union lagged behind the USA, even the USA of the witch-hunt era, of which he himself was a notable victim, and he went so far as to condemn Russia's denial of freedom of speech and assembly to the *enemies of socialism* as "a flagrant violation of civil liberties".[40] But reconsidered, this phraseology could equally suggest that the potential opposition inside Russia was exclusively confined to "enemies of socialism".

Hindus was again frank: in 1933 he referred to "the small group of men who rule the country"[41] – but he didn't suggest it could be otherwise. Edgar Snow was no more prone to hazy sentimentality, describing Stalinism as "socialism by knout instead of by common consent". Yet it had beaten the stubborn peasants out of the morass and it was a dynamic, exciting and important enterprise which only "came to be and ... persisted because it had firm foundations in the collective mind...."[42] A whole range of extenuating and exonerating circumstances were available in the alibi-armoury: the weight of the Russian past, foreign hostility, imperialist encirclement. Russia had no democratic tradition, Upton Sinclair pointed out, so don't complain, just concentrate on the future. The British Labour MP, Konni Zilliacus, blamed early bolshevik ruthlessness on the menshevik trouble-makers, middle-period ruthlessness on the fascist trouble-makers, and recent ruthlessness on the Western, NATO trouble-makers. He forgot to add that where trouble-makers didn't exist, as in the Red Army of 1937, Stalin invented them.

77

Bernard Shaw was a different case. He exulted in the bolshevik dictatorship. In an article published in October 1921, he defined the Soviet system as an oligarchy founded on the will of an energetic minority of political doctrinaires. Fine! Why give people the vote when they will inevitably use it on behalf of their oppressors? Genuine progress was always autocratic. A real *proletarian* revolution would be sheer chaos. Democracy in Russia? A nonsense notion. If a soviet were to oppose the Government, the Government would promptly dissolve the soviet. As for the Marxist clap-trap of the bolsheviks, it didn't interest him, only their actions interested him. Thirteen years later he called Russia "a really free country – that is to say a country which belongs to its people. . . .",[43] but he still did not mean a country *governed* by its people. What appealed to him was Russia's emulation in ten years of what it had taken Britain a century to accomplish, and this had been achieved not by a crude dictatorship or a bloody Committee of Public Safety but rather by "a self-dedicated democratic priesthood organizing a democratic Church Militant and an Inquisition held together by a common faith and by vows of poverty and chastity" – one of the longest definitions in modern political science. Like the other fellow-travellers, Shaw therefore viewed and articulated the Soviet phenomenon in his own, private, non-Marxist language. But it would be a mistake to assume that this razor-sharp intellect was immune to deception or gullibility, for it was he who described Stalin as "simply secretary of the supreme controlling organ of the hierarchy, subject to dismissal at ten minutes' notice if he does not give satisfaction".[44]

Back from a recent trip to Russia, Shaw visited the Webbs in August 1931 and offered them good news: workers' control had been jettisoned in Russia in favour of their own famous threefold structure of separate institutions representing citizens, producers and consumers. Beatrice noted in her diary that what was *not* Webbsian in the USSR was the domination of an indifferent, lukewarm or hostile population by two million faithful Party members. This might excite Shaw, but not her. However this reservation was soon to be dislodged by her own encounter with the Soviet reality. In the meantime she was pleased to notice that the "vocational" or trade union element in Russia had now been placed in the subordinate position she had so long recommended. In 1932 the Webbs visited Russia, and Sidney returned to check their references in 1934. The outcome was the massive *Soviet Communism: A New Civilisation?*, from which the question mark was removed in the second edition.

The Webbs were formalists, blueprint addicts. Inevitably they began their description with an account of the formal political and administrative structure of the USSR, very rarely pausing to check the theory against the practice. So Soviet man and woman first appears in his or her three-fold capacity: as a citizen, represented in the hierarchy of soviets; as a producer, represented in the trade unions; and as a consumer, represented in the 45,000-odd consumers' co-operatives. Turning to the mechanics of power, they decided that Russia's refusal to separate the executive and administrative branches of government from the legislative was on the whole an advantage and an advance. Democratic centralism, they explained, was an "upwards stream of continuously generated power . . . transformed at the apex into a downward stream of authoritarian laws".[45] Thus the effective, working constitution was rooted in a million or two local meetings held each year. Within the village, the "*selosoviet*" was sovereign: "this does not look as if the Soviet Government was afraid of the peasant, or distrustful of popular democracy!"[46] But wait. The Webbs had to admit that both the village soviet and the "rayon" congress above it could be and often were overruled from above. Unlike local authorities in Britain and America, they enjoyed absolutely no legal rights. So this "sovereignty" emerged a trifle battered. As for elections, the Webbs confessed to being a little disturbed by the unanimous votes for single candidates – but not deeply disturbed. After all, elaborate sifting really did take place at preliminary meetings. So it was all an expression of the popular will.

The Webbs then ascended higher up the hierarchy of "continuously generated power". The reader should study the next few lines carefully, for they have a story to tell. The All-Union Congress of Soviets elects the Central Executive Committee (TSIK). The Congress meets *only once a year*; at all other times its sovereignty resides in TSIK. But TSIK meets *only three or four times a year*. One of its main functions is to appoint Sovnarkom, the Council of People's Commissars, whose decisions it invariably ratifies when it does meet. Now Sovnarkom also appoints its own Presidium. . . . But the Webbs missed the italics and the fable as well.

What of the Party? They acknowledged its power and its influence, but this could be justified as the natural "vocation of leadership". One must not imagine that the Party *imposed* its will; it exercised its influence only "by persuasion". (And that was what the Enlightenment tradition was all about – rational, comradely discussions leading to persuasion and ultimately consensus.) As for the Party's internal structure, it was deeply democratic. Stalin himself had emphasized that supreme authority rested with the Central Committee and that he himself could answer the letters of farmers only within the guidelines laid down by the comrades. The Webbs came away convinced that nowhere were personal decisions more distrusted than in the Soviet Union. Everything was decided by groups and committees (in the best Fabian manner): the USSR was nothing less than "government by a whole series of committees".[47] So what of Stalin? Was he, as Shaw contended, to be dismissed at "ten minutes' notice"? Here the Webbs had a brain-storm. Something indicated to them that the leader of the CPSU becomes with time "practically irremovable against his will . . . without a catastrophic break-up of the whole administration".[48] One would have thought that this admission exploded the whole delicate and sublime structure of democratically delegated authority. But no: the Webbs retracted nothing, and left this honest observation stranded in lonely isolation.

They, like Shaw, had no patience for Marxian clap-trap, preferring to draw their vocabulary from Bentham or even Rousseau, as here: "But the term dictatorship is surely a misnomer for this untiring corporate inspiration, evocation and formulation of a General Will among so huge a population."[49] Reactions to their book in Britain were predictable. R. Palme Dutt hailed its publication as an event, while *The Times* regretted in November 1935 that they had "said goodbye to the free life of the human spirit". Nor were they later inclined to retract a word of it. In their *The Truth about Soviet Russia* (1942), they described the USSR as a fully-fledged democracy, and though they indicated some reservations about the *cult* of Stalin they had none to offer about Stalin. They missed, of course, the heart of the matter: that the Soviet Union was run by co-optation from above; that its power-structure closely resembled that of Renaissance Italy; that elections were devices for rubber-stamping Party decisions; that public criticism was always directed at the ranks below the top leadership; that the Central Committee had long since been castrated. And if they had been around to read Milovan Djilas's *The New Class*, their indignation would no doubt have matched their astonishment. Indignation against Djilas, of course.

There is a revealing story about Sidney Webb which happens to be true. He used to relate how during the First World War his housemaid had been afraid of falling bombs. So to set her mind at rest he one day took paper and pencil, noted down the population of London and the average number of bombs dropped in a week; then performed a quick calculation which proved that the housemaid's chances of survival were statistically so high that she could regard herself as virtually immune. But she continued obstinately to be afraid of bombs! Sidney used to tell Labour Party colleagues this story to demonstrate what a rational man had to contend with in his efforts to overcome popular superstitions. The Webbs were comfortable bourgeois who belonged as much to the nineteenth century as to the twentieth.* They were energetic, ambitious worthy, intelligent, unimaginative and impatient with the vagaries of human emotion. Their literary output was prolific.† The arts didn't interest them. Only facts, statistics and blueprints interested them, although their life's work was dedicated to the emancipation of the working class, which is commonly supposed to consist of people. Heirs to Benthamite Utilitarianism, they sought a model, a plan, a scheme of society, which would conform to the "greatest happiness of the greatest number" principle. The solution lay in socialism, which for them meant public ownership, planning and state power. Distrustful of Marxian or Hegelian theories of history, they experienced no need to propose an alternative of their own. Nor were they revolutionaries; the Fabians borrowed their name from the Roman Fabius because he was a gradualist, an evolutionary. For this reason Lenin had no time for them, once describing Shaw as "a good man fallen among Fabians".

Beatrice was much the more remarkable, original and perceptive of the couple. Beautiful in her youth, bold, emancipated, strong-willed and ambitious, she was also a snob whose drawing-room had always been filled with men of power and influence, and not necessarily socialists either. (From Robert Owen they inherited the desire to convince the exploiters by rational argument that exploitation was irrational.) Nevertheless their *The Decay of Capitalist Civilisation* (1923) describes the tyranny exercised by small classes of rich men in the capitalist democracies. Capitalism burnt into the wage earners, dooming them to perpetual penury and recurrent destitution through unemployment. "The capitalist ... does actually stand convicted of moral inferiority before the working classes."[50] And even if Marx was guilty of "pretentious blunders" in abstract economic theory, he had at least shown up the iniquitous villainy of the bourgeoisie. And they spoke of an intensifying class war. Yet in 1924 Sidney turned up in top hat and tails with other members of the first Labour Government, to kiss hands at the Palace. He was President of the Board of Trade in Ramsay MacDonald's short-lived Government, whose main aim was apparently to prove that socialists are worthy to govern in a sober, responsible and non-socialist manner. The Webbs were élitists, technocrats. They believed in an independent labour movement but often wondered whether the working class was worthy of it. When the working class took the law into its own hands, their sense of responsibility rebelled. Granting the miners a strong case in 1920, they

* Sidney Webb was born in 1859, his wife, *née* Beatrice Potter, in 1858.
† Their books include: *The History of Trade Unionism, Industrial Democracy, The Consumers' Cooperative Movement, English Local Government* (in ten volumes), and *A Constitution for the Socialist Commonwealth of Great Britain.*

felt large-scale strike action could not be justified "from the national point of view". In 1926 Beatrice noted: "We have always been against a General Strike . . . such methods cannot be tolerated by any government."[51] Their natural sphere of empathy lay with the governors. In words that Winston Churchill would have been proud to make his own, she described the General Strike as the work of a "militant minority" starving the majority into submission. It was a "monstrous irrelevance" and she could only hope it signalled the death gasp of the "pernicious" doctrine of workers' control. When after ten days the strike failed, or was betrayed, she hailed this event as a victory, as proof of the sanity of the British people. As for the families of the strikers, she noted frankly that neither she nor Sidney would have given "a penny" to them "if no one would have been the wiser". However, on this occasion her courage failed her and she sent along a cheque for ten pounds. She called British workmen pig-headed, jealous, stupid, vulgar and undisciplined.

In the 1920s the Webbs were fiercely critical of the Soviet Union. They disparaged the October Revolution as the work of anarchists. Beatrice refused to go to Russia to see for herself, as Wells suggested she should do, and she scornfully swept aside M. Philips Price's suggestion that the CPSU had something in common with the Fabians. In 1926 she noted: "*We* regard Soviet Russia and Fascist Italy as belonging to one and the same species of government. . . ."[52]

She began to study Soviet documents more seriously in 1929. By the following year, despite lingering reservations, she doubted "the superior virtue of the British over the Russian socialism".[53] She read and was impressed by Hindus's *Red Bread* as well as by the pro-bolshevik reporting of the American correspondent W. H. Chamberlin. In August 1930 Soviet Ambassador Maisky, who was to play an important role in their conversion, paid the Webbs a visit and impressed them with his accounts of Soviet workers accepting low wages to save money for capital expansion. He explained to Beatrice that this psychology of sacrifice was possible because "equality" now prevailed. Nor should it be forgotten that at this time the second Labour Government, of which Sidney was a member, was floundering before foundering, thus providing the context-contrast which was the necessary prerequisite for serious fellow-travelling. Philip Snowden, the right-wing Labour leader and now Chancellor of the Exchequer, began to remind Beatrice of a "West End clubman or prominent manufacturer", and in February 1931 she recorded her growing scepticism about the possibility of changing from a capitalist to an egalitarian civilization by means of gradualism. The schoolmistress in her was aroused by reports of altruism among the Soviet young, their puritan respect for honesty and punctuality. Yet the traditions of a lifetime could not be dissipated overnight, and in December she confessed herself baffled by this "strange combination of science without free thought, and fanaticism without religion".[54] She was always herself. Wicksteed records that in 1921 she told him that the Russians needed fifty thousand second-grade civil service clerks. In 1933 he asked her whether her view had now changed. Yes, she said; they need a hundred thousand second-grade civil service clerks.

Meanwhile, as this conversion progressed and the great journey of investigation drew closer, Sidney Webb was indulging his only recurring vice – governing. As Secretary of State for Dominion Affairs and the Colonies, he found himself advised to sanction the withdrawal of land rights from the natives of Southern Rhodesia, and to impose there a segregation policy. Clearly he was in the hands of his civil servants (not the second-grade ones). As regards Kenya, he explained that he could not move faster than his officials in the matter of reform, although he did issue a White Paper in June 1930 which argued that the interests of the natives must be paramount. But he did nothing effectively to check the avaricious demands of the Kenya Whites, and Gandhi came to London and went without India moving a step closer to independence. Sidney was no bolshevik.

The fall of the Labour Government in disastrous and humiliating circumstances left the old pair with time to travel. In May 1932 they set out for Leningrad by boat.

"No elections could be fairer," a demobilized Red Army soldier remarked to Nadezhda Mandelstam in 1937. "They put up the candidates and we elect them."[55]

The Webbs' book, of course, came out before the famous Stalin Constitution of 1936 was promulgated, but the impact of this new Constitution provides an interesting footnote to the general issues of democratic centralism. Needless to say, the reactions of foreign fellow-travellers were unreservedly and unanimously enthusiastic. Much enthusiasm was generated over the informal referendum which had been conducted throughout the Soviet Union on the basis of the draft Constitution, the sounding of the popular will. Stephen Spender observed this with pleasure and expressed confidence that the Constitution had "removed the main barrier to real liberty of thought and discussion: terror".[56] Anna Louise Strong called the preliminary nation-wide discussions "the most spectacularly widespread . . . in connection with any government action in history".[57] The fact that only forty-three of the 154,000 amendments sent in had been approved did not fray the seal of her enthusiasm.

Although the system of one-party rule and unanimous elections from a single list remained in operation, both Samuel Harper and Hewlett Johnson felt this was defensible if you remembered the preliminary soundings of the popular will. The Dean added, with his usual dexterity, that the Constitution was proof not only of Stalin's "genius" but also of his willingness to relinquish power. Feuchtwanger agreed that not all 146 articles of the Constitution were fully operative, but work at a fair wage and the right to leisure, to pensions and to education were all firmly realized in practice. In other words, the substance of freedom was guaranteed, in sharp contrast to the West where you found "the breath of freedom and equality . . . but only the breath". This said, he hurried back to the West to stifle. Meanwhile, in the London School of Economics, Harold Laski was awarding the Constitution alpha minus. "It is true that the dominance of the Communist Party is maintained. But that is the logic of any system which, retaining the coercive power of a state, does not allow its fundamentals to be jeopardized. The new legislature will be a very interesting body. It is not clear just what its relation to the executive will be. . . . The gains in individual freedom this draft represents are wide and notable; they are politically inconceivable in Germany or Italy; they are socially inconceivable in a capitalist state. Russian economic success is producing a profound sense of internal security, and this, in its turn, is naturally producing a relaxation of political control."[58] Laski wrote these words in June 1936, at the beginning of a twelve-month period in which the first group of old bolsheviks was tried and executed, senior generals were summarily sentenced and shot, and a great purge swept through the population. But can Laski be blamed for failing to foresee that? He was not, after all, a soothsayer, and the LSE graduate seminars on the relationship of the Soviet legislature to the executive would continue undisturbed.

Meanwhile in America the radical press went to town over the Constitution and Walter Duranty, the *New York Times*'s Pulitzer Prize-winning Moscow correspondent, sent news of the flowering of Soviet democracy. Corliss Lamont paid his tribute, adding to those sent from all quarters of the globe by Madame Sun Yat Sen, Romain Rolland, Pierre Cot, D. N. Pritt, Norman Angell and many others. But the loudest voice was that of Anna Louise Strong who treated the Constitution as if she had personally given birth to it. One-party democracy? Of course. Stalin had explained that all class antagonisms had now been abolished in Russia; therefore there were no further cleavages of interest; therefore more than one party would be superfluous. (An ingenious argument, were it not for the fact that previously one-party rule had been justified precisely because there *were* internal class antagonisms.) Reminding the world that of twenty-six European countries sixteen were now fascist or semi-fascist, and that in Spain democracy was already threatened by armed force, she urged democrats everywhere to welcome the Soviet Union into the fold. After all, Stalin had told Roy Howard that universal suffrage would now "be a whip in the hands of the population against the organs of government which work badly".[59] Furthermore the Supreme Soviet (usual rigmarole) could remove the People's Commissars any time, the judiciary was fully independent, and freedom of speech, assembly and the press were securely guaranteed. Why, the Constitution even put printing shops, paper supplies and buildings at the disposal of the working people! Of where else could that be said? Sidney Webb was absolutely right, said Anna Louise, to call all this "truly a unique and unprecedented conception of public freedom".[60] But there was one further point, widely misunderstood in the West, which she was determined to clear up once and for all. Articles 127 and 128 guaranteed that: "No person may be arrested except by decision of court or the sanction of a state attorney." And that guarantee was as good as gold. (It is not clear whether her own interrogation in the Lubianka in 1949 came under article 127 or article 128.) Louis Fischer sent home to *The Nation* the message that the Constitution marked the beginning of true democracy and civil liberty in Russia. The journal's editorials agreed. But Fischer didn't believe it. At the time when the Constitution was being drafted he told Karl Radek: "The question of the Constitution is a question of the GPU." Radek had apparently agreed, thunderstruck.[61] Fischer also knew that public sentiment had been overwhelmingly against the new anti-abortion law; the law nevertheless went on to the statute book with only minor amendments. But he was not yet ready to air his doubts to the Western public; as a leading fellow-traveller he abided by military discipline.

Shaw was cynical. Most of the new Constitution, he advised "The Intelligent Woman", might have been written by Tom Paine. "It may be dismissed as a feat of window dressing to conciliate Liberal opinion in Europe and America."[62] Right on both points. And the Tom Paine analogy was particularly acute, referring as it did to a British radical who helped to make the American Revolution and then fellow-travelled with the French one. Paine was an ultra-democrat and a rationalist, but not a socialist. It was precisely this combination of the ideals of the old political Enlightenment with the achievements of the new economic, or socialist, Enlightenment which proved irresistible to the fellow-travellers.

For communists the absolute rectitude and justice of Stalin's case in his quarrel with Trotsky was an article of faith and a canon of dogma as demanding as the divinity of Christ is for a Christian.* The slightest indication of doubt incurred instant expulsion and ignominy. The fellow-travellers were naturally much slower to recognize that the hero of the Civil War, the man who had stood at Lenin's shoulder in October 1917, had latterly become the agent of international reaction and the Gestapo's most favoured collaborator. Faced with such improbable theology, they responded in differing ways.

After Lenin's death in 1924 it was not immediately clear that the conflict lay between Stalin and Trotsky. M. Philips Price noted in January 1925 that Lenin's will, which praised Trotsky and warned against the growing power of bureaucracy within the Party machine, had been suppressed. But Price was unaware that Stalin himself had been condemned in the will, and his own strictures were directed against Zinoviev and Kamenev. (All the fellow-travellers loathed Zinoviev, who was Secretary-General of the Comintern; perhaps they recognized his own scathing contempt for them.) Price assured his readers that Stalin, "one of the big minds in Russia today", was against heresy hunting and would prove tolerant of Trotsky's point of view even if not in agreement with it.[63] Toller was in Russia at a time when Trotsky was already under heavy attack but not yet disgraced or exiled. The playwright didn't like it. Had not Trotsky organized the Red Army? Why was his successor, Frunze, now given the credit? He heard an orator quote Trotsky's phrase "we must chew the granite of science" and then hastily add: "as our great Frunze has said".[64] Then hearing Trotsky himself speak, Toller was lost in admiration for his passionate temperament, his logic, his clarity, his knowledge and his originality. However in later years he naturally declined to step forward on Trotsky's behalf; but neither did he join in the witch-hunt.

Shaw admired both Stalin and Trotsky and enjoyed saying so. He was always delighted to twist the tail of communist dogma. To Molly Tompkins he wrote: "For good sense, unaffected frankness and educated mental capacity give me Trotsky all the time."[65] Comparing him as a writer to Lessing, he generously described Trotsky as "the inspirer and hero of all the militants of the extreme Left of every country". At the time of the Moscow trials Shaw declared himself to be no more convinced that Trotsky was an assassin than that Stalin was "a vulgar gangster". Nor was he alone among fellow-travellers in refusing to subscribe to the orthodox fulminations. Even at the time he entered on his three-week adventure in the CPGB, Spender honoured Lenin and Trotsky in the same breath as the two inspirers of the October Revolution. Gide had a number of young

* That is to say, for those Soviet and foreign communists who did not defect in the wake of Trotsky's disgrace.

Trotskyist friends, notably Claude Naville, whom he refused to disown. Although he felt that Trotsky had somehow been disloyal in sowing dissension within the Party, he was distressed by the crudity of the attacks inflicted on him. But it was not until his own disillusionment with Stalinism that he began to express forcefully admiration for Trotsky's critique – an admiration, incidentally, quite unreciprocated. Trotsky despised the Western fellow-travellers as a fine painter despises the mob which gathers round a vulgar painting; but they were bound to respect an intellect as sharp and learned as his. Harold Laski referred in 1935 to his "fire and audacity" and to his "superb" *History of the Russian Revolution*.[66] On the other hand Trotsky in Laski's opinion lacked Stalin's grasp of Party management, he was too arrogant, he made too many enemies and in any case it was not he but Stalin who had been right during the debates of 1924–7. Nevertheless the current rewriting of history to obliterate Trotsky's role in the Civil War was more than Laski could stomach.

Laski was not alone in deploring Trotsky's arrogance. Louis Fischer admitted that after 1928 Stalin had largely adopted his domestic policies, but he could not forgive Trotsky for his unrelenting attacks on the USSR, his insistence that Stalin was always wrong – which in turn forced the regime to insist that Stalin was a genius. (One notices that Stalin's genius did not diminish after the ice-pick put paid to Trotsky.) Lincoln Steffens echoed this point of view and also Gide's. "Trotsky," he wrote in October 1934, "was a hero to me once too, but when he put 'right' above unity and broke our front to be right ... I recognized that he was not of the New Day, but of the Old. He says to the world what is only fit for the Party...."[67] Here the non-Party individualist sternly rebukes indiscipline within the ranks. And Samuel Harper of the University of Chicago decided in 1926 that Trotsky was no longer in touch with the Russian masses. Paying his first visit to the USSR (but not to Russia) in that year, he concluded that the younger, Russia-oriented communists were sick and tired of the oratory of the cosmopolitan heroes of the Revolution, whom they dismissed as wind-bags. Anna Louise Strong came round to this point of view reluctantly, for she had once given Trotsky English lessons and he had thereby become one of those "important" Russian "husbands" who meant so much to her. Besides, Marxist theory was never her forte. As she confessed to a Russian friend: "I never quite saw why he was thrown out; I couldn't see so much difference between those theories. Everybody wanted to build this country, didn't they?"[68] Mum and Dad had begun inexplicably to quarrel and the unity of the happy home was imperilled. But in an unconscious way she was right: Trotsky's exile was not primarily the result of a theoretical controversy.

However, Anna Louise Strong's loyalty to the regime finally led her to "realize" that Trotsky had refused to listen to the workers, who wanted an alliance with the peasants, because he was so full of his own ideas. Whereas Stalin kept his ear to the ground. And so – mesmerizing logic – it was not Stalin himself who threw out Trotsky but the working class acting through him. Yet we have evidence that privately she remained troubled. She confided her doubts to Lincoln Steffens, who in October 1934 sternly rebuked her: "Your difficulties with Trotsky are the sign of your failure. The great man matters with both you and Max [Eastman]."[69]

Trotsky wanted a permanent world revolution and the fellow-travellers didn't. That was the root of their complaint. Anna Louise Strong put it simply: Trotsky had agitated for "adventurous escapades among the nations whose workers were not ready to revolt".[70] Upton Sinclair breathed a sigh of relief now that all that rubbish about world revolution had been discarded along with Trotsky. Samuel Harper could never forgive Trotsky (and Zinoviev) for the fate which befell his liberal friends in 1917, and Stalin's concentration on *domestic construction* enormously recommended itself to him. This was a key-word for the fellow-travellers: "construction". According to Lion Feuchtwanger, Stalin was the constructor, the builder, the enlightened organizer – whereas Trotsky was good only in time of war. Like Shaw, Feuchtwanger agreed that Trotsky was a great writer; perhaps he was also a tragic personality, which is praise indeed from a dramatist; but he lacked "moderation, strength of character, and an eye for reality".[71] Moreover – to revert to a theme already familiar – he had shown only hatred and contempt for Stalin whereas Stalin – here Feuchtwanger displays his own "eye for reality" – had instructed that a portrait of Trotsky should be included in the *History of the Civil War*, edited by Gorky. The Webbs, being what they were, leant strongly in the same direction. Though they set out the history of the Stalin-Trotsky controversy with an objectivity unattainable for a loyal communist, they ultimately characterized the choice as one between patient construction and flamboyant iconoclasm. Trotsky had stuck his oar into British waters and Beatrice in particular found that hard to forgive. The fate of the English working class was hers to determine, not that of some upstart Jew from Russia. And, despite the antics of his minions in the Comintern, Stalin left one with no doubt that this was also his private opinion. Stalin ran deep; he understood.

The corollary to the rejection of Trotsky* was a vulgar adulation of

---

* In the US a small group including both communists and fellow-travellers broke with Soviet communism in 1936 and became temporarily Trotskyists. The *Partisan Review*, edited by William Phillips and Philip Rahv, turned in that direction. The disaffected group included

Stalin quite common among fellow-travellers, though they rarely caught the note of messianic fervour achieved by some foreign communists. A few moments in Stalin's presence could produce miraculous results. Anna Louise Strong was deprived of this privilege for almost ten years, but when embroiled in a dispute over the editorship of the *Moscow Daily News* she was suddenly summoned to the Kremlin. "His eyes were kind yet grave, giving rest and assurance." She found herself in the presence of "a man to whom you could say anything; he knew almost before you spoke; he wished to know more clearly and to help." People never waited for Stalin's *command*, as they did with dictators; no, it was his analysis they were interested in. "The Soviet Union is the only country where this function of analyst ranks highest."[2] More comfort for all the philosopher-kinglets. For that was Stalin's appeal: pipe-smoking back-room boy; did his homework; prodigious worker, up all night, mastering the statistics; listened to others, took his time, but once his decision was made he never flinched. At last – scientific government. As Bernard Pares, one of England's most distinguished Russian scholars, put it: "He has shown that his heart is in his own country, that he has set his reputation on a purely practical object of vast scope, [Russia's] radical transformation for the benefit of all."[3] Once more the uncomfortable vision of proletarian revolution in the West is wafted away. Practical chap: calls himself a Marxist and no doubt he's sincere, but actually doesn't bother his head about all that metaphysics. "I backed Stalin the way you back a horse," explained Walter Duranty. The horse never stumbled.

An oriental despot? The Dean of Canterbury put this myth to rout in 1942. Three years later he flew to the USSR and was granted an audience. "Stalin was calm, composed, simple. Not lacking in humour. Direct in speech, untouched by the slightest suspicion of pomposity. There was nothing cruel or dramatic . . . about Stalin's face. Just steady purpose and a kindly geniality." The Dean found himself face to face with "a man who had helped to plan a new order and a square deal for the masses. . . . The man whom no assault could terrify and no atom bomb intimidate or deflect from his purpose of building the world's first socialist country." The Dean told Stalin that he had stood bareheaded before the tomb of his mother in a church above Tiflis. The following exchange then took place:

" 'My mother was a simple woman.'

Dwight MacDonald, Edmund Wilson, Lionel Trilling, James T. Farrell, Sidney Hook and James Burnham, many of whom later became hard-line Cold War liberals. In France *"le vieux"*, as Trotsky was affectionately known, picked up some notable supporters, including Pierre Naville, André Breton and Victor Serge.

" 'A good woman,' I added.

" 'A simple woman,' he repeated."[74]

Just how long they plugged away on these two notes the Dean does not record. Then Stalin made a complaint: the Western press gave a prejudiced version of events in the Soviet Union. Hewlett Johnson agreed and then, as the Soviet tanks swept into Berlin, the spirit of the former Wadham College oarsman revived in his large, seventy-one year old frame, and he challenged his girl interpreter to a bicycle race round the Great Square in Leningrad. What the onlookers made of this one can only guess: unlike the Romans they can scarcely have cried, "An honest priest, he should be our Pope!"

Romain Rolland and Bernard Shaw were also granted audiences with Stalin. Rolland felt he had "a firm and supple hand" which could be relied on to defend "*les droits de l'esprit*". Heinrich Mann, who would certainly have been ushered into the presence had he ever gone to Russia, told himself that Stalin, although a great realist, would rather renounce the title of Marshal than that of intellectual. In terms of Mann's most cherished calculus, this meant putting *Geist* above *Macht* – the highest tribute of all. As for GBS, he discovered in 1931 that Stalin was a good listener, though whether Stalin was left with the same impression of Shaw one does not know; it was a question posed by H. G. Wells. But Shaw was twenty years the senior and had known Friedrich Engels, which must have stirred in Stalin a suitable humility. The Irishman, however, was unimpressed by all those Marx-Engels-Lenin-Stalin dogmas, the divine right of interpretative succession, and in 1934 he let loose a volley of iconoclasms, calling Stalin the "Pontifex Maximus of the new Russo-Catholic Church of Communism". But he was poking fun less at Stalin than at his communist acolytes lower down the hierarchy. For many years Stalin remained beyond the reach of criticism. "It's good," Arnold Zweig wrote in 1952, "that the wheel of history is forced forward by men like Lenin and Stalin. Only here is the welfare of millions of toilers so assured – by the socialist achievements of a gigantic state."[75] One would press the point that these non-Marxist fellow-travellers were pleased to remove the burden of historical initiative from the shoulders of the proletariat, were it not for the fact that the communist intellectuals also put this aspect of Marxism into cold storage by attributing each and every achievement to one man.

If Shaw refused to blame Stalin for the crude hero-worship of his minions, he only expressed a common attitude. Georges Friedmann deplored the cult but explained that the Russian masses still needed icons – a mausoleum for the embalmed Lenin, a high pedestal for the living Stalin. And then, of course, imperialist encirclement of the USSR made it necessary to focus loyalty on a single figure. The Webbs were sure Stalin was not "the sort of person" to covet arbitrary personal power, and if the cult was deplorable he himself was guiltless. Feuchtwanger concluded that however vulgar the cult had become, it was nevertheless sincere, natural and organic, a naïve human expression of love for social- ism and the regime: "nowhere have I found anything to indicate it is in the least artificial or ready-made." More than that: "It is manifestly irksome to Stalin to be idolized as he is. . . ."[76] When Stalin confided to him that Trotskyist wreckers might be behind it all, the German writer swallowed the bait. A few months after this interview *Pravda* celebrated the twentieth anniversary of the Revolution by mentioning Stalin's name eighty-eight times in a single issue; no doubt the wreckers had got hold of *Pravda*. Some years later Corliss Lamont held Stalin personally blame- less for the adulation surrounding him and for the rewriting of history in his honour. Oddly enough, the fellow-travellers were victims of their own intelligence and high education. Having learned in the best Enlight- enment manner that there is a material or environmental cause for everything, they were not to be taken in by obscurantist hocus-pocus about one man's megalomania and paranoia. This emphasis on environ- mental determinism only began to play a useful analytical role when, after Khrushchev had virtually attributed all the evils of the last thirty years to Stalin's personality, not only fellow-travellers but also many communists, including Palmiro Togliatti, demanded a more scientific analysis.

What most perturbed the rationalist mind was the prevalence in the Soviet Union of conformity and uniformity reinforced by a propaganda which ceaselessly reiterated orthodox dogmas. Dreiser was overwhelmed by the "endless outpour and downpour of propaganda", by the paternal- istic posters, the monotonous slogans hanging from buildings and by the ubiquitous portraits of Marx, Lenin and Stalin. Even so he preferred it to "the lies of the British and American capitalists and their selfish propaganda for purely personal and plutocratic reasons".[77] Remarking that Marx and Lenin "are respectively the Old and New Testaments of Bolshevik Russia", Maurice Hindus noted that in Stalin's time recanta- tions in the style of the medieval Church had become commonplace. Toller warned: "one ought not to underrate the danger that socialist doctrines may become an article of faith which will be accepted mechan- ically. . . ."[78] And Waldo Frank, after hearing a communist professor hold forth, concluded: "Without knowing it, he had given voice to a pure mystic sense of life: he had pleaded that the writers serve the Dialectic Law as his forebears served the Torah."[79] Anyway, one can guess what Frank meant. As for Stephen Spender, so many things distressed him about the country he felt compelled to admire: "A verbal conformity imposed from without only encourages vindictiveness and ambition"[80] – Spender was right. During his three trips to Russia Georges Friedmann encountered an overdose of sterilizing polemic: this pitiless war of partisans must ultimately be waged at the expense of science and philosophy, and indeed the negative by-products were already only too apparent to him: ignorance about the West and a lazy taste for ready-made formulas. Even Feuchtwanger baulked when confronted by the officially-fostered universal optimism with its standardized phrases.

The Enlightenment *philosophes* bequeathed to their heirs a plain but sacred message: liberty is the precondition of progress. Whereas the militant communist was a monist determined to impose *the* single truth, and considered it a militant's duty to extirpate heresy, the typical fellow-traveller recoiled from so draconian an amputation. Even so, some made the effort and therefore deserve our attention. Apparently resolved that no one should damn him as a petty bourgeois sentimentalist, the young John Lehmann reported from Tiflis in 1936 that Georgian writers were not offended by the censorship – because they favoured it. Only manifestly counter-revolutionary propaganda was denied publication. Lehmann then offered a second *plaidoyer* which threatened logically to sabotage the first: a society building socialism along scientific lines was entitled to compel authors to alter their texts when they were guilty of misrepresentation or *misunderstanding*. But if Lehmann was merely engaged in a youthful imitation of the *enragé*, the Webbs were growing thick skins in the sunset of their lives: "an indulgence in unlimited freedom of discussion especially if accompanied by unlimited duration of debate, has the drawback that it is apt to militate against the effectiveness of corporate action."[81] Hewlett Johnson was of the same mind: one could not stop to debate the construction of a bridge in midstream. He contrived to argue both that Soviet censorship was vitally necessary and that it didn't really exist, for the simple reason that "the public no more questions the communist creed than we question antiseptic surgery". But lest the word "surgery" arouse unfavourable associations, the Dean hastened to explain that the Party put across its point of view entirely by persuasion and "not by sending the artist to Siberia".[82]

Sidney and Beatrice Webb made in this context one fundamental error, if error it can be called. They asked their Western readers to believe that there was no country in the world "in which there is actually so much widespread public criticism of the government, and such incessant revelation of its shortcomings, as in the USSR".[83] But had they ever seen or heard a word directed personally against Stalin, Molotov, Vyshinsky,

Voroshilov or Kaganovich? Did they ever pick up an issue of *Pravda* or *Izvestia* containing an editorial critical of the latest Politburo decision? No. When the Webbs said "the government", they really referred not to those who governed but to those who implemented the policy of the rulers, those who in the lower ranks of the Party or administrative hierarchy were constantly reprimanded, removed and punished. If the British Chancellor of the Exchequer were to make a habit of blaming all fiscal disasters on his Treasury officials, this would scarcely constitute criticism of the government. The Webbs were really far too experienced as political scientists to blur this distinction innocently. Hardly less disingenuous was their plea of last resort – that intellectual freedom was equally restricted in the West. In their view no British teacher would keep his job if he called for communism, atheism, the abolition of parliament or the dissolution of the empire. But they must have known that normally crises occurred only where and when a teacher carried such opinions into the classroom; the Webbs were definitely mistaken in maintaining that even in the British universities lecturers prudently withheld ideas which ran counter to the current orthodoxy. What of Laski and what of Cole? What of the scientists Needham, Haldane, Huxley, Bernal and Waddington? Indeed in the late 1930s a young communist historian was elected a fellow of All Souls College, Oxford, and the establishment did not turn a hair. To emphasize and condemn limitations on intellectual freedom in the West was one thing; blandly to talk the very real freedom available out of existence was a shabbier exercise.

Feuchtwanger re-phrased the Webbsian apologia for the "by no means ideal" predicament of the Soviet press: "the establishment of socialism would never have been possible with an unrestricted right to abuse."[84] And when you really came down to brass tacks, continued Feuchtwanger, there were only two opinions banned outright in the USSR: that socialism could not be built in a single country; and that the Soviet Union was bound to lose the coming war. (Presumably reporting the Ukrainian famine of 1931–2 would violate the first article of faith, and doubting the Judas-like treachery of Karl Radek the second.) Implicitly equating a profound analysis with a disarmingly simplified one, Feuchtwanger explained the only feasible alternatives for Russia: either *"weniger Fleisch, Brot und Butter"* for the masses, with more freedom of expression accorded to the writers; or alternatively *"weniger Schreibfreiheit"* and more meat, bread and butter for the masses. You can't have everything. Konni Zilliacus excused Soviet press control on the grounds that in the West the public was maddened and duped by propaganda; and the Dean of Canterbury pointed out with justice that the Western press was controlled mainly if not exclusively by the rich. Nevertheless he had to concede that the *Daily Worker*, which he so admired, was for some time permitted to appear even when it was opposing the war against Hitler, and he was kind enough to concede that the editorial policy of the *Manchester Guardian*, the *News Chronicle* and the *Daily Mirror* justified a press freedom which would have been out of the question under fascism. He might have added: under Soviet communism also. But of course he was not the only fellow-traveller to give his blessing to a style of dictatorship in *Russia* which he was happy to do without *at home*.

Artistic censorship tended to distress the fellow-travellers though the Webbs made no mention of it. Toller was upset to discover that a satire written by the German communist Egon Erwin Kisch had been cut by a humourless Russian censor, and that both Wagner and Pirandello were banned. Stanislavsky told Dreiser that he would have willingly produced his plays in Russia had the censors not intervened, and a writer thus thwarted usually concludes: if they censor *me*, something must be wrong. The American novelist also saw productions of Schiller's *The Robbers* and of *Uncle Tom's Cabin* which had been "edited" and mutilated for propaganda reasons, leaving him with the impression that the Soviet Government was enslaving and betraying the arts. Describing the appalling effects of the RAPP dictatorship on the arts, Hindus hoped that the dissolution of RAPP in April 1932 would bring about a freer climate. Huxley was offended by the flood of second-rate literature distributed for propaganda reasons, and when he was taken to see a play vitiated by long and tedious political discussions he grew bored and then hostile. Feuchtwanger admitted that writers who failed to reflect the official optimism had "a hard time" and that state intervention was damaging the arts. "The Soviet Union has a fine theatre but no drama." Spender was consistently courageous and outspoken about Soviet artistic policy, the sectarianism of RAPP, and the climate of bullying which banned Zamyatin's *We* and drove Yessenin and Mayakovsky to suicide. It was no use, he complained, dismissing Max Eastman's *Artists in Uniform* as the work of a counter-revolutionary, nor would the hectoring tone encouraged at the international Writers' Congress held in Kharkov in 1930 produce a single good poem or novel. He feared the onset of a new ice age in the arts. Elsewhere he attacked Christopher Caudwell for his crude collective anathemas against so-called "bourgeois" and "petty-bourgeois" writers, while putting in a word himself on behalf of those writers who distrusted panaceas and detested violence. "I am a communist because I am a liberal," Spender explained.[85] The conjunction may seem obscure but the confrontation was honourable.

In the longer run even the scientists had cause to think again. In 1932 Huxley had concluded that only time would tell whether Soviet censorship served a useful purpose. By 1949 Stalin was officially supporting the charlatan theories of Lysenko and suppressing biologists of the opposite school: time, for Huxley, had told. In the interim the biologist Vavilov, whose expeditions and researches were widely admired in the West, had disappeared in the purges.

Feuchtwanger's self-appointed role was to repair the damage inflicted on the Soviet image by Gide's sudden and violent apostasy. Every Luther demands an immediate Council of Trent and a reaffirmation of infallibility. And if it be asked why the opinions of political simpletons like Gide or Feuchtwanger should have become so prized and paraded, the question is a good one. The writer whose life work has been the exploration of human values and motivations, the learned amateur with no obvious axe to grind, is likely to be regarded as an incorruptible witness, rigorous in his honesty, fearless in judgment and acknowledging only a single binding obligation: to the truth. But when he exercises these qualities in a critical spirit he is immediately transformed into a dupe, a liar and a boot-licking stooge of the bourgeoisie.

André Gide's immediate heritage was that of the ultra-conservative French Protestant bourgeoisie. But the effect of his religious upbringing (he was born in 1869) was apparently to intensify his natural temperamental estrangement from "everyday reality", from life as most people experience it. Fascinated by the exceptional individual, by the artist *sui generis*, he revealed in his early work strong moral preoccupations but not social or political ones. And, like the majority of writers who despise politics, he was a conservative: to do nothing is to subsidize the *status quo*. In 1916 he went so far as to join the ultra-rightist Action française. It was not until he fully came to terms with his own personal problem, accepted pederasty as a norm and integrated it with his writing to his own satisfaction, that he found sufficient emotional energy to tackle the "social question", that stubborn predicament which generation after generation stoically lies in wait for ageing writers. Even so, with Gide the private and public aspects of life remained densely entangled: and it is no slander to point out that his latter-day commitment to communism was partly promoted if not originally prompted by personal regard for certain young friends, particularly the Dutch communist Jef Last. And since Trotsky's supporters also included the young and attractive, the author of *Strait is the Gate* felt obliged to travel simultaneously in directions widely regarded as incompatible.

In 1925 he toured the French Congo and returned repelled by the gross exploitation of the Africans. Although *l'Humanité* chided him for failing to advocate the complete abandonment of colonial territories, it was Gide's encounter with the ugly behaviour of his own civilization over-seas that launched his short career as a radical. Haunted by his own privileged position, he began to accept at least superficially the Marxist critique of capitalism as rapacious, inefficient and bellicose. "When faced by certain rich people," he commented in 1928, "how can one fail to feel communistically inclined?" But he also had to face himself: for Gide work had never been a financial necessity. In confessional mood at a meeting of the Union pour la Vérité in 1935, he explained: "What brought me to communism with my whole heart was the fact of the privileged position which I personally enjoyed – that seemed to me pre-posterous and intolerable."[86] Not so intolerable, however, as to oblige immediate remedial action; he could wait until the avenging angel of the revolution, perhaps decoratively represented by a handsome young commissar, subjected him to a cruel but sweet justice. Meanwhile he had rejected both the dogma and the cult of Christianity, while adhering to the essential moral creed now reborn as communism. He dissociated Christ from the Church to present Him as an example of what man is capable of becoming without the help of any illusory divine grace – a charming fable, were it not for the fact that Christ rested rather heavily on divine support. His Catholic *frères-ennemis*, particularly Henri Massis, François Mauriac and Paul Claudel, attacked him relentlessly: more than anything it was this private vendetta with his peers in the upper house of French literature which strengthened his commitment to communism.

His doubts and tribulations were confided in silence to his Journal. "Emotionally, temperamentally, intellectually, I have always been a communist," he discovered in February 1932. "But I was afraid of my own thought and, in my writings, strove more to hide than to express it. I listened too much to others and gave them more credence than I did myself ... through fear of 'being entirely of my own opinion'."[87] Even so, he reflected the following year that conversion to communism, as to Catholicism, implied an intolerable abdication of free inquiry and a sub-mission to orthodoxy. Twisting in the net, he asserted, again privately, that the personality truly asserts itself in renouncing itself. As a public man this he could not do. When in December 1932 the Alliance Euro-péenne des Amis de la Russie invited him to join them, he refused on the ground that he could not write according to the principles of someone else's charter – which they were not in fact asking him to do. Two years later his friend Roger Martin du Gard wrote: "How incautious to attach so much importance to the adherence of a man who, by his very nature, is unfitted to hold firm convictions...."[88] And Gide himself later claimed that he repeatedly warned Paul Vaillant-Couturier, the Party's spokesman on intellectual affairs, that intellectuals like himself provided unstable and untrustworthy allies. Why? Because "it is to the truth that I attach myself; if the Party deserts it, at the same moment I desert the Party."[89]

Nevertheless he turned up at the appropriate meetings and congresses, and in 1934 he flew to Berlin with André Malraux to urge Goebbels to release the imprisoned communist leader Thälmann. Gide's prestige as a fellow-traveller was of the highest. At the celebrated Soviet Writers' Congress, Gorky named him and Rolland as writers worthy, in Stalin's phrase, to be called "engineers of souls". (Not that either of them ever wrote a line of socialist realism; but then neither did Gorky.) Gide did not himself travel to Moscow for the occasion, but Louis Aragon ended his speech with a message of greetings from "our great friend André Gide". At the Congress for the Defence of Culture held in Paris in 1935, Gide received the longest ovation. And although his books were not for Everyman, his name at least was known to the French public. Ramon Fernandez recalled an incident during the left-wing demonstration of 12 February 1934, when a building worker blurted out: "We ought to have rifles and go down to the rich quarters...then we need a man to march at our head, a leader...a fellow of Gide's type."[90] Anatole France had indeed led demonstrations, but Gide was of frailer stuff.

And so to the great collision. Royally received in the Soviet Union, he broke away from the conducted tour and the entourage of officials as often as he could. Yet many of his criticisms were the products less of direct, first-hand observation than of quotations from sources available to him in France. On the prevalence of shoddy goods in the shops he quoted *Pravda* and *Izvestia*; he relied on the same source for the discovery that in one quarter of Moscow a single chemist's shop served sixty-five thousand people. For housing conditions he relied on Sir Walter Citrine. For first-hand evidence of low wages he quoted the French worker Yvon, who had lived for some years in the USSR. Likewise the criticisms that clothes were too dear and that the choicest houses and sanatoria were monopolized by bureaucrats. He castigated the average Soviet worker as indolent, conformist, ignorant and acquisitive. So pure was the rich man's idealism that he was appalled to discover that the poor in holy Russia cared more for material objects than for the communal spirit. But he complained about the lack of toilet paper.

What really got under Gide's skin (and here his own direct experiences were crucial) was the prevailing conformism. Pictures of Stalin everywhere; morning after morning the press taught the people what to think. To talk to one Russian, he felt, was to talk to them all. And the standard of foreign languages disappointed him; the new Soviet citizen

assumed he had nothing to learn from abroad. Gide had always believed
that nonconformism is the hallmark of a true writer, and indeed he had
in his own way been as good as his word. But he found the Russian
writers all swimming with the same current. They had no patience with
minority art and they were scornful of formalists – an unintended insult
for him. Gide believed that the only works of art which survive are
those which rise above temporary preoccupations (like the building of
socialism, for example). One can't dispute this; but, as Sartre later said,
why write for posterity? Above all, one asks why Gide had been able to
veil his head in illusion for so long. Soviet aesthetic policy was certainly
no carefully guarded secret.

It now dawned on him that Soviet democracy was a farce, that the
unions were powerless and that the workers were tied to their factories or
farms on pain of losing their right to ration cards or lodgings. (Yet this
also was common knowledge long before 1936.) Elections meant nothing, voting was a joke. Russia was governed, as Citrine had said, by a
handful of men. Those Western workers who believed the rosy tales their
Communist Parties told them were being duped. As for Stalin, he was
divorced from his people, elevated on a pedestal; when sending him a
telegram Gide had been advised to avoid the plain *"vous"* in favour
of something like "you leader of the workers". Terror everywhere prevailed. The least protest was heavily punished; it could scarcely be worse
in Hitler's Germany; a one-man dictatorship; if all opposition was
systematically suppressed, then terrorism was to be expected. Only the
most lazy, servile time-servers prospered, while the Barbusses and
Rollands of Russia were exiled or exterminated. One incident in particular left its mark on Gide. Bukharin had come to see him at the Hotel
Metropole but the conversation had been abruptly interrupted; Bukharin
tried again at Gorky's funeral but the same sinister termination
recurred. So Gide felt a duty to speak out, to warn that things were getting worse not better, and also to re-draw the ethical map: the failure
of communism as attested by Gide now restored to Christianity its revolutionary implications. "Man cannot be reformed from outside – a change
of heart is necessary."[91]

His erstwhile friends and allies certainly experienced a change of heart.
He had expected abuse, but less than he got. Romain Rolland's comments
pained him, for though he had never cared much for Rolland's writing
he had always held his moral personality in high esteem. Once again the
élitist and spiritual aristocrat in Gide rendered him acutely sensitive to the
judgments of the select few whom he regarded as peers. When *Pravda*
described him as "a mixture of old French writer and lively White
Guard", he could not have cared less. To be accused of serving the

diabolical composite beast "Trotsky-Gestapo" was merely risible, but accusations of personal cupidity touched him on a raw nerve, particularly when the *jeunesses communistes* of the 7th *arrondissement* wrote asking their Honorary President whether he had published his *Retour de l'URSS* to make money. He needed to retain the esteem of the young. Naturally he was charged with aiding and abetting fascism and with stabbing Spanish democracy in the back by his untimely sabotage, but he gave as good as he got. As each new Moscow trial hit the stage he exposed it as a sham and a fix. Nor were friendly voices lacking. Marcel Martinet, until 1926 an ardent communist and always a left-wing socialist, wrote thanking him for providing the world with so honest and sincere a report. (In fact Gide had earlier found favour with the ex-communist opposition in France by publicly speaking up on behalf of Victor Serge in 1935.) And though he could expect little comfort from the other fellow-travelling celebrities of the time, the maverick Shaw came out with an unexpected tribute, praising the *Retour* as "a really superfine criticism of Soviet Russia ... Gide's complete originality and sincerity, sensitiveness and comprehension ..."[92] – amazing, really, since GBS carried on as before resolutely backing Russia. It was the communists who would never forget or forgive, for not a few of the pre-war fellow-travellers who took Gide to task were later to tread the same painful path of apostasy and renunciation. When he was awarded the Nobel Prize in 1949 the PCF commissioned a hatchet-job describing the eighty-one year old writer's face as a death mask and depicting his young admirers deriving from his work the same "liberation" others picked up in the Place Pigalle. And when his life ended *l'Humanité* announced: "a corpse has died." It was the Anatole France story all over again but in a more gruesome mode.

Even Gide was taken in by one showpiece during his visit to Russia, and he was not the first: Laski, the Webbs and many others had already succumbed to the model, GPU-run prison at Bolchevo. This raises the question of Soviet prisons and labour camps in general, carrying us forward into the era of purges, political trials and indiscriminate terror. Once again the fellow-travellers, with the single major exception of Gide, were not found wanting. With the best of intentions they began by lauding humanitarian prison reform and ended by ignoring or condoning the creation of a new hell on earth. They rejoiced over the abolition of capital punishment in a country where a human life was often not worth a death certificate. So absorbed were they by the renunciation of the old, vengeful, bourgeois "hang a sheep-stealer" principle of justice, so charmed by the Soviet recognition that the common criminal is more often than not the victim of an underprivileged environment, and is therefore potentially an honest, productive citizen, that they failed to recognize the emergence of a penal system characterized by vindictive brutality.

This was indeed the "conducted tour". Visiting a farm prison, Maurice Hindus found every effort being made to increase the comforts of the inmates; girl friends were allowed in from outside and wives could visit their husbands in conditions of marital privacy. Here, remarked Hindus "the dictatorship . . . actually overflowed with kindness". Shaw observed that whereas an English delinquent entered prison an ordinary man and emerged a criminal, in Russia he entered a criminal and emerged an ordinary man "but for the difficulty of inducing him to come out at all". He had seen Soviet prisoners taking the greatest delight in making tennis rackets. The Webbs relied heavily on the testimony of the French lawyer, P. Guiboud-Ribaud, who had apparently been accorded a free hand to visit prisons alone and without warning, and found them to be on the whole much more humane and rationally conducted than their French counterparts. A statement made by Gorky in 1933 also stirred the Webbs: "Out of the ranks of the law-breakers of fifteen years there were salvaged, in the colonies and communes of the OGPU, thousands of highly qualified workers and more than 100 agronomists, engineers, physicians and technicians. In the bourgeois countries such a thing is impossible. . . ."[93] (Whether the Webbs might thus have been "salvaged" is a non-verifiable hypothesis, since bourgeois Britain omitted to commit them to prison.) But if M. Guiboud-Ribaud really did have a free hand to conduct his own investigations, the majority of visitors were led straight to Bolchevo with its model factories, libraries and educational facilities. Such a visit only strengthened Laski's conviction that the Soviet legal system, by bringing judges, social workers and trade union officials into close consultation, was now a model for all the world. At Bolchevo they told him that "all punishments are in the hands of the prisoners themselves. . . ." They introduced him to a prisoner who had bought a fine balalaika for his wife out of his prison wages; the professor immediately realized that the prisoner was "a different human being by reason of that achievement".[94] At Bolchevo, wrote Ella Winter, one sees no guards, no walls, no convict uniforms, "no bent heads". The young director of the prison was "kindly faced" in the general prevailing spirit of "ease and easy-goingness". It was only after his return to France that Gide discovered that Bolchevo was packed with privileged informers.

But Ernst Toller had himself been a political prisoner and he was not so easily taken in. No smugness eroded his capacity for empathy, his ability to visualize the human misery behind the well-scrubbed faces. The Russians told him a tale of Soviet justice, expecting to impress him, but he was nauseated. A young woman who had once worked for the Tsarist police turned over a new leaf and made a voluntary confession to the Cheka (predecessor to the GPU). She was none the less imprisoned – for failing to confess on behalf of her husband as well. Toller's hosts had perhaps forgotten that he was the author of *Masse-Mensch*, which deals with precisely such a conflict of loyalties and which comes down resoundingly on the side of compassion and the sanctity of the bond between people who love one another. Later Toller visited a prison and leafed through the visitors' book. Someone calling herself "Lucas, Vienna" had written: "Many European working women would be glad to lead the sort of life which is led in this reformatory."[95] Toller wished he could reach out to strangle Lucas of Vienna, not because the reformatory was itself bad but because free men can never know what it is like to be a prisoner. Readers of Alexander Solzhenitsyn's novel, *The First Circle*, may remember the icily depicted scene where a big white-wash is put on for the benefit of an important foreign lady, Mrs R. (Mrs Roosevelt?). The Prison Governor deliberately infuriates the prisoners, causing them to shout and swear; he then translates their oaths as a unanimous protest against the oppression of the negroes in the USA. To dismiss this episode as far-fetched is to forget the bitterness felt by Russian convicts towards the bland, benevolent smiles of the Western progressives who came for an afternoon to inspect New Harmony, Soviet model. Solzhenitsyn closes the novel with a cruel metaphor for the long line of professional foreign dupes. The Moscow correspondent of the Paris fellow-travelling paper, *Libération*, is driving to a hockey match when he sees a neat, clean van with the word "MEAT" written on it in four languages. He makes notes for an article on the high standards of hygiene prevailing in Moscow food transport. But the van is in fact packed with political prisoners.

As for the forced-labour camps, we naturally have to distinguish between what we now know and what a perceptive, open-minded foreign observer could reasonably have been expected to know "at the time". In this connection it is worth noting that as early as 1931 Prime Minister Molotov, replying to growing foreign criticism, had boasted of the excellent conditions prevailing in the forced-labour camps employing convicts on communal construction projects – their lot, said the Soviet Premier, was indeed a happy one when contrasted with the unemployed of the capitalist world. Not long afterwards the Webbs referred to a vast aggregate of prisons on the shores of islands of the North Sea where (they said) "every form of cruelty and torment" had been perpetrated: beatings, torture and killings. However, they expressed the unsubstantiated belief that such barbarities had ceased after 1930 as a result of a world outcry, though they imagined that conditions in these camps and prisons continued to be "inhuman". The Soviet Government, they complained, had not deigned to reply to allegations of cruelty: "the sum of human suffering involved is beyond all computation".[96] So the Webbs too were aware that socialism should wear a human face. Yet, having hinted at the scale of the outrage, they managed to devote as many lines to the show-place prison at Bolchevo, with its pleasant countryside and unlocked gates, as to the whole phenomenon of labour camps! Nevertheless their comments are instructive in one respect: if they knew that much, then it was knowable. In 1934, moreover, *Izvestia* published a decree signed by President Kalinin authorizing a Special Board (OSSO) within the new NKVD to banish an individual by administrative procedure (i.e. without normal trial) to a labour camp. Yet Hindus contrived to describe Siberia simply as "a new world for a new humanity" without offering a word about the many camps it contained. *On the subject of slave labour the fellow-travellers of the 1930s maintained an almost unanimous silence.*

By the early 1940s the testimonies of Polish prisoners released after the nazi attack on Russia were adding weight to the accounts provided earlier by Soviet defectors. Then came the evidence of fugitive NKVD officials and those employed in camp administration, backed up by documents captured first by, then from, the Germans, which for the first time revealed the enormous budget of the NKVD as a major economic department of state. There were many things one could not know with any degree of accuracy, just as the actual death toll in Auschwitz and Treblinka remained conjectural while the war was on. But no alert observer could any longer justify complete agnosticism or the version so favoured by Soviet sympathizers, that the camps were essentially rehabilitation centres to which a delinquent could be sent by a regular court for a period of a month. Nor would it be easy to justify the behaviour of the sinologist Owen Lattimore who accompanied Vice-President Wallace on his Soviet Asia tour in the summer of 1944 and was taken to see Kolyma Camp (or part of it). On returning to America, Lattimore wrote a favourable report about Kolyma and its friendly commandant, Nikishov, in the *National Geographic*. Replying years later to those who criticized this action, Lattimore explained: "So the only editorial pressure on the text of my article was for the addition of friendly human touches. Hence the appearance of the names of Mr and Mrs Nikishov. It is hard, sometimes, to remember those days when the Russians were saving us all."[97] Another who harped relentlessly on the Russia-as-our-Saviour theme was Alexander Werth, a brilliant journalist whose native language was Russian and who became one of the most favoured Western reporters inside the Soviet Union. In 1947 David Dallin and Boris Nicolaevsky, working from irrefutable documented evidence, published a book in which 125 camps were named and located on the map. They concluded that the total labour camp population at that time was between seven and twelve million. Rallying to Russia's defence, Werth first misquoted their estimate as twelve to fifteen million and then proposed that the actual number of inmates "might conceivably amount" to one and a half or two million. Many years later he was publicly challenged about this by Leopold Labedz. Werth's reply to Labedz in October 1967 is indeed interesting: "I did 'minimize' the number of 'slave labourers' in camps by saying that there were probably 'only' two million of them, though even that was bad enough. But how many actually were there? Does Mr Labedz know? . . . My estimate was lower than most, I admit. But there was a very good reason for this. In 1948 the Cold War was at its height, and there were no end of people in Britain and especially in the US who were advocating a preventive war against Russia: and the 'slave labour' (the more the better) was their pet argument. . . . Yes, I had every reason to pull my punches. . . . And I don't regret it."[98] For some reason he continued to put the words "slave labour" in quotation marks, which is normally a way of indicating "so-called". Actually Alexander Werth fellow-travelled on some issues, but not on others. His feeling for and understanding of the Russian people ran deep, and it was only one of the more common tragedies of the epoch that for such men the Russians who vanished in their anonymous millions ceased to be people.

When the Kravchenko controversy hit France in 1949 the full magnitude of the Soviet forced-labour system had been established beyond reasonable doubt. Kravchenko was a Soviet defector of 1944 vintage whose crude exploitation by American Intelligence justified a certain distrust. The communist weekly, *Les Lettres françaises,* boldly announced that his book, *I Chose Freedom,* was not only a tissue of lies but had actually been forged on his behalf by the aforesaid Americans. Kravchenko promptly sued for damages. The generous and elastic notion of testimonial evidence entertained by the French court enabled this trial to be transformed into a full-scale punch-up in the Cold War. (Soviet generals were flown from Moscow on behalf of the defendants, the weight of their medals alone enough to sink a plane.) Into court came a famous array of communists and fellow-travellers, the latter including Louis Martin-Chauffier, Vercors, Emmanuel d'Astier de la Vigerie, Pierre Cot, Jean Cassou, Yves Farge, Konni Zilliacus and the

Dean of Canterbury. All were willing and "able" to refute Kravchenko's venomous contention that slave labour was practised in the Soviet Union. Not that all of them had led sheltered lives: Martin-Chauffier, for example, had been a prisoner in Bergen-Belsen, but this almost mortal experience did not lead him to think twice before exonerating the Soviet Union from having joined in the *"univers concentrationnaire"*. The prosecution for its part produced witnesses who had actually survived Soviet camps, notably Frau Neumann, widow of the liquidated German communist leader Hans Neumann. But the Reds remained unshaken: indeed they wanted to know what *Germans* like Frau Neumann were doing in a French court continuing to play the nazi game by slandering the USSR. The court awarded Kravchenko minor damages and declared its incompetence to form a legal judgment about the state of the world.

In her novel, *The Mandarins,* Simone de Beauvoir describes a heated debate among the French left-wing intellectuals on the vexed issue of Soviet labour camps. In the novel the debate takes place in the years 1945–6; in reality, as the author herself has pointed out, it occurred between 1949 and 1952. She justifies this transplant on the ground that the relevant documents existed at the earlier date. Precisely! Indeed – earlier than that. What is therefore astonishing is the reluctance to face the issue, the continual deferment. Simone de Beauvoir recalls how Louis Fischer, for whom the god had now failed, took Sartre into a corner "and explained the horrors of the Soviet regime. . . . Eyes burning with an aberrant fanaticism, he related breathlessly stories of disappearances, treason, liquidation, doubtless true, but neither the meaning (*sens*) nor the implication (*portée*) of which one understood."[99] Why not understood? In *The Mandarins* the hero Debreuilh insists that the only relevant question is whether, in denouncing the camps, one is working for mankind or against it. He prevaricates, arguing that to publish figures about the camps would be to indict the Soviet regime and thereby to help the Right in the forthcoming referendum. In real life the real Sartre put the case cogently during his controversy with Albert Camus in 1952: "Yes, Camus, like you I found these camps inadmissible, but equally inadmissible is the use which the so-called bourgeois press makes of them every day. . . . I am saying that you cannot utilize the sufferings inflicted upon the Turkestani to justify those to which *we* subject the Malagasy. I have seen these anti-communists rejoice in the existence of these prisons." Yet he, Sartre, confessed himself appalled that "a socialist government, supported by an army of bureaucrats, could systematically have reduced men to slavery".[100]

The dilemmas raised here go well beyond the specific issue of the camps. In a sense we have to consider whether intellectuals acting as such make effective politicians; in other words, whether the tactical compromises and evasions which are committed in the name of the greater good are legitimate activities in the realm of *l'esprit*. The answer is no. But this "no" has nothing to do with supra-human purity or even the innate desirability of clean hands. The intellectual's proper function is a critical one: his theories require factual support, but if he fixes the facts then the theories lose all credibility. This is precisely what very rapidly occurs in practice. Sartre (or Werth) defends a socialist regime (theory) by suppressing the facts about slave labour. As soon as we discover they have done this, we have to ask whether men who can put ten million slaves in cold storage can claim to represent authentic socialist theory. Once they have debased their own coinage in this way their credibility and therefore their utility (not to mention their personal reputation) are destroyed. In the obsessive search for an objective over-view, for a global context, in which to measure their yes and their no, Sartre, Simone de Beauvoir and their friends spiralled into a form of madness. This is revealed when Sartre laments that "a socialist govern-ment, supported by an army of bureaucrats, could have systematically reduced men to slavery". The madness lies in the inability to ask a simple question: what does a regime have to do before it becomes no longer useful to call it socialist? And if public ownership of the means of produc-tion had traditionally been taken as a rough definition of socialism, then surely facts such as those then coming to light should have indicated that this *is a necessary but not a sufficient* definition. Yet, oddly enough, at the very moment he made this damning criticism, Sartre was putting aside his earlier reservations and entering on his four-year marriage with the Soviet Union and his love affair with the PCF. Why? Because of those ill-treated Malagasys? Because of France's war in Indo-China? Because of American global imperialism? No doubt. But a choice between two evils is a tenable temporary expedient for an intellectual only if he continues fearlessly to expose those evils – both of them. Once he argues that the lesser evil is really no evil at all he is back in bankruptcy. As for those Bad Men who rejoiced at news of the Soviet camps, here the response of the fellow-travellers and sympathizers was absurdly self-righteous. Did they not derive a certain *Schadenfreude* on hearing of the execution of Julius and Ethel Rosenberg? Of course they did. Who can resist pointing at his enemy with the words: "I told you so"?

As late as 1963 Simone de Beauvoir continued to argue that the size of the camps, the length of sentences, the number of deaths as well as – once again – the *sens* and the *portée*, remained in doubt. She remained a captive of that state of mind which can come to terms with Soviet realities only when they are spelt out from a podium in the Kremlin by the most authoritative political voice in the USSR. And since no Soviet leader had yet dared to tell the whole truth, the whole truth did not yet exist. Hence her astonishing remark: "no one, neither in the USSR nor elsewhere, has yet satisfactorily explained the Stalin period."[101]

"I wish all fellow-travellers could be induced to read this book," wrote Bertrand Russell in an introduction to Freda Utley's *Lost Illusion* (1949). "She depicts ... the nightmare atmosphere of terror and mutual suspicion, in which colleagues are engaged in an infamous race to be the first to launch untrue accusations which may lead others, rather than themselves, to undeserved death by execution or starvation or forced labour in inhuman conditions."[102] One fellow-traveller who didn't read the book but apparently met its authoress was Sean O'Casey. Living quietly in Devon after the war, he was visited by a lady called "Creda Stern", an ex-communist whose Russian husband had been arrested by the OGPU and then disappeared – precisely Freda Utley's unhappy fate. Sean regarded her behaviour as distinctly hysterical. Evidently she wanted him to believe her and to do something (maybe just to stop blarneying and blathering about "Red Mirror of Wisdom", etc.), but he wasn't having any of it. "Lady," said Sean softly, "I have been a comrade to the Soviet Union for twenty-three years, and all she stands for in the way of socialism, and I don't intend to break that bond for a few hasty remarks made by one who obviously hates the very bones of the Soviet people."[108] So Russell hoped in vain.

Another widow, another vanished husband, another testimony: Nadezhda Mandelstam recalls the GPU motto of the purge era: "Give us a man and we'll make a case." But the GPU didn't wait for gifts, they took all they needed. "For people of this extraordinary human type, human blood is like water and all individuals, except for the victorious ruler, are replaceable." At the height of the terror (1937–9) "denunciations poured into every institution on a quite unmanageable scale". One suspected everybody; everybody suspected one. Terror-stricken intellectuals sought the protection of a powerful "prince" in the Party hierarchy, as perhaps in the time of Caesar Borgia. "Pilnyak comes to see us," said the wife of Yezhov, the future tsar of terror, "whom do you go to see?" Osip Mandelstam calmed his wife's indignation when she reported this incident to him. "Everybody goes to see someone," he said. "We go to see Nikolai Ivanovich [Bukharin]." Even the nazi terror was basically confined to certain well-defined categories of victim: Jews, communists, active socialists and democrats, political rivals. But if you were a "good German" or just an obedient one, you could sleep soundly. Not so in Russia. The purge gutted whole apartment blocks like a fire. "Anybody who breathes the air of terror," writes Mrs Mandelstam, "is doomed. . . . Everybody is a victim – not only those who die, but also the killers, ideologists, accomplices and sycophants who close their eyes and wash their hands. . . ."[104] Of course, by O'Casey's definition, she clearly hated the very bones of the Soviet people; he told her kind what Stalin implicitly told them, that once persecuted they were excommunicated from "the people". Imagine, then, what such Russians felt about the foreign visitors who also closed their eyes and washed their hands, but in complete immunity, untouched by the cold finger of fear: Feuchtwanger, for example, who spoke in 1937 of "the individual's feeling of complete security, his comfortable certainty that the State is really there for him and not he for the State. . . . Indeed everywhere in that great city of Moscow there was an atmosphere of harmony and contentment, even of happiness."[105] About which Mrs Mandelstam has a comment: "It was essential to smile – if you didn't, it meant you were afraid or discontented. This nobody could afford to admit."[106]

In the year during which Feuchtwanger visited Russia about six to eight million arrests were made. During the same short period between a half and one million people were shot, while about two million more died in camps. At a conservative estimate the labour camp population was eight million by the end of 1938. Given an average death rate of about ten per cent per annum in the camps, the total number of such deaths between 1936 and 1950 would be in the region of twelve million. This does not include the executions (above), the three and a half million who died as a result of collectivization, plus others lost during the deportation of whole nationalities. Again it could be said: we know this now but how could Feuchtwanger and his brethren have known it then? Granted that the present estimated figures could not have been accurately gauged then, we are once more unable to avoid the conclusion that there was evidence enough for those who wished to see it. Published testimonies, for example.* Or take Orwell's summary written in June 1938: "All real power is concentrated in the hands of two or three million people," (Orwell's comma here should be a semi-colon) "the town proletariat,

---

* These testimonies included: Anton Ciliga, *The Russian Enigma*, London, 1940; Walter Krivitsky, *I was Stalin's Agent*, London, 1940; Louis Fischer, *Men and Power*, London, 1941; Alexander Barmine, *One Who Survived*, London, 1945; D. J. Dallin and B. I. Nicolaevsky, *Forced Labour in the Soviet Union*, London, 1948; Margarete Buber-Neumann, *Under Two Dictators*, London, 1949; Freda Utley, *Lost Illusion*, London, 1949; Eleanor Lipper, *Eleven Years in Soviet Prison Camps*, London, 1951; Alexander Weissberg, *Conspiracy of Silence*, London, 1952; Victor Serge, *From Lenin to Stalin*, London, 1954; Alexander Orlov, *The Secret History of Stalin's Crimes*, London, 1954.

This is by no means a complete list. It should also be remembered that in several cases English was not the original language of publication, and that the first editions of these books appeared earlier than the dates given.

theoretically the heirs of the revolution, having been robbed of the elementary right to strike; more recently, by the introduction of the internal passport system, they have been reduced to a status resembling serfdom. The GPU are everywhere, everyone lives in constant terror of denunciation.... There are periodical waves of terror, sometimes the 'liquidation' of *kulaks* or 'nepmen',* sometimes some monstrous State trial at which people who have been in prison for months or years are suddenly dragged forth to make incredible confessions.... Meanwhile the invisible Stalin is worshipped in terms that would have made Nero blush."[107] So Orwell got it right *at the time*. Was he wrong to be right? "The sin of nearly all left-wingers," he wrote in 1944, "is that they have wanted to be anti-fascist without being anti-totalitarian."[108]

But there was more to it than that; the attempt to come to terms with terror had begun with the Revolution itself, albeit hesitantly. In 1918 Arthur Ransome had accepted the bolshevik view that the suppression of the Moscow anarchists was tantamount to putting down common criminals. Two years later Arthur Holitscher spared a sad thought for the fate of the Cadets, mensheviks and socialist revolutionaries who had "made the Russian Revolution" and who now found themselves incarcerated as under the Tsars. Then he drew a deep breath: "This would be a totally inexplicable cruelty on the part of the Government, a shame on the word communism, did it not appear in the last resort profoundly reasoned and indeed unavoidable...."[109] For the next thirty years or more fellow-travellers perpetually accorded Soviet actions the alibi of "the last resort". In 1925 the American Civil Liberties Union was asked to lend its weight to a campaign on behalf of political prisoners everywhere. But the Chairman, the Rev. Harry F. Ward, objected: "Besides, you will do more harm than good. A campaign on behalf of 'all political prisoners in all countries' will be interpreted by anti-Soviet elements as an attack on Russia.... Furthermore most of the politicals in Russia have been arrested *for overt counter-revolutionary acts,* and not merely for expression of opinion.... We must also remember that in civil war the expression of opinion may be equivalent to the firing of a gun. The Civil Liberties Union as such must keep out of this business."[110] In other words: the Civil Liberties Union will regard the Soviet Union as in a state of civil war for as long as there are political prisoners there. Even Toller proved insensitive to what one might call the sub-plot of the Soviet drama. He discounted reports of GPU tortures as "fairy-tales"; ex-prisoners had assured him on that. After his second visit to Russia in 1934 he took issue with H. G. Wells and insisted that there was growing intellectual freedom in Russia. There is evidence that the cruelties of

* Traders or profiteers during the New Economic Policy period (1921–8).

Stalinism upset him[111] but he never spoke out against them. Others were inclined to pat the GPU on the back for doing a good job, much as Americans have learned to trust the stern paternalistic hand of J. Edgar Hoover. Referring to the GPU, Alexander Wicksteed intended no humour when he observed: "I should doubt if anywhere in the world you could find so much ability collected in one establishment." Certainly innocent people lived in fear of the secret police, "but it would be a very liberal estimate to put them at 0.01 per cent of the population".[112] However, it was amazing how often even a visitor in transit ran into that one man in a thousand.

John Dos Passos arrived in 1928 for his second visit to Russia, bringing with him a sense of history: "The train ran into the [Finland] station and stopped; an empty station without bustle, broad clean asphalt platforms. ... This was where Lenin, back from hiding in the marshes, had landed ... eleven years ago. ... Could it have been only eleven years ago?"[113] He soon encountered a terrified Englishman with a Russian wife who spoke of his early idealism and his growing fear of the GPU. Dos Passos was so impressed by this human incident that he decided to draw absolutely no conclusion. Dreiser was more outspoken, complaining about "the inescapable atmosphere of espionage and mental as well as social regulation which now pervades every part of that great land. The prying. The watching."[114] The GPU, he said, were everywhere; an accused man was considered guilty until proven innocent and the chances of a fair trial were slim. But even in Dreiser's case the law of compensation, adjustment to a new context, was soon in full operation. Six years later, when Max Eastman solicited his support on behalf of Trotskyists imprisoned in Russia, he replied: "... I am so much interested in the present difficulties in Russia and Russia's general fate, that I am not prepared without very serious consideration to throw a monkey-wrench such as this could prove to be, into their machinery."[115] Waldo Frank had an experience similar to Dos Passos's. On visiting an old bourgeois couple on behalf of long-lost friends abroad, he found them terrified that this would bring down on their heads the wrath and vengeance of the GPU. Though he saw evidence of cruel repressions, Frank contrived to pass it off as an aspect of the necessary struggle against the bourgeois factor *in all people*. A perpetual, universal cleansing operation. Stephen Spender was always sensitive to the uses and abuses of the spiked knout. The savage reprisals which followed the murder of Kirov in 1934 provoked him to deplore Soviet police methods at a meeting of British communist writers. They abused him. "I listened with disgust to the dogmatic crowing of inferior talents."[116] He at least had the courage to say: enough is enough. It was a rare quality.

Julian Huxley preferred a clinical diagnosis. The foreign intervention of 1918–20, he said, fully justified the Russians' long memories: "Hence the censorship; hence the arbitrary powers of the GPU; hence the violent suppression of political and economic opposition...."[117] Discovering Russia to be caught between its medieval past and the needs of its planned, communist future, he saw no alternative to strong measures. So it was "hence" all the way. Meanwhile Lincoln Steffens, like Shaw, played in his last years the strong man of the Terror Circus, determined not to be caught with the pants of sentimentality dangling round his ankles. In July 1934 he explained to readers of the *New Republic* that he was "not incensed at tyrannies and idiocies inevitable in the early stages of planned evolution". Two months later he chided Anna Louise Strong: "Get the notion of liberty out of your head and out of the heads of your (American) readers. It is false, a hangover from our Western tyranny...."[118] Neither Steffens nor Shaw doubted that the head-bashing was aimed at the unregenerate mob as well as the "enemies of the people": indeed who more inimical to the true, ultimate people than the corrupted, present-day people?

The Webbs dithered over the terror – though their visits were completed before it gathered its full impetus. They were incapable of the strident, I-love-to-be-hated tone which both Steffens and Shaw relished. The prosecution of Professor Ramzin and others in 1930 started, they lamented, a reign of terror against the intelligentsia which left no one beyond suspicion and filled the jails. As Louis Fischer had pointed out in his *Machines and Men in Russia* (1932), the fact that some engineers had engaged in espionage was no warrant for condemning them all. The Webbs described as "abhorrent" the practice whereby the GPU organized their own courts, procurators and trials, during which the defendant was denied a lawyer. The summary trials which followed the murder of Kirov struck them as an act of vengeance, a way of removing surviving opponents of the present policy. But wait. They began to backtrack. After all, when the GPU struck it was usually with good reason, *n'est-ce pas*? After all, did not the destitute and the unemployed in America live in fear, whereas the victims in Russia generally belonged to the privileged classes? After all, between 1917 and 1935 the USSR had achieved what it took the West from the sixteenth to the nineteenth centuries to accomplish. After all, the political, industrial and religious revolutions had been navigated down one single stretch of the Russian river. Consider (they urged) the religious persecutions in England, the enclosures, the evictions of the Highland crofters, the enslavement of handicraftsmen in mines and factories, child labour, filthy prisons, workhouses, paupers deported to penal colonies, the status of Africans in the colonies, the Indian mutiny and the overflowing prisons of present-day India.

This is a powerful argument worthy of every respect and one, moreover, widely adopted by the Soviet Union's friends in the West. One notices that many liberals have reversed the argument: the cruelties practised in blind ignorance by past generations or by economic forces beyond their comprehension could not be equated with those deliberately inflicted, as a matter of conscious policy, by a dictatorship bent on moulding humanity to its own pattern. Many such liberals would rather have the Indians starve in "freedom" than acquire the necessary calories under a Maoist dictatorship. Such a controversy cannot be resolved in a few words, if resolved at all. It does, however, seem self-evident that "freedom" is a mirage for a man who cannot feed his family and whose average life-expectancy is thirty. Western democracies quickly resort to military discipline and martial law when they go to war; the chips are down; but for a country hovering on the subsistence level and periodically decimated by famine and plague, the chips will remain down until this predicament is a thing of the past. One is reminded of what Lenin said to Lincoln Steffens when told that the statesmen assembled in Paris, the gravediggers of millions, were demanding an immediate end to the atrocious Red Terror. On the other hand in the field of totalitarian politics the ends are used to justify the means to a point where the means themselves become ends. The fellow-travellers' cardinal mistake was to visualize the Stalin regime as a dispassionate surgeon wielding the social scalpel with scientific detachment. Nothing of the sort. They should have known that wherever a large police force is running amok, it means that a great number of nature's thugs have acquired uniforms and a licence to kill. One cannot therefore disagree with Raymond Aron when he writes: "How many intellectuals have come to the revolutionary party via the path of moral indignation, only ultimately to connive at terror and autocracy?"[119]

The Webbs did so, and likewise their friend Harold Laski. Following a lecture-tour in Russia, he published in 1935 a remarkable tribute to Soviet justice. The observant reader might have noticed a single sentence in Laski's preface warning that the author would say nothing about the OGPU's legal activities or the military courts (or the three-man tribunals which sentenced people behind closed doors). This was very much like writing a study of justice for the blacks of the Southern States without mentioning the Ku Klux Klan. Much impressed by an earlier book written by "my friend, Mr D. N. Pritt, K.C.", Laski discovered that Soviet lawyers "do not feel inhibited even in defence of persons accused of counter-revolutionary activity". As for the judges, "though they are civil servants, they no more regard themselves as servants of the executive than a judge in France or pre-Hitlerite Germany". He had an interview with Andrei Vyshinsky, who had been a menshevik until 1921 and then forged a career in the legal world as an academic politician which culminated in his appointment as Procurator-General. In this role he later exacted a terrible revenge on the GPU men who despised him, wringing confessions from them in purge after purge and executing the executioners. But this inferno had no place in Laski's pursuit of the Enlightenment reborn. "The office of procurator in Russia is one that has no analogue in this country. On one side, he is a public prosecutor. . . . The judge, the investigator, the advocate, even the police, are all, in a real degree, under his jurisdiction. . . . I may add that he has a personal representative in the office of the OGPU to safeguard the public interest there. . . . The public undoubtedly feels confidence in him; the stream of visitors to his office is evidence of that."[120] It is interesting that a system which puts judges under the authority of the public prosecutor should not have aroused Laski's distrust: evidently all those years studying the Anglo-Saxon legal and constitutional systems had not taught him so elementary a lesson. As for that "stream of visitors" – where do people turn for news of arrested relatives except to the power that arrested them? And Vyshinsky himself, although his great perfor-mances during the 1936–8 wave of trials still lay in the future, had already shown his vindictive side in earlier show trials. But Laski found him to be a man "whose passion was law reform. . . . He was doing what an ideal Minister of Justice would do if we had such a person in Great Britain. . . ."[121] Vyshinsky, in short, was carrying on the great reforming tradition of Jeremy Bentham. Laski said so.

The lesson is clear. Though a clever intellectual and a scholar of some learning, Laski patently lacked the ability to distinguish wish from reality, the shop window from the cells in the rear. One night in the Lubianka would have taught this professor of politics more about politics, and perhaps about human nature, than ten thousand books read, lectures heard and officials interviewed. Even in 1940, when the Nazi-Soviet Pact had sharpened his awareness of the "crimes and blunders" of Soviet Russia, he still refused to believe that torture was practised there. Not that. Impossible.

As for Shaw, when the bolsheviks shot down their old comrades and (in his own words) "fellow-sufferers" of the Tsarist era, the anarchists and syndicalists, he refused to reproach them. Shaw understood history, as he was the first to admit, but he was an insensitive observer of contemporary Soviet history. In 1931, at a time when the persecution of the intelligentsia was gathering a new furious momentum, he explained that it had not lasted long. It was also necessary. Grinning from ear to ear, he contemplated the justice of his own liquidation: "I levy tolls on railways I never saw and to whose construction and upkeep I have never contributed a farthing." Tucking his British passport into his coat, he exulted in the murder of the kind of people who filled his theatres and made him rich. How – he wanted to know – could we, who had gloried in the slaughter of millions of innocents during the war, honestly become squeamish when the USSR "judiciously liquidates a handful of exploiters and speculators to make the world safe for honest men"? But suppose "we" didn't glory in the slaughter? And suppose it weren't "a handful"? But the old bird enjoyed snapping his beak: "Every Russian knows," he declared in a broadcast, "that unless he makes his life a paying proposition for his countrymen he will probably lose it."[122]

He was born in 1856 and he discovered socialism in the 1880s when he read Henry George and Karl Marx. He collaborated with Sidney Webb in drawing up the Fabian *Plan of Campaign for Labour*, which was accepted in principle by Keir Hardie after the founding of the Independent Labour Party in 1892. But after the formation of the Parliamentary Labour Party in 1906 the Shaw–Webb proposals were forgotten or shelved, a crime which Shaw attributed to the negative outlook of trade unionists whose shabby greed for immediate gains and whose refusal to collaborate in the root-and-branch renovation of society only proved that they were blind victims of the capitalist ethos. The termites who ignored the dictates of reason aroused his contempt and disgust. And although he had been against a violent revolution before 1914, the syndrome of upper-class stupidity and hypocrisy portrayed in *Heartbreak House* shortened his temper and sharpened his eye for uncompromising solutions. War maniacs had destroyed liberty, the masks of civilization had been torn aside, braying asses exulted in German losses, profiteers flourished and the politicians indulged their ignoble distemper at Versailles. In 1921 he described the capitalist system as "the defiance of Nature in the name of liberty: the apparent freedom to be idle. It is useless to demonstrate that no such freedom is possible for all." Nevertheless he echoed almost to the word the Webbs' scorn for the foolish fetish of strike action. "This folly reaches its climax in the panacea of the general strike. . . . A general strike is general suicide."[123] A truly socialist state would never tolerate it. It was, after all, only another form of idling. So once again we see how weak was the democratic and how strong the paternalistic, élitist impulse among budding fellow-travellers.

He wanted to get things done. In 1919 he was interviewed by Max Eastman's *Liberator*: "A Bolshevik as far as I can tell is nothing but a socialist who wants to do something about it. To the best of my knowledge I am a Bolshevik myself."[124] Lenin, who had heard Shaw speak in England, told Arthur Ransome: "He may be a clown for the bourgeoisie in a bourgeois state, but they would not think him a clown in a revolution." For his part Shaw admired Lenin, particularly the short shrift he had made of ballot-box democracy. Nevertheless the local British communists found his idiosyncrasies and unpredictability worthy of reproach. In October 1921 William Paul wrote: "When Shaw gets one or two things straightened out he may find himself like Anatole France, Barbusse, Gorky, etc., etc., compelled to stand forth as a champion of communism."[125] It was Paul's complaint that Shaw refused to subordinate his personal views to communist ideology; but in fact neither Gorky nor Anatole France had done so either, and GBS remained confident that he would do history a greater service by subordinating communist ideology to Shaw's. Once the clamour of the Civil War and the Allied intervention had abated, he found little in the years of the New Economic Policy to admire. Besides, once the world revolutionary tide of 1917–20 had receded, the postures and petty piracies of the Comintern looked merely ridiculous. In 1926 he described the Soviet leaders as "a handful of Russian novices". Zinoviev was the worst. As for ideology, authentic socialism had left Marx as far behind as science had left Moses. The Fabian-ILP* heritage was the only tradition fit for Britain. Commending Wells for deriding Moscow's Marxian idols, he praised his *Outline of History* as far in advance of *Das Kapital.*

He never put a premium on consistency. This lively mind constantly changed its clothes, its face – and its mind. His was the syllogistic intellect run amok. In *Man and Superman* the touted Shavian solution for mankind's ills was selective eugenic breeding; in *Back to Methuselah*, artificially preserved longevity. (Said the famous actress to Shaw: "We should breed together. Imagine a child with your brains and my body." Said Shaw: "But what if it had my body and your brains?") As a playwright he was only occasionally seduced by specifically socialist solutions. The sober Beatrice Webb complained to her diary that her friend's abrupt changes of outlook were becoming increasingly disconcerting: ten years ago, she noted in 1925, he had insisted that children should grow up uninfluenced by their elders, but now he was praising the Soviet practice of indoctrinating children with a rigid communist gospel. She wished he would just for once pursue a process of reasoning through to its conclusion, but she was even further vexed when in 1927 he warmly recommended the revolutionary energy of Mussolini's fascists (as Steffens had also done). Shaw promptly incurred a violent attack by the communist

* Independent Labour Party.

W. Gallacher, "Shaw as Bourgeois Philistine". Ten years later he still admired Mussolini's early actions in smashing the proletarian parties and the trade unions, but he regretted that subsequently the dictator had balked before the big capitalists and landowners. So poverty, parasitism and the dole continued unchecked in fascist Italy. Even so, "Fascism is better than Liberalism . . . in so far as it produced a United Front with a public outlook. . . ."[126] and in so far as it had suppressed the ridiculous practice whereby one party attempted to stop the other governing.

Then he fell in love with Russia and became another Nobel-Prize catch: he had done more to persuade people to think than any other British writer of his time. His wit was brilliant, his intelligence prodigious, his culture broad and deep, and he wrote a kind of prose which led people to gobble his books like ripe strawberries. His plays were performed all over the world to packed theatres and deserved to be. But when he went high on Soviet Russia his old friend and rival H. G. Wells accused him of gross inconsistency. Shaw had a facile answer: it is not I who have changed, he said, but Russia. Had the bolsheviks shown the good sense to take their lessons from the Webbs and the Fabians at the outset, they would have avoided the disaster which resulted in the New Economic Policy, and so saved wasted years. But they had learned from their mistakes: "Stalin has delivered the goods to an extent that seemed impossible ten years ago." For their part, the bolsheviks welcomed him to Russia with every possible display of respect, but they remained on their guard. "We realize Bernard Shaw is our ally," Lunacharsky wrote in *Izvestia*. "Yet we know quite well that he may sometimes execute some amazing zigzag . . . indulging in witticisms at our expense. . . ." Here was "one of the most untrammelled minds of the civilized world . . . a free mind, a free man", yet too free, said Lunacharsky, because always suspicious that a good cause would produce a new dogma and a new slavery.[127]

Henceforward Shaw chipped away at the dogma and ignored the slavery.

It had happened before: the Shakhty trial of 1928, the Industrial Party trial of 1930, the Menshevik trial of 1931, the Metro-Vickers trial of 1933. Each trial was accompanied by a purge. By the early 1930s the GPU had become a state within the state; Party members, far from being immune as in the days of the CHEKA, were now favoured targets. On 1 December 1934 the Leningrad communist leader and Politburo member Kirov was assassinated, probably on Stalin's instructions. In the first instance the old bolsheviks Zinoviev, Kamenev and the other "Zinovievites" were accused of indirectly instigating the assassination by contaminating the ideological atmosphere. By the time they were brought to trial in August 1936 the charges had become more specific: they were accused of organizing a terrorist centre under Trotsky's guidance. All except one of the prisoners publicly confessed their guilt in court. All were shot. In January 1937 a second show trial took place, with Radek and Piatakov the principal accused. On this occasion the charges included a plot to dismember the USSR with the connivance of Germany and Japan. All but four were sentenced to death, but naturally none of them lived for long. Then in June the press announced the arrest and execution of a number of military leaders, notably Marshal Tukhachevsky, on similar charges. The last act was played out in March 1938 when Bukharin, Rykov, Krestinsky and sixteen others faced sentence. Not the least remarkable fact of this trial was the presence among the accused of Yagoda – until very recently the head of the OGPU and therefore the engineer if not the architect of the earlier trials. He was now accused of poisoning Gorky on Trotsky's instructions! But the most spectacular element was the elaborate and mutually corroborative confessions. Rykov, for example, admitted having worked for Polish intelligence while Soviet Prime Minister! Krestinsky said he had been a German spy since 1921. Then suddenly he retracted his confession in court. But the next day he reverted to his plea of guilty.

Those foreign observers who believed the whole drama was a frame-up offered two types of explanation for the confessions. The more subtle contention was that these old bolsheviks were performing a last loyal service to the Party by objectifying their guilt, by demonstrating to the Soviet public how even mental reservations about Stalinist policy inevitably led to acts of sabotage and collaboration with hostile foreign powers. The more obvious explanation was that the accused had been beaten to their knees by torture, threats and promises. And this was indeed the case. In his famous speech to the Twentieth Congress of the CPSU in 1956, Khrushchev spoke of "application of physical methods of pressuring him [the prisoner], tortures, bringing him to a state of unconsciousness, deprivation of his judgment, taking away of his human dignity. In this manner 'confessions' were acquired." Mass arrests, deportations and executions without trial, said Khrushchev, created "insecurity, fear and even desperation".[128] And although he did not specifically confirm that such methods had accounted for the public confessions of the old bolshevik leaders, it is surely significant that the 1957 official history of the Party described Zinoviev, Kamenev, Rykov and Bukharin as having been "mistaken" and therefore "objectively" anti-Soviet. One scarcely needs to read between the lines to realize that this way of phrasing things comp-letely explodes the specific charges on which the trials were based.

Again we must emphasize: it is easy to be wise after the event. Communists and fellow-travellers were not the only contemporary witnesses to have been taken in. The American Ambassador to Russia, Joseph E. Davies, a self-confessed God-fearing capitalist, attended the Radek trial and reported to Washington: "There was nothing unusual in the appear-ance of the accused. They all appeared well nourished. . . ." For Davies's money, the State had uncovered a widespread conspiracy directed against the Government. "To have assumed that this proceeding was invented and staged . . . would be to presuppose the creative genius of a Shakes-peare and the genius of a Belasco in stage production." Then in March 1939 a rather greater strain was thrown on his credulity, for there, a few feet away in the court room, sat Krestinksy, Under-Secretary of State, "to whom I had presented my credentials a year ago"; there sat Rosengoltz, former Commissar of Trade, "with whom I lunched just a year ago . . . at his country home"; there sat Dr Pletnov, "the heart specialist who had treated me professionally. . . ."[129] All guilty of hideous crimes? All traitors to their fatherland? Yes, yes, concluded the sadder and wiser Ambassador, they must be. After all – they confessed. Later, in 1941, no one sang louder than Davies the popular song, "There's No Fifth Column in Russia Today!" (In fact there was one.) His book, *Mission to Moscow*, enjoyed enormous popularity. Thomas Mann wrote to his brother Heinrich describing it as "extraordinarily interesting": *"ich empfehle es Dir sehr* – I strongly recommend it to you."[130]

The Moscow correspondent of the London *Observer* reported on 23 August 1936 that the Government's case again Zinoviev, etc., was genuine. The Russia-expert Sir Bernard Pares, who had for years sus-tained his initial hostility to bolshevism, reported after a visit to Moscow that the guilt of the accused was established beyond doubt. "Zinoviev was now finally brought to book and died, still fawning, like the coward he had always been. . . ."[131] Warming to the cumulative rhythm of the trials, Pares later printed Radek's elaborate confession in *The Slavonic Review* (April 1937). Another respected scholar of Russian affairs, Sir John Maynard, who had already been taken for a conducted ride over collectivization, explained that the sinners had simply made "a clean breast" of their sins.

We must therefore recognize that on this occasion gullibility was not necessarily the child of political bias. On the other hand there were at the time too many sane and sceptical reactions to permit the thought that the show trials were utterly convincing. Both the *Manchester Guardian* and the orthodox Labour press in Britain refused to be taken in; the Labour Party promptly published Friedrich Adler's brilliant denunciation of the "new witch-hunts". Nor could H. N. Brailsford swallow it all. Orwell was, of course, scornful. And Kingsley Martin, editor of the *New Statesman*, refused to suspend his disbelief even though he was steering that journal on what Dwight MacDonald later called a "Stalinoid" tack. But, as Martin afterwards recalled, to express doubts about the trials was to incur immediate odium, to be hounded as a kind of Gestapo agent, witting or unwitting, and as an assassin of Republican Spain. Listen for a moment to the voice of Louis Aragon, the budding communist poet: "to claim innocence for these men is to adopt the Hitlerian thesis on all points...they reprieve Hitler and the Gestapo of the Spanish rebellion, they deny fascist intervention in Spain."[132] On the Left tribal reflexes were uppermost.

So to the fellow-travellers. Let us mention first the handful of cases where some doubts were expressed, where a note of hesitation was sounded. Samuel Harper confessed himself mentally routed by the cumulative speed of the trials; he suspended judgment since he had none. Spender refused to run with the pack: "These men were found guilty of a crime which may only have been criticism of the Government."[133] Immediately one of the Party's pet literary Alsatians, Randall Swingler, leapt at his throat in *Left Review*. In France the classics scholar and man of letters, Jean Guéhenno, thrashed about to reconcile his sense of loyalty with his sense of feasibility. "It seems impossible," he wrote in February 1937, "to doubt the guilt of the accused, the condemned." On the other hand the confessions had been improbably theatrical and he wondered what "intolerable constraint" could have impelled the old bolsheviks to pass from opposition into treason. He wished the bloodshed would end. At once he was set upon and banished from the club.

But for the most part the chorus of assent was deafening. Jean-Richard Bloch had watched the funeral of Kirov in 1934 from the Hotel Metropole, and the following day he found himself only a few steps from Stalin as he passed carrying the urn with three others. "I will never forget the picture of rigid sorrow on the face of this man, falsely reputed to be impassive."[134] Therefore he naturally rejoiced when Kirov's assassins, assassins' accomplices, accomplices' accomplices, and so on, were brought to book. With the exception of Gide, now self-excommunicated, the French fellow-travellers like their communist colleagues spoke with one voice. In England the Webbs reaffirmed their admiration for Soviet justice: besides, said Beatrice, the Soviet leaders *must* be right, they *must* know....And an intellectual of comparable stature, Heinrich Mann, reflected: "...many earlier supporters, even Party members, have been disillusioned to the point of falling out with the Party, if not with the Revolution, by events, particularly the Moscow trials, which have revealed to other, more hesitant observers, evidence of an intellectuality unique in the world."[135] This "*Intellektualität*" particularly manifested itself, Mann explained, in the Dostoyevskyan manner in which both prosecutor and accused worked together to clarify the truth. When Prosecutor Vyshinsky reached a dead end, could pursue the chain of evidence and the logic of motivation no further, then the prisoner Radek would leap to his aid and help him to uncover his errors. The cross-examination of Radek thus became "a psychological struggle for the possession of subterranean truth".* So here Mann, a lifelong apostle of non-violence, celebrated as the ultimate display of "intellect", "spirit" and "reason" in politics what was in reality a matter of brutal physical and psychological intimidation.

Mann was one of many who relied heavily on the British lawyer D. N. Pritt's assurances that the trials had been conducted according to the best traditions of law and justice. Pritt made a great play of the fact that Stalin and his associates were really not the sort of men to engage in a conspiracy to liquidate rivals – an assertion he showed no sign of retracting when two of Stalin's leading associates, Yagoda and Yezhov, successive heads of the GPU, both involved up to their necks in the trials and purges, themselves confessed to the usual fantastic range of crimes. Like Corliss Lamont, Pritt was adamant that a splendid social system automatically possessed a splendid judicial system. And if the defendants had appeared in court without counsel, this was because they had specifically renounced counsel. *Why?* But his most convincing argument was this, and to some extent it is one which still defies an answer. How, even after months of meticulous rehearsal, could so many defendants have sustained so great a body of detailed evidence in court? How could the intricate cross-corroborations have been woven together if they were bogus? As for torture and other fatuous rumours, did the prisoners when they appeared before the world's press look anything but alert and healthy? Besides, these men were tough, hardened revolutionaries whose resistance to torture would be high.† (But not to threats against their families and children?) Another left-wing lawyer, Dudley Collard, who had observed the trial of Zinoviev and who spoke Russian, wrote to the *New Statesman* dismissing theories of threats, drugs, torture and promises

---

* This was written in 1942. Did Mann not know that thousands of German communist refugees had been arrested in Russia during the purges? That four members of the KPD Politburo, Remmele, Neumann, Schulte and Schubert, had been liquidated? That nine members of the KPD Central Committee also went to the wall? The score here compared favourably with that of the nazis, who managed to kill only three Politburo members and eight Central Committee men in the whole period 1933–45.

† See D. N. Pritt, *The Zinoviev Trial*, London, 1936.

as ridiculous. Upton Sinclair was quite sure that proven bolshevik revolutionaries would not confess to crimes they had not committed. If they had withstood the worst that the Tsar's police could throw at them, what kind of terror could now persuade them to confess?

A good question, a question which preoccupied many ordinary newspaper readers; it became the emblem of public incomprehension. Not only had the GPU perfected techniques of interrogation in which the old Tsarist Third Section had been mere novices – the bright lights day and night, the salty food without water, the strait-jacket and the inexorably patient cross-examination by relays of fresh-eyed interrogators – they had also developed new ones: a glimpse in the corridor of a blood-stained prisoner seeming to resemble a wife, father or relative; voices on records crying out, again resembling some loved one. Not for nothing had Stalin by way of preparation for these inquisitions promulgated a decree rendering all children over the age of twelve liable to the death penalty. And no doubt the kind of complex ideological persuasion depicted in Arthur Koestler's *Darkness at Noon* did sometimes take place. But probably the main factor of inducement which the Upton Sinclairs of the West could not comprehend was this: Tsarist Russia was an autocracy; Stalinist Russia was the ultimate *totalitarian* autocracy. Which means there was no way out. The system was closed, the edges of the net were tightly sewn both physically and psychologically, and the victims knew they had once helped to build at least the foundations of the machine which now swallowed them. A man (a radical) may find the heart and the will to fight *them* (the Tsarist police), but the master strategy of the Stalin–Yezhov purge was to erode and eradicate that distinction between "us" and "them". The political boundaries and allegiances on which the careers of the defendants had been logically founded, vanished. A Bukharin or Radek did indeed find himself in the situation of Frankenstein. The promise of clemency both for the victim and his family was probably the ultimate weapon, even though, as one trial followed another, the chances of it being honoured must have appeared increasingly improbable.

Meanwhile the Western fellow-travellers explained why these culprits had fallen into the pit of iniquity. Said Pritt: a frustrated craving for power and a sense of personal injustice had demoralized ambitious men. Said Collard: since the Soviet people were unanimously behind Stalin, his opponents had to resort to terrorism. Samuel Harper, who had never forgiven Trotsky for signing the Treaty of Brest-Litovsk, thought it quite likely that he was once again collaborating with Germany – a pathological egoist who acknowledged no fatherland except himself. The *New Republic* drew its own conclusion: the deepest lesson to be learned from the Russian trial was the profound, unchangeable stubbornness of human nature. Dreiser announced that Trotsky was guilty of all the charges levelled against him, while Maxwell Stewart returned from Russia and reported in *The Nation* that the Russian masses themselves were instigating the purges and killing off unpopular leaders. In March 1937 eighty-eight American intellectuals published a letter in *Soviet Russia Today*, urging non-co-operation with John Dewey's Commission of Inquiry: "Should not a country recognized as engaged in improving conditions for all its people, whether or not one agrees with all the means whereby this is brought about, be permitted to decide for itself what measures of protection are necessary against treasonable plots to assassin- ate and overthrow its leadership and involve it in war with foreign powers?"*[136] In September the Dewey Commission decided that the trials of August 1936 (Zinoviev) and January 1937 (Radek) had been "frame-ups".

No defence of the trials was more exploited by communists than that of the novelist Feuchtwanger. He later recalled how, viewed from France, the Zinoviev trial had seemed to him ludicrous, but as soon as he set foot in the court room where Radek was on trial "my doubts melted away as naturally as salt dissolves in water. If that was lying or prearranged, then I don't know what truth is."[137] A shrewd penetration of human motives was, after all, the constant glory of his many admirable novels; he prided himself on his capacity to puncture sham and imposture, particularly as practised in the courts of his native Bavaria. The German communist writers whom he and Ludwig Marcuse met in Moscow, Johannes Becher, Friedrich Wolf and Willi Bredel, celebrated the trials with the noisy stridency of men whose comrades were begin- ning to disappear and who believed, perhaps, that the moment the optimistic smile left their own lips would also be the moment of a more sinister departure. "For all this we thank Comrade Stalin," Becher cried, clinking glasses. When Feuchtwanger met Stalin he discovered that "for many years he has been striving to win over competent Trotskyists rather than destroy them. . . ."; it was, he felt, "affecting to see how doggedly he is endeavouring to use them for his work".[138] But to no avail; either Trotskyism would be stamped out or there would be war.

Many aspersions have been cast as to Feuchtwanger's integrity. The legend has grown that both his trip to Russia and his eulogistic account of it were quickly engineered to counteract the effect of Gide's indict-

---

* The signatories included such fellow-travellers as Malcolm Cowley, Dreiser, Louis Fischer, Rockwell Kent, Corliss Lamont, Robert Morss Lovett, Carey McWilliams, Dorothy Parker, Raymond Robins, Margaret Schlauch, Rev. William D. Spofford, Donald Ogden Stewart, Anna Louise Strong and Nathanael West.

ment. But in fact Feuchtwanger had contemplated the trip for some time; as early as 1935 he was proposing to Heinrich Mann that they make it together. Recently a more serious allegation has been levelled by Elizabeth K. Poretsky, the widow of "Ignace Reiss", an NKVD agent who defected in the West and was subsequently murdered. She tells the following story: The writer Fedin reported to her that he was present as interpreter when Feuchtwanger had a first interview with Stalin. The German writer boldly expressed shock at the massive adulation of Stalin in Russia, Stalin became angry, and the interview was abruptly termin- ated, with Feuchtwanger leaving the Kremlin pale and shaken. According to Fedin, a second interview later took place at which *Fedin was not present*. But he had been informed that Feuchtwanger "had agreed to write an apologia for the trials . . . but in exchange asked that Radek and other Jewish defendants be spared".[139]

Feuchtwanger himself recorded only one meeting with Stalin and added: "No arrangement had been made as to what I was to discuss with Stalin." Really the whole plot seems an improbable one and is less interesting as an account of actual events than as a reflection of the anger which this flying visitor's wand-waving benedictions aroused among people who had reason to know what was going on. For Feuchtwanger, not content with writing his own report, pursued Gide as if it were his duty to do so, publishing in *Das Wort* an acid-and-dagger attack called "The Aesthete in the Soviet Union". Gide's conversion to communism, he wrote, had been sentimental not logical; it was a mere accident that he had chosen communism rather than Catholicism. He had confused the genuine Soviet democracy with the purely formal democracies prevailing in the West, and then had reacted petulantly when he discovered they were not identical. Egoist and eccentric, he assumed that Paris was the centre of civilization. Fussed by tastelessness and the lack of toilet paper in Russia, he had entirely overlooked the sublime *"Planmässigkeit"* and *"Vernunftmässigkeit"* of the new order. (Meaning: "high plan-content" and "high reason-content".) Gide had behaved as if Russia were not threatened by war and as if Spain were not in danger, freely giving comfort to the enemy while sanctimoniously withdrawing into his own privileged ivory tower. And so on.

A few voices were raised in protest against the trials but they were drowned by the cohorts of approval. Waldo Frank was sufficiently perturbed to suggest an international socialist inquiry, had to forfeit the presidency of the League of American Writers as a result, agonized further, decided that the trials were probably valid and then in 1940 stigmatized Stalin's methods of "blood and guile" while expressing continuing faith in Russia's future. Edmund Wilson made a clean break.

Having read the proceedings of the Zinoviev trial while on the Volga, he smelled fear and decided they were faked. Shaw took the line that the accusations levelled against each other by both Stalin and Trotsky were fatuous. But these were voices crying in the wilderness. Even those whose first-hand knowledge of the terror in Russia gave them cause to distrust the whole operation were inclined to preserve a tactical silence. Louis Fischer later explained his attitude towards the trials: "I suspended judgment because I was not sure in my own mind what they were."[140] And he claimed never to have written a word justifying the trials *after 1936*.[141] But according to Isaac Deutscher, Fischer like Walter Duranty vouched for Stalin's integrity and the GPU's humane methods, not to mention Prosecutor Vyshinsky's veracity, in obtaining authentic confessions from Zinoviev, Kamenev, Piatakov and Radek.[142] In fact the last two were not tried *until January 1937*. It is also the case that Fischer signed the petition denouncing Dewey's investigating commission, which did not meet until 1937. Well, Fischer later explained, "it is not easy to throw away the vision to which one has been attached for fifteen years".[143] Which would seem plausible enough had his family not lived in August 1937 in a Moscow block of 160 flats on more than half of which "the GPU had laid its hand". He read press reports in which husbands and wives denounced each other, he knew that many Polish, Hungarian and German communists had been arrested and that suicides were multiplying, and he heard even loyal communists beginning to refer to the regime as "they", instead of the old "we". One would have thought that this "veritable holocaust" would have plucked the vision of fifteen years from his head, yet Fischer's stubborn rearguard action conformed to the rule of the age rather than the exception. The prospect of being denounced and pilloried by erstwhile comrades was in itself a hard one to face. Besides, everything was linked to everything else. Fischer had to consider the situation in Spain and the morale of the Left in America. Thus in April 1938 about 150 American intellectuals issued a statement linking support for the Moscow verdicts with the cause of progressive democracy in the United States; here again the leading fellow-travellers of the day were to the fore.*

In France a similar confrontation between pro- and anti-Stalinists occurred when the *Cahiers* of the Ligue des Droits de l'Homme refused to publish an article by the ex-communist Magdeleine Paz denouncing the trials. The Ligue, now packed with fellow-travellers, had come a long way since the Comintern put it on the index in 1922, and even

* Among the signatories were the fellow-travellers Dashiell Hammett, Dorothy Parker, Paul de Kruif, Harry E. Sigerist, Nelson Algren, Harold Clurman, Cowley, Lamont, Schlauch and Samuel Putnam.

further since it had first risen to the defence of Dreyfus. In November 1937 seven members of its Central Committee resigned in protest against what they called its cowardly subservience to Stalinist tyranny – by now the heirs of the democratic Enlightenment were mesmerized by the Soviet system's capacity for continuous dramatic action. Nor did their own humanitarian traditions induce them to petition the Soviet authorities for clemency. Pritt recalled that the miscreants had already been forgiven for past misdemeanours and then reinstated after they had offered assurances of future good conduct. Heinrich Mann turned the executions to mystical advantage: "Out of every strong revolution emerges a pitiless literature."[144] Upton Sinclair believed Tukhachevsky and the other generals shot in 1937 had got only what they deserved. As for Trotsky's supporters, "If the medicine they had to swallow is bitter, the answer is that they got their own medicine."[145]

Upton Sinclair belonged to an early generation of American radical writers, the one which included Lincoln Steffens and Jack London and was associated with muckraking exposures in an era when the rising Socialist Party was the great hope.* His novel *The Jungle* (1906), with its powerful portrait of working-class misery and capitalist exploitation in the Chicago meat-packing yards, closed with a didactic sermon calling for a socialist solution. But when the Bolshevik Revolution came Sinclair deplored its bloody excesses and what looked like its collaboration with Germany. Like Steffens, who also settled in California, he was a fiercely independent, even quixotic writer who was readily attracted by quack solutions. For such men the Enlightenment was a huge box of colourfully wrapped chocolates, some soft-centred, some hard, and you could take your pick. For many years he was no friend of the Soviet Union. In 1934 a *New Masses* cartoon depicted him as an insect perched on the boot of a capitalist marching straight for fascism. He ran for Governor of California pledged to End Poverty in California (EPIC), as an independent Democrat in the face of communist opposition; they called him a "social-fascist". But the Popular Front mood affected him deeply. He had watched Gorky all these years from afar, his sufferings and waverings, but in the end Gorky had made his choice and now a little belatedly Sinclair felt compelled to make the same one. His appeals on behalf of Republican Spain were published in Russia, and the whole

* A socialist by conviction since 1903, he was an SP candidate for Congress in 1906. In 1917 he resigned from the SP, declaring his support for the US Government's war policy. After the war he re-joined, ran for Congress in California in 1920, for the US Congress in 1922, for Governor of California in 1926 and 1930, and again, this time as Democrat, in 1934. In 1938 he joined the National Progressive Party.

structure of his outlook now conformed to the fellow-travelling mould. He liked to recall how Lenin had condemned him as "a sentimental socialist without theoretical background" – a badge he was happy to wear. He was glad that Stalin had repudiated world revolution: "it means that events have forced Stalin to a wiser and saner point of view". He didn't think that bolshevik-style solutions were suitable for America and he kept his independence from the American CP. In an affidavit addressed to the House Un-American Activities Committee in December 1938, he drew the classic fellow-traveller's distinction: "Bolshevism ... advocates the overthrow of capitalist governments by the workers and the establishment of a dictatorship of the proletariat. That was the method used in Russia, and from the time that it occurred I have defended the right of the Russian workers to settle their own affairs. ... But in discussing the domestic affairs of the American people, I have invariably argued that, since they enjoy democratic institutions ... they should make the necessary changes by democratic and orderly process, and under the Constitution. ... This is a perfectly obvious distinction which any honest person can understand at once."

His devotion to the Stalin regime was beyond question: he once spoke by direct wire from Pasadena to a mass meeting in New York, supporting the sentences passed on the old bolsheviks. But after the Nazi-Soviet Pact the old patriotic anti-German attitudes which had possessed him during the First World War revived and he found himself again adrift. In 1950 he attended the first Congress of the (anti-communist) Congress for Cultural Freedom, and in his *Autobiography* (1963) he says little about Russia, while his references to the American communists are both sparse and disparaging.

When the Germans invaded the Soviet Union in June 1941, those who had celebrated the Moscow trials felt themselves vindicated. D. N. Pritt argued that Russia's capacity to resist was the result of the eradication of the fifth column in the years 1936–8. Heinrich Mann agreed, and even his nephew Klaus Mann, who was by no means a fellow-traveller, was so impressed by the heroism of the Soviet people and the Red Army that he wondered whether his earlier doubts about the trials and purges had been ill-founded. The Dean of Canterbury explained that the purges had rid Russia of her potential quislings. In his *Moscow '41* (1942), Alexander Werth argued that although the purges involved "thousands of probably innocent people", the old bolsheviks if permitted to survive would have "undermined or delayed the growth of Russia's military strength". Tukhachevsky was "going to sell out to Hitler". As for the excesses, these were not the work of Stalin but of "Yezhov and his gang". Challenged in 1967 to justify these remarks, Werth replied: "This book was written at the height of the war, with the Russians fighting with their backs to the wall at Moscow and Leningrad." And Britain's "very existence depended on whether the Russians held out or not". As for being wrong about Tukhachevsky, if Beneš of Czechoslovakia had fallen into the Gestapo trap and handed on to Stalin the incriminating documents planted on him, how could an ordinary citizen like himself be expected to know the truth?[146] But what is most odd in all this is that Russia's performance in the war against Finland, and again in 1941 against Germany, surely indicated disastrous military weakness rather than strength. An army which had lost in the purges three out of five marshals, thirteen out of fifteen army commanders, and 110 out of 195 divisional commanders, not to mention half its officer corps, was scarcely likely to recover its efficiency overnight. And if so high a proportion of the Red Army's leading cadres really had been traitors willing to sell out their country's vital interests to the nazis, this ought logically to have indicated a deep-rooted sickness in the Soviet system itself.*

But the majority of fellow-travellers emerged in 1945 grinning like cats of rectitude. Faced with the malevolent proposition that Stalin had systematically eliminated all the old bolsheviks, Hewlett Johnson put the charge to rout by citing a single exception: Kalinin. As for D. N. Pritt, he confessed many years later that he had been "shocked and disappointed" to learn in 1956 of the "grave irregularities" which had been perpetrated in the USSR. But he saw no reason to abandon his faith in the Soviet people. Thus in the course of a three-volume autobiography, he devoted only one page to a reconsideration of the gargantuan crimes for which he had made himself over the years the unremitting apologist. "Grave irregularities": such is the force of pride.

Probably no intellectual of high distinction suffered such internal conflicts and torments over the trials and purges as Romain Rolland. He was indeed one of the most celebrated fellow-travellers of the 1930s. Born in 1858, his education and values were shaped by the University of Paris and the Ecole Normale Supérieure. These values, confirmed by the Second Empire, insisted on the separation of art and intelligence from the muddy maelstrom of plebeian life. The European avant-garde was at that time effecting its famous retreat into the ivory tower. Like Anatole France, Rolland had learned to scorn the vile multitude; when he visited the Socialist Congress of 1900 it was as an artist, a detached observer, "to study a revolutionary crowd". And there he found only

---

* The fellow-travellers perhaps cannot have been expected to know that particularly in the Ukraine there existed a popular "fifth column" of formidable proportions.

"l' éternel peuple de Shakespeare, braillard, irréfléchi, sans aucune suite dans les idées"[147] – brawling, thoughtless, without consequence in their ideas. Unlike Anatole France, he was not ready in 1905 to hail the first Russian Revolution; admiring Tolstoy and holding both politics and politicians in contempt, he preferred some quasi-Nietzschean revolt of *l'esprit*. Few can have employed that word more regularly than Rolland: *l'esprit*.

But whereas Anatole France succumbed to patriotism in 1914, Rolland with remarkable singularity of conviction and courage of purpose refused to do so. Removing himself to Switzerland, he formulated a position which was certainly not revolutionary in the Leninist sense, but rather "religious" and pacifist as befitted one who admired Tolstoy and later Gandhi. The author of the *Jean-Christophe* novels saw the bastion of civilization, Europe, demented and gripped by a manic lust for destruction before the force of which political, spiritual and cultural leaders had abandoned their trust and their duty. Though he regarded the three empires (Russia, Germany and Austria-Hungary) as the principal villains of the piece, he denounced every warring Power for its own brand of imperialism, whether military or financial, republican or feudal. For his part he was determined to stand *au-dessus de la mêlée*, nor was he entirely alone, for Heinrich Mann, Gorky and Russell were of the same mind. In 1916 he recognized in Gorky, with whose writings he was not very familiar, a *"cher et bien estimé camarade"*. Although Anatole France and Gide called him traitor, and though the legions of the *union sacrée* in France daily covered him in calumnies, his own army of supporters grew in strength as the war extended. He was widely respected and even loved. Stefan Zweig met him in Geneva and discovered a feeble, delicate man whose health was then badly threatened, who could speak only in low tones and always struggled with a slight cough, who needed the protection of a shawl if he entered a corridor and had to rest after every step. Nevertheless, working night and day, always alone, without a secretary, he kept in touch with all efforts everywhere, conducted a vast correspondence with people who asked for advice on matters of conscience and wrote copiously in his diary every day. Some years later Jane Addams, President of the Executive Committee of the Women's International League for Peace and Freedom, and the founder of the famous Hull House, a philanthropic mission to the poor people of Chicago, sent this tribute to Rolland: "It is hard to convey to you the sense of rescue which your challenge to war brought many of us in the United States throughout the dark years of violence and denial."[148]

Many of Rolland's young admirers were intellectuals who were destined to become founder-members of the French Communist Party, but Rolland himself did not hear of Lenin until April 1917; his first contact with Russian socialists in exile had been with Lunacharsky whose position at that time, unlike Lenin's, was for an immediate peace and a return to the *status quo ante bellum*. (Not until July 1917 did Lunacharsky transfer his allegiance from the menshevik faction led by Martov to the bolsheviks.) Rolland greeted both Russian Revolutions of 1917 warmly. In February 1919 he launched a series of articles denouncing the unholy alliance of the German Majority Socialists with the Freikorps and the Entente Powers in crushing the German Revolution. In reality his own political position, in so far as it could be institutionalized by analogy, was closest to that of the USPD in Germany (Eisner, Haase, Toller) and of Jean Longuet's "Minoritaires" in France: he sympathized with the communists where they were crushed but kept his distance where, as in Russia, they were palpably doing the crushing. He could not, of course, tolerate the Allied intervention in Russia; about this he and his fellow Nobel Prize winner Anatole France were of one mind. But when in 1920 the French socialist movement split and a new Communist Party was created, there the two writers parted company. Rolland refused to take sides.

More than any other intellectual, he symbolized the short-lived alliance of illusions between the pacifist idealists and the Leninists – an alliance which was to be rebuilt with reinforced concrete in the era of the Five Year Plans. He even refused to collaborate with Henri Barbusse in Clarté once its narrow political orientation became clear. Fastidious and aloof, perpetually washing his hands of the grime of human nature, he returned to the *internationale de l'esprit*. This was the one international which bore no number; it was sublime and timeless. In 1920 he published *Clérambault, or One Against All – History of a Free Conscience during the War*. Here he was less concerned to justify his *au-dessus de la mêlée* position with regard to the war than with regard to the subsequent Bolshevik Revolution. Gunfire came at him from the pages of the magazine *Clarté* but, undeterred, he drafted a "Declaration of Intellectual Independence" which was later signed by Croce, Jane Addams, Russell, Israel Zangwill, Stefan Zweig and others. "The mind knows no master," Rolland wrote. "It is we who are servants of the Mind. ... We raise above ... blind battles the Ark of the Covenant – the unshackled Mind, one and manifold, eternal."[149]* Thus the inheritance of the Ecole Normale had reasserted its sovereignty, and the Enlightenment of the eighteenth century, of the *philosophes*, continued to defy Karl Marx.

* Here the word "mind" serves as a poor translation for the French *"esprit"* which, like the German *"Geist"*, suggests spirit, soul and sensibility as well as cerebration. There is no French word corresponding precisely to "mind".

He noted that Gorky had quit Russia and he drew his own conclusions. In December 1921 Barbusse fired the first salvoes in what was to prove to be a lively campaign. Acknowledging Rolland's moral courage and literary genius, Barbusse described the role of the pure moralist as purely negative and always wise after the event. As for the violence about which the Rollandists made so much fuss and palaver, it should be disregarded as a "provisional detail", a short-term necessity. Replying, Rolland complained that in bolshevik Russia humanity and liberty had been sacrificed to crude *raison d'état*. "Militarism, police terror, brutal force are not sanctified for me because they are the instrument of a communist dictatorship instead of being that of a plutocracy."[150] He insisted that means counted for more than ends; perhaps Lenin alone of the bolsheviks was capable of grasping this, surrounded as he was by minions and "scribes of the law". The debate grew bitter. Barbusse accused the Rollandists of egoism, self-love and a purely ornamental role. Rolland rejoined: "Party thought, caste thought, instruments of every oppression." He recommended Gandhi's strategy of passive resistance as the only viable revolutionary tactic, the only philosophy of social action which did not rush headlong into perversion and self-denial. An evolutionist by reason and instinct, Rolland counselled patience; time, "the master mason", and the spirit of self-sacrifice, would gradually fashion a better world.

Certainly Rolland's later reconciliation with Soviet communism did not entail any change in his basic philosophy. Indeed in the cases of nine fellow-travellers out of ten, the philosophy of a lifetime was merely coaxed and twisted a little to yield a different ideology. Thus the fellow-traveller does not declare: "Eureka, the Marxist light has dawned and leads me to the East." He says: "Whatever theology the Russians may claim for themselves, it becomes increasingly apparent that they are at last putting into practice what we progressives have always preached." By 1928 Rolland was convinced that the League of Nations had betrayed its mission by making itself the servant of two or three Great Powers; at the same time the unrelenting hostility of France and Britain towards the USSR placed the bolshevik dictatorship in the light of a defensive necessity. Rolland feared a new war. While urging the Russians to open their political prisons, and while not (yet) sweeping the "crimes and blunders" of the regime under the carpet, he was at least prepared to describe the Russian Revolution as the most fruitful and hopeful effort for social regeneration made in modern Europe. These remarks were offered in February 1927. The alert Lunacharsky at once held the door open, inviting him to contribute uncensored to the Moscow-based journal, *Revolution and Culture*. Rolland noted: "*La barrière, dès lors, était rompue.*"[151] And though never a Marxist himself, he discovered that Marx's critique of "bourgeois ideology" had a pitiless lucidity which he could well imagine applied to himself, the result being a protracted "autocritique" directed very largely at someone else, the Cartesian philosopher Julien Benda! He used Benda's recent *La Trahison des Clercs* as a trampoline for bouncing on his own past errors, particularly the elevation of *l'esprit* into a mere abstraction of no avail to empty stomachs. But naturally autocritiques turn out less painful when one is able to plaster the word "sophist" on one's faithful disciples rather than oneself.

His first and only visit to Russia occurred in 1935. Because of his frail health the journey took six days and was interspersed with many pre-arranged stops. He was received, of course, by Stalin. He met Gorky. Publicly he spoke of this being one of the great hours of history with a whole people climbing to the summit of destiny and ushering in a new world epoch. And on his departure he wrote to "dear comrade Stalin", assuring him that the progress of the world was linked to the fate of the Soviet Union.

But Rolland's real thoughts were of a different order. On meeting Stalin, he not only appealed for the release from prison of Victor Serge, which was granted, he also expressed general fears on behalf of Soviet intellectuals. When he asked for permission to publish the transcript of his interview with Stalin, it was not given: loyalty led him to respect the interdict. But he did keep a journal of which he published only carefully selected portions. In 1937 he noted privately: *"C'est le régime de l'arbitraire incontrôlé le plus absolu ..."*, a regime permitting not a shadow of elementary liberty, a regime violating the most sacred rights of human justice. Hearing in himself the rumblings of grief, anger and revolt, he suppressed them: "I stifle the need to say it and to write it." Why? Because – he reasoned – the raging enemies of the Soviet Union would seize and capitalize on his words with criminal bad faith.* No argument could be more familiar. In public he remained staunchly loyal towards the USSR: *"j'aime son invincible essor."* His castigation of Gide's book as "mediocre, poor, superficial, puerile and contradictory"[152] – a five-adjective indictment worthy of Thomas Hobbes – appeared to reflect a divergence of opinions; but what was really at issue between them was the decision to speak out or to keep silent.

Rolland felt that his own power to intervene on behalf of maltreated Soviet intellectuals had ceased abruptly with the death of his friend Gorky. In 1938 he told Hermann Hesse that a friend he had known

---

* See Jean Pérus, *Romain Rolland et Maxime Gorki*, Paris, 1968, pp. 319–22. Pérus has been able to examine Rolland's unpublished private journal.

for twenty years, a Leningrad doctor, had been under arrest for eight months without trial or explanation. Twice Rolland had written to Stalin about it, but had received no reply. As for the trials themselves, he expressed only orthodox opinions and one cannot gauge what he really thought. Writing to an English friend in October 1938, he said: "I have no occasion to doubt the condemnations, which strike down in Kamenev and Zinoviev, persons long despised, twice renegades and traitors, on their own word. And I do not see how one can reject as invented or extorted the declarations made publicly by the accused. . . . I regret not being able to share your confidence in the vindictive diatribes of Victor Serge. . . ."[153] The same Serge whom he knew to have been unjustly imprisoned. One cannot fathom this and it is idle to speculate further.

3

The Popular Front Era

The fellow-travelling odyssey really requires a new calendar based on B.H. and A.H. – before Hitler and after Hitler. One of Willi Müzenberg's elastic-sided creations which bounced safely over that great divide was the League against War and Fascism, also known as the Amsterdam-Pleydel Movement. Launching this enterprise in 1932, Willi was in his best form, marshalling into the "Organizing Committee" (*he* did the organizing) Gorky, Shaw, Rolland, Barbusse, Heinrich Mann, Upton Sinclair, Dreiser, Paul Langevin, Madame Sun Yat Sen and Albert Einstein. John Strachey was treasurer for the British delegation. The Congress* produced a manifesto denouncing aggressive capitalism and the lie of the so-called peace-keeping organizations like the League of Nations (a line quickly dropped in 1934 when the Soviet Union became a member). It also proclaimed the duty of defending the USSR against attack by means of mass agitation against war. In Germany alone five hundred thousand copies of the Amsterdam manifesto were distributed. To perpetuate the good work Willi created the World Committee for the Struggle Against War, the directing committee of which included the Russians Chvernik and Stassova; anti-war councils were also set up in each major country. Münzenberg succeeded in pitching the appeal on a sufficiently broad and liberal basis to evoke a letter of support from Russell and Havelock Ellis. It was now that he established a foothold across the Atlantic. The American delegation to Amsterdam included two reliable fellow-travellers, both New York academics, H. W. L. Dana and Margaret Schlauch. The Congress which met in

* The Second International on the advice of its Secretary, Friedrich Adler, boycotted the Congress. According to Romain Rolland, of approximately 1,200 delegates, 830 were communists, and 315 socialists or independent socialists. But these figures are not conclusive since a large number of "trade unionists" and "syndicalists" were listed as a separate category, and these designations do not indicate political allegiance. Similarly the sociological breakdown should be treated with scepticism. Rolland gives the figures as 1,865 workers, 72 peasants and 249 intellectuals or members of liberal professions. But where are the bureaucrats and functionaries? It is an old strategy to classify as a "worker" any militant of remotely working-class origin. No doubt Münzenberg himself attended as "a worker". The figures for nationalities represented at the Congress were: 75 German, 458 Dutch, 318 British, 585 French, 55 Czech, 42 Belgian, 37 American, 35 Italian.

September 1932 to launch the American League against War and Fascism was chaired by the most energetic fellow-traveller of the day, J. B. Matthews, and was addressed by the Secretary of the American Communist Party, Earl Browder.

After February 1933 there were no communist front-organizations in Germany and there was no Willi Münzenberg. The bird had flown in the nick of time: he had escaped from Germany on the night of the Reichstag fire. Although speaking no language except German he set up his headquarters in Paris and rapidly designed and scaffolded that expanding, multi-chambered palace of pro-Soviet sympathy which in 1938 provoked an exasperated comment from Leon Trotsky: "Under the pretence of a belated recognition of the October Revolution, the 'left' intelligentsia of the West has gone down on its knees before the Soviet bureaucracy.... A new era has opened with all sorts of centres and circles ... with the inevitable epistles by Romain Rolland, and with subsidized editions, banquets, and congresses...."[1] Quite so.

Arthur Koestler recalls working for the man who more than any other was responsible for Trotsky's legitimate frustration: shortish, square, heavy-boned and friendly, Münzenberg dictated, says Koestler, a stream of messages to his secretary: "Write to Feuchtwanger.... Ask him to do a pamphlet for us, ten thousand copies to be smuggled into Germany, upholding cultural heritage and so on, tradition of Goethe and so on, leave the rest to him, love and kisses."[2] Arriving in Paris, he quickly set up the World Committee for the Relief of the Victims of German Fascism, patronized by the usual galaxy of celebrities. Within his own Paris secretariat, located first in the Rue Mondetour and later at 83 Boulevard Montparnasse, he maintained a tight and loyal communist caucus consisting of his wife Babette Gross, Otto Katz, and his secretary, driver and bodyguard. He never went anywhere without an armed bodyguard. This was not paranoia: there was no refugee whom Goebbels would rather have disposed of. At one stage Koestler, still in the KPD, worked for him, at another he had the help of the talented communist novelist Gustave Regler. In the Münzenberg battleship – to change the metaphor – the engine room was manned by communists and the captain was Willi himself, but both the admirals parading the deck and the young ensigns enthusiastically hauling up the flags were fellow-travellers and sympathizers. This combination scored a series of notable victories. But before examining some of these, we should take note of the chief of staff, Otto Katz.

The perfect complement or foil for the blunt, monolingual German proletarian, Katz was a suave, persuasive operator who was equally at home speaking fluent French, German, English, Russian or his native

Czech. He had been manager of the Berlin liberal weekly journal, *Das Tagebuch,* and subsequently business manager for Erwin Piscator's Volksbühne – indeed it was Katz who persuaded the millionaire Louis Katzenillenbogen to put up the money to sponsor Piscator's lavish productions. He acted as agent for a Moscow film distribution company but he was equally adept at raising funds and support for Spanish Relief. He knew his way around and the intellectuals found him charming company; he also knew when and with whom to talk Marxism, but he could beguile a fellow-traveller with a non-orthodox (in communist terms) appreciation of Franz Kafka. Hitler's occupation of Europe later drove him across the Atlantic to Hollywood and Los Angeles where he quickly brought a new flair and efficiency to the front-organizations. When FBI surveillance became too hot for comfort he made his way to Mexico, and then in 1945 returned to his native Prague where he became chief of the Government Information Service. Like other cats, he tended to land on his feet. But seven years later his luck ran out in a situation which Kafka would instinctively have understood. Now bearing the name André Simon, he stood trial with Slansky, Clementis and twelve others, most of whom were, like himself, Jews. And he confessed: "For thirty years I defended the bourgeois ideology, disrupted the unity of the working class ... movement in various capitalist countries." He had, he said, "pledged" himself to the French Minister Mandel (a Jew) in 1939, and also to British Intelligence. From 1947 he had maintained espionage contacts with the well-known British spy – Alexander Werth! Nevertheless, as we shall see, his execution came fully twelve years after Münzenberg's.

Willi's first task on arrival in Paris was to set up the famous counter-trial to prove that the nazis had themselves burned down the Reichstag as an act of provocation. He moved so fast that the counter-trial was staged and its report published before the actual trial got under way in Leipzig. The British lawyer D. N. Pritt was appointed President and the imprisoned communists Dimitrov and Torgler were "acquitted". An anti-nazi indictment known as the *Brown Book* was quickly compiled and six hundred thousand copies distributed in twenty-three languages, sponsored by communists such as Barbusse, Mike Gold and Kisch, as well as by fellow-travellers like John Heartfield, J.-R. Bloch, Rolland, Toller and Steffens. The whole enterprise proved to be immensely effective propaganda, the more so since the case the *Brown Book* made against the nazis was undeniable, and very possibly it saved Dimitrov's life. Münzenberg's publications carefully avoided communist phrase-mongering. His *White Book*, documenting the events of the "night of the long knives" (30 June 1934) in Germany infuriated the Hitler regime as much as did his *Nazi Leaders, Look at Yourselves*. He had meanwhile set up a publishing house, Editions de Carrefour, which in turn sponsored the book club, Universum Bücherei. These enterprises employed communist refugees from Germany like Regler, Katz, Kurt Kersten and Alfred Kantorowicz, while the journal *Arbeiter Illustrierte Zeitung*, which Münzenberg had transferred from Berlin to Prague, published articles by the more persuasive and esteemed fellow-travellers: Rolland, Heinrich Mann, Arnold Zweig, Louis Fischer, Bloch and Ilya Ehrenburg. Willi also arranged that the Free German Library in Paris should enjoy a "directing committee" headed by Mann, Feuchtwanger, Toller and the left-wing socialist politician Rudolf Breitscheid. Moving nimbly from one national crisis and culture to another, he created for the French comrades the Institut pour l'Etude de Fascisme, to which Aragon, Langevin and Frédéric Joliot-Curie lent as much time as they could spare. Willi didn't mind about time; he wanted the names. In 1934 he arranged for Malraux and Gide to travel to Berlin to petition Goebbels for Thälmann's release, but on this occasion the enterprise failed. Refusing to admit defeat, Willi drummed up an international campaign, roping in Alfons Goldschmidt, Waldo Frank, Granville Hicks (not yet a communist), Sinclair Lewis and the renowned underdog's lawyer, Clarence Darrow.

Willi was as foul-mouthed as a cab driver but they all loved him. His financial genius never deserted him. He went about his work, as Regler recalls, with the calm intensity of a chess master moving from board to board, playing twenty games simultaneously. Equally remarkable, he was almost immune to the self-justifying delusions which plague professional propagandists. While many of his exiled communist colleagues believed their own rhetoric about the imminent revolution in Germany, Münzenberg had taken stock of Hitler's strength and knew it to be formidable. His whole effort was geared to fighting the menace of war, so that he soon switched his propaganda drive from Germany to the democracies. This shift of emphasis produced in turn a change of priorities within him; his allegiance was now to anti-fascism first and to communism only second. He saw only too clearly the folly of the intrigues engineered by the power-hungry KPD bureaucrats Ulbricht and Pieck, whose primary aim was to secure the Party's paramountcy within the Volksfront. Walter Ulbricht, for his part, had a score to settle with Willi, whose independence infuriated him. Systematically setting about weakening his position within the Comintern, Ulbricht began to accuse him of fraternizing with dubious elements and of refusing to explain his actions to the KPD Central Committee. Summoned to Moscow in 1936, Willi was interrogated. His position was weak. His former sponsors and protectors, Jacob Mirov-Abramov and Ossip Piatnitzky, had disappeared in the first show trial. Ordered to remain in Moscow, he pleaded to be allowed to finish his work on behalf of the Spanish Loyalists; only Togliatti's intervention got him a passport and an exit permit.

From a communist point of view, Ulbricht's complaints had some justification. In the summer of 1937 Willi actually joined another party – the new Deutsche Freiheitspartei. Summoned to Moscow again, he refused to go. He knew only too well his inevitable fate. But, unwilling to face a complete break with the movement he had so long and loyally served, he wrote personally to Stalin: "If, contrary to Party custom, I address myself to you directly and personally, I am inclined to do so by my absolute and unlimited faith in you as the head of the world communist movement. . . . This letter is intended to be a cry for help . . . to draw your attention to the danger I believe I can see . . . ."[3] But Stalin sent no flowers and Willi plunged even deeper into heresy, setting up a new paper, *Die Zukunft*, with the now disenchanted Koestler as editor and another ex-communist intellectual, Manes Sperber, as a leading collaborator. Some of the contributors were fellow-travellers with impeccable credentials: Arnold Zweig, Heinrich Mann, Feuchtwanger, Toller, Werfel, Benda and the Italian socialist leader Pietro Nenni; but others must have aroused suspicion even at a time when the communist movement was still working for the broadest possible anti-fascist alliance: Clement Attlee, who had helped to frustrate the Popular Front in Britain, the Catholic novelist François Mauriac, the anti-communist Wells. Willi tried to stave off the inevitable with a letter written in June 1938 to the Secretary-General of the Comintern, Dimitrov – the same Dimitrov whom his counter-trial and *Braunbuch* had done so much to save. "I know that my political concepts are communist and correct. But at the same time I also know that I have gravely offended against Party discipline."[4] By March 1939 the KPD was accusing him not only of opportunism but – worse – of outright betrayal. He was expelled from the Party. After the Nazi-Soviet Pact was signed the dam of his indignation broke and he accused the Soviet Union of having betrayed peace. Furious attacks on the German communist leaders Ulbricht, Pieck and Dahlem continued to appear in *Die Zukunft* until May 1940, when Willi was interned as an alien by the French authorities. As the German army approached the camp in which he was held, he made his escape and set out on foot, apparently in the company of two young men. His body was later found hanging from a tree. The relevant police documents were subsequently destroyed – but he was not the suicidal type. Stalin had no doubt finally responded to his "cry for help". Willi was in his lifetime a charmer with the face of a wood-cutter from a sixteenth-century German engraving, and he really did admire the great men of *Geist* and *esprit* whose talents he so skilfully harnessed to the cause. None of them would, in retrospect, disown him; as Ludwig Marcuse recalled, he was a man with whom one felt one could make a better world.

It would, of course, be nonsense to attribute every one of the thousands of front-organizations which sprang up in the West after Hitler came to power directly to Münzenberg's intervention. But he was the presiding genius who set the pattern and gave a nudge where a nudge was needed. In these years Friendship Societies flowered and flourished: for example the Society for Cultural Relations between the British Commonwealth and the USSR, whose journal, *Soviet Life and Work*, was edited by D. N. Pritt. According to Pritt, the aim of the journal was not at all political – merely to show British people how members of their own profession fared in Russia: but naturally they tended to fare well. The communist Andrew Rothstein took care of the Society's relations with the Party, a function performed by Pat Sloan with regard to the British-Soviet Friendship Society. Harold Laski put the case for co-operating with such organizations persuasively: "are we not all, as socialists, friends of the Soviet Union, even if we are also critics?"[5] In March 1937 a National Congress of Peace and Friendship with the Soviet Union was held in London, with such speakers as the Dean of Canterbury, Eleanor Rathbone and a short-term fellow-travelling recruit from the aristocracy, the Duchess of Atholl. In France Les Amis de l'URSS prospered under the patronage of Barbusse and the fellow-travelling architect Francis Jourdain. (Later, after the war, this friendship principle was to be extended to embrace the Popular Democracies through the Organisation de Rapprochement avec les Pays Démocratiques and the Combattants de la Paix.) In the United States Corliss Lamont guided the Friends of the Soviet Union (FSU) through their many victories and defeats. Nor, even in these early days, was the communist portion of China overlooked: J. B. Matthews helped to launch the American Friends of the Chinese People, of which Maxwell Stewart, one of the editors of *The Nation* and a prominent fellow-traveller, became chairman. As in Britain and France, there was a proliferation of magazines, journals and news-sheets. From the FSU came *Soviet Russia Today*, which enlisted the collaboration of Malcolm Cowley, Dr John Kingsbury, Maxwell Stewart and Robert W. Dunn. In 1937 the FSU prepared a *Golden Book of American Friendship with the Soviet Union*, collecting several thousand signatures and laying on a gala meeting at the Carnegie Hall where the *Book* was ceremonially turned over to representatives of the Soviet Government. The speakers on this occasion included Louis Fischer, H. W. L. Dana and a young historian whose attitude towards the Soviet Union was strongly sympathetic, F. L. Schuman.

In France several strategies were employed by the PCF, the most fruitful one being to create front-organizations whose homogeneity was professional, academic or cultural. Paul Vaillant-Couturier had an early success with the Association des Ecrivains et Artistes Révolutionnaires (AEAR), founded in March 1932. Its journal, *Commune*, was edited by two reliable communists, Aragon and Paul Nizan, but once again the flagpole carried illustrious fellow-travelling names, Rolland and Gide, alongside that of Henri Barbusse. But such "directors" never directed: they were too old, busy or venerable for the day-to-day administration which really counts. Just how the AEAR operated can be illustrated by a small incident which occurred in May 1934 when the novelist Edith Thomas wrote to Vaillant-Couturier. (She was then moving into a fellow-travelling position; later, from 1942 to 1949, she was in the Party.) Referring to people like herself, she asked: "Is it not better, despite their good will, to abandon them as incurables to their petty-bourgeois individualism – or to their egoism?" No, no, replied Vaillant-Couturier in a generous open letter, "without doubt, comrade, you can join the AEAR."[6] That was the style of the day: fellow-comrades. Whereupon Edith Thomas threw herself into writing for *Commune* and for the pro-communist paper, *Ce Soir*.* Then, broadening its base, the Party moved from the writers, painters and musicians to their audience, creating throughout France Maisons de la Culture, which by 1937 claimed a total membership of seventy thousand. Federated to these popular Maisons were the AEAR and other front-organizations representing the arts such as the Union des Théâtres Indépendants de France, the Fédération Musicale Populaire, the Alliance du Cinéma Indépendant – and so on. In these years the word "independent" could usually be assumed to mean the opposite, just as after the war any organization calling itself "national" was taking its cue from Moscow in nine cases out of ten.

A second obvious tactic was to penetrate and tacitly assume control of organizations with a venerable history of progressive militancy, notably the Ligue des Droits de l'Homme. This was the Trojan Horse principle – permeating the progressive middle class under the cover of names long since respected for their independence. Thus the famous physicist Paul Langevin, himself a founder-member of the Ligue, became in the 1930s its vice-president. But the men who realized that Dreyfus had been framed could now be relied upon to realize that Zinoviev, Radek and

* *Nouvel Age, Vendredi* and *Europe* were fellow-travelling journals not under direct communist control. After the war the PCF took over *Europe*.

Bukharin hadn't been. Leading members of the Ligue, including Langevin himself, Victor Basch, Félicien Challaye and Jacques Kayser, are reputed to have played down the Ligue's findings on the inhuman methods employed during Soviet collectivization.[7] At the same time the shadow of independent judgment was sustained by offering Moscow occasional rebukes about minor infringements of human rights.

In the United States the proverbial native energy was channelled into the creation of a staggering range and variety of new front-organizations. If one were to select a single man qualified to represent that energy, it could well be the artist and writer Rockwell Kent. He was a landscape and figure painter, a wood engraver and a lithographer whose pictures hung not only in the Metropolitan Museum in New York but also in the Pushkin Museum in Moscow. He was an out-of-doors frontiersman in fact and spirit, the kind of radical Pilgrim Father who will never forget England's effete corruption and whose books reek "of the good earth": *of Men and Mountains* and *It's Me O Lord* were just two of his many titles. He painted Eskimos and spoke of man with a capital "M". He was hot for lower taxes in Essex County and he preached this and other causes in an utterly heroic prose derived eclectically from Homer, the Bible and maybe Mark Twain. "The heavens are brightly starred, and peace is in our land. So keep it, for in the morning we begin: to build America."[8] People used to write to him saying go back to Russia but he didn't. Instead he said – and here we return to front-organizations – all honour to the Civil Liberties Union, to the Southern Conference for Human Welfare, to the Committee to Aid Spanish Democracy, all honour, as he put it, "to every liberal organization in America".[9] Rockwell Kent was an attorney general's list all on his own. He was a member of the American Artists' Congress, which he addressed in New York Town Hall in February 1936, attacking war, racism, nazism, and praising the Soviet Union. He became in time its vice-chairman. He was president of a Congress of Industrial Organizations local, he was a member of an American Federation of Labour local, he was a member (though born in 1882) of the American Youth Congress, of the Descendants of the American Revolution (not to be confused with the Daughters of the same) and of International Labor Defense. He was chairman of the National Committee for People's Rights, a member of the League of American Writers, and vice-president of the International Workers' Order; he served on the national committee of the American League for Peace and Democracy, he was a member of the American Committee for Democracy and Intellectual Freedom, he sat on the Spanish Refugee Relief Campaign. He was a fellow-traveller. And really even Corliss Lamont would have to admit defeat when faced with that record. But one should mention that Kent later became Chairman of the National Council on American-Soviet Friendship and that at the age of eighty-five he was awarded the Lenin Prize for work "permeated with warmth and respect for man – the toiler and fighter". By the time he died he had put all the latter-day George IIIs to rout and ruin.

Not all of these organizations were children of the thirties. International Labor Defense, for example, had been founded in 1925. Presently it came under the leadership of Vito Marcantonio, a self-made man who arrived in the House of Representatives under the curious joint auspices of the right wing of the Republican Party and the left wing of the American Labor Party. For many years one of New York's "Republican" Congressmen, he travelled resolutely with Soviet policy and became one of the *Daily Worker*'s long-serving heroes, though a hostile commentator claimed that Marcantonio's appreciation of the finer points of New York politics also led him to address Italo-American pro-fascist meetings.[10] By 1937 ILD claimed three hundred thousand members distributed through eight hundred branches. One thing it never did was to defend the rights of labour in the Soviet Union, any more than the American International Political Prisoners Committee defended the rights of Soviet political prisoners in the thirties. One says "in the thirties" because it had indeed once aspired to do so: in the mid-1920s its meetings were broken up by communists because the menshevik Russian refugees had raised the whole question, and not without passion. But after further pressure, penetration and persuasion, the Committee came to understand that Soviet political prisoners were not really "political" at all, and therefore not properly speaking prisoners. Similarly the National Federation of Constitutional Liberties concentrated its energies on keeping America in step with the (often imagined) intentions of the Founding Fathers, while resting assured that the USSR was in the hands of Fathers whose devotion to liberty was beyond question.

The attempt to penetrate the young was made principally by two fronts, the American Youth Congress and the National Student League, whose national committee included such student fledglings as J. B. Matthews, H. W. L. Dana, Corliss Lamont, Scott Nearing, Margaret Schlauch and Robert Morss Lovett. Possibly the most influential front-organization, however, was the League against War and Fascism, a product of the Amsterdam-Pleydel Movement masterminded by Münzenberg. In October 1937 it changed its name to the League for Peace and Democracy (LPD), acquiring also a brand-new chairman, the Rev. Harry F. Ward, to replace the renegade Matthews. At its peak the League claimed 1,023 affiliated organizations, with two million members.[11] The LPD's vice-chairman, Robert Morss Lovett, naïvely claimed that Ward's election as chairman was a recognition of the fact that the communists could not carry the enterprise alone, and Ward himself appeared voluntarily before the Un-American Activities Committee to deny that the LPD was communist-dominated. Roger Baldwin argued that the LPD's policies were arrived at by democratic consultation, but the salient fact was that Earl Browder sat permanently on the council of seventeen and could always impose an effective veto in the event of a challenge to the Party line. And when the challenge became ungovernable, as after the Nazi-Soviet Pact, the LPD was soon dissolved. Lovett himself later admitted that, like the League of American Writers, the LPD had existed on sufferance and had been consistently at the service of a foreign power – an experience which in retrospect he found chastening.

A former religious fundamentalist from Kentucky, Joseph Brown Matthews became, like Roger Baldwin, a prodigiously active fellow-traveller. On his own testimony, he held official positions in fifteen organizations and committees, and delivered 105 speeches on behalf of causes most of which had communist support. In 1929 he had become an executive secretary of the pacifist Fellowship of Reconciliation, and it was in the same year that he joined the Socialist Party (SP). Like Heywood Broun, president of the American Newspaper Guild and a contributor to the New York *World-Telegram*, he soon ran into trouble with the SP on account of his participation in United Front activities and his contributions to such periodicals as *The New Masses* and *Soviet Russia Today*. He was also instrumental in the merger of the National Student League and the Student League for Industrial Democracy into the new front-organization, the American Student Union, which promoted annual anti-war demonstrations on the campuses. In addition he was active in the National Committee to Aid the Victims of German Fascism (set up in 1933 and affiliated to International Workers' Relief), alongside A. J. Muste, Dos Passos, Dana and George Soule, of *The Nation*. In 1934 Matthews angrily resigned as chairman of the League against War and Fascism, largely as a result of communist disruption of a meeting held in honour of the socialists of Vienna, but he accepted membership of the League's Bureau until he also resigned from that, in September 1935, apparently because the CP was set to destroy Consumers' Research, of which he was vice-president. And there, evidently, ended his odyssey as a fellow-traveller.*

The League of American Writers (LAW), which attracted a brilliant assembly of left-wing literary talent, served as a counterpart to the AEAR in France, although it came on the scene three years later and was

* For discussion of Matthew's later career as witch-hunt consultant, see Chapter Nine.

therefore more obviously a product of the Popular Front era and of the new tactical emphasis on democratic literature, as distinct from the proletarian model favoured earlier. (When the Proletcult, or proletarian art, was abandoned in Russia the John Reed Clubs, despite the genuine enthusiasm they had stimulated among many young intellectuals, were snuffed out like the flame of a candle.) The LAW was born at the first American Writers' Congress, convened at the Mecca Temple, New York, in April 1935; Earl Browder assured the delegates that the Party had not the least intention of instructing such distinguished writers how or what they should write. A second Congress was held in 1937, "called for" mainly by fellow-travellers* but stage-managed by the Party's cultural commissar Alexander Trachtenberg, who was also boss of International Publishers. In the style approved by Münzenberg, the innocuous Waldo Frank was elected chairman, Hemingway spoke and President Roosevelt was elected an honorary member. Meanwhile on the West Coast the screen writers, directors and stars of Hollywood were doing their bit, embracing the only left-wing party which took the trouble to embrace them. The Hollywood Anti-Nazi League, whose chairman was the ever-active Donald Ogden Stewart, revealed the extent to which it was at Russia's beck and call by politely changing its name to the Hollywood League for Democratic Action after Stalin agreed to share the spoils of Eastern Europe with Hitler. The League served mainly as a kind of Rotary Club whose four thousand members, many of them earning one or two thousand dollars a week, were able to contribute as much to Party funds as the whole American working class. They were naïve enthusiasts without political experience, and many of them had a cruel fate awaiting them.

Münzenberg's own talents were fully extended in co-ordinating front activities at an international level. The first International Congress of Writers for the Defence of Culture was held in Paris in 1935 and assembled a truly impressive galaxy of talents.† Indeed if the proverbial pen had been more powerful than the sword, Hitler would there and then have raised the white flag. The prevailing mood was of course that of the democratic alliance, and the star performances were carefully reserved for fellow-travellers. Gide earned the longest ovation while Jean-Richard Bloch, whose agonized wrestling with the god-demon of communism

---

* Including Lovett, Archibald MacLeish, Vincent Sheean, Donald Ogden Stewart, Jean Starr Untermeyer and Ella Winter.

† Alain, Aragon, Barbusse, Gide and Malraux led the French delegation. Heinrich Mann, Becher, Brecht and Kisch headed the German contingent. Greetings were also sent by Gorky, Rolland, Benda, Toller, Dreiser and Hemingway. But the search for prestigious names from England could produce nothing more radical than two liberal sceptics, E. M. Forster and Aldous Huxley.

filled many notebooks, reported to thunderous applause that nowhere was a writer's pride and independence more secure than in the USSR. As for the Soviet delegation, while the *Pravda* journalist Mikhail Koltsov did the deals in the background, that born master of ceremonies Ilya Ehrenburg urged Moscow to dispatch without delay Isaac Babel and Boris Pasternak. This strategy proved effective: Babel charmed his audience with Jewish tales and the shy Pasternak was finally coaxed from his hotel room to read a poem about the truth lying at one's feet in the grass, and not in the clouds. The Westerners were thus treated to a *bal masqué*. So deep had the communists buried the red flag that when Gustav Regler delivered a speech which deliberately stirred the delegates to rise and sing the Internationale, he ran into trouble. Johannes Becher, on his way to becoming the little Stalin of East German letters, caught up with Regler in the wings of the Mutualité: "You must be mad. . . . You've ruined everything. . . . The Congress can't pretend to be neutral any longer. . . . You're a saboteur." Two days later Regler was hauled over the coals at a cell meeting of the KPD in Paris, earning a sharp rebuke from Anna Seghers and a reminder from Abusch, later a State Secretary in the German Democratic Republic, that: "We are at present in an under-cover phase. Whoever breaks cover is a counter-revolution-ary."[12]

International gatherings of the left-wing intellectuals continued almost up to the moment when Hitler and Stalin came to an accommodation. A second Congress for the Defence of Culture was held in July 1937 and became a travelling road show as it moved from Valencia, Madrid and Barcelona to Paris. By now the line-up was as flexible as in an American football team: the former Dadaist high priest Tristan Tzara represented the French squad at Valencia, Jean Cassou and Malraux stepped in at Madrid, with Benda, Claude Aveline and André Chamson appearing in Paris. Messages of support and encouragement from Anna Louise Strong, Heinrich Mann, Feuchtwanger *et alia* thronged the wires of Europe in formulas which became as stereotyped as invitation cards. In the background Münzenberg was still at work, but time was running out for Europe, and for Münzenberg too, and in the aftermath there would be only swarms of well-meaning words left hovering aimlessly in the hot summer air of war.

In Germany the books were burning. In a single year the Third Reich arrested about 160,000 communists and murdered at least 2,500. Exile became the fate of almost the whole left-wing intelligentsia,* of many

---

* Of course not all German intellectual refugees were left-wing. Consider, in the field of academic politics, the cases of Hans Morgenthau and Henry Kissinger; in scientific politics,

liberals and, of course, of a great number of Jewish writers, scholars and scientists, whatever their political persuasion. For the writer particularly, so often dependent on close contact with his native soil, language and community, exile can be a form of death. Yet Voltaire had suffered it for forty-two years, Mickiewicz for twenty-six, Heine for twenty-five and Victor Hugo for nineteen – and few who left Germany in 1933 imagined that Hitler would last that long. So, bravely making a virtue out of necessity, the exiled writers took pride in having their complete works consigned to the flames by the SS and SA men. When in 1933 Goebbels's Reichskulturkammer banned only one of Oskar Maria Graf's books and recommended the rest as true *Blut und Boden* literature, Graf wrote a celebrated letter of protest: *"Verbrennt Mich"*.

The exiles naturally chose different roads of departure. Those who really believed in Russia with their whole souls went to live there,* but not surprisingly few if any fellow-travellers accompanied them. Toller, Heinrich Mann, Feuchtwanger, Arnold Zweig and Alfred Kerr – among the most prestigious of post-Hitler fellow-travellers – all preferred to love the Soviet Union at a distance. Kerr had been the most influential drama critic in the Weimar Republic, and as early as 1930 he had written in the bourgeois *Berliner Tageblatt* of "the new, daring human order of the Soviets". When he fled from Germany in 1933 all seventeen of his books were banned there, a reprisal which may partially account for his comparison of Soviet society with the greatest of Beethoven's symphonies. At the age of seventy, in 1937, he declared: *"Für Sowjetrussland empfand ich höchste Bewunderung* – I felt the highest admiration for Soviet Russia."[13] He nevertheless preferred to live in Switzerland, Paris and London. Whereas the minor writers and journalists had to hang around Paris or Prague scouting for jobs and part-time editorial work on émigré journals, the more famous and prosperous writers tended to gravitate towards the less frenetic environment of the French Mediterranean coast. Heinrich Mann lived in Nice, in the same house as Joseph Roth and Hermann Kersten, but it was Sanary-sur-Mer which became a veritable colony of distinguished fellow-

---

of Edward Teller; among economists, of Hayek and Mises. Schumpeter, Freud and Cassirer were scarcely political radicals. Others underwent interesting mutations: Karl August Wittfogel, once the KPD's leading China expert, later informed on his American sponsor to the McCarthy Committee!

* The communists who settled in Moscow included Becher, Willi Bredel, Alfred Kurella, Theodore Plivier, Friedrich Wolf, Erich Weinert and Adam Scharrer. In Moscow they earned their keep by working for the International Union of Revolutionary Writers and by editing such periodicals as *Internationale Literatur* and *Das Wort*. Some of them, like Plivier, only narrowly survived the purges. Others, like Kurella's brother Heinrich, didn't, though Kurella himself finally returned to East Germany in 1954 as a Soviet citizen.

travellers. Situated between Toulon and Marseilles, this picturesque fishing village with its single hotel, two or three cafés and a handful of smart villas, witnessed in the spring of 1933 a meeting of Thomas, Heinrich and Klaus Mann, Zweig, Feuchtwanger, Toller and Brecht. Of these it was Lion Feuchtwanger who came to stay. In the late 1930s Sanary could boast no more faithful or productive a resident.

Feuchtwanger was born in Munich in 1884 and was subsequently educated at a humanistic gymnasium. He studied philosophy and philology at Berlin University where he wrote a highly commended dissertation on *Der Rabbi von Bacharach*, a novel-fragment by Heinrich Heine, whose triple fate of German, Jew and refugee was one which Feuchtwanger was destined to share in full. After founding a literary bi-monthly, *Der Spiegel* (Thomas Mann and Jacob Wassermann were contributors), he was conscripted in 1914; only short-sightedness earned him a reprieve after an experience of six months he was never to forget. In 1915 he published *Lied der Gefallenen*, one of the first anti-war poems to appear in Germany during the First World War. But much as he detested militarism and chauvinism, he was too physically timid a man to take up arms as a revolutionary. He witnessed the Munich Revolution and its suppression as a trembling spectator, torn between his conviction that Toller, Eisner and Landauer were intellectuals unfitted for politics, and his indignation at the way the revolutionaries were treated when the Revolution was suppressed. Observing the Bavarian courts distributing farcically light sentences to the most blatant murderers,* Feuchtwanger took refuge in the pen, in biting satire and in the comforting notion that the Right traditionally resorted to murder because the Left had a monopoly of intelligence. Like Heinrich Mann and Romain Rolland, indeed like many later fellow-travellers in their formative years, he was convinced that the true vocation of art and intelligence is incompatible with politics – an attitude cultivated under the German Empire where the scribes were permitted to doodle ineffectually in the margin of history. In fact none of those prominent French and German humanists who embraced the Soviet Union late in life ever quite overcame the inbred apartheid of *Geist* and *Macht*.

In 1925 Feuchtwanger moved from Munich to the new cultural capital of Germany, Berlin. Though his chief claim to fame and fortune were his novels, which enjoyed a prodigious success in the Anglo-Saxon countries, in Berlin he was able to indulge his passion for the

---

* As late as 1970 a deputy in the Bavarian Parliament objected to a street in Munich being named after Kurt Eisner on the ground that it might offend the widow of Eisner's murderer, Count Arcos!

theatre, both as critic and writer. In 1918 the young Brecht had sought his advice about his play *Spartacus,** and later he brought him the text of *Baal*. But it was Brecht, fourteen years the younger, who possessed the natural talent as a playwright, and by 1925 it was he who was helping Feuchtwanger to prepare *Warren Hastings, Gouverneur von Indien* for the stage. They collaborated together on Brecht's *Leben Eduards II*, and although Feuchtwanger's ideology stopped well short of Marxism, he did allow Brecht to coax him away from the dramatic-realist forms he employed as a novelist towards an alienated and epic conception of theatre. It was in this mode that he wrote *Die Petroleum-Inseln* (1925), a parody of American capitalistic enterprise. But his was the kind of party-less intellectual radicalism cultivated within the circle gathered round *Die Weltbühne* (for which he wrote theatre reviews), and his general political posture during the twenties gave few clues to his later affection for the USSR. In *Erfolg* (1930) he wrote: "In Russia Bolshevist judges executed supporters of the Tsarist regime for acts of espionage of which they were probably innocent, after brow-beating any defence that was offered."[14] He put bolshevik authoritarianism on a par with the imprisonment and execution of innocent socialists and Jews in Rumania, Hungary and Bulgaria, and with the imprisonment for unproven offences of communists in Paris. In other words – an aristocratic plague on all your houses. But the philosophers tumbled from their turrets as the landscape of Weimar civilization began to tremble and erupt. Standing in protest at the gate of the prison into which Ossietzky was led in May 1932, Feuchtwanger remarked to Zweig: "The true Republic is going to prison." Within a year it had also gone into exile.

Hitler drew his attention to the virtues of the Marxist analysis of history. The illusion that *Geist* could defend itself unaided against *Macht* was no longer tenable. Already in *Erfolg* he had depicted the big capitalists and landowners as the real mentors of early fascism in the era of the 1923 Munich putsch, but Feuchtwanger had nevertheless committed himself through his hero Tüverlin to the liberal, democratic tradition of justice, reason and progress. Now the political balance of his fiction began to change. In *Die Geschwister Oppermann* (1934), Gustav Oppermann is depicted living in an unpolitical universe, smugly assured that the values of the Enlightenment must ultimately prevail; nazism hurls him into a fight for survival. Here again the capitalistic substructure beneath and behind the Hitler movement is exposed. Yet Feuchtwanger's journey towards orthodox Marxism continued to be a "two steps forward, one step back" affair, and in his *Wartesaal* trilogy he fell precisely into the trap which orthodox Marxists like Wielande Herzfelde warned

* Later known as *Trommeln in der Nacht*.

against – the view that what had occurred in Germany was, as in the Thirty Years' War, the triumph of barbarism over reason. Though he emphasized in the afterword to the last novel of the trilogy, *Exil*, that the reign of the irrational, of naked power, can be overcome only by violent social struggle, it was not a point of view that he was psychologically or intellectually capable of *integrating* into his fiction. Privately he could only visualize Voltaire challenging the King of France; the notion of a proletarian revolution rubbed against the deepest sources of his scepticism.

When the nazis took power and ransacked his apartment, he was abroad on an American lecture tour. All his manuscripts and notes for work in progress were lost. Gallantly and without a pause he resumed his literary labours at Sanary, working imperturbably in a pretty house overlooking the sea and greeting visitors like Ludwig Marcuse with the Chinese smile which blended Western rationality with Oriental tranquillity. He was proud to be Jewish and, confronted by rampant anti-semitism, his answer was to calculate just how many readers round the world were reading his books at any moment of the day. Like Gide he believed ultimately in a single reason; that it resided in his own head he was the first to admit. When the drums of barbarism sounded too loud he was able to wall himself off within the citadel of world literature, communing serenely with the great minds of the past. He was an epicure, ate well, loved well, told anecdotes and was his own most appreciative listener. To protect his remarkable capacity for work* he maintained a rigorous domestic routine: visitors who telephoned from the Marine Café were told: "Herr Feuchtwanger will be delighted if you come from 4.30 to 6.15." These visitors included the Mann brothers, Marcuse, Zweig, Toller, Brecht, Otto Katz, Koestler and Alfred Kantorowicz.

The problematic of the Soviet Union is echoed in *Exil*. Here we find a contrast between the character Trautwein, who is anti-fascist but averse to the dictatorial aspects of communism, and his son Hanns who is eager to help build socialism in the USSR. Hanns's mentor Merkle explains that the father represents a generation (Feuchtwanger's own, no doubt) which has not yet grasped the fact that humane ideals cannot be realized until society has first passed through a preliminary phase of dictatorial power. Thus the writer Feuchtwanger attempts to expose and transcend his own "false consciousness". But he couldn't. Really he was bound to remain the father. And yet he was convinced that communism alone had the guts to resist fascism in the democracies and to check its expansion

---

* At Sanary he completed five major novels, *Die Geschwister Oppermann* (1934) and *Exil* (1939), both belonging to the *Wartesaal* trilogy, as well as the second and third parts of the *Josephus* trilogy, *Die Söhne* (1935) and *Das gelobte Land* (1938). He also wrote *Der falsche Nero* (1936).

abroad. Hence his struggle to translate *"wollen"* into *"können"*; hence also, I would suggest, the lack of moderation with which he embraced most if not all aspects of Soviet life under Stalin. He even accepted Soviet criticism of his earlier novels as "formalist". In 1937 he sent a message to the International Writers' Congress to the effect that the so-called freedom of art and thought under the formal Western democracies was merely a dangerous play on words. He damned the West, lauded Russia – and lived in France.

The Nazi-Soviet Pact must have shaken him to the core. One does not know. At the outbreak of war he was briefly interned as an alien, and then released. But in the summer of 1940 he was again taken into captivity, this time at Les Milles camp. After some weeks he was released. Later, in *Unholdes Frankreich* (1942), he complained about the monotonous work in the camp, the aimless piling and unpiling of bricks, the bureaucratic routine and the general thoughtlessness which prevailed. So the arch-apologist for the Soviet Union, the visitor who saw Moscow smiling under the purges, howled when he experienced the mildest taste of regimentation, of imprisonment. Would that other familiar names, shielded by the English Channel or the Atlantic Ocean, had shared this short seminar in slavery!

He escaped with Heinrich Mann and others from France, via Spain and Portugal, to California. And there he was to remain. After the war he produced a book whose tactless title convinced Moscow that he had indeed turned renegade: but in fact *Waffen für Amerika* (Weapons for America) was a novel set in the time of the American Revolution – Feuchtwanger was again seeking refuge in the historical novel and the bourgeois Enlightenment. In East Berlin Alfred Kantorowicz came under pressure to reprint the *Novy Mir* attack on Feuchtwanger in his own magazine, *Ost und West*, but after some negotiating with the cultural officers of the occupying Red Army he was allowed to publish instead an appreciation by Heinrich Mann. Still rumours continued to circulate in Eastern Europe that Feuchtwanger had somehow turned his coat in the course of the American witch-hunts, and Arnold Zweig recalled that when he visited Moscow in 1952 he had to "break several lances" on his behalf, explaining that Feuchtwanger had really supported Thomas Mann and Chaplin against the witch-hunts. Then the tide turned. In 1953 he was awarded the National Prize for Literature in the German Democratic Republic, and the following year the Humboldt University in East Berlin awarded him an honorary degree. Large editions of his work began to reappear in Russia and the Popular Democracies. Nevertheless, Feuchtwanger would not budge from California. One of his last books, *The House of Desdemona*, surveys the scope of the historical novel from a standpoint which is fairly scornful of Lukács and the Marxist critics – as if he had come full circle to the 1920s, as if the entire fellow-travelling phase had been simply a passing aberration. He died in 1958.

For the majority of German left-wing émigré intellectuals, some form of collaboration with the KPD, so long avoided or resisted, became inevitable. Certainly the communists did their level best to make it so. Gone were the days when Johannes Becher and his comrades blasted the social-fascists, social pacifists and class-collaborators through the columns of *Linkskurve*. Though the communist (and Comintern) leadership took their time in recognizing the full extent of their error in pursuing sectarian, pseudo-revolutionary tactics, by 1934–5 the KPD was working hard alongside its French and British counterparts to form effective United and Popular Fronts (Enheitsfront and Volksfront). At the Brussels Conference of the KPD held in October 1935, past mistakes were admitted and the formula accepted that nazi persecution had rendered the Socialist Party more amenable to joint anti-fascist action. The KPD henceforward called for a broad-based, worker, peasant and middle-class alliance committed to a democratic programme. But the majority of SPD leaders in exile were having none of it, though left-wingers like Rudolf Breitscheid, Alfred Braunthal, Max Braun and Rudolf Hilferding were prepared to associate with the communists in a Volksfront. In December 1936 the KPD issued an appeal signed by the entire Party leadership, by twenty socialists, by nine members (including Willi Brandt) of the Sozialistische Arbeiterpartei, by prominent communist intellectuals and by such fellow-travellers as Feuchtwanger, Heinrich Mann, Arnold Zweig, Toller, E. J. Gumbel, Rudolf Olden, Alfons Goldschmidt and Rudolf Leonhard.

The attitude of non-co-operation adopted by the SPD leaders increased the importance of the fellow-travellers' mediatory role. Feuchtwanger, admittedly, was not very active in this respect, while Zweig had taken himself off to Palestine. The key figure was undoubtedly Heinrich Mann. In 1934 he issued a general reproach to those of his fellow-émigrés who could not forget old tribal loyalties: "Here you forget that you are republicans. . . . The individual is not primarily a Marxist, a Jew, a head worker or a hand worker; above all he is an emigrant."[15] This was not Marxism, but it was useful. Constantly emphasizing that if the leaders of the two German workers' parties had not fought one another, there would have been no Hitler regime, Mann hailed the formation of the Front populaire in France and welcomed the new orientation of the Comintern towards a democratic alliance. However in time he began to find the distant Stalin more congenial than the little German Stalins closer to hand. When a Volksfront congress was convened in Paris in April 1937, Ulbricht manoeuvred to sow distrust and to ensure KPD domination. Willi Münzenberg openly opposed such tactics, while Mann's indignation was enormous. He wrote to Max Braun complaining that Ulbricht was nothing but an intriguer and a power-seeker one could no longer deal with. But efforts towards unity continued – there was no alternative except passive acceptance of Hitler. In September 1938 the German Friends of Freedom in Paris published an appeal for unity signed by a number of fellow-travellers, including Georg Bernhard, Hermann Budzislawski, Bruno Frei, Alfons Goldschmidt, Arthur Holitscher, Rudolf Leonhard and Arnold Zweig. In May 1939 Heinrich Mann wrote to his brother Thomas: "... the German rising must come before the war . . . by the turn of the year Hitler must lie under the ground."[16]

Paris was naturally the centre of émigré activity. But life was not easy. The refugees were not wholly welcome in France and few found jobs commensurate with their abilities or professional qualifications. Official work permits were simply not available (the economic depression began to hit France just in these years), the result being that some were forced to do "ghosting" for French professional men, who took most of the pay – a situation analogous to the one which occurred in America during the post-war witch-hunts. Nevertheless the outlook was not entirely black: the French communists gave some help, Münzenberg was adept at conjuring jobs out of thin air, and although the German domestic market was obviously closed to émigré writers, the Dutch publishers Albert de Lange and Querido began to specialize in German-language editions of the works of refugees.

The main front-organization for German writers living in Paris was the Schutzverband deutscher Schriftsteller (SDS – usually translated as the Association of German Writers in Exile), roughly a counterpart to the AEAR in France and the League of American Writers. Originally founded in 1908 as a writers' trade union, the SDS was dissolved by the nazis and then re-founded in Paris by the communists Kurella, Kantorowicz, Regler, Anna Seghers, Kisch, Bodo Uhse, Koestler and Sperber. The communist members were accustomed to meet in private caucus once a week, often under the supervision of Otto Abusch, alias Ernst Reinhardt, a member of the Central Committee and a former editor of *Rote Fahne*. But the usual front-tactics were pursued and a fellow-traveller, Rudolf Leonhard,* was elected first president. If he was the model of the easily manipulated sympathizer, so another

* Born in 1889, Leonhard had been a minor poet, pacifist and revolutionary. While in exile he published two books in French. He collaborated with many Soviet- or communist-

littérateur of minor talent, Alfred Kantorowicz,* was the model communist manipulator, busy-body and general secretary. Meanwhile the SDS required an honorary president: Heinrich Mann was the automatic choice. He was now the honorary everything, a living statue of democratic rectitude, a kind of Hindenburg of the Left. But the SDS had real work to do, and on more than one front. It helped out when writers found themselves in dire financial straits, it bargained for decent royalties and tried to defend copyright, it organized meetings and demonstrations, and it agitated ceaselessly on behalf of those imprisoned in Germany, sometimes successfully, as with Ludwig Renn, and sometimes not, as with Carl von Ossietzky who died in 1936 in semi-captivity, a year after he was awarded the Nobel Peace Prize. Each major nazi propaganda event, like the Nuremberg Rally of 1936, evoked a counter-demonstration from the SDS. Presenting to Europe the healthy face of Germany, many of its members fought and died in Spain, their unremitting and selfless activity on behalf of the anti-fascist cause earning them the respect of their European colleagues.†

The different shades of opinion within the German emigration were reflected by the several German-language periodicals published in exile. Perhaps the most "liberal" of these was *Die Sammlung*, founded in 1933, published by Querido of Amsterdam, and edited by Klaus Mann (whose energetic sister Erika married W. H. Auden). The official patrons of *Die Sammlung* were Gide, Heinrich Mann (the editor's uncle) and Aldous Huxley. Twenty-four issues appeared between March 1933 and August 1935, the main emphasis being on politics and literature viewed from a left-democratic standpoint.‡ Also independent was *Das Neue*

sponsored organizations, periodicals, etc. Interned in France in 1939, he managed to join the French Resistance. In 1950 he settled in East Germany and in the following year published a collection of essays and poems praising the DDR.

* Born in 1899, the son of a Jewish Berlin merchant, Kantorowicz had been a volunteer in 1914. Later a theatre critic and editor, he joined the KPD in 1931. In Spain from 1936 to 1939, he was interned in France in 1940 but escaped to New York where he worked in the foreign news department of CBS. After the war he founded the magazine *Ost und West* in East Berlin, but it was suppressed in 1949. He made it his business to know the more distinguished fellow-travellers well. In 1957 he fled to the West.

† As examples of the unremitting activity, one could mention the creation of the Deutsche Kulturartell, the Frei Künstler-Bund, the Verband deutscher Journalisten unter Emigration the Vereinigung deutscher Bühnenangehöriger (theatre people), and the Deutsche Volkshochschule, which taught a wide variety of scientific, sociological and aesthetic subjects. Foreign sympathy was reflected in the collaboration of Rolland, Gide, Wells and Lévy-Bruhl in sponsoring, along with Feuchtwanger and Heinrich Mann, the Deutsche Freiheitsbibliothek, founded in May 1934. Mann, inevitably, was president.

‡ Contributors to *Die Sammlung* included: A. Huxley, Gide, Maurois, Ehrenburg, Sforza, Cocteau, Hemingway, Rolland, Bloch, Spender, Silone, Croce, Isherwood, Pasternak, Brod, Doblin, Frank, Giraudoux, Kerr, Mann, Romains, Schickele, Wassermann, A. Zweig, S. Zweig. This list of names is interesting in so far as it shows that the effect of Hitler's

Tage-Buch, launched in July 1933, three months after its editor Leopold Schwarzschild escaped from Germany determined to resurrect his *Tage-Buch* of Weimar Republic days. Here contributions were to be found not only from fellow-travellers like Heinrich Mann, Feuchtwanger, Zweig, Toller and Ehrenburg, but much more typically and frequently from the cream of the European liberal intelligentsia. Schwarzschild adopted a friendly attitude towards the Soviet Five Year Plans and campaigned vigorously for the United and Popular Fronts, but the first Moscow trial seems to have had an extraordinary effect on him, bringing from his pen venomous invective against anyone who had ever collaborated with the communists. In 1939, for example, he called Klaus Mann, who had written for *Das Neue Tage-Buch* until 1937, "an old Soviet agent".

Moving leftwards and closer to communist influence, we find four magazines published in exile. *Der Gegenangriff*, (Counter-attack), a title inspired by Goebbels's own *Angriff*, was subsidized by Münzenberg's Editions du Carrefour, published in Prague and Paris, and edited first by the communist functionary Abusch and later by the fellow-traveller Bruno Frei. Another Prague-based journal was *Neue Deutsche Blätter*, edited by the communist intellectuals Wielande Herzfelde and Anna Seghers, in collaboration with the left-wing writer Oskar Maria Graf. Hard-line communists dominated the list of contributors, notably Becher, Bredel, Herzfelde, Weiskopf and Uhse, but less orthodox Marxists such as Brecht and Ernst Fischer were welcomed along with fellow-travellers like Feuchtwanger and Holitscher and some left-wing liberals. The first editorial in September 1933 warned that, "There is no neutrality. For nobody. And least for the writer. Whoever is silent takes part in the struggle." The writer (the editors insisted) must neither be frightened back into private introspection, nor use words as toys, nor depict fascism as an anachronistic retreat into medieval barbarism; he must insist on its quality as an organic product of dying capitalism. No other force could conquer this tyranny except the proletariat. The battlefront thus defined, the editors then relapsed into gentler tones: there would be no question of imposing a single viewpoint on contributors, and comradely discussions would be held.[17] Grasping this friendly hand, Holitscher fired off with an amusing satire of nazi Germany based on Gulliver's travels. Evidently *Neue Deutsche Blätter* could accommodate itself to the fellow-travellers. The only thing which ran out was the money.

Die Neue Weltbühne, heir to the great radical journal of the Weimar

---

seizure of power was not automatically to throw German émigrés into the arms of Russia or the KPD. Klaus Mann's magazine was certainly friendly towards the Soviet Union, but many of its contributors were not.

Republic we have already discussed, turned out to be considerably more Marxist than Tucholsky and Ossietzky had allowed its predecessor to be.* Published variously in Vienna, Prague, Zurich and Paris, it survived until 1939. The first editor, Willi Schlamm, stopped just short of the KPD line, but in March 1934 the widow of the previous owner, Jacobsohn, dismissed him largely because he had solicited and published an article by Trotsky in an early issue. The editor who replaced him, Hermann Budzislawski, was a fellow-traveller who adhered closely to the Party line (thus yielding the substance but blurring the image) and who in later years was to settle at the University of Leipzig in the DDR. Unlike the old *Weltbühne*, its successor never criticized either Soviet policy or the KPD: it also endorsed the Moscow trials.

But the most orthodox of all Popular Front periodicals was one which first appeared in 1936 and was published in Moscow – *Das Wort*. The composition of the editorial committee was a perfect example of the "front" principle: Willi Bredel, a Moscow-based, hard-line communist; Brecht, a Danish-based, non-Party communist with a growing international reputation; and Lion Feuchtwanger, of Sanary-sur-Mer. The funds necessary for the enterprise were apparently promised to the Germans during the 1935 International Writers' Congress by Mikhail Koltsov, director of the Soviet publishing house Jourgaz (and later a victim of the purges). After a year as effective resident editor, Willi Bredel departed for Spain, leaving Fritz Erpenbeck in charge. Though Erpenbeck dispatched all incoming articles to the three nominal editors, the facts of geography and the limitations of transport usually compelled him to go to press before he received their comments. When he finally met Feuchtwanger during his Moscow visit, the famous novelist was much too preoccupied with interviewing Stalin and negotiating the Soviet editions of his works to bother about *Das Wort*. As a distracted general might treat a beavering adjutant, he merely thanked Erpenbeck for his good work and told him to carry on. Clearly, the way to handle both fellow-travelling and plain liberal contributions had been carefully worked out in the Moscow editorial office. If a fellow-traveller like Feuchtwanger were vigorously to toe the Party line in a language all his own, so much the better: give him prominence, give him space. But generally the German communists in Moscow handled the hottest political issues, for they alone understood the exact phraseology and nuances of emphasis required. You could not, for example, trust a fellow-traveller to break the news that Gorky had been poisoned by Trotsky. On the other hand many of the fellow-travellers were writers and scholars whose

* Contributors included Barbusse, Brecht, Fischer, Graf, Kisch, Leo Lania, Heinrich and Thomas Mann, Heinz Pol, Silone, Sinclair, Agnes Smedley and Toller.

broad culture was now a highly profitable asset, since the question was constantly posed: which is the authentic Germany? So ask them to write about the revolution of 1848, about Lessing, Goethe and Heine; invite them to satirize fascism. When Toller gives a speech in New York on the fundamental unity of German culture and its binding force on all émigrés, then print it. Meanwhile let the editorials refer to the USSR as a state constantly threatened by nazi Germany "but which does not respond chauvinistically, but rather with love and respect for the true, human, German spirit which has contributed so much to the world".[18] And when a star like Hemingway releases a couple of paragraphs about the two Germanys currently fighting one another in Spain, then publish the whole piece in italics without questioning just where this famous American stands on the issue of communism.*

In America the exiled Germans were also active. The Aurora Press was established to publish their work in their native language. In October 1938 a Schutzverband deutsch-amerikanischer Schriftsteller was set up with Thomas Mann as honorary president and Oskar Maria Graf as first president. Graf was something of a character. Having fought on the Russian front in the First World War, refused orders in the field, been court-martialled and sentenced to fourteen months in prison, he became a socialist. His best-known work was *Wir sind Gefangene* (We Are Prisoners) which appeared in 1926 to warm praise from Gorky and Rolland. After his Munich home was raided and his papers seized in 1933, he moved to Vienna and there witnessed the bloody suppression by Dollfuss of the workers' rising. Thence to Prague. In 1936 he published *Der Abgrund* (praised by Feuchtwanger in *Das Wort*), the second part of which depicted Austria during the rise of Catholic fascism and which laid the whole blame for the collapse of the workers' movement on the shoulders of the social democratic leadership. Accordingly he was held in increasingly high esteem in communist circles and began to take on the appearance of a candidate fellow-traveller. Stout, witty and good-natured, he appeared in Moscow in 1934 for the Soviet Writers' Congress and walked the streets in Bavarian *Lederhosen*, followed by an army of astonished children. He was delighted to meet the great Gorky at last, but refused to inspect Lenin's tomb: "Snow White", he called it. He then unburdened himself of a speech to the effect that the Russians indulged in too many military parades and too little dancing and singing. When his hosts invited him to sign the usual book contract, he dumbfounded them by asking for the money there and then. By the time he

---

* A. Zweig, H. Mann, Rudolf Olden, Leonhard, Toller and E. J. Gumbel were among *Das Wort*'s most favoured fellow-travellers. Also popular were A. Kerr, O. M. Graf, S. Zweig, L. Marcuse, M. Brod, T. Mann, A. Döblin, W. A. Berendsohn, W. Benjamin, K. Mann.

reached New York it was apparent that he was travelling with nothing and nobody except himself.

In America, the Germans experienced varying personal fortunes. Hollywood was the scene of a "we never close" tragicomedy. Feucht-wanger, Heinrich Mann, Franz Werfel, Bruno Frank and Leonhard Frank all worked there, as did the director Leopold Jessner and at least five top-rank actors and actresses. The most farcical events occurred. Carl Zuckmayer was working on a screen version of Arnold Zweig's anti-war novel, *Sergeant Grischa*, when Hal Wallis told him to forget it: the Soviet-Finnish war had just broken out and Zweig was known for his Red sympathies. The venerated Heinrich Mann, the film of whose early novel had presented Marlene Dietrich to enchanting advantage in *The Blue Angel*, found himself like others employed on a yearly contract by MGM at a salary of six thousand dollars – many American screen writers earned as much in six weeks. Obliged to clock-in at the office, he twiddled his thumbs all day or fiddled with scripts he knew would never be used. Then he was fired. Short of money, he had to move to a small apartment in Los Angeles and to rely on his brother's financial help. It could, of course, have been worse.

The era of the Popular Fronts provided an exception to the general rule, or tendency: that fellow-travellers prefer to collaborate with the Soviet Union rather than with their local Communist Parties. The CPs were, after all, cultivating a non-revolutionary, democratic image; everywhere they were the driving force behind the United and Popular Fronts; the struggle against fascism at home and in the international arena had become one and indivisible. This was certainly what many French left-wing intellectuals felt after the alarming right-wing, anti-parliamentary riots of 6 February 1934. Within a few weeks the PCF was integrating the fellow-travellers (many of whom were only now emerging as such) into its master-plan: to form an effective electoral alliance first with the Socialist Party (SFIO) and then with the middle-of-the-road radicals. In March 1934 a large meeting was held in the Latin Quarter, presided over by Jean Cassou. Paul Rivet and Paul Langevin issued an *Appel aux Travailleurs*, urging solidarity between workers and intellectuals. Rolland appealed to the people of Paris. André Chamson's diffidence began to wither away as he experienced "growing anguish before the rise of totalitarian regimes" (the USSR not included) and "the decisive shock of 6 February".[19] Veteran scientists like Aimé and Eugénie Cotton joined anti-fascist organizations and began to move within the communist orbit. Jean-Richard Bloch, who only a year previously had publicly preferred the SFIO to the PCF, now blamed the socialists and radicals for failing to encourage the necessary revolutionary solution, the "Fourth Republic". Like many German intellectuals living through the last months of the Weimar Republic, he came to the conclusion that the socialists feared the communists more than they did the police. Richard Cobb, an English historian living in Paris at the time, recalls: "My first sight of France was an Action Française strong-arm team in full spate, beating up a Jewish student. And this was a daily occurrence. It is difficult to convey the degree of hate that any decent person would feel for the pimply, cowardly *ligueurs* ... France was living through a moral and mental civil war ... one had to choose between fascism and fellow-travelling."[20] And so, stimulated by a new sense of urgency, of time running out, a growing legion of fellow-travelling intellectuals worked to clear the path towards left-wing unity. The Comité de Vigilance des Intellectuels Antifasciste (CVIA), founded on 5 March 1934, with Rivet and Langevin as joint presidents, organized a second *Manifeste aux Travailleurs* signed by more than 1,200 intellectuals, including such prominent fellow-travellers as Gide, Benda, Cassou, Friedmann, Guéhenno and Vildrac. In 1935 Rivet was elected deputy for the 5th *arrondissement* of Paris on a United Front platform; the Party had a few months earlier brought the CVIA and the Ligue des Droits de l'Homme together at a large meeting in the Salle Bullier. It was Langevin who presided over the meeting of 8 June which voted to create a Comité du Rassemblement populaire. When the three-party Popular Front was formally consecrated at the Buffalo Stadium on 14 July, all the communist front-organizations were represented. And it was symbolic of the prevailing strategy that a distinguished intellectual, Victor Basch, should be elected figure-head president of the Popular Front.

Naturally the communist literary monthly, *Commune*, vigorously roped in fellow-travelling contributors. But there were also tensions. In November 1935 three fellow-travellers of the milder variety, Charles Vildrac, André Viollis and Jean Guéhenno, had founded the weekly cultural review, *Vendredi*. (Chamson was, in his own words, "more and more devoured by political passions" and had moved so far towards Russia that he felt able to tell an audience at the Maison de la Culture that French peasants would ultimately adopt a system of agriculture analogous to the Soviet one.) *Vendredi*'s funds came not from communist but from radical sources, which permitted a degree of editorial independence the communists could not tolerate. When Chamson, out of his great regard for Gide, decided to publish the foreword of his *Retour de l'URSS*, all hell broke loose and the communists tried to take *Vendredi* over. The paper at once backtracked and published a scathing attack on Gide written by Sartre's young communist *copain*, Paul Nizan. Eleven months later the editors refused to publish Gide's exchange with *Izvestia* about communist suppression of the Spanish anarchists. Whereupon Gide accused the editors of being slaves to the Party line, an arrow which apparently stung; it was not long before political issues disappeared from *Vendredi*, which was re-named *Reflets*. Obviously the fellow-traveller serves the communist cause more usefully and safely as a contributor subject to communist editorial control than as an editor periodically overtaken by the old "bourgeois" respect for open controversy.

Although the British CP remained throughout this period comparatively weak and ineffectual, it began to play an increasingly crucial role in the consciousness of left-wing intellectuals. (It lacked only one ingredient: workers.) The Party reversed its line on social-fascism in strict tempo with the Comintern. In June 1934 R. Palme Dutt, an ideologue of Jesuit-like subtlety who in 1971 celebrated his fiftieth year as editor of *Labour Monthly*, was still describing Sir Stafford Cripps, G. D. H. Cole, George Lansbury and other leading figures in the Socialist League as "chatterers" and as blood-brothers to the French, right-wing "neo-socialists". (The comparison was singularly inapt.) By September he had executed a complete volte-face and was calling on the Socialist League and the ILP to collaborate with the CP in returning a Labour government to power. In October 1936 Dutt renewed an old campaign for CP affiliation to the Labour Party. For its part, the parliamentary Labour leadership was adamant in its rejection of such overtures; Dalton called them "clotted nonsense", Attlee also said no, and in April 1938 the National Executive of the LP flatly and finally rejected all talk of a Popular Front.

It would be a mistake to label all those who campaigned within the Labour movement for a Popular Front as fellow-travellers. Although Cripps voiced doubts about reformist socialism, he was no Marxist and he regarded the Soviet experiment with some scepticism. In 1939 he was expelled from the Labour Party Executive and from the Party itself for continuing to advocate a Popular Front in defiance of Party policy,* but he was not a fellow-traveller. Nor was Aneurin Bevan, who went with him. George Strauss and Charles Trevelyan, who were purged at the same time, were closer to the mould. The two most ardent fellow-travellers of the LP National Executive, D. N. Pritt and Harold Laski,

* Cripps was reinstated in the LP in 1945, and thereafter became President of the Board of Trade, then Chancellor of the Exchequer, in the Attlee Governments. As such he carried his old, left-wing load singularly lightly. Those who had gone to the wall with him in 1939, and remained faithful to their principles, naturally viewed his career uncharitably.

were able to sit tight and avoid expulsion. Pritt believed, as he put it, that a United Front would have brought "all the enthusiasm, devotion and political education of the communists into the centre of the political struggle. . . ."[21] Among less publicized names, we find several fellow-travellers who in 1939 suffered for their Popular Front convictions by expulsion from the Labour Party. One of these was Edgar P. Young, parliamentary candidate for North-West Hull. Although not a brilliant political intellectual like Cripps, nor a popular working-class leader like Bevan, nor a distinguished academic like Laski, nor a successful profes-sional man like the lawyer D. N. Pritt, Young was in many senses representative of a considerable body of middle-class opinion which travelled resolutely and enthusiastically with the Soviet Union both before and after the war. It is easy to forget that while Heinrich Mann was accepting yet another honorary presidency, and Romain Rolland was sending yet another message of greeting to a Party Congress, and Upton Sinclair was addressing a New York rally by direct line from California, and the Webbs were being read all over the world – that in the background many humbler English, French and American people were licking brown envelopes, subscribing small sums of money for this cause and that, eagerly buying tickets for the forthcoming visit of the Red Army dance ensemble, gazing approvingly up at the Dean of Canter-bury from the crowded auditorium of the Albert Hall or the Salle Bullier or New York Town Hall, reading the news from Spain with hope then despair, borrowing Sholokhov's *Virgin Soil Upturned* from the local lending library, subscribing to the Left Book Club, marching with their fellow Parisians on 12 February 1934, raging with anger and disgust at the hypocritical policy of appeasement pursued by the Chamberlain and Daladier Governments – hating Hitler and investing in Stalin their hopes for a better, more peaceful world. In other words there was a cake beneath the marzipan.

In 1937 Cripps took the initiative in founding a new left-wing weekly, *Tribune*. From the outset the tone of this paper was distinctly pro-Soviet and only marginally more mutedly pro-communist. It published an article by Harry Pollitt on the need for working-class unity, it offered Palme Dutt review space to eulogize the published letters of Lenin, and it commissioned the communist Pat Sloan to demolish Trotsky's *The Revolution Betrayed*. When the fellow-traveller Hartshorn replaced Mellor as editor, these tendencies were reinforced. J. R. Campbell's apologia for the Moscow trials, *Soviet Policy and its Critics*, was favourably reviewed, Trotsky was incessantly denounced, and Stalin's unscrupulous re-drafting of recent history, *The History of the CPSU* (1939), was praised in lavish terms. Both in *Tribune* and elsewhere the

British fellow-travellers campaigned vigorously for a Popular Front and for CP affiliation with the Labour Party. Spender adopted this cause and tried to embody it in his verse play, *Trial of a Judge*, while another budding poet, Cecil Day Lewis, published a pamphlet in 1937, *We're not going to do nothing*, calling for a Popular Front, a peace front and an alliance with France and the USSR. Though a member of the Party for three years, he had written with some justice in 1935 that poets and artists like himself were likely at best to be "fellow-travellers"; in taking on the role of militant and disciplined communist, he was doing violence to an essentially gentle and reflective nature. Presently he abandoned the struggle.

The most articulate proponent of a British Popular Front was Harold Laski, a brilliant teacher who exercised a profound influence on several generations of students at the London School of Economics. His case is in some respects a remarkable one, yet also symptomatic of a general pattern whereby the changing landscape of domestic and international politics could rapidly propel an intellectual into impassioned refutation of the very arguments he had previously advocated with equal passion. Kingsley Martin commented that when Laski died he bequeathed to posterity no single "Laski", as there had been a single J. S. Mill or T. H. Green, but only a series of developing and sometimes inconsistent positions. Laski was indeed a brilliant bird in perpetual migration, guided by the changing political climate and singing all the way. In the late 1920s he was in communist eyes a typical "social-facist"; T. H. Wintringham derided Laski's Marxism as being that of the intellectual who agreed that capitalism was warlike and exploitative, yes, agreed that the pattern of history was much as Marx had understood it, yes – yet wanted to do nothing about it. Ralph Fox wrote of "Professor Laski at the service of capitalism", while T. A. Jackson mocked his pale hope that capitalism would reform itself in time to stave off violent revolution. Much of this abuse was occasioned by a small book he published in 1927, *Communism*, and it is this text which most clearly reveals the degree of his inconstancy. About one thing we must however be clear: a changing political environment can very well legitimize a change of tactics; whereas collaboration with the communists might seem unnecessary in a time of economic prosperity and democratic security, it might equally reasonably assume the force of an urgent imperative in the face of irredentist fascist power. But Laski contrived to turn much more spectacular somersaults than that, finally denying his own premises and asphyxiating his own analytical axioms. In *Communism* he "discovered" (in private letters he celebrated his flash of insight) that the Leninist technique of *coup d'état* as exemplified in the October Revolution stemmed from a particular élitist tradition which originated in Gracchus Babeuf's "Conspiracy of Equals" of 1796, was transmitted by Babeuf's disciple Buonarroti to the lifelong communist revolutionary Auguste Blanqui (with whom Marx quarrelled), and was later picked up again by the bolshevik faction in Russia. In fact Laski had made no discovery: Rosa Luxemburg and others had raised the same argument twenty years earlier. Nor, as an analysis of ideological derivations, was it anything but over-simplified: the local, *narodnik* tradition in Russia also had its impact on Lenin. But that is not germane here; the conclusions Laski drew from his theory are. He described the bolsheviks as a "doctrinal aristocracy" all too easily corrupted by the acquisition of power: "The leaders who seize power for one end may choose to maintain power for quite different ends."[22] Futhermore the national CPs of Western Europe were dominated by Moscow which manipulated them for its own ulterior motives. "Quite intelligibly and logically the Labour Party looks with suspicion at proffers of alliance with communists on the ground that they propose to do within its ranks what they would not permit within their own. Their policy . . . of an allegiance which does not admit of open-minded cooperation with alternative views, naturally promotes distrust of the very united front they hope to secure. . . ."[23] So far so good. But by 1936 Laski was convinced that collaboration with the CPGB was an urgent necessity. Such a change of strategy in the context of a worsening international situation was, as we have suggested, not in itself illegitimate. But, by a most probably unconscious coincidence, Clement Attlee now argued against any such collaboration in terms almost identical to those employed by Laski ten years earlier. Had the basic nature of communism changed? Certainly Laski didn't pretend that it had – he simply performed as if *Communism* had never been written. Attlee called the communists a self-proclaimed "intellectual aristocracy", a phrase as close to Laski's "doctrinal aristocracy" as to make no difference, but Laski replied: "I am not sure I know just what that phrase implies. If it means that communists believe in leadership by those who understand Marxism, rather than by those who come to political decisions without any philosophy of action at all, I think they are right."[24] (But had not Laski himself "understood Marxism" in 1927?) He then put to rout the other "pitiful" arguments voiced at the 1936 Edinburgh LP Conference. The communists were said to be dictatorial, but this was "a mere blind. . . . No communist, to my knowledge, believes in dictatorship for its own sake."[25] (Oh – what had happened to the Babeuf-Buonarroti-Blanqui-

Lenin élitist tradition in the interval?) Attlee and others insisted that communists always employed machiavellian tactics and would disrupt the internal democracy of the LP – again precisely Laski's own accusation in 1927. But no : "I know full well the clarity of diagnosis the communists have. I admire their courage and devotion. But they are often bad psychologists. . . ."[26] In other words they were merely clumsy and gauche about respecting the susceptibilities of their friends. Only one objection did he concede to be "more solidly grounded", the charge that the CPGB was Moscow-dominated. But (he racked his brains for a retort) were not British Catholics equally devoted to the Vatican? Did the Labour Party consider that to be sufficient ground for excluding them from its ranks? This is easily answered; British Catholics do not act as a cohesive political unit and are not instructed to do so by the Vatican. Laski knew this; he had known it in 1927, and that is why he had not then thought the excuse worth the paper it would consume. The best conclusion one can draw from this remarkable case of self-contradiction is that in political controversies you can't afford to shuffle the pack without also pretending the cards have changed.

We can certainly sympathize with Laski's indignation about Labour's failure to adopt a vigorous policy on Spain, disarmament, collective security and unemployment. Despite the shattering lesson of 1931, the LP was still plagued by its perpetual search for respectability, by the fetish of "responsible opposition". And he was overwhelmed by what had happened in Germany – as a democrat, as a neo-Marxist, as a Jew. When Palme Dutt welcomed the erstwhile social-fascist into the columns of *Labour Monthly*, even permitting him to chide the CP for "grave errors of judgment and policy and of tactics. . . .",[27] Laski was the more easily convinced that communist democracy was genuine after all. Explaining in *Tribune* that the communists did not at heart believe in a minority seizure of power, he conveniently recalled that *Lenin had set out a powerful case against Blanquism*![28] In 1934 he had visited Russia on a lecture tour and there met the new Bentham of Soviet legal reform, Vyshinsky. The short account he published after his return, extolling Soviet justice, provoked questions in the House of Commons and threats to reduce the grant to the London School of Economics, where he held a chair in political science. But it blew over. And Laski continued to sing the Internationale, attributing (in March 1938) the remaining negative aspects of the Soviet system to hostile imperialist encirclement. Yet only a few months after the Nazi-Soviet Pact he attributed the Soviet dictatorship to the corruption of Stalin and his associates by power. With the rediscovery that power corrupts and absolute power corrupts absolutely, the professor graduated again. Perhaps the deepest layers of

Laski's mind rested on the nineteenth-century tradition of Benthamite radical rationalism (though he also admired Disraeli), but he extrapolated that tradition further to the Left than any other British thinker except J. A. Hobson. He was never wholly a Marxist. The generous and most attractive aspect of his character was seen in his tireless grappling with the problem of creating a genuine democracy in a time of economic crisis and fascist coups, and it was this which made him so popular with the constituency Labour Parties which voted him on to the National Executive.

One Popular Front project with which Harold Laski was closely associated was the Left Book Club.[29] Completely independent of CP control, the Club was launched in March 1936 with a panel of book-selectors composed of one non-Party communist, John Strachey, one fellow-traveller, Laski, and one convert from Judaism to Christianity who had boarded the Moscow express but who was soon to show that he knew where to get off, Victor Gollancz. This successful publisher put up the capital for the Club and remained its effective boss throughout. The inexpensive LBC paperbacks in their familiar vermilion covers and magenta lettering soon enjoyed a great success with the progressive intelligentsia, and by 1939 membership of the Club was put at fifty-seven thousand, representing an actual readership of about a quarter of a million for each title. A Popular Front in microcosm and by default, the Club soon established links with the LP, the ILP, the Liberal Party, the Socialist League, some unions and, of course, the CP. It organized Russian language classes, it showed the films of Eisenstein and Pudovkin and it arranged tours of the USSR. In addition it published *Left Book News* (later *Left News*), which carried reviews by Strachey and Laski of the latest Club publications. Hundreds of discussion groups were set up throughout the country, poetry readings by Spender and Day Lewis were sponsored, a Theatre Guild was formed and left-wing scientists like Haldane and Bernal toured the country on its behalf. From September 1938 *Tribune* carried by formal arrangement a weekly two-page supplement on Club news. At the same time a deal with the communist publishers, Lawrence and Wishart, enabled Club members to buy their books at reduced prices. The political balance struck by the Left Book Club occasioned much controversy both at the time and subsequently. According to Dalton, the Club toed the CP line. In denying it, Gollancz and Strachey pointed to the publication by the Club of books by Salvemini and Attlee, as well as George Orwell's *Road to Wigan Pier*. (But, of course, his *Homage to Catalonia* was beyond the pale.) Apparently Joseph Freeman's *An American Testament* also gave a healthy quantity of offence to communists, as did R. Osborn's attempt to reconcile Freud with Marx in his book *Freud and Marx*. On the other hand the publication by the LBC of Attlee's *The Labour Party in Perspective* was accompanied by specific instructions to group conveners to contrast it unfavourably with the relevant Marxist works on the same theme.[30] The author of a master's thesis on the Club has pointed out that nearly one third of the Club choices before the war were written by communists, most notably Thorez and Dutt, while the list of optional choices included such communist authors as John Gollan, J. R. Campbell, Otto Katz and Emile Burns.[31] One must also take account of such events as the mass meeting the Club organized in the Empress Hall in April 1939, when Hewlett Johnson spoke of Russia's moral strength, equal educational opportunity for all, and the "effective franchise" enjoyed by all her citizens. Gollancz, Strachey, Pollitt and Paul Robeson attended the meeting. Even so, strong as communist influence on the LBC may have been, it was strictly moral and ideological, dependent entirely on the goodwill of the fellow-travellers, and when the Nazi-Soviet Pact intervened there was nothing the CP could do, in the face of Gollancz's indignation, not to mention the defection of Laski and Strachey, to save the Club. In the event a new series of popular paperbacks, the Penguin Specials, soon eclipsed the vermilion covers, achieving a much larger circulation and not one confined to the converted. Bernard Pares's *Russia,* for example, sold 273,000 copies as a "Special", and Pritt's *Light on Moscow*, 150,000. But as a fellow-travelling enterprise directed at a broad, Popular Front audience, the Club enjoyed a much greater success than the short-lived politico-literary periodicals of the time like *Left Review*. Founded and edited by communist intellectuals,* this magazine conducted a tempestuous love-affair with the younger fellow-travellers like Spender and Day Lewis, only to collapse in May 1938, four years after it had been launched.

If Day Lewis was a fellow-traveller temporarily within the Party, John Strachey should be regarded as a communist who never joined.† But, as with other marginal cases like those of Brecht and Malraux, Strachey's is worth discussion briefly if only to reinforce the portrait of the fellow-traveller by means of negative exposure to the portrait of the communist. We may notice straight away that in the thirties Strachey referred to himself as a communist, which to the best of my knowledge no fellow-traveller

---

* It was founded by Montagu Slater, Amabel Williams-Ellis and Tom Wintringham. In January 1936 Edgell Rickword became editor, and in July 1937 Randall Swingler.

† Neal Wood calls Strachey "a fellow-traveller strictly adhering to the Party line".[32] This is the usual confusion resulting from the fetish of the Party card.

ever did. Later he attempted to blur this self-designation, arguing in April 1940 that "for nearly ten years" he had given himself no label: some had called him a communist, some a social democrat. The truth, he could now reveal, was that he had been a Marxist – but not a social democrat. But really this tightrope act was superfluous. As far back as October 1934, *Labour Monthly* was calling him "comrade", and if a man cannot be held responsible for what others call him it is sufficient to note that in October 1935, writing in the *New Statesman*, he used the word "we" when referring to the communists, as indeed he did throughout *The Theory and Practice of Socialism* (1936).

The Popular Front era was a time when many fellow-travellers buried their reservations about the local CPs, but Strachey went much further, justifying in October 1935 the entire history of the Comintern's policy towards social democrats since 1919. (Not even Laski could be persuaded that he had indeed been a "social-fascist" until September 1934.) Then in October 1936 Strachey upheld the CPGB as the "embodiment" of the Marxist conception of working-class politics explained in his new book, and as "the only body of persons who possess a knowledge of the science of social change".[33] This, too, was a step further than Laski was prepared to go. Strachey was unstintingly and undeviatingly loyal to every aspect of Soviet policy, describing the USSR in 1934 as the centre of life in the world, lauding its public election system, confining the victims of the GPU to the irreconcilable enemies of socialism, and so on. Years later, garlanded with the respectability of the disillusioned, he wrote in *Encounter* that in 1935 he had been "staggered" by the Webbs's inability to analyze Russian society critically.[34] It so happens that at the time he called their book "the definitive study of the political, economic and social life of the Soviet Union",[35] deploring, moreover, their scepticism about both the concept and the reality of the proletarian dictatorship. In 1962 he saw fit to blame the Webbs for having closed their eyes to "the nightmarish features of Stalinist Russia", but these same nightmares he had himself described at the time as "the inevitable birth pangs of a new civilization".[36] In fact the Webbs had more to say, little though it was, about the ruthless exercise of dictatorial power in Russia than Strachey did. Had either of them been alive in 1962, they might have pointed this out. And pointed out, also, that Strachey had totally endorsed the Moscow trials, applauded the death sentences, constantly denigrated Trotsky and propagated the rubbish about Trotskyist-POUM collaboration with the Gestapo in Spain (he had interviewed the venomous Pasionaria at CP headquarters).

But the crucial, defining aspect of Strachey's outlook in the thirties was his theoretical-ideological position. What distinguished him most vividly from the run of fellow-travellers was less his orthodoxy on current affairs than his total commitment to Marxism-Leninism. About the nature of history, of capitalism, of imperialism, of state power, and about the origins of the First World War he took it all from the classical texts. In the obligatory manner he pursued yesterday's bogeymen, the famous revisionists Bernstein and Kautsky – this was the kind of theological-polemical enterprise for which fellow-travellers had neither inclination nor talent. *They* shrank from violent revolution on the October model in the West, but Strachey wrote in 1934: "The assumption of power by the workers can occur by revolution alone."[37] He specifically enumerated the factors which would precipitate a British revolution and the subsequent working-class dictatorship. Only Shaw of the British fellow-travellers touted a future dictatorship, but he, after all, wanted to put himself in power not the stinking rabble of idlers and trade unionists. When Laski and ILP showed some timidity on the issue of revolution and dictatorship, Strachey took them to task. The areas in which he deviated from the orthodoxy of the day mostly concerned minor cultural matters. His criticisms of Lawrence, Proust, Huxley, Joyce and Eliot, though clearly Marxist by inspiration, were happily lacking in that abrasive, sloganeering abuse widely regarded as the mark of true militancy. To Joyce's powers of innovation he attached genuine value; he regretted *The Waste Land*'s reactionary orientation but nevertheless found it to be a good poem, thereby earning a rap on the knuckles from that Oddjob Observer of the British cultural scene, Dmitri Mirsky. Otherwise Strachey's only deviationary indulgence concerned his admiration for Freud. Strachey was the most influential communist theorist of the 1930s and his books were widely read not only in Britain but also in America, where he was in considerable demand as a lecturer. His case reminds us that what separates communists from fellow-travellers is only partially the *degree* of commitment, the red instead of the pink, and much more the *structure* of commitment: commitment *to what*? And yet with Strachey as so many others, one blow could bring the whole reinforced edifice down; if an event in the field of foreign policy (the Nazi-Soviet Pact) could lead an apologist for the trials and purges to the conclusion that savage repression had begun in 1935, one wonders whether a part of his mind had not entertained doubts all along. Thus the god also failed for the future Secretary of State for War in the Attlee Government.

The American CP began by denouncing the New Deal and the National Recovery Administration as phoney, as perfect examples of world-prevailing "social-fascism". But in 1935 Roosevelt turned leftward with the Wagner Act and more extensive social security, and this coincided with the Comintern's own change of line. In its search for a United or Popular Front, the CP had to rule out the Socialist Party; its ranks were too heavily permeated by Trotskyists. So we find Rockwell Kent calling Roosevelt's victory in 1936 a victory for the "United Front". There was no other option.

The Party's cultural organ, *The New Masses*, founded in 1926, did its level best to throw off the old sectarianism and to embrace not only fellow-travellers but also liberals willing to collaborate in the Popular Front spirit. Into the pages of *The New Masses* came Sherwood Anderson, Dreiser, Dos Passos, Erskine Caldwell and, later, Hemingway. (Dreiser was the only one to last the course.) *The Nation* also campaigned for a Popular Front, though its front pages were redder than its back ones. Louis Fischer contributed regularly on Soviet affairs, and in 1938 *The Nation's* publisher and editor, Freda Kirchwey, wrote: "With all their faults, the communists perform necessary functions in the confused struggle of our time. They have helped to build up and to run a string of organizations known as 'fronts' by their opponents – which clearly serve the cause not of 'totalitarian doctrine' but of a more workable democracy."[38] *The New Republic* was likewise friendly to the Popular Front idea, but somewhat cooler in tone. An editorial dated June 1938 remarked that one's attitude to the communists depended on what causes they upheld, but, it added: "In instance after instance, the communists have fought and are fighting for civil liberties, for union principles, for social legislation."[39] Nothing could be more true. And as the appeal of American communism gathered momentum, not, it should be stressed, for the great bulk of the working class (American and British communism were two of a kind in this respect) but rather for the progressive intelligentsia of the East and West Coasts, so there was a tendency for individuals to pass through a youthful fellow-travelling phase only to wind up committed communists. One such was Granville Hicks, a New Englander who taught at Harvard and who moved gradually from the ethos of *The Nation* and *The New Republic* to that of *The New Masses*. In 1935 he joined the CP which stood in his eyes for social justice, patriotism and, indeed, moderation. In so far as communism in the Western democracies projected a democratic-reformist and anti-fascist image in the late 1930s, and in so far as this policy or image attracted into its ranks many middle-class people who neither before nor subsequently would have considered joining, then the CPs in these years can in a sense be said to have been packed with fellow-travellers. Which is only one reason why the demonology of the McCarthy era, the Pavlovian equation of the word "communist" with cloak-and-dagger conspiracy, would have been comic had it not also been for the victims tragic. This was indeed the "Red Decade" but the scale of communism's appeal should be kept in strict perspective; as Hicks later pointed out, "There never was a time when anti-communism wasn't a vastly easier road to success than communism. . . ."[40]

Lincoln Steffens did not live to confront the Nazi-Soviet Pact, but this professional Strong Man, this scourge of sentimentality, would no doubt have welcomed it as another iron bar to bend. Famous before the First World War as the muckraking author of *The Shame of the Cities* (1904), he had occupied a room in the heroic age of Washington Square, mixing with Reds, poets, bohemians, radical labour leaders like Big Bill Hayward, socialists like Eastman and Dell, and anarchists like Emma Goldman. John Reed, whose father he knew, occupied the room above his own, and it was Steffens who steered him into journalism. Born in 1866 of pioneering stock on his father's side and of an English mother, he inherited a buccaneer's temperament softened by an abiding respect for European culture and civilization acquired during protracted studies in Berlin, Heidelberg, Leipzig and London. Money fascinated him almost as much as revolution, the strange gentlemanly codes of London clubs almost as much as a good brawl plus court case involving the "Wobblies" and their brutal employers. Rather like Shaw, he thrived on paradoxes, on turning official morality upside down. It was he who had once described the Fourth of July oration as "the 'front' of graft". An early estrangement from his own class left him with a lasting predisposition towards rebellion – if only as a sympathetic observer of its physical manifestations. Muckraking had finally seemed to him a mistake: it merely improved the graft system; besides, the people were less easily shocked than the muckrakers like himself. He loved to travel: 1914 found him in Mexico, 1917 in Russia – in each case holding out a sensitive but somewhat untutored ear to the rapid heartbeat of revolution.

We have already discussed his initial reactions to the Bolshevik Revolution, how he returned to Paris in 1920 to declare, "I have been over into the future and it works". But having seen the future he preferred to settle in the past, in old Europe, marrying a charming and intelligent bride more than thirty years his junior. Ella Winter had been brought to the Versailles Conference by Felix Frankfurter, then enrolled at the London School of Economics. Settling in a villa at San Remo, holidaying in Switzerland, and sitting about the large, sunlit verandah of the Villa Montagu at Alassio, the Steffens ménage took a town house at Karlsbad, often visited the sculptor Jo Davidson at the Manoir de Becheron, Touraine, and then finally withdrew to a house called "The Getaway" at Carmel. It was during these years that he wrote: "I am for them to the last drop, I am a patriot for Russia; the Future is there. ... But I don't want to live there." Less confident of his own identity than Shaw, he sometimes guiltily described himself as "a liberal" and not "a real red". Though he was a fine orator who could swell the hearts of young audiences with visions of that distant, better world, his own feet would not follow his tongue: "... though we had been to heaven, we were so accustomed to our own civilization that we preferred hell."[41] Still, he did pay one more visit to Russia in 1923 and concluded correctly that the NEP was only a tactical retreat. But he was no Marxist and the paternalist-authoritarian streak in him was gaining the upper hand as the years advanced. Like Shaw, he began to turn hopefully to Mussolini with whom he was granted an interview: "... here was a man and that ... man knew something and meant something and had the will and the way to do something."[42] He decided that Lenin and Mussolini had done "opposite things" but were employing the same methods. Steffens explained: "But Mussolini's power and his triumph came not only out of his strength and his character and his frightening contempt, but from his faith, his scientific confidence, in facts and in history. Like Lenin."[43] Luckily such insights are rare among men of intelligence; Mussolini cared nothing for science and happened to have no philosophy of history. But he had stabilized the lira "in a week": Steffens liked that – and as for the Italian parliamentary democracy which Mussolini liquidated, the American ironside had a short answer: what fails must go. The clarity of his analysis surpassed all understanding: "I recommend to ... British liberals a study of Mussolini, as a leader trying by bolshevik methods to avoid a revolution and by evolution to establish the state as the sovereign ruler of private business, privileged classes and labour."[44] Without wishing to speak for them, it is hard to imagine that these were precisely the ideals of Cobden, Mill and Gladstone, but Steffens, you see, wanted to cut right through those old cobwebs of obscurantist tradition, he wanted to inject a little of his own youthful vigour into dessicated veins: "It was a bracing sight to see the young black shirts walk through the streets ... heads up, shoulders back, in command of the world."[45]

In the years 1927 and 1928 it dawned on him that a new style of managerial capitalism was really working in America, really delivering the goods. To frustrate this new insight, the year 1929 dawned. But the insight at first refused to be frustrated. Trusts, combinations and mergers, he wrote in 1930 in semi-Saint-Simonian fashion, were steps towards the organization of all business and industry into one unit which would replace political government. A new culture had to be learned, he told Alfred Harcourt, the new scientific, experimental culture. But the Great Depression persuaded him to transport this vision back to Russia, the Russia of the Five Year Plans – which was also really delivering the goods. And Russia did him a good turn too, lending the autobiography he was now writing a shape, a destiny roughly parallel with his own. After twenty years of comparative obscurity with the American public, his *Autobiography* came out in 1931 and became a best-seller. Once again he enjoyed the admiration of spell-bound audiences to whom he explained that Soviet communism was just one thing – the logical extension of scientific technocracy. Meanwhile his wife Ella made several journeys to Russia and also discovered the future.

Steffens had a keen eye for talent. "My dear Whittaker Chambers," he wrote in June 1933, "my hat came off while I was reading today a short story of yours."[46] At the same time renewed success with the public encouraged him to indulge even further in rather shallow self-criticism. "Dear Mike Gold," he wrote in July 1935 to one of America's most aggressive communists, "I fell for you first when you got me right and roasted me to a turn for a sentimentalist who liked everybody."[47] He continued to insist – virtually parodying the fellow-travelling mentality – that Russia under Stalin was experiencing planned evolution, not bloody revolution, and that this policy was merely a logical extension of the liberal tradition. In an article published in *Soviet Russia Today* (January 1936) he called Lenin "the greatest of Liberals", just as Shaw might have called him the greatest of Fabians. But though Steffens called for a United Front in 1935 and was generally friendly to the CP, he kept his prudent distance from it. This aspect will be examined later.

Already unpopular with his neighbours at Carmel, he received in 1935 an offer from the Soviet Government to live in the Crimea and to report events "without authority". In February 1936 he wrote to a communist friend that he and his family intended to apply for a passport – but his health gave way and he died in August 1936, too soon to take in the trials and purges. It is hard to believe that he would have wavered: some of Upton Sinclair's later utterances would surely have echoed his own. Max Eastman recalls: "His deathbed at Carmel, California, was a place of pilgrimage for devotees and dupes and fellow-travellers of Stalin's tyranny from all over the country."[48] If this obituary is ungenerous, so also was the one Steffens accorded the victims of Mussolini.

So much has recently been written about the Spanish Civil War, and particularly its impact on foreign intellectuals, that one hesitates to add

169

more. Yet it cannot be bypassed, if only because it did so much to shape the attitudes of the younger fellow-travellers. Here at last was the Soviet Union giving practical assistance – human, military and economic – to a Western democracy threatened by a military-fascist rising. And Russia's ostensible policy stood out in sharp relief to the vacillations of the democracies. "Non-Intervention" was a farce and everyone knew it. "The Spanish war," wrote André Chamson, "was a shock still more profound than that of 6 February. We saw there the symbol of liberty in peril and the prefiguration of our future."[49] The cause of Russia and the cause of liberty had become indivisible. *"A notre secours! A votre secours!"* pleaded Rolland. *"Au secours de l'Espagne."* Blum's decision to close the Pyrenees frontier aroused passionate resentment: one Popular Front was failing to help another. Within the ruling coalition the communists were adamantly in favour of supplying arms to Spain, as were left-wing socialists like Zyromski and the Radical Minister for Air, Pierre Cot. Among the intellectuals of the Left, virtual unanimity prevailed. Bloch believed England was solely responsible for Blum's policy, and he concluded that British fears of a general European war were a sham: the real fear was inspired by Largo Caballero's leftist social policy in Spain. He rightly pointed out that neither Germany nor Italy were militarily prepared for a full-scale conflict; the bluff of the dictators could easily have been called, had the will existed. Bloch now perceived both in the Soviet Union and in Republican Spain the emergence of a new type of man, the man no longer divided against himself. (The term "alienation" was not then in fashion.) At the same time the Spanish-born essayist, poet, art critic and later Director of the Paris Museum of Modern Art, Jean Cassou, quoted President Azaña as saying that he had needed only fifty additional planes in the first weeks of the Civil War in order to crush the rebellion, yet France refused to provide them. Chamson, Bloch and Cassou became confirmed fellow-travellers. Meanwhile in America Upton Sinclair and others protested that while the US was pretending to be neutral in imposing an arms embargo, it was all the while selling munitions to Germany and Italy.

The Communist International resolutely threw its weight against any revolutionary developments in Spain. It claimed, simply, to be defending democracy. Every attempt, anarchist, syndicalist or left-socialist, to collectivize agriculture, to bring factories under workers' control, or generally to infuse class war into the Civil War, was ruthlessly stamped out by the Spanish communists and the ever-proliferating army of Soviet agents. This general procedure was warmly applauded by the fellow-travellers, even if, as on other occasions, some of them preferred to ignore the blood which made the heart beat. Returning from a visit to Spain in the company of other men of faith, Hewlett Johnson reported in 1937 that the communists were imposing the order so essential to a secure democracy; he accepted the Republican Minister of Agriculture's denunciation of the revolutionary collectivists and "doctrinaires" who were simply causing trouble. A sermon the Dean delivered in Canterbury Cathedral on the subject of Spain provoked hot remonstrances from Archbishop Lang and two Suffragan Bishops in Church Assembly, but Johnson was not deterred and returned for a second visit to Spain in 1938.

Dolores Ibarruri (La Pasionaria) became for them a symbol of gallant heroism in the cause of democracy (the same Dolores who remarked on 9 August: "The Trotskyists must be exterminated like beasts of prey"). About this lady the French fellow-traveller Edith Thomas had written the following lines:

> Pasionaria, Pasionaria,
> il n'est plus temps que les hommes t'aiment
> ils t'écoutent
> comme ils écoutent le vent chanter,
> ils te regardent
> comme ils regardent la flamme monter,
> ils t'entendent
> comme ils s'entendaient eux-mêmes.[50]

Deaf ears were turned to those who complained about the murderous campaign waged by the GPU against Spanish anarchists, the POUM and even left-wing socialists. When the French Trotskyists Daniel Guérin and Colette Audry, along with Gide and Paul Rivet, protested against the bloody repression which occurred in Barcelona during the first week of May 1937, they were denounced all round the French intellectual Popular Front as saboteurs. One eyewitness of the Barcelona events was George Orwell, who had served with the POUM militia at the front and been seriously wounded in the neck. The *New Statesman* turned down an article and a book review he wrote on the subject of Spain on blatantly political grounds, and there was no question of the Left Book Club publishing his *Homage to Catalonia*. "Gollancz," he wrote bitterly, "is of course part of the communism racket...."[51] *Tribune* meanwhile proved again its commitment to a fellow-travelling position when it declared in May 1937: "There is no doubt that since the liquidation of the Catalonian rising Republican Spain has become not weaker, but definitely stronger."[52] (There had been no "rising"; there had been an intervention from Valencia and Madrid, and then a suppression.) Meanwhile Upton Sinclair applauded the putting down of left extremists and anarchist individualists on the grounds that "these enemies" were working hand in glove with spies and provocateurs to undermine "the people's government". Even so gentle and humane a spirit as Jean-Richard Bloch returned from Spain convinced that stern measures were the only appropriate ones.

Born in Alsace in 1884 of a Jewish family, Bloch had been in 1914 a patriot committed to the *union sacrée*. But here again direct experience of the war produced a total change of emotional and ideological metabolism. In *Carnaval est Mort* (1920) he wrote of his own growing humility before the spectacle of dumb and infinite suffering, of spiritual anguish, explosions, gangrene, mutilation, fear and doubt – and before the stoical courage of ordinary men and women. He himself had fought on the Marne and at Verdun where he was seriously wounded. Subsequently he turned to socialism, but to a socialism which owed more to Péguy, Jaurès and Rolland than to Marxism-Leninism. He set his pen against capitalist values, the "egotistical disorder" of bourgeois anarchy, and he insisted that in a just society men would be born free and equal; but he avoided Marxian historical determinism, the emphasis on the economic motor, and clung to the faith in free choice which had pervaded the pages of the journal he had founded in 1910, *L'Effort Libre*. Like others, he embraced "reason", not class violence.

For some years he found no existing social system which matched his ideals, and he was content to lead the life of a highly respected, if not world-renowned, writer. Then came Hitler: the old story. And, like Feuchtwanger, Mann and other future fellow-travellers reared in an idealist-rationalist tradition, he at first regarded nazism as a barbaric disease, a medieval anachronism, a hurricane sweeping the geography of elemental passions. He hesitated to embrace Russia and in 1933 he still preferred the socialist to the communist way. Then came the second shock, the riots of 6 February, and Bloch joined the general stampede to the left. He read *Mein Kampf*, with its prophecy of a destiny-fulfilling assault on Russia, he watched Mussolini running amok in Abyssinia, and he found no alternative but to conclude: "Communism, place of refuge, the proletariat, bastion of hope, such are the colours of this autumn of 1935."[58] The law of adjustment and compensation now governed him. In 1933 he regarded the predicament of the Soviet writer with trepidation; in 1934 he had himself attended the Moscow Writers' Congress where the speeches of Zhdanov and others might well have reinforced such fears; yet Bloch was now psychologically compelled to banish these fears, to express his admiration for the free climate in which his Soviet colleagues worked. The advance of fascism kaleidoscoped the value structures of the liberal mind. He was invited to collaborate with Louis Aragon in editing the communist-front paper, *Ce Soir*, and in January 1938 he found himself addressing the CP Congress at Arles. It took only the final blow of Munich to persuade him to join the Party. Once committed, he never looked back, graduating to the status of communist in the fullest sense. Having escaped from Paris in 1940, he spent the war years in the Soviet Union, broadcast regularly to the French Resistance on Moscow radio, and wrote a book depicting Stalin in hagiographical terms. He returned to France after the war and died there in 1947.

We have mentioned Orwell's difficulties in getting his eyewitness accounts of communist behaviour in Spain published. Although his hostility to the CP dated, as he explained, from "about 1935", he declined to criticize the young communists who fought and died in Spain, such as John Cornford, Ralph Fox, Christopher Caudwell and Charles Donnelly, if only because he admired genuine courage, commitment and self-sacrifice. Orwell's scorn was reserved mainly for the "parlour bolsheviks", notably Spender and W. H. Auden, whom he regarded as fashionable, effete dilettantes. Orwell's strictures seem all the more relevant when one considers the extraordinary legend, partly self-congratulatory and partly self-wounding, which this particular generation of British intellectuals has sustained in later years. In his semi-historical, semi-fictional memoir of the period, *Fellow Travellers,* T. C. Worsley accurately captures the naïvety prevailing at that time. The character Martin, clearly modelled on Spender, reflects: "The fact is we are absurdly cushioned from the realities in comfortable, safe, blind old England. All our political dilemmas and questionings and wonderings are a sort of make-believe game."[54] So the train to Spain was boarded in search of "real reality", the true frontier of the age – but for many the make-believe element remained transcendent. It remains so today, although the generation in question produced only one major talent, Auden, and he clearly wishes to forget the legend. Meanwhile others, who failed to die at Madrid or Almeria, periodically renew the search for their own Spanish graves.

Recently Spender has written: "Members of the 'Auden generation' tended to be fellow-travellers partly for personal reasons to do with their background, but mainly because they had already formed in their own minds sets of values which were not capable of being converted into communist ideology...."[55] True enough. Spender himself had left Oxford in 1930, a "vague socialist", then read Maurice Hindus and Louis Fischer and become marginally less vague. Familiar with Germany, Austria and the German language, he was well placed to take stock of the European crisis. Then Spain beckoned. Harry Pollitt apparently enrolled him in the CPGB in the hope that a quick death would give the Party its Byron, but when Spender did depart for Spain under the auspices of the *Daily Worker*, the mission lacked a fully Promethean dimension: to track down the fate of a Russian merchant crew whose ship had been sunk by the Italians. In Barcelona he heard the voice of his friend and fellow-poet David Gascoyne blaring out encouragement over street loudspeakers – further make-believe. His second trip, in 1937, seems to have been facilitated by a false passport procured by Malraux, but Spender's plan to become the English-language broadcaster on Valencia radio came to nothing. So he toured the trenches, visited International Brigade HQ, and attended the Madrid Writers' Congress. On his return he complained in the *New Statesman* that volunteers were being enrolled in the Brigades without being informed that it was a communist-controlled organization, but despite such hideous deceptions he trailed along, continually mystified by the air of dogmatic certainty which filled the lungs of his communist colleagues. As late as April 1939 he was refuting charges of communist malpractice in Spain.

In January 1937 Auden went out as a stretcher-bearer. By March he was back in England. But he did produce his famous poem, "Spain", which proves that you don't have to feel deeply about something to write about it well. Orwell called him a "sort of gutless Kipling" and his friends "the nancy poets". Auden's line in the poem which spoke of "The conscious acceptance of guilt in the necessary murder" led Orwell to remark that such words could be written only by someone "to whom murder is at most a word", by the sort of person "who is always somewhere else when the trigger is pulled".[56] In 1940 Auden changed the line to, "The conscious acceptance of guilt in the face of murder", but in later editions of his poetry "Spain" vanished, while other of his neo-Marxist poems of the period took on a Christian symbolism with a few deft strokes of the pen. Auden was not really ever a fellow-traveller. Certainly the CPGB interested him not at all. And he steered clear of the fellow-travelling international literary gatherings. About the Russian Revolution he had little to say; one searches in vain for a single positive reference to the USSR in his writings; he praised Gide for telling the truth as he saw it. Though works like *On the Frontier* show a paddler's willingness to splash about on the shores of the revolutionary ocean, unlike Spender and Day Lewis he had no time for the daily bread of politics. Soon he had put another ocean – the Atlantic – between him and the whole business.

About forty per cent of approximately four thousand Americans who volunteered to fight in Spain were communists. The majority joined the

Abraham Lincoln Brigade. About half did not return. The issue of Spain further cemented the unity of the American Left. Within the Aid and Relief Committees which sprang up, fellow-travellers like Archibald MacLeish and Malcolm Cowley did more than their bit in composing petitions and organizing fund-raising rallies. Cowley, whose pipe-smoking style and military moustache reminded his friends of Hemingway, had been a student at Harvard in Dos Passos's day, then an ambulance driver in France, a companion of Hart Crane in the Village, and an occasional companion to Hemingway in Paris. Having attended the 1937 Writers' Congress, he sent reports to *The New Republic,* of which he was then literary editor, disparaging the POUM and the anarchists. A stream of distinguished visitors crossed the Atlantic. Hemingway went to Spain as a war correspondent, Dorothy Parker made the trip, and so did Caldwell and Dos Passos. But for the last it was not to be a happy one.

With Hemingway, Edmund Wilson, Cowley and E. E. Cummings, John Dos Passos belonged to that distinguished company which served in the ambulance corps in Europe during the First World War. A Harvard graduate who developed a "behaviourist" style of prose writing based on words run together, punctuation omitted, normally separate thought-clauses juxtaposed in original ways, and chunks of documentary material dovetailed with newspaper headlines, his big, sprawling novels of American society were destined to exert an enormous influence on public and writers alike, not only in America but throughout Europe. (Sartre's novel, *Le Sursis,* for example, owes its biggest stylistic debt to Dos Passos.) An inveterate traveller, he happened to be in Georgia and Armenia in 1921 when the Red Army incorporated those regions, but he was not yet ready to blow the trumpet. Then in 1925, in company with Waldo Frank and Van Wyck Brooks, he grew enthusiastic about the idea of a Proletarian Writers' League in the USA. When *The New Masses* was founded, the executive board included a number of sympathetic non-communists: Freda Kirchwey and Dos Passos were among them. He visited Russia again in 1928 but declined a total conversion; he valued his independence of mind and didn't want to find himself in any collective bag. His writing style by no means conformed to the canons approved in Moscow, and speaking of *The New Masses* he advised: "I don't think there should be any more phrases, badges, opinions, banners imported from Russia or anywhere else. Ever since Columbus imported systems have been the curse of this country.... I want an expedition that will find what it's not looking for.... I'd like to see a magazine full of introspection and doubt that would be like a piece of litmus paper...."[57] Naturally Mike Gold rebuked him. But he joined hands with Gold and John Howard Lawson in setting up a new radical theatre in the Village. Some of his own plays were performed there, though generally they enjoyed less public and critical success than his novels. What in his case provoked the most profound political disturbance was not the rise of Hitler, it was the Sacco and Vanzetti case. He covered its closing stages as a reporter and his poem about it, which appeared in *The New Masses*, is said to have moved a whole generation of progressives.

Between 1930 and 1937 appeared the three parts of his masterwork, *USA*. This epic provides a fair indication of both the extent and limitations of the author's radicalism. John Reed is honoured in its pages, and also his love for Soviet Russia; Wilson is harshly mocked; anger and passion over the suppression of the "Wobblies" constantly flickers and burns; capitalists of great wealth and irresponsible power like Henry Ford are put to rout. But one also perceives that Dos Passos was drawn less to the spokesmen of mass movements than to the lone-wolf protagonists of unorthodox radical solutions – to Thorstein Veblen, for example. The word "individualist" is so much used and abused as to have become virtually meaningless, but his novels, as well as his reaction to the Sacco and Vanzetti case, show clearly that Dos Passos's imagination and therefore his commitments were most readily excited by the singular rather than the plural. The singular, it should be added, always understood in the collective context; Dos Passos turned Joyce's world upside down and inside out. One significant episode of *USA* concerns a fictional hero, Ben Compton, a Jew from Brooklyn who joins a strike committee, reads Marx, is beaten up by the police and jailed. Later, having embraced the USSR, he becomes a communist and throws himself into the great causes and confrontations of the early years of the Depression. But then the story of Ben Compton takes a surprising turn: he is expelled from the Party as an opportunist, though the reader is left in little doubt of his innocence. All faction fights and schismatic manoeuvres were foreign to Dos Passos. At the very close of *USA* we are left in the company of a new character, the poor worker Vag who is trying to hitch a lift on a highway while the rich sweep past in their cars and in their aeroplanes overhead – a bitter vision of America's betrayed promises, a clear indictment of capitalist civilization, but nevertheless a commitment to the individual rather than to any party.

Even at the height of his friendship for the American communists Dos Passos was liable to act in unreliable ways. When in 1934 the CP disrupted a Madison Square Garden meeting held to honour the fallen Austrian social democrats, he, with Lionel Trilling, Wilson and John Chamberlain, denounced "the culpability and shame of the communists" for their "disruption of working-class action in support of the Austrian worker".[58] Then in April 1937 he arrived in Spain to help Hemingway with the film script of *The Spanish Earth*. Though already cooling towards communism, he came as a staunch Loyalist and as one who believed still in the Popular Front. What finally turned him was the affair of José Robles, an old friend and Professor of Spanish Literature at Johns Hopkins. Though Robles had a brother on Franco's side, he was believed by Dos Passos to be totally firm in his commitment to the Republic. But Robles had disappeared, and Dos Passos eventually learned from the chief of Republican counter-espionage in Madrid that he had been executed. Hemingway apparently took a cool line: in civil war individuals were bound to be sacrificed. But his friend could not see it that way: had not Sacco and Vanzetti also been "individuals"? In a novel he published subsequently, *The Adventures of a Young Man*, Dos Passos depicted his hero joining the CP in Harlan County only to discover that the Party was exploiting a strike for narrow political advantages. The hero protests. Though he joins the International Brigade, communist vindictiveness dogs him – Dos Passos himself had crossed his Rubicon. Supporting the Trotsky Defence Committee, he also put in a good word for the Spanish anarchists and recalled how he had watched the Soviet staff officers in Madrid, polished, efficient and with no feeling for the population that "formed the raw material of their human engineering". (But this was a judgment too generalized and too subjective to be fair.) Apparently in Barcelona he had met an honest man; only later did he discover that it was Orwell. So the CP dropped Dos Passos and adopted Hemingway as their white hope, but again they had little luck since Hemingway's own novel about the Civil War, *For Whom the Bell Tolls*, contains a scathing portrait of communist intrigues and power-hunting as represented by the International Brigade's Commissar, André Marty. Even so, Hemingway was disinclined in later years to adopt the extreme anti-socialist, anti-union posture for which Dos Passos became faintly celebrated. Generally speaking, the communists and fellow-travellers who experienced ultimate disillusionment divided into two categories: those who regretted the erosion of brave perspectives; and those who became obsessed by the conviction that Stalinism had been a trap designed solely to destroy them.

Then came Theodore Dreiser to Spain, the scourge of the Catholic Church, on his way to attend this congress and that. He explained to Yvette Szekeley how it all came about: "Last Sunday wires from the League of American Writers and the American League for Peace and Democracy began to arrive asking me to attend – all costs paid – the International Convention for International Peace. . . . All I had to do was to go and say I represented them and that I believe in peace. That seemed easy, so, since I needed a lot of peace just then, I decided to do it. So here I am in the grandest candy box ever set afloat."[59] In Spain, where he arrived in July 1938, he was royally received and granted interviews with Azaña, Premier Negrin and Foreign Minister Alvarez del Vayo. A farewell party was flung on his behalf at the Hotel Majestic and attended by Malraux, Louis Fischer and others who had done more than cursorily inspect the Civil War as if it were the Eiffel Tower. Toller was there too, smiling his sad refugee's smile as Dreiser ranted interminably, blaming everything on the twin conspiracies, the Masonic and the Catholic. (By Masonic, Dreiser also implied Jewish.) He was a big shot and expected the world to know it, but when he got to London no one of practical importance would see him. "England is an autocracy," he wrote. "The masses are underpaid; stupid, silent. The gang at the top wants not only to rule England but the world."[60] But when he returned to America he was granted an interview with the President himself, and so it turned out that "the gang at the top" back home contained good fellows after all.

Of those who listened with astonishment and some dismay to Dreiser's droll harangue in the Hotel Majestic, two particularly claim our attention. Louis Fischer knew communism in both its Soviet and Spanish scenarios more intimately than any other American fellow-traveller; Anna Louise Strong had lived as long in Russia, but her naïvety was an incalculable factor. Fischer was anything but naïve. Born in 1896, he had become a regular visitor and virtually a resident in Russia since the early twenties. He knew many bolshevik leaders and enjoyed their confidence. When writing his two-volume *The Soviets in World Affairs* (1930), he had been granted privileged access to bolshevik archives regarding the Treaty of Brest-Litovsk and the internal disputes it generated. The Commissariat for Foreign Affairs permitted him to inspect the documents captured from Kolchak by the Red Army, while Chicherin, Litvinov and Rakovsky as well as several German diplomats reconstructed for his benefit the hidden story of the Genoa Conference and the Rapallo Treaty of 1922. He wrote regularly for *The Nation*. According to Eugene Lyons, *Izvestia* liked to quote the favourable opinions he expressed there as being those of "a bourgeois American economist". In the late 1920s he sailed too close to the Trotskyist wind, but was forgiven. Then in Spain he became *commandante* and quartermaster of the International Brigade, while his family remained in Moscow. His relationships with leading politicians like Largo Caballero, as well as with Soviet officers, diplomats and journalists, were close, and undoubtedly both his heart and his mind were now invested in the Spanish outcome. Even after his defection he wrote: "The Bolsheviks who worked and fought for Spain were glorious human beings. . . . They identified with Spain. It was their adopted country."[61] (Perhaps he was less familiar with the GPU agents.) But eventually he found the burden of working under André Marty an impossible strain, and he took time off touring the US on behalf of Spanish Relief. When he returned to Spain it was as a correspondent, firmly believing that the measures taken to quell spontaneous collectivization were vital if the landowning peasants and the anti-Franco portion of the middle class were not to be antagonized. It was not until the Nazi-Soviet Pact that he finally stepped off the train.

Another of Dreiser's amazed interlocutors in the Hotel Majestic, his face ravaged by the perpetual nervous tic which many wrongly took for a sign of irritation, was the authentic romantic hero of the Spanish Civil War, the composite artist and activist, André Malraux. He was never a Party member and he was certainly not a communist in so orthodox a sense as, say, Strachey, even though he was widely regarded (and paraded) as the most glittering jewel in the tiara. Yet to describe him as a fellow-traveller would make little sense. Admittedly fellow-travellers tend to adapt their image of communism to their own philosophical systems, and Malraux did precisely that. But whereas they were predominantly scribes and yogis, he was an extrovert adventurer in search of an ideal Promethean hero: T. E. Lawrence, Trotsky and De Gaulle all filled the role at one time or another. He never really cared about Plans, about social security benefits, about production statistics and easy-to-come-by abortions. The heirs of the Enlightenment did. He was not of their number. The title of his Spanish novel, *L'Espoir*, is ironical in so far as he regarded hope and death as constant companions. Whereas they cared about the destination, he cared more about the journey itself, the struggle, the heroic *camaraderie*. As for the proletariat, this elemental force represented to him not so much an agent of history as a symbol of humiliation, of oppression and also of purity. The very poor are by definition pure, or so it sounds good to say. The proletarian cause was a giant whetstone on which his heroes (Garine, Kyo, Katow, Mangin, Garcia – himself) could sharpen their swords, and also the gravestone over which their bloody corpses would finally be thrown. The fellow-travellers weren't so keen on violence; he was. The apocalypse tautened his nerves, he involved himself in the Indo-Chinese revolution, in perilous flights over the Arabian desert, emulating Saint-Exupéry, in the Spanish Republican airforce, in the Resistance against nazi occupation. He wrestled with Nietzsche and Spengler more strenuously than with Marx and Lenin, and he never said things the way a communist said them. Signing petitions and doing good bored him.

Between about 1933 and 1939 his relations with the communist movement were close ones. His novel *Le Temps du Mépris* (1935) celebrates
in the shape of the hero Kassener a type of communism which restores to
the individual all the buried creative potentialities of his nature. At the
same time Malraux detested fascism, the exaltation of race, nation and
political leadership as hierarchical and irreducible biological entities. In
later years his critics called him a fascist, but this was a mistake; never
could he say, like General Millan Astray, "Death to intelligence, long live
death". But he was in no sense a Party man. The *camaraderie* and
discipline he valued were of the spontaneous variety, ignited by pressing
crises, by the light in the eyes of the enemy. Though he could and did
organize efficiently, he was not an organization man. In *Les Conquérants*, the fictional hero Garine complains of the "Roman" mentality of
the Stalinists and accuses Borodin, the chief Comintern agent in China,
of wanting to manufacture revolutions as Ford manufactured cars. But
the majority of fellow-travellers were also spiritual Romans, engineers of
souls, building straight roads to the future along which a grateful and
regenerated humanity would march in step. Malraux was a mystic and
an aesthete; often it seemed as if the gesture counted for as much with
him as the deed. He was not impressed by the Marxian anthropology
or by any other historical determinism, and as a naïve existentialist he
insisted that man is whatever he makes of himself in the burning moment,
whether it yield victory or defeat. He cared greatly for human justice
and dignity, he abhorred exploitation, but his socialism was skin deep.
Soon after the war he and James Burnham were exchanging notes on the
disappearance of the class war.

Socialist realism and Soviet literary dogmas merely exasperated him.
He told the first Congress of Soviet Writers that Soviet communism had
shown more confidence in "man" than in its own writers. In his opinion
Soviet literature did a good job revealing the external facts about the
USSR, but a poor job in the sphere of ethics and human psychology. "*Le
marxisme, c'est la conscience du social, la culture, c'est la conscience du
psychologique.*"[62] He insisted that the living man of flesh and blood always
intervened between dogma and authentic art. Radek rebuked him for these
observations and Malraux listened, his face twitching – which Radek mistakenly assumed to be a manifestation of guilt or irritation. The fact was
that he did not need to please or obey. International communism needed
him more than he needed it. He was capable of riding roughshod over
sacred territory. Although he had quarrelled with Trotsky over *Les Conquérants*, he contributed to a committee which collected money to pay for a
bodyguard and thus ensure Trotsky's safety while he was living in France.
Even in 1937, when "Trotsky-Gestapo" had become a double-barrelled

watchword of the faithful, he told the guests at a fund-raising banquet laid on for him in New York by *The Nation*: "Trotsky is a great moral force in the world, but Stalin has lent dignity to mankind; and just as the Inquisition does not detract from the fundamental dignity of Christianity so the Moscow trials do not detract from the fundamental dignity of communism."[68] One can interpret that as one will, but the direct challenge to sacred dogma is obvious. Time was running out. The Nazi-Soviet Pact told him all he needed to know; in Paris he remarked to Louis Fischer, "we are back at zero". And quite soon he adopted the view that Soviet communism was a mixture of Russian chauvinism and Asiatic despotism totally alien to authentic Western culture. But in the same motion of rejection he swept aside the whole socialist tradition and the whole concept of rationality in politics. He was therefore not so much back at zero as back with Oswald Spengler.

"Peace and Disarmament": these two words link comfortably together by convention and logic. So it was natural for the Left in the late twenties and early thirties to demand in one breath: "*A bas la guerre!*" and "*Désarmement!*" For if Britain and France, the victors of 1918, the main beneficiaries of the Treaty of Versailles, the two capitalist powers which still possessed vast overseas empires, were regarded as the potential agents of aggression in any future conflict, then any high military capability on their part was to be resisted. Thus when in the late twenties the Soviet Government entered the round of international disarmament conferences and extravagantly proposed total abolitions of this and that, and when such suggestions were pooh-poohed as phoney, then it was not communists and fellow-travellers alone who insisted that the Russians be taken seriously. But after 1933 it was no longer logical to shout: "*A bas le fascisme*" and "*Désarmement!*" in the same breath – although some, by inherited reflex, were indeed still doing this. Here lay a gruelling dilemma for those many fellow-travellers (and others too) in whom the experience of the First World War had implanted a determined pacifism or, if less doctrinaire, a hatred of war. Now they were forced to reappraise the nature of the British and French politico-economic systems. Could capitalist democracy be trusted to rearm *against nazism*, or would it inevitably employ its tanks and planes against the Soviet Union? Naturally the willingness of these democracies to enter into an effective diplomatic and military anti-aggression pact with Russia was taken as the touchstone of good faith in this matter.

Before 1935 many fellow-travellers adopted a position which in retrospect appears somewhat self-contradictory, given the nature of fascism.

Rolland, like Barbusse, believed the real alliance lay between capitalism, fascism and the Church against the working class. In America the League against War and Fascism during its first two or three years of life (after 1932) demanded concerted action to prevent war by means of boycotts, embargoes and disarmament. But these did not work in practical experience; either they were only nominally applied, as against Japan in Manchuria, or they proved impotent, as against Italy in Abyssinia. With pain and doubt Rolland found himself obliged to abandon the notion of Gandhian passive resistance to Black Shirts and Brown. Turning against his own position, he attacked those, like Georges Pioch and Russell, who believed that anything was preferable to war. In March 1933 he delivered a speech: one must either fight shoulder to shoulder with the workers and with the Soviet Union or go under. Gide travelled the same road. In July 1932 he had described himself to Félicien Challaye as a "pacifist", and the following year he wanted to know how any capitalist system could combat what was ultimately vital to its own existence – war. But by 1936, to the dismay of his pacifist admirers, he had followed Rolland into demanding a viable military alliance between France, the USSR and Britain. Four years later Jean Guéhenno relinquished his own cherished position when he wrote: "one must accept the eventuality of war to save the peace".

The career of Pierre Cot throws this predicament into sharper relief. A professor of International Law at Rheims, he entered politics as a radical in 1928 and later served as Minister of Air in the Herriot, Blum, Chautemps and Daladier Governments. As a delegate to the 1932 international conference on arms reduction, he argued in favour of a citizens' militia (as once recommended by Jaurès) supported by an international force at the disposal of the League of Nations, a formula designed to rid military power of its chauvinistic professional castes. But this was utopia: one had to work within the established realities. Therefore, while co-president of the International Peace Campaign, he began to enter into secret negotiations with the Soviet Union. In Blum's Government he conducted a small purge of the air force, pushing Popular Front sympathizers towards the top, and he also broke the arms embargo ordered by his Prime Minister by illegally dispatching a number of planes to Republican Spain. But as his own Radical Party increasingly turned its back on the Soviet alliance and committed itself to appeasement, he saw no alternative but to become a *compagnon de route* of both the USSR and the PCF. After the war he sat in the Chamber of Deputies as one of those "*progressistes*" who voted with the PCF on practically every issue.

When the Munich crisis arrived, only the communists and a handful of socialists resisted the general stampede towards capitulation.* The fellow-travellers were more than ever confirmed in their commitment to the Soviet and communist positions. Georges Friedmann drew attention to Litvinov's statement of 17 March 1938 that Czechoslovakia could count on Soviet support provided France lived up to her engagements by the 1935 Franco-Soviet Pact. On 24 June Litvinov had repeated this pledge. He even negotiated a passage for Soviet troops across Rumania in the event of a German attack on Czechoslovakia. Georges Bonnet, the French Foreign Minister, had in Friedmann's opinion deliberately suppressed news of the Soviet-Rumanian agreement, so anxious was he to fend off the Russian embrace. And Julien Benda asked early in August 1938 whose fault it was if the PCF led the anti-fascist movement and had for the past three years been the only party to defend the frontiers of French democracy. (Thus another convert from the fastidious ranks of the *clercs de l'esprit*.) In response to the Munich débâcle, Langevin, Albert Bayet and Victor Basch, strongly supported by Rolland, formed the Paix et Démocratie group to campaign for an effective Anglo-French-Soviet alliance and to drum up support for the PCF's foreign policy.

In Britain the perspectives were even bleaker. France at least enjoyed for a time a socialist-led Popular Front Government, but the 1935 general election in Britain returned the Conservatives to power with a huge majority. The only line the CPGB could adopt was as follows: let the LP, the CP, the unions and all progressive forces compel the reactionary Government to defend Spanish democracy, to abandon appeasement and to form a binding pact with France and the USSR. This was easier said than done. Inevitably the Left became schizoid about British rearmament. Spender, for example, called for a collective security pact (which required teeth, i.e. armaments, to be effective) yet could not escape the conclusion that any militarization of the capitalist democracies would merely precipitate fascism at home. (Interestingly enough, Orwell took the same view in the late thirties.) Day Lewis spelled out the choice of evils: on the one hand democracy must be armed; on the other huge armaments could not safely be placed in the hands of an imperialist government. Shaw, the Webbs and Laski were all baffled by the dilemma, convinced as they were that Paris and London hoped to divert Hitler eastwards. Pritt spoke at numerous meetings, unmasking the collusion existing between the Federation of British Industry and the Reichsgruppe Industrie. Hewlett Johnson and Konni Zilliacus campaigned for an alliance with Russia but would not contemplate rearming Britain until the Government's honest intentions were

* In the Chamber of Deputies the seventy-three communists, one socialist and one conservative voted against the Munich Agreement.

proven. Edgar Young, Labour parliamentary candidate for North-West Hull, called on London to associate with the Franco-Soviet, Czecho-Soviet and Franco-Czech pacts of mutual assistance, but he then argued that the British Government could not possibly do so since it was already quasi-fascist. So what then? Get the Government out? But the Tories had just won a general election by a handsome margin. As an ex-naval officer, Young insisted that British sea power was fully capable of blockading Spain and crushing Mussolini in the Mediterranean, and indeed should do so forthwith, yet at the same time he vigorously opposed both conscription and rearmament! In 1937 he embarked on a tour of Eastern Europe with credentials signed by Harry Pollitt sewn into the lining of his jacket, and warned Beneš that London intended to sell out Czechoslovakia. But, so he recalls, the Czech Premier couldn't believe it – and what if he had? What practical measures of defence could he have taken if Soviet support was conditional on Western collaboration?

The American fellow-travellers tended to view Britain as the villain of the piece. Samuel Harper noted that Chamberlain, speaking in the Commons as late as 14 April 1939, did not even mention the USSR until a question was asked from the floor. Rockwell Kent, Dreiser, Ward and their comrades detested Britain's social system, her empire, her ruling class and her Government. It was no doubt due to such antipathies that they never recommended that the United States should guarantee Europe's national integrity against fascism. Nevertheless, it is a poor philosopher who cannot distinguish the bad from the worse.

4

The Pact and the War

The Nazi-Soviet Pact* was signed in Moscow on 22 August 1939. Western communists and fellow-travellers now faced their greatest trial of faith and loyalty. The anti-fascist mission to which they had dedicated themselves for six years appeared to have been cancelled, obliterated by Stalin with the stroke of a pen. But here one must distinguish between a number of different issues and phases which trod in rapid succession on each other's heels. There was the Pact itself; there was the Comintern line on the war which became clear only a month later; there was the question of Russia's winter war with Finland and her annexation of the Baltic States; there was the phoney war followed by real war; finally the whole situation was transformed by Hitler's invasion of the Soviet Union in June 1941.

First, the Pact itself. In general and despite notable defections, the line was held more resolutely in Britain and America than in France. The Webbs concluded that Stalin had no alternative and that it was not for them to criticize Russia's life-and-death decision. Pritt, though temporarily stunned, was soon in full possession of his loyalties, rushing out a "Penguin Special" explaining everything. The Dean of Canterbury laid the blame squarely on Britain and France while offering a notable item of misinformation: that the Pact contained no provision for the partition of Poland between Russia and Germany. The Soviet invasion of Poland he found perfectly defensible; the new frontier was close to the old Curzon line, was it not? (Yes, but the new frontier with whom? Not with Poland, which had ceased to exist.) Later in 1947 he denounced as a lie the version that Russia had handed over a number of anti-fascist refugees to Germany at the time of the Pact, and he refused to budge from this position even when confronted with the victims in person, notably Frau Neumann and Alex Weissberg. Joseph Needham, who knew Poland well, reported that his scientific friends in the area of Soviet occupation enjoyed excellent working conditions, in contrast

* Ostensibly a non-aggression pact, it secretly provided for the division of Poland between Germany and the Soviet Union.

to the lot of their colleagues in the German zone. Sean O'Casey's imagination as usual worked wonders: "The Nazis got a shock when they came to the River Bug, for there, on the opposite bank, stood battalions of Red Army men watching them...."[1] Inscrutably, no doubt. In America, Dreiser, Anna Louise Strong, Lamont, Kent and Ward all rallied staunchly, the latter explaining that the Pact had given Hitler "more of a check than it had helped him".[2] When Granville Hicks broke with the CP as a result of the Pact, Anna Louise Strong wrote to him: "Don't you know in your soul that Stalin and Molotov are our comrades?"[3] Rockwell Kent rejoiced over the discomfiture of Tory Britain: "Good. They've served that perjured double-crossing Allied outfit right." The fact that Hitler hadn't exactly been "served right" evidently did not disturb him. When the USSR grabbed half of Poland, he said, "everyone with a grain of common sense and human decency was glad. *Those* Jews ... would be safe."[4] Corliss Lamont found that the circumstances completely justified Russia's actions, and Samuel Harper explained to his notebook that the Soviets had annexed only those territories which Poland seized by force in 1920. They had not seized "ethnic Poland", and in any case Moscow was rushing social workers of the highest calibre to the scene while pursuing a mild economic policy analogous to the NEP of the twenties. As for the Nazi-Soviet declaration of 28 September whereby those two Powers announced their intention to settle all matters in Eastern and Central Europe between them, Harper congratulated Russia and Germany on putting an end to the Anglo-French system of client states.[5] (Which is rather like blessing the death of one's child on the ground that it will no longer have to suffer the pains of asthma.) Logic had gone berserk.

Born in 1882, Samuel Harper inherited an interest in Russia from his father, the President of Chicago University. As a young man he was actually an eyewitness to the Bloody Sunday massacre in St Petersburg in 1905. Later he met up with the British scholar Bernard Pares and together they conducted field-work interviews with Russian politicians at the time of the first Duma; they interviewed Miliukov alone ten times. Pares taught at Liverpool University and Harper was invited there in 1911 for a two-year spell as visiting lecturer, travelling to Russia during vacations. His Russian friends were basically the liberals, some more left-wing than others, but none of them bolsheviks. Believing strongly in the Allied war effort, he toured the Russian front-line trenches, as Pares also did, learning all he could and at the same time trying to raise morale. In 1916 he sailed to Russia in the company of David R. Francis, whom Wilson had just appointed Ambassador to

Russia – a sign of Harper's increasing tendency to frequent the corridors of power, particularly those of the State Department, even when they were in transit. In 1917 he returned from Russia prophesying that Kerensky would hold out until the Constituent Assembly met; consequently the Bolshevik Revolution struck him as a personal affront, a refutation of his own expert judgment and a lethal attack on his Russian friends. Establishing personal connections with Colonel House, Secretary of State Lansing and Justice Brandeis, as well as businessmen interested in the Russian market, he threw his weight angrily and insistently against the counsel of Colonel Raymond Robins and the fellow-travellers of *The Nation* who wished to recognize the bolshevik regime. Pares adopted the same attitude, referring to bolshevism as bearing "all the marks of the beast...." It was not until 1926 that Harper's curiosity as a Russia-expert, and his natural desire to keep up to date in his field of specialization, finally persuaded him to pay his first call on the Soviet Union.

In Russia he travelled with the knowledgeable Hindus, studied new methods of civic training and published a book on the subject which received a favourable review in *Izvestia*. He was in! One should not underestimate the professional factor here: Western experts on communist regimes naturally benefit from the official goodwill of those regimes,* but this goodwill is dependent on the attitude they adopt. Harper's lectures at Chicago were beginning to excite protests from alumni and trustees, but in 1930 he returned to the Soviet Union, toured the villages and interviewed American and German engineers working there. The prevailing enthusiasm of the young impressed him. Furthermore like so many other potential fellow-travellers, he was struck by the change of mood, by the transition from what seemed iconoclastic nihilism to practical economic construction. He went again in 1932, acknowledged that living standards had fallen, but justified the balance sheet. Meanwhile Pares remained entrenched in his anti-bolshevik hostility – his "journey to Damascus" was deferred. When in 1933 Roosevelt decided to formally recognize the USSR and arrangements were put in hand for the arrival of Litvinov as the first Ambassador, Samuel Harper at last came into his own and was closely consulted by the State Department on a wide range of sensitive issues. From that time on until his death in 1942, he moved ever deeper into the fellow-travelling orbit, pursued belatedly but finally overtaken by a Bernard Pares who now beheld in the Soviet Union "that material of character and purpose out of which true democracy can be made".[6]

* More recently a generation of American China scholars has suffered from non-access to China and the relevant sources of information.

The German fellow-travellers were scarcely in a position to express opinions about the Pact. While their communist brethren in Moscow suffered grotesquely, they held their breath as they became enemy aliens living in a France now nominally at war with Germany. Heinrich Mann wearily convinced himself that Russia was buying time, and that France's non-conduct of the phoney war proved Stalin's wisdom. (This was certainly true.) But he could not subscribe to the Comintern's anti-war line of 1939–41; his basic liberal affection for British and French democracy was too strong, and he read reports of the Battle of Britain with both anxiety and admiration. Britain, he reflected, hated no one; it possessed a proud record of civic peace and harmony; the Battle of Britain had decided the fate of Europe. So here Mann lapsed into heresy.

In France the line did not hold; indeed the fellow-travellers who had brought such lustre and prestige to the Soviet cause in the thirties rebelled violently. On 29 August 1939 the Union des Intellectuels Français issued a statement expressing "stupefaction before the volte-face which has reconciled the leaders of the USSR to the Nazi leaders at the very hour when the latter simultaneously threaten both Poland and the independence of all free peoples".[7] When one considers that this protest was signed by such top-flight fellow-travellers as Frédéric and Irène Joliot-Curie, Langevin, Jean Perrin, Victor Basch and Aimé Cotton, one sees the magnitude of the blow to the Party. Nor did the rot stop there. On 1 September Luc Durtain condemned Stalin's tactics in *L'Oeuvre* while Benda concluded that the Pact was a suicidal action in terms of the credibility of international communism. Rolland fell silent; presently he sent a message to Premier Daladier supporting the French national war effort. Privately he reflected that neither dialectical materialism nor the class struggle could compensate for the abandoned religious spirit, for the loss of contact with the primal instincts of morality dwelling in the depths of the human soul. The old man now withdrew into his shell, ruminated with himself and waited.

One might have expected the French fellow-travellers, with their greater loyalty to the powerful PCF, to have held the line more staunchly than their Anglo-Saxon colleagues. But no doubt those who lived on the Continent of Europe felt more closely the menace of the nazi beast poised to strike. It would be wrong, however, to suggest that the Anglo-Saxon world did not experience some spectacular defections. For Lehmann and Spender the Pact was the last straw. Laski reacted violently. Cowley, Frank and MacLeish dissolved their marriages with the Soviet Union. For Hindus, "red bread" was no longer digestible. To Gollancz the Pact was "a great shock", but the thought weighed on him that Britain and France were ultimately responsible. In January 1940 he wrote: "I have had many grave differences of opinion with communists since more than a year before the war; but their single-minded devotion to the cause of human liberation is such that it should make every supporter of capitalist and fascist abominations hang his head in shame."[8] And he warned that "a war against the Soviet Union would be the vilest of crimes" – a reference to the fact that Anglo-French opinion seemed more incensed by Russia's attack on Finland than by Germany's record of aggression. But the most important camel whose back was broken by the Pact was Louis Fischer. The version of recent history he put forward in his *Stalin and Hitler* (1940) was perhaps more original than convincing. Appeasement, he argued, really stopped in March 1939 with Chamberlain's speech about Czechoslovakia. As soon as Moscow recognized this, it decided to jettison the collective security strategy because, with Anglo-German hostility assured, it was free to manoeuvre for the best possible bargain with either side. The British refused the Russians any concessions with regard to the Baltic States, whereas the Germans accorded them a free hand. That clinched it: the Pact became inevitable. What seems wrong with this theory is that appeasement was by no means abandoned in March 1939; Britain showed no serious intention during the summer of concerting military arrangements on which Russia could effectively depend, and Moscow's assessment of Anglo-French military capability must have forced the conclusion that even in the event of a formal alliance being signed, Russia would be left to bear the brunt of the fighting against the Wehrmacht.

The Pact also gravely weakened the front-organizations. One third of the League of American Writers' officers resigned, although quite a few of these, like Thomas Mann, were by no means fellow-travellers. Some stalwarts hung on, like Donald Ogden Stewart, Dashiell Hammett, Edgar Snow, Samuel Putnam and Rockwell Kent, but the League was so weakened that it did not meet again until June 1941. The League for Peace and Democracy was also split down the middle, and the compromise formula arrived at – "we neither condemn nor approve the actions of the Soviet Union" – was scarcely likely to satisfy lively minds. Four months after the Pact the League was dissolved; the American Friends of the Soviet Union suffered the same fate. Within the American Civil Liberties Union a bitter struggle ensued, and when some communist members were expelled, Harry Ward loyally resigned in protest. The American Youth Congress stood the strain better, condemning "war hysteria" and opposing defence aid to Britain. The Left Book Club was shattered (though it was not formally disbanded until 1948).

No longer able to present a cohesive, fellow-travelling image, it resorted to publishing different sides of the case as represented by the Dean's *The Socialist Sixth of the World* and Leonard Woolf's *Barbarians at the Gate,* the first attack on the Soviet Union to appear in vermilion covers.

Meanwhile the British weekly *Tribune* went through a time of torment. Its 25 August headline announced: "Soviet Peace Move Exposes Chamberlain", and a week later an editorial congratulated the Russians on reinforcing peace in Europe. They had apparently "smashed the fascist war making alliance". Wallowing deeper in astrology, the paper declared on page five: "Russia has not given Hitler a free hand." By the following week, confronted with the fact of war, *Tribune* adopted the line that it had to be fought, but on behalf of the workers not the bosses. Zilliacus, who went out on a limb and condemned the Pact, recommended that the war be fought with energy and determination "but without illusions". Still basking in ignorance of what the Pact implied, the paper's foreign affairs editor stated categorically on 15 September that Poland remained free to purchase war materials from the USSR. (Unfortunately a few days later the Red Army imported them free of charge.) Desperate in the face of these escalating events, each one shattering another illusion, the paper again rallied, this time putting Stafford Cripps into bat with the interesting thesis that Russia had not really stabbed Poland in the back by occupying her Eastern territories. On 6 October another astounding blunder was perpetrated, this time *after* the event: six days after the French communists in the Chamber of Deputies called for an immediate peace on Moscow's orders, *Tribune* protested against the suppression of the PCF and claimed that it stood for a vigorous prosecution of the war. Swivelling to catch its own tail, *Tribune* now called for an end to the war – or for a revolutionary socialist war under a revolutionary socialist government. When this miracle didn't occur, *Tribune* began to have doubts: maybe an immediate peace would be Hitler's peace – a devastating flash of insight.

Then came the additional misery of Russia's war with Finland, which released yet another flood of recriminations and "last straws". The Soviet Union had demanded a strip of territory in the Leningrad region and Finland had refused. On 30 November the Soviet attack began, and disastrously too, so that the Finns were able to hold out for four months. Then – to leap ahead by several months – pacts of military assistance were imposed on the three independent Baltic states, followed by coups in each and a shotgun wedding with the USSR in June 1940. Once again Russia was not without her friends. The American Student Union college chapters in New York City defended the invasion "of a puppet state created and maintained by imperial powers from abroad" – as if describing what Finland became after her defeat and the installation in power of the pro-Soviet Kuusinen Government. Rockwell Kent judged the border between the two countries to be "arbitrary" and Russia's demands "reasonable". As for his observations about the annexation of the Baltic States, they seemed totally unfathomable: "Lithuania, Esthonia, Latvia. 'Stalin has grabbed them,' screamed our press. 'The Soviets won't grab them,' said the communists. Well – they didn't."[9] But they did. Samuel Harper, noting that the Finnish war had pro- duced an upsurge of crude anti-bolshevism, took resort in the thought that whatever crude anti-bolsheviks opposed must be good. In any case Stalin had accorded the Finns "a rather decent peace". As for the Baltic States, their "reabsorption" had always been a likely event: "Moscow did indeed carry out its frank warning of some twenty years before, that it would respect the independence of its small neighbours only if such independence were genuine."[10] By such Alice-in-Wonder- land logic the fellow-travellers laid to rest Lenin's principle of national self-determination and justified every new Soviet annexation on the ground that where the Tsars had once ruled Stalin too had a right to sit. But Samuel Harper's views were not popular with his university col- leagues, who apparently regarded him as a kind of nazi-Soviet agent, bringing on in him the acute nervous breakdown from which he never recovered.

As far as Sidney and Beatrice Webb were concerned, each Soviet attack was explicable as an act of self-defence. Pritt, ably served by his legal training, darted into print at every crisis, rushing about the country to defend Russia's war against Finland and asserting that the Finnish guns had fired first, killing seven Soviet soldiers. (One recalls that the Chinese were well known to have provoked the Japanese in 1937, and that a notorious Polish cavalry charge deep into the Third Reich had compelled Hitler to defend his country.) His book *Must the War Spread?* led to his expulsion from the Labour Party. He showed himself a master of the convenient euphemism, referring for example to "the change in status of the Baltic States", but he was also capable of the most blatant logical contradictions, as when he argued that British reactionaries "openly paraded their affection for the Baltic fascist regimes by refusing to recognize the decision of those States to enter the Soviet Union".[11] Hewlett Johnson approached the Finnish crisis on an unconventional note: "From the moral standpoint the Finnish invasion by the USSR is indefensible and bitterly regretted by her warmest friends"; he felt bound in this instance to consider whether the Soviet regime lacked certain Christian qualities. However he then made out an excellent strategic case for Russia's war and warned all progressives to remain devoted to the only State which had achieved "the abolition of the exploitation of man by man".[12] So it was all right after all. Certain professional embarrassments ensued. On the last day of the year Archbishop Lang attended a service in the Cathedral where special prayers for Finland were offered. The Dean was obliged, *ex officio*, to attend the Archbishop. On 13 March all five Canons of the Cathedral, frustrated beyond endurance, wrote to *The Times* complaining that Johnson's political activities "gravely impair the spiritual influence of the Cathedral in the City and diocese" and were quite "incompatible with the proper discharge of the trust which has been committed to him".[13] But the Dean noted with some justification that if they and the Archbishop could say prayers for Finland he could say prayers for Russia. Meanwhile in the United States a kindred spirit, Corliss Lamont, described the invasion of Finland as "an act of aggression and a terrible mistake", and then proceeded to justify it without reservation. Finland hit the nerve-racked staff of *Tribune* below the belt. It was the last straw. The fellow-traveller Hartshorn was removed as editor and replaced by Raymond Postgate, the war against Finland was condemned, the verdict about Poland was amended to "rape", and the absorption of the Baltic States finally traced back to the deal Russia made with Germany in August 1939. One can however sympathize with those who smelt much hypocrisy in the atmosphere. As Louis Fischer remarked, the seizures of Austria, Czechoslovakia and Memel had never even been *debated* in the League of Nations, yet Russia was promptly expelled from the League over Finland. "If the world had been humane to Spain," he wrote, "Finland might never have been invaded."[14] In December a distinguished group of British intellectuals,* many of them fellow-travellers, warned that certain circles would gladly divert the so-called war effort against Russia, and that such a diversion would be interpreted by the working class as an assault on socialism.

The anti-war line adopted by the Comintern in September 1939 was not of course an issue separate from the Pact; on the contrary it was Russia's method of rationalizing at the ideological level its own *Realpolitik*. Nevertheless we are compelled to treat it as a separate issue in so far as some intellectuals found the Pact digestible but the Comintern line not. Even within communist circles there was at first widespread confusion about the implications of the Pact for the European working-class movement. On 2 September, for example, the PCF's parliamentary

---

* Including Sidney and Beatrice Webb, Bernard Shaw, Charles Trevelyan, P. Chalmers Mitchell, Hewlett Johnson, Richard Acland and Sybil Thorndike.

group actually voted for the war credits; neither the French, the British nor the American Parties realized that they were obliged to condemn the war as "imperialist" until specific instructions from Moscow reached them at the end of the third week of the month. The PCF and the CPGB thereupon demanded an immediate peace, while the American CP opposed lend-lease, all aid to Britain and conscription. The full implications of the Comintern position were exposed in an article written by Walter Ulbricht and published in *Die Welt* on 9 February 1940. An Anglo-French military victory, he said, would only mean that the City of London would harness Germany as a workshop for its intended war against the USSR. *British imperialism had revealed itself as the main culprit by refusing Hitler's peace offer which the USSR supported.* In Britain Palme Dutt took up this line, attributing London's declaration of war to one fact alone – Germany had made peace with Russia. Meanwhile in the USSR all anti-fascist references disappeared from the Soviet press and Premier Molotov delivered a speech to the Supreme Soviet to the effect that one could take Hitlerism or leave it, it was a matter of taste.

For many this was too much. Georges Friedmann had just about reconciled himself to the Pact itself, but what followed disgusted him. Gollancz called the Comintern line "fatuous" and spoke of Ulbricht with contempt. A year later Laski reminded the CPGB that all talk of a "people's government" in Britain was utopian in present circumstances and that a nazi military victory would merely bring Britain the benefits of a Vichy-style regime. Although he distrusted Tory war aims and himself looked forward to a socialist Europe, a "free India" and a radical solution to African colonialism, the logic of the situation was for him very much as Cecil Day Lewis expressed it:

> It is the logic of our times
> No subject for immortal verse,
> That we who lived by honest dreams
> Defend the bad against the worse.[15]

After some months of hesitation, Strachey came off the fence, pointing out that although Chiang Kai Shek was more repressive than Churchill, the Chinese communists continued to support him against the Japanese. He saw current communist policy as leading to a nazi-dominated Britain, and he blasted the *Daily Worker* for characterizing the German invasion of Norway as an inevitable response to British aggression. Thus for Gollancz, Laski and Strachey the Comintern line on the war signified a final and irrevocable break with communism. Day Lewis and Spender had also quit.

Other fellow-travellers adopted a *faute de mieux* form of patriotism without actually emphasizing their disagreement with the communists. Lecturing at Cornell in 1940, Joseph Needham criticized Britain and France for having aspired to turn Hitler eastwards against Russia. But, like Strachey, he drew attention to the united stand of the Chinese against Japanese aggression: surely Hitler, too, had to be resisted even if the weapons were not ideally clean. O'Casey, perhaps aware that the nazis might not understand that he was a friend of their Soviet friends, came out with a play, *Oak Leaves and Lavender,* the hero of which was a Battle of Britain pilot who claimed to be fighting not for England but for "the people" against fascism. In the circumstances, a distinction not lacking in sophistry. As for the Dean of Canterbury, he lurched about these stormy seas like a ship bereft of its rudder. In December 1940 he told Gollancz that he rejoiced at news of Italian defeats and British victories and, according to Gollancz, he followed this up with a letter in January 1941 saying how "appalling" it was that he had unwittingly lent his good name to the defeatist policy of the CP. But if Hitler was enemy number one for Johnson, he nevertheless reacted with indignation when Home Secretary Herbert Morrison closed down the defeatist *Daily Worker* (to which the Dean continued loyally to contribute). He praised the "valiant spirit" of the *Worker*'s editor, William Rust, and in June 1943 accepted honorary membership of the paper's Board. But by that time, of course, the hatchets had been buried.

Other fellow-travellers brought more comfort to the communists. In an inflammatory article, "Uncommon Sense about the War", published in the *New Statesman* on 7 October 1939, Shaw asked: now that Poland is gone, what are we fighting for? He couldn't visualize Chamberlain or Churchill as champions of democracy, and in any case neither Roosevelt nor Stalin would permit Hitler to conquer the world. (But suppose their conception of "the world" did not include Western Europe and Britain?) Said Shaw: we are making mischief instead of making peace. Stalin knew what was best for everyone; in flouting his advice the British were simply abolishing what little democracy they still possessed. Predictably, this article provoked a storm; on this occasion the heat seems to have driven Shaw out of the kitchen. In a letter written a month later he expressed continuing scepticism about the war effort, but yielded a grudging reconciliation to it. Thereafter he subsided.

Even more faithful to the Party line, in spirit if not always in phrase, were D. N. Pritt and Edgar Young. Young wrote to *Tribune* in February 1940 suggesting that Munich and its aftermath had disposed many good people "to accept the policy of revolutionary struggle against Imperialism – Franco-British no less than German – which the

Communist Party has enunciated . . ."[16] Pritt for his part tended not so much to enunciate the Party line as implicitly to condone it; by constantly emphasizing that all military confrontations with Hitler were really a masquerade, he managed to exclude from his writings and speeches the over-riding desirability of defeating Hitler. In later years, donning the patriotic hat, he was to claim that he had supplied vital intelligence about the coming German invasion of Norway which the Government had failed to use. For once, the Government could scarcely be blamed.

In January 1941 the CP launched a new campaign and a new front-organization, the People's Convention, with fellow-travellers like Pritt, Young and Harry Adams occupying prominent positions, and the white-haired head of the Dean towering serenely above the rest. The Convention announced a six-point programme, but the defence of blitzed Britain against Hitler was conspicuously not one of them. Gollancz tried to persuade the Dean that what the CP meant by a "people's government" was not necessarily what the Dean meant: but who knew with certainty what the Dean meant? Edgar Young, who had greeted the absorption of the Baltic States into the USSR enthusiastically, and was now writing anonymously as the *Yorkshire Post*'s naval correspondent, was arguing that as a sea power Britain could not win a Continental war without Soviet help. In 1941 he published a pamphlet upholding the People's Convention, calling for an end to the Empire and for the creation of a people's government which would appeal to the German people to throw off their rulers. Confronting the remote possibility that the German people might not thus generously respond, he warned them that they would thereby face "the disastrous possibility of being engaged with a fresh and powerful belligerent on another very vulnerable front . . . Historical memories would . . . evoke in their minds the spectre of defeat."[17] When this was written Hitler was already in triumphant occupation of half of Europe; as for the "powerful belligerent" and the "historical memories", the answer was rather clearly provided on 22 June 1941.

The anti-war line was much easier to accept in America, where no bombs were falling, no jackboots goose-stepped and no invasion was imminent. Even in June 1940, after the fall of France, a meeting of the German American Writers in New York adopted a majority view that the war was merely another inter-imperialist crisis with Britain as culpable as Germany. Both the Youth League and the rump of the League of American Writers took up this position, while the Hollywood Anti-Nazi League dropped "Anti-Nazi" from its title and assumed another more innocuous, the Hollywood League for Democratic Action. To prop up this position the American Peace Mobilization was created in September 1940, nominally headed by the Rev. John B. Thompson of Oklahoma and staffed by the usual mixture of communists and fellow-travellers. (After the nazi attack on Russia the word "Peace" went out of the title and the word "People's" came in.) In April 1940 John Dewey's Committee for Cultural Freedom listed twenty-five new front-organizations created since January 1939, although such a figure is deceptive in so far as it partly reflected a plurality of local initiatives rather than a stack of separate national organizations. Rockwell Kent now advised Americans to cultivate their own garden (since Stalin was cultivating his, admittedly an expanding one). In May 1940 Dreiser poured ridicule on the notion that Britain and France were in any sense democracies. "If England is not a totalitarian state there never was one. It has been for the last three hundred years a landed and primogeniture legalized and titled and high financed autocracy. The clerk and labor classes in England have no more opportunity to express themselves democratically than the Germans, the Russians or the Italians."[18] In February of the following year he wrote to the Soviet Ambassador enclosing a copy of his own *America is Worth Saving* with the request that it be delivered to Stalin. At about this time Edgar Snow met Dreiser in a radio studio. The great novelist took the younger man home and explained to him that the British, the French, the Dutch and the Belgians did nothing on behalf of their colonized natives; they had made no move to save Spain, Abyssinia or China. Chamberlain and Daladier had miscalculated and Stalin simply beat them at their own game. Later, through Dreiser's influence, Snow was invited to address a conference sponsored by the League of American Writers, but when it was dis-covered that he planned to recommend aid for both China and Britain, the invitation was withdrawn. Dreiser's hatred of England proved un-quenchable even after June 1941 when the vast majority of fellow-travellers returned to the Popular Front and collective security themes of the thirties with an inward sigh of relief. "I mistrust England as much as I mistrust Hitler," he commented in July, but in September of the following year he really exceeded himself: "I would rather see the Germans in England than those damned aristocratic horse-riding snobs there now. The English have done nothing in this war thus far except borrow money, planes and men from the United States."[19] And he warned the world that should Russia go down "due to any connivance on the part of England", he hoped Hitler would "invade England and drive that upper ruling class – not the sadly misruled and betrayed English mass – into the sea".[20] Gas chambers strictly for dukes.

The whole movement went into reverse in June 1941 when Hitler crossed the Soviet frontiers. The malevolent City of London vanished almost overnight from the lexicon of political science. The Hollywood Writers' Mobilization threw off the isolationist toga and armoured itself in patriotic military fervour. The People's Convention in Britain dropped its demand for a people's government: evidently one such in the new alliance was enough. Orwell commented in August: "... the 'Communism' of these people amounts simply to nationalism and leader-worship in their most vulgar forms, transferred to the USSR",[21] a good point spoiled by its failure to explain why these emotions had been transferred to Russia. Hewlett Johnson became chairman of the Joint Committee for Soviet Aid, with Mrs D. N. Pritt as vice-chairman and the fellow-travelling scientist Sir Peter Chalmers Mitchell a prominent activist. Pritt's relentless propagandizing earned from Orwell the title of "perhaps the most effective pro-Soviet publicist in this country", but Edgar Young's activities closely paralleled those of the lawyer. "For all practical purposes," he wrote in October, "we have been looking on for the past four months while our Ally has borne virtually alone the weight of the Nazi war effort", thereby squandering "the prospect of a victorious peace by Christmas."[22] That Russia had looked on for nearly two years while Britain bore the weight was not of course an argument he considered relevant. But he was entitled to point out that Russia was now fighting 240 German divisions while Britain was engaging twenty at most in Africa and facing only thirty more in Europe. He explained to a meeting in Penzance that Britain's role, as part of the new team, was to draw the nazi defence while the Ally scored the goals, but his own military solution differed appreciably from the conventional communist call for a full-scale second front. Young didn't regard a massive invasion of the Continent as militarily feasible, proposing instead a series of scattered commando raids involving units of up to ten thousand men.

In France the Party's outstanding role in the Resistance enormously enhanced the power and prestige of the communist movement. Intellectuals gathered into local clandestine groups and were later federated into the communist-controlled Union Nationale des Intellectuels, with a claimed membership of one hundred thousand.* An influential clandestine press sprang up, notably *L'Université libre, L'Art Français* and most influential of all, *Les Lettres françaises clandestines*. The military Resistance produced a new and younger type of activist fellow-traveller

---

* The affiliates of the Union Nationale included the Front National Universitaire, the Comité National des Médecins français, the Comité National des Ecrivains, the Comité National des Juristes, the Front National des Arts.

attracted by fighting organizations such as Libération, perhaps the most influential being Emmanuel d'Astier de la Vigerie. Backed by Albert Bayet, one of the last of the dying species of Jacobin, Dreyfusard fellow-travellers, d'Astier worked energetically to affiliate Libération with the communist Front National, only to be thwarted by Malraux, André Philip and others for whom distrust of the PC had become a primary principle of action.

Rolland was too old to fight: he lived in great trepidation, nervously (and tragically) burning large parts of his correspondence with Gorky, and daily expecting the arrest or assassination which never came. Paul Langevin fared less well. Having swallowed his distaste for the Pact to the extent of testifying on behalf of the communists arraigned before a Paris military tribunal in March 1940, he was interned by the nazis on 30 October, an event which sparked off student riots and inspired his young communist admirers Jacques Decour, Georges Politzer and Jacques Solomon (Langevin's son-in-law) to found *L'Université libre*: all three were later killed. After thirty-eight days of intensive interrogation in the Santé, the old physicist was released, but in 1942 he was again arrested for a period. Then, under the assumed name of Léon Pinel, engineer, he began to work within the Resistance until, totally exhausted, he escaped over the Jura frontier in May 1944, carried by two *francs-tireurs*. His family suffered terribly: not only was his son-in-law executed but his daughter Hélène was deported to Auschwitz. Both were communists. When after the war he finally joined the Party it was partly in tribute to their heroism and martyrdom. Generally the nazi authorities in France shrank from exterminating eminent and venerated intellectuals and scholars, so that Aimé Cotton, President of the Academy of Science, and the left-wing mathematician, Professor Borel, although arrested, were ultimately released. Picasso worked on in Paris, disturbed only by those many Wehrmacht officers whose appreciation of great art had carried them to the farthest corners of Europe.

In October 1940 the writer Vercors met with the philospher René Maublanc, the physicist Joliot-Curie, Francis Jourdain and the psychologist Henri Wallon to discuss the possibilities of intellectual resistance. The high historical temperature was soon to carry them all, except Vercors, into the Party. Joliot-Curie's position within the Collège de France enabled him to manufacture incendiary bombs for the *francs-tireurs,* and his wife Irène was also active in the Resistance, finally escaping, like Langevin, to Switzerland. At the same time the Resistance promoted a new militancy among fellow-travellers, many of whom were destined to enjoy an uneasy and sometimes harrowing relationship with the Party during the glacial years of the Cold War. Intellectuals who had found the Pact and the Comintern line of 1939–41 abhorrent, like Friedmann, Cassou and Louis Martin-Chauffier, now buried the past, accepted the communist embrace, and joined the Comité National des Ecrivains (CNE). Cassou had been relieved of his job as *conservateur* of the Musée d'Art Moderne in September 1940, was arrested in 1941, spent a year in prison, emerged to become the leader of a southern zone Resistance network, and was later brutally beaten up in Lyons by the quasi-fascist French *milice*. The communist poet Louis Aragon, who was drawing the broadest possible spectrum of left-wing opinion into the CNE, encouraged Martin-Chauffier, Claude Aveline and Vercors to join in 1942. Albert Camus, who had seven years earlier passed into the PCF and out again, returned from Algeria at this time, joined the southern zone network, Combat, and also entered the ranks of the CNE – but not as a fellow-traveller. Jean-Paul Sartre was no less reticent. Grossly maligned by the communists in 1941 following his release as a prisoner of war (the reason was ill-health, the communists shouted "collaboration"), he entered the CNE in 1943 to loud apologies and fraternal greetings. Soon he was writing for the roneo-typed *Les Lettres françaises clandestines*. Of these writers, Vercors rose to early prominence, if not notoriety, with a short novel called *Le Silence de la Mer*, wrongly interpreted by some as an invitation to passivity if not collaboration with the Germans. The clandestine publishing house, Les Editions de Minuit, which he helped to found, published several excellent works of fiction, notably *Les Temps Morts*, a collection of stories depicting the horrors of arrest, interrogation and deportation. (The pseudonymous author, "Minervois", was in reality Claude Aveline.) About such horrors Martin-Chauffier soon learned all there was to know: deported to Bergen-Belsen, he was liberated in the nick of time, almost mortally ill from typhus.

About sixty thousand communists died during the four years of the occupation. With justification the PCF called itself *"Le Parti des Fusillés"*, and it emerged from the war a heroic whale surrounded by shoals of pilot fish. But three or four years later new storms and tidal currents were to carry them apart.

Part Two: Beliefs

5

Revolution, Go East

It is worth attempting at this stage to examine more systematically the basic characteristics of the fellow-traveller, the universe of inherited assumptions, Enlightenment values and moral expectations which created so attractive an image of communist Russia and China in the minds of Western intellectuals, the majority of whom aspired to become neither communists nor revolutionaries. Running right through the history of fellow-travelling is the assumption, implicit or explicit, that what is good, progressive medicine for the backward East might kill the patient in the advanced, industrialized West. This was not an iron law and it needs to be qualified, but the tendency is obvious enough to demand the first claim on our attention.

It was, for example, the conclusion that Arthur Ransome formed during the early months of the Bolshevik Revolution: excellently invigorating for Russia, but quite irrelevant to his native England. He knew little about British socialists like H. M. Hyndman or Keir Hardie, he cared even less, and he had no qualms about telling Lenin and Bukharin flatly that their expectations of permanent revolution were ill-founded. This, of course, was to reject the whole Marxian prognosis that proletarian revolution would first establish its dominion in countries where advanced capitalism had reached the final stage of unresolvable internal contradiction – but what Ransome and his kind admired in Lenin's Russia was not exactly *proletarian* revolution. Alexander Wicksteed was convinced that British people would never tolerate the privations and sacrifices demanded of the Soviet citizen, nor did he think they should. The same double standards gradually emerged in Germany in the 1920s. Adolf Grabowsky, writing in *Die Weltbühne* in 1925, commented that the Soviet system, while doing an excellent job in Russia, "fits into Europe the way a street organ fits into a chamber orchestra".[1] At about this time Jean Guéhenno experienced a "religious" joy at the thought of vast, desperate Russia bringing to birth the long-awaited Marxist revolution, but when he came to consider his native France he discovered that he believed in "Jaurès, in truth and justice". Studying

Lenin's career, he was overcome by the guilt of a "petty-bourgeois Girondin"; reason and even expediency apparently justified the idea of a French proletarian dictatorship but "an explicable refusal of consciousness prevented me" from accepting it.[2] In 1927 Georges Duhamel returned from a trip to Russia full of enthusiasm, but nevertheless insisted that the communist solution could be averted in France by "judicious reforms". Like Luc Durtain he was convinced that the ends had fully justified the means in Russia, but reflecting on the French scene he preferred Léon Blum's counsel: French socialism should be independent – and French. Ten years later Charles Vildrac embraced, with only minor reservations, the Soviet Union's flattering portrayal of itself, but he nevertheless maintained that some other road to socialism would have to be engineered in those countries where the population was more mature, critical and democratic. Maurice Hindus impressed on his readers in the early thirties that the Soviet Government (good) was not to be confused with the Comintern (irrelevant). Apparently Stalin recognized that solutions necessary in backward Russia were inapplicable in the West, and had sensibly confined his energies to building socialism in one country. According to Hindus, the middle class in the West was too powerful, resolute and socially open-ended to permit a violent revolution; therefore if communist ideas were to have any impact on the capitalist world they would have to rely on the force of example and emulation. The idea of planning might prove infectious. Upton Sinclair appealed in *The Way Out* to American capitalists to rescue the United States from the spectre of revolution by timely reforms. When running for the governorship of California, he explained: "I am one of those old-fashioned persons who still have hope that in countries such as Britain and the United States where the people have been accustomed to self-government, the change from capitalism to socialism can be accomplished without the overthrow of the government."[3] Admittedly he was not yet fully committed to the USSR, but that commitment was not destined to change his attitude in this respect.

In March 1932 Beatrice Webb wrote: "Russian communism is the only hope for China."[4] In other words: go east, young revolution, go east. But not west. When in 1929 the Labour Government, of which Sidney Webb was a leading member, refused to allow Trotsky to enter Britain, Beatrice wrote to Trotsky offering to send him books and periodicals. "My husband and I are very sorry that you were not admitted to Britain. But I am afraid that anyone who preaches the permanence of revolution, that is carries the revolutionary war into the politics of other countries, will always be excluded from entering those other countries."[5] So she wasn't so very sorry after all. Nothing the Webbs saw and admired in the USSR altered their opinion that the Labour Party was the authentic, indigenous agent of social change in Britain. Strachey remonstrated with them: what about the British communists? The Webbs shrugged contemptuously. Louis Fischer complained in 1935 that their agnosticism about where, when, how and with what modifications Soviet communism would spread was "honest but feeble". Yet his own solution remained obscure: certainly his regular message to the readers of *The Nation* was not "Stalin is coming". On the contrary, it was "Trotsky would have come", rejoice in his downfall. In April 1933 Gide noted that it was inconceivable that France should attempt to adapt her system to the Russian model. Thirty years later the whole proposition, distinction, schizophrenia if you like, was stated with impressive clarity by a lifelong admirer of Maoist communism, Edgar Snow: "It seems to me that any nation which has achieved a democratic system compatible with civil liberties would undergo unmitigated tragedy and evil if it were to lose them. . . . That one form of dictatorship or authoritarianism should replace an existing one, however, in a nation which has never known a democracy or free choice between the *status quo* and the legal opposition, cannot be said to threaten to rob the people of any treasure they already possessed. . . ."[6] That sums it up. "Our democracy, valuable though it is and a thing to fight for. . . ."[7] The words are Hewlett Johnson's, the date 1941, the theme being that the existence of a legal parliamentary opposition is an indispensable element of British society. Though he wanted to bury British capitalism and introduce planning, he promised the small traders of Britain that they would survive and prosper even if their Russian equivalents had not. Since a peaceful transition to socialism always recommended itself to him, his way of evading Marxist theory without quarrelling with it was to transform virtually the whole British population into "workers": "The forty-three millions of the working class can and must work for their own deliverance."[8] Thereby leaving only a couple of million exploiters to suffer undeliverance. Turning to agents of British progress, he listed the unions, the Labour Party and the Co-operative Movement, while leaving the CPGB out of account. When the enraged Canons of Canterbury finally sprang at his throat, he wrote to *The Times* protesting that he had never advocated Russian methods of change for Britain.

No doubt these attitudes represent what Shaw called uncommon sense. On the other hand those who cherish the civil liberties which emerged gradually in the Western democracies, regarding these liberties and rights as inalienable from the dignity and well-being of the individual, surely put themselves in an untenable position when they recommend crash courses and military discipline in quarters of the globe furthèr afield. To deny these liberties to the Russian or Chinese people ın their own interests is merely to treat whole races of adults like history's retarded children. Admittedly some fellow-travellers approached the problem of freedom and violence in the West with more ambiguity. This question increasingly obsessed Laski after Hitler seized power. In 1933 he recommended a form of socialism which "pays reasonable tribute to the established expectations of vested interest" as preferable to one "which insists on their forthright destruction".[9] But then he began to believe that in an epoch of economic crisis and contraction hallowed ideals of toleration, rationality and assent could readily vanish, and he also began to criticize Labour leaders for assuming too blandly that their opponents were committed to constitutional action. He almost said: we must use force if they do. But this of course was a defensive position and had little to do with the positive assault recommended by Lenin and Trotsky. On discovering the success of the New Deal, Laski's natural faith in tolerance and "insistent liberalism" was easily revived, and those communists who had earlier accused him of accepting the Marxist analysis of history but not the Marxist solutions appeared once again justified.

Some affected a revolutionary stance which was only skin deep. In 1920 Anatole France derided parliamentary institutions, declaring boldly: "If I am told that a revolution would bring suffering, I would nevertheless accept it although I hate suffering . . . But, more than that, I hate mediocrity, sterility. To suffer is to live, to live intensely . . . if one wishes to see an era of justice established, one must be resigned to what may come to pass in its accomplishment – of injustice, of cruelties, and of blood. . . ."[10] Yet he cried out in protest against the trial of the Socialist Revolutionaries in Russia, and when the next French general election dawned he voted for the reformist Cartel des Gauches. Ten years later Gide began bravely to prophesy the inevitability of revolution – unless the bourgeoisie reformed itself in time. But he also prayed privately that the extreme Left in France would not voice its aims and claims prematurely, lest Hitler be encouraged to pay a visit. Dreiser was capable of dismissing the whole history of reformism as a wash-out, but he declined to draw conclusions. Spender castigated the Labour Party for its betrayal of revolutionary socialism, for its pathetic fetish of ballot boxes and parliamentary majorities, yet almost simultaneously he wrote to Aldous Huxley: "I should add that I sympathise with all your objections to violence and to certain features of the Russian system. . . ."[11]

Where there is guilt among intellectuals there is liable to be masochism. To visualize one's original bourgeois sin flayed and flagellated in those Eastern temples of righteousness was a form of emotional doodling not unattractive to the fellow-travellers. Ever since 1905, confessed Wicksteed, I have been trying to liquidate my class pretensions. "If the Bolsheviks can liquidate what remains I shall certainly be grateful." (But a voluntary camping expedition is not the same as compulsory military service.) Travelling round Russia, Waldo Frank became increasingly enthralled by the contrast between the timid, phrase-mongering, shoulder-glancing intellectuals, and the bold, fearless, "organic" proletarian communists: "perhaps the want of that flabby relativism which goes by the name of liberalism in the West and which is often nothing but a want of conviction, is not an unmixed evil."[12] But when he came face to face with a stern Red Army man in a train, who told him bluntly that in the West there were only communists and bourgeois, and nothing in between, Frank answered indignantly that the United States had quite a different history to Russia: the "revolution" there would take a different form. He wrote later that whereas Marxist materialism was liberating the Russian and Chinese masses from the oppressive grasp of priests and magic, only a new idealism could liberate the American workers from the shallow materialism they rubbed off their bosses. Lincoln Steffens declined to complain if in Russia "our group, the intelligentsia, got some of the medicine they gave other groups and classes".[13] But crucifixion by proxy is not crucifixion. In politics the masochistic impulse was demonstrably weaker among fellow-travellers than among the many young middle-class communists who submitted to rigid discipline and scorched their own inherited culture from their brains in order to acquit their guilt. In Sartre's *Les Mains Sales*, the young bourgeois Hugo remarks: "I am in the Party in order to forget myself." The fellow-travellers on the whole had no wish to forget themselves or to abandon their own independence.

The Iron Revolutionary was Shaw. But was Shaw for real? In October 1921 he consigned the British constitution to the rubbish heap, and called for a new type of socialist conscience which would legitimize "the ruthless extirpation of parasitic idleness". He predicted that when the warring classes finally came to blows in Britain (the sooner, the better), then Reds and Whites would argue in the Russian style. Maybe he was playing the clown, but Lenin estimated that the bourgeoisie would laugh on the other sides of their faces if Shaw ever got into a revolutionary situation. One can't be sure. In July 1932, writing to Laski, he described reformist social democracy as the new "official opposition to Communism, which now means Socialism plus the utilization of the new constitutional discoveries of the Soviets in Western politics. On which issue I am a communist."[14] This is an extremely important statement, not only because it provides a perfectly accurate assessment of what a genuine communist stood for, but also because it is without precedent or parallel in the history of fellow-travelling. So why not call Shaw a communist? He had, after all, returned from Russia with the news that he was "a revolutionist ... in the light of the accomplished revolution in Russia". But the definition of "revolutionist" he offered suggested the mandarin more than the arsonist: "one who has adopted the study of the history and practice of revolution as a profession".[15] He could scarcely in honesty claim more: had he ever torn up paving stones, hidden in the marshes, carried a gun, plotted a coup? Not only did he never contemplate joining the Communist Party, but even in the mid-thirties he could not resist mocking the local British specimens of the tribe in his play, *On the Rocks*. It was all very well to warn Wells that capitalism could be overthrown only by men who *hated* it, and that this meant "smashing its institutions ... the defensive, humanitarian, palliative and popular brakes and ... liberties ...",[16] but the people who worked in the post office in the village of Ayot St Lawrence knew their famous neighbour as a gentle old man who liked to take regular consitutionals and didn't eat meat. Probably they were closer to the truth about Shaw than Lenin was – or Shaw was. A sense of humour such as his is by definition cathartic: a subversive wit is irreconcilable with totalitarian government – except at a distance. The fellow-travellers regarded the Comintern apparatus in the West with scepticism. Radek complained in 1934 about "writers of Western countries who are sympathetic to the USSR, full of contempt for decaying capitalism ...", yet looked down their noses "patronizingly upon the young Communist Parties of the West, and see only their mistakes ..."[17] Even Anna Louise Strong (who liked to portray Soviet life in a breezy, outward-bound style) could scarcely bring herself to do her homework among the dry, turgid periodicals put out by the Comintern agencies, "so dull, so heavy", she complained, "so angry with the world".[18] All those furious polemical attacks on foreign renegades, social-traitors, revisionists and social-fascists shattered her vision of the happy, struggling family. The British fellow-travellers were particularly sensitive to foreign intrusions. When the Red Trade Union International (Profintern) began to interfere within the British unions, M. Philips Price tersely called for its liquidation. The Webbs had time for neither the Profintern nor the Comintern, and the frenetic vituperation which emanated from the sixth Comintern Congress in 1928 aroused in them horror and impatience. Palme Dutt later complained that Sidney and Beatrice wanted an international composed entirely of statesmen, completely excluding revolutionary agitational groups. This was precisely what they wanted, provided experts like themselves were regarded as honorary statesmen. They pointed out that, all pretensions notwithstanding, the Executive Committee of the Comintern was consistently dominated by its Russian caucus: "The peoples of the Western democracies will not stand government, or even authoritative direction, from a foreign capital ..."[19] If Russia wanted to convert the world, they said, let her do a fine job at home and exert her influence by the force of example. In 1937 Sidney brusquely insisted that Englishmen who had once thrown off the domination of Rome would not tolerate domination from Moscow. He and Beatrice fully endorsed the Labour Party's refusal to accept CP affiliation, advising the Russians to concentrate on the good work of the Society for Promoting Cultural Relations, on Intourist, on music festivals and international conferences for doctors and engineers. The sooner the Soviet Government disassociated itself from the Comintern's inflammatory rhetoric, the better. Even during his campaign for a Popular Front, Laski had to admit that the Comintern had never understood British life, history or psychology. Shaw laughed off the Comintern as "a church" and proposed "a final conflict between Church and State in which the State had to get the upper hand ..."[20] He meant the Soviet State.

As regards the attitudes of fellow-travellers to their local CPs perhaps the best generalizations are these: that friendship thrives during "soft", *main tendue* phases when united or popular fronts are the order of the day and the general strategy is defensive, that is to say designed to defend democratic liberties against the threat of fascism either at home or abroad; and, finally, that a large, dynamic, electorally powerful, proletarian-based Communist Party naturally presents a more attractive image to fellow-travellers than a skeleton sect containing more leaders than led. But this last point requires one qualification. The KPD was apt by its violent and dramatic displays of bull-like virility to feminize its potential fellow-travelling supporters into chaste withdrawal. In other words, where the first factor (revolutionary sectarianism) is operating unfavourably, the third factor (size) may appear a frightening rather than an attractive asset. That is why the PCF enjoyed such prodigious success between 1934 and 1939, and again between 1941 and the late forties, in harnessing fellow-travelling support notable both for its quality and quantity. Not only was the Party within sight of acquiring one hundred parliamentary deputies during the Popular Front period, and almost two hundred immediately after the war, but in both these phases the Party line was national, coalitionist and non-revolutionary. Yet one further factor should be mentioned when accounting for the unique attraction of the PCF for fellow-travellers, the factor of historical traditions and historical myths. In the thirties the Party discovered that by claiming to be the heir of Robespierre, Saint-Just and the Jacobins, it resurrected not so much the spectre of the guillotine as a proud and peculiarly French heritage compounded of *liberté, égalité, fraternité,* of the revolutionary *mission civilisatrice,* of secular education, social progress and, above all, of defence of the eternal Republic against all the latter-day Bourbons and Bonapartes in their many disguises. Furthermore, the Marxist vocabulary was not alien to the French philosophical *langage,* and still less so to the German, in the way it was to Anglo-Saxons whose vocabulary and concepts were empiricist, positivistic, utilitarian, or pragmatic. Which is not to say that the French and German fellow-travellers actually *became* Marxists. It is, however, to suggest that they could more comfortably graft selected fragments of Leninist ideology on to their own humanism, and that their local Party theoreticians sounded to them less like foreigners or Yahoos than they did to the Anglo-Saxons.

Take, first, the situation in the Weimar Republic. What the left-wing intellectuals of the *Weltbühne* circle really wanted was an Independent Socialist (USPD) regime without the Bavarian-style popular putsches. They wanted, therefore, to work within a democratic and Republican framework while simultaneously avoiding the gross capitulationism of the Majority Socialists (SPD) and the élitist, Leninist violence which the Communist Party (KPD) only reluctantly abandoned in 1923-4 after it had been clobbered once too often. But the USPD disappeared in the early twenties and so they were left floating free, compelled to make a virtue out of their independence, marooned in limbo. In 1925 *Die Weltbühne* tentatively proposed some form of socialist-communist co-operation, but enthusiasm was lacking. Only the rise of a violent extreme Right could nudge them towards the KPD, persuading Tucholsky and Ossietzky that a Volksfront alone could save democracy. Yet they, along with Heinrich Mann, Arnold Zweig, Toller, Graf and Feuchtwanger, were all the while being remorselessly attacked in *Linkskurve* by Becher, Wolf, Renn and Lukács. Despairing, Ossietzky dropped his plan of running Heinrich Mann for President of the Republic in 1932 and announced that, *faute de mieux,* he would vote for the communist Thälmann. Early in 1933 Mann, Käthe Kollwitz, Einstein and others signed a call for the immediate unification of the SPD and the KPD – but it was too late. So the Weimar Republic produced virtually no fellow-travellers of real stature; for that, one had to wait until the years in exile already described.

Nor was the situation much better in France. In 1923 the PCF began expelling heretics in waves and droves, often in the name of minor theological subtleties which were less obscure in Moscow than in Paris precisely because they were basically extensions of internal tensions within the bolshevik leadership. Distrust between the Party and the intellectuals became mutual. Not until the early thirties, when Thorez assumed command, were the first hesitant steps towards *rapprochement* attempted. Rolland responded, though his admiration was mainly directed towards the USSR, and others like Langevin, Joliot-Curie, Jourdain, Bloch and Benda followed his lead, but with varying degrees of caution. By the time the Popular Front was consecrated the hymns were stirring all feet to march in step. In 1937 Rolland addressed a letter to the National Conference of the PCF assuring it, in a phrase Heinrich Mann would have been proud to make his own, of his "entire sympathy". Later, addressing the ninth Party Congress amidst adulatory tributes, he described himself as linked to the Party "by reason and by the heart" (but not, of course, by membership). And great though his sorrow and bitterness was after the Pact, the old spirit revived in him when he welcomed Thorez back from Russia in December 1944, a gesture the Secretary-General repaid a month later by personally attending Rolland's funeral.

The older generation of French physicists who moved into the Party's orbit comprised a brilliant group knit together by ties of family, marriage, educational institutions, and by the progressive political tradition of the Dreyfusards. There was Irène Curie, whose husband, Frédéric Joliot, had been a pupil of her parents, Pierre and Marie Curie; the two Joliot-Curies were jointly awarded the Nobel Prize in 1935 for their work on radio-activity. Then there was Paul Langevin, who had recommended Joliot to Marie Curie and later directed him towards the Institut du Radium. There were other friends of the Curies, Jean Perrin, Aimé Cotton and his wife Eugénie, all scientists of high distinction. Despite her political allegiances, Irène Joliot-Curie became Director of the Institut du Radium after the war, guiding the training of hundreds of young scientists and earning from the French Academy of Science the Albert of Monaco prize as "a feeble homage of gratitude". When she died in 1956, a victim of leukaemia, she was succeeded in the chair of nuclear physics at the Sorbonne by her husband. The growing commitment of these scientists to the PCF was highly prized and advertised. In a message to the Gennevilliers Congress of 1938, Langevin declared: "It is the honour of your Party to unite tightly thought and action ... it has been said that a communist ought always to teach himself, but I wish to say to you that the more I am taught, the more I feel myself a communist ... your Party ... is a sort of expansion of the French Revolution as the doctrine of Marx-Engels-Lenin is an expansion of the great French thinkers of the eighteenth century."[21] Then came the Pact. But the Resistance once again fired the kiln, baking soft-edged fellow-travellers into hard-glazed communists. "I have become a communist because I am a patriot", announced Joliot-Curie in 1942, in words as memorable as Spender's "I am a communist because I am a liberal". In 1944, after the Liberation, Langevin joined the Party at the age of seventy-two, as did the eminent psychologist Henri Wallon and the architect Francis Jourdain, all of them fellow-travellers of long standing. Eugénie Cotton entered the Party at the age of sixty-four. Irène Joliot-Curie chose to remain outside, but in 1951 she announced that she would vote communist since all other parties were leading France to war and ruin. The PCF, she said, was the only organization which stood for a rational utilization of French scientific resources. In the Cotton family it was the husband, Aimé, who stayed out, but he too announced his intention to vote communist and busied himself in such front-organizations as the Association France-URSS and the Comité d'aide à Grèce. As a member of the Scientific Council of the Atomic Energy Commissariat he warned more than once that he would not be a party to the exploitation of science for aggressive purposes.

These old scientists were sharp-witted not senile: but once the decision, the commitment, had been made in the autumn of their lives, they drifted through the turbulent battlefields of the Cold War like sleepwalkers, virtually unmoved by the recriminations and resignations occurring around them. It was the younger generation of fellow-travellers who discovered that the marriage or liaison they had formed with the PCF during the war could not be a tranquil one unless they abandoned all pretensions to independence and objectivity of judgment. Writers like Friedmann, Aveline, Cassou, Vercors and Martin-Chauffier acknowledged their common dilemma and their unity of principle by collaborating in publishing two collections of essays which drew clear lines of demarcation between their own position and the Party's. In 1946 Friedmann had praised the PCF on the "of the people, for the people, by the people" principle, and pointed to it as the only party likely to create in France a society based on justice and dignity. Soon he was not so sure. Aveline complained that the communists had become like the anti-communists: they seized on the slightest criticism, however guarded and modulated, as proof of anti-communism. *"Je m'élève solennellement,"* he wrote, *"contre cette absurdité."* A few years later he came wearily to the conclusion that the Party's submission to the USSR was total and inhuman. How, he wanted to know, could the

PCF mimic Stalinist methods of debate and bullying while claiming to defend old liberal values? Cassou was also disenchanted: the choice between the two power blocs was a choice between two lies, and the PCF would permit not the slightest deviation from the Soviet position on any subject whatsoever. The Party, he said, wanted to turn its supporters into machines lacking intelligence, conscience and intuition. It all reminded him of the old black and brown shirts. Martin-Chauffier described the Party in the late forties as dominating, peremptory, solitary and malicious. And Simone de Beauvoir reflected: "I often asked myself what my position would have been if I had not been linked to Sartre. Close to the communists, certainly, out of horror for everything they fought; however I loved truth too much not to demand freedom of inquiry; I would never have entered the CP. Sometimes I asked myself whether we ought not to stamp on our intellectuals' scruples and become militants within the CP. Sartre also passed through these oscillations.... We discussed it often."[22] One cannot fully appreciate the strains and humiliations these fellow-travellers suffered by concentrating on the political issues of the day alone; it was also a matter of style, of mood – the harsh vituperation, the gendarme-lunges and baton-charges of the small-time sub-intellectuals who served as the Party's hatchet men: Casanova, Hervé, Wurmser, Garaudy....

The Party was no longer a warm, loosely-knit family holding perpetual open house and chatting with the neighbours. It was an army at war. This, of course, is the proverbial or mythological image of a Communist Party and it reminds us once more of the most widespread of all conceptions of the fellow-traveller: the pink who dare not become a red, the timid free-lance radical who shies away from discipline and organized dedication; a commitment which will not openly commit itself. This image is well expressed in T. C. Worsley's *Fellow Travellers*: "but joining the Communist Party was something different," reflects one of his hesitating fellow-travellers. "It was an act of Faith. The Party, like the Catholics, demanded absolute obedience ... you had to renounce the freedom of thinking for yourself.... So it was an act of Renunciation as well...."[28] One approaches here the demonology of Whittaker Chambers, the mystique of the fanatical Conspiracy, but the truth of the image is as partial as its depiction of what is involved in becoming a Catholic. It held good for some fellow-travellers, but not for all.

The intellectual for whom such considerations were most obviously paramount was Gide. The prospect of formally committing himself to any organization produced in him symptoms of paranoia. He gladly presided over meetings of the AEAR, but he would not join. After all, he reasoned, would people not assume that he was writing under orders? In June 1933 he noted that since Hitler had taken power he had received a dozen or more solicitations from groups whose objectives he fully agreed with. But no, he could not bring himself to join any of them. Nor would he sign anything he had not himself written. "Do not therefore ask me to belong to a party." No doubt many fellow-travellers and sympathizers were put off by a factor more mundane, the dreary ritual of concerted tributes, concerted anathemas, the plodding mono-tone of world-improving drum beats, the revivalist clichés, the slogans. It will after all be recalled that this aspect of things in the Soviet Union itself disturbed many otherwise sympathetic visitors: but what they could condone or excuse at a distance, in "backward Russia" with its proverbial "backward masses" and its need for icons, mausoleums and tsars, they certainly could not live with at home. The very thought of it provoked a man like Shaw to the most savage verbal iconoclasm.

This brings us back to the question of the Anglo-Saxon outlook and temperament, with its particular resistance to communist doctrine and discipline. At the time when their enthusiasm for the Soviet Union was approaching its peak, the Webbs invited to their home not Pollitt, Dutt or Gallagher, but Arthur Henderson, Walter Citrine, Clement Attlee and Arthur Greenwood. Few communist feet, unless very young and therefore excusably naïve ones, crossed the threshhold of Passfield; unless, alternatively, they were the Soviet Ambassador's. Maisky was always welcome because he was (a) Soviet and (b) an ambassador. When Herbert Morrison led the Labour Party to victory in the 1934 London County Council elections, Beatrice was delighted, calling it "a Fabian triumph". In 1939, at the age of eighty-one, she became president of the Fabian Society, and "bolshevik" though she was, she never wavered in her conviction that an authentic *British* Labour movement must embrace a wide spectrum of opinions. She had long despised the CPGB and her belated admiration for the Soviet Union did nothing to alter her opinion. In October 1924 she had hoped that the "communist gang" would once more be discredited and "the blister pricked".[24] In 1927 she called the communists futile but a nuisance, in 1929 she described them as silly but sinister, and in 1931 she dismissed the *Daily Worker* as "an absurd little paper". Later, in their *Soviet Communism*, the Webbs complained that the Western CPs were not composed "of the right sort of people", contrasting them with the "elaborately instructed, strictly disciplined and willingly obedient" men and women whom Lenin had enrolled as professional revolutionaries between 1903 and 1914.

What could be more revealing of the fellow-travelling mentality than the Webbs's dismissal of modern Western communists as rebels who gave no thought to "social construction"? As Strachey remarked, they revered the calm, constructive Soviet statesmen as a different organic species to the rude, crude agitators of the West. (But they conveniently forgot that Lenin's bolsheviks had themselves once been rude agitators and rebels – which was precisely why Sidney and Beatrice had declined to visit Soviet Russia for fifteen years.)

There was another aspect to this. Power was attractive – not so much power in itself, but the power to get things done, to reshape the world, to master destiny. The Western Parties were impotent. When Anna Louise Strong first raised with her Russian friends the idea of joining the Soviet Communist Party, they laughed and told her she was at heart a sentimental bourgeois. Why, they suggested, didn't she go home and join the American Party? Whereupon she promptly lost interest. "Especially did I respond to advice from Russian communists. Not from American communists – I almost never took their advice. I saw them as quite fallible human beings who knew less about my life and work than I did. . . . I saw Russia and its communists mystically, as that group of creators in chaos into which all my efforts were unable to break."[25] When she witnessed the class struggle in California in the early thirties her admiration for the American communists increased, but she could never get over that feeling – "if I must have a lifelong boss, let it be a big one . . . like a woman wanting an important husband".[26] Although Edgar Snow's experiences in revolutionary China did not turn him into a frustrated bride (or groom), the sheer power and scale of the Chinese achievement, when contrasted with the sectarian squabbling over tiny campaigns at home, made a lasting impression on him. "The truth is that a revolutionary party in a country nowhere near a revolutionary situation is basically a political anachronism."[27] The high moments of his life were his meetings with Mao, but power has more than one face, and when Franklin Roosevelt read *Red Star Over China* and warmly summoned its author to the White House, Snow was both delighted and impressed. Indeed which fellow-traveller has ever turned down an invitation to the White House? More than a few received one.

In Britain and America there were those whose temperament inclined them to flirt with a CP they never intended to marry. In the course of the Presidential election of 1932, fifty-three American intellectuals publicly endorsed the communist Foster-Ford ticket. To explain their position, the League of Professional Groups for Foster and Ford issued a pamphlet, *Culture and Crisis*. The names of those involved were certainly distinguished ones,* but the element of irresponsible flirtation should not be under-estimated. Edmund Wilson was prepared on this occasion to vote communist but not to entertain any relationship with the CP, while John Dos Passos rationalized his own support for Foster and Ford thus: "It was because I knew they had no chance of winning. It was the old protest vote."[28] The playwright Elmer Rice recalled the event in similar terms: though he inclined at the time towards Norman Thomas's Socialist Party, he felt it had failed "to take the strong affirmative position the crisis demanded". As for the CP "if I had believed it could win, I would have opposed it".[29] What he really hoped to do was to galvanize Congress into action by means of a big protest vote.

Neither can one take Steffen's vote seriously. He knew as well as any that what was sauce for the Russian goose was not sauce for the American gander. Reminiscing about "Jack", he wrote to John Reed's mother in May 1932: "He ceased to be the free soul that you (and I) remember. He lived the life of a party communist at the end."[30] Six months later he wrote: "I am not a communist. I merely think that the next order of society will be socialist and that the communists will bring it in and lead it",[31] just as Rockwell Kent explained that he was not a communist but did not feel "the least abhorrence of those Socialist principles" which the CP was promoting. (Such fellow-travellers usually supported domestic movements with a broader base than the CP. Robert Morss Lovett, for example, backed La Follette for President in 1924 and Norman Thomas in 1936. The Committee of Forty-Eight, the Farmer Labor Party and, later, the Wallace Progressive Party were the organizations he *joined,* though he was content to collaborate with communists in these or any other progressive causes.) Clearly enjoying his prestige as a fellow-traveller and his teasing reticence towards the Party's embrace, Steffens wrote to his wife Ella Winter in 1933: "You might come home to protect me from the communists who pester me for appearances.... They act as if they were glad that I'm not a communist."[32] But the naïvety was false. He knew his value. Steffens replied in 1934 to a CP California District Organizer who had proposed that he join the Party: "As a lifelong liberal.... I had not thought I was up to that.... Too many of my kind and class have had to get out after being in.... I could quote you something Lenin once said to me...."[33] – the final Shavian thrust, though it was with news

* Including Steffens, Dos Passos, Frank, Caldwell, Anderson, Cowley, Hicks, H. W. L. Dana, Matthew Josephson, F. L. Schuman, and Ella Winter, all fellow-travellers at that time. Other signatories were soon to turn to Trotskyism and subsequently to anti-communism: Sidney Hook, James Rorty, Edmund Wilson and Felix Morrow.

of Engels that Shaw had flabbergasted Moscow. We, said Steffens, "who have fitted successfully into the old culture . . . are corrupted and unfit for – the kingdom of heaven". When *The New Masses* congratulated him on demolishing Max Eastman's *Artists in Uniform,* (an account of what life was like for the "liberals" in the Russian "kingdom of heaven"), Steffens coyly told Joseph Freeman: "I never expect to get such things right in the eyes of the Party." But let there be no doubt that he would "back up" the thoughtful, loyal, daring communists working "out in the field". The communists were accused of splitting the trade union movement? Sure, but not enough for Ironside! It was time they "chiselled off all the old pacifist, liberal, socialist labor leaders whom the big-business leaders find 'reasonable' and can 'do business with' ".³⁴ In the same year, 1934, he endorsed the CP candidates for the State elections and called for an American CP on the Russian model – trained, united and disciplined. Only he'd rather not join it, thank you. And Theodore Dreiser, too, proved to be a reluctant bride.

As a child Dreiser had endured much; he had seen suffering in New York in the nineties, he was to see it again in the 1930s, and in between he had surveyed the bleak, dreary defeat of Britain's industrial slums, visualizing those horse-riding snobs skimming the cream in Constable's lush pastures. He was right, of course: take Blake, take Lenin, and you have it: this green and pleasant land – for whom? Dreiser developed a hatred of capitalism and his was an important hatred: the stature of *Sister Carrie* and *An American Tragedy* is established beyond dispute. Yet his philosophy, his ideology, was eclectic. He owed a lot to Her[bert] Spencer, his imaginative universe was aroused by Horatio Alge[r], his psychological notions derived largely from Elmer Gates. As he was prone to swim towards the deep end; the moralizi[ng] which closed novels like *The Titan* were pretentious, ri[ch in clas]sical allusions, and generally the waters closed over h[im.] he remarked: "In short I catch no meaning from pass quite as I came, confused and dismay[ed.] Ranke said it, the effect would be impres[sive.] Dreiser's case the choice between the fac[t] determinism was raised to the level of with communism could be interpret[ed] the claims of the collective and action and the exceptional int[e]himself an "incorrigible i[ndividual]nism", and certainly wh[en] of joining hands wit[h]

came and he found himself involved in the coalfield strikes of Pennsylvania, Ohio, West Virginia, Indiana and Illinois. Dos Passos recalled serving on a committee investigating the strife in the Kentucky pits in the face of the violent opposition of the proprietors to communist efforts to form a union there: "Theodore Dreiser, shy, opinionated, sensitive and aware as an old bull elephant, headed the committee. He looked like a senator, he acted like a senator and he got himself into a thoroughly senatorial scrape."[36] Dreiser did indeed announce flatly that America needed communism. When, along with Sherwood Anderson, he was indicted by the Harlan County grand jury in Kentucky for criminal syndicalism, he experienced first-hand the class war disguised as law.

Though he didn't return to Russia, or perhaps because he didn't, the passage of the years worked their benign alchemy on the impressions he had recorded at the time, winnowing out the chaff and ripening the wheat to gold. In 1943 he wrote to H. L. Mencken: "As for the communist system – as I saw it in Russia in 1927 and '28 – I am for it – hide and hoof. For like Hewlett of Canterbury ... I saw its factories, its mines, its stores, its Komissars [sic] ...

American communists "have never interested me and I have never been interested by their gyrations and genuflections. I am – and have been – content to deal with the Russian Government direct. . . . I have written for *Pravda* often. . . ."[40] Soon afterwards, he wrote to Madame Chiang Kai Shek, regretting that her husband did not favour "some sort of communism" in China, which he thought would be a good thing – for China. Finally, to cap it all, by a final gyration of his own, he joined the American CP in 1945 and soon afterwards died.

What may occur if a fellow-traveller joins the CP is cogently illustrated by the case of M. Philips Price. Whereas "radicalism at one remove" normally translated itself into a distinction between East and West, Price regarded revolutionary communism as suitable for both Russia and Germany, but not for Britain. In November 1923 he gravely violated CP discipline by getting himself adopted as Independent Labour Party parliamentary candidate for Gloucester. In July of the following year he answered his critics with the argument that it was no earthly use the CPGB adopting the sectarian language of the Soviet comrades: the task was to help the sincere, anti-imperialist elements in the ILP to radicalize the Labour Right and the Labour Government. The objective was to "capture by stages . . . the parliamentary and administrative machinery of capitalism".[41] Lenin may have been right about tactics for Russia, and Rosa Luxemburg for Germany, but neither was right for Britain. In reply, Palme Dutt accused Price of Fabianism, vacillation and social pacification. J. R. Campbell also levelled charges against "Comrade Price", who was now described in *The Communist Review* as "the most ordinary peddler of little reforms"; finally Karl Radek accused him of wishing to liquidate the CP. While insisting that British capitalist society was more complex than the Comintern appreciated, Price continued to admire the Soviet Union and indeed to criticize the Continental social democrats for pursuing reformist policies very similar to the ones he advocated in Britain. Finally in 1929 he was elected to Parliament as a Labour member.

Although this case further demonstrates the incompatibility of the fellow-traveller with the ideology and discipline demanded by the CP, the more common relationship in Britain, particularly in later years, was the diametrically opposite one: instead of working for the ILP or LP from within the CP, a number of fellow-travellers faithfully pursued *aspects* of the CP line from within the ILP, the Socialist League and the Labour Party itself. Such men are often called "crypto-communists", but that term, it seems to me, is more usefully descriptive of those who accept the communist ideology *in toto*, yet prefer for tactical reasons to conceal or blur their allegiance. It may be useful at this stage to examine in some detail the formation and development of a fellow-traveller whose close involvement in communist causes never prompted him to take the plunge and join the Party.

Edgar P. Young* was educated at Tonbridge School, joined the Royal Navy as a regular in 1917 and served in the Black Sea Fleet during the anti-bolshevik intervention of 1919 – an event which made no negative impression on him since he knew very little about bolshevism and was content to accept the stereotyped image of it common among imperialists like himself. Perhaps surprisingly, the British General Strike of 1926 applied a depth charge to his Tory patriotism: it didn't look like fair play on the part of the authorities. Then in 1929 he was posted to the Far East as Communications Officer on the staff of the Commander-in-Chief (having begun to learn Russian to increase his technical proficiency), and it was there that the failure of the Powers to check Japanese expansionism finally torpedoed his navy-blue conservatism. Back in England, he happened one day to pick up Dutt's *Labour Monthly* at a station bookstall: thereafter he read it regularly, though the editor's fulminations against "social-fascists" both perplexed him and failed to deter him from taking a native Englishman's cautious first step into the ranks of the Fabians. It was now, while still a Lt-Commander in the Navy, that his eye fixed on Sir Stafford Cripps as someone whose combination of radicalism and worldly experience might be of help. "I wonder," he wrote to Cripps in August 1933, "if you would be good enough to give me some advice about how I should set about embarking on a political career as a socialist." Young confessed that he had never entered the Commons and until recently never attended a political meeting; nevertheless the financial problems of maintaining a family if he left the Navy, quite apart from a fairly resolute ambition, dictated that he should keep his apprenticeship in the ranks of Labour brief and so quickly re-enter the officers' mess as an MP. As for his opinions, he confessed that he was not sure whether they were "left-wing socialist or communist...." He explained: "I am not hankering after a revolution, unless, of course, the fascists force us to it.... So I cannot, strictly speaking, call myself a communist – the more so as I have no fault to find with the Monarchy."[42] A year later he indicated other misgivings typical of the fellow-traveller: "I personally should like to see the Socialist League working with the CP, if only the latter would be less intransigent in their policy and less abusive in their personal denunciation.... The CP misestimates the British psychology ... they

* Commander Young has kindly allowed me to study his personal files and collections of documents, speeches, articles and reviews relating to his career.

see signs of a revolutionary feeling and of a mutinous spirit where none exists."[48]

By July 1934 he was out of the Navy and making inquiries at Transport House about available constituencies. It was a gloomy outlook: a newcomer to the scene was inevitably shown a list of safe Tory seats – it was, in any case, a period of low fortune for Labour. (Cripps had been helpful, but he was busy with his law practice and he could hardly plonk Young straight into the Commons.) When Young was finally adopted as candidate for North-West Hull, the financial problems which had preoccupied him reared up menacingly, since he was promptly sacked from what he described as "probably the greatest sinecure in London", the job of Assistant Secretary to the Institute of Naval Architects. Young – as he reported to Cripps – treated the retired admirals of the Institute to a lecture about it being "sound patriotism" to ensure that *our* revolution was run on sounder lines than the one in Russia. But he was destined to lose on both fronts, suffering defeat soon afterwards in North-West Hull during the general election. The problem now was how to maintain the political activities for which he had forsaken a secure naval career, while earning a decent living. He wasn't a brilliant journalist by any means, jobs were scarce, no national newspaper would take him on and even Cripps could not find a space for him on the staff of *Tribune*.

He had in the meantime moved closer to both the USSR and the Communist Party. Standing as a Labour candidate for Marylebone in the 1937 local elections, he shared platforms with communists like Jack Gaster; he also told an audience in Hull that co-operation with the CP in an ever widening field was imperative. He now envisaged the future British socialist state as similar to that of the USSR but "modified to suit national temperament and conditions" and less harshly intolerant towards opponents. The question was: do such men occupy a legitimate place within the Labour Party? Just how far Young's expulsion from the LP in 1939 was due to his continued advocacy of a Popular Front, and how far due to his close connections with the CP, it is difficult to judge: certainly only the former reason was officially given. In March 1939 the LP's National Agent, G. R. Shepherd, explained in a letter to Young that once the National Executive had taken a decision subsequently endorsed by the Party Conference, it was intolerable for groups and factions within the Party to continue to fight that decision. This sounds reasonable enough; on the other hand the principle has usually been invoked by the LP bureaucracy against the extreme Left rather than the Right; one recalls that the Parliamentary Labour Party frequently abjures the authority of Conference, and that, when Leader of the Party, Hugh Gaitskell vowed to "fight and fight again" a Conference decision he disapproved of. So the Popular Fronters were right in suspecting that politics coloured principle. In September Shepherd offered Young reinstatement if he signed a document expressing regret for past misdemeanours and undertaking to participate in no further campaigns contrary to Party policy. No, said Young: "Intolerance of constructive criticism and rigid restriction of democratic rights are indicative of a sense of weakness...."[44] Which would sound more plausible as a declaration of principle were it not for the fact that he did after the war heartily approve, with a keen eye for discipline on board ship, all expulsions and purges which took place within East European communist and national front groupings, notably the one staged in Czechoslovakia in February 1948. Obviously, then, there was more than a touch of opportunism in his attitude towards the Labour Party: outside it, he had no hope of ever entering Parliament. Repeatedly (in 1942 and again in 1944) he applied unsuccessfully for reinstatement, the second failure provoking from him a spate of letters to the press protesting that he was "an Englishman, a Democrat, and a Socialist". Rebuffed, should he therefore join the CP? He recalls that "sometime during the war" he raised the question with Pollitt, who advised him he would be more useful outside the Party. But one cannot doubt that he chose to steer clear of the doctrinaire discipline he so enthusiastically recommended for post-war Eastern Europe. And there, in papers like *Viata Sindicala,* of Bucharest, and *Tvorba,* of Prague, he remorselessly bombarded the French socialists and British Labour leadership, firing salvo after salvo at Bevin and occasionally putting renegades like Laski to rout with a whiff of grapeshot.

Young never achieved the status of political office, his journalism was confined mainly to obscure publications and to an interminable stream of letters to the press. D. N. Pritt, on the other hand, was a big shot, a "King's Counsellor" (a high and remunerative honour for a lawyer) and one of those who succeeded in using the LP as a Trojan Horse. Though he joined the LP during the First World War, he had not immediately become active within it. The General Strike made an impression on him, as on Young. Invited by MacDonald to become a Law Officer in the 1929 Labour Government, he declined. In 1932 he visited Russia with the Webbs, Margaret Cole, Dalton and Postgate, all members of the Fabian Research Bureau. Impressed, two years later he became chairman of the Society for Cultural Relations with the USSR. Like the Webbs, he befriended Soviet Ambassador Maisky, while his analysis of Soviet developments owed much to the communist, Robin Page Arnot. In 1935 Herbert Morrison told him he was wanted in the Commons, but would he please "drop all this left-wing nonsense". Pritt entered the Commons without dropping the "nonsense", and he was to remain MP for North Hammersmith until 1950. At that time – in the mid-thirties – he still did not know many communists well; Pollitt was the exception, but the General Secretary of the Party was an exception well worth knowing.

For a month or two Pritt sat on both the National and Parliamentary Executives of the LP, but he soon lost his seat on the latter where he was unprotected by the left-wing sentiment of the rank and file. Increasingly pro-communist, a frequent contributor to the *Daily Worker*, and an ardent advocate of a Popular Front, he visited the USSR again in 1936 and became, as we have earlier seen, a major apologist for the show trials. Meanwhile he deployed his professional skills as an outright champion of British liberties as threatened by reactionary judges and myopic courts. He acted as defence counsel in one political case after another: in Hong Kong, on behalf of arrested British communists; in defence of Welsh miners prosecuted for riot and Nottinghamshire miners charged with disorder, and so on. None of his clients produced elaborate confessions in court, as Zinoviev *et al.* had done, so presumably they were innocent. Surviving many storms within the LP, he was finally expelled in 1940 as a result of his pro-Soviet stand over the Finnish war. From 1944 onwards he was almost convinced that his reinstatement would follow naturally from world events, but it didn't. He did, however, enjoy a notable personal success when in 1945 he fought the North Hammersmith election against both the official Labour candidate and a Tory, sweeping home with a majority of sixty-one per cent. A cable of congratulation from Mao Tse Tung followed. Pritt was, indeed, to be increasingly honoured in the communist world; in 1954 he was awarded the Stalin Peace Prize, and later the medal of the (East) German Peace Council.

Since he openly stated his preference for the policy of the CPGB, how did he justify his continued application for Labour membership? He did so on the ground that Labour was the only mass workers' party enjoying trade union support in Britain. Certainly some of Pritt's causes and campaigns were admirable, as when he protested that even after the war, fascistic, anti-semitic rallies were being staged in Hackney and Dalston with the same old police passivity or even connivance which had been so alarming a feature of the Mosley era. And to defend Jomo Kenyatta and five other imprisoned Kenyan militants, as he did from 1952 to 1955, was altogether admirable – one need hardly stress again that Soviet Russia's millions of slave labourers were talked out of existence by the same powerful advocate of justice. But the Cold War really meant the end for Labour's fellow-travellers. In 1948 John Platts-Mills, MP was expelled from the Party, and a year later the axe fell on Konni Zilliacus, Lester Hutchinson and Leslie Solley. All lost their seats in the 1950 general election, as did Pritt himself. Their consistent opposition to Bevin's foreign policy, to the Marshall Plan, to NATO, conscription, devaluation, the wage freeze and the stationing of American military personnel and air bases in Britain, finally overtaxed the patience of the Party leadership. Their best friends abroad were the Nenni socialists in Italy. In 1948 thirty-seven Labour MPs signed the "Platts-Mills telegram" supporting Nenni's Popular Front coalition with the communists, while in September Pritt took part in the sixtieth anniversary celebrations of the Italian Socialist Party (PSI) in Genoa. Indeed Pietro Nenni was in those years Western Europe's leading fellow-traveller among professional politicians.

For the British fellow-travellers, the orientation of the West European socialist movement after the war was both a crucial and a cruel phenomenon. Zilliacus regarded the anti-communism of Saragat in Italy, Schumacher in Germany and the SFIO leadership in France as a disastrous repetition of the errors made by the mensheviks and the SPD in the years 1917–20. Naturally he deplored the pro-American, anti-communist stance adopted by Attlee, Bevin, Dalton and indeed Cripps. The CPs, he insisted, were not wreckers, not subversives; until driven out of the post-war French and Italian ruling coalitions by American intervention, they had thrown themselves energetically into the task of domestic reconstruction. And this was true; Stalin was content with a division of Europe into spheres of influence; it was also true that though no European social democratic party owed the same kind of formal allegiance to Washington as the CPs owed to Moscow, any historian who looks closely into the ties and condition of dependence developed during those years may find the distinction more nominal than real. But by 1950 such fellow-travellers as Pritt, Zilliacus and Young had been driven to the periphery of politics and ostracized as a potential fifth column.

6

Alternatives to Marx

The authentic communist is a Marxist. So too is his Trotskyist enemy. Each, of course, will accuse the other of distorting or abandoning Marxism, but we are not concerned here with adjudicating who is a "good" Marxist and who is not. The question is: who regards himself as a Marxist? And we quickly discover that the vast majority of fellow-travellers made no such claim on their own behalf.

When Marx said "the philosophers have only interpreted the world, the point is, to change it", his gunsights were focused on a peculiarly German tradition which, itself a product of Germany's hesitant and fragmented progress towards national unity and political democracy, insisted on separating thought and action, spirit and power. *Faute de mieux,* even the critical intellectuals had accepted a separation of functions imposed on them by a military and landed aristocracy which was prepared to yield to them the shadow but not the substance of an effective historical role. The greatest of German fellow-travellers, Heinrich Mann, was a true heir to this tradition. Mann saw the typical German petty-intellectual as slavishly serving the *Weltanschauung* of the Prussian State, craving respectability, greedily gobbling the small titles and honoraria thrown to him, and so abandoning the proper critical function of the *Geist,* of intelligence itself. Consequently Mann drew the conclusion that the intellectual should stand aloof from State patronage in order to assume his proper role as custodian of the categorical imperative – the legacy of Kant. But this standing aloof worked both ways, separating Mann and his friends both from the State and its revolutionary opponents, who also dealt in the merchandise of power. In 1918–19, he presided during the Munich Revolution over a "soviet of brain workers" which remained a powerless spectator to a great social convulsion. This abstentionism, which was by no means confined to Germany and which Rolland himself shared in full measure, was most cogently defended by Julien Benda in his famous *La Trahison des Clercs.* Defining the *clerc* as he who speaks to the world "in a transcendental manner", Benda complained that in recent times the *clercs*

225

had ceased to stand aside, to formulate principles of ideal behaviour, and had begun to indulge themselves in the game of gross political passions. Though he found it hard in this connection to explain away Dante and Petrarch, he insisted that when Rousseau, de Maistre, Lamartine or Michelet committed themselves to political causes, they did so in an elevated, generalized style, disdaining immediate results. (But what of Burke?) Alternatively, said Benda, it was legitimate to intervene on occasion, as Zola had done, but that did not involve a continual huckstering in the market place. Now all priestly authority had gone. (Yet Benda, like Mann and Rolland, was to become in his time a fellow-traveller.)

Mann's perspective in his essays was historical but the style was significantly abstract, avoiding concrete details and gusting along on the winds of high abstraction: *"Macht, Vernunft, Unvernunft, Geist, Verstand* – power, reason, unreason, spirit, intelligence". A whole generation of which he was part was convinced that *Macht* and *Geist* can only work to each other's disadvantage: his brother Thomas believed this, as did Feuchtwanger, Arnold Zweig, Hesse, Döblin, and Stefan Zweig. Indeed Feuchtwanger explained that the central theme of his own books was the split between *"Tun"* (doing) and *"Nichttun"* (not doing), between power and knowledge, action and contemplation. Even in the 1930s he could make an old Jew in *Josephus* tell the young hero: "... power is always suspicious of the spirit. But the spirit is resilient. ... They will destroy our State and our Temple; we shall build instead our doctrine and our law."[1] In Feuchtwanger the Western or Faustian tradition of acting on the world to change it was offset by the deeper (so it seemed to him) values inherent in Oriental and Jewish mysticism. The two philosophies, he remarked in *Jud Süss*, had collided in the land of Canaan, in Israel; to choose between them was also the dilemma of the modern Jew in the diaspora. Marx, of course, had made his choice, but in *Erfolg*, Feuchtwanger's hero Tüverlin answers Marx's celebrated challenge with the retort: the only way to change the world is to explain it – in a silent way – *"durch fortwirkende Vernunft"*. Indeed he went further: men try to change by force only what they cannot explain. The enormous gulf between this doctrine and Marxism, with its crucial notion that force is the midwife of history, is obvious.

The Marxian dialectic of history was alien to these humanists. Hegel likewise. What they were inclined to borrow from Marx was his critique of capitalism as warlike and exploitative – but of course Marx was only one of many socialist theorists who said as much. Marx believed in historical reason, that is to say in the progress of reason through a number of distorted historical phases, linked at each stage to the egotistical will of a dominant class, and achieving universality only in its final, communist form. But the humanists could not agree. Like the *philosophes* of the eighteenth century, they believed in a single reason, graspable by means of knowledge, experiment and intelligence. When Paul Nizan spoke of proletarian philosophy in his *Les Chiens de Garde*, Gide confessed himself baffled : like Benda, he knew of only one philosophy, the truth. Was there more than one mathematics? Did not the famous Cartesian *cognito ergo sum* apply equally to all men, regardless of class? Loyally though he ploughed his way through *Das Kapital* and *Anti-Dühring*, Gide emerged both stifled and convinced that the authentic Western tradition insisted on the autonomy of thought. "What leads me to communism is not Marx, it is the Gospel." And in 1934 he added : "But, I beg of you, if I am a Marxist, let me be so without knowing it."[2] And Rolland, too, was beyond the age when he could reverse the philosophy of a lifetime; like Gorky he always insisted that Marxism as an explanatory system left too little room or scope for the role of both conscience and consciousness. The only concession he made during the fellow-travelling stretch of his road was to turn a blinder eye to the philosophical potholes.

In *Erfolg*, Feuchtwanger faced both ways, mocking the history books which simply list the dates of kings and wars, but also chiding those who catalogued everything in accordance with economic and sociological concepts. Nor did he leave any doubt as to whom he referred : "They attempted, too, to organize on the Sixth part of the earth's surface, a state in accordance with the sociological doctrines of K. Marx and N. Lenin, the so-called Union of Soviet Republics, generally called Russia."[3] Benda condemned a socialist philosophy which "solely desires to obtain possession of material advantages for the benefit of its class".[4] The Marxian concept of a scientific theory of history based on class struggle struck the humanists as distinctly unscientific. Anatole France had never swallowed historical determinism or scientific prediction in human affairs, and Benda was no less sceptical. (Shaw for his part pointed out that the fact that the Revolution had come first to Russia and had lodged in one state alone, belied Marx's prediction. Besides, he added, the Revolution was *an accident*, the result of a "foolish" war, and not the culmination of pre-determined social evolution.) Heinrich Mann's major political and artistic statement of the thirties, *Henri Quatre,* subordinates sociological analysis to reason, toleration and peace. The use of force is admittedly vindicated, but it is wielded in the novel by a king of France on behalf of a whole people, not a single class alone.

The Anglo-Saxon fellow-travellers tended to ignore Marxism as a philosophical system, content as they were to echo its strictures against capitalist civilization. Or, alternatively, they resorted to gross Marxian simplifications uttered as if searching truths. According to Joseph Needham, the purpose of the First World War was "to exhilarate the steel and nickel shares",[5] while the English Civil War had simply been a clash between feudal royalism and the City of London. It was all, he said, a matter of thesis, antithesis, and synthesis – terms used by generations of "Marxists" who scarcely read Marx. Needham was also attracted by Engels's naïve formulations about the dialectical relationship of quantity and quality, the negation of the negation, the unity of opposites, etc., all of which he claimed (wrongly) were now commonplace in the field of natural science. In fact Needham's admiration was really captured by masters of modern science who barely gave a thought to Marx or Engels: by Einstein, Freud, Frazer, Roux, Hopkins, Warburg, Sherrington and Pavlov. Laski at least *understood* Marxism but, like most Englishmen schooled in the Utilitarian tradition, he regarded Marx's theory of value and surplus value as ethically useful but technically wrong. (Shaw agreed.) Even in 1935 he referred critically to dialectical materialism "in that dangerously rigid form it often assumes in orthodox communist hands".[6] In his opinion Marxism did not provide "a true theory of political obligation" – a marginally different formulation of the Rolland-Gorky complaint about "conscience" and "consciousness". And just as the authentic scientist in Needham admired Einstein, Pavlov and Freud, so the social scientist in Laski reached out to Sombart, Weber and Pirenne, the sweeping Marxist attacks on whom he could not but resent. Though the younger British fellow-travellers of the thirties made gallant efforts to understand Marxism, these efforts need not detain us. Day Lewis read the texts and boldly quoted the more challenging propositions, but got it all vaguely mixed up with D. H. Lawrence and romantic humanism. Spender was at sixes and sevens, occasionally refining gems of confusion such as this: "The materialist conception of history, the theory of surplus value, the idea of crystallized labour: all these are solids, they are material subject matter and yet move in the world of ideas."[7] Gamma minus for that.

The whole Marxian vocabulary was alien to the Anglo-Saxon ear, and more than one fellow-traveller said so. Alexander Wicksteed put it nicely: few Anglo-Saxons, he said, could carry any theory to its logical conclusions, irrespective of practical considerations, whereas Marxists could – and did. Julian Huxley could cope with the phrase "dictatorship of the proletariat" only by translating it into more familiar East African tribal terms – "a rather high-sounding phrase meaning roughly that paramountcy must be given to working class interests".[8] Roughly, it didn't mean that. The overriding reaction towards Marxism was one of impatience, and the simplest solution of all was to ignore it. "Youth is an ardent time," wrote Rockwell Kent, explaining his intellectual development, "I read the New Testament, and Tolstoy, and Thomas Paine, and that book whose philosophy was such close kin to that of Thomas Jefferson, Rousseau's *Social Contract*."[9] He added Wordsworth to the list, but not Marx. Explained Sean O'Casey: "communism isn't an invention of Marx; it's a social growth, developed through the ages, since men banded together to fight fear of the unknown...."[10] He saw mystic analogies to this burgeoning communism in Blake's vision of Jerusalem and Shelley's unbound Prometheus. Sean also had memories of Keir Hardie's cloth cap, as well as Lenin's, but that Germanic dialectical business was not for him. Wicksteed considered the matter more generously: Marx was an important thinker even though he "may have been right or he may have been wrong" – scarcely the credo of a fanatical devotee. As for Lenin, what really counted in him was his "inspired and ever vigilant common sense, a most unusual quality in a Slav". Marxist doctrine is here regarded as a kind of cerebral narcotic for addicts, a shot in the head, useful only in so far as it keeps them on their feet and working. The Russians, Wicksteed said, had "searched the scriptures and picked on the phrase 'dialectical materialism' ... but all they mean in nine cases out of ten is just plain commonsense."[11] Hewlett Johnson also put Russia's vast achievement down to a judicious mixture of science and common sense. Lincoln Steffens hurled bucket-loads of common sense over his gasping audiences, fashioning allegories and anecdotes as he proceeded: in 1933 he told an audience in the Scottish Rite Hall, San Francisco, a story about the hansom-cab horse who sat down, open-mouthed, at his first sight of an automobile on Fifth Avenue. The audience laughed. Then Steffens told them they were the horse – communism was the automobile. Common sense for Americans: get yourselves wheels *and move* like "them Russkies".

Waldo Frank complained that the materialism contradicted the dialectic – and then he ran for cover. Dreiser had a more practical objection to any hot gospelling of Marxism in the USA: it frightened the horse and threw the rider. He preferred to talk about "equity and balance"; as a self-taught positivist and disciple of Herbert Spencer, he couldn't fathom the Hegel business, and felt no less a man for that. Shaw wielded the lance with more aplomb, demanding in 1921 that the Marxists cease "their intolerable swallowings and regurgitations of Marxian phrases which they do not understand".[12] Twenty years later he put it more circumspectly, deferentially and pragmatically: "I should always write on the assumption that the English are brain-lazy, fatheaded and politically ignorant in the lump, and not on the assumption that English men and women are German university students going through a Hegelian course in the year 1840. But I should, I hope, maintain socialism in its integrity as Mr Palme Dutt has maintained it."[13] Of the Fabians and neo-Fabians, Shaw and Laski were considerably more tolerant and appreciative of aspects of Marxist theory than the Webbs, who remained convinced to the last that Marx had tried to impose a transcendental, metaphysical pattern on history, and without success. They regarded all historical theories as "hypotheses" at best, and certainly felt no urge to come up with one of their own. (Shaw claimed that the materialist theory of history had been "knocked into a cocked hat by the history of Peru".) Persuasion and education, the Webbs insisted, were the only valid instruments of progress, not class struggle. From the Benthamite Radicals they inherited the emphasis on "specific ends", and though they rejected Comte, they were not unaffected by Comtean positivism. Beatrice called Bentham "Sidney's intellectual god-father". Only the dynamic and practical enterprise of social engineering in Russia interested the Webbs: the struggle with nature, the faith in science, the belief in knowledge, the experimental method of trial and error, the constant soundings to ensure that the order of thinking corresponded to the order of things. The Russians would surely recover from the "disease of orthodoxy". As for those Soviet articles entitled "The Dialectics of Graded Steel", "We Stand for Party in Maths . . . in surgery . . . in the fishing industry, etc.", what, they asked, could be more ludicrous. In an introduction to Pat Sloan's *Russia Without Illusions* (1938), Beatrice proposed substituting for Marxian dialectics "the utilitarian calculus, by which I mean the greatest good of the greatest number, a calculus which I believe controls the Soviet Gosplan, in its planned production for community consumption".[14] As Shaw explained to an ILP summer school in August 1931, "the Fabians have turned out to be perfectly right, and the system which has established itself [in Russia] is a Fabian system".[15] Apparently it was also a Shavian system, for Edgar Snow recalled that it was not Marx, Lenin or Mao who set him on the road to socialism – it was the complete works of GBS purchased, believe it or not, in Peking. So the most distinguished and influential of pro-Chinese fellow-travellers "accepted the Fabian view of history from here on out", though on account of later observations it merged with "a general view of present history as man's last world where civilization begins".[16] While recognizing how vital a source of inspiration and analysis Marxism represented to Mao, Snow felt able to sell Mao's great practical achievements without buying wholesale his philosophy.

Out of the Anglo-American political emporium there emerged no fellow-traveller more devoted to the Soviet cause, yet more stubbornly determined to plod his own philosophical path, than Corliss Lamont. Though Professor of Philosophy at Columbia University, it has to be admitted that his claim to philosopher's status was not noticeably supported by any other criterion. His efforts to persuade Marxists that John Dewey's pragmatic and instrumentalist view of knowledge was a great improvement on William James's were generally as inept as they were superfluous – likewise his unheeded reminders to Marxists that they were at heart pragmatists too. Furthermore, Lamont advanced a popular, normative and ethical philosophy which not only bore little logical relation to his admiration for the aforementioned Dewey, but which advertised as its most illustrous sponsors Einstein, Freud, Laski, Thomas Mann, Herriot, Nehru and Sun Yat Sen. Lamont called it "scientific humanism", described it as "a philosophy of joyous service for the greater good of all humanity in the natural world", and then proceeded to assure those who had built up the Soviet Union that, did they but know it, this was the philosophy which had guided their unforgettable actions. Ecumenical by nature and wishing to leave no "progressive" soul out in the rain, Lamont generously included the "religious humanists" (sic) among the natural or scientific humanists, especially if they were Unitarians. And really, when you came to study the matter dispassionately, you discovered that Jesus also had been a humanist because some of his utterances "can be given a this-worldly interpretation"; for how otherwise should one comprehend "Ye shall know the truth, and the truth shall make you free"? In later years Corliss Lamont went on to publish a Humanist Funeral Service and a Humanist Marriage Service, though a Humanist Christening has not so far been forthcoming.

Few fellow-travellers were impressed by the claims of latter-day Marxists to lay down the law on aesthetic taste and artistic creation. Of course it was not necessarily "Marxism" which was wielded like a cudgel, it was a Party line which ran through a succession of conflicts and suicides until, in the early 1930s, it settled into the dogma of socialist realism. All "modernist" literature and painting was condemned as formalist, abstract, passive and therefore objectively counter-revolutionary. At which moment the political and artistic avant-gardes of Europe finally parted company. The fellow-travellers who cared about art rejected both the theory or dogma itself and the censorious, repressive spirit in which it was imposed not only on Soviet writers but also, in so far as imposition by persuasion was possible, on their Western comrades as well.

Dreiser couldn't take it; besides, the censor had banned one of his plays in Russia. Hindus reported that Soviet fiction had become as hard and heavy as steel or coal. Georges Friedmann was alienated by the incessant Soviet condemnations of formalism, which led to minor persecutions of artists as talented as Pasternak and Shostakovitch; he called it a stifling of creativity. All those appalling coloured statues of Stalin depressed him – in 1933 he visited a Red Square exhibition of Five Years of Soviet Art and found nothing but flat, meaningless portraits of leaders and panoramas of the Civil War. These negative impressions were somewhat offset by admiration for the relevance of the writer to the masses in the USSR – a Soviet writer was a national figure, Gorky almost a god. Even so, socialist-realism won few friends among Western fellow-travellers. In 1927 Dreiser had told Eisenstein that the drama of the individual is primary, and a year later he wrote to Mike Gold: "Personally I can never see Protest as literature. . . ." Gide's recoil on this issue was ultimately total. Though he had said in 1932 that his admiration for the Soviets' organization of education, leisure and culture was great, he was thinking perhaps more of quantity than quality, and certainly no message could have been more unwelcome than the one he transmitted to the first Soviet Writers' Congress: "If the USSR triumphs, and she must triumph – her art will soon disengage itself from the struggle; I mean to say: will emancipate itself."[17] Asked in the course of a debate in Paris whether his individualism was really compatible with orthodox communism, he replied: *"la chose à laquelle je tiens le plus, c'est mon art."*[18] And he added that he had not written anything of value for four years because he had not found a way of reconciling his art with communist doctrine. Earlier he had refused to allow *Les Caves du Vatican* to be filmed in Russia, lest it be *"dénaturé"* in the cause of propaganda.

Spender felt that art must remain speculative, disinterested and free; Dos Passos wanted literary adventures with unpredictable destinations; Jean-Richard Bloch told the Soviet Writers' Congress that the good writer was always in a posture of opposition since he only made himself ridiculous if he became a court minstrel. Nor was minority art reactionary of itself; some authors wrote for millions of readers, some for a few thousand, and both approaches were valid. When Karl Radek informed the Congress that Joyce's *Ulysses* was a dunghill swarming with worms seen through a microscope held upside down, even the communist Wielande Herzfelde rebelled. Radek held his ground: Joyce was morbid, backward-looking. But, protested Herzfelde, had not the admired progressive Dos Passos learned much from the Irish writer? That, said Radek, was precisely the trouble with Dos Passos. He then heaped on to the same dunghill as *Ulysses* the works of Proust, Eliot,

Faulkner, and Kafka. In the face of such philistine idiocy, the fellow-travellers and not a few of their communist brethren could feel only miserable. Spender could not stomach the equation of poetry with propaganda and the Party line. "Poetry is the conditioning of emotional truth, a way of relating the poet's feelings to objective reality."[19] When the Group Theatre presented his verse play, *Trial of a Judge*, the regular Unity Theatre audience, reared on Soviet "girl-meets-tractor" stuff, stayed away, and those communists who did attend criticized the play as too liberal and too mystical.

In fact John Lehmann was to my knowledge unique among fellow-travellers in attempting to keep up with the Zhdanovs on matters of art. Though he found the emphasis of *Left Review* too obsessively political, and therefore in conjunction with Christopher Isherwood set up *New Writing,* he actually produced an acceptably Marxist study of modern English writing for *International Literature,* of Moscow. In January 1937 he published in *Left Review* an article, "Should Writers Keep to their Art?" – a question so simplistically posed that the inevitable answer, "no", looked legitimate. Praising the epic quality of Soviet writing, he flatly contradicted those who suggested that the officially inspired and applauded Russian poetry was sterile.

Only fools deny the legitimacy of political commitment in art. The inevitable stumbling block was the Party line, that narrow prism of virtue through which no writer has ever attempted to pass without emerging mauled beyond recognition. This was precisely Toller's point: committed art must not be anchored to short-term Party ideology, it must tackle the eternal problems of proletarian experience. He saw himself as justly and inevitably two men: the political activist and the artist. "In my political capacity, I proceed upon the assumption that groups ... various social forces ... have a real existence. As an artist, I recognize that the validity of these 'facts' is highly questionable."[20] In *Masse-Mensch* he therefore presented the "real" sequences in the same visionary atmosphere as the "dream pictures". Indeed many of the young militants of the USPD were influenced by the powerful expressionist current flowing in German art and theatre in the early twenties: Toller, Landauer, Mühsam, the young Becher, Brecht and Wolf are obvious examples. Later Georg Lukács pronounced a harsh judgment on them: "Subjectivity, honest, mostly immature, unclear and confused in their convictions."[21] But the virtue of these writers, subject as they were to mutual influence and even ephemeral fashion, was nevertheless to speak with their own voice. Day Lewis too, could pull off didactic poems because they were genuinely his own: even the injection of clumsy ideograms like "freedom is the knowledge of necessity" added to their impact because they entered the verse not as ritual climaxes to ritual melodies, but in the poet's own, interior time. He had, also, a knack for doggerel verse which in its utter unpretentiousness and sincerity wears well with time:

> The hooters are blowing,
> No heed let him take;
> When baby is hungry
> 'Tis best not to wake.
> Thy mother is crying,
> Thy dad's on the dole:
> Two shillings a week is
> The price of a soul.[22]

Insisting against the orthodoxy that a T. S. Eliot could be both reactionary *and* a fine poet, and rejecting blanket condemnations of non-political poetry, Day Lewis drew the same kind of distinction as Spender: "A poem appeals to the mass through the individual; a slogan, a political speech, appeals to the individual through the mass."[23] Inevitably he was jumped upon by the demon avengers of *Left Review*, Montagu Slater complaining that his poems expressed "a sweet smell of cleanliness and empty space".

The great novelists and playwrights among the fellow-travellers made virtually no attempt to bring their creative writing into line with the canons of Moscow orthodoxy. In 1895 Bernard Shaw commented that when a play deals exclusively with a social question, nothing can prolong its life beyond the life of that question. Shakespeare and Goethe were of course keenly engaged by political causes and passions, but their ultimate theme was humanity as a whole: according to Shaw, the great dramatic poet was never any sort of "ist". Though by no means afraid of using the stage for short-term didactical purposes (he claimed *Widowers' Houses* was written to get people to vote Progressive at the next London County Council election), his last frontal attack on capitalism in dramatic form, *Mrs Warren's Profession*, was written early in the century. Less a hero-builder by instinct than a debunker, he was thereafter mainly preoccupied as a dramatist by the struggle between human vitality and artificial systems of morality. But that vitality never assumed the face of a party. Shaw's disciple, Sean O'Casey, *écrivain engagé* though he was, remained as a playwright anchored to a style of sceptical naturalism which belied the fervour of his polemics in prose. A champion of the worker and the poor man, he could nevertheless not hold down his doubts about heroes, rhetoric and theories. In *The Plough and the Stars*, the characters Peter Flynn, the Young Covey and

Fluther Good chase each other in circles, prattling ridiculously of God and other great matters, delighted by the pomp and patriotism of their Irish time, yet mindful of their own skins and getting in a bit of looting during Easter Week. We are not invited to despise or condemn them. O'Casey did, later, try his hand at one or two naïvely tendentious plays, but he was obviously doing violence to his own talent. A critic once remarked that in *Purple Dust* O'Casey delighted in the eccentricities of individuals: was this not an uncomfortable position for a revolutionist? O'Casey replied: "A dramatist is one thing, a revolutionist is quite another: one looking at life in the form of individuals, the other as part of the collective urge and thrust forward of men ... so when he's working on a play, the dramatist is neither Tory nor communist, but only a playwright, setting down his characters as he knew them...."[24] Nevertheless, not once did he express sympathy for the fate of the writers who shared and suffered for this philosophy in the Soviet Union.

The most distinguished Marxist critic of the age, Georg Lukács, grouped together Shaw, Anatole France, Rolland, the Mann brothers, Feuchtwanger and Dreiser as "critical realists" – meaning progressive writers who in their creative writing exposed the hypocrisy of capitalist society while hesitating to embrace the solution of revolutionary socialism. To the first Soviet Writers' Congress Radek explained that pacifist writers like Rolland and Arnold Zweig had exposed in full the horrors and deceits of imperialist war, but not its fundamental causes. They were, he said, able to show only "the fate of human atoms, caught up in the vortex of the war events, as impotent and helpless ... through tear-stained eyes".[25] Indeed Zweig's major novels* never transcended Lukács's definition of "critical realism". On each occasion he returned to the First World War for his material, and on each occasion he, or his fiction, failed to yield the Leninist solution, though the minute and scrupulous detail in which he depicted the social mechanism and military apparatus of the time brought warm praise from Lukács, Hans Mayer, Paul Rilla and other communist critics. Mayer felt that Zweig's historical-concrete realism collided with certain psycho-analytical obsessions (his admiration for Freud was enormous) and with certain "comic-philosophical" aims. Zweig himself explained in 1938 that fantasy is the poet's method of evoking a unity of emotion, and his own admiration was directed towards the cool humour of Dickens and Stevenson, the comedy of Chaplin, towards the art where the laws of fable corresponded to the laws of life. When Zweig became an honoured citizen of

---

* *Der Streit um den Sergeanten Grischa* (1927), *Junge Frau Von 1914* (1931), *Erziehung vor Verdun* (1935), *Einsetzung eines Königs* (1937).

the German Democratic Republic and president of its Academy of Art, naturally his virtues as a novelist had to be emphasized, so that Lukács cunningly resorted to praising him for clearly posing in his fiction the question, "what should we therefore do?" The fact that Zweig provided no answer was now discreetly passed over.

Feuchtwanger made a more strenuous effort in the thirties to transcend critical realism. From a Marxist point of view, the limitations of a historical novel like *Jud Süss* (begun in 1923 after the murder of Walter Rathenau by right-wing, anti-semitic extremists, and set in the Duchy of Württemberg in the eighteenth century) were obvious. The novelist showed himself imaginatively much more at ease with the upper classes he criticized than with the lower orders whose plight theoretically aroused his compassion. Indeed the urban poor appeared only as a stupid, ignorant, bigoted mob, easily inflamed by drink and demagoguery, while in Book Two, "The People", the people appeared only as a faceless backcloth. In truth, the bourgeois littérateur of the Munich cafés knew little or nothing about them. But the novel gave even worse offence to Marxists by clogging itself with mystical episodes relating to the wandering Rabbi Gabriel, and ultimately portraying political history as a succession of intrigues and manoeuvres in the palaces of power. The novels of contemporary Germany, *Erfolg* and *Die Geschwister Oppermann,* written before he entered his fellow-travelling phase, attacked nazism from a semi-Marxist perspective, but no solution beyond the reaffirmation of rational, progressive values was provided. When Feuchtwanger was driven into exile, the first part of his *Josephus* cycle, *Der Jüdische Krieg,* was already published. Now, in completing the cycle, he took stock of it in the light of the new situation: "I had learned a great deal more about the theme of *Josephus* – nationalism and world-citizenship – the material burst its earlier mould...."[26] But to what extent? In the long run the novelist's approach changed much less radically than either he or his new communist friends liked to imagine. Admittedly he criticized his hero Josephus because he ran from "the difficulty of the attainable into the comfortable dream of never attainable dreams", and because he "betrayed the today and the tomorrow in favour of a misty future", yet Feuchtwanger remained incapable of breaking into the provinces of popular life he did not know (and Sanary-sur-Mer was no place to learn about them). The costume-artist in him was still drawn and delighted by the castles of iniquity, by the courts, aristocrats, lavish spectacles and subtle debates of ancient Rome. He still dealt in intrigues, in the poker-game of vice cheating itself, of lust thwarting its own greedy desires. Nor could he really disassociate himself from the hero he wanted to transform into an antihero, the cosmopolitan, sold-out, quisling Jew, Josephus, who falls in love with the power of Rome and the polish of Greek culture, trailing in the wake of Titus's army as it besieges Jerusalem, betraying his own past as a leader of Jewish armed resistance in Galilee. This was the Josephus who wrote a seven-volume history to fortify Roman rule and to discourage further Jewish revolts, the urbane citizen of the world whose Psalm declared:

> Cast thyself free from thine anchor, said Jehovah,
> I love not them that dally in the harbour.

Josephus's bourgeois urbanity and weakness of character represented much that the communist movement in the thirties, with its stress on popular and national resistance to fascist imperialism, wished to combat. Yet Feuchtwanger could not stamp out his own love for the universal, the detached, the singular, the cultivated. He attempted to compensate by spasmodically injecting small nuggets of Marxist-sounding doctrine into his fiction. The financier Claudius, for example, remarks: "Society is a pyramid ... but it isn't the man at the top that revolves it, but those at the bottom ... his fifty million subjects prescribe his actions."[27] Fine: then demonstrate it! But Feuchtwanger couldn't. Indeed his hero's career became a symbol of the accident-factor in history: "The amnesty, the edict of Caesarea, the revolt, the burning of the Temple to ashes, all these were links in one chain. And he himself [Josephus] was the first link."[28] In the last volume Feuchtwanger made a titanic effort to concentrate his narrative and his sympathies on the leaders of Jewish armed resistance like John of Gishala, who tells Josephus that the causes of the struggle are not Jehovah or Jupiter but the price of oil, wine and figs. Josephus replies that there are no statistics in Homer: the destiny of nations is shaped by concepts and spiritual drives. But with whom did the novelist himself really identify? It was obvious with whom he felt duty-bound to identify – but it went against the grain.

Heinrich Mann was considerably older than Feuchtwanger when he embraced the Soviet Union, and even less able to change the literary outlook of a lifetime. Yet again the effort was made. Published in two parts, in 1935 and 1938, *Henri Quatre* is a novel depicting the sixteenth-century wars of religion as a mirror held up to Hitler's Europe. Attempting to move from abstract humanism to political realism, historicity and active sympathy for violent popular struggle against class tyranny, Mann produced a novel hailed by Feuchtwanger, Zweig and Lukács as the summit of anti-fascist literature, as occupying that place at "the table of the immortals" left vacant by Anatole France. Yet Mann crystallized the will of the people in a single figure, the king of France fighting the rapacious nobles of the Catholic League, and unless Henri IV was intended to represent a post-Reformation Stalin, the failure to progress to socialist realism was clear. Mann himself later wrote: "Rather compromised than eliminated, a banker can be driven to that by necessity, but not a novelist.... Literature can only travel where the spirit itself is a power, unless it abdicates and bows to powers hostile to the spirit."[29]

Heinrich Mann was born in 1871, the eldest son of a Lubeck senator. His first novel was published in 1894.* Living variously in Munich, Berlin, Italy and the Côte d'Azur during the pre-war years, he displayed as a young writer a rich mastery of language and a wide range of narrative forms. Critical of German society, even abrasive, in a sense he anticipated the "Weimar spirit" before its time – unless, as is legitimate, "Weimar" is traced back to the ethos of Wedekind, Hasenclever and Kandinsky. For years he was attacked in conservative periodicals as a blend of traitor and pornographer; only with the débâcle of 1918 did he suddenly become revered as a prophet. In *Geist und Tat* (1910), he deplored the lynching estrangement prevailing between classes of men in Germany, the total lack of corporate love, and the way in which the *"Herrenstaat"* systematically fostered this enmity. "No great people," he complained bitterly, "only great men."[30] And what appalling harm these great men had done! And how readily the intellectuals in Germany had collaborated with "dumb, unclean power".

The title of "traitor" was flung at him by no less a person than his brother Thomas. Assuming bravely the role of Romain Rolland in Germany, Heinrich published in 1915 his celebrated *Zola-Essay* in René Schickele's *Weisse Blätter,* a journal of the anti-war movement published in Zurich to evade the German police. Like Rolland, he upheld the spirit against power – and the Powers – which failed to serve the causes of freedom, truth and justice. Describing Germany as a *"Kaiserreich"* containing only commanders and commanded, he called for an end to the ghastly war. Though Wedekind, Hesse and others approved of his stand, he, like Rolland, was furiously abused, not least by Thomas Mann, whose *Gedanken im Krieg* represented the most noxious and mystical form of pan-German chauvinism, lauding the war as an effort to unify in manly dedication the German *Volk,* and so to complete the work launched in the great soul of Frederick the Great. Small matters like the seizure of Belgium he justified as "the right of

* His early works included: *Professor Unrat oder Das Ende eines Tyrannen* (1905); *Die Kleine Stadt* (1909); *Die Armen* (1917); *Der Untertan* (1918).

rising power". Then in 1918 he published his *Betrachtungen eines Un-politischen*, the highly political reflections of a self-named "un-political" man. In this work he defamed his brother Heinrich as a "Sunday preacher", a *"Vernunftrepublikaner"* (reason-republican), even sneering at the popularizing, money-making scribblings of this cultivated but shallow bourgeois pen-pusher, this *"Zivilisationsliterat"* who was blind to the depths of the German soul and who sacrificed the power of *Kultur* to superficial humanitarian optimism. Heinrich was deeply wounded; in 1917 he attempted a reconciliation but Thomas curtly refused "to sink sobbing on to your breast". Only in 1922 were they fully reconciled, by which time Thomas had become an ardent republican and also a democrat of the aristocratic variety. Yet it is interesting to note that during the war Heinrich was not driven into exile, despite the general unpopularity of his views; instead he frequented the Luitpold café in Munich where he would chat with Wedekind, Mühsam, Feuchtwanger and others, and indeed his plays continued to be published and performed in Germany.

When the first news of the Bolshevik Revolution reached him he was not impressed: "One hears that Lenin is an agent of the German General Staff."[31] Later he noted: "The great General Staff sent in its time Lenin and his stormtroopers against a still weak Russian democracy and conquered it."[32] But by 1920 he was reading Lenin's works with some admiration, in the light of the eclipse of the German Revolution which, he felt, had been crushed by "a blind hatred ... of human association as the work of creative reason"[33] – a typically abstract formula. Reason alone, he had said in *Zwischen den Rassen* (1907), could overthrow the existing power system, and it was armed with this "reason" that he and Feuchtwanger sat back as troubled spectators to the real revolution in Bavaria. On 16 March 1919, in the interval between Eisner's assassination and the onset of the Red dictatorship, he paid tribute to Eisner's mild regime as incarnating the powers of thought and reason, and he defined the true revolution as "an association of all friends of truth, which is the way of humanity – and no war after the war, no civil war!"[34] But that came soon enough and he didn't like it. He recoiled. He could not comprehend how any "economic-technical conception of the pivot of all existence and all events could be made"[35] – a complaint which emphasized not only his divorce from Marxism but his total miscomprehension of it. In retrospect the Bavarian Revolution appeared to him a "class revolt, nothing more", having failed in "its vocation to bring about a new epoch of German spirituality".[36] Which really was hot air. On the other hand he was against "the retention of an unlimited capitalism", on the other he opposed a "communistic universalization of the proletariat". Like many other fellow-travellers, both before and after their conversion as such, he shrank from the idea of *proletarian* rule; no, he wanted the working class to be raised up, educated and awarded true citizenship by means of "social economy". And this vision of his required that the bourgeoisie become liberated from its own self-hating quest for domination, ultimately discovering, embracing and merging with the workers.

France was his passion. Where, he complained, was Germany's Stendhal, Hugo, Flaubert, Zola and Anatole France? In the French radical-republican tradition he caught sight of the precious, the unique "dictatorship of reason". The German mentality was all wrong – in 1931, as the nazi menace grew, he became more than ever convinced of this: the French had fought for their democracy, whereas the Germans had had theirs thrust upon them. He saw other countries wrestling with the general economic crisis, but only Germany was disintegrating politically and morally: "in Germany it is now evening, if not already midnight". And later, when the Second World War was over, he returned to the same line of speculation, viewing German history as a constant but unsuccessful struggle to capture the democratic spirit of 1789, to overcome the irrational, romantic *Blut und Boden* impulse to destruction. Alas, all that Germany had accepted from France was the brief Napoleonic episode. This was not a Marxist approach, and indeed his friends in the twenties were not Marxists; those statesmen whom he most admired were those whom he visited – Masaryk in 1924, Briand in 1931. He prayed for European reconciliation, but his vision of Europe was quintessentially Western: it excluded Russia. He was an honoured guest of the Ligue des Droits de l'Homme, he was the foreigner naturally chosen to speak in the Palais du Trocadéro on the centenary of Hugo's birth, and he also loved beauty . . . the dancing of Anna Pavlova.

As a playwright he was most happy in the company of pretty actresses: one of them led him to her husband, the half-Japanese, crackpot class-reconciliationist Count Richard N. Coudenhove-Kalergi, whose pan-European movement (America, out! Russia, out!) temporarily engaged Mann's imagination. Mann saw little hope in the USSR; in 1930 he, with Zweig and others, protested against the trial of forty-eight specialists. Meanwhile he enjoyed the gay, the cultivated, the elegant life of Berlin. In 1912 he had married the Prague actress Maria (Mimi) Kanova. But in 1930 they were divorced, and though he was to survive the war, she died in 1947 as a result of her internment in Theresienstadt concentration camp. In the meantime, even if it was "evening, if not already midnight", the artificial lights burned brightly, bringing his early novel *Professor Unrat* to the screen under the more famous title of *Blaue Engel* (*The Blue Angel*). He constantly petitioned the film company to award the leading female role to his dear friend, the Berlin cabaret star Trude Hesterberg, but Dietrich got it. When old Marshal Lyautey met Mann in Paris in 1931, he exclaimed: "Ah, you're the fellow who wrote *The Blue Angel*!" Carl Zuckmayer had in fact written it.

After 1933 it was a different thing. He renounced his German citizenship. His articles written (in French) for the *Dépêche de Toulouse* led to nazi demands that the Quai d'Orsay suppress the paper, but the owner, Albert Sarraut, happened to be the Minister of the Interior. Of Mann's strenuous and unremitting labours in the cause of the Popular Front we already know. His was the great name of the German left-wing emigration. When in 1935 he rose to speak in the Mutualité, Paris, all five thousand delegates stood in his honour. In Germany he was number one on the book-burning list (*Verbrennungswürdig*) and was known to be, among other things, a "Jewish knave". He lived convinced that the nazis would assassinate him. Oddly enough, he never made the trip to Russia, though in October 1935 he wrote to Thomas suggesting they make together "the obviously necessary journey of investigation. ..."[37] and proposing that they take the Constantinople route. Feuchtwanger, he added, was pressing him to accompany him to Russia the following May. But something held him back, and so he remained mainly in France, a patrician eminence with a large moustache and a pointed beard, reserved and unpretentious in manner, convinced that "the enemies of my enemies are my friends".[38] And that, of course, was one key to the fellow-travellers' lock.

In September 1940 Heinrich, Nelly (his wife) and Golo Mann, accompanied by Lion and Martha Feuchtwanger and Franz and Alma Werfel, fled on foot over the Pyrenees to Port Bou in Spain, and thence by train to Barcelona, Madrid and Lisbon, where they took the Greek ship *Nea Hellas* to New York. He was not happy in California: there was the humiliating drudgery of the MGM period, the poverty, and then the suicide of his Nelly which left him utterly alone. Now in his infirm old age the world was choked by physical menace: military power, desperate flight, death; doggedly he clung to his old thought-system, his only grasp on reality, twisting that reality to fit the system and contriving to describe the Allied war effort as representing "the higher authority of the intellectuals in the realm of power". Russia would triumph, of course, because of its "love of truth", but he was generous and various in his admirations, viewing Sir William Beveridge's social security plan (1942) as being "already half way to Moscow". When the war ended his hopes were pinned on a salvationary friendship between his old love and his new, between France and Russia, but there is no doubt that his thinking, while retaining its characteristic abstractness, was becoming confused. How otherwise could he bracket Lenin and Masaryk together as proponents of thought-power, and put Churchill, Roosevelt and Stalin under the same umbrella as intellectuals?

His final dilemma was Germany. Whether to return. The East Germans held out a friendly hand. Becher urged him to come, to see, to settle. By 1949 a villa in Berlin stood waiting for him and a presidential office in the new Academy of Art had been specially fitted out. But still he hesitated. Time was running out and he knew it, bringing him increasingly to consider his own stature as a writer. On the last page of his manuscript of *Der Atem* is scribbled in German: "finished Saturday the 25th October 1947, at 11.30 a.m.". Evidently he saw the eyes of history, of archivists and research students, upon him, but he was not to know that the name Mann would endure more through the work of his brother. By 1950 he was resolved to leave for East Germany, a cabin reservation had been made, but he died instead.

If the fellow-travellers were not Marxists, it should occasion no surprise that many of them were Christians. That the message of Christ was a socialist one is a view one can take or leave: certainly it convinced the Hussites, the Anabaptists, the Diggers, the Christian Socialists and the worker priests of many Catholic countries. On the other hand, Marxism really is a materialist philosophy; what Marx, following Feuerbach, said about supernatural religion is well known. Furthermore, and perhaps more relevant here, militant atheism, iconoclasm and the closing of churches were activities officially encouraged for more than a decade after the October Revolution. So when a Dean of Canterbury jogs round this desecrated land of sacrilege, bobbing and blessing, one has to sit up a bit. Certainly Christian fellow-travelling was predominantly, if not exclusively, an Anglo-Saxon and a Protestant phenomenon. Catholic fellow-travellers like Louis Martin-Chauffier appear on the scene more rarely – bearing in mind, of course, that fellow-travelling is not the same thing as a commitment to socialism or even neo-Marxism, which was quite common in Catholic Europe.

The most prominent fellow-traveller among British clergymen was obviously Hewlett Johnson, and among Americans the Methodist, Harry F. Ward, Professor of Christian Ethics at Union Theological Seminary.* He was, in Walter Goodman's phrase, "the model of a model fellow-traveller". Consistently he claimed complete innocence about communist domination of the front-organizations he joined or headed, notably the League for Peace and Democracy: "my position on communism is that of a critical student, sir".[39] A vice-chairman of the League was the Rev. B. Spofford, of the (Episcopal) Church League for Industrial Democracy, while the Rev. William Howard Melish served as chairman of the National Council of American-Soviet Friendship. Melish was a friend of Johnson's, as was the Congregationalist minister John Darr, a prominent activist in the Peace Movement. He too was a "critical student" of Marxism, the result being that he took copious notes wherever he travelled in the communist world; misunderstanding his motives, the Chinese assumed he was a spy. Indeed a "critical student" could come to grief in all manner of ways. For the distinguished Rev. Dr John Haynes Holmes, it was the Nazi-Soviet Pact which generated a Sunday sermon of repentance: "We were wrong because in ... our vision of a new world springing from the womb of the Russian experiment ... we defended, or at least apologized for, evils in the case of Russia which horrified us wherever else they appeared...."[40] As for those radical pastors who saw no wrong and kept their gaze faithfully fixed on the hopeful womb, they were later to encounter another form of grief, the hostile attentions of the House Un-American Activities Committee and its rival vigilantes of the witch-hunt era.†

In 1931 Ward had published his *Which Way Religion?*, an intelligent and well-written argument which contrasted with the appallingly turgid tediousness of his accounts of life in the USSR. Attracted by the anti-sacramentalist school within Anglo-Catholic socialism, Ward too wished to dethrone the priest as mediator between God and people, and to reinstate him as the people's representative before God. But, as a Protestant, his main emphasis was predictably on a return to the fundamental scriptures, the fundamental Jesus. As a socialist, he emphasized Christ's ethic of sharing; as an anti-Romanist, he believed that Protestantism alone could accommodate the scientific method, the search for truth. Then, turning to capitalist civilization, he most effectively exposed the conventional social morality preached by the contemporary churches, the ritual subscription to a general egalitarian ethic of property

---

* Reinhold Niebuhr, of the Union Theological Seminary, exerted influence on a significant clerical group, the United Christian Council for Democracy. But he was not a fellow-traveller. Capitalism, he wrote, was possessed by "the demon of hypocrisy"; communism, by the "demon of vengeance". Political fanaticism of the communist variety, he wrote in 1933, "shuts the gates of mercy on mankind".

† See Chapter Nine.

but the evasion of any precise practical application. Religion was used to cloak imperialism's motives under a masquerade of benevolence; theology and life itself were carefully divorced, and people were taught resignation to the evils of the world by making them dependent on a transcendent power. Above all, Ward insisted, Protestantism must divest itself of the capitalistic ethic of self-interest.

This point of view naturally had its passionate adherents in England also. Joseph Needham quoted the Bishop of London's address to the plantation owners of the Southern States in 1727: "Christianity and the embracing of the Gospel does not make the least alteration to Civil Property ... it continues Persons just in the same state as it found them."[41] To which Needham found an answer in the Proper Preface for Trinity Sunday: "neither afore nor after them, without any difference or inequality". He was convinced that the England envisaged by Thomas More and William Blake could not come into being until the curse of a class-stratified society had been lifted. He, like Ward, saw a close alliance operating between big business, nationalism, militarism and, ultimately, fascism. (Needham was working in the Kaiser-Wilhelm Institut für Biologie when the nazis took power.) Ward pointed out that in modern America inequality of income was increasing and civil liberties were in jeopardy, while black lists and Red-hunters had proliferated since the First World War. Socialism was the answer, substituting as it did industry for use for industry for gain, the will to serve for the will to profit. But what of socialism in its communist, agressively materialist form? Well, said Ward, I too am a materialist to the extent that I see man's historical activities conditioned mainly by economic factors. Marx was right about this, as also about wages, surplus value and prices. Admittedly surplus value still existed in the USSR, but it was at least invested in the development of the workers' own state. But what of the militant atheism prevailing there? This Ward sidestepped.

Confronted by such dilemmas, Hewlett Johnson became more the bull than the matador. Jesus, he said, "was a materialist" – a proposition which annoyed the left-wing Methodist, Donald Soper, as well it might. Johnson quoted no less an authority than Archbishop William Temple to the effect that "if materialism once becomes dialectical, its own dialectics will transform it into Theism".[42] This is amusing stuff, but it reminds us that politically the Dean stood not entirely alone in the upper reaches of the Anglican hierarchy. Even more radical than Temple was Bishop Barnes of Birmingham, who liked to remind his congregations that early Christians were also communists, that Lenin was a truly great man (if not strictly a Christian), and that the spiritual basis for communism was "lofty humanism".[43] One sees how the words "humanism" and "humanitarianism" tended towards benign confusion in the mouths of the fellow-travelling priests. Nor was this the only confusion. Ward admitted that the Christian attitude towards violence differed from the bolshevik one, yet then justified or disregarded every act of Soviet violence on the ground that (a) it hadn't happened and (b) was fully understandable. But generally a strict focus on the ideal doctrine enabled the Christian fellow-travellers to leave in the cupboard the thorny crown of Soviet practice. Thus Needham argued that communist principles of racial equality reflected the essential Christian ethic – which having been said, there was apparently no need to comment on the deportation of whole nationalities.

In fact Needham was an unusual combination: a scientist, Marxist and Christian, who owed debts variously to Pavlov, Marx and Conrad Noel, the Red Vicar of Thaxted.* He believed that if by accident of birth he had come into the world a Confucian rather than a Christian, he would none the less have recognized the virtues of communism – but not if he had been born and bred a resigned Buddhist. "One must show that communism, in a sense, completes and extends Christianity, just as Christianity, in a sense, completed and extended the civilization of the Mediterranean paganism."[44] (The words "in a sense" were well chosen: what follows chronologically is not necessarily "an extension of", particularly if it directly and aggressively refutes the basic premises of.) Needham did not regard the Church as a necessarily eternal institution, and considered that it perhaps had only a limited historical role to play: "When that which is perfect (the just social order) is come, that which is imperfect (the ecclesiastical institution) shall be done away."[45] It was all foreseen in the Scriptures: "Thy Kingdom come, Thy Will be done, in earth as it is in heaven." But really all this is neither serious nor plausible theology, and it completely ignores the fact that even the most radical Christian, to deserve the name, must wish to preserve the divine creed, if not the cult and the church as well. But that creed – God, Jesus, divinity, the supernatural, the after-life – had no place, except as a diminishing relic of the past, a small concession to toleration, in the Soviet Union. Nor could the Dean's clumsy juggling

* Like Noel, Middleton Murry, editor from 1932 of *Adelphi*, was a major influence of the time. As a Christian he spoke of an inevitable revolutionary crisis and of the need for the Labour Party to adopt Marxist programmes. Marx, he said, belonged to the Judaeo-Christian passion of *disinterested* sympathy. But his political position was equivocal. He believed that self-liberation by the proletariat would be self-seeking, unethical and conducive of "inhuman horrors", such as occurred in the USSR. The progressive bourgeoisie must take the lead, in that disinterested spirit — not a Marxian notion. Orwell thought at one time that Murry was a fellow-traveller, but Murry suffered an extraordinary number of crises of conscience and reversals of opinion.

rescue logic from itself. The communists, he declared, had "recovered much of the core of real belief in God". Oh why? Because the communist "feels himself to be an instrument in the hands of a Power ... which here and now is working to achieve its purpose of creating the brotherhood of mankind".[46] Interestingly enough, this is precisely the kind of analogy recommended by anti-Marxists who wish to prove that Marx psychologically translated the messianic impulse and the Second Coming from one code (theology) to another (social philosophy). But let that not be held against the Dean.

Hewlett Johnson was born in 1874, in a well-off suburb of Manchester, one of a family of nine. He trained as an engineer, offered his services to the Church Missionary Society, studied theology at Wycliffe Hall, Oxford and became in 1904 captain of the Wadham College Boat Club. He was a tall man and a big one. In 1908 he became a vicar. He was then already thirty-four, and one notices that his career was making the slow start it was later to maintain. Socialist influences implanted themselves gradually but steadily: the works of Tawney, the impact of the Pankhursts and the suffragettes, and membership in 1918 of the Union of Democratic Control. He was now a "ninety per cent Pacifist", although the other ten per cent always governed his soul whenever a just war had to be fought. But apparently the real evangelists of his original conversion were two apprentices working at the Ashbury Railway Carriage Company, Manchester, who had got the message from Robert Blatchford's *Merrie England*. Yet it was in a wealthy, bourgeois parish that he settled as vicar, which limited for some years his scope for practical radical action. He was already fifty when in 1924 he was appointed Dean of Manchester; seven years later the left-wing Bishop Temple proposed to Ramsay MacDonald that Johnson be appointed Dean of Canterbury, and so it was done. Henceforward the socialist masses of the world could easily be persuaded that the Head of the English Church was a communist.

Now came his first serious trouble. At Johnson's invitation, Gandhi visited the Deanery in 1931. The pig-headed Canons were upset. After a visit to China in 1932 (not communist China, at that time physically blockaded), the Dean returned home, patched up his relations with the Canons, became a governor of the King's School (rather against his principles, but it was in the line of duty), fell under the influence of the crackpot Major Douglas and the panacea of social credit, and spoke on behalf of the Major up and down the country until he noticed that Douglas was backing Franco in Spain. To which country the Dean hurried, returning to preach thereon, and bringing mighty attacks upon

himself from Archbishop Lang and two Suffragan Bishops in Church
Assembly (it generally being thought at the time that the Republicans
in Spain were raping nuns, etc.). Then in 1937 he travelled at last to
Russia: his enthusiastic and well argued report, *The Socialist Sixth of
the World* (called *Soviet Power* in America), sold several million copies
in twenty-five languages, even appearing in Belgium during the German
occupation under the not altogether incongruous title, *Recipes of Aunt
Mary*. More trouble came from the Canons at the time of the Soviet-
Finnish war. But when accused of mixing politics with religion, Johnson
had a good answer: the Anglican Church had two Archbishops and a
whole Bench of Bishops installed in the House of Lords with just that
purpose, to mix religion with politics. (Clearly Johnson himself was no
longer a candidate for that Bench of Bishops.) There were attempts to
get him out of the Deanery, but England loves the law and he could be
found guilty neither of heresy, nor neglect of duty, nor immorality.
Apparently the statement "Jesus was a materialist" was no heresy,
though only God knows why. In fact during the war his troubles
diminished due to the convergence of two factors; Russia was an ally
at war, and Archbishop Temple was also an ally, or a friend at least, at
all times. When Temple died in 1944 and was succeeded by the rather
dry, severe, prim Geoffrey Fisher, relations were bound to deteriorate
sharply, and they did.

Not that Johnson ever willingly quarrelled with anyone, for his was
both a generous and an innocent nature, and he had a friendly smile
and a warm handshake for any other mortal who would accept them.
The King, for example. Shortly after telling Stalin how closely he resembled his mother ("a good woman"), he told George VI how closely
his father George V had resembled – Henry IV. But did the King know
that the five hundred thousand dollars received from America to re-
store the bomb-damaged Cathedral was the fruit of Johnson's friendship
with Corliss Lamont, whose father was Thomas W. L. Lamont, a banker
belonging to the house of Morgan? (The Dean picked up smaller sums
for the cause of peace where and how he could; in Hollywood, Chaplin
greeted his arrival on set with a backward somersault and then wrote
out a cheque.) But such beneficence did not appease Geoffrey Cantaur
(as the Archbishop's signature then ran) when Johnson began lauding
Russia all over America and referring to Lord Halifax as a lackey of
Hitler. The Dean, declining to apologize, explained that he had been
misquoted: the words had in fact been used in his presence by Masaryk.
Nevertheless the Archbishop asked the Dean to resign and the Dean
declined. Then he flew to Paris in 1949 to give evidence at the Kravchenko trial: no slave labour in the USSR. In April he was back there

for a congress of the World Peace Movement. Still he maintained his poise and equilibrium between two worlds, and his pleasure in simple English traditions: "The [Canterbury] Festival play was a revival of *Zeal of Thy House* by Dorothy Sayers, and once again the Cathedral Choristers sang Sir Sydney Nicholson's delightful boy's opera, *The Children of the Chapel.* There was a lecture by John Betjeman on 'Looking at Churches'."[47]

1950, to Australia. There the leading spirit in the Peace Council was Mrs Street, the wife of the Lord Chief Justice, further proof that the establishment was cracking at the seams. Thence to Canada, where he addressed more than a thousand people in the Maple Leaf Gardens, Vancouver. Five hundred hoodlums stoned the hall, the Dean turned the other cheek, and Fisher was incensed (by the Dean, not the hoodlums). Already the Archbishop had written to the Mayor of Auckland: "My advice to overseas Anglican Churches is completely to ignore the Dean's visit."[48] However, Stalin didn't ignore it and awarded Johnson the Peace Prize the following year, along with Joliot-Curie, Eugénie Cotton and the Rev. Arthur Molton. By 1952, following his denunciations of germ warfare in Korea, the Dean was in the hottest water ever, Fisher making a really determined effort in the Lords to get his Royal Charter revoked, but Churchill, who may secretly have admired the Dean's spirit if not his cause, pointed out that it couldn't be done – due to an oversight the Elizabethans had omitted all mention of germ warfare when framing the Thirty-Nine Articles, the Victorians likewise when drafting the Church Discipline Act of 1840. Four years later Johnson invited Malenkov to visit the Cathedral (to the fury of guess who), and so great was the mutual admiration of the Dean and the Soviet authorities that, to his slight embarrassment, he was accorded more lines in the *Soviet Encyclopaedia* than Jesus Christ.

But his great love did not extend to Russia alone. In the post-war years he travelled the length and breadth of Eastern Europe; in 1960 it was East Germany, in 1963 Cuba, in 1964 China, but we are making no real effort to keep up with his itinerary in utopia. Chou En Lai provided the ninety-year-old fellow-traveller with a special plane equipped with a bed and oxygen apparatus to facilitate his expeditions across China where, to his delight, he ran into a mere youngster of seventy-nine, Anna Louise Strong. Both had much, when all is considered, to be thankful for. Johnson died in 1968, and though we have without shame or scruple mocked him for his block-headedness, his blindness, it is not altogether contradictory to insist that there also was a good man, a Christian in spirit and in his dealings with others, who wished the world well. He had seen more in a long life than most:

picture him, always smiling, beside "Living Buddhas", the Iman of Tashkent, the Head Lama of Ulam Bator, receiving the Peace Star of Mongolia, standing outside the Deanery under a huge "Ban Atomic Weapons" sign (the sign under which the Headmaster of the King's School forbade his boys to pass, even though the Dean was the chairman of the governors, a most unusual situation). One suspects that his pride was great, which is not normally accounted a Christian virtue, for rarely did he admit his mistakes and not even Khrushchev's revelatory speech in 1956 could convince him that he had erred in his judgments. The ultimate impression is that of the sublime merging with the ridiculous, as when this hugely tall figure with the puffs of white hair billowing over his ears stood on-stage with the minute, masked members of the Peking Opera, clapping with them, smiling, clapping. . . .

7

A Postscript to the Enlightenment

In its more serious intellectual aspects, the phenomenon of fellow-travelling can best be understood as a postscript to the Enlightenment. It represented, to adapt Peter Gay's admirable phrase,* a re-recovery of nerve, a reaffirmation of values once boldly proclaimed and universalized but subsequently eroded. It signified a return to the eighteenth-century vision of a rational, educated and scientific society based on the maximization of resources and the steady improvement (if not perfection) of human nature as visualized by objective, unprejudiced brains. Knowledge and morality are once more viewed as complementary; the prejudice- and tradition-crippled past is joined to a brave new future by the high road of "progress". For the fellow-travellers, Stalin's Russia represented the mental and physical will to revive the great experiment, whereas the Western democracies were seen to have betrayed their own ideals and to have foundered in the mire of self-interest, revived superstitions and class egoism. Furthermore, both the values and the assumptions of the Enlightenment had been formidably challenged by the philosophers, writers and social commentators of the late nineteenth century, and this challenge demanded a bold reply, an affirmation of faith. One need only recall the influence of Kierkegaard, Schopenhauer and Nietzsche in the field of philosophy, of Pareto and Michels among sociologists, and of Freud and Jung among psychologists, to perceive the extent of the challenge, not forgetting the immense impact of the second-rate popularizers who exalted myth, instinct, racial superiority, blood and soil in a deliberate attack on what Nietzsche called the feminism of the Enlightenment. If – so the message emerged – man was inherently aggressive, emotional and libido-dominated, then his virile nature should be accepted if not positively celebrated. Rimbaud, Verlaine, Stefan George, Proust, Kafka, d'Annunzio, Barrès and Joyce offered little comfort to those who still believed that "knowledge liberates and absolute knowledge liberates absolutely". And while modernist writers, including the greatest, were

* See Peter Gay, *The Enlightenment: An Interpretation*, vol. 2, London, 1969.

depicting human consciousness and behaviour as a labyrinth of distortions and repressions, so other philosophers were busily engaged in challenging the rationality of language, of human communication itself, and in proposing that words were as much the masters as the servants of human thought and indeed perception. From the *Weltanschauung* of the anti-Enlightenment man emerges as no more free than a slave crawling east across the deck of a ship travelling west. Even advocates of social revolution like Georges Sorel were now capable of deriding those *philosophes* who discerned in history a coherent pattern of evolution, and of exalting violence as an end in itself, as a component of a necessary collective myth, as a gesture of catharsis in the face of an irredeemably hostile environment.

Leninism furiously rejected the anti-Enlightenment as retrograde, obscurantist and reactionary. But so long as bolshevism presented itself to hesitant Western observers in the colours of a quasi-Asiatic anarchism, the potential fellow-travellers refused to discover in Russia a new Enlightenment. Only when Stalin turned towards positivistic social engineering did they identify Soviet communism with a re-recovery of nerve, with a reaffirmation of man's capacity to master his environment and his own nature. Yet their own spiritual ancestors were Condorcet, Bentham, Owen and Saint-Simon rather than Marx or Engels. They were heirs to the pre-Marxian Enlightenment. Not only did the Hegelian or dialectical aspects of Marxism-Leninism leave them cold, but they also rejected the cruel instrumentality of Marxism, its emphasis on class conflict and class reason. And they had little difficulty in convincing themselves that what was taking shape in Russia in the thirties was not the dictatorship of the proletariat but the benevolent despotism of enlightened, disinterested pedagogues working for the common good. If they had read Robert Michels* they would of course have learned by analogy a good deal about the new bureaucratic formations within the State and Party, coagulations of power which were very far from disinterested, but the fellow-travellers had inherited an ideal thirsting for fulfilment and they readily discounted pessimistic accounts of the Soviet reality as being jaundiced by envy, fear or bad faith.

Anatole France, for example, was steeped in the spirit of the *philosophes* and their Encyclopaedia. No less than they did he insist that knowledge and wisdom accumulate with time and that progress was represented by the republican and democratic principle fighting authoritarianism, Catholicism, duty and tradition. France himself constituted the last link in the chain of French writers whom Heinrich Mann most

---

* Austrian sociologist, author of *Political Parties,* and student of bureaucratic-élite formations.

admired, a roll of honour which included not only Victor Hugo and Zola but also non-democrats like Flaubert who nevertheless believed that government should be conducted according to the precepts of Intelligence and Science. It was this article of faith which linked in Mann's mind Voltaire, Rousseau, Fourier and Saint-Simon with Lenin and Stalin. For Marx, irrationality was a symptom of the decadence and desperation of a declining ruling class; for those who, like Mann himself, continued to carry the torch of an earlier Enlightenment, irrationality represented a kind of innate mental curse comparable to the Calvinists' conception of original sin. For the *philosophes* the primary, generative theatre of human endeavour was the mind itself; thus Mann, resuming a lifelong obsession, began to trace the origins of the Second World War back to the influence of those intellectuals who had scorned the power of intelligence and rationality, notably to Sorel who, in his opinion, had laid the foundations for all forms of fascistic state capitalism and *"Synarchismus"*,* and to Martin Heidegger whose detestable *Sinn und Form* represented a kind of existentialism which robbed both past and future of all meaning.

But the name of Heidegger reminds us that not every fellow-traveller rigorously conformed to the same cultural tradition as Mann: Sartre's existentialism was forged at the expense of the blander optimism of the Enlightenment, while Shaw had many years earlier announced his admiration for theories of will-power and creative energy expounded by Lamarck, Schopenhauer and Nietzsche. Shaw was even capable of the remark that life is the attempt to satisfy a passion we cannot explain, rather than a rational process. Nevertheless his Nietzschean side was easily domesticated by the Utilitarian heritage transmitted through Bellamy and the Webbs, and by Wells's positivistic scientism. It was this dimension of his mind which governed his appraisal of the USSR in the 1930s. And if, as is possible, he recognized in Stalin both Man and Superman, then it should not be forgotten that since the time of Diderot, Voltaire, Rousseau, Owen and Fourier, the *philosophes* of progress had acknowledged that words and thoughts do not translate themselves into deeds without the intervention of wills sterner than their own. Indeed the fellow-travellers harboured no prejudice against power as such provided that, in Saint-Simon's phrase, the government of people was progressively replaced by the administration of things. That Stalin should have appeared to so many superior brains as the embodiment of this mutation reminds us of the hopeful journeys made by the French *philosophes* of the eighteenth century to the courts of autocracy, notably

---

* Meaning the anarchism of syndicalist and corporate power.

St Petersburg. It was, after all, to be some time before Robert Owen would despair of securing the support of the Tory lords of the reactionary Liverpool administration, while Fourier in turn was always waiting for his Napoleon. A long journey often demands a short cut.

Even so, the fellow-travellers' vision of the Soviet Union under Stalin represented a remarkable reversal of the prevailing Western image of Russia. In the nineteenth century russophilia in England normally went hand in hand with anti-intellectualism, with a taste for the primitive, the exotic and with the cult of ruthless authority. And not only in England: in 1854 Ernest Coeurderoy (a name too good to be true) published his *Hourra ou la révolution par les Cosaques,* applauding Russian primitivism as a vital ally for Western traditionalists in their struggle against decadence and incipient democracy. Yet after 1928 russophilia became *the* gospel of progress. Brailsford had already called the Revolution "a great and heroic attempt to shorten the dragging march of time...."[1] Both Shaw and Steffens saw the bolshevik experiment as the best available example of creative evolution, while the hallowed word "progress" sprang readily from many pens. In assuming that bolshevik Russia had firmly dispensed with both religion and the family, Gide concluded that she had put paid to "the two worst enemies of progress". The communist experiment was interpreted by Joseph Needham as proof that human history is a continuation of natural history in the sense that individual cells are compelled to renounce their primitive autonomy in order to unite in higher, more complex organisms. Mann wrote a good deal about "progress", which he equated with freedom, justice and equality, while the same "progress" emerged as the tragic hero of Feuchtwanger's novel *Waffen für Amerika* – discovered in the eighteenth century, recognized and prized in the nineteenth, and then denied and slandered in the twentieth. Edgar Snow remarked that communism, though frequently compromised by its methods, "retained its human connections, its lineal relationship to the evolution of mankind as a whole, and to the ends of *liberté, égalité* and *fraternité*".[2] Whereas, said Rockwell Kent, the nations which had first proclaimed these values had subsequently betrayed them: "Where, I ask of Capitalism, are your promises? Where are the promises of our Declaration – for which men fought and died – which you confirmed?"[3]

The unifying principle of the Enlightenment was Reason. It replaced God. Man was now prepared to worship his own, unaided potentialities. The *philosophes* did not regard themselves as omniscient or infallible, but they confidently expected their grandsons to become so, since only relative ignorance temporarily clouded the clear crystal of Reason. Marx challenged this proposition by emphasizing the distortions imposed on thought in class society and by insisting that pure reason first demands a classless, non-antagonistic society. The fellow-travellers remained unconvinced. Like the Holy Ghost, Reason was at large: the right mental net could catch it, preserve it, cultivate it. *Cognito, ergo sum,* protested Gide and Benda, was equally true for aristocrat, bourgeois and proletarian. Heinrich Mann admired the French aristocrats of the eighteenth century and their Russian successors of the nineteenth whose love of truth had ultimately wrought their own destruction as a class.

Gorky was devoted to reason, knowledge and science. He wrote bitterly of the impotence of reason in the old church-dominated Russia, of the "dark abyss" and the "elegiac submissiveness to fate". What initially alienated him from Lenin's regime was the conviction that it was suppressing the light of reason and perpetuating in a new form the dark abyss. For Rolland, the authentic *esprit* was above all a rational one. Shaw, like the Webbs and like the Welsh utopian socialist Robert Owen, whom the Fabians had latterly discovered as an intellectual ancestor, was a fierce rationalist. Like Owen, the Fabians condemned ignorance, waste, dislocation, booms, slumps and unemployment as essentially irrational. Was racism, Needham asked, anything but irrational? Was not the Soviet Union the most determined opponent of racism? "The subjective and irrational are anti-democratic, they are the instruments of tyranny."[4] Georges Friedmann described the Soviet Union as "the most magnificent effort towards the rational transformation of institutions ... that humanity has ever attempted".[5] So here "reason" becomes simultaneously a system of logic or cerebration immaculately synthesized with a set of moral values. No one voiced the liberating claims of reason more fervently or consistently than Heinrich Mann with his perennial argument that the greatest weapon of the *Geist* in its struggle with arbitrary power was reason (*Vernunft*): indeed he published in 1923 a collection of essays collectively titled *Diktatur der Vernunft.* In 1937 he wrote of the USSR: "At last a state undertakes to make out of men what we have always wanted: a rational existence, the collective working for the benefit of each individual, and out of that individual shall something higher and better develop within a totality that further predicts itself."[6] But here rationality is interpreted as a common heritage not a class monopoly, as a matter of *Geist* not of *Macht*: he spoke of the "deep, fundamental intellectuality of the Revolution" and he pleaded that it was "in the last resort no rebellion of some against others. Basically it asks for and receives the agreement of all."[7] This was indeed the dream of the Enlightenment. Mann's friend Feuchtwanger continued to regard reason as the preserve of an enlightened minority, a treasure destined to be distributed to the populace at large but so far withheld from them in all countries except the Soviet Union. "I sympathized inevitably with the experiment of basing the construction of a gigantic State on reason alone. . . ."[8] He stressed the ethical "*Vernunftmässigkeit*" of the Plans, and later he wrote of his belief in "a slow, slow yet sure growth of human reason between the last ice-age and the next".[9] Similarly, "reason-through-knowledge" was the formula recommended by the Webbs and finally identified by them as operational in Russia. They were convinced that under socialism the problem of who gives orders to whom would progressively diminish since the combination of what they called "measurement with publicity" and the "searchlight of public knowledge" would burn out unreason, ignorance and apathy among the public, freeing it from its false dependence on traditional or arbitrary power. This had also been Saint-Simon's belief.

It is of course easy to criticize the philosophical naïvety of the fellow-travellers. Too blandly did they incorporate subjective, ethical premises into the general concept of reason, and in this respect they were little in advance of Thomas Paine, who described history as a periodically interrupted progress from the government of priests and conquerors to the government of pure reason – this reason being defined simply as the antithesis of ignorance. When Owen declared: "Train any population rationally, and they will be rational",[10] he virtually spoke for a later generation separated from him by a hundred years. Yet what sounded enlightened in 1830 could only be judged as naïve in 1930. When Condorcet and Owen argued that idleness, poverty, crime and punishment were merely, in Owen's words, "the necessary consequences of ignorance", they could not reasonably be criticized for lacking a concept of alienation or anomie, whereas the fellow-travellers turned their backs not only on such concepts but blandly ignored a century of psychological inquiry. It was time to recognize that formulas such as Bentham's "the greatest happiness of the greatest number" had an ethical rather than a rational basis, yet the fellow-travellers continued to elect Unitary Reason to the throne once occupied by God, complete with all the court ritual of the fall, redemption and salvation. One can at least partially sympathize with Marx's scorn for the endeavours of Saint-Simon and Owen to convert humanity, including the rich and powerful, to socialism by means of rational persuasion; it was this aspect of their thought rather than the building of model settlements like New Harmony which provoked him to brand them as "utopians". Admittedly the later fellow-travellers occasionally acknowledged that the knout had become a frequent messenger of reason in Soviet Russia, but they refused to draw conclusions about the motivation of the knout-wielders, preferring to judge them as benevolent schoolmasters occasionally resorting to sterner discipline out of love for their pupils. Though they were anti-capitalist, and though some of them, like Shaw, recognized the necessity of force, the fellow-travellers still inhabited the mental universe of Auguste Comte, with his vision of history as being synonymous with the progress of the human mind towards the final, rational stage of universal positivism. No doubt the immense upheaval which took place in Russia during forced collectivization was in a sense positivistically inspired; but what appears ruthlessly rational is not necessarily reasonable, and the fellow-travellers lacked not only Kant's insight into the necessity of an inner, moral revolution within men but also the vital gleam of cautionary wisdom offered by Voltaire when he remarked: *"Le monde avec lenteur marche vers la sagesse."*

For the fellow-travellers, as for their ancestors the *philosophes,* science represented the most glorious incarnation of rationality. How often did they refer to Soviet policy in the era of the Plans as a gigantic experiment! The very fact of Russia's relative scientific and technological backwardness made it the ideal experimental laboratory for the new positivists. In May 1917 Gorky had lamented that Russia remained a nation dominated by disease and ignorance, incapable of cultivating its land according to modern methods or of installing viable sewerage systems in its cities. In the eyes of Europe, he said, we resemble African negroes. "Full realization of the ideals of socialist culture is possible only in the presence of a wide-based technological development and strictly organized industry."[11] When this development and organization became an absolute priority in the age of construction it immediately evoked enormous enthusiasm among Western scientists including many of the most distinguished.* According to Harry Ward, the Soviet religion of science and the passion for following "facts" to their conclusions represented a journey of human investigation comparable to that of the seers and prophets; moreover socialism emerged now as the authentic religion of science by directing it solely towards the end of human well-being.

Meanwhile the capitalist economies were falling apart. Not only was the law of supply and demand in disgrace, but the face of Soviet communism gained in beauty for many scientists when they regarded the vile features of nazism with its crude doctrines of racial supremacy, its persecution of Jewish scientists, its war mania. Whereas in the Soviet

* In Britain, communist and fellow-travelling natural scientists of the 1930s included J. Crowther, J. Haldane, R. Calder, J. Needham, C. Waddington, P. Chalmers Mitchell P. Blackett, H. Levy, L. Hogben and J. Bernal.

Union – so the nuclear physicist Klaus Fuchs later put it during his interrogation by British security officials – "man understands the historical forces and he is able to control them, and ... for the first time he will be really free".[12] But the fellow-travelling scientists were no more inclined to integrate Marxism with their own creative work than were their colleagues the philosophers. Julian Huxley confessed that he did not see how Marxism helped one to become a better chemist, physicist, biochemist, geologist, ecologist or palaeontologist. Even the fervently pro-Soviet fellow-traveller J. G. Crowther admitted in 1932 that it was by no means clear how dialectical materialism actually assisted a scientist once he was inside the laboratory. About this C. H. Waddington was equally sceptical, confining himself to endorsing the Marxist interpretation of history in its broad economic outlines. Crowther attempted to work his way out of the difficulty by reversing the whole proposition: "The social philosophy of the Soviet Union ... is founded on modern physical and biological investigation. Natural science is an organic part of Marx's philosophy."[13] (Thus a good cause makes a monkey out of a good man.) Meanwhile in France a group of kindred red-heads* formed the fellow-travelling Commission Scientifique du Cercle de la Russie neuve, but a study of the reports offered to the Cercle in 1933–4 reveals little evidence of Marxism being employed in the course of creative research; rather it was invoked to explain the history of science in terms of social formations. Occasional pious utterances of a general nature scarcely detract from this impression. In the post-creative years of his life Paul Langevin became increasingly prone to such remarks as, "the more I progress in my own science, the more I feel myself become a Marxist", but this was just about as carefree and incantatory a testimony as the nowadays familiar "the more I make love, the more I make the revolution". Neither Langevin's distinguished pupil Frédéric Joliot-Curie nor his wife Irène claimed that Marxism had been of theoretical service to their experimental work in the field of radium.

What really turned so many scientists into fellow-travellers in the thirties was the notion that the most rapid scientific advances are made by a system which methodically relates research to the solution of urgent social problems. Having visited Russia in 1928 and 1931, Langevin concluded that Soviet science was unique in its single-minded dedication to the material, intellectual and moral liberation of man. The psychologist Henri Wallon contrasted the unco-ordinated specialization, the cloistering, isolation and disequilibrium of scientific research under capitalism with the integration of theory and practice achieved in a

---

* Notably P. Langevin, physicist, H. Mineur, astronomer, P. Labérenne, mathematician, H. Wallon, psychologist.

planned society. P. M. S. Blackett put it this way: "The advantages on the side of Soviet science are unlimited resources, the advantages of doing things on a big scale, the planning of the relation between industry and science, together with enormous enthusiasm."[14] Huxley complained that in the West pure science remained esoteric and unrelated to popular needs and awareness, noting in passing that while the Labour Chancellor of the Exchequer had recently slashed the scientific budget, the proportion of the Soviet national income devoted to science was rising rapidly. Visits to Russia and first-hand encounters with the work of the biologists Vavilov, Koltsov and Zavadorski, or the physicists Joffe and Hessen, deepened the admiration of Western scientists. Chalmers Mitchell spoke of the lavish scale on which research facilities were provided, while the Cambridge embryologist Waddington argued that only in Russia were scientists enabled to pursue experiments for more than a few months at a time. "Of all the political systems which are alive at the present day, communism is almost the only one whose influence is mainly due to the force of its ideas."[15] Needham, at that time Reader in Biochemistry at Cambridge, returned impressed from a visit to the 1935 Moscow Physiological Congress, and Ruscoe Clarke, whose speciality was medicine, declared that in Russia, where practice was the criterion of truth, science truly belonged to the people. "Human nature is being changed in the process of building the future. Mankind itself as a biological species is being transformed in relation to the new society"[16] – an extravagant claim yet one consistent with the central vision of the Enlightenment. The idea of changing human nature was naturally attractive to those who inherited Rousseau's wish that men should be forced to be free, and the degree of force employed did not always awaken scruples: overwhelmed by the virtues of the Soviet medical system, Dr Edith Summerskill MP told a rally: "When I read about Ivan the Terrible, I was not so impressed by the fact that Ivan used to gouge out people's eyes but that he imported four German doctors into Russia."[17]

The physicist Crowther, who made seven visits to Russia in as many years, became one of the leading propagandists for the USSR as the incarnation of scientific progress, explaining that super-high-power and high-pressure steam turbines could be afforded and used with confidence only in a socialist productive system. Since Soviet research owed no obligation to shareholders, it was accordingly free of the burden to yield immediate results (a curious reversal of the argument that practical results were the yardstick of Soviet scientific endeavour whereas Western university research was too esoteric). In fact the fellow-travellers intended to have it both ways, depicting the typical new

Soviet scientist as doing his own private thing for months on end without interference and simultaneously hurrying about the streets questioning citizens, "how can I help you here and now?" But the aspect of this highly partial enthusiasm worth closest attention is its emphasis on the positive role of an intellectual élite reorganizing society according to the most advanced principles of scientific rationality and out of devotion to the greatest good of the greatest number. The Soviet system was thus transformed into one great, thriving school or polytechnic with the pupil-masses awakening from centuries of slumber to grasp thankfully the miracles of creative knowledge offered them by the élite.

The history of the Plans, Ludwig Marcuse commented bitterly, was the unhappy story of the planned. This went too far. It would however be fair to comment that, until the purges of the late thirties wreaked their indiscriminate havoc, the history of the Plans was the happy story of the planners. The fellow-travellers of the West, themselves frustrated planners and pedagogues, were not slow to grasp this. "See, see, it works!" murmured Sidney Webb, ecstatically, beaming at his companion Barbara Drake during his second visit to Russia. He meant: the planning. Without doubt, in making planning a fetish the fellow-travellers accorded themselves the relevance and dignity of which they felt deprived at home. Julian Huxley announced in 1934 that conscious and scientific planning marked the fourth great step in history (a step viewed somewhat less optimistically by his brother in *Brave New World*), and he went on to explain: "As an individual organism man is inherently selfish; but as a social animal he is also inherently altruistic."[18] "Inherently?" – well, given a little persuasion and planning. The new philosopher kings rejoiced that the impedimentary dross of the old society, the middlemen and parasites, had been cut away, leaving a single immense experimental farm planned, guided and controlled from the centre.

Rolland, Gide, Mann, Feuchtwanger – they all worshipped at the temple of planning. Overwhelmed by the USSR's *"Vernunftmässigkeit"*, Feuchtwanger was positively knocked down by its *"Planmässigkeit"* – which is really intolerable even to contemplate translating, but emerges literally as "planfulness". As for the Webbs, the most significant social trend for them in the USSR was "the deliberate planning of all the nation's production, distribution and exchange . . . for increasing the consumption of the whole community".[19] Of the early experiments in workers' control they were entirely contemptuous: how, they asked, could single factories recognize the community's needs or the general requirements of production? They recalled the "splendid peroration" delivered by L. B. Krassin to the Fabian Society as early as 1920 when he announced, to applause, that the bolsheviks had discovered the "philosopher's stone" – planning based on the collation of statistics and the prediction of needs. (But the stone had to be buried beneath thin soil during the NEP interim period.) Sir Daniel Hall put it succinctly in 1933 when he described the Soviet master-plan as "an engineer's lay-out to obtain maximum efficiency of production ... without any hampering conditions other than those imposed by soil and climate".[20] It all required, he went on, a kind of authoritative directive skill attempted in the West only in wartime – so this was it, a new form of martial law, with the experts rather than the generals in the saddle. Orwell commented harshly: "In Russia the capitalists were destroyed first and the workers were crushed later."[21] In his view, and it is not one appreciably spoiled by exaggeration, the British russophiles were primarily intellectuals, scientists, teachers and bureaucrats eager to acquire more power and prestige for themselves by eliminating the old ruling class yet keeping the workers in their place. Only after the USSR became fully totalitarian, he observed, did large numbers of the intelligentsia in England warm to it. The imbalance of Orwell's account was twofold: first, large numbers of German and French workers revered the Soviet Union, and it was they who gave the CPs their power and militancy; secondly, the "crushing" of the Soviet workers has to be set against the remarkable development of the welfare state of which they were the main beneficiaries. It was nevertheless true that the passion of the fellow-travellers for order, planning and controlled experimentation, for the absence of "hampering" elements, exposed one of the deepest contradictions of the post-Enlightenment Left: the rage for order always implies the firing squad for individual liberty. But then ... after all ... the freedom to be mistaken is no freedom at all. Is it?

But here again fellow-travelling thought echoed closely the tenets of the early nineteenth-century Enlightenment, particularly that faith in progress, productivity and planning represented during the French Revolution by the luckless Condorcet and later by his more fortunate successors, the scientists and *idéologues* of the Institute de France. In fact many early socialists such as Malby, Morellet and Babeuf had shown no enthusiasm for greater productivity, which they associated with the Mammon-principle of bourgeois economics. It was rather Voltaire, Mandeville, Montesquieu and the Encyclopaedists who associated increased wealth with progress, a point of view vigorously adopted by the English Utilitarians. Saint-Simon was perhaps the first to adapt this enthusiasm to a socialist blueprint, and it was he more than any other theorist who anticipated the ideology of the fellow-

travellers, which might be described as left-wing technocratic totalitarianism. Admittedly the fellow-travellers of the twentieth century were
more wholeheartedly anti-capitalist than either Saint-Simon or Owen,
both of whom tended to classify masters and men as members of the
productive classes in contrast to aristocrats, priests and soldiers. But it
is worth noting that in a work published in 1825 Saint-Simon envisaged
scientists, *industriels* and artists as members of a projected administrative élite presiding over the future socialist state, a vision elaborated later
by his former secretary, Comte, who naturally entrusted the guidance of
a scientific and industrial society to those who understood science and
production – the *savants*. And if the distinction between the two words
is understood, many of the latter-day fellow-travellers can better be
understood as frustrated *savants* rather than as *philosophes,* although
this is more true of the scientists and the Webbs than of Mann, Rolland
and Feuchtwanger.

Undoubtedly Owen and Saint-Simon were élitists. They aspired to
change society from above: but they also desired to change the nature
of that "above"; out went the theological and metaphysical past with
its hereditary castes, and in came a modern-minded, rationalist élite.
Owen differed in spirit little from the Webbs when in 1849 he denounced those "Red Republicans, Communists and Socialists" whose
seditions led to "universal disunion, opposition . . . a pandemonium state
of society". As early as 1832 the *Poor Man's Guardian* had complained
that the Owenites spoke "sneeringly and contemptuously" of political
rights, and Owen himself later displayed no sympathy for the Chartist
movement. If one finds a shade of difference between this emphasis and
that of the Webbs it lies in this: that whereas Sidney and Beatrice could
scarcely disown the political gains and claims of the British working
and lower middle classes, they had absolutely no patience when similar
claims were voiced in Russia. For his part Owen paternalistically inspired at least sixteen utopian communities all based on the belief that
a properly engineered environment and a properly educated population
would produce a happy human race. A hundred years later New
Harmony finally took root in one sixth of the world's land surface. But
Owen did not elaborate the future administrative hierarchy as rigorously as Saint-Simon, who envisaged a three-chamber system, the first
encompassing artists and engineers who would formulate general plans,
the second containing scientists who would both examine these plans and
control the educational curriculum, and the third consisting of entre-
preneurs and managers who would put the finalized plans into operation. For class conflict he had no sympathy: his thought was as much
a reaction to the excesses of the French Revolution as an extension of its

principles. Proper corporatism, proper leadership and proper planning would, he insisted, obliterate the resentments, the envy and the yearnings for a spurious freedom which had brought Europe to turmoil. Did the individual members of a well-run choir, orchestra or rowing boat squabble over their roles or precedence? "An enlightened society needs only to be administered." What stood between Saint-Simon and the fellow-travellers was solely his continued reverence for the creative role of the capitalist entrepreneur, but after his death his disciple Bazard made good the fault, launching a general attack on private property and including only workers, scientists, sociologists and *savants* in the ranks of productive virtue. With this modification the heritage was virtually complete for transmission, but before the fellow-travellers could take up (albeit unconsciously for the most part) the Saint-Simonian legacy there intervened a century dominated by Marxism, anarchism and the more mundane but equally influential democratic reformism embodied in social democracy. When Saint-Simonianism once again came into its own in the 1930s, its trustees endorsed one form of violence (the omelette and eggs kind) while nervously repudiating another (permanent revolution). Indeed the fellow-travelling *savants* obviously felt for Trotsky the same repugnance that Robespierre, Marat and the proponents of permanent guillotine had once inspired in Saint-Simon.

To which one footnote should be added. Was rationality and scientific administration enough? In his last years Saint-Simon evidently had doubts, emerging with a new motivational ideology, the cloudy pantheism of *Le Nouveau Christianisme*. Among his followers the cult of the leader-prophet-artist, of the messianic superman not subject to any written code of laws (since he was himself the living law) and bound to the people by love alone, ran amok, resulting in the bizarre worship of Bazard and le Père Enfantin. A century later, confronted by a similar phenomenon represented by the embalmed, en-statued, en-quoted Lenin, and by le Père Stalin in the Kremlin, the fellow-travellers took explanatory refuge in Russia's past, perhaps forgetting that when you divest all trade unionsts of their rights and uproot whole populations, then the juggernaut Plan has to be invested with a divine form. And divinity requires a human face.

The majority of fellow-travellers did not really understand the Soviet power structure. Many of them wishfully believed, with Ruscoe Clarke, that "scientists are an integral part of the leadership of the [Soviet] State ...", but in fact Soviet scientists were honoured and patronized only so long as they didn't step out of line. As for the non-scientific intelligentsia, they were periodically decimated. The fellow-travellers did not appreciate how rapidly a new political and bureaucratic caste, institutionalized in the Party but extending, in the manner of Djilas's "new class", beyond its ranks, solidifies and defends its privileges. They saw what they wanted to see, the rise of a new breed of experts bridging, as Needham put it, the gap between the old scholar and artisan, a new élite no longer studying history, literature, and the classics, as in the West, but steeped in science, technology, statistics and mathematics. Crowther revealingly commented that the Soviet State Planning Commission not only attracted the most able students but enjoyed more prestige than the Foreign Office. Here the grammar school declares war on the private school,* the grey flannel trousers on the pin-stripe. But the masses are also kept in their place. As Edmund Wilson explained in 1932 : "I too admire the Russian communist leaders because they are men of superior brains who have triumphed over the ignorance, the stupidity, and the short-sighted selfishness of the mass. . . ."[22] The Revolution had thus become the dictatorship of superior brains, of engineers of every sort – of souls, of matter, of men. It was, said Harry Ward, "one of the greatest bits of human engineering ever achieved". In his *If I Were Dictator,* Huxley concluded that the good society had to be the work of wise men; Steffens agreed; both believed that full democratic rights remained irrelevant until the good society had been introduced.

The Webbs regarded the CPSU approvingly as an Order or College, trained, disciplined, immensely self-controlled, leading by enlightenment and example. Reflecting on the constitution of a future socialist Britain, they (like Laski in Fabian Tract number 235) were careful to stress that the expert would only advise, not give orders; apparently they placed all their hopes "in the working class, served and guided, it is true, by an élite ... of experts who, without claiming any superior social status, would be content to exercise the power conferred upon them by their science and their long administrative experience".[23] In other words : we neither aspire to riches nor to cutting off your heads. In fact the socialist schemes they rejected and the ones they endorsed precisely reflected their answer to the question: who shall rule? Workers' control, "the mines to the miners", revolutionary syndicalism and de-centralized Guild Socialism – all these were vigorously opposed in favour of a centralized state structure which would automatically transfer power from the capitalists to themselves. Trotsky's judgment was rough: the Webbs, he said, found in the USSR neither Chartism nor the October Revolution nor communism, they found only an administrative mechanism and a bureaucratic plan.

---

* In Britain the so-called public school.

When some Soviet factory workers engaged in an argument with his companion, Lady Astor, Shaw said aloud, in English: "The more I see of the proletarians the more I thank God I am not one."[24] He had never believed that socialism would be built by the working class, for too many of its members were ignorant, corrupted and sycophantic; on the contrary he like the utopian socialists before him regarded the socialist cause as the preserve of the vital, enlightened spirits within all classes in their struggle against the mechanicals, the pre-conditioned. Wells characterized the real proletarians as the chorus to the October Revolution; and that, he believed, would always be their lot. Both men were élitists. "What we call democracy," Shaw told the ILP summer school in 1931, "instead of creating responsibility, absolutely destroys it...."[25] And later, while recoiling from some of the crudities of Chinese socialist realism, Simone de Beauvoir revealed the same pedagogic spirit when she reasoned that since the Chinese were a people who took every written word for gospel truth, it was imperative "for the regime to see to it" that the people "is given a wholesome diet".[26] Shaw derided Owen for ruling out the use of force, but he nevertheless stood squarely in the paternalist tradition which ran from Owen to Ruskin, preaching order and authority and utterly rejecting the quasi-medieval, libertarian vision presented by William Morris in his *News from Nowhere*. For Shaw it was *noblesse oblige*; his model gentleman assumed the responsibility conferred on him by knowledge instead of abdicating to the law of supply and demand, as the liberals did, or to the laws of nature, as the anarchists did, or to God, as Christians did. Russia, he said, had found what no other political movement had produced since the days of Stein and Hardenburg in Prussia: "leaders who had been specifically and scientifically educated for their job."[27] He also predicted that communism would not alter "the natural division of mankind into ninety-five per cent who had their work cut out for them and five per cent who can cut it out".[28] He agreed with Wells that the world was divided into commanders, obeyers and thinkers – but in Russia the thinkers were now the commanders. The Soviet worker felt respected because the best seats at the opera or ballet were offered to him, but he didn't always want to be bothered "to attend committees that are thrust on him by the managers...." When a job has to be done in the Soviet Union, Shaw announced enthusiastically, "it is always done by a dictator". This provoked a warm response in other fellow-travellers. "So many of us," confessed Wicksteed, "call ourselves democrats when all we are really doing is sitting on a fence built entirely of words. Bernard Shaw with his hatred of folly and inefficiency has quite definitely got off the fence into the garden of dictatorship."[29]

True: except the Shaw's tongue was one side of the fence and his feet the other. He called himself a "totalitarian democrat"; the Webbs could with equal justice have termed themslves corporate democrats. But it was Wells – a fellow-élitist, though by no means a fellow-traveller – who put their own case most unashamedly: "For the purposes of revolutionary theory the rest of humanity matters only as the texture of mud matters when we design a steam dredger to keep a channel clear."[30] Who, then, did matter? The "questioning, planning brains". Where Wells differed from Shaw was in his belief that communist fanaticism in Russia had suppressed the questioning, planning brains, the experts; he told Stalin during an interview in 1934 that it was no use preaching class war propaganda to the technical intelligentsia. Shaw could not swallow that; he was hot for class war – so long as it was not conducted by the lower classes themselves – and he accused Wells of repeating Comte's mistakes all over again, of believing in purely technical solutions within the context of class collaboration. Hating capitalism and capitalists, he himself preferred an élite led by Lenin and Stalin to one led by Ford and Rockefeller. But the dispute between Shaw and Wells was essentially a family quarrel, a wrangle over the proper contemporary interpretation of the Owenite-Saint-Simonian legacy.

Fascinated as they were by the new meritocracy emerging in the Soviet Union, it is scarcely surprising that few fellow-travellers were disturbed by the considerable inequalities of income prevailing during the Five Year Plans. According to Marxist theory, the "'from each according to his abilities, to each according to his needs" formula would become viable only in a future, classless, communist society, but it is doubtful whether the fellow-travellers looked forward to such a future with either confidence or enthusiasm. More congenial to them was the solution recommended by Saint-Simon's disciple Bazard, "a state in which all individuals will be classed according to their capacities and remunerated according to their work...." Georges Friedmann noted that Soviet specialists and engineers were now receiving wages five to seven times as great as those of unskilled workers; such workers might earn 350 roubles a month while successful film directors received seven thousand and famous writers ten thousand. That friendly witness, Ambassador Joseph E. Davies, reported to Secretary of State Hull: "The Government itself is a bureaucracy with all the indicia of a class, to wit: special privileges, higher standards of living, and the like...."[31] In a recent novel, Solzhenitsyn describes two of his characters: "They belonged to that circle of society where such a thing as walking or taking the metro is unknown ... where there is never any worry about furnishing a flat.... Not a breath of the sorrow of the world fanned the cheeks of Innokenty and Datoma."[32] Admittedly the spectrum of privilege had shifted its centre of gravity. Charlotte Haldane recalled that when she and J. B. S. Haldane first visited Russia in 1928, "the élite had been the scientists, engineers and skilled factory workers ...", whereas by 1940 "it was tending more and more to be composed of the bureaucrats and the NKVD".[33] But the fellow-travellers had good reason to believe that no breath of material sorrow fanned the cheeks of their professional kith and kin inside Russia. As a fellow-traveller Gide celebrated the equality of *opportunity* prevailing in the USSR; only when he made his break did he wax indignant about high wage differentials. Heinrich Mann could define communism as "a technical means of achieving true common equality among men", but he paused to reflect that "it remains undecided whether nature favours equality".[34] In fact the left-wing middle class has always condemned with fervour the profits exacted by industrialists and shareholders, but has responded in uneasy silence to the equitable proposition that its own earnings should not exceed those of the working class. After all, argues the capitalist, the risks I take and the productive initiatives for which I am responsible deserve their rewards; after all, argues the *savant,* the long years of educational training I have undergone and the high abilities implicit in my professional qualifications deserve their rewards. After all, argue both, where would the workers be without me? And where would I be without proper incentives?

But it was not really wealth which interested the fellow-travellers. Power, social relevance, status and prestige counted for more: to see the workers flocking into the hall when Gorky was due to speak; to watch the populace hurrying from work to the open meetings of the Academy of Science. The Webbs described it: "In the body of the hall the proletariat, fresh from factory, plant, technical school, docks. On to the spacious stage file the academicians amid thunderous applause from the gathering."[35] Now *that* was something.

Part Three: Conflicts

8

The Cold War

Henry Wallace was a native of Iowa, a specialist in the breeding of hybrid corn. In 1932 Roosevelt plucked him from political obscurity and made him Secretary of Agriculture. From 1940 until 1944 he served as Vice-President, but in that year he was narrowly defeated for re-election by Harry Truman at the Democratic Convention (Roosevelt had in fact manoeuvred him out) and so had to step down to become Secretary of Commerce. Two years later, in September 1946, following a speech at Madison Square Garden, he was forced by President Truman to resign. He had become America's leading fellow-traveller among politicians – and perhaps the last two words are superfluous.

Yet the conversion was scarcely predicted in bold strokes on the tablet of his past. In 1935 he had said: "Communism and fascism have a striking similarity . . .", and in April 1941 he had denounced "the communists, the nazis and the defeatists. . . ."[1] He had always been careful to placate business interests. Though his *Sixty Million Jobs* (1945) looked like a manifesto for a second, left-wing New Deal, it also called for a balanced budget, business tax reductions and *no* planned economy. What Wallace wanted was "a people's capitalism". Indeed as Secretary of Commerce he conspicuously appointed conservative businessmen to the top jobs in his department. Though during the 1946 coal strike he advocated public ownership of the industry, the gist of his argument was that as federal employees the workers in vital industries would automatically lose the right to strike.

An official visit to Soviet Asia, at Roosevelt's request, seems to have set him on the fellow-travelling course for which he later became famous, though much of the conservative behaviour already described occurred subsequently. With him as advisers went certain pro-Soviet experts whose interpretations no doubt coloured his own: Owen Lattimore was one, John Carter Vincent, Chief of the Division of Chinese Affairs in the State Department, was another. Lattimore pointed out to Wallace the superior economic development of Soviet border areas, when compared to those on the Chinese side, and the Vice-President was impressed. The Mongolian People's Republic also struck him favourably. Without doubt Wallace was perfectly sincere in his desire to perpetuate good relations between his own country and Russia, and equally without doubt he was bitterly disappointed when Truman reversed the policy which (Wallace and many liberals assumed) Roosevelt would have pursued. But obviously other disappointments sharpened his polemics: had he not been defeated by Truman at the 1944 Convention, he would automatically have become President of the United States the following year.

So he began to denounce Red baiters, yet stressing, in typical fellow-travelling style, that the East is not the West, that Russian solutions had no place in American life. "When you look at Russia, you have to consider the historical background. Compared to what they had under the Czar, the Russian people are well off today.... Of course I'm not a communist, I'm an idealist, the communists are materialists. ... I wouldn't want communism over here, but it makes more sense in Russia."[2] No one ever stated the proposition with greater clarity. Wallace, in fact, was a fellow-travelling radical only in the field of foreign policy, and even after the Progressive Party was formed under his leadership he ignored the socialist convictions of its majority and continued to call for a people's capitalism. But his whole foreign policy stance ran counter to that of the Truman Administration in which he served. In September 1945 he had proposed to a cabinet meeting that the US should reveal its atomic secrets to Russia as a "peace insurance". Frequently he referred to Russia's fear of encirclement, and one fifth of his book, *Toward World Peace,* was devoted to a defence of Soviet foreign policy, as well as to a whitewash of the suppression of the opposition, of the trials and labour camps. In his fateful Madison Square Garden speech, he said that even if Soviet actions in Eastern Europe offended democratic opinion in America, that was nevertheless Russia's sphere of influence and Americans had no business interfering. He was in effect clinging to the spirit of Teheran and Yalta as he interpreted it. Oddly enough Truman had approved this speech in advance* (while the *Daily Worker* reacted to it with hostility), but Secretary of State Byrnes blew his top and made it a resignation issue. Either Wallace went or he went. Wallace went.

Two years later he ran as a Presidential candidate against Truman

* Wallace clearly adjusted parts of the speech he had shown to the President. He omitted a passage which referred to "native communists faithfully following every twist and turn in the Moscow Party line", and another urging the Russians "to stop teaching that their form of communism must... ultimately triumph over democratic capitalism". He also extemporized the words which attributed the threat of war to imperialism rather than communism.

and Dewey. To his cause rallied not only the older generation of fellow-travellers and communists, but also many college students and people who were simply afraid of a new war. At last the American Left had a leader from within the hierarchy of the political establishment. Dwight MacDonald spoke on a number of campuses at this time and discovered that the Wallaceite students did not deny the gruesome facts about the USSR, they simply insisted that America was just as bad and that in any case Soviet reactions were the result of imperialist encirclement. MacDonald was upset: "Stalinoids" were everywhere. Not only had Wallace himself become editor of *The New Republic,* but the paper *PM*, under its editor-in-chief, Ralph McAllister Ingersoll, was also boosting his cause. Nor was the appeal confined to communists and fellow-travellers alone. That impeccably democratic socialist, much the noblest American journalist of the post-war era, I. F. Stone, reasoned to himself in August 1948: I'm for Wallace: because I'm a dupe: if the communists came to power here, I'd be in a concentration camp. But which is the bigger question: the role of the communists in the Progressive Party, or whether there will be another war? Stone decided a vote for Wallace would be a vote for peace. Even so, he was disturbed by the extent of communist influence in the Progressive Party, and complained of "the stultifications and idiocies, the splits and heresy hunts, which make the communists so ludicrous a spectacle half the time".[3] Yet the communists inevitably took on the lion's share of the organizational and propaganda work, and if one had to sup with the devil, long-handled spoons weren't practical. Wallace himself was the first to realize this. Congress's prime fellow-traveller, Vito Marcantonio, was congratulated by him in 1946 for having "the best voting record of all the 435 members. . . ."[4] When MacDonald asked him whether communists should be excluded from the Progressive Citizens' Association, Wallace replied: "Well, I think it would be undemocratic to discriminate against people just because they hold communist beliefs."[5]

Part of his appeal lay in his ability to be different things to different men. Speaking in America, he depicted British imperialism as the evil genius seducing the US into the Cold War, but in the spring of 1947 he got an enormously enthusiastic reception in Britain when he urged the British not to be seduced by the Truman Doctrine. (Because made on foreign soil, this speech provoked an uproar in Congress.) When he moved across to France, it was the *progressistes* grouped round Pierre Cot who organized his itinerary, the result being that he spoke on the same platform as the PCF leaders Thorez, Duclos and Cachin in the Sorbonne. He also addressed the communist-front Union Nationale des Intellectuels, under the chairmanship of Louis Aragon. *But* when he addressed the Paris chapter of the American Veterans' Committee, he took care to criticize communism and lay himself straight down the capitalist line. He was nothing if not an all-American politician.

Naturally the fellow-travellers rolled and rallied. Fresh from a Peace Rally, Hewlett Johnson spent the weekend on the large Wallace farm, later recalling with touching inaccuracy that he had been "a close runner-up for the Presidency" (Wallace got just over one million votes, less than two per cent of the total). Corliss Lamont, Harry Ward and Robert Morss Lovett were in on the movement – no progressive could fail to become a Progressive. But once the 1948 bid had failed dismally, the whole enterprise was doomed as the Cold War approached the trauma of Korea. Increasingly Wallace drew the line between himself and the communists, while promising not to purge them from the Party – if he had, it would have disappeared. But increasingly, too, the figurehead lost the substance of command, and at the 1950 Chicago Convention he could do nothing to prevent the voting down of a perfectly sensible resolution which ran: "it is not our intention to give blanket endorsement to the foreign policy of any nation." That action, that gesture, tells us a good deal about the mentality of the Progressive Party. When the Korean War began, Wallace fell broadly into line with Government policy, and so it was he who had to purge himself. Whereupon he returned to the obscurity from which Roosevelt had plucked him eighteen years earlier.

Returning to Western Europe in the post-war era, we find an old friend, Russia, staunchly cherished, new friends to admire, the Popular Democracies – and a new arch-enemy: the United States. The fellow-travellers unanimously blamed Western policy for the break-up of the wartime alliance and the onset of the Cold War. Chained to their imperialist, anti-bolshevik heritage – so the argument ran – American and British leaders were determined to revive and expand their spheres of influence, while bitterly resenting the new power and dignity acquired by the Soviet Union in the course of her heroic struggle against nazism.

On the French Left, Russia was more than ever idolized: "One morning," recalled Simone de Beauvoir, "I saw in the metro unknown uniforms, decorated with red stars: Russian soldiers. Fabulous presence. Lise, who spoke her native language fluently, tried to chat with them; they asked her in a severe tone what she was doing in France, and her enthusiasm stopped short."[6] A cautionary tale for fellow-travellers in the metro. As for anti-Americanism, it was at first contained by optimism, gratitude and a sense of fraternity: but not for long. In her

novel, *Les Mandarins,* Simone de Beauvoir depicted the American prag-
matist Preston attempting to manipulate the editorial policy of a French
newspaper by supplying scarce newsprint on the black market. Interviewed in May 1948 after being held by immigration officials on Ellis
Island, Irène Joliot-Curie told journalists that America preferred
fascism to communism because it respected the sanctity of money. The
Catholic writer Louis Martin-Chauffier was one of many who accused
the American capitalists, politicians and generals of preparing the way
for war by means of vicious anti-Soviet propaganda. The Atlantic
Pact, he said, turned European soldiers into mercenaries; the Socialist
Parties, like the Labour Government, had finally delivered themselves
into the arms of capitalism. Fellow-travelling scientists like Irène Joliot-
Curie and Aimé Cotton joined their communist colleagues in warning
that they would not put their skills at the service of military aggression,
a threat which alarmed Washington since many of them were members
of the Commissariat à l'Energie Atomique.

The fellow-travellers within, or on the fringes of, the Labour Party
vigorously attacked Ernest Bevin as a lackey of American imperialism.
The Webbs had enough energy between them to denounce Western
policy in Italy, Greece, Turkey and China. Zilliacus, Pritt, Young and
their comrades continually demanded the removal of all American military bases from British soil, Zilliacus accusing the Labour Party officials
at Transport House of trying "to split and ruin European Socialist
Parties" and of making the LP "officially the enemy of the great
majority of the European working class".[7] When in January 1948
Churchill in the House of Commons praised the Attlee Government for
maintaining the broad outlines of his own foreign policy, Zilliacus
eagerly seized on the tribute: "The Foreign Office, like the Mounties,
has the reputation of always getting its man."[8] He meant, of course,
Foreign Secretary Bevin. Indeed the drum-beats of the American military establishment and the recurrent hysteria of the American press
did give legitimate cause for alarm, particularly the October 1951 issue
of *Collier's* magazine which carried the hair-raising caption: "Russia's
Defeat and Occupation 1952–60, Preview of the War We Do Not
Want". Profusely illustrated, mapped and diagrammed, and claiming
the co-operation of high Washington officials, the October issue envisaged a three-and-a-half year war climaxed by a rising of the Soviet
people against Stalin. Soviet casualties were coolly predicted at thirty-
two million dead. But, as Corliss Lamont pointed out, *Collier's* was by no
means the first journal· to offer the scare-crazed American public this
kind of spectacular: in 1948 the *New York Times, Newsweek, Look,
Life* and the *Saturday Evening Post* had all published long articles on

how most effectively to bomb Russia from the air. But it was *Collier's* which made the greatest impact. Arnold Zweig had been in Vienna for the World Peace Congress at the time it appeared; later, in Moscow, he talked over the scandal of it with James Aldridge, Paul Eluard and some Russians, coming to the conclusion that the real operators (*Hintermänner*) of the West had never wanted peace, determined as they were to make good the failure of their armed intervention in Russia in 1918–20. Would, he asked, Master Adenauer's Urals-stormers first come to their senses on the bones of their predecessors?

Russia desired only peace. About this the fellow-travellers were adamant. Argument was widely conducted at this time by means of quotation: the blood-curdling threats of American generals and senators were scrupulously filed (if not always scrupulously used) while *The Times* of London was quoted as frequently "admitting" Russia's desire for peace – the ploy here being that if a "bourgeois" paper "admitted" such a fact then the evidence for it must be irresistible. In fact *The Times*, though an honorary national institution, was neither more nor less than the men who edited it at any given time: while E. H. Carr was in the saddle its bias was distinctly pro-Soviet. Other less famous papers, but ones with which we are already familiar, writhed on the horns of a dilemma, suspecting Soviet intentions only slightly less than they suspected the intentions of the chief suspectors. *Tribune* was such a case. Accused by Zilliacus of criticizing Bevin's anti-Sovietism while quietly pushing its own brand, it was simultaneously berated by Orwell for always finding Bevin wrong even when he did what *Tribune* had advocated a week earlier. Meanwhile Corliss Lamont found the best proof of Stalin's desire for peace to be his professions of peaceful intentions; Arnold Zweig summed up Soviet foreign policy since 1917 in a single word: peace. As for Soviet territorial expansion in Eastern Europe, the same mechanisms of explanation and exoneration now came into play as in 1939–40. The USSR, said Zilliacus, had merely "recovered" territories wrested from her by Allied intervention twenty-five years earlier. Had not France re-expropriated Alsace-Lorraine in 1918, even though its population was predominantly German-speaking? Hewlett Johnson protested that with the exception of one "small item", East Prussia, Russia had taken back only what had been hers at the time of the Revolution, but in any case it didn't matter since "any constituent nation not entirely enclosed in the Soviet Union may secede". But why had the territories been expropriated? "Largely," explained the Dean, "through military necessity." In which case how could they be permitted to secede? Bessarabia, said Lamont, had been "stolen" from Russia in 1918 by Rumania. As for East Prussia, this came under the heading "spoils of victory", and moreover the USSR had a legitimate historical claim to all its new conquests "through the expansion of the Tsarist empire". (One suspects that a British attempt to recapture Eire on the basis of a similar historical claim would have met with less sympathy.)

The dominant attitude was one of guilt and a sense of gratitude to Russia for her immense sacrifices. Clearly the USSR could not tolerate for a second time a ring of hostile states on her borders. And the fellow-travellers were able to ask a very good question indeed: if the Western democracies had watched unperturbed the proliferation of semi-fascist dictatorships in Eastern Europe between the wars, why the cries of rage and horror as soon as communist regimes were established there? A revival of the old Wilsonian idealism? Hardly. Senator Vandenburg and his kind were not seen to have made themselves the champions of Polish democracy during the Pilsudski dictatorship, and the British and American statesmen who sent troops into Greece to rescue it from communism had never contemplated sending troops into Spain to rescue it from Franco. The fellow-travellers were right: the Western passion for freedom was too partial, too inconsistent, to be convincing. On the other hand they themselves were nothing if not blind to the crudescence of Great-Russian chauvinism. So deeply was the Soviet nationalities policy admired, so impressive was that vast plurality of cultures, languages and costumes, so much taken to heart were the folk-dance festivals, so unquestioningly accepted was the concept of cultural autonomy balanced by the advantages of economic union, that it became virtually impossible to recognize the extent to which Stalinist policy revived and exploited the heritage of Great-Russian domination. The Webbs had insisted that "no other area containing an analogous diversity of races and nationalities" could boast of a complete absence of discrimination and of complete equality of opportunity. Needham had singled out this aspect of Soviet life as the greatest achievement of "the genius . . . of Joseph Vissarionovich Stalin". Heinrich Mann had rejoiced that in the sixteen (as then) Soviet Republics the Russian language was merely taught, merely offered, not imposed. Feuchtwanger agreed. But nothing at all was said, or maybe even noticed, of the huge deportations of Crimean Tartars, Poles, Balts, Caucasian nationalities and Meskhetians.

The issue of a divided Germany soon became both the touchstone and flashpoint of the Cold War in the West. There is no disputing the fact that the occupying Western Powers failed to implement the economic measures agreed upon at Potsdam. Zilliacus pointed out that since 1942 the Labour Party had been pledged to nationalize key industries in

Germany, and he quoted (most legitimately) Bevin's statement of November 1946 that "the heart of the General Staff in Germany was the industrial lords of the Ruhr, and the Ruhr must not go back to their possession. . . ."[9] Yet it did. When the socialist majority of the North Rhine Westphalia Parliament called for large-scale nationalization, and the British Military Government subsequently vetoed the project, Zilliacus with apparent justice cited this as further proof of Britain's subservience to the United States. Pritt wanted to know why the Labour Government staffed the vital Control Commission in Germany with non-socialists, anti-socialists and downright capitalists. Young complained about the almost total absence of land reform in the Western zones, whereas the Soviet authorities and the East German Socialist Unity Party (SED) were faithful to the Potsdam policy of extirpating fascism at its economic roots. And when the German Democratic Republic (DDR) was created, he reacted with enthusiasm. In 1951, writing in a Paris newspaper, he described the *Volkspolizei* as democrats, trade unionists and well educated in politics and economics: no honest man had any reason to fear them. As for Russia's draconian reparations policy, it delighted him. Admitting quite candidly in 1955 that Russia had taken away fifty per cent of East German industry and expropriated thirty-two per cent of what remained (the victors of Versailles were obviously a timid lot!), Young concluded: "The ultimate net result of this harsh treatment, however, has been to the advantage of the Germans." Ignoring the workers' rising of June 1953, he explained that the East German grumblers were now confined "very largely to the same kind of rather selfish middle-class people as grumble in Britain. . . ."[10] For years he continued to regard the German and Hungarian people as infected by the disease of fascism, and no Soviet measures taken to eradicate this cancer were too harsh for his taste.

Another Western journalist, the Australian Wilfrid Burchett, believed that the Russians really did want a unified Germany, and attributed the abandonment of Ruhr socialization to American pressure. One of the most colourful, adventurous and intrepid of fellow-travellers (and never a man to seek comfort at home while advocating discomfort at a distance), Burchett was also one of the few to have missed a middle-class upbringing. Self-taught, an avaricious reader and by unstinting effort a competent linguist, when family bankruptcy forced him to leave school prematurely he tried his hand as carpenter, bricklayer, bush-clearer and cow-hand. When the depression hit Australia news also reached him that there was no unemployment in the USSR. Having launched the left-wing Poowong Discussion Club near Melbourne, and having as a cane-cutter experienced at first hand the class struggle on the land, he found his hero, his myth, his model when the famous German "red reporter" Egon Erwin Kisch visited Australia and was subjected to the most ludicrous obstruction by the authorities. In later years Burchett certainly lived up to his hero's example, becoming by hours the first Allied staff reporter to reach Hiroshima after an incredible journey involving a train ride from Tokyo in the company of glowering, humiliated and samurai dagger-carrying Japanese officers – and not an Allied soldier within miles. Earlier it had been the Burma Road; later it was to be the Vietcong jungle trails in Indo-China. It was under the aegis of the Beaverbrook press (which took an almost sadistic delight in hiring radical contributors to its reactionary pages) that he came to Germany, but the mood at the time of the Berlin airlift was so tense that the *Daily Express* was no longer willing to publish his pro-Soviet reports. A colleague, John Peet of Reuters, found the strain so great that he walked across to East Berlin and promptly treated his former colleagues to a press conference. He is still there. Burchett himself later became a "stringer" for *The Times* in Eastern Europe; we shall encounter him again in Korea where he first gained his notoriety.

For the pre-war German fellow-travellers, East Germany generally proved more attractive as a place of return and residence than the West. But not necessarily attractive enough. Admirable as many of the regime's industrial, agricultural and educational reforms were, notably in their dedication to the root and branch destruction of nazism, nevertheless a National Front dominated by a Unity Party controlled by its communist component under the leadership of men like Pieck and Ulbricht was scarcely likely to reassure someone with Mann's unhappy memories of these gentlemen during the Volksfront era. And easy as it might have been for Feuchtwanger to congratulate Soviet writers on their enjoyment of "true" freedom, it was no less easy to reconsider one's enthusiasm when contemplating living and working in a cultural atmosphere dominated by Johannes Becher and the poet Kuba. Becher: Stalin Prize, National Prize (first class), President of the Kulturbund, member of the Central Committee of the SED, Honorary Doctor or Honorary Senator of this university and that, schools named after him, his face in every bookshop window, a power maniac, the prototype, as Alfred Kantorowicz later described him, *"des Quislings am Geist"*. Nor was life with Kuba (Kurt Barthel) an appealing prospect: Secretary of the Writers' Union, member of the People's Chamber, National Prize winner. Quote: "When we let our trousers down in the name of louder self-criticism, holding our behinds up to the enemy, we can't complain when he skins us."[11]

When the DDR was founded in 1949, a joint telegram addressed to Pieck and Grotewohl arrived from Herrn Mann and Feuchtwanger: "We need not assure you with what deep involvement we watch the fate of the young Republic under your leadership."[12] But it remained involvement (*Teilnahme*) at a distance. Though he received his share of literary honours in the DDR, Feuchtwanger no doubt never regretted his decision to stay away; such at least is suggested by the fact that his last act in 1957 was to intervene on behalf of his East Berlin publisher, Walter Janka, who had been condemned to five years' imprisonment as an enemy of the State. For his part, Mann deeply distrusted the Western attitude towards Germany. "Only one fear exists," he wrote to Eva and Julius Lips in March 1945, "that Germany could become 'chaotic' or, to speak more honestly, bolshevik. Therefore it must once again be 'built up', industrialized, and with that Hitler II brought into being."[13] In August 1946 he wrote to Kantorowicz to report that he had three or four times been urged to settle in the Soviet zone, but he foresaw only an intolerable round of public appearances and speeches. The wooing persisted: in May 1947 he was invested in his absence as an Honorary Doctor of Philosophy, Humboldt University, and soon afterwards came the National Prize (first class) as well as the offer of a job: President of the newly founded German Academy of Art in Berlin. But evidently his qualms and suspicions were not easily allayed, for in the same year he again wrote to Kantorowicz saying that reliable witnesses told him that East Germany was characterized by "capriciousness" and "independability", two words which, stripped of their euphemistic wrapping, spell fear. Finally he decided to take the plunge: he would go back. Instead he died. And his brother Thomas noted that not a single word of respect came forth from Bonn, Frankfurt, Munich or the family town of Lubeck.

The one who did return was Arnold Zweig. The son of a food merchant who was ruined when Jews were forbidden to supply the Prussian army, Zweig was born in 1887. He published his first story in 1909. In 1912 there followed *Novellen um Claudia* and in 1914 the drama *Ritualmord in Ungarn* which showed an early preoccupation with the identity problem of the European Jew. In 1915, the year in which he received the Kleist Prize, he volunteered for the army. Having served on the Eastern front and at Verdun – where he was almost blinded – he became a pacifist. From these experiences sprang the "Sergeant Grischa" novels which made his name and which depicted the attempt of a group of German idealists to save just one Russian prisoner from being mistakenly executed, a single act of humanitarianism amidst the holocaust of mass death. Scathingly depicting the German ruling caste, notably Ludendorff, whom he likened to a brightly lit telephone exchange, Zweig took his place within the bourgeois, anti-war, rationalist intellectual family with which we are by now familiar, the family of Rolland, Shaw, Jean-Richard Bloch, Mann and Feuchtwanger.

Like the latter he wrote in the twenties for *Die Weltbühne* and was a close friend of Tucholsky; no less than Rolland, Gorky and Mann was he alienated by the repressive and vindictive aspects of Soviet domestic policy. Joining vigorously in the condemnation of the show trial of the forty-eight Russian specialists, in November 1930 he published an article warning that it was a mistake to treat human beings like ants or bees, and criminal to sacrifice the living masses in the name of a doubtful collectivist theory. To kill individuals in order to save a class was a falsification of the socialist idea: "Every man has the right freely to sacrifice his own life for ideas; but every man has the duty to fight against those who ... squander the life of the masses for aims which were or are worthy of neither life nor death."[14] At that moment in time Mann and Feuchtwanger were in entire agreement with him. None of them subsequently renounced the principle involved, they merely decided that it wasn't involved. In the case of Zweig not even the nazi seizure of power immediately transformed his antipathy for bolshevism into sympathy. In 1934, writing from Palestine whither he had emigrated in 1932, he published his *Bilanz der deutschen Judenheit, 1933*, a work in which he put the Russians, the Poles, the Italians and the Germans in the same bag: "Neither the Soviets, which have been in power for fifteen years, nor yet the fascists, who are now celebrating their tenth anniversary, have produced a vigorous intellectual life."[15] And for Zweig a vigorous intellectual life was the thermometer of social health. Besides, his intense preoccupation with the plight of the Jews inclined him more than ever to prize the quality which the Jews most obviously exemplified – individual brilliance.* The Jew, he believed, had become the authentic proletarian of Europe; even the well-off, right-wing Jews were discovering that medieval barbarism was always lurking round the corner. It was therefore time for all Jews to recognize that only *social democrats* truly and sincerely believed in those liberties, those civil rights, that respect for the individual, upon which their survival depended. His analysis of the history of anti-semitism was preponderantly psychological and only thinly Marxist; he was less concerned with economic factors than with dark collective

* He reminded his readers that Toller, Mehring, Döblin, Werfel, Feuchtwanger, Kraus Kafka, Ernst Weiss, Kisch, Brod, Roth, Schnitzler, Stefan Zweig, Mühsam and Tucholsky were all Jews.

forces of the soul, with "the dethronment of reason and the abdication of intelligence" with which we are also familiar. The incensed, corrupted mob appeared to him as the great enemy, whereas true individuality was "the highest significance of life on earth".

Nevertheless one had to consider who it was who corrupted the furious horde, and he was enough of a Marxist to believe that "so long as the rule of the capitalism of dominant classes continues . . ." so also would exploitation and racism. But socialism of itself would not automatically eradicate racism; an inner, psychological revolution was also needed, one which Marx, with his spurious claims to scientific comprehensiveness, had ignored. Indeed of the masters of modern thought it was not Marx but Freud whom Zweig most admired. In 1929 he launched an exchange of correspondence with the eminent psychoanalyst thirty years his senior, declaring how greatly he had benefitted from psycho-analytical treatment and describing Freud as a thinker of Plato's calibre, a scientist such as mankind had never before produced.

For sixteen years Zweig lived in Haifa, but with muted enthusiasm. Though he regarded the Jewish settlement of Palestine as a necessary step of self-preservation, he was never a zealous Zionist; increasingly the Soviet Union assumed in his mind the leading role in the resistance to nazism. He began in the thirties to associate with the radical humanists who wrote for *Das Wort* and pinned their hopes on a Popular Front of all democratic forces, and although his contributions were mainly literary rather than political in nature, and though his own sources of inspiration continued to emanate from the Enlightenment, one notices that as the years passed his references to Luxemburg, Liebknecht and Lenin became increasingly favourable. He too came to the conclusion that the Western democracies were incapable of defending the heritage they supposedly incarnated. He helped to found the Levant Publishing Company which published anti-fascist literature, predominantly of Soviet origin, in four languages, and he was also active in Liga v whose aim was to mobilize Palestinians in support of the Red Army. (Apparently seven ambulances were dispatched to Russia via Teheran.) After the war Palestine seemed more than ever a backwater and in 1948 he decided to settle in East Germany, convinced as he was that former nazis were prospering in the West; later, the creation of the Bundeswehr in the Federal Republic confirmed his fears.

Honoured as he was by the regime (he became President of the Academy of Art), he could never fully integrate himself with its cultural norms. His sources of literary inspiration remained entombed in the past; his *Die Zeit ist reif*, written in Pankow, was set in 1913. And then, not long after the workers' rising of 1953, he stepped defiantly out of

line with a heterodox speech delivered in Dresden to the Kulturbund:
"We ... must protect our most valuable possession, the young people,
and people in general, from the damaging intrusions of the social
Apparat. It is not only that our language is changing or threatens to
change into gibberish. It is also the case that many ideas no longer
exist which were self-evident to us when we grew up; for example ...
that a person must be capable of cutting himself off or sitting down
alone on a bench to read something, without that leading to a repri-
mand, without him being asked whether it's compatible with some duty
involved in the basic situation of the DDR. ... Humanism and tight
organization have always contradicted one another. The Jesuits themselves ... were less strained in their organization than we in the building
up of the DDR ... don't let our German be turned into a bureaucratic
language, with commands and rhetorical phrases, which brings you into
conflict with your own essence."[16] The publication of this speech was
forbidden, and one editor who did have the temerity to publish it was
so persecuted by the State Security Forces that he fled to the West.
Zweig, having had his say, stayed put, a deputy in the People's Chamber
and, in 1958, the recipient of a Lenin Prize.

Reuters' correspondent John Peet also made his life in East Germany
where he became editor of the English-language *German Democratic
Report*, a role which he still discharges with verve and wit (provided
the target is suitable). Here the journalist fellow-traveller commits himself to the single function for which he is fitted: political propaganda
of a type illustrated by the following themes and headlines which appeared in the *Report* during the period May 1968 to April 1971:

Kiesinger's nazi record; new economic system in the DDR; top Bonn
general 150 per cent nazi; President Lübke's shady war record; the
new DDR Constitution, article by article; SED resolution on Czechoslovakia, 1968; Ulbricht says; details of Bonn's bug-warfare plans;
former nazi judges still working within West German legal profession;
former nazis among West German diplomats working abroad (full list
provided); five Müller babies born on the day the DDR was established, and what has become of them; Ulbricht on this and that; what
is popular reading in the DDR?; Rita, the prize cow, is the first in the
DDR to crash the hundred ton barrier (of milk not of flesh); Walter
Ulbricht has "indicated", "said", "stated"; typical timetable of DDR
nursery school; does the DDR need Women's Lib?; "Must Socialists
be Slim?" by Susanne Statkowa. And so on. The back page of the *Report*,
written by Peet himself, takes a diary form and is full of engaging chat,
answers to readers and amusing reflections on the current development

of the English and American languages. A good many of the allegations about former nazis and neo-nazis in the Federal Republic have been documented with impressive rigour, and it is also possible to learn something about life in the DDR from these pages, though on all essential questions the Party line is rigidly respected, often by means of direct quotation from *Neues Deutschland*. Peet's value as a fellow-traveller lies in his ability to avoid turgid Marxist phrase-mongering, in the freshness of his style, and in his ability to project an image of the DDR as the Germany which all decent men of good sense should support. Having twice met Peet, I wrote asking him some questions about the circumstances of his life and work in the East, to which he replied: "when did *you* last beat your wife?"

Eastern Europe now offered the fellow-travellers a new happy hunting ground. In Hungary the Dean of Canterbury came across a children's home: ". . . it was full of young girls; the airy buildings were on the lake shore . . . and the sun-browned children played in and out of the water."[17] The sun also shone on a galaxy of charming mini-Stalins. In 1947 Johnson met Rákosi at a reception: "So fresh in mind, and so unembittered after fifteen years in gaol."[18] Oddly enough, these words were written twenty-one years later, further proof that the Dean was a Bourbon. Police states? Nonsense. In Rumania he met Patriach Justinian who assured him that "freedom of conscience and freedom of creed are guaranteed by the State".[19] Konni Zilliacus declared challengingly that the US was a police state for its coloured population (true), that Ulster had been a police state for a quarter of a century (true), and that the police in Eastern Europe directed their attentions solely against the old ruling classes, the enemies of the people (untrue). In Zilliacus's opinion, if post-war democracy had crumbled in the East, then the communists were not to blame. He accused Bevin of backing right-wing Polish émigrés when he demanded an election in Poland even before a constitution had been adopted and while forty thousand terrorists were still fighting the Coalition Government because it was friendly towards the USSR. Hilary Minc, Minister of Industry, had assured Zilliacus in Warsaw that democracy would be preserved, but by 1948 "Anglo-American intervention had changed all that". Naturally the tougher communist elements then took over, it was only to be expected, but their toughness caused him no sleepless nights.

The argument about the nature of genuine democracy was now revived: in 1948 Irène Joliot-Curie told New York reporters that the shift to communism in Eastern Europe was the result of a "democratic process". Edgar Young adopted the cause of the Popular Democracies with so much fervour that his articles began to appear in the pro-communist press of Czechoslovakia, Bulgaria and Hungary, one consequence being that Bevin instructed British legations and consulates in the area to afford him no assistance. "Why be Unjust to Bulgaria?" Young asked in April 1947 – in other words, why claim that the recent election there violated the spirit of Yalta? As an eye-witness to the election, he himself had seen no evidence of terror or intimidation (in fact twenty-four electoral agents of the Agrarian Party had been assassinated, while opposition leaders had been condemned by military tribunal on the eve of the election). As for the new Fatherland Front which dominated the Bulgarian scene, "I have never met leaders more, ... deserving of the popular love and confidence which they undoubtedly enjoy",[20] he declared on the BBC Overseas Service. Except perhaps in Rumania. When Ion Mihalache, vice-president of the National Peasant Party, was arrested in July 1947, Young explained that Mihalache had been preparing to fly illegally to rejoin the "Green International", the State Department's pet counter-revolutionary project. The Rumanian Peasant Party was presently dissolved by force, though it had received 872,972 votes in 1946, an act of repression vindicated by Young on the ground that not one genuine peasant was included among its parliamentary deputies. (Would the former naval commander, if elected to Parliament as a Labour MP, have been transformed into a proletarian?) In time Young was to become chairman of the British-Rumanian Friendship Association.

But not before he had justified the communist coup which ended Czechoslovak democracy in February 1948. When one considers the outcry raised among fellow-travellers after Stalin launched his attacks on Tito, the response to the Czechoslovak coup appears surprisingly mild and docile. The action of fellow-travelling socialist leaders like Fierlinger in delivering themselves permanently into the hands of the communists was endorsed by Zilliacus as "closing the ranks". The coup itself he described as "a bloodless semi-revolution carried out in constitutional forms".[21] While admitting that civil liberties had subsequently diminished, he felt this was more than atoned for by the new energy in construction; tales about terror and a police state were "ludicrous". Corliss Lamont regretted that the Czechoslovak CP had taken "such drastic action" but insisted that the new Government "could not have been successfully established unless the internal situation ... favoured it",[22] a remark which reduced political analysis to tautology and which could be applied with equal justice to Hitler's seizure of power. Anyway, said Lamont, the CPs had led the anti-nazi struggle in Eastern Europe and could not be blamed for turning "their new-won power to political advantage". Meanwhile Young celebrated the eclipse of that Czechoslovak democracy which he had so vigorously defended at the time of Munich. As early as 1945 he approached his old friend Cripps, now President of the Board of Trade, with a plea that Britain should extend generous credit terms for trade with Czechoslovakia, but Cripps deflected this approach to an official, who gave Young no joy. When the coup itself came, Young called it no coup, even though Beneš, whom he so admired, obviously accepted it with a sick heart and resigned as President four months later. What had really happened? On 12 February a majority of the coalition cabinet in Prague ordered the communist Minister of the Interior, Nosek, to stop packing the police with communists; when Nosek, backed by Gottwald, ignored this instruction, a number of ministers resigned on 21 February. Young did not deny that Nosek had done this: on the contrary, "the transformation of a country from capitalism to socialism involves the necessity radical changes in the character and personnel of the police...." Western democrats, he insisted, should thank the Czechoslovak CP for having preserved the old State against the violent passions of the workers (which in fact the CP had whipped up by means of action committees and demonstrations). Gottwald had saved constitutional democracy and Beneš fully approved, as did "that other courageous individualist and staunch democrat, Mr Jan Masaryk".[23] Events were soon to belie these propositions: Beneš resigned, constitutional democracy disappeared and Masaryk committed suicide. Yet Young remained unabashed. Masaryk, he explained, suffered from ill-health and insomnia. As for the new Constitution, all the democratic liberties were guaranteed and the judiciary remained secure in its independence; the fact that all the "official" parties henceforward appeared without distinguishable labels on a single electoral list to which there was no opposition, in no way detracted from his enthusiasm for the new democracy. Why was there no opposition? Terror? Certainly not. The general public would simply no longer tolerate the enemies of socialism. (Obviously the Government, in Brecht's famous phrase, had elected a new people since the coup.) Two years later Young reflected contentedly in the *Daily Worker*: "Thus Czechoslovak democracy was saved from the 'democrats' by the communists and those who accepted their leadership."[24] It is indeed worth remembering how instrumental were the "Youngs" of Eastern Europe in obliterating the democratic socialist heritage and in fostering the shot-gun weddings which invariably worked to the permanent advantage of the communists. These rites were performed in Czechoslovakia (April 1948), Hungary (June 1948), Poland (December 1948) and Bulgaria (the same month). When recalcitrant socialist leaders like

Kelemen, Puzak, Petrescu and Pastukhov were arrested, no murmur of protest was heard from their former colleagues; nor, of course, from people like Young.

For many fellow-travellers the emergence of the Soviet-Yugoslav conflict presented an agonizing dilemma, but not for him. In January 1947, after a visit to Yugoslavia, he eulogized the genuine democracy prevailing there. But six years later, speaking on behalf of the mothers of airmen everywhere, he complained: "The Meteor crash at Duxford is the second fatal air accident which has occurred in showing off to Tito. Surely it is absurd to go on risking our airmen's lives in the hopes of persuading a bankrupt to buy jet aircraft from us and paying for them with money which we borrow from the Yanks to lend him."[25] (Sic.) Yet though the Western communists accepted with well-drilled discipline the new image of Tito as a lifelong agent of the Gestapo, the whole volte-face was too abrupt for the taste of many fellow-travellers. Zilliacus rebelled, but it was in France that massive resistance developed. Jean Cassou called Tito "a moment of the human conscience", thereby provoking the Party hatchetman André Wurmser to remind him that Tito was really "the vilest agent of American strategy and espionage".[26] As a result of their Titoist sympathies both Cassou and J-M. Domenach were forced out of the Peace Movement. Sartre was not alone in welcoming the prospect of a genuinely neutral socialist "third force" pioneered by Yugoslavia, and when Simone de Beauvoir paid her first visit to a communist country in the fifties, it was to Yugoslavia. "For the first time in my life I did not see opulence side by side with poverty" – and the people themselves impressed her as friendly and courteous but never obsequious. Indeed the trials and executions in Eastern Europe made an unhappy impression on both her and Sartre, as did the behaviour of the French *"sympathisants à tout prix"* who justified everything on the ground that *il faut bien croire à quelque chose.* One of them told her: "The communists can kick me in the neck as often as they like: they won't discourage me."[27] Another whose uneasiness gained ground was Martin-Chauffier: why, he demanded to know, had the communist leaders suddenly discovered in 1948 that Tito had worked for the Gestapo since 1936? Vercors shared his curiosity, while Aveline pointed to the whole affair as one more example of the attempted suppression of national independence by Russian chauvinism. If Tito was an American puppet, asked Cassou, why did Yugoslavia vote for the admission of communist China to the UN and refuse to ally with the Western bloc over Korea? Aveline returned from a trip to Yugoslavia and reported having witnessed a true socialism built "with a courage and a maturity of spirit perhaps unique in the world".[28]

Obviously Tito's appeal for these Frenchmen had a lot to do with their own resentment of Great Power domination in its American form, but one also notices that they themselves soon succumbed by inversion to the communist logic that any opponent of Stalin was inevitably an opponent of Stalinism – they tolerated both the cult of Tito and the rigorous suppression of dissent within Yugoslavia with apparent equanimity.

By the time a new wave of political trials struck the communist *imperium* in the late forties, the French fellow-travellers were in a markedly less tolerant mood than in the late thirties. The glaring inconsistencies in Rajk's faked confession, though vehemently denied by the communist intellectuals, were painfully obvious. "Each new trial," wrote Aveline, "in copying with too much servility the preceding ones, only further persuades free minds that the communist church is no more than an Inquisition."[29] To Cassou it all seemed like a bad dream; he interpreted the trials as sinister fables. Vercors, who had swallowed the Moscow trials, could take no more (something which happened to him time and again; but, like Donald Duck, he invariably emerged from the pond bone dry). Edith Thomas, for some years a fellow-traveller until she joined the Party in 1943, quit its ranks in disgust. In her view the only operative factor was Russia's unquenchable thirst for domination. *L'Humanité* responded with the usual personal abuse. Meanwhile, across the Channel, D. N. Pritt, resolute as ever, doubted nothing, though Zilliacus lay low over the whole issue. The execution of the Bulgarian opposition leader Petkov had met with his approval, but when the Party leadership decimated its own ranks he began to hesitate. Then in 1952 came the Slansky trial in Prague, in the course of which fourteen leading communists, eleven of them Jews, were accused of Zionist espionage and sabotage. Slansky and ten others were subsequently executed. Young leapt into the fray with news of "cases of treachery in high places. . . ." The facts, he asserted, "can be established beyond question". How? One need only believe the case so persuasively made out by the prosecution. For readers of the *Pakistan Times* (3 December 1952), Young had a scoop of his own to offer, a most elaborate rigmarole story of Gestapo files, buried boxes, American blackmail and clandestine comings and goings across the Czech border.

That Moscow had launched a concerted anti-semitic campaign was obvious. In 1949 nearly all Yiddish publications as well as the Yiddish theatre in Moscow had been closed down, and three years later the majority of Yiddish cultural leaders were shot after a wave of mass arrests. Finding himself suddenly unpublishable, Ehrenburg expected every night the front door bell to ring. "These symptoms were familiar. ..." But not, however, to many kindred spirits in the West; they never grasped the symptoms and never feared the front door bell. For just as the Soviet Union was famous for its enlightened nationalities policy, so too was it renowned for its abhorrence of anti-semitism. Feuchtwanger had joyfully reported in 1937 how successfully the USSR had assimilated its five million Jews, placing at the disposal of others the vast, autonomous territory of Birobidjan. All those he had met were "deeply grateful for the new order", for instead of pogroms they now lived under a regime which valued Yiddish no less than the other national languages. Had not Stalin himself told him, man to man, how highly he esteemed the Jews? He had indeed – but in a curious fashion. "You Jews," Stalin remarked, "have created one eternally true legend – that of Judas." But the Germans refused to see the blood on the Temple wall: "It was strange to hear a man, otherwise so sober and logical, utter these simple, emotional words."[30] What was strange was that Arnold Zweig, for example, could indignantly protest against the despoliation of a Jewish cemetery in the Federal Republic, yet say nothing about the campaign of persecution raging in the Soviet bloc between 1949 and 1952, nor comment upon the circumstances which drove the chairmen of the Jewish communities of Leipzig, Dresden, Erfurt and other centres to leave the DDR. What was strange was that, in the face of all this, Lamont should have declared not only that anti-semitism had long since "disappeared" in Russia but also that Jews as a race enjoyed greater democratic rights in the USSR than in any country except Israel. Yet today Soviet Jews in their tens of thousands are hammering on the doors of the emigration offices while their brethren in the West show no comparable enthusiasm for mass exodus. But here again the French fellow-travellers showed the most sensitivity to the facts. When Serge Groussard submitted to the Comité National des Ecrivains a motion condemning Soviet anti-semitism, the communist majority naturally rejected it, the consequence being that Aveline, Martin-Chauffier, Vildrac, R. Laporte and P. Bost, all friendly towards communism in their time, resigned.

In the post-war period the international communist movement took up with new energy the work left in abeyance when Willi Münzenberg was found swinging from a French tree: the harnessing of fellow-travelling support in the West through front-organizations. Of the new fronts operating on an international scale, among the most important were the Women's International Democratic Federation, founded in Paris in December 1945, the World Federation of Scientific Workers, of which Irène Joliot-Curie became president in 1953, and the World

Federation of Democratic Youth. Founded in 1945, the Federation at first claimed to be non-political, but by 1949 it was in overt rivalry with the non-communist World Association of Youth. In 1951 the Federation's secretariat was moved to Budapest. The International Union of Students (secretariat, Prague) also lost in time its non-communist national affiliates, and it increasingly collaborated on particular projects with the Federation of Youth – as in the case of the Youth and Student Festival held in Warsaw in 1955. Every penetrable profession or vocational group was penetrated: in America the National Lawyers Guild acted as a counterpart to the French Comité National des Juristes, and in 1955 D. N. Pritt was elected president of the International Association of Democratic Lawyers, in a sense the successor to the old International Juridical Association. While such organizations often sported a fellow-travelling president, the engine-room work was performed by the general secretary who was in nine cases out of ten a communist: thus while Pritt was president of the Democratic Lawyers the secretariat was controlled by the communist jurist Maître Joe Nordmann.

Obviously the broad-based or patriotic titles were preferred to blatantly partisan ones: for example in France the old Jeunesses communistes were replaced after the war by the Union de la Jeunesse républicaine. At the same time the emergence of the Popular Democracies signalled the proliferation of new "friendship associations"; in France these included the Organisations de Rapprochement avec les Pays démocratiques, France-URSS and France-Vietnam. In America, the National Council of American-Soviet Friendship campaigned under the leadership of Rockwell Kent and Corliss Lamont, its press organ being *Soviet Russia Today* (after 1951 *New World Review*), edited by Jessica Smith. Lamont also acted as a sponsor of the Cultural and Scientific Conference for World Peace which was convened in style at the Waldorf Astoria in 1949. The Friends of American-Soviet Unity could count on the support of distinguished politicians or former politicians like Henry Wallace and Joseph Davies, while the Dean of Canterbury was always a welcome guest. Naturally all of these organizations were soon to figure prominently on the Attorney General's list, as did the Civil Rights Congress, founded in 1946 out of a merger of the old International Labor Defense and the National Federation of Constitutional Liberties. Vito Marcantonio, Lee Pressman and Harry Ward were prominent among its supporters. The witch-hunts themselves prompted the establishment in 1951 of the Emergency Civil Liberties Committee, which of course promptly assumed its own place on the Attorney General's list. Ten years later another defence organization was set up, the National Association for Democratic Rights, with Kent to the fore alongside communists like W. E. B. Du Bois and Benjamin Davis.

But what could not be done in the climate of the Cold War was to establish any viable successor to such immensely prestigious fronts as the League of American Writers. In this respect the French communists, benefiting from a much more favourable domestic climate (or one in which the opposing forces were more evenly balanced), had a notable success with the Comité National des Ecrivains (CNE), originally a Resistance grouping but increasingly a rallying point for the pro-communist intellectual Left. In the first months after the war the CNE took the initiative in pursuing collaborationist writers, presses and publishers, but soon the rapidly shifting climate of opinion drove it on to the defensive. Normally a fellow-traveller was appointed president. Cassou, Martin-Chauffier and Vercors succeeded one another. Only in the post-Hungary crisis of 1956–7 was the Party forced to show its hand to the extent of appointing Aragon himself to the post. The CNE organized "Battles of the Book" throughout France; not only celebrated writers and artists like Eluard and Picasso made public appearances, but so also did show business personalities such as Yves Montand and Simone Signoret. In 1954 l'Humanité claimed record sales amounting to about £8,000 worth of books.*

But far and away the most notable success scored by international communism in the field of propaganda was its virtual expropriation of the word "peace" as interpreted by the World Peace Movement. And though the Movement was guided by an efficient organizational nucleus, it soon achieved the status of a world crusade, a harnessed climate of global opinion. Over-all direction of this super-front was invested in a Council which in 1955 had 417 seats (only seventy-seven of them filled by representatives from communist countries) and a "governing body" called the Executive Bureau which contained fifty members. On this Bureau sat representatives of all the main international front-organizations, the women, the scientists, the lawyers and, of course, the trade unionists. In 1954 Joliot-Curie became president and Laffitte, also a communist, general secretary.

When the World Congress for Peace met at Wroclaw in Poland in August 1948, by far the strongest and most distinguished Western contingent was the French one. The Russian delegation, which included the redoubtable Fadeyev, the painter Gerassimov and the inevitable

---

* Equally important were new journalistic ventures such as *Libération*, a daily paper with a definitely fellow-travelling orientation. Party journals heavily employing fellow-travellers both as contributors and editors included *France Nouvelle, Défense de la Paix* and *Horizons,* directed by the "*progressiste*" Pierre Cot.

Ehrenburg, was in an uncompromising mood, causing the milder Western spirits to blench and quail by their fiery metaphors of denunciation. Ehrenburg, whose function was apparently to reassure the intimidated or alienated that Fadeyev's life was a strained one but that he was an honest fellow at heart, was approached by the bewildered old French philosopher Julien Benda, who complained to him: "But I don't understand anything any longer. Tell me, what became of Babel, of Koltsov? When I ask I get no answers. One of your comrades in his speech referred to Sartre and O'Neill as 'jackals'. Is that fair or, to put it at its lowest, wise? And why do we have to clap every time Stalin's name is mentioned? I'm against war. I'm against the policy of the USA. I'm all in favour of co-operation, but what I'm being asked to do is to swear allegiance. I'm seventy-eight, you know – a bit too old for an elementary school."[31] Benda was in fact eighty-one, a minor error we can attribute not to his own but to Ehrenburg's memory, but the mistake reminds us that Benda's words are here paraphrased after a passage of time. A Parisian Jew and a Cartesian rationalist, his name had been made in the late twenties when he published *La Trahison des Clercs*. Although this book was often construed as an indictment of political commitment as such, a closer examination shows that his strictures were mainly directed against those who abandoned universal values for the narrow yet sacred egoisms of nationalism. The subsequent history of Benda as a political animal is a familiar one – another heir to the Enlightenment pushed increasingly far to the Left by the rise of nazism and the failure of the democracies to evolve an adequate response. Incensed by Italy's attack on Abyssinia, he found himself expressing his indignation through the columns of *l'Humanité* and *Commune,* and when he discovered that the communists were in the vanguard of the anti-fascist movement within France, a lifetime of logical training dictated that he accepted the facts as they were. But Marxism never captivated him, and neither temperament nor ambition inclined him to assume a national role as prominent as that of Rolland, Gide and Langevin. In October 1947 he explained that though he had little time for communist doctrines, he harboured a good deal of sympathy for communist actions. Possibly the Party did, as was widely feared, pose a threat to liberty – but if so it was in order that everyone might have bread, not on behalf of the satraps of money. But: *"Je garde le droit de les juger. Je garde mon esprit."*[32] Obviously the judgment he formed of the regimented virulence displayed at Wroclaw was an unfavourable one, but he was not inclined to express his misgivings publicly.

When in 1949 a second congress met in Prague and Paris, two

thousand delegates were present, including a brilliant galaxy of artists, writers and intellectuals.* The peace campaign was already canvassing universities, professional bodies and women's organizations for support: 550 million signatures were claimed. Ehrenburg in later years protested that it was by no means a communist congress: could the ex-President of Mexico, the Queen Dowager of the Belgians, Heinrich Mann, Matisse, Chagall and Chaplin be called communists? Of course not; but who is fooled? Also present were leading politicians of the pro-communist Left, notably Pietro Nenni and Konni Zilliacus. The Stalin Peace Prizes first introduced in 1949 were of course frequently awarded to non-communists. "Peace" was the word. But "peace" had a specific thrust, as every congress made clear: it meant à bas the Marshall Plan, the Atlantic Alliance, Western rearmament and the new West German State. It meant à bas the American bomb – but not the Soviet bomb. So when Pablo Picasso explained his commitment to the Peace Movement – "I stand for life against death; I stand for peace against war" – he could perhaps be accused of simplifying if not his own aims at least those of the Movement. When he uttered these words the great painter had reached Sheffield to find the Peace Congress due to be held there completely sabotaged by the Labour Government's last-minute decision to turn back a majority of foreign delegates at the ports of entry. The Congress retired at once to Warsaw where there was some compensation for Picasso, a peace prize.

"Then a miracle happened: the appeal which we had worked out in the basement room of that Stockholm restaurant circled the world."[33] Thus, Ilya Ehrenburg. It was certainly consistent with his life-style to launch peace from a café, but the miracle may have had something to do with the fact that these obscure, coffee-sipping partisans were supported by the propaganda machinery of the entire communist movement as well as a highly efficient secretariat located in Prague. The Stockholm Appeal did indeed gather millions of signatures throughout the world. By 1954 the propaganda magazine called in France *Défense de la Paix*, directed by Pierre Cot, was appearing in thirteen languages. Here again the sympathy of fellow-travellers was heavily exploited. A writer like Vercors, for example, was permitted to express reservations about the Party line on, say, Korea, so long as he compensated by associating Soviet foreign policy in general with peace and Western policy with war. This simple dichotomy was tirelessly emphasized by the most active French fellow-traveller within the Peace Movement, Yves Farge. Publicist, amateur painter and the author of a book about Giotto, Farge had

* Including Fast, Laxness, Aragon, Anna Seghers, Zweig, Guillen, Alberti, Neruda, Andric and O'Casey.

emerged at the time of the Popular Front as a champion of the miners. At one time a member of the SFIO, and a leader of the Resistance, he was later dispatched by Foreign Minister Bidault to represent France at the second A-bomb test. Meanwhile he wrote a play, organized the Combattants de la Liberté, a forerunner of the Peace Movement, and in 1946 became briefly Minister of Food, in which capacity he apparently fought a hopeless battle against speculators and black marketeers. Farge had already survived Greece, Korea and China when in 1952 he was killed driving from Gori to Tbilisi in a chauffeur-driven car. The rumour went about that this had been no accident. But in fact the car had hit a stationary lorry and his wife, who was with him, emerged unscathed, which makes the insinuation look extremely improbable.

Hither and thither travelled the partisans of peace. The Dean of Canterbury in festive mood took his children to greet a Peace Ship at Margate, following its epic journey from London. But less festive was the journey undertaken by Monica Felton with other peace-loving women to Korea. A former member of the London County Council town planning committee and then chairman of Stevenage New Town (until her return from Korea, that is), Mrs Felton recalled how she prepared for her investigation of American war crimes by buying two smart dresses. When she arrived at the airport a friend of hers proved to be no friend at all by remarking: "Well, at least ... you don't look like a fellow-traveller."[34] Visiting a Prague school *en route*, she was asked by the pupils to convey their good wishes to the children of Korea, a ritual incantation which impressed her: "I smiled wryly, making the inevitable comparison between the lively, critical, indoctrinated kids and the docile blankness of English girls. I knew whose minds are being kept antiseptically free from the injection of any contemporary ideas."[35] Then in Moscow Mrs Felton came upon the Soviet members of her delegation, and here the first dissensions arose. She wanted to visit South Korea as well as the North: but this was rejected as ridiculous. Then she refused to sign anything in advance: if this was really a fact-finding tour, let the facts first be found. Finally she bravely stood up to the Soviet and Chinese ladies by objecting to the anti-Western statements which were being issued in the name of the delegation before they had even arrived in Korea. Most of the non-communist women agreed with her, but were too timid to raise their voices – a scenario which illuminates the relationship of communists to fellow-travellers (except the most eminent) within front-organizations. But after the rift embraces followed, though Mrs Felton frankly was averse to being hugged by members of her own sex.

To discuss the intrinsic validity of the Peace Movement would entail a discussion of the whole range of international relations beyond the scope of the present study. But its appeal, both in terms of scale and intensity, is beyond doubt. Had it not been for its nagging attraction, such fellow-travellers as Martin-Chauffier, Benda and Vildrac would long since have broken definitely with all things communist. And when Sartre entered upon his four-year *rapprochement* with the Soviet Union and the PCF (1952–6), the initial appeal of the Peace Movement for him was by no means a negligible factor. In 1952 he addressed the Vienna congress and was heard respectfully by his erstwhile revilers; he even refused a Vienna theatre permission to stage his own play, *Les Mains Sales,* in case it should be interpreted as Cold War propaganda. Returning to France, he declared: "What I have seen in Vienna is peace." So now, under the umbrella of peace, the "jackal" Sartre and the communist politician Duclos could be seen exchanging smiles on the platform of the Vel' d'Hiv' (*"piquant"*, Simone de Beauvoir called it), and the sad, time-worn eyes of Russia's leading fellow-traveller Ilya Ehrenburg would henceforth focus appreciatively on the brightest star of the French literary Left as once, twenty years earlier, they had settled on André Malraux.

Of Soviet communism, Ehrenburg knew more than any other living fellow-traveller. Unlike his Western colleagues he lived and worked mildly dazed by the miracle of his own survival, permanently anchored to the original sin of his bourgeois background and recalling with faint surprise the time when, at the age of fifteen (in 1906), he had first engaged in clandestine political activity on behalf of the bolsheviks. But his true love had been art or, rather, the arts, and it was this passion which carried him westwards to Vienna where, discovering that he loved the decadents, he abandoned political activity. When the Bolshevik Revolution took place he was still living in the West. At first he did not recognize that this was what he had been fighting for ten years earlier – probably it wasn't. Yet he returned to Russia, curious and timid, only to be informed by a lieutenant at a police station that the Red Army didn't need him, it already had more than its share of windbags. If such an insult hurt very little, Mayakovsky's description of him as "a frightened intellectual" was more wounding. He was not happy; he searched for his idol Alexander Blok but without success; "I searched for a hundred different truths and bewailed a world which had never been mine".[36] At the height of the Civil War he found himself in Kiev: "Sometimes I felt as if I were watching a film and could not understand who was whom. . . ."[37] Later he came into contact with the great director Meyerhold who decided that Ehrenburg's recent experience in supervising the aesthetic education of handicapped children qualified him to take charge of Russia's children's theatre.

And then, when the Civil War was over, he had had enough. He went abroad on a Soviet passport: few Soviet citizens can have left the USSR more frequently than Ehrenburg. His first novel was published in Moscow much to the indignation of *Rote Fahne,* which described it as disgusting. Weighed down by the doubts of the old Russian intelligentsia, he moved from one project to another, editing a journal in collaboration with the artist Lissitzky, whose "formalism" made his work unacceptable in Russia, visiting the poet Nezval in Prague, travelling to Italy to find Gorky, harassed by the police of countries which still declined to recognize a Soviet passport. But after 1924 it became possible to settle in Paris, his first love among cities, and there he happily passed his days in the streets and cafés, talking and writing. Paris was to be the scene of many delights and adventures: it was there that ten years later the poet André Breton slapped his face after he had published a book describing the surrealists as pederasts endlessly pursuing their own dreams. It was an *acte* not entirely *gratuit.* Garrulous, inquisitive and sociable, Ehrenburg lived in perennial conflict with his own innate laziness. For him travel was a drug. Meeting famous artists was another. He knew Durtain, Duhamel and Vildrac well, and he used to discuss with Bloch whether the Bolshevik Revolution could be reconciled with Nietzsche and Tolstoy – which was Bloch's temporary hang-up, not his own.

His own concerned the increasing intolerance displayed by the Soviet regime towards the futurist and modernist art he personally admired. Many of the treasures of modern art were secreted away in Soviet museums behind locked doors: "You cannot abolish a link in a chain," he complained. His own style as a writer actually owed less to Parisian influences than to American ones; though he revered Babel's work, he borrowed the staccato disharmonies of short sentences and rapidly shifting scenes from the novels of Hemingway and Dos Passos, but that won him no approval at home. When in 1924 he visited Kiev to see a stage adaptation of his *Julio Jurenito,* he found himself depicted on the stage with an American "Mr Cool" astride his shoulders shouting, "Faster, faster, my bourgeois steed!" (Yet apparently Lenin liked the novel.) Striving to reform himself, to quench the "doubting Thomas" within, he travelled in 1932 through the USSR to observe the new contruction work, finally producing what he considered to be a committed novel, *The Second Day.* The Soviet press damned it as "negative", and one critic wrote in the *Literary Gazette:* "the people are lost in the chaos of the new construction, they have lost their way among the ditches, excavators, the cranes."³⁸ Ehrenburg kept trying. In 1934 he visited a lumber camp near Archangel in search of virtuous inspiration, but his heart sagged when he heard Tairov, Meyerhold and Eisenstein condemned for formalism and when he saw writers like Alexei Tolstoy recanting their errors at public meetings. Believing as he did in progress, in Soviet progress, but not in phoney or manipulated optimism, he himself received his share of abuse: "a candidate for the title of the Russian Spengler" was one such offering. The *Shorter Soviet Encyclopaedia* described him as an exponent of "the neo-bourgeois wing of literature" lacking faith in the capacity of scientific socialism to change the biological nature of man.

But his knowledge of foreign languages had its uses and in the thirties he worked as a foreign correspondent for *Izvestia,* first in France and then in Spain. How often he must have hesitated before embarking on the return journey! He later reflected in 1961 that of the seven hundred who, like himself, had attended the first Writers' Congress in 1934, only about fifty had survived. Returning to Moscow in 1937, he visited the *Izvestia* building: "I could not see a single familiar face." Two old friends, Meyerhold and Pasternak, assured him that Stalin would soon end the purges if only someone would tell him about them.

After the German occupation of Paris, Ehrenburg left the city with the Soviet embassy staff. Returning to Russia, he wrote the novel, *The Fall of Paris,* and became chief correspondent of the army newspaper, *Red Star.* But he soon discovered that it was impossible to publish anything critical of Germany or nazism. Then Stalin telephoned him one day to say that he liked the second part of the novel and would "try" to get the third part published despite its anti-fascist passages. This modest intervention succeeded. Undoubtedly Ehrenburg was a first-class journalist; during the war few writers were more popular with the men of the Red Army.

In 1947 he visited the USA. The Cold War atmosphere struck him like Breton's blow in the face; also, as an old European, he could not stomach the hectic, brittle culture of the New World – the other hostile New World. He took temporary respite in the garden of Einstein's house in Princeton. The physicist wanted to know what Stalin was really like. "Of course," he said, "I'm not a Marxist." Later, visiting Henry Wallace's farm, Ehrenburg found the Presidential candidate cultivating Russian strawberries. Back in Russia the censors were once again cutting chunks from his books and by 1947 he had reason to fear that the purges were going to stage a repeat performance. For Jews things looked particularly bad. *Einigkeit* was dissolved along with the Jewish Anti-Fascist Committee, though it was a communist not a Zionist paper and its only crime was to publish in Yiddish. As the campaign against "rootless cosmopolitans" spread, Ehrenburg had good reason to reflect, who more rootless and cosmopolitan than I? Attempting to save himself, he published an article in *Pravda* attacking Zionism and discounting a genuine common bond between the Jews of different countries. It was now that he waited every night for the front door bell to ring. Finally, desperate, he wrote to Stalin. Silence. Then one day Malenkov telephoned him in a tone of utter innocence: apparently accounts of anti-semitic discrimination had just been brought to his notice. Once again Ehrenburg had survived. But he still found it difficult to accommodate to the prevailing chauvinism, to the critics who complained that his novels portrayed Frenchmen as superior to Russians, to those who accused him of excessive subjectivity and to those who accused him of excessive objectivity.

Once again he travelled, an ambassador at large, an inevitable presence at every international front meeting and peace congress: "Trains shrieking through the night, rough, pitted roads ... confidences at wayside halts, unfinished conversation...."[39] His friends abroad included all the stars of the intellectual Left: Joliot-Curie and Bernal, Renato Guttuso and Carlo Levi, Aragon and Sartre. And when Togliatti talked to him about the film *Bicycle Thieves*, Ehrenburg briefly tanned himself under the warm cultural sun of Italian communism. So much time did he spend in congresses and committees, he later reflected, that he had scarcely any left over for his own "professional work": but the distinction is obscure.

He was, of course, never a Party member. But in 1950 he was elected a deputy to the Soviet of Nationalities by one of the Riga districts, and in 1951 to the Supreme Soviet of the RSFSR by the town of Engels.

Why was Ehrenburg so disliked and despised in the West? "Western journalists ... accuse me of tendentiousness, of subjecting truth to narrow ideology and even to directives from higher up."[40] Orwell, implying that he did it all for money, called him a literary prostitute. He was, perhaps of necessity, a trimmer. Nor could he be accorded a fanatic's licence. Over Trotsky, he ran with the pack. Even in his later memoirs he criticizes only what has been officially criticized. Referring, for example, to "the events in Berlin" of 1953, he quickly adds: "I do not intend to go into the German situation.... But I must recall the Rosenbergs' execution."[41] Even at the end of his life he could never be quite sure ... liberal thaws were invariably pursued by conservative reactions. At the Twenty-second Congress of the CPSU in 1961, when the early volumes of his memoirs had already appeared, Vsevolod

Kochetov lashed out at "morose compilers of memoirs who look to the past ... and ... rake around the rubbish dump of their very fuddled memories in order to drag out into the light of day moldering literary corpses...."[42] One could never be quite sure. After a period in favour, he suddenly found Khrushchev and his aide Leonid Ilyichev abusing him with anti-semitic remarks. Both his nature and a lifetime's experience inclined him to bend slightly with the wind. The style in which he lived exacerbated suspicions both in Russia and the West. He passed his last years in a comfortable flat in Gorky Street surrounded by the trophies of many expeditions, by paintings worth perhaps a million pounds – early Chagalls, Modiglianis, Légers, Matisse drawings, half a dozen Picassos. For lunch, Alexander Werth recalls, there was iced Chablis and blue Gauloises. Ehrenburg had once proudly brought home from Normandy the recipe for authentic Camembert, but after a Moscow dairy boldly went ahead with the project of producing it locally the city's newspapers were flooded with letters of complaint.

It is very far from true that Ehrenburg was a man lacking courage. Let those who have lived in security, protected by the rule of law, hesitate to judge him. In his speech to the first Congress of Soviet Writers he boldly complained that red and black lists of authors had replaced serious criticism, and he raised his voice against the slavish imitation of nineteenth-century literary forms. No testimony about his character is more salient than that of Nadezhda Mandelstam, whose poet husband Osip was a victim of the purges and who herself lived through years of hell. Constantly she refers to Ehrenburg's courageous sympathy and help for intellectuals upon whom the shadow of the GPU had fallen – and this was at a time when every man, however decent, was compelled to avoid compromising himself. In 1952, at the time of the phoney "doctors' plot", he said to her on the doorstep of his apartment: "I am ready for anything." When two years later he published *The Thaw*, he was taking a risk, so unflattering were many of his portraits of citizens who had learned to prosper under the regime. The character Volodya remarks: "Everybody trims his sails, manoeuvres, lies, only some are smarter at it, some less smart."[43] Then in 1958 he rose courageously to the defence of Pasternak. He protested against the trial of Daniel and Sinyavsky. He always gave encouragement to unorthodox young writers and to the *samisdat* method of privately circulating unpublishable manuscripts.

He had never been thick-skinned and a deep anger glowed inside the old man. In 1968 he said to Werth: "But God knows why our so-called statesmen have to stick their necks out and lay down the law" on books and paintings. Khrushchev's absurd peasant arrogance had infuriated him. "The trouble is," he went on, "we've got only one Party, so *every-body* gets in, even a fascist like Sholokhov."[44] Well said – but too much to say publicly. In a sense the final testimony to the balance of his career was his funeral. Scarcely an official representative was present, but several hundred young people turned up to pay tribute, and if he meant something to these young Russian intellectuals then all the abuse he had received in both East and West could be laid to rest with his body.

Those fellow-travellers who have collaborated within communist front-organizations are often described as dupes or worse. We should pause to consider how true this is. And if it is indeed true, recent events have demonstrated clearly that such gullibility (or corruption of *l'esprit*) has by no means been confined to the friends of Soviet Russia. Consider the following quotation : "Use legitimate, existing organizations; disguise the extent of ————— interest; protect the integrity of the organization by not requiring it to support every aspect of official ————— policy."[45] Guess the word omitted on two occasions. "Communist?" Wrong. The word is "American", and the whole quotation belongs to Thomas W. Braden explaining in retrospect* how, under the patronage of Allen Dulles, he arranged for CIA penetration of the (American) National Student Association, the Institute of International Labor Research, the American Newspaper Guild, the American Friends of the Middle East, the National Council of Churches and the Congress for Cultural Freedom (CCF). One of the publications of the latter was the London-based magazine, *Encounter,* which was therefore the indirect beneficiary of CIA funds through dummy foundations like the Hoblitzelle Foundation from 1950 until 1964. Nor was the scale of this subsidization inconsiderable: between 1961 and 1966, at least 430,700 dollars reached the Congress for Cultural Freedom from the CIA.

Frequently we have come across those hard-faced communist functionaries, the *Hintermänner,* manipulating their unsuspecting fellow-travellers. When the CCF was set up in 1950 its two most active organizers were Michael Josselson, a former employee of the US Office of Strategic Services, and Melvin J. Lasky, who had served with the American Information Service and edited *Der Monat,* which was sponsored by the US High Commission in Germany. Presumably the point is made. It was also the case that when the scandal broke in 1966–7, a number of gentlemen who were in a position to know the facts (notably Lasky himself) published denials, though a year later, on 9 May 1967, when the facts were established beyond doubt, Lasky admitted in the

* *Saturday Evening Post,* 20 May 1967.

New York Times that he had been "insufficiently frank" with colleagues and friends.[46] In May 1967 John Kenneth Galbraith conceded in an interview that he had got a convincing hint of CIA involvement in the affairs of the CCF as far back as 1960, while Arthur Schlesinger Jr said quite frankly at about the same time that he had been aware of the position since he joined the Kennedy Administration in 1961. (But, of course, those who swim in the Bay of Pigs must learn to hold their breath.)

The year or so during which an accusation became an incontrovertible fact was filled with many bizarre episodes some of which the present writer was pleased to witness at close quarters. Let them rest. But great indeed was the wailing and gnashing of teeth among those who, having in all innocence collaborated with *Encounter*, felt themselves to have been duped and betrayed. I recall a somewhat exotic gathering in a New York TV studio (a debate between Schlesinger and Conor Cruise O'Brien) during which Stephen Spender and Dwight MacDonald fumed with rage and misery in the face of Schlesinger's ice-cold, contemptuous *Realpolitik*. For Spender in particular it was no doubt too much: duped by the communists in the thirties, duped again by the anti-communists in the fifties and sixties. And the misery of such intellectuals was compounded by the thrusts of their opponents, the anti-anti-communists. Cruise O'Brien, for example, had written in 1966: "... the beauty of the operation ... was that writers of the first rank, who had no interest at all in serving the power structure, were induced to do so unwittingly."[47]

Now this analysis – much as I sympathize with Cruise O'Brien's general political position – seems to me mistaken. Certainly the facts about CIA financial support had been withheld (one now supposes) from Spender and others, but the extent to which in any fundamental sense they had been duped seems doubtful. Common sense and the history of *Encounter* since the scandal both indicate that CIA funds were not the *cause* of the magazine's anti-communist, pro-American orientation, merely a materially supporting factor. The men who edited and wrote for *Encounter* were anti-communists by conviction, and they would have been complete fools to imagine that the general tone of the magazine was anything but comforting to the American political establishment. Can one not equally well "serve the power structure" (in Cruise O'Brien's phrase) when no subsidy is involved? Indeed, so obsessed by the CIA has the Left become that it has virtually forgotten its ancient analysis of capitalist society as the creation of capitalists – if the subsidy had come from the Ford Motor Company there would have been no outcry. In short, the history of this subsidy, as well as the involvement of hard-faced men close to the corridors of power, does not seem particularly important, except in so far as it shows how those who ceaselessly denounced communist fronts willingly adopted their methods.

Particularly in an era of major confrontation there are no "clean hands" in politics, just as there is no "clean money". Too conspiratorial or manipulative an analysis has the disadvantage of blurring the motivation which lies behind most writing: conviction. Very probably not all those who wrote for *Encounter* wished, as a priority, to serve the American establishment, but they must have realized, as fellow-travellers have also realized, that my enemy's enemy has, *faute de mieux,* to be my friend. In his last years Bertrand Russell, a lifelong anti-bolshevik, came very close to the communist position on the Vietnam war. Writing in the *New York Times,* C. L. Sulzberger accordingly described him as "a sounding board for Communist drum beats". But this was not the case; Russell remained his own mental master, choosing his allies according to the circumstances. From this general argument one main conclusion emerges. If the fellow-travellers were at fault, if they did on occasion act as dupes, it was not because they served a cause, a creed slightly different and more ruthlessly directed than their own. It was because the causes they adopted were often bad ones. Did that Anglo-American tribe whose reputations foundered in 1966–7 really serve a better one? The answer seems to depend on which aspect of political life one considers: Soviet labour camps and purges suggest a "yes"; the Vietnam war with its accompanying atrocities suggests a "no".

The communists in the West claimed that South Korea had attacked the North. So did D. N. Pritt: "South Korea attacked North Korea with American aid and encouragement. . . ."[48] Speaking at a Peace Committee meeting he exposed "the swindle" by means of copious quotations from Syngman Rhee's speeches and secret letters as well as from purported statements by the US Ambassador to South Korea. But one document he did not quote was the dispatch published by *Izvestia* on 10 June 1950, to the effect that the Central Committee of the North Korean Patriotic Front had called for the unification of the country by 15 August, the fifth anniversary of the liberation. Hewlett Johnson fully shared Pritt's insights. When she reached North Korea, Monica Felton, president of the British National Assembly of Women and vice-president of the Women's International Democratic Federation, was shown documents supposedly captured in Seoul, including letters from Dulles, which "proved" Rhee's intention to make war. Yet she felt unable to reach a definite conclusion as to what had really happened on

25 June, a reticence perhaps encouraged by the fact that if the North had indeed been the victim of aggression it had staged the most rapid and successful counter-attack in the history of modern warfare. Corliss Lamont found the logic of events unanswerable: the North must have struck first; as for its continued advance southwards, he considered this to have been an immoral blunder. Edgar Snow also adopted a different view from the official Pyong-yang/Peking version of the origin of the war. The fact was that both Syngman Rhee and Kim Il Sung wanted to unify the country by force of arms and to achieve total supremacy for their own systems; but the North possessed a superior army supported by a population with superior cohesion and morale.

Among this war-ravaged population Mrs Felton and her investigating colleagues pursued their distressing researches, witnessing the aftermath of the destruction of Pyong-yang, the mass graves and the genuine outrage of the North Korean population. She was told that women had been seized for brothels during the brief American occupation; she heard of atrocities; but she also found "an astonishing, almost incredible, expression of belief in the humanity of the human race. . . ."[49] The facts, as she saw them, "added to a total picture of ruthless brutality that was beyond imagination". Not long afterwards Pablo Picasso produced his *Massacre en Corée,* showing a squad of semi-robot soldiers being ordered to fire on a group of naked women and children.

The most vigorous Western champion of the North Korean position (leaving aside communists) was Wilfrid Burchett,[50] an active member of both the Peace Council and the Democratic Rights Council in his native Australia at a time when the Menzies Government was leaving no stone unturned in its efforts to outpace Senator McCarthy. Working beside Alan Winnington of the London *Daily Worker,* Burchett was for two years based at Kaesong, whence he reported that the American negotiators at the peace talks were deceiving their own journalists about their actual bargaining demands. According to Burchett, the Americans repeatedly bombed the headquarters of the North Korean and Chinese delegations and refused an immediate ceasefire even after a ceasefire line had been agreed. But what of the notorious torturing of United Nations prisoners, the brainwashing? None, said Burchett: all lies. He was proud of having personally secured an improvement in the prison conditions of the captive General Dean (according to Dean, he always referred to the communist forces as "our side" or "we"). Brash in his self-righteousness, Burchett could not understand why his periodic visits to British, American and particularly Australian prisoners of war aroused such violent resentment – especially among the POWs themselves.

The war was the high point of East-West tension, and as such generated a rash of charges and counter-charges. Of these "germ warfare" ranked in the forefront alongside "brainwashing". Burchett was adamant: from 1951 onwards the US had been air-dropping over North Korea smallpox germs via insect and rat carriers. In March 1952 the International Red Cross and the World Health Organization's offers to investigate on the spot were turned down by the North Koreans. The communist-front International Association of Democratic Lawyers naturally confirmed the allegations, but purely on the basis of statements submitted to it. Then the World Peace Council appointed an International Scientific Commission to investigate, including Joseph Needham, president of the British-China Friendship Association, and a number of distinguished communist and fellow-travelling scientists from Russia, Sweden, Italy, France and Brazil. In September 1952 the Commission issued a 330,000-word report, based on its visits to Manchuria and North Korea, describing its investigation of thirteen Korean and twenty-seven Chinese incidents involving germ-warfare allegations. Of these, nineteen were discussed in great detail, the conclusion being an absolute endorsement of the allegations. Since the integrity of the scientists was no more in doubt than their expertise, anti-communist commentators like John Clews suggested that the evidence had been planted by Soviet bacteriological teams. Meanwhile a series of captured American pilots "confessed". Burchett himself claimed to have interviewed captured South Korean agents dispatched to the North to check the effects of the bacteria, as well as Air Force lieutenants Quinn and Kniss. However in October 1953 Dr Charles Mayo reported to the UN Political Commission that these and other American officers who had "confessed" now claimed that they had done so under physical and mental torture.

From Korea to Vietnam Burchett soldiered on, visiting Ho's HQ, living in Hanoi from 1954 to 1957, publishing friendly accounts of the campaigns waged by the Vietminh and later the Vietcong, moving to Moscow for a spell of pseudonymous reporting for the *Daily Express* and the *Financial Times*, and then, though already in his fifties, sharing the forced marches, jungle hammocks and precarious existence of the Vietcong. For fourteen years he campaigned without success to recover his Australian passport; Castro gave him a Cuban one instead, a fitting tribute to a fellow-travelling guerrilla.

9

The Witch-Hunts

During the decade which followed the Second World War, American communists and fellow-travellers were persecuted, victimized and sometimes imprisoned. The mood prevailing in the American political superstructure, in the courts, in commercial and academic institutions and to some extent in society at large was one of hysteria and sickness. But what occurred in America was in no way comparable to the Soviet experience under Stalin. Julius and Ethel Rosenberg were executed, but Stalin's policies may have accounted for twenty million deaths. Not all the victims of the witch-hunts got a fair trial, but at least they got one. It took a grand jury investigation and two jury trials to send Alger Hiss to jail for five years. He came out after four. The attentions (and intentions) of the FBI may have been exceedingly unpleasant, but J. Edgar Hoover's displeasure had less fatal consequences than Yezhov's or Beria's. In the United States there were no forced labour camps for political prisoners, no queues outside the Attorney General's office waiting for death certificates. The balance sheet of repression and terror was so weighted in one direction that comparisons are futile.

Although our main preoccupation is with fellow-travellers and their fate, their predicament obviously cannot be understood in isolation since the witch-hunts to which they fell victim were directed mainly against "communists", with whom they were frequently confused. A climate of demagoguery, fear and indeed superstition does not encourage nice distinctions.

The witch-hunts of the forties and fifties were by no means the first suffered by American radicals. The Alien and Sedition Acts, the Know-Nothing Movement and the Palmer raids remind us of that. A wide-ranging repression followed the Espionage Act of 1917. Robert Morss Lovett recalled citizens profiteering on patriotism by bearing tales of the disaffections of friends and neighbours. Eugene Debs was sentenced for opposing the selective service law and Congressmen Victor Berger was expelled from the House. One hundred members of the IWW went on trial for obstructing the war effort. And then with the consent of President Wilson, the Quaker-vigilante Attorney General A. Mitchell Palmer instigated the notorious raids which bear his name. In December 1919, 249 radicals including Emma Goldman and Alexander Berkman were deported. In January 1920 five thousand political arrests were made. The ranks of the Communist Labor Party were decimated. In the same year the blacklisting habit received a boost when the Lusk Committee, appointed by the New York State Legislature, issued a four-volume report naming as subversives such innocuous figures as Jane Addams, the founder of Hull House and chairman of the National Women's Peace Party. In fact the witch-hunts of the Truman and Eisenhower years were merely the culminating performance of a drama often rehearsed.

Yet, oddly enough, they were distinguished from their predecessors by their virtual irrelevance. The IWW and the old Socialist Party had at least represented a genuine force among the American working class; the Communist Party never did. In twenty-five years it could boast of the following achievements: the election of the Mayor of Crosby, Minnesota (pop. 3,500) in 1932; the election of two members of New York City Council in the 1940s; and an estimated Party membership which climbed from about 57,000 in 1938 to a meteoric 80,000 in 1944. During the Presidential election of 1940, the communist ticket of Browder and Ford attracted the votes of only 46,251 Americans. Furthermore the CP emerged from the war torn by dissension, recantations and, finally, the expulsion of Browder himself. By 1950 membership was down to about 40,000* – yet the fewer American communists there were to find, the more frenetically were they hunted. It is interesting to note that a 1954 opinion poll discovered that only three per cent of a national cross-section of the population had ever known a self-admitted communist. It is this factor which makes the term "witch-hunt" so apposite; since there are no real witches, they have to be invented. A further ten per cent of those questioned in 1954 had their suspicions about certain individuals – the woman who never went to church, the man who wore shabby clothes or the one who "travelled a lot". It was as bad as that. The enormous dislocation of the collective American psyche which took place in these years can be illuminated by comparison. The strength of British communism was relatively just as great, indeed greater, yet no comparable persecution or loss of perspective took place. France and Italy, both members of the Atlantic Alliance and both incapable of defending themselves against the Red Army,

* In October 1949 the *Daily Worker* confessed that its circulation was only 23,400.

possessed Communist Parties capable of collecting twenty-five per cent of the national vote; yet in both countries the purges which took place were trivial in comparison to the ones staged across the Atlantic. The average French bourgeois did indeed fear the Soviet Union and its local friends, but since every fourth person he passed in the street voted communist certain demoniac illusions about communists were barred to him.

Nevertheless a conspiracy on behalf of a powerful foreign Power cannot be measured in terms of numbers alone. One Philby or Fuchs can do as much for Russia as fifty communist MPs. Post-war investigations in America disclosed *not one* certifiable communist working within any Government department.* But they did bring to light the presence during the Roosevelt era of persons in high places owing allegiance to the Soviet Union and co-operating with Comintern agents. Both Whittaker Chambers and Elizabeth Bentley, themselves former communist spies, took the lid off genuine espionage rings. Between 1933 and 1935 the Federal establishment expanded by as much as fifty per cent, and for the first time government service became more attractive than private enterprise for the clever young graduates of the East Coast colleges, not a few of whom were extremely radical in outlook. Yet no historian of repute has estimated the number of communists working within the huge compass of the Administration at more than a hundred, and the vast majority of these, of course, were not spies but simply men who hoped to influence policy, which is perhaps a democratic right.

Among fellow-travellers working in government, two notable cases of espionage came to light after the war. One concerned Julian Wadleigh, the son of an Episcopalian minister, an MA from Oxford, a BSc from London and a graduate of Chicago. Initially drawn to the left by Fabianism, he had served in the Federal Farm Bureau, the State Department, the Department of Agriculture and UNRRA in distinguished capacities. Protected by the three-year statute of limitations, he confessed in complete immunity after the war to having passed State Department documents from March 1936 onward to two agents, one of whom was Chambers. At Hiss's second trial Wadleigh owned up to having passed over about four hundred such documents. Late in 1937 he had met Chambers's boss, whom Chambers called Colonel Bykov and Wadleigh remembered as Sasha (just as he remembered Chambers as Carl Carlson – it was all in the best cloak-and-dagger tradition, with surreptitious meetings on street corners). Apparently Wadleigh was told

---

* Although on 6 March 1949 Judith Coplon, a Barnard graduate in the Justice Department, was arrested in the act of a rendezvous with an attaché of the Soviet delegation to the UN.

on this occasion that he was suspected of holding back certain documents. He promised to do better, shopped around the State Department desks and might well, he said, have been the source of some of the papers which Chambers attributed to Hiss. After the Nazi-Soviet Pact Wadleigh dropped the whole thing. According to his own published account, he had never joined the fronts, was not a convinced Marxist and was not interested in overthrowing the Government. These were not untypical traits in a fellow-traveller. Wadleigh's peculiarity was to have deliberately disguised his left-wing views in order to engage in espionage. The irony of the situation lay in the fact that while Hiss was standing trial for perjury, that is to say for crimes he claimed he did not commit, Wadleigh was simultaneously publishing in the *New York Post* twelve articles on "Why I Spied for the Communists". If Hiss had only confessed, there was no law under which he could have been sent to jail. Asked in court what his impression of Hiss had been in the thirties, Wadleigh described him as a moderate New Dealer with markedly conservative instincts.

According to Chambers, the main source of information in the Treasury was Harry Dexter White. White, like Wadleigh, was a fellow-traveller not a communist. "These men and women communists and fellow-travelers who staffed the Fifth Column," wrote Chambers, "were dedicated revolutionaries...."[1] Indeed, continued Chambers, "the fellow-travelers who cooperate to the point of espionage ... in effect ... have become communists, whatever fictive differences they may maintain."[2] This sounds like good sense: when a man passes a document it makes no difference whether he carries a card or not. But the point missed by Chambers (and most of America) was this: the Soviet State has never hoped to bring down the US Constitution or impose a communist regime in America *by means of espionage*. When the Russians extracted State Department documents from Wadleigh, it was not in order to plan a "Pearl Harbour", it was to find out what was going on, what the deals with other foreign Powers were, to protect the interests of the USSR. And one can be sure that American spies like Wadleigh appreciated this and regarded themselves as the protectors of a weak and vulnerable Russia rather than as potentially raising the red flag over the White House. Furthermore the authentic fellow-traveller (and both Wadleigh and White were of the breed) by no means desired a Soviet-style dictatorship at home.

In August 1948 Harry Dexter White came before the House Un-American Activities Committee (henceforward called the Committee) at his own request, to clear his name. He had entered the Federal Service in 1933, rising subsequently to the post of Assistant Secretary to the

Treasury with responsibility for matters concerning foreign relations in which the Treasury was involved, and later for all Treasury relations with the Army and Navy. In fact, a big fish. In February 1946 he had been nominated by Truman as executive director of the International Monetary Fund. But his record did look suspicious. He had intervened on behalf of a certain Silvermaster when he was accused by the Office of Naval Intelligence of being a communist, and when action was started to remove him from the Board of Economic Welfare, Elizabeth Bentley claimed that White gave classified information to Silvermaster, who passed it on to her. Holding his head high before the Committee, White refused to renounce "seven or eight years of friendship" with Silvermaster until a court proved him guilty. About ten of the people named as spies by Elizabeth Bentley had worked for White. Chambers claimed he had received documents directly from White, and produced a four-page memo in his handwriting. According to Chambers, after he himself had broken with the CP in 1937 he had warned White that he would denounce him if he did not terminate all relations with communists. But White took no notice. "He thoroughly enjoyed," said Chambers, "the sense of being in touch with the Party, but not in it, courted by it, but yielding only so much as he chose."[8] Chambers was a pathological liar but too many of his revelations were corroborated by other sources for his evidence to be automatically discounted. The case against White was a strong one. A few days after testifying before the Committee he died of a heart attack; Hiss told the Committee they had killed him and Henry Wallace said much the same, calling White his own "good friend and associate on many New Deal committees".

It didn't add up to very much. America soon became the victim of its own publicity machine(s). Words like "espionage", "subversion" and "agent" buzzed like hornets across the nation's mental landscape, inducing fears out of all proportion to the threat. Indeed if the US Constitution was menaced during the decade 1945–55 it was predominantly by those who claimed to defend it. Democracy is more than majority rule. The twelve members of the CP National Board who were tried in January 1949 on a charge relating to the overthrow of the Government by force were condemned under the Smith Act, but the Smith Act was no more consistent with democracy and minority rights than were Senator McCarran's Internal Security Act (1950) or the Communist Control Act of 1954 (which the noted liberal Hubert Humphrey considered not stringent enough). It was the McCarran Act which compelled both "communist-action" and "communist-front" organizations to register with the Attorney General – who was given discretion to label organizations according to these categories. No one group or person ever registered; the Attorney General and his legion of "consultants" simply compiled their own lists. But it was not innovatory legislation which most menaced the security and livelihood of American radicals in these years, it was "contempt" (usually of Congress) and "perjury". In other words either refusing to answer questions by pleading the First or Fifth Amendments, or, alternatively, holding fast to a version of events which a court judged to be untrue. And "contempt" was the sword employed in the first major post-war purge, the scything of Hollywood's remarkably powerful left-wing ranks.

As early as 1940, forty-two Hollywood personalities had been named to the Committee as fellow-travellers or communists. A retaliatory meeting held in Hollywood's Philharmonic Town Hall staged a skit written by the militant fellow-traveller Donald Ogden Stewart, satirizing the chairman of the Committee, Martin Dies of Texas. Some of the films produced in Hollywood during the war and scripted by communists and fellow-travellers offended conservative sentiment: J. Edgar Hoover described *Mission to Moscow*, based on Ambassador Davies's book, as "a prostitution of historical fact", while Congressman J. Parnell Thomas took exception not only to this film but also to *North Star* and *Song of Russia*. In 1947 a California State Senator on the make, Jack B. Tenney, testified to the Committee that Chaplin, John Garfield, Edward G. Robinson, Frank Sinatra and Fredric March had been aiding or abetting communism. The atmosphere became increasingly menacing and the members of the Committee were not such as to inspire confidence. Rankin of Mississippi, a rampant anti-semite, associated Hollywood with the insidious power of Jews; for J. Parnell Thomas of New Jersey, Hollywood symbolized the whole virus of the intellectual New Deal. And for all members of the Committee an investigation of Hollywood meant excellent publicity for themselves.

The actor Fredric March and his wife Florence Eldridge March soon encountered the mounting virulence of the witch-hunts. A seven-page FBI report called March a "Communist Party fellow-traveler" who had been connected with the Institute for Democratic Education, and reported that in December 1945 the actor had addressed a New York rally protesting against atomic weapons. (Henry Wallace had been present.) According to this report, he had also played the part of a Russian soldier in a skit staged during a Madison Square Garden meeting of the American Society for Russian Relief. Soon he and his wife found the doors of film studios closed to them. Subsequently they brought a libel suit for half a million dollars against the newsletter

Counterattack: the case was settled out of court and the newsletter withdrew its allegation that they were communists.

Pressure was intensified by the right-wing Motion Picture Alliance for the Preservation of American Ideals which published Ayn Rand's *Screen Guide for Americans*, with its famous "Don'ts": "Don't Smear the Free Enterprise System"; "Don't Glorify the Collective", etc. In fact the communists and fellow-travellers within the Screen Writers' Guild had ridden high during the war, and they had also been active in the long, violent and ultimately unsuccessful attempt to form one industrial union out of the several existing craft unions. In the end the Conference of Studio Unions, which led the strike, was destroyed.

In 1947 the Committee subpoenaed nineteen Hollywood personalities (thirteen of them Jews) to testify before it. In the event only ten were asked to take the witness stand. Each refused to declare whether or not he was a communist; as each stepped down an FBI agent read out the number of his Party card. In December the Ten were indicted by a grand jury for contempt of Congress. In June 1950 the Supreme Court refused to review the case and so the Ten went to jail for one year. Though Henry Wallace championed their cause the New York financial interests behind the film industry didn't, the result being that in November fifty-seven movie executives declared they would "discharge or suspend without compensation" the Ten. The situation escalated, the blacklist became a tapeworm, the nine witnesses who had not in the event been asked to testify found it hard to get work, and even those Hollywood personalities who had protested against the whole procedure or who had subscribed to the Committee for the First Amendment* were lucky not to lose their jobs. No one dared employ them, whatever the value of their talents. After this initial success the Committee moved in on the ex-communists and fellow-travellers. If the victims chose to take the Fifth Amendment, their careers ended there; the repugnant alternative was to inform on old friends. The Hollywood branch of the Council of the Arts, Sciences and Professions, an offshoot of the Progressive Party and therefore swarming with fellow-travellers, backed those who took the Fifth, but the terrified Actors Equity refused to intervene. The Screen Actors Guild (president, Ronald Reagan) also refused to help actors who had "offended public opinion" and by 1951 the Association of Motion Picture Producers was vociferously supporting the Committee. The Committee for its part did not lack the assistance of enthusiastically hostile witnesses. (Ayn Rand, the director Sam Wood, the actors Adolphe Menjou, Robert Taylor, George Murphy, Ronald

* Prominent members of the CFA who survived professionally were Thomas Mann, Danny Kaye, Humphrey Bogart, Katharine Hepburn, Burt Lancaster and Irwin Shaw.

Reagan and Gary Cooper, to name only a few.) Needless to say, the intellectual level of these exchanges left much to be desired; the light-headed Mrs Lela Rogers, mother of Ginger, testified that she and Ginger had turned down a part in a film of Dreiser's *Sister Carrie* because it was "open propaganda".

The implicit deal made between the Committee and the industry bosses was clear: an attack on a film could be financially ruinous; therefore the Committee would henceforward confine its attacks to individuals provided the executives co-operated. They did. In 1951 they agreed to investigate over two hundred employees listed on the American Legion's bad books. A climate of utter despair and degradation soon established itself. Elia Kazan, once a communist in the thirties, refused to provide the Committee with names then changed his mind (he wanted to make films): "The American people need the facts and all the facts about all aspects of communism...."[4] José Ferrer took out paid advertisements pleading that he was no communist; appearing before the Committee he profusely praised its work. John Garfield depicted himself as a political simpleton who had once been inveigled into some fronts. Edward G. Robinson was glad the Committee had exposed the communist conspiracy (he wanted to act). Soon American Legion head-quarters were swamped with pleas from Hollywood writers and actors for political "clearances", but their pleas were ignored. The Legion enjoyed putting names on lists more than taking them off. A smaller America was working off its petty resentments and inferiority complexes. Inquisitions and firings continued without interruption. One actor was on set during MGM's production of *Julius Caesar* when he was summoned, still wearing his toga, by the studio executive. Refusing to say whether he was in the CP, he was fired on the spot. By 1956 he had not found a single new role.

The blacklists certainly remained effective until the late fifties. Many writers were forced to work for low fees under pseudonyms. Among those directors who felt they had a chance of working abroad, an exodus of considerable proportions took place. The screenwriter Donald Ogden Stewart, one of the most organizationally energetic fellow-travellers of the thirties and forties, settled in England, later testifying: "The thing that made so many Hollywood people leftists, radicals, Reds, I think, was guilt – the fact that we were getting all that money – when thousands of other Americans were on the breadline. I think that's an encouraging thing, especially when I think of it in relation to myself, a lawyer's son from Ohio who went to Yale and had the American Dream dumped in his lap and still swung left."[5] The director Abe Polonsky had reached a peak of success with his *Force of Evil* when the subpoena came, followed by the refusal to betray friends and associates, and the inevitable blacklisting. His next film as a director had to wait twenty years. Carl Foreman emigrated to Britain in 1952, again as a consequences of blacklisting, another talent drained from the American film industry at precisely the time when it had to meet the combined challenges of television and the European studios. Foreman recalls: "I knew one writer who was hounded out of the business, took a job on a department store counter, but they got him there as well, so he wound up digging ditches to support his wife and kids, and then he died. He was a man who might be alive today if he had been an informer."[6]

Why were such men persecuted? The superficial answer is that they were communists, had been communists or, more frequently, had taken part in front-organizations and signed good-cause petitions during the era of the Popular Front and the war. Such activities were now interpreted as tantamount to subversion or the intention to subvert the American way of life. Ludicrous though this proposition was, it compelled the majority of victims to resort to the First or Fifth Amendments* not only out of personal honour but because the maximum sentence for contempt was one year whereas "perjury" (which was whatever prejudiced juries and judges made of it) could incur five – as with Hiss. Unfortunately the resort to either Amendment was generally interpreted as a tacit admission of Party membership. Sidney Hook claimed in 1957 that "almost all who invoked the privilege, *independent evidence shows*, were present or former members of the Communist Party".[7] This was not accurate: many fellow-travellers refused to testify. Besides, America in these years was neither a perceptive nor a discriminating society. As Justice Douglas of the Supreme Court pointed out, a confession of any kind of affiliation to communist causes usually led to professional ruin and social disgrace. For sheer arbitrariness, the American notion of guilt by association was fast pursuing its Soviet counterpart.

The front-organizations were a prime target for the Committee, the Attorney General's office and other investigators. Early in 1947 the executive board of the Joint Anti-Fascist Refugee Committee, headed by Dr Edward K. Barsky, went to prison for contempt, for refusing to provide the Committee with lists of contributors and members. At the

---

* The First stipulates that Congress shall not, among other things, abridge freedom of speech or the press, or the right to peaceful assembly and petition. The Fifth affords citizens the right to say nothing self-incriminating.

time members of the Committee were suspected of pro-Franco sympathies; when in 1963 Moe Fishman, executive secretary of the Abraham Lincoln Brigade, was subpoenaed it emerged that the Committee had turned over to Franco's police the names of families being cared for by the Refugee Committee and the Veterans. In 1946 Corliss Lamont was subpoenaed as chairman of the National Council of American-Soviet Friendship, and though he was subsequently cited for contempt the case was dropped. Later, in May 1954, the National Council* was brought before the Subversive Activities Control Board (SACB) set up by the Internal Security Act of 1950. The American Committee for the Protection of the Foreign Born was investigated and in 1955 the Jefferson School of Social Science in New York dissolved itself after being adjudged a front by the SACB. In the early sixties the Committee turned its attention to the Fair Play for Cuba Committee and Women Strike for Peace, which demanded an atomic test ban and included in its ranks some fellow-travelling and communist veterans of the past. In 1960 Senator Dodds's Senate Internal Security Subcommittee investigated the National Committee for a Sane Nuclear Policy, as a result of which the SANE sanely purged itself of communists, something which Mrs Dagmar Wilson, leader of the Peace Women, disdainfully declined to do.

The pursuit of individual fellow-travellers was a sport already popular in certain circles before the war. When J. B. Matthews, himself a former fellow-traveller but later a professional investigator, told the Committee that Rockwell Kent was a communist and that the Department of the Interior had scandalously paid this communist forty thousand dollars for a mural, Kent felt obliged to write to the Committee denying both that he was a Party member and that his opinions had been influenced by the CP. Another case concerned Goodwin Watson, a fellow-travelling faculty member of Columbia, a social psychologist and a member of a number of fronts including the Workers' Alliance and the Consumers' Union. When the Federal Communications Commission hired Watson as an analyst the Committee kicked up a fuss – and he lost the job. The same occurred when Malcolm Cowley was hired as chief information analyst of the Office of Facts and Figures (the Committee listed seventy-two connections between Cowley, the CP and its fronts). Then in April 1943 Robert Morss Lovett was called before a subsidiary committee of the House Committee on Appropriations three years after he had been

---

* Its witnesses included Dr John Kingsbury (chairman), Rev. William Howard Melish, R. M. Lovett, Prof. Arthur Upham Pope, of the Asia Institute, and Prof. Ralph Barton Perry, Emeritus Professor of Harvard.

appointed to succeed his friend Robert Herrick as Government Secretary of the Virgin Islands.

A student at Harvard from 1888 to 1893, Lovett had worked as a
teacher, an editor, a consultant literary critic and as a general activist
for good causes. Apparently the Spanish-American war had been the
first international event to fire his imagination and indignation; thereafter he leaned strongly towards pacifism. His pupils at Chicago University had included names with which we are familiar such as Samuel
Harper and Anna Louise Strong. No great scholar and something of
a gentleman of leisure, he did not seem destined to make much impact
on the world; between long, pre-war trips to Europe and climbing
Swiss mountains in the company of his son, he invested in a fruit-tree
scheme in Bitter Root Valley, Montana, ending up with seventy-five
thousand trees – but not with the expected yield of seventy-five thousand
dollars per year. It was the First World War which drew him "from
academic seclusion ... into activities which I had hitherto avoided".
Once started with these activities, he could never have enough of them.
Certainly the death-in-action of his son Robert profoundly shocked him.
Every good cause beckoned him: Russia, Ireland, India, Tom Mooney,
Sacco and Vanzetti, birth control, capital punishment and Spain. For
a while he lived appropriately in Jane Addams's Hull House in Chicago,
a saintly place for middle-class philanthropists but not, as the Lash
Committee believed, a centre of subversion. President of the League for
Industrial Democracy, Lovett was arrested in 1933 while observing a
strike and then faced an Illinois subversion committee. He joined the
League for Peace and Democracy and the League of American Writers,
invariably favouring collaboration with communists whom he regarded
as human beings capable "like the rest of us, of giving aid to
human and generous causes".[8] Lovett was both a muddled and
saintly old fellow. While Government Secretary of the Virgin Islands
he received a letter from the militant fellow-traveller Jack McMichael,
chairman of the American Youth Congress, calling on him to sign
a petition to preserve American neutrality. Lovett signed. Then he wrote
to McMichael arguing that China and Britain deserved American economic support in their war efforts, later reflecting: "I have constantly
held that the possibility of freedom and peace in the present world is
bound up with the victory of Great Britain. With Hitler in power the
United States will never be free from the fear of war...."[9] During the
First World War he had "fought for peace" while somehow refusing
"to oppose the war"; time, evidently, had not lessened his confusions.

Lovett's action in signing the McMichael manifesto provoked a
rocket from Secretary of the Interior Harold Ickes, yet when Lovett

was summoned before a House committee in 1943 Ickes loyally defended him (reminding us how enlightened was the mood of the Roosevelt era compared to the dark ages which followed). "Mr Lovett," said Ickes, "has simply typified one of the best traditions in American life, that in every generation there should be a group of disinterested and active liberals who should labor prodigiously to remove the imperfections of the contemporary society. Thomas Jefferson, Thomas Paine...."[10] But Lovett's accusers were not convinced. They cited a speech he had made on behalf of Norman Thomas in 1936, an article of his in *The New Masses* criticizing State Department policy in Spain, a letter written to Mother Bloor of Iowa on her seventy-fifth birthday, and a letter in which he had once described all governments as "rotten". So :

"Mr Nowell: You made the statement that the United States Government is rotten.

"Mr Lovett: That was an unguarded and extreme statement, which, as I say, appeared in a private letter and would be understood by the man to whom it was written."[11]

Lovett had to go. Congress made it a condition of a financial appropriation. But in 1946 the Supreme Court unanimously found that this action had been unconstitutional because it amounted to a bill of attainder.

After the war the Committee launched an attack on Dr Edward U. Condon, Director of the National Bureau of Standards and a distinguished authority on quantum mechanics, microwave electronics and radioactivity. In 1940 he had been appointed to the National Defense Research Committee, and subsequently he was closely associated with the development of the atomic bomb. But he was also associated with the Soviet-American Friendship Society and with Harlow Shapley, one of the Progressive Party's leading scientists. Condon had given offence in certain quarters by calling for a freer flow of scientific information and by suggesting in March 1946 that the US should welcome Soviet scientists into its laboratories. He regretted that certain people evidently had Russia in mind as a target for the next war. In March 1948 a subcommittee of the Committee issued a press release accusing Condon of associating with alleged Soviet agents, and calling him "one of the weakest links in our atomic security". The Committee demanded to see his file: Truman refused. In July 1948 Condon was cleared by the Atomic Energy Commission but the witch-hunters on the Committee tried again in 1952 when they summoned him to explain his left-wing friendships at the University of California Radiation Laboratory during the war. Condon, however, survived intact, and so highly esteemed was he among his peers that in the same year he was elected president of the American Association for the Advancement of Science.

As Senator Joseph McCarthy's star rose in the political firmament witch-hunting became a highly competitive enterprise with the various investigating committees and agencies engaged in constant demarcation disputes like prospectors during a gold rush. For McCarthy in particular it was a case of "if communists didn't exist we would have to invent them". Certainly he invented more than existed. He hurled charges against Judge Dorothy Kenyon, a fighting lady who was forever in and out of communist front-organizations, but who denied explicitly that she was a fellow-traveller, calling herself an "independent, liberal, Rooseveltian Democrat". In 1953 he grilled Cedric Belfrage, editor of the *National Guardian,* along with James Aronson, executive editor of the same left-wing weekly. A British resident alien who had lived in the US for sixteen years, and a former SHAEF press officer in Germany, Belfrage took the Fifth on a number of questions including his alleged membership of the CP in 1937. After a two-year legal battle he was finally deported in April 1955. As for the unfortunate Lamont, he was too good to ignore. In September 1953 he faced the McCarthy Committee (officially the Senate Permanent Subcommittee on Investigations) represented on this occasion by the Wisconsin Senator alone. The pretext? Communist infiltration – believe it or not – of the US Army. Lamont had contributed to a publication called *USSR, a Concise Handbook,* which McCarthy claimed was being used to indoctrinate the troops. Apparently the Senator possessed sworn testimony that Lamont had been a member of the Party, but as usual he declined to say who had sworn. But his underlings had done some useful research, coming up with two *Daily Worker* editions of February and July 1938 which contained photographs of Lamont in Russia as well as a report of a broadcast he had delivered over Moscow short-wave radio, condemning John Dewey for questioning the validity of the Moscow trials. Then in December 1952 he had signed an appeal to Truman calling for an amnesty for the CP leaders jailed under the Smith Act. Questioned about his knowledge of such academic fellow-travellers as Ernest J. Simmons and Frederick L. Schuman, both experts in Russian affairs whom McCarthy naturally described as communists, Lamont declined to answer. But he did describe himself as a loyal American who had never joined the Party. Otherwise he reached for the First Amendment. The Senator reached for contempt. The US District Court and the US Circuit Court of Appeals supported Lamont (the courts in general were by now recovering their nerve) and in August 1955 Judge Edward

Weinfeld dismissed the whole indictment.* But this case did illustrate the mood of cowardice prevailing in the Senate; only Senators Langer, Lehman and Chavez voted against Lamont's citation for contempt, while the liberal heroes of the 1960s, including Kennedy, Johnson and Humphrey, voted for it.

In the days of Martin Dies, the House Un-American Activities Committee had honoured Lamont with the title of "perhaps the most persistent propagandist for the Soviet Union to be found anywhere in the United States". In the context of his family, he was certainly a fish out of water, the son of a millionaire banker, Thomas Lamont, and the brother of a businessman who became a member of the Harvard governing body. As a student at Harvard in the early twenties, Lamont had shown his later aptitude for controversy and confrontation, editing the *Crimson* and leading a campaign against President Lowell's proposal of a *numerus clausus* for Jewish students. As vice-president of the Union he invited Eugene Debs and Upton Sinclair to speak on the campus, and though his passion for free speech married oddly with his admiration for the Soviet system there is no doubt that it was genuine. Not only did he insist that even fascists should be allowed their say, but in 1956 he pointed to Britain as the country which had achieved the most in the field of civil liberties, the USSR not excluded. "I am repelled," he admitted in 1952, "by the dictatorial and repressive aspects of the Soviet regime...."[12] Which presents an apparently impenetrable paradox, the more so as he was fully capable of quoting Macaulay's *Essay on Milton,* with its reflections on the emergence of basic liberties out of the English Revolution, as in every way relevant to the history of the USSR. Probably Lamont enjoyed his own image as a maverick; what others might regard as schizophrenia he termed "the independent mind". Accordingly he periodically announced his disagreement with the communists, on one occasion informing reporters that discord prevailed on some fifty separate issues. When the communists called George Santayana a fascist, Lamont defended him; and, as we have seen earlier, he never tired of rebuking them for failing to perceive the genius of Dewey as a philosopher. In 1952, already deprived of a passport, he became a candidate for US Senator on the American Labor Party ticket – with what success can be imagined.

Things were not good in America. The stage was soon reached whereby six million citizens were officially covered by civilian personnel security

---

* Lamont's lawyer, Philip Wittenberg, challenged the Senate's indictment of Lamont not on First Amendment grounds but on the argument that McCarthy had been delegated no authority to conduct his own, one-man subversion probes. Wittenberg's contention was upheld by Judge Weinfeld and, in July 1956, by a three-man appeals tribunal.

programmes and a further three million by their military counterparts –
figures which do not include those involved in *ad hoc* Congressional
investigations or purges of teachers launched by individual States, let
alone those caught up in the proliferating racket of municipal investigations. By 1955 the US Customs Mail Division in Boston was consign-
ing to the incinerator *Peace News* of London as well as pamphlets issued
by the Movement for Colonial Freedom and the Union for Democratic
Control. An organization designated "communist-action" or "communist-front" by the Attorney General was legally obliged to stamp the fact
on its mail, and it was a criminal offence for members of such organizations to apply for a passport. Lamont was only one of many to lose their
passports. It happened to the Presbyterian, Dr J. Henry Carpenter, to
Clark Foreman, director of the Emergency Civil Liberties Committee, to
Arthur Miller and to the Nobel Prize-winning chemist Dr Linus Pauling
– none of whom had been communists. After Charlie Chaplin and his
family left for a trip abroad the Attorney General ordered the Immigration Service to prevent his re-entry, pending a hearing on his beliefs
and associations. It is perhaps not surprising that so sober a judge
of men and events as Thomas Mann saw in McCarthy a new Hitler
and in Eisenhower a kind of Hindenburg preparing the ground. Annoyed and harassed by charges that he too was a fellow-traveller, Mann
left the US in 1952 and never returned, fearing his passport would be
taken from him if he did. A year later he described the new American
conception of "loyalty" as "compulsion to conformity", and he complained of "spying out people's opinions, mistrust, training people to
denounce others. . . ."[18]

The style in which the term "fellow-traveler" was increasingly employed offered a measure of the escalating hysteria and of the lack of
scruple of those who accelerated it. In 1950, for example, the Democratic State Central Committee of Pennsylvania published a pamphlet
entitled: "Fellow Traveling Pa. GOP Congressmen Follow Red Party
Line." Vice-President Nixon announced: "We're kicking the communists and fellow-travelers and security risks out of the Government . . .
by the thousands." In the early 1950s vigilante bodies like the American
Legion enjoyed and exercised the power to make or break. There was
no appeal but there was plenty of competition from the Catholic War
Veterans, the Veterans of Foreign Wars and the American Jewish
League against Communism led by Rabbi Benjamin Schultz. The
Legion's magazine was ever open to the professional, self-styled "Red-
baiters" like J. B. Matthews who specialized in non-specific charges
relying on words like "affiliated", "supporting" and "connections". The
hysteria penetrated every segment of society, including organized labour,

317

for the simple reason that silence was interpreted as connivance which in turn implied active involvement. Thus in 1952 a Wage Earners' Committee picketed a cinema in Los Angeles with the placard: "Communists are killing Americans in Korea. Fellow Travelers support Communists. Yellow travelers support Fellow 'Travelers. Don't be a Yellow traveler."[14] Capitulation followed capitulation. In 1955 Muhlenberg College cancelled a Chaplin film festival after an intervention from the local branch of the Legion. The Girl Scouts purged their own handbook under pressure from the same quarter.

The investigators, experts, consultants, informers and snoopers proliferated. In 1798, in the course of a speech opposing the bill introducing the Alien and Sedition Acts, Edward Livingtone had predicted the appearance of a swarm of "informers, spies, relators, and all the odious reptile tribe that breed in the sunshine of despotic power...." The prediction would have been equally apposite in the America of Truman and Eisenhower, an America which, though by no means a despotism, gave full rein to minor despots. The new tribe relied mainly on former communists, like Louis Budenz (who became a professor at Fordham University), specializing in caucus room consultations and in a rigmarole of skulduggery built up by repeated "I was there" allusions to the conspiratorial past – conspiratorial more often in the case of the consultant than of the victim. In July 1948 the Canwell Committee investigating the University of Washington allowed an incredible freedom of denunciation to the ex-communist "experts" George Hewitt and Howard Rushmore, the last of whom worked for the Hearst press. When the Broyles Committee turned its attention to the University of Chicago, Rushmore appeared as the star witness, alleging fifty cases of "fellow-traveling" on the part of seven professors. Yet only eleven of the thirty-eight organizations which Rushmore listed as "subversive" actually appeared on the Attorney General's list. Twenty-one either did not exist or were unknown to the seven professors. The Justice Department was only one of many agencies which hired such people as Paul Crouch on regular salaries, deploying them as expert witnesses during trials: the less they knew about a case the more they generally claimed to know. About eighty ex-communists pursued such public careers: most of them had scores to settle. In 1955 a scandal broke when Harvey Matusow published his book, *False Witness*, confessing how he had ruined people by providing false evidence. The Justice Department immediately hauled before a grand jury Matusow himself, his publishers, and the printers and staff of *The Nation*, which had already published an article on the informer racket. This was a confirmation of the old principle – the greater the truth, the greater the libel.

Perhaps the most interesting and complex of the "consultants" was Joseph B. Matthews, from Kentucky, who had in the early thirties been one of the most prominent fellow-travellers of the time. Matthews had passed from religious fundamentalism to the "social gospel", thence to humanitarianism and political reform in the style of the elder La Follette, thence to pacifism, socialism and fellow-travelling.* He was proud of his scholarly achievements, his knowledge of Sanskrit, Hebrew and Malay (he had taught in Java), and of his meeting with Tagore in Geneva. He was widely travelled and evidently restless; in 1938 he reported that he had served on the faculties of forty-two institutes of higher education, both American and foreign. As late as 1935 he warned that big business, government and blind liberals were opening the way to fascism, but within the space of a few months it had been revealed to him that the blind liberals were really opening the way to communism. The "Jekyll, the scholar", as he put it, had now finally triumphed over "the Hyde, the revolutionary". But with obvious *Schadenfreude* the Jekyll enjoyed scaring his new public with newspaper accounts of how Hyde-Matthews had previously been honoured in the palaces of evil. He now revelled in the familiar, witch-hunting vocabulary of "fellow-travelers", "stooges" and "innocents", further alarming his readers with the thought that although many of the leftist organizations which innocent Americans joined were un-American, the act of joining itself was typically American. He described the Marxian code of ethics as "the most cold-blooded pragmatism the world has ever seen", praised Randolph Hearst, and announced that political and economic conservatism had now become for him "a personal faith". A demagogue, he wrote in 1938, "by whatever political name, who deliberately seeks to prejudice the public against business, as such, is as dangerous as any communist could be to the welfare of the people of America."[15] He testified before the Dies Committee and began to compile on its behalf immense lists, ferreting out old newspapers and periodicals, and making sensational appearances at investigatory sessions. (By 1950 the Committee employed a staff of seventy-five and possessed about six hundred filing cabinets containing records and dossiers on about one million people.) In later years Matthews worked for the Hearst press and, within it, on behalf of McCarthy. The Senator liked to reward such services. In 1953 he and some three hundred self-styled red-baiters paid twelve and a half dollars per head to honour Matthews at a testimonial dinner at the Waldorf Astoria. Soon after-

* See Chapter Three.

wards McCarthy gave him the job of executive director of the staff of the Senate Permanent Subcommittee on Investigations. Almost immediately Matthews published an astonishing attack on the Protestant churches in the July issue of *American Mercury,* claiming that seven thousand clergymen and three thousand college professors had been enlisted in the cause of the CP. The reaction from within the establishment was fierce: even Eisenhower was moved to condemn as "alien to America" general attacks "that sweepingly condemn the whole of any group of citizens". So Matthews, too, was un-American. McCarthy loyally fought to retain him on his staff, but he soon had to abandon the struggle.

Unfortunately we cannot examine the causes of the purges, the political mechanisms deployed, the role of events abroad and the manner in which the Truman Administration anticipated the worst excesses of the McCarthyism which Truman himself later denounced. But the consensus of opinion among historians is already this: that the hysteria, far from emanating in the bowels of the general public, was artificially stimulated at a national and local level by competing political élites, and fanned in turn by mass media motivated both by panic and opportunism. Bombarded by scare stories, the public's reaction to the word "communism" ultimately became one of conditioned reflex. Likewise with the word "fellow-traveler". This conclusion is supported, for example, by a poll taken in 1952. Asked to name the *"two or three* biggest problems facing the country", only thirteen per cent spontaneously mentioned communism as being one of them. Yet when in another poll a sample of 4,933 people were asked to attach one of several offered measurements to the communist danger, forty-three per cent replied "a very great danger" or "a great danger". All poll evidence in the post-war era showed unskilled workers and small businessmen adopting the most violently anti-communist positions; the US political élite, in effect, was competing for the votes of the ignorant by drenching them in a climate of obsessive and neurotic prejudice.

The field of education was bound to suffer. Since the First World War academic persecution had by no means been unusual in America. As a result the Association of University Professors was formed in an attempt to protect academic freedom. Yet investigations or purges were not uncommon between the wars, and much depended on whether the heads of educational institutions with an independent foundation were prepared to stand firm against the local politicians and pressure groups. But many schools and colleges, of course, enjoyed no independence from the edicts of State legislatures. By 1949, twenty-two States had adopted oath of allegiance clauses for teachers, thirty-eight States had general anti-sedition laws on their statute books, twenty-one forbade seditious teaching, and thirty-one forbade teachers to belong to organizations advocating sedition. Twelve States authorized the dismissal of teachers for undefined "disloyalty". More than half the nation's nine hundred thousand public school teachers lacked the protection of tenure and could be dismissed without notice or explanation. In 1949 Governor Dewey of New York signed the Feinberg Law, which was later upheld as constitutional by the US Supreme Court, Justice Black dissenting. School principals were required to file a report on the loyalty of all teachers and clerks in their schools with the Superintendent of Schools. The loyalty of the principals was to be checked by assistant superintendents. By 1950 eight teachers had been suspended for refusing to answer questions. The general terror of collaborating with the Left hindered the emergence of concerted opposition to the Law, which was widely deplored: Catholics refused to co-operate with the representatives of the American Labor Party, while the Teachers' Guild (AFL) would have nothing to do with the leftist Teachers' Union (CIO).

On other occasions the Committee itself would descend on some locality, with its large retinue of hangers-on, like a medieval court or army engaged in a punitive expedition against dissident enclaves. In 1957 the Committee wrought havoc among the school-teachers of California.

Within the universities faculty staff tended to argue that a teacher should be judged on his actions, not on his private beliefs or associations. But trustees (overwhelmingly composed of businessmen) and state legislators took a different view. It was they who normally called the tune. The Association of American Universities, which spoke for the heads of thirty-seven major institutions, resolved that present membership of the CP automatically "extinguishes the right to a university position". By 1949 the American Association of University Professors was swamped with complaints that academic freedom was undergoing its most severe attack in the history of American education. But the shadow of unemployment fell on fellow-travellers as well when it was also resolved that a teacher who took the Fifth Amendment must bear the burden of proving his fitness to teach.

At Rutgers two professors who had taken the Fifth were fired despite the support of a faculty review committee. Such firings had occurred in at least six universities when the Association of University Professors censured them. George F. Parker, an assistant professor of religion and philosophy at Evansville College, Indiana, was dismissed in 1948 because he had served as chairman of Vanderburgh County Citizens for Wallace. In February 1949 the president of Oregon State College, Dr A. L. Strand, annulled the contracts of Dr L. R. La Vallee, assistant professor of economics, and of Dr Ralph W. Spitzer, associate professor of chemistry, on the ground that they had supported Wallace in 1948. Strand also reported to the faculty that Spitzer had published a letter in *Chemical and Engineering News,* supporting the views of the Soviet geneticist Lysenko. This, said Strand, was "because he goes right down the party line without any noticeable deviation...." In fact Spitzer had not endorsed Lysenko's theories about the inheritance of acquired characteristics but merely suggested that there might be some truth in them, and that they deserved the attention of American scientists. He also commended the public planning and financing of research in the Soviet Union. When Dr Linus Pauling, president of the American Chemical Society, wrote protesting against the sacking, President Strand replied: "... how much impudence do we have to stand for to please the pundits of dialectical materialism ... academic freedom entails some discipline in regard to truth...."[16] If Strand was thereby joining fellow-travellers with communists in the category of those ineligible to teach, the State of Oklahoma attempted to systematize the same principle by enacting an oath which demanded of all key administrative personnel such as deans and heads of department the statement on oath that, "I am of the opinion that no member of the faculty in my department ... is a member of the Communist Party, a communist sympathizer or so-called 'fellow-traveler'.... Those about whom my information is insufficient, or whom for other reasons I do not wish to include, are as follows."[17]

Some private universities adopted a more principled position. When the Harvard physicist Wendell Furry took the Fifth and told the Committee he did not believe that the USSR started the Korean War, he kept his job, provoking McCarthy to attack the "smelly mess" at Harvard. On another occasion, Frank B. Ober, an alumnus of Harvard Law School, wrote to President Conant explaining that he had not subscribed to the Law School Fund because of "extra-activities of professors giving aid and comfort to communism". He objected specifically to the appearance of an assistant professor of English, John Ciardi, at a Progressive Party rally in Maryland. The rally was designed to raise funds to fight the anti-communism laws sponsored by a Maryland legislative commission, of which Ober was chairman. Ober also complained that Professor Harlow Shapley, director of the Harvard Observatory, had taken part in the Cultural and Scientific Conference for

World Peace, held in New York in 1949. The senior member of Harvard Corporation, Grenville Clark, replied to Ober that a purge could and would have no limits, that it would embrace students as well as staff, and that it would rapidly destroy morale on the campus. Harvard's neighbour, the Massachusetts Institute of Technology, also made a determined stand in the case of a fellow-traveller, Professor Dirk Jung Struik. A mathematician and executive director of the Massachusetts Council of American-Soviet Friendship, and also a member of the Progressive Party, Struik had denied to the Committee that he was in the CP but had taken the Fifth on all other questions. He kept his job. Yet in schools and colleges literally hundreds of teachers, having taken the Fifth, were dismissed, suspended or forced to resign.

Speculating about this issue, Sidney Hook (like Norman Thomas) was quite sure that a communist had no right to teach, but hesitated with regard to those who had taken the Fifth. Much, he concluded, depended on individual circumstances; any friend of communism could in his opinion be said to have the same relationship to truth as a real estate lobby had to a judiciary post. But anyone who is really familiar with the behaviour of communists and fellow-travellers within Western academies will recognize that in nine cases out of ten, particularly in a climate of persecution, they will take every care to separate their roles as teacher and citizen, their educational responsibilities and their political commitments. And if by chance a teacher were tentatively to propose that the USSR did not begin the Korean War (or impose communal prostitution on all its womenfolk) would the free society be in jeopardy? Were Gorky, Shaw, Rolland and Heinrich Mann unfitted to teach had they chosen to do so? What a group of professors at Columbia clearly recognized at this time was that the main threat to academic integrity was posed not by those who took the Fifth but by "an atmosphere of apprehension and distrust that is jeopardizing the cause of free inquiry and threatening the right to dissent".[18] A step towards sanity was taken in 1967 when the Supreme Court ruled that mere Party membership is not a legally valid reason for dismissal unless "specific intent to further the unlawful aims of the Communist Party" could be demonstrated. But even this formulation is very far short of the democratic ideal.

A less dramatic procedure than expelling teachers, but one considerably more conducive to rigid conformity, was the practice adopted by many colleges and universities of not admitting a teacher to the faculty unless he signed a disaffiliation oath, swearing his non-membership in the present or the past of any organization listed by the Attorney General. This was precisely the strategy which hurt fellow-travellers and sympathizers the most, since the list finally extended to at least three hundred organizations.*

Witches were discovered not only in the academies but also in the churches. In 1948 the Rev. Richard Morford spent ninety days in jail after refusing to provide membership lists of the American-Soviet Friendship Society. Kenneth Leslie, a Canadian fellow-traveller who edited first *The Protestant* and then *The New Christian*, was another who must have found Arthur Miller's play *The Crucible* all too relevant. Matthews claimed in 1953 that seven thousand clergymen had been "enlisted" by the CP: "Party-members, fellow-travelers, espionage agents, Party-line adherents and unwitting dupes".[19] How had he arrived at this startling conclusion? Mainly by adding up the names of those who signed the Stockholm Appeal, petitions for clemency for the Rosenbergs and the like. Five of those he named had indeed contributed prominently to communist causes for many years: Harry Ward, Kenneth Ripley Forbes, executive secretary of the Episcopal League for Social Action, Jack R. McMichael of the Methodist Federation for Social Action, Willard Uphaus, co-ordinator of the American Peace Crusade, and Joseph F. Fletcher, Professor of Christian Social Ethics at the Episcopal Theological College, Cambridge. Fellow-travelling, as we have said, was an almost exclusively Protestant phenomenon: Catholics were conspicuous by their absence from these blacklists. Accused of having been a member of the Young Communist League and the CP in the thirties and early forties, McMichael denied it. As for Uphaus, he had supported charges that the US was using germ warfare in Korea. In 1956 he told the Committee: "Jesus stood before Pilate and He didn't answer a single question when asked."[20]

Symbolic of the disease sweeping America were the ubiquitous black-lists themselves. Here again there were precedents. We have mentioned the Lusk Committee's report of 1920. Then in 1934 an otherwise obscure housewife, Elizabeth Dilling, produced *The Red Network*, furnishing data on 460 organizations (including the YMCA and the YWCA) as well as on 1,300 individuals, among them Dewey, Felix Frankfurter, Freud, Gandhi, Eleanor Roosevelt, Wells and Thornton Wilder. Einstein himself later got six citations in Jack B. Tenney's report sponsored

---

* The State of Texas continued to impose such an oath on the University of Texas as late as 1967. The list of prescribed bodies in fact makes highly comic reading. It is all the more absurd in that it naturally omits many genuinely violent radical groups and parties of modern vintage, and this at a time when the main threat to stability in universities comes not from friends of the USSR but from militants of the New Left. One sees that the list makes a strenuous attempt to balance leftist with rightist organizations. However one might think that members of the Shinto Temples, or the Silver Shirt Legion of America, or the Veterans of the Russo-Japanese War are infrequent candidates for university teaching posts.

by the California State Senate. Late in 1944 Matthews came up with *Appendix ix,* a seven-volume report on communist fronts. The seventh volume contained twenty-two thousand names and became virtually a bible for intelligence officers in the witch-hunt era. It was of course a mine of misinformation and mis-insinuation. But the most cruelly damaging list compiled during the witch-hunts was *Red Channels,* subtitled "The Report of Communist Influence in Radio and Television". A purely private project, *Red Channels* was published by *Counterattack,* a weekly, four-page newsletter founded in May 1947 by former FBI men calling themselves American Business Consultants of New York. On the cover there appeared a microphone surrounded by a red hand. Again the habitual smear technique employed was to list names (151 of them) without specifically calling any of them communists (scarcely surprising in such cases as Leonard Bernstein, Aaron Copland, Burl Ives, Arthur Miller, Dorothy Parker, William L. Shirer, Orson Welles and Gypsy Rose Lee). An incident illustrates the consequences of this "red-listing": when the playwright Elmer Rice proposed a number of actors for the leading role in his *Counsellor-at-Law,* an attorney for the Ellington Advertising Agency, which controlled the production, objected that they all appeared in *Red Channels*: Lee J. Cobb, Edward G. Robinson, Sam Wanamaker, José Ferrer and John Garfield.

Faced with a choice between profit and principle, the business concerns did not hesitate. CBS appointed a vice-president solely to ensure that no one upon whom suspicion had fallen was employed by the System; at NBC a legal department took care of the same operation. In 1950 CBS imposed a loyalty oath on all its employees. Rice wrote in 1951: "Crass commercial cowardice has become more important than standing up for the principles of liberty." Not pleased by this remark, *Counterattack* promptly announced that Rice had supported eleven fronts in the late thirties and early forties, and recently four more. (In fact he had backed the exclusion of communists from the Civil Liberties Union.) In 1954 the actor Joe Julian brought a suit which showed that radio and TV industries were systematically blacklisting everyone whose name appeared in *Red Channels.* A production director, Charles E. Martin, testified in court: "We quarantine everybody in the book. We cannot take any chances." One actor spent four years trying to prove that he could not have served in the Abraham Lincoln Brigade. So degrading did the situation become that blacklisted writers had to employ "fronts" or covers who received public credit for shows they had not written and who tended to demand more and more by way of a fee. To all this Broadway, with its relative freedom from advertising pressures, remained happily immune. In 1955 the Committee held hearings on communists and fellow-travelling influence on Broadway, and though twenty-two of the twenty-three subpoenaed witnesses took the Amendments, they all resumed their work without difficulty. Arthur Miller was blacklisted from movies, radio and TV, but money was always forthcoming for the production of his plays on Broadway. Having signed the Civil Rights Congress statement censuring anti-communist legislation and the activities of the Committee, Miller finally was brought before the Committee in 1956. Saying that he had associated with communists in the 1940s but would no longer wish to do so, he refused to name names and received a citation for contempt. But it was not upheld in court. It was all a matter of chronology; the Supreme Court was by now becoming the bogy of paranoid conservatives and the whole judicial system was engaged in recovering some of the ground earlier forfeited by democracy. But for many it was too late. The numerous suicides which can be safely attributed to the effects of blacklisting and investigations were a striking feature of the time. The actor Philip Loeb, for example, had played the father on the TV Goldberg Show with success, but then *Red Channels* listed his front associations and he lost the part even though his contract had two years to run. His wife had died and it cost him twelve thousand dollars a year to keep his schizoid son in a private institution. He got some theatre work but it was not enough. A devoted fellow-traveller since the thirties, he told a Senate Committee that though he had never been in the Party he intended to go on working with anyone he admired. A brave man. But in the end the strain proved too great and he committed suicide in the Hotel Taft.

The American "liberals", those intellectuals obsessed by their hatred of Stalinism or by the guilt associated with their own Stalinist pasts, did little to check the steady erosion of democratic liberties. While libraries were purged and the FBI ran amok, they kept their gaze rigidly fixed on the enemy in the East and on the many shades of red in which his sinister flag appeared on American soil. It all began in the mid-thirties when many of them broke with Stalinism, toyed briefly with Trotskyism – then cashed the whole Marxist cheque at the bank for all-American dollars. In 1939 John Dewey, Sidney Hook and others had created the Congress for Cultural Freedom, attacking "Stalinism together with all fronts, stooges and innocents" – unpromising language in the higher reaches of intellectual life. Typical of the "god that failed" mentality were the editors of the *Partisan Review*, William Phillips, Philip Rahv and Dwight MacDonald, all of whom showed varying degrees of unreality in their assessment of the prevailing balance of political opinion.

(Orwell, who during the war wrote the "London Letter" for *Partisan,* actually claimed in 1948 that it took courage to criticize the USSR and that it was "fashionable" to agree with Zilliacus and the fellow-travellers ... who were about to be expelled from the Labour Party!) Rahv wrote to Orwell warning that *Animal Farm* might be less well received in the US than in England because "public opinion here is almost solidly Stalinist, in the bourgeois as well as the liberal press".[21] This was in 1946, the same year as *Partisan* printed an editorial called "The 'Liberal' Fifth Column" denouncing all those who favoured an accommodation with the Russians, including Mrs Roosevelt. At that time MacDonald disagreed, the immediate consequence being that *Partisan* accused him of having made "in objective terms ... a complete surrender to Stalin". But MacDonald was soon moving into line, describing in his turn Kingsley Martin as a "liberal Stalinoid". What had happened to these men and their kind was well analysed by Isaac Deutscher: the ex-communist, he wrote, reverses his old mentality without changing; "As a communist he saw no difference between fascists and social democrats. As an anti-communist he sees no difference between nazism and communism."[22] Such intellectuals resembled the embittered ex-Jacobins of the Napoleonic era like Wordsworth and Coleridge; Shelley kept a more balanced head but there were few Shelleys in post-war America. Phillips solicited material from Whittaker Chambers, an unfastidious gesture, and invited Schlesinger to explain in *Partisan* how fellow-travellers were allies of Russia's fifth column. When the Congress for Cultural Freedom met in West Berlin in 1950, the leading inverted Stalinists were present together with the "stooges and innocents".* From this gathering there emerged in the following year the American Congress for Cultural Freedom on the initiative of Burnham, Farrell, Schlesinger, Hook and others.

If one of the most obvious mistakes of well-meaning fellow-travellers had been initially to justify Soviet repressive measures as being directed exclusively against the class enemy, failing thereafter to perceive that repression had become an end in itself, a permanent system of government, then the American liberals were guilty of precisely the same blindness in reverse. Thus in August 1952 Dianna Trilling wrote that "the idea that America is a terror-stricken country in the grip of hysteria is a communist-inspired idea".[23] Irving Kristol wrote in *Commentary*

---

* Like any good communist front, the Congress elected successive presidents with impressive reputations: Croce, Dewey, Jaspers, Maritain, Russell. But the hard-line, god that failed, element was provided by such men as Hook, Koestler, Farrell, Dos Passos, Fischer, Malraux and Gollancz. But when one considers that messages of support also came from R. Niebuhr, C. Levi, Mrs Roosevelt and A. J. Ayer, one recognizes the "innocents".

that "if a liberal wishes to defend the civil liberties of communists and communist fellow-travelers", he must display his awareness of an organized subversive movement threatening "the concensus on which civil society and its liberties are based".[24] According to Peter Viereck, professor of history at Mt Holyoke College, American communists and fellow-travellers constituted "a murderous Red army of invasion on behalf of a Russian fascist ruling class". Dos Passos, who detected a conspiracy of assassins all around him, warned sternly that "a living organism that fails to react to danger is sick or dying", and complained about "the moral lynching of Whittaker Chambers by the right-thinking people of this country. . . ."[25] Granville Hicks testified about his former communist colleagues on the ground that every American communist "is actually or potentially a Soviet agent" – a proposition which nowadays looks as good as "every anti-communist is actually or potentially a CIA agent", and which in any case married poorly with his own recollections of local meetings of his Party branch in Troy: it was "more like a meeting of the Roxborough Parent-Teacher Association than it was like a gathering of conspirators".[26] Quite so. But for those who deplored the prevailing loss of perspective, the blotting-paper absorption of Chambers's apocalyptic tears, Schlesinger had a damning label: anti-anti-communists: "They just have a feeling that a communist is a rather noble, dedicated fellow, who deserves special consideration in a harsh and reactionary world."[27] On the contrary: the "special consideration" was immanent in the Smith and McCarran Acts. And in the execution of the Rosenbergs.

On 28 March 1951, the day that the Rosenbergs' jury deliberated their verdict, the *New York Times* carried the following headlines: "Acheson Exhorts America to Meet Soviet Peril Now"; "Danger of Atom Bomb Attack is Greatest in Period up to this Fall, Expert Asserts"; "Ferrer denies he is Red".[28] In summing up, trial judge Irving Kaufman deployed arguments that many liberals would have endorsed: "It is so difficult to make people realize that this country is engaged in a life and death struggle with a completely different system ... which is challenging our very existence." And he spoke of "this diabolical conspiracy to destroy a God-fearing nation".[29] "Fearing" was indeed the key word. The American liberals, in short, failed to recognize that legislation like the Smith Act put the clock back to the eighteenth-century Age of Absolutism and that its provisions on the advocacy of force and violence were not even in line with the "clear and present danger" doctrine of Holmes. Hook, admittedly, thought the Act required modification, but he nevertheless insisted that the investigating committees had "educated" the public. When protests did arise from the liberal ranks they were both too little and too late. As soon as McCarthy turned on conservative institutions like the Voice of America and the Army, the more liberal elements in the American Congress for Cultural Freedom decided, much to the disgust of James Burnham, that enough was enough. When the respected Oppenheimer fell from grace, it was time to call a halt. When they themselves could no longer receive *Pravda* through the US mails, the cause of freedom was clearly in jeopardy.

The case of Owen Lattimore was one of the most interesting of the witch-hunt era. It showed among other things how a person who held certain opinions about X was automatically assumed to hold "corresponding" opinions about Y and Z. Denials were to no avail; the assumption became insistence, and once the charges had been made they stuck. Not only was the victim guilty until proven innocent; in this category of thought-crime innocence could never be proven.

Owen Lattimore was born in Washington but his parents moved to China when he was only one year old. He spent the next twelve years in China, then went to schools in Switzerland and England. In 1919 he returned to Shanghai, entered an import-export business, then turned to travel and journalism, exploring in 1926–7 little known parts of Central Asia. He received an award from the Royal Geographical Society. Not until he was twenty-eight did he return to America to pursue graduate work in anthropology at Harvard. He then returned to China and witnessed the Japanese invasion. A linguist of high calibre, he became an acknowledged expert on China and Mongolia as well as on Soviet Asia and adjoining areas.* In 1938 he took up a post at the Page School of Johns Hopkins University.

Big trouble hit him suddenly. For some time after the war members of the "China Lobby" had been sniping at him – he regarded the industrialist Kohlberg as his arch-persecutor – but it was not until 1950, when he was working abroad, that the wire services began to hum. McCarthy was at work. First he called Lattimore both "the chief architect of our Far Eastern policy" and "an extremely bad security risk", and then, like the narcotics addict who requires ever greater doses, stepped up the accusations to sensational levels. Lattimore, said the Senator, had been "Alger Hiss's boss in the espionage ring in the State Department" and he remained, moreover, the top Soviet espionage agent operating in the US. Lattimore flew home and engaged Abe Fortas as his counsel.

* His books include: *Manchuria, Cradle of Conflict; The Mongols of Manchuria; Inner Asian Frontiers of China; America and Asia; China, A Short History;* and several other works.

Let us look back very briefly at Lattimore's career. From 1934 to 1941 he had been a member of the Institute of Pacific Relations and editor of one of its journals, *Pacific Affairs*. During his time as editor the journal published contributions from both pro- and anti-communist commentators. However the IPR's left-wing orientation offended some: when Professor David Rowe of Yale resigned from the Board in 1950 he remarked: "I have for a number of years labeled Lattimore as a fellow-traveler."[30] Certainly Frederick V. Field, executive director of the American branch of the IPR from 1928 until 1940, was virtually a communist (he pleaded the Fifth on this issue to both the Tydings and McCarran Committees in 1950–1). Lattimore himself made a number of trips to the USSR in the thirties, while Edward C. Carter, general secretary of the IPR, was on record as justifying the Moscow trials against the slanders of the American Trotskyists.

Then in 1941 FDR selected Lattimore to work with Chiang as personal political adviser. From 1942 until 1944 he served as head of Pacific operations for the Office of War Information. In 1944 he accompanied Vice-President Wallace on his trip to Soviet Asia, and the following year he was a member of the Pauley reparations mission to Japan. He was never actually a member of the State Department but his links with it and his influence over the younger China officers were considerable. And then, in the frenetic post-war atmosphere, presumably innocent or accidental coincidences like the following suddenly assumed sinister dimensions: FDR's adviser Lauchlin Currie admired Lattimore; Lattimore's successor as editor of *Pacific Affairs*, Michael Greenberg, later shared an office with Currie in the White House; Elizabeth Bentley claimed that she had recruited Greenberg into her wartime spy ring. Furthermore Republican hypersensitiveness had been rendered more acute by the *Amerasia* case. The editor of *Amerasia*, Philip Jaffe, a warm supporter of the Chinese communists, received documents from State Department employees and published them. In fact this was merely one more manifestation of the "leak" as a means of scoring in interdepartmental rivalries, but Jaffe was assumed to have acted as some kind of agent for Mao. The China Lobby was convinced, or said it was, that the State Department was riddled with Maoists. And who had exercised more influence on these bright young men than Lattimore? So the climate of suspicion built up, mounting to hysteria after the fall of China to Mao or, as some might say, to the Chinese.

By the time Lattimore reached Washington to face the Tydings Internal Security Committee, McCarthy's grandiose charges of spying had completely evaporated. Nor could anyone swear with certainty that Lattimore was a communist (he wasn't). But the informers were present in force. Freda Utley, whom he had met in Moscow and London in 1936, to whom he had given hospitality in the US in 1939, and who apparently believed that he was capable of pulling strings to secure her Russian husband's release from a Soviet concentration camp, came forward at the Tydings hearings with the statement that Lattimore's function "has been to lead us all unknowingly to destruction". The ex-communist professional "expert" Louis Budenz, who had apparently been in touch with the China lobbyists Kohlberg but who had never met Lattimore, attempted to prove that Lattimore's many anti-communist utterances over the years were an integral part of the cover, the conspiracy. Which was a big step towards the spiritual universe of *Darkness at Noon*.

Lattimore himself testified for 189 pages of the public record. *The Nation* called his performance "magnificent", and it was indeed excellent. But David Dallin attacked him in the *New Leader* under the heading "More Harmful than Spies", while Eugene Lyons surfaced with an article, "Lattimore: Hiss or Dreyfus?" Senator Tydings himself was not unduly hostile to Lattimore (he had his own quarrel with McCarthy). He told Lattimore that four members of his committee, having had a complete summary of his file read to them in the presence of the Attorney General and J. Edgar Hoover, concluded that there was nothing to show that he was either a communist or connected with espionage. Moreover, General Elliot R. Thorpe, chief of counter-intelligence under MacArthur, called Lattimore "a loyal American citizen". But within the Tydings Committee itself Senator Hickenlooper acted virtually as McCarthy's representative, at one point asking Lattimore whether he thought of six named people as being communists. Lattimore said he didn't. The Senator then gave a good example of the intellectual level of the witch-hunters by remarking that it was strange that so intelligent a man as he "would fail to sense or appreciate the leftist leanings of these particular people".[31] Lattimore himself commented on his ordeal: "As it builds up, it creates the wolf-pack psychology that made the old New England witch-hunts into a reign of terror."[32]

In essence he disowned both Marxism and communism, denying having any communist connections. Both democracy and capitalism, he said, possessed vitality and adaptability. He recalled that at a time when the CP was hostile to Britain, he had praised Britain's recovery after Dunkirk. And he described American Marxist writings as "mechanical uses of slogans and ready-made social, political and economic formulas borrowed from Europe and Russia".[33] He claimed to be no friend of the USSR: when the Russians had expelled the Living Buddha of

Mongolia, he had brought him to the US and helped to support him. Furthermore the issue of Mongolia had precipitated several minor quarrels between himself and the Russians in the thirties, and he recalled having written to Admiral Henry E. Yarnell in September 1940: "I do not think it is practical politics to negotiate with the Russians about their ideas and our ideas of the future of the Far East. There is too little in common between the two nations...."[34] In the Soviet press he had more than once been called "a learned lackey of imperialism", etc.

So here we have an apparently irreconcilable conflict of evidence. Was someone lying? Which was the true Lattimore? Leaving aside the demagoguery of McCarthy, the hysteria of Freda Utley and the cynical rubbish of Louis Budenz, we do indeed find two Lattimores – unless, that is, we recall the varieties of ideological duality which generally characterize fellow-travellers. In Lattimore's case, mainly due to the bias of his professional interests as a Far-Eastern expert, this duality of outlook had an unusual basis. Undoubtedly his over-all appreciation of the Soviet Union was more friendly than he made out to the Tydings Committee: he was, after all, trying to save himself under the judgment of unreasonable men in circumstances which must seem to any democrat illegitimate. In his *The Situation in Asia*, published in the previous year, he pointed out that Russia was envied throughout Asia for her schools, universities, hospitals, industry and modern farming. But he also pointed out that the Asians were less shocked by "the virtual civil war of the collectivization drive and the harshness of the political purges" than were "Russia's neighbors in Europe".[35] By which he implied clearly that he too was shocked by them. The pattern of his thinking begins to emerge. And then, turning to Eastern Europe, he argued that the vital, unstoppable forces were local ones: nationalism in that region was now directed against the classes who had supported the Germans and the forms of property they depended on. Expropriation of such property had been endorsed not only by communists but also by socialists and militant nationalists. Clearly, Lattimore also identified with this point of view. Though he did not employ a Marxist vocabulary, "landlord" was invariably a bad word in his lexicon, and "peasant" a good word. In fact he was an "indigenist". He believed both that local communism provided the only solution in certain post-war contexts, and also that such a communism could maintain its independence. Unless, of course, the West persisted in its efforts to maintain old spheres of influence: "We must chasten the feeling of unlimited power with which we came out of the war."[36] If the West supported reaction in the Near East, naturally the local populations would turn to Russia. If not, not. Great Power domination from either side was to be avoided.

Like Edgar Snow he believed that China was emerging as beyond the control of either Power; Tito had already shown the way. But if the US supported little Chiangs in Korea and Indo-China and cut off trade with China, the Asians would automatically turn to the Russians. He admired the North Korean regime as a genuinely popular one, whereas the US in the South was relying on collaborators who had formerly worked with the Japanese. Similarly he regarded Ho as the authentic leader of nationalist forces in French Indo-China. Above all – and this is the distinguishing feature of his thought – he foresaw and hoped for the emergence of a group of "third countries" which would be puppets of neither side: he was a prophet of the Third World concept. His thinking was joined as much to the partisans of the Third World in the fifties and sixties as to the old fellow-travellers of the thirties.

As regards China itself, under the pressure of the witch-hunt he undoubtedly blurred the outlines of his own convictions. *The Situation in Asia* contains an historical account highly favourable to the communists and highly disparaging of Chiang and the Kuomintang, which he depicted as the slave of monopolies, feudal thought and nepotism. Modern-minded Chinese capitalists, technicians and managers had thereby been driven into the arms of the communists. He stressed the KMT's debt to nazi training, its massive waste of US aid and its outrageous policy in Manchuria. It is therefore painful to find him pleading in the wake of the Tydings ordeal that in 1945 he had described Chiang as "a world statesman of real genius" and "never ... a dictator or fascist".[37] He also protested, now, that if the State Department had adopted his own ideas China would not today have been in communist hands: timely democratic reforms would have checked Mao's accession to power. This was neither convincing nor edifying; frightened, he was pandering to public emotion. But one might hesitate to blame him, for the personal menace behind these investigations was only too real.

But the Tydings Committee was by no means the last of Lattimore's "ordeal by slander". In 1951 the Senate Permanent Subcommittee on Investigations, chaired at that time by the reactionary Democrat Senator Patrick McCarran, described Lattimore as "from some time beginning in the 1930s, a conscious, articulate instrument of the Soviet conspiracy". Subpoenaed in February 1952, Lattimore arrived armed with a long statement which charged McCarran with smearing the innocent and conducting "a reign of terror" among American diplomats abroad. But so frequently did committee members interrupt that Lattimore got through only eight sentences in three hours. They seemed determined, as the Washington *Post* put it, to beat him "into sheer physical exhaustion. ...." But by now his persecutors had their hands on a valuable new haul of evidence – the files of the Institute of Pacific Relations lifted in a cloak-and-dagger fashion from a Massachusetts barn owned by Edward C. Carter. They contained, for example, a letter dated July 1938 from Lattimore to Carter, general secretary of the IPR, advising that it would be "the good scoring position" for the IPR "to keep behind the Chinese communist position – far enough not to be covered by the same label – but enough ahead of the active Chinese liberals to be noticeable".[38] The whole letter was impregnated with a concern for tactics and manoeuvre. It also came to light that in the course of a clash with William Henry Chamberlin in 1938, Lattimore had even defended Stalin's purges.

The McCarran Committee report accused him of lying on five points, and in December 1952 a federal grand jury in Washington indicted him for perjury, mainly about errors of recollection concerning events which had transpired ten to fifteen years earlier. (McCarthy's aide Roy Cohn had a hand in the indictment.) In May 1953 District Judge Luther W. Youngdahl, a Republican and a former Governor of Minnesota, threw out four of the perjury charges and let three stand despite "serious doubts". In July a Court of Appeals reinstated two of these four counts. US Attorney Lee A. Rover took the case before a new federal grand jury and obtained a new indictment in October 1954. It detailed twenty-five topics in which Lattimore's own opinions were said to parallel those of "the communist line". In January 1955 Youngdahl, whom Rover had unsuccessfully urged to disqualify himself, threw it all out. In June 1955 the Justice Department announced, after two-and-a-half years, that it was dropping the case.

A happy ending? These events involved for the victim five years of constant strain, loss of livelihood, public vilification and high legal costs. And what (one might ask the liberal anti-communists) was really happening? In theory, of course, the charges related to "perjury". But in reality a man was on trial for his thoughts and beliefs. In Hiss's case, at least, the substantive accusation behind the perjury charge was of having *done* something, and something very serious, but Lattimore was for five years in danger of going to prison for what he had thought, written and advised in the field of international politics. It is scarcely surprising that he decided to settle in England.

J. Robert Oppenheimer was born in 1904 of a wealthy New York merchant family. He was a brilliant student (not until he went to Göttingen did he encounter young scientists of comparable calibre), he read Latin poets in the original, he enjoyed Dutch poetry and he studied Sanskrit. Things came easily to him and his students adored him (from 1929 he taught at the University of California) to the point of imitating his manner and gestures. Haakon Chevalier, who first met him at Berkeley in 1937, recalls: "His fine curly hair, which he let grow rather long, formed a misty halo on his head." Brilliant as he was, he never in fact made a fundamental contribution to his chosen field, physics. Unlike Heisenberg, Fermi, Dirac or Joliot-Curie his name is not attached to any system, theory or discovery.

Disturbed by the Spanish Civil War, he moved into those Californian circles of the Left which held parties, often with a Hollywood celebrity present, to raise funds for Spain. He joined Local 349 of the Teachers' Union and the American Association of Scientific Workers. According to Chevalier, he favoured the Nazi-Soviet Pact as well as Soviet action in Poland and Finland, while remaining opposed to American involvement in the war. If so, he was close to the Party line. We learn more about his attitudes at this time from the accusations levelled against him in General Nichols's letter of 23 December 1953 which, as Oppenheimer's own reply made clear, was substantially correct except on one count – Oppenheimer denied ever having been a secret member of the CP. We learn that in 1940 he was listed as a sponsor of the Friends of the Chinese People, that he served on the national executive of the American Committee for Democratic and Intellectual Freedom, and that he was also a member of the Consumers' Union. (All of which, incidentally, were named by the Committee as fronts in 1944.) In his reply to Nichols, Oppenheimer explained that he had been influenced by the Webbs's book, which he read in 1936; on the other hand the purge trials had influenced him the other way, as had the personal testimony of three scientists who had lived in Russia. The Pact, Poland and Finland, he said, had also disturbed him (but here his version is flatly contradicted by that of Chevalier). When interrogated in 1953-4, he at first claimed that he had ceased to be a fellow-traveller in 1942, but he later changed the date to 1939. When this was pointed out to him by a member of the Board, he qualified his explanation: after 1939 he had continued to sympathize with *certain* communist aims like the organization of the valley workers and helping Spanish refugees. "That seemed to me fine at the time. I am not defending the wisdom of these views. I think they are idiotic."[39] But were they?

Oppenheimer himself had volunteered the term "fellow-traveler" as self-descriptive during a conversation in 1943 with a security officer, Colonel Lansdale. By fellow-traveller he meant "someone who accepted part of the public programme of the Communist Party, but who was not a member of the Party". He told Lansdale that this had been his own position from late 1936 or early 1937, tapering off after 1939 and definitely renounced after 1942. Certainly his communist connections had been both close and numerous: friends, a sweetheart who died, his wife's first husband, his wife, his brother, his brother's wife – all were at one time communists. His younger brother Frank, also a physicist, had been in the Party from 1937 to 1941, while a student*; Frank's wife Jackie was a Party member in 1938, and even after the war they both associated with the California Labor School, listed by the Attorney General. Oppenheimer's wife had apparently been in the Party from 1934 to 1936, but it was his communist woman friend, Dr Jean Tatlock, who had introduced him to a number of fronts. Yet subsequent history – fate would be an appropriate word – made Haakon Chevalier the most damaging of his left-wing friends. A specialist in French literature also teaching in the University of California, Chevalier had first become interested in politics in 1932 when he travelled to New York and met Cowley, Hicks, Calverton, Freeman and other leaders of the literary Left. A year later he met Malraux, Aragon, Gide, Barbusse and Bloch in Paris, an even more distinguished galaxy and one which greatly fired his imagination. He later became Malraux's American translator.

By early 1943 the Security Agencies had refused to clear Oppenheimer. Nevertheless he was chosen by Vannevar Bush, James B. Conant and General Leslie R. Groves to direct the laboratory at Los Alamos. In later years he was accused of having employed on the atom-bomb project communist and fellow-travelling scientists, but this was symptomatic less of sinister intent than of a scientist's natural desire to get the best men for the job. The success of the Los Alamos project launched him on a second and even more glittering career in the corridors of power and prestige. He became State Department adviser on atomic strategy under Acheson's tenure; the Acheson-Lilienthal plan for international control, which the Russians rejected, was largely his work; he was appointed to the General Advisory Committee of the US Atomic Energy Commission, and was later its chairman; he became Director of the Institute for Advanced Study in Princeton and he received both a Presidential Citation and the Medal of Merit. No scientist-in-government had wielded greater influence. The image of him as a dreaming idealist, a cerebral saint, an unworldly mandarin finally making a brave gesture against the power machine, demands substantial modification. He was, on the contrary, one of those who put the science of destruction

---

* As he publicly admitted to the Committee in June 1949, having previously denied the fact in secret session. The University of Minnesota promptly fired him. In Colorado he decided to raise cattle.

at the service of government, and when in June 1945 seven leading scientists sent a letter to Secretary of State Stimson warning against the ill-considered use of the bomb, their report was sent for comment to Oppenheimer, Fermi, Lawrence and Compton – who declared themselves incompetent to make a decision of a politico-military nature. It was only later, as we shall see, that Oppenheimer entered into a limited conflict with the military establishment, or part of it. But the Oppenheimer castle was built on sand. Because of the climate of the age.

In 1943 George Eltenton, a left-wing British scientist who worked in the US for Shell, and who had previously worked in Leningrad, apparently proposed to Chevalier that he approach Oppenheimer with a view to improving scientific collaboration between America and Russia. *According to Chevalier*, he merely passed on to Oppenheimer what Eltenton had said at a moment when Oppenheimer was fixing drinks from an ice-box. Oppenheimer had looked rather shocked: that was all. Nothing more was said. Early in 1946 Chevalier was interrogated by the FBI in San Francisco. The agents, who had a file on him, told him that three scientists who had worked at Los Alamos had sworn that he had approached each of them three times with a view to securing information on behalf of the Russians. Chevalier denied it. When they next met he told Oppenheimer about this unpleasant incident. Oppenheimer apparently looked worried. In October 1947 Chevalier was subpoenaed by the Tenney Committee in California and accused of having approached Oppenheimer for scientific information, whereupon Oppenheimer issued an equivocal statement withholding comment. But later he appeared before a House subcommittee and told what Chevalier regarded as the true story of their ice-box conversation. This apparently put Chevalier in the clear, but his career was now suffering in view of his political past* and he couldn't get a passport. In February 1950 Oppenheimer wrote to him: "As you know, I have been deeply disturbed by the threat to your career, which these ugly stories could constitute...."[40] After a period of estrangement they were now friends again; indeed in 1953 Chevalier introduced Oppenheimer to Malraux in Paris, an event which produced a crass reaction typical of the times when a member of the investigating Gray Board referred to this "Dr Malraux" as a well-known communist. So they were friends: there was still something Chevalier did not know.

The crisis came about after Oppenheimer – whose career had long been a matter of interest to the FBI, the Committee and other guardians of national security – had in December 1953 been denied access to

---

* And not merely because of his 1943 conversation with Oppenheimer, as he was inclined to insist.

classified material on the instructions of Eisenhower himself. The physicist himself subsequently chose to submit to what turned out to be a three-week-long interrogation by the Gray Board, appointed by the Atomic Energy Commission.

It was now that Chevalier discovered what he had not known. In point of fact one must add that the evidence remains at some points obscure, shrouded as it was in the cloak-and-dagger atmosphere generated by the security agencies. Nor would it seem very important but for the fact that Oppenheimer's accusers used it as proof that he was and had all along been a security risk. In August 1943, some time after his "ice-box" conversation with Chevalier, Oppenheimer had informed a security officer that an "intermediary" had approached three scientists, mentioned using microfilm, and explained that the information obtained would be transmitted to Russia through the Soviet consulate. But Oppenheimer had not divulged the intermediary's name. In a further interview he apparently altered the number of scientists approached from three to two. Still later, when General Groves, Oppenheimer's superior on the Manhattan Project, ordered him to supply the name of the intermediary, he had provided Chevalier's. Had he, in doing this, explained that Chevalier had approached him alone, and not other scientists as well? Chevalier later thought not (hence his post-war troubles), but Oppenheimer told the Gray Board that he had indeed explained to Groves that his earlier version was cock and bull, and that he had invented it because "I was an idiot".

How did those who now sat in judgment on Oppenheimer view the matter? It became clear that they believed, or wanted to believe, that in the first instance (August 1943) Oppenheimer had indeed told the truth (although omitting Chevalier's name), and that he had thereafter been falsely minimizing Chevalier's activities in order to protect an old friend. Taken in this light, his decision not to report these activities for several months, together with his initial failure to reveal Chevalier's name, indicated that, though not disloyal, he was on account of his associations and temperament a genuine security risk.

But Oppenheimer's earlier left-wing connections were undoubtedly the pretext rather than the cause of his downfall. They had, after all, been known to the security authorities since 1943. The salient issue was a quarrel over nuclear strategy. Oppenheimer had come to favour a tight defensive network supported by an early warning system, with less emphasis on striking power and big bangs. This the Air Force did not like. They preferred Edward Teller's H-bomb emphasis and they had their way. Familiar rivalries were involved, the Air Force believing that Oppenheimer's plan would reduce their own preponderant share of fissionable materials. Furthermore Oppenheimer had with characteristic arrogance humiliated Lewis L. Strauss, chairman of the AEC, before a Congressional committee, thus accumulating powerful enemies all the way. And when in 1953 he complained that the public was kept in the dark on the major issues of nuclear strategy, comparing America and Russia to "two scorpions in a bottle", he did not increase his popularity with the authorities.

They were out to get him and they did. His interrogation by the Gray Board in 1954 was a highly humiliating one. Some of the evidence supplied to the Board was kept from him and he himself was forced to rely largely on memory. Would he now employ a fellow-traveller on a secret project? No, because it "manifestly means sympathy for the enemy". And in 1942 or 1943? "I would have thought it was a question of what the man was like, what he would or wouldn't do."[41] Desperately he tried to minimize his own radicalism: "I had no clearly formulated political views." He stressed his unworldliness, his ignorance of economics and politics, even of radio and newspapers. This highly privileged man found himself compelled to stumble through doors his interrogators opened for him – then slammed on his fingers. The atmosphere was not unlike that of the Tudor Star Chamber, and his fall reminiscent of that of Cromwell or Essex – with the difference that Savonarola-McCarthy was also ranting in the background. Nevertheless, he may have drawn some comfort from the massive support extended to him by his fellow-scientists, notably Vannevar Bush. (On the other hand his enemy Edward Teller described him as a security risk.) It is significant that the only scientist on the three-man Gray Board, Ward Evans, rejected the verdict of his colleagues. "To damn him now and ruin his career and his service, I cannot do it."

But Oppenheimer was scarcely ruined. He remained Director of the Institute at Princeton, surrounded by esteem and patronized by the liberals who recognized that he had indeed put his fellow-travelling past behind him. Sir John Cockcroft, at that time Britain's leading atomic scientist, remarked to Sir Solly Zuckerman that it would be years before America recovered from the Oppenheimer case, climaxed as it was by the verdict of the Gray Board that, though his loyalty was sound, "fundamental defects of character" and social relations with communists "far beyond the tolerable limits of prudence and self-restraint" made him a "security risk". One cannot fully agree with Cockcroft. The Oppenheimer case served a useful function, revealing as it did how the witch-hunt mentality could rob the nation of its most valuable and eminent brains. And if subsequently many scientists did avoid government service it was certainly not science or its reputation which suffered.

This at least may have been the implication of the presentation by President Johnson of the Fermi Award to Oppenheimer in 1963.

"He used constantly to be reading seditious publications in the back shop; – it was there, in that cathedral of sedition, that he sat like a spider, weaving his filthy web to ensnare the unwary."[42] The prosecutor at the Rosenberg trial? Freda Utley accusing Lattimore? No: an English sedition trial which took place in 1793. Anyone who doubts that the witch-hunts were unworthy of a twentieth-century democracy would do well to compare the events in America with those which took place in Britain not after the Second World War but during the decade of hysterical reaction which followed the French Revolution. (Or, as Justice Black pointed out, in the reign of Elizabeth when it became policy to attaint all Catholics unless they subscribed to test oaths incompatible with their religion.) The British radicals, nonconformists and democrats like Paine, Priestley, Price, Tooke and Hardy no more desired the rule of the guillotine in England than the later fellow-travellers desired the rule of the concentration camp in America. Yet they did, like their successors, challenge both the social system and their Government's policy towards the foreign revolutionary Power, so that Pitt the Younger largely anticipated the behaviour of Truman and Eisenhower – Edmund Burke would certainly have been applauded at any meeting of the Congress for Cultural Freedom. These parallels are not farfetched; any historian who studies the two periods will be surprised by the coincidences of mood and action. Above all, the instinct to suppress was paramount on both occasions. When Paine's *The Rights of Man* appeared in 1791, the *Critical Review* (*The New Leader?*) called for police measures: "The evils arising from inflammatory publications are great and extensive ... writers of this class are more fit to plan 'treasons, stratagems and spoils'."[43] In the following year the vigilantes banded together to form the Association for preserving Liberty and Property against Republicans and Levellers: "Considering the danger to which the Publick Peace and Order are exposed by the circulating of mischievous opinions. ... It appears to us, That it is now become the duty of all Persons, who wish well to their Native Country ... to suppress seditious Publications...."[44] In 1792 Paine was sentenced *in absentia* and banished although, as Erskine said in his defence, he had by no means advocated defiance of the law. When the King's speech in Parliament turned out to be a model of McCarthyite scaremongering, Fox answered in much the same spirit as the pro-Soviet industrialist Cyrus Eaton was later to answer the Committee: "The next assertion is, that there exists at this moment an insurrection in this kingdom. An insurrection: where is it?"[45] The "front-organizations" of the Jacobin period provoked similar reactions to their communist successors.

The word "disloyal" was as common in Pitt's England as in Eisenhower's America (though "sedition" later became "subversion"). Anticipating the various Congressional committees of investigation, the House of Commons set up a Committee of Secrecy which dispatched informers to reformers' clubs and conferences. The informers naturally played their role in the trials which followed. In 1793 the Scottish lawyer Thomas Muir was charged with a seditious visit to Paris, while the Rev T. F. Palmer was accused of publishing an address calling for liberty and parliamentary reform. Muir received a sentence of fourteen years' transportation, Palmer one of seven years. But if anything the British juries of the time tended to a greater independence of judgment than their American successors: the cases against Horne Tooke and John Thelwell were both thrown out by juries.

The Smith and McCarran Acts also had their precedents. A report of 1792 reads: "When Mr Burke adverted to the [Aliens] Bill ... he said he would give it his most cordial support, as being calculated to keep out of England those murderous atheists, who would pull down the state and church, religion and God, morality and happiness. The extraordinary power it would give ministers was necessary and even proved the people who gave it to be free."[46] The French war, of course, provided a climate similar to that of the Korean War. And just as the First and Fifth Amendments came to count for nothing, so England suspended habeas corpus. Just as the US post office banned subversive publications, and organizations on the Attorney General's list were obliged to say so on their envelopes, so the Newspaper Act of 1798 compelled all newspapers to furnish the Stamp Office with details about publishers, printers and proprietors, together with copies of every issue. The radical Cartwright spoke of a "system of proscription and terror like that of Robespierre".

But between the England of Pitt and the England of Clement Attlee one would find few parallels in this respect. Strachey became Secretary for War and Cripps Chancellor of the Exchequer: their political opponents did not accuse them of crypto-communism or drag up their past. It was generally accepted (a) that a man had a right to his youthful follies and (b) that when he sobered up, he sobered up. The security programme launched in 1948 was confined only to those sections of the civil service connected with security. Additional procedures introduced in 1952 affected only 14,000 individuals. The defection of the diplomats Burgess and Maclean to Moscow did, it is true, lead to tighter security in the foreign service, defence and atomic energy: perhaps 120,000 were screened or affected. Between 1948 and 1961, 163 civil servants were involved in cases: thirty-two were reinstated and eight-three transferred to non-security positions. Furthermore great care was taken that security programmes should not be publicized and therefore the person involved (perhaps innocently) not stigmatized. The population of the United States is approximately four times as great as that of Britain; what such measures would have implied in America can therefore be visualized by multiplying the figures by four. The contrast is clear.

The treason committed by Nunn May and Fuchs was certainly no less militarily significant than that of which the Rosenbergs were accused; the two British scientists, moreover, confessed. Yet while the American couple were executed, Nunn May and Fuchs received sentences of ten and fourteen years respectively. There were no rampaging committee-men, no tribe of informers, no blacklists, no Attorney General's list, no persecution of actors and no purgings of colleges. In her *The Meaning of Treason,* Rebecca West, it is true, engaged in warnings almost as irrational and apocalyptic as those of Chambers (who reviewed her book approvingly in *Time*), but obviously some controlling mechanism operated in British politics, a tacit code of restraint, so that when Churchill tried his hand in 1945 at associating Labour "totalitarianism" with the word "Gestapo", the gesture rebounded to his disadvantage. In 1950 the Conservative candidate in the Greenwich election attempted to paint his Labour opponent red; the local Conservative chairman immediately refused him all facilities until he withdrew the offending poster.

Communists continued without challenge to teach in the universities, judged by colleagues and students alike according to their abilities: at worst, a commitment to the Party was regarded as eccentric, as rather odd. One case stands out: in 1950 the communist Andrew Rothstein was dismissed as a lecturer in the School of Slavonic Studies on the official pretext of "inadequate scholarship". In 1953 London University Convocation condemned this action, but the Senate made no move to reinstate him. And the schools in Britain, too, were almost immune from political interference. When in 1950 the Middlesex County Education Authority barred past or present communists and fascists from the post of head teacher and from staff positions in Teacher Training Colleges (a provision which applied only to applicants, not to incumbents), the decision was criticized by successive Ministers of Education. The National Union of Teachers opposed it militantly, none of the other 145 Education Authorities followed suit, and in 1955 Middlesex climbed down.

One rather amusing incident typified the British view of things. In

1952 Edgar Young, a leading official of a number of front-organizations and friendship societies, and about as dedicated a fellow-traveller as one could find, received a letter from the Admiralty informing him that on account of his political conduct he had been struck off the list of retired officers and could therefore no longer call himself "Lt Commander, RN, Retired". Nor wear uniform on ceremonial occasions. But his pension remained unaffected and if he really insisted on calling himself "Lt Commander, RN, Retired", then there was nothing anyone could legally do to stop him! This petty gesture produced an uproar in the House of Commons, evoking protests not only from Labour MPs but also from the ultra-conservative Colonel Clark, of Portsmouth: what, he asked, if a future Labour Government were to decide to divest him of his own rank? Another retired naval commander, Stephen King-Hall, editor of the crusading anti-communist *National Newsletter,* called the Admiralty decision wrong and foolish. The National Council for Civil Liberties expressed consternation and papers up and down the country published letters from Young in which he stated that though he was not in the Party he was ready to co-operate with it in all good causes.

The leaders of opinion evidently understood the difference between the 1790s and the 1950s.

The Reckoning

If Jean-Paul Sartre was never a communist, he was certainly no ordinary fellow-traveller, though the cap fitted closely during the years 1952–6. Unlike most fellow-travellers he not only took Marxism seriously but increasingly wrestled with its propositions as an integral part of his own creative philosophy. Again, he was unusual in so far as he accepted the historical inevitability of class struggle in the West, temporarily embraced a violent solution for the proletariat, and completely rejected the paternalistic, social-engineering-from-above approach so frequently encountered in these circles. Indeed his guilt at being a bourgeois ran deeper than the superficial posture adopted by Steffens, Gide or even Shaw. Taking the Communist Party more seriously than they did, he pondered gravely the contrary claims of practical unity in action and independence of judgment.

As a student and teacher in the early thirties, Sartre had regarded literature as an end in itself. Although not unsympathetic to his friend Nizan's commitment to communism, he remained more a rebel than a revolutionary or, if a revolutionary, one of anarchist convictions who believed "society could change only globally, at one blow, by a violent convulsion". The artist being a stranger in every society, the integration demanded by Soviet communism was accordingly suspect; the USSR was merely "a civilization of engineers". In 1936, while hoping for a Popular Front victory, he did not bother to vote. "The political pretensions of the Left intellectuals made him shrug his shoulders."[1] But Sartre's capture by the Germans and his subsequent career in the Resistance (which was admittedly more mental than physical), imposed on him a harsher, more immediate confrontation with the society in which he lived. The Resistance experience crystallized his concept of guilt and responsibility (a key term), and brought him into closer contact with the communists. Yet he could never run with the herd or hunt with the pack. His own singular philosophical evolution had to be reconciled (or not) with the dogmas loudly trumpeted on the communist Left. Both Marxist communists and fellow-travellers who were not Marxists shared in common the optimistic assumptions of the Enlightenment; the Marxists gave this social optimism a final determinist polish: absolute, scientific certainty about the outcome of history. To the existentialist in Sartre this was alien, wrong; man being condemned to an absolute freedom of choice, he had therefore to fashion his own destiny.

In Sartre's political evolution, three crucial turning-points stand out. The first occurred during the nazi occupation of France, when he extended the phenomenological system of *L'Etre et le Néant* to embrace a socialist humanism, absorbed a number of Marxist premises, and accepted the proletariat as the revolutionary embodiment of the universal ideal. The second turning-point came in 1952, when at a practical level he abandoned his reservations about French and Soviet communism. The third occurred between 1956 and 1961, at a time when a renewal of these reservations coincided with the recognition that the revolutionary initiative had passed from the European working class to the peasant masses of the Third World.

Moved by his experience of the occupation, Vichyite collaboration, the Resistance and civil war, Sartre forced by a series of philosophically arbitrary steps his existentialism to a socialist conclusion. Rejecting all determinisms, whether Marxian, Freudian or Pavlovian, he insisted that man is free, that man is nothing other than what he makes of himself. But if, as slave-owner, dictator or capitalist, he insists on using whole categories of men as objects, if he rids them of their potential for free action, then he has destroyed his own freedom. He accepted as undeniable that capitalism is based on exploitation, that colonialism is its logical extension, and that the struggle between the bourgeoisie and the proletariat could be settled only by violent means. Why, then, did he refuse his allegiance to the Communist Party? For Sartre, as for Marx, the proletariat was the universal Subject of history, the agent of its own emancipation. In theory, the same conviction held true for the communists. But practice belied the theory. Step by step those who adhered to the heritage of Lenin had transformed the proletariat from the Subject to the Object of the historical process. Like Bernard Shaw, they wanted to haul the worker to his feet by the collar. Increasingly, impulses of militancy and social solidarity were absorbed, disciplined and re-shaped by a new transcendental Subject, the Party.

Sartre could not accept the validity of this substitution. When the writer Louis Aragon described the Secretary General of the Communist Party, Maurice Thorez, as a "professor of energy", or when a communist writer insisted in print that "for a communist Stalin is the highest scientific authority in the world" – when he observed such ceremonies,

345

he felt sickened by what seemed to be a wilful abnegation of critical intelligence. At a time when French communists were insisting that Tito had been an agent of the Gestapo since the 1930s, Sartre upheld the Yugoslavs in their struggle against Russian domination. He was no more convinced by the charges laid against Rajk and Kostov in 1949 than he had been by the pre-war Moscow trials. In 1947 he regretted that the Russian Revolution had congealed into a conservative and defensive nationalism. He accused the French Party of having entered the infernal cycle of means, of developing an overriding preoccupation with tactics and the acquisition of key positions. Its intellectual atmosphere, which he described as evasive, cryptic, scornful and threatening, and its religious attachment to Zhdanovism in the cultural sphere, led him to the conclusion that "the politics of Stalinist Communism in France is incompatible with the honest practice of the literary craft".[2] As a writer, he believed that language was the human act of revelation by which objects were brought from the shadows and integrated in purposeful activity. But if literature was potentially a method of action, action by disclosure, this potential depended on autonomy, on an unfettered penetration of the possibilities of freedom, and on an absolute refusal to underwrite the official dogmas of any temporal power whatsoever. As a writer, he insisted on penetrating awkward episodes in the history of the Party which communist novelists like Aragon preferred to distort or ignore. The third volume of *Les Chemins de la Liberté* probes the duplicity and calculated ambivalence of the Party's policy after 1939. The contrast Sartre drew between the sincere militant Brunet and the scheming Party bureaucrat Chalais is reminiscent of Malraux's juxtaposition, in *Les Conquérants,* of the revolutionary ardour of Garine and the Roman, administrative mentality of Borodin. *Les Mains Sales,* although by no means the anti-communist play it is sometimes taken to be, explored with equally unacceptable rigour the machiavellian manoeuvrings to which the Party leadership so frequently resorted. Although Sartre was inclined on balance to endorse the necessity of dirty hands in politics, the very act of exploration infuriated the communists and provoked the theatre critic of *l'Humanité* to describe him as a "nauseous writer", a "hermetic philosopher", a "Third Force demagogue", and – supreme vilification – "an understudy for Koestler". "Every class," wrote the communist Roger Garaudy in 1947, "has the literature it deserves. The big bourgeoisie in decay delights in the erotic obsessions of a Henry Miller or the intellectual fornications of a Jean-Paul Sartre."[3] The following year Sartre was described in the Soviet press as "the servile executor of a mission confided to him by Wall Street".

Sartre's reservations about communism have also to be explained in terms of what he knew but did not immediately choose to comment upon. It was not until January 1950 that Merleau-Ponty persuaded him to break silence on the subject of Soviet labour camps. In a joint article, the two principal editors of *Les Temps Modernes* acknowledged that Soviet citizens were deported without legal process and that the number of detainees could be established beyond doubt at between ten and fifteen million. They condemned the police terror, the top-heavy bureaucracy and the distinctly un-socialist salary differentials established in the USSR.

This was in 1950. Yet only two years later Sartre committed himself without reservation to the cause of Soviet communism. His conversion, which was sudden and virtually unheralded, took both communists and anti-communists by surprise. The first thing to note is that the conversion was stimulated by practical, historical considerations rather than by a theoretical re-orientation. Although his observations of the predicament of the working class inclined him to lay increasing stress on historical materialism, he never abandoned his objections to the materialist philosophy as such. He continued to insist that monist materialism dissolves man into the universe and logically makes of his actions nothing more than mechanical responses to external stimuli. Insisting as he did on the absolute liberty of the Subject, it followed logically that the real ideology of the proletariat was revolutionary idealism. In 1947 he had argued that the Party, by stifling idealism and by setting up the Party as the repository of all wisdom, was in effect diverting a great historical force into whatever tactics of expediency Moscow's interests might dictate. Yet in 1952 we find that while the philosophical objection remains unamended, the practical consequence is no longer held to follow.

Why? In 1947–8 the possibility of a third way, a Third Force, of a policy which was both truly socialist and truly democratic, remained feasible not only to Sartre but also to Camus. By 1952 not only Sartre, but Camus and Merleau-Ponty as well, were agreed that it remained feasible no longer. As Sartre later put it in the course of a posthumous tribute to Merleau-Ponty, "our slowly accumulated disgust made the one discover, in an instant, the horror of Stalinism, and the other, that of his own class".[4] He had never believed that the Soviet Union planned to attack Western Europe. Refusing to credit Western statesmen with stupidity, he concluded that the Atlantic Alliance was created in bad faith. Its purpose could only be war. At home the growing power of de Gaulle's Rassemblement du Peuple français, which might seem illusory in retrospect, appeared at the time to carry with it the menace of fascism. The socialist leaders, having jettisoned Marxism lock, stock and barrel, had firmly embraced the Atlantic Alliance. Force Ouvrière, the socialist trade union confederation, received substantial financial support from the AFL. The parliamentary elections of 1951 resulted in a victory for the pro-American Right. The predicament of the Communist Party, now almost completely isolated in its opposition to the war in Indo-China, seemed desperate. American military intervention in Korea appeared to Sartre as part of a plan for global war. The spectre of McCarthyism had arisen in the United States. The crocodile tears of governments which lamented Soviet injustices yet maintained fascist regimes in Spain and Portugal and ruthlessly repressed national independence movements in Africa and Asia left him unmoved. He became increasingly convinced that the Moscow-inspired Peace Movement had to be accepted at face value. Then a small incident occurred. In May 1952 the French Communist Party organized a demonstration protesting against the arrival of General Ridgway as the new NATO commander-in-chief. The demonstration flopped. The workers failed to turn out. Within days the Pinay Government arrested a communist trade union leader, the editor of *l'Humanité* and, despite his parliamentary immunity, a top-ranking communist, Jacques Duclos. Sartre later recalled: "But after ten years of ruminating I had come to the breaking point, and only needed that one straw. In the language of the Church, this was my conversion."[5]

In those ten years, he had written eight plays and three novels. In the following ten years, he was to write three plays and no novels. Weighed down by historical crisis, convinced that art was an enterprise he could no longer afford, he wrenched his mind and imagination into provinces hitherto foreign to them, into history, economics and sociology. In a long, personal statement of faith, *Les Communistes et la Paix*, he argued that working-class morale in France had suffered from a protracted crisis of under-production. "The world changes and France does not move; the French proletariat asks itself whether it has not fallen outside history."[6] When Sartre insisted that the French worker was more interested in concrete freedoms, in work, wages and production, than in the state of intellectual freedom, abstract painting and genetical theory in the USSR, he crossed one Rubicon. He passed finally from the subjectivity of one class to that of another.

The French worker found himself in a Republic where even nominal democratic rights had been eroded. As a consequence of the new electoral law introduced for the 1951 elections, five million votes were required in order to send 103 communists to the Chamber of Deputies; to send 104 socialists, only 2,700,000 were required; to send 95 MRP deputies, only 2,300,000. Thus two and a half million communist votes had in effect been suppressed. Yet by and large the working class voted communist. The workers had learned through bitter experience that short-term economic agitation was not enough; the proletariat had to define and fortify itself through political action. Rejecting Bukharin's Marxist yet essentially passive or structural definition of a social class, Sartre insisted that *"les classes ne sont pas, on les fait"*. He struck an almost Sorelian note when he observed that for the worker the political strike was a manner of becoming a man. Furthermore, in identifying the tactics and ideology of the Party with the revolutionary interests of the working class, he crossed a second Rubicon. He reasoned that if the proletariat voted for the Party, then it was logically impossible to believe simultaneously in the historical mission of the one and the treason of the other. The logic of this is obviously suspect, but it was the logic he now embraced. The French worker had become a revolutionary without a revolution; only the Party could bridge the gap. "The working class recognizes itself in the trials of strength which the Party institutes in its name."[7]

Long passages in *Les Communistes et la Paix* are devoted to the international situation, and the impact of the world crisis on Sartre's new vision of the Communist Party should not be underestimated. Although he explicitly declined the title, he was from 1952 until 1956 virtually a fellow-traveller. In his opinion the Soviet Union, where some of his plays were now performed, and from which he returned after his first visit in 1954 with a favourable verdict, stood for peace. The USA, which was increasingly sustaining France's war in Indo-China and which was increasingly committed to the containment of communism in France and Italy, did not. His comment on the execution of the Rosenbergs indicates his abhorrence of American domestic and foreign policy in the age of Dulles. The execution, he wrote, was "a legal lynching which has covered a whole nation with blood.... According to whether or not you [the Americans] spared the Rosenbergs, you were clearing the way either for peace or for world war.... You have allowed the United States to become the cradle of a new fascism ... fascism is not defined by the number of its victims, but by the way it kills them."[8]

But what of the way the Soviet Union killed its victims? Fear of American foreign policy had thrown Sartre off balance. At that time the physical liquidation of the Yiddish-speaking intelligentsia in the Soviet Union was still in progress. The labour camps, to which he had drawn attention in 1950, had not disappeared. The power of the police, the censorship and the bureaucracy remained substantially undiminished. About all this Sartre now lapsed into relative silence. When pressed, he answered that every social crime reflected a crime elsewhere, a converging pressure, and that the extension of freedom in the Soviet Union depended on an attenuation of the external military threat. Having rejected the subjectivity of his own class, he remained unimpressed by Raymond Aron's classic argument that the ultimate virtue and safeguard of Western society lay in its tolerance of opposition and dissent. Sartre had to agree that in the Soviet Union he would long since have been gagged and imprisoned, but he insisted with some justice that the orphans of Vietnam and Kenya were not interested by the liberal climate of Paris or London.

In November 1956, he abruptly revised his position, entering then the third phase of his political development. The new phase, considerably more complex than the two which preceded it, entailed in the first place a simple negation – an absolute condemnation of Soviet armed intervention in Hungary and of its French apologists. Within two or three years there followed a more discreetly expressed and reluctantly accepted disenchantment with the French working class. Out of this second negation, and out of the historical events which provoked it, there developed a new, neo-Marxist philosophy whose primary orientation was towards the peasant masses of the Third World.

In Khrushchev's speech to the Twentieth Congress in February 1956, Sartre had found grounds for optimism. That the new, and seemingly more liberal, regime in the Soviet Union should nevertheless crush by force a legitimate and popular movement demanding democratization of a socialist state, was a shattering blow. In an interview published on 9 November he declared: "I condemn entirely and without any reservation the Soviet aggression." He denounced the Party's "repugnant lies" and its utter subservience to Moscow. "With the men who at this moment direct the French Communist Party, it will never be possible to resume relations. Each of their phrases, each of their gestures, is the outcome of thirty years of lies and sclerosis."[9] Yet only four months previously he had publicly lauded the same men for their wisdom, their lack of pride and their ability to champion the short-term demands of the working class without ever losing sight of the ultimate revolutionary ideal. Now the old antipathies and suspicion, so frequently expressed before 1952, broke through with volcanic force. He could not, of course, advocate a massive desertion of the Party by the working class; the fact that a socialist Premier, Guy Mollet, had launched the Suez operation with the almost total support of the SFIO served as a reminder that all other options remained closed. The problem henceforward would be to de-Stalinize the de-Stalinizers.

Sartre's reactions to the Hungarian Revolution shed much light on his underlying attitude towards social violence. It was precisely on this issue that he and Camus had joined battle in 1952. In his powerful moral tract, *L'Homme Révolté*, Camus argued the case for an ethic of moderation which he had already dramatized in his play, *Les Justes.* Camus's principal target was the Germanic philosophy of history, the obsession with ultimate ends and the justification of organized violence and repression in the name of these ultimate ends, whether they be national or social. The alternative to authoritarian revolution he recommended was rebellion – the act of individual negation or refusal which, even when it assumes a violent form, scrupulously limits its objectives, never loses sight of the humanistic values it strives to foster, and guarantees its own purity by an emphasis on personal sacrifice rather than on personal power. Sartre was not impressed. Camus, he said, had chosen to opt out of history; he had made his Thermidor. Camus's fastidious emphasis on means would gratify the consciences of those who preferred to criticize the *status quo* rather than to change it: "To merit the right to influence men who are struggling, one must first participate in their struggle, and this first means accepting many things, if you hope to change a few of them. . . . It is not a question of whether history has a meaning or whether we should deign to participate in it, but to try, from the moment we are in it up to the eyebrows, to give history that meaning which seems best to us, by not refusing our participation, however weak, to any concrete action which may require it."[10] In certain contexts, the bourgeois mind accepts the legitimacy of violence. This is true of national wars, and in some cases of Resistance movements, depending of course on who is resisting whom. In his play, *Morts sans Sépulture,* Sartre depicts a group of French Resistance fighters who kill and are killed. The play proved to be acceptable. But in *Le Diable et le Bon Dieu,* the most overtly socialistic of all his plays, certain passages evoked a lively scandal. The revolutionary Renaissance general Goetz reflects: "I wanted pure love: ridiculous nonsense. To love anyone is to hate the same enemy; therefore I will adopt your hates. . . . On this earth at present Good and Evil are inseparable. I agree to be bad in order to become good." At the close of the play he declares: "There is this war to fight, and I will fight it."[11] The war Goetz intended to fight was not national, but social and revolutionary; hence the scandalized reaction. In aligning himself with the communists from 1952 until 1956, Sartre, to quote his own words, had no doubt accepted many things in order to change a few of them. The repression of the Hungarian rising was more than he could accept. The Marxian revolution, as represented by the Red Army, was on this occasion employing violence not in order to eradicate violence, but in order to sustain an oppressive *status quo*. Sartre withdrew his allegiance from the Party. Camus might have been forgiven a smile.

Sartre's quarrel with the Party and the USSR was bad enough; it entailed a return to the unrewarding isolation of the years before 1952, the sense of living in the margin of history. But within a few years he had experienced a second and perhaps more profoundly desolating disenchantment. His faith in the French working class turned sour. The scene of this drama was the Algerian revolution. The whole white population resented FLN terrorism in France; the Party was compelled to denounce it. Young communists were now fighting in Algeria; how could the Party survive if it came out in favour of the FLN? Roger Garaudy complained that Sartre and his friends favoured "a conspiracy organizing itself in the shadows or an external intervention doing violence to the majority of our people". He accused Sartre of distrusting the proletariat; for once Garaudy was right. Henceforward Sartre's primary commitment, at both the practical and theoretical levels, would be to the revolutionary movements in the Third World, in Algeria, the Congo, Cuba, China and Vietnam.

In a renewed attempt to penetrate and assimilate the subjectivity of the universal under-dog, he turned his back not only on his own class but on his own people, his own race. From Frantz Fanon he accepted the thesis that the revolutionary class in the Third World is not the proletariat but the dispossessed peasantry – *les damnés de la terre*. Fanon believed that in a colonial situation hatred of the white man is both inevitable and necessary. Sartre agreed. Our victims, he said, know us by their wounds. We need to be ashamed, for shame is a revolutionary sentiment. Events elsewhere confirmed Sartre in his new alignment. After a visit to China in 1955, he told an interviewer: "I was overwhelmed by the unity of purpose shared by the people and their leaders. I call it the auto-determinism of the masses."[12] He believed that the Chinese peasants had been convinced of the value of joining collectives by practical demonstration and not by coercion. Meanwhile chaos in the Congo in 1960 and 1961 drew his attention to a neo-colonialism no less devastating in its effects and predatory in its motives than the old direct imperial rule. In the late 1950s he felt the need to incorporate these events into a wider theoretical framework, to re-totalize, as he would put it, his philosophy. The result was a massive volume which appeared in 1960 under the title *Critique de la Raison Dialectique,* about which three points need to be made here. First, the *Critique* demonstrated the extent to which Sartre had in the course of a decade and in the heat of many political engagements torn free from existentialism and come to terms with Marxism. Secondly, we can see how he had developed a sociological analysis which might explain the partial degeneration of the Soviet system and of the Communist Party. Thirdly, he had revised the Marxist interpretation of history in order to account for the transfer of revolutionary impetus from the European working class to the peasantry of the Third World. In the *Critique*, Sartre declared Marxism to be *the* philosophy of our time and dialectical reason to be the only sound method for the study of history. Relegated to the function of explaining the psychology of the individual and the influence of the family, existentialism was replaced in the *Critique* by man's dialectical relationship with matter, by praxis confronting what he called the practico-inert, by man's continual modification of the world and his continual modification by it. The shedding of existentialist categories led to another important change of emphasis. Sartre had earlier maintained that the source of freedom is simultaneously the source of anguish; hence the famous phrase "hell is other people". But he now moved closer to the Marxist conception of alienation, identifying its source in two interrelated factors: scarcity and need. In a world where needs outstrip the means of satisfying them, the praxis of one man inevitably conflicts with the praxis of another. Hence alienation. Sartre tentatively suggested that if alienation was born of praxis it may ultimately be suppressed by praxis, by social action. This would impart to history a profound symmetry.

Secondly, there is the question of his sociological categories and his attitude towards organized communism. He proposed a sociology of series, collectives and groups which, although they coexist, represent the progressively heightened states of awareness and common purpose in which human beings associate with one another. A social class – the proletariat – may achieve the cohesion and sense of common purpose of a collective, but never the dynamism and tight identity of a group. To a limited extent this exploration had been anticipated by the Italian communist Antonio Gramsci, who endeavoured to modify the simple Marxist dualism of the individual and the social class in order to account for the role of active minorities in the revolutionary movement. But Sartre's conclusions went much further. If a collective cannot rule, then the dictatorship of the proletariat is a contradiction in terms. Only a group – in this case the Party – can rule. The group may rule on behalf of the class which it represents, but at the same time it possesses vested interests of its own which lead it to disperse, serialize and make passive the same class. The historical problem of the group, according to Sartre, is that it is born in a moment of revolutionary apocalypse, at a time of high historical temperature, but is then defeated by its own victory. Faced with the danger of inertia, it degenerates into an organization with a new rationale and a new suspicion of individuals who propose further changes. Sartre stated explicitly that this is what has happened in the Soviet Union and within the Communist Parties. Finally, he attached revolutionary significance to the antagonisms generated by the original needs-scarcity dichotomy. Following this line of argument, he pointed to the growth of socialist movements in relatively undeveloped economies and also to the process whereby the Western proletariat, when confronted by a more radical scarcity, by the claims of the very poor, by the peasant masses of the Third World, temporarily develops a collaborative alliance with the bourgeoisie against the common adversary.

In 1960 he visited Cuba. His sympathy for Castro's revolution was no doubt a foregone conclusion. The political and economic analysis which he offered of Cuba's past and Cuba's ills, in some respects similar to that of C. Wright Mills, and in many respects unchallengeable, need not detain us here. Arriving in Cuba with the *Critique* already completed and his head heavy with labyrinthine formulations, he discovered in a blaze of sunlight their almost perfect embodiment and justification. Plunged into a world of youthful energy and idealism, he was again overcome by the humility that he had once expressed when he reflected that those who merely wrote for the service of the Resistance felt inferior to those who had fought for it. Here he is talking with Castro: "I thought I recognized in Fidel an idea which was too important to me to speak about. Except with him. . . . I said to him, 'All those who ask, no matter what they ask, have the right to obtain?' . . . Fidel didn't answer. I insisted: 'That's your view?' He puffed on his cigar and said loudly: 'Yes. Because demands, in one manner or another, represent needs!' "[18] For the revolutionary élite in Cuba he felt great respect: it not only provided the most effective means of controlling the environment in the context of scarcity, it also embodied the absolute end of pure freedom for men struggling against alienation. But would this élite, like others before it, surrender to inertia and organization? He was optimistic. "What protects the Cuban revolution today – what will protect it for a long time, perhaps – is that it is controlled by the rebellion."

In November 1956, at the time of Hungary, he had taken an oath never to resume relations with the communist leaders in France. But this short, squint-eyed, ugly and brilliant man, about whom so many semi-scandalous stories had accumulated but whose life was really one of single-minded and even austere devotion to his work, was perhaps too serious to be consistent. Praxis subverts posture. And so, although he broke with France-URSS, he remained within the CNE and the Peace

Movement. His plays continued to be performed in the communist countries and he himself continued to visit Leningrad and other socialist cities for conferences. Simone de Beauvoir explained: "It was an important innovation, that one could attack the USSR on a particular point ... without being considered a traitor."[14] Then in 1961–2, when Algérie française terrorism was at its height and Sartre's own assassination seemed all too probable, he began to feel the strains of isolation. "When one leaves the marginal zone of the CP," he commented, "one has to go somewhere; one walks for a time and then one finds oneself on the Right.... An anti-communist is a dog, I do not depart from that, I shall never depart from it." Nine months later he added, almost as if he were writing an obituary for the by then almost extinct fellow-travelling species: "Collaboration with the CP is both necessary and impossible."[15] Had he been Italian he might have felt differently; he respected the Italian CP for its lucidity and its relative lack of dogmatism. He would never forget once dining with Palmiro Togliatti in Rome: the restaurant musician proudly showed them his Party card and sang old Roman songs in their honour. One was, momentarily, absorbed into the great people.

The great high road of the pro-Soviet fellow-travellers finally turned to dust and desert in the year 1956. The Hungarian Revolution and its forcible suppression by Soviet tanks, following hard on the heels of Khrushchev's revelatory speech to the Twentieth Congress of the CPSU, had the effect of making the journey no longer worth pursuing. This is not a moral judgment but a historical one. Henceforward idealism-at-a-distance would be focused on China, on Cuba, on the Third World. Naturally a few diehards, whose pride was locked to their past, marched on among mirages and oases all their own. In his last years Hewlett Johnson was pleased to observe the climate of Soviet opinion swinging back in Stalin's favour. Anna Louise Strong, in her *The Stalin Era* (1957), argued that the evils of the time were caused by (a) Russia's past, (b) hostile encirclement, (c) Hitler's fifth column and, (d) "in part, from the character of the man who led". But mainly by the recalcitrance of the Western workers in leaving the building of socialism to an illiterate, backward peasant people. Pritt, for his part, regretted nothing. He has seen no reason to alter his account of the Moscow trials. Admittedly he felt in 1956 "shocked and disappointed" to learn of "the grave irregularities" which had taken place, but he saw no reason to abandon his faith in "the Soviet people". About this one need not comment. But it does reinforce the impression that the French fellow-travellers of the post-war era belonged to an altogether more intelligent, self-aware and sensitive breed than their British counterparts. Their autocritiques may have been on occasion tediously elaborate, and their recognition of simple errors of judgment may have been accompanied by unnecessarily complex philosophical speculations, but at least they made them. In fact the year 1956 proved that the best brains and souls of the pro-Soviet Left in Britain were inside the Communist Party rather than on its fringes, the irony being that in the wake of Hungary almost every intellectual of calibre quit its ranks while the diehard fellow-travellers, few though they now were, clung to their myths.

A simple fascist counter-revolution: enter the Red Army in the nick of time to save socialism. Thus did Pritt interpret the events of October-November 1956 in Hungary. The Dean also saw an "attempted counter-revolution" encouraged by Khrushchev's immoderate and unwise speech and, of course, by that perennial alibi, Radio Free Europe. The brutal suppression which took place he described simply as "the return of Soviet troops to Budapest".[16] Edgar Young went so far as to rebuke the *Daily Worker* for initially publishing the pro-rebel dispatches of its reporter Peter Fryer, reminding the confused editors *who these people really were* (the rebels): the sons and daughters of Horthyite fascism. Though he admitted that the Rákosi regime had its "sins and shortcomings", he maximized the disruptive role of Radio Free Europe, the Voice of America and the BBC, laid the onus of blame on reactionary émigrés and prophesied joyfully that they would be "wiped out, unfortunately with some students and some workers whom they have misled".[17] And if there had indeed been some legitimate grievances then the Russians were in no way to blame: it was all due to "the foul outlook inculcated during twenty-five years of the old order".[18]

But in France the events in Hungary left the PCF completely isolated. Sartre, Simone de Beauvoir, Vercors and Louis de Villefosse joined with some dissident communist intellectuals in signing an open letter which, after a protestation of friendship for the USSR, strongly denounced the use of force to break "the revolt of the Hungarian people and its will to independence". Certainly right-wing elements had exploited the revolt in its final stages: but who was to blame? Cassou, Aveline and Edith Thomas petitioned Tito to intervene with Russia to secure Hungary's genuine independence as a socialist state. Within the CNE a storm broke after news was confirmed of the arrests of leading Hungarian writers. On 8 November the Directing Committee had called on Kádár to protect the physical and mental interests of Hungarian writers, while admitting that the Committee itself was deeply divided over the general interpretation of what had taken place. On 13 January an extraordinary general meeting was held at which Francis

Jourdain, who had succeeded Vercors as president, attempted without success to arbitrate between the two factions, but so embittered was the atmosphere that no compromise was possible. Jourdain was replaced by Aragon: the Party was compelled to display its fist without the calf-skin glove. Then another front-organization, the French National Council of the World Peace Movement, exploded in the face of its creators by demanding the withdrawal of Soviet forces and the full restoration of Hungarian sovereignty.

But over in Devon, England, a playwright from whom we have not heard for some pages decided the Soviet actions were necessary – "a sad necessity", as he explained to his uncomprehending son. O'Casey was perhaps the only writer of genuine talent among the fellow-travellers who doggedly persevered.

Sean O'Casey was born in 1880 in Dublin, of working-class Protestant parents. Treated to a religious upbringing, he was confirmed in the Church of Ireland at the age of seventeen. Hating Catholicism, he began to drift away from religion entirely in his early twenties, finding a preferred identity in the Gaelic language and the movement for an Irish Ireland. At one time a member of the Republican Brotherhood, in 1914 he was actually secretary of the Citizen Army, but subsequently resigned over a dispute. In fact he took no part in the rising of 1916 or in the fighting against the Black and Tans which took place from 1918 to 1921. When it came to civil war his was a voice raised on behalf of moderation and peace – only in retrospect did the blarney stone transform him into a fiery militant. He later reflected that he had abandoned a romantic nationalism during the first years of the century and had discovered the real Ireland of poverty and disease when he read Shaw's *John Bull's Other Island*. And this meant socialism. But there was no Irish socialism, only Russian socialism, so the Soviet Union became Sean O'Casey's Other Ireland. "The terrible beauty," he wrote in 1949, "had been born there, and not in Ireland. The cause of the Easter Rising had been betrayed by the commonplace bourgeois class, who ... were now decorating themselves with the privileges and powers dropped in their flight by those defeated."[19]

For O'Casey the pen proved more attractive than the gun. After years of toil and poverty as an unskilled labourer, literary success came to him comparatively late; not until 1924, with the production of *Shadow of a Gunman*, was his reputation as a playwright made. The phrase "the literary side of the movement" was in fact employed somewhat derisively in Ireland to refer to those who talked and wrote about "the Revolution" but kept out of it in practice. Most of his

357

militant contemporaries regarded him in precisely such a light. Furthermore the naturalistic mode he favoured as a playwright blunted the impact of his political commitment, conveying an over-all impression of the artist's benign neutrality, so that left-wing Republicans defeated in the Civil War reacted with some hostility to *Gunman, Juno and the Paycock* and *The Plough and the Stars*. Meanwhile the establishment applauded him on the ground that these dramas proved the cruel and sordid futility of the whole Rebellion. This was not exactly the impression O'Casey wished to transmit, but there is no doubt that the closing scenes of *The Plough*, for example, saturated as they are by tragedy and death and the irony of fate, stand far removed from the tradition of agitational theatre.

So he quit. He went to live in England; to be a revolutionist in the peace of the English countryside and to fantasize nostalgically about an Ireland with which he was increasingly out of touch (in *The Bishop's Bonfire*, Dublin working men are depicted drinking gin instead of pints of stout). More than ever he felt the need to parcel up his plays and send them off, inscribed with fervent good wishes, to the USSR, and he did. Occasionally aspiring to wield practical influence, he remained a prisoner of whimsy: in 1932 he wrote to the utterly discredited Prime Minister, Ramsay MacDonald, "as an effort to entice him to where an Irishman and a Scot could sit together quiet, and talk things over".[20] As a professional Irishman O'Casey had become a bore. Orwell certainly thought so. Reviewing *Drums Under the Window*, he wrote: "W. B. Yeats once said that a dog does not praise its fleas, but this is somewhat contradicted by the special status enjoyed in this country by Irish Nationalist writers."[21] Orwell pretended to be surprised that an Irishman whose "life-work is abusing England" should choose to live there and look for support to the English people. O'Casey wasn't pleased: like many writers who relish handing it out, he couldn't take it. Orwell's remarks were "a jingo snarl"; he protested that he, Sean, had "a great and consuming love for England's culture", for the "broad, the vital, the everlasting England".[22] Of which Orwell, it need hardly be added, had no part. But still his pen would not rest: "And Orwell had had quite a lot of feeling for himself; so much, that, dying, he wanted the living world to die with him. . . . He yearned to drag all life down with himself into his own stony despair,"[23] turning men into beasts in *Animal Farm* and writing a new "Doomsday Book" in *1984*. Had not Gower in his poem *Vox Clamantis* expressed his fear of Wat Tyler and John Bull by turning the crowd into beasts led by a Jay (Tyler) who demagogically harangued them?

Orwell thus dispatched, off went O'Casey in 1949 to the World

Peace Congress, to show some of the fight, the refusal to run away and yield, of which he had discovered Orwell to be incapable. Apart from Ireland, his professions included Optimism. He would tolerate no pessimistic anti-humanists in literature – Beckett for example, within whose work "there is no hazard of hope". How "dowdy and doleful" were Camus, Kafka, Orwell, Greene, Huxley and Eliot, how poorly they compared with *our* witnesses, Copernicus, Newton, Beethoven, Shelley, Whitman, Balzac, Faraday and Shakespeare. These were impressive credentials, precisely the ones held aloft by Soviet critics, and O'Casey never tired of blowing a silver trumpet towards the distant steppes. "The great achievements of the Soviet Union; touching material possessions, deprived of all by one war, and most by another, having to start afresh twice with little more than a few flint hammers and a gapped sickle or two. Their inexhaustible energy, the irresistible enthusiasm of their Socialistic efforts, were facts to Sean; grand facts ... calling all men to a more secure destiny in which all heads shall be anointed with oil, and all cups shall be filled."[24] But if he ever visited Moscow, his "holy city", his voluminous autobiographies make no mention of it; whereas the pleasures of life in New York are vividly recounted.

The epilogue: Prague, 1968. The great fellow-travellers were dead; others had fallen by the wayside; and the younger generation, galvanized by the values, heroes and life-style of the New Left, provided no successors. Approaching seventy, Edgar Young was left almost alone to defend the indefensible even though communists as hardened and dedicated as Roger Garaudy could take no more. Weeks before the Soviet intervention Young was sounding the alarm signals, describing the *Two Thousand Words* manifesto, signed by some seventy Czech and Slovak intellectuals, as "a blatant call for anarchy, followed by counter-revolution".[25] How, he protested, could Dubček *allow* such a document to be published? Or fail to take action against the Party members who signed it? (Once again the non-Party man calls for discipline within the ranks.) Soon it all began to remind him of February 1948, and he urged "healthy" elements to act decisively and rapidly as they had on that occasion. When in 1938 and 1939 German troops invaded Czechoslovakia and extinguished democracy there, Young had been mortified; when in 1968 the East Germans repeated the operation he was delighted. Could one really blame the Soviet Union and its allies "for taking firm steps to save the Czechoslovak people from the folly of their rulers, before they have to shed their blood in the streets to save their factories from passing into the hands of the international cartels?"[26] The Czechoslovak people, he commented in November, had been "in a state of euphoria conjured up for them by cunning word spinners...." Then followed a surprising remark: the Czechoslovaks, apparently, had "suffered for close on twenty years a regime backed by brutality and blatant injustice".[27] Even so, they didn't know what they wanted and had no right to want what they did want. He revisited the country: "With most of the younger people, say under forty years of age, it was rather hopeless to argue." Quite so. Yet he was sure of one thing: those among them who had engaged in "dangerously provocative behaviour towards the incoming armed forces" were for the most part the children of nazi collaborators. But he did find at least one kindred spirit in the streets of Prague: a Soviet major.

Whenever a satellite people provoked the Russian tanks, Young had easily located the original sin of that people. In the case of the Germans and Hungarians it was the legacy of fascism, but with the Czechoslovaks some other explanation had to be offered. In 1969 he condemned the whole nation for having "featherbedded" itself at the expense of the Russians, and now for "going slow", as if the world owed it a living. The sooner the Czechoslovaks grasped the fact that they were in the socialist "union" to stay, and stopped trying to change the rule book to their own advantage, the better for them.

So much for socialism with a human face.

II

Into China

"Every ticket sold had a seat number printed on it and there was no crush or standing. . . . The conductors, instead of looking for bribes, looked after aged people."[1] Thus Wilfrid Burchett, travelling from Canton to Peking in February 1951, reflecting contentedly on the new China and the old. For here in China, People's China, new creators were emerging from chaos, flowers were budding in the desert and pilgrims heard the beckoning call in the distant West. The pro-Chinese fellow-travellers who claim pride of honour as well as precedence in time were those intrepid spirits, like Edgar Snow and Agnes Smedley, who first made contact with Mao's Red Army a decade and a half before communism established its dominion over the whole of mainland China. They experienced dangers and privations generally unknown to foreigners even in Civil War Russia.

After the failure of Stalin's strategy of urban revolution and class collaboration, and after Chiang Kai-shek's successful but murderous coup against his communist allies in 1927, the only hope for Chinese communism lay with Mao's peasant organizations which at that time numbered approximately two million men. By 1930 the Red Army was engaged in full-scale fighting with the forces of the Kuomintang (KMT), and in the following year Mao was elected chairman of the Central Executive Committee by the first All-China Congress of Soviets held at Juichin. In 1932 the Chinese Soviet Republic declared war on the Japanese invaders at a time when Chiang was manifestly more interested in crushing the Reds than in expelling the foreigners. Two years later the communists were compelled to evacuate Kiangsi province, where a Soviet Republic had been established in November 1931, thus precipitating the epic, six-thousand-mile Long March which began when 100,000 Red soldiers broke out of their encirclement and ended when 20,000 of them reached safety. Not until December 1936 was a truce with the KMT arranged; thereafter the Red Army became the Eighth Route Army and the Sino-Japanese war began. "Adventure, exploration, discovery, human courage and cowardice, ecstasy in triumph, suffering, sacrifice and loyalty, and then through it all, like a flame, an ... amazing revolutionary optimism."[2] Edgar Snow's description of the communists' experience in his celebrated *Red Star Over China* (1938) was in no sense an exaggeration.

Born in Missouri in 1905, Snow* set off on a journey round the world at the age of twenty-two and did not leave the Far East for a further thirteen years. For seven of them he lived in China, studying the language and teaching at a missionary college called Yenching University. Unlike Anna Louise Strong he was not a convinced radical when he left America. On first arrival he worked for J. B. Powell, editor of *China Weekly Review*, who supported Chiang as the embodiment of authentic nationalism and as the man who had saved China (i.e. Shanghai) from the mob. Snow adopted this view. After a trip to Russia, Powell wrote a number of anti-Soviet reports, the results being that Snow's subsequent application for a visa was turned down. Instead, lusting for travel, he visited Japan, Formosa, Hanoi, Burma and India, where he met Gandhi and Nehru and became an ardent proponent of the nationalist movement. Meanwhile he earned his living as a correspondent for the *Chicago Tribune*, the *New York Sun* and the *New York Herald Tribune*; meanwhile, also, he picked up Shaw's collected works in Peking and began his mental voyage to the Left.

Getting to Mao's Red Army in the north-west in 1936 was his most famous achievement – for a Westerner, a unique one. His arms and legs punctured by injections against smallpox, typhoid, cholera, typhus and plague, feeling ill but elated, he set out by train from the Forbidden City to territories "hundreds of years and hundreds of miles" removed. But of course it was not a journey one could complete by train, and it was only the circumstance that the KMT Manchurian army was then preparing for a United Front with the communists which enabled him to cross the KMT lines and enter Red territory – from which, according to popular belief, no foreigner could emerge alive. Finally he left the last KMT outpost behind him. "For four hours we followed a small winding stream and did not see any sign of human life.... It was the perfect setting for the blotting-out of a too-inquisitive foreign devil."[3] Pursued or shadowed by White bandits, he was indeed lucky to reach the communist capital of Pao An alive. But there he was gently received, one of his first delights being a meeting with Chou En Lai, already a legend, who spoke good French and some English. During the four months Snow spent in Red territory (he quit in October 1936)

* Edgar Snow died in February 1972.

he discovered a social system which was not yet fully Marxist but was moving steadily in that direction. He emerged from this experience a devoted fellow-traveller, but one with a difference: he knew intimately the world he described and his enthusiasms were never naïve, were always tempered by the shrewd appraisal of a first-class reporter. His prose resisted Marxist jargon while contriving to convey, sometimes drily, sometimes in flights of superlative language, the mental universe of revolutionaries who had adapted Marx's basic propositions to Chinese conditions. Here he describes a heroic episode in the course of the Long March, the crossing by Red troops under pursuit of a bridge spanning the river Tatu:

No time was to be lost. The bridge must be captured before the enemy reinforcements arrived. Once more volunteers were called for. One by one the Red soldiers stepped forward to risk their lives, and, of those who offered themselves, thirty were chosen. Hand grenades and Mausers were strapped to their backs, and soon they were swinging out above the boiling river, moving hand over hand, clinging to the iron chains. . . . Probably never before had the Szechuanese seen fighters like these – men for whom soldiering was not just a rice bowl, and youths ready to commit suicide to win. . . . In an hour or two the whole army was joyously tramping and singing its way across the River Tatu into Szechuan. Far overhead angrily and impotently roared the planes of Chiang Kai-shek, and the Reds cried out in delirious challenge to them.[4]

Earlier Snow had made the acquaintance of China's own most distinguished fellow-traveller, Madame Sun Yat Sen. In the early twenties her husband had brought the KMT into close collaboration with the USSR and reorganized its ranks using the CPSU as a model. It was after Sun's death in 1925 that the KMT under Chiang's leadership became increasingly anti-communist. Chiang approached Sun's widow, who declined his hand; whereupon he married her sister, determined as he was to legitimize his own succession. Madame Sun Yat Sen was no more a Marxist than her late husband, but she held fast to his principles of nationalism, democracy, livelihood for the people and friendship for the communists. When Snow first got to know her she lived in a house guarded by the KMT and the French concessionary police – she could not permit him to quote her directly – nursing her scorn for Chiang's betrayal of 1927 and for her sister's action in lending the Soong name to it. Always attractive to visiting Western fellow-travellers (such as Anna Louise Strong, who in the late twenties was darting back and forth, like a bee, between one red flower and another), Madame Sun Yat Sen was later honoured by high state positions in communist China.

In 1936 Snow returned to Peking, published his unprecedented interviews with the enigmatic Mao, and was anxiously interrogated by both Nanking and Japanese agents. The Chinese edition of *Red Star* came out first, providing many Chinese with their first authentic account of life in the Red territories; thirty-odd years later Snow was to meet lowerechelon Party leaders whose first knowledge of Mao was acquired from his book. Indeed the scale of Snow's scoop is reflected in the fact that no original Chinese text of Mao's autobiography exists, merely the account Snow took down and published in *Red Star*, the Chinese version of which is a re-translation from the English. In 1939 he revisited Yenan but thereafter Chiang's renewed military blockade of the Red areas sealed them off. Working as a war correspondent for the *Saturday Evening Post*, he returned in 1942 to Nationalist China where he helped to found, in co-operation with the New Zealander Rewi Alley, the Chinese Industrial Co-operatives. Alley, who had first met Snow in 1929, was a modern missionary figure who organized the self-sufficient Sandan community and who later lived in the People's Republic as New Zealand's resident delegate to the International Peace Commission, apparently turning down, *en passant*, a knighthood offered to him by London.

When the United States decided to quarantine communist China, Snow's green passport prevented further visits, though for several years he applied fruitlessly for a visa, hampered by officials in both Washington and Peking. The breakthrough came in 1960: he spent five months in the State whose painful and protracted birth he had witnessed twenty-four years earlier. Both his *The Other Side of the River* and *Red China Today* were hailed as classics by American China scholars such as Harry Schwartz and John K. Fairbanks – never has a fellowtravelling reporter been taken more seriously in academic circles, or deserved to be. No one has more effectively dissipated many of the myths clouding the West's appreciation of the nature of the regime. In 1936 Snow had immediately understood the virtue of Mao's struggle against the landlords. Unlike the Government in Nanking which was content with pious but mainly unimplemented resolutions, the Reds had implemented real, substantive social progress for the peasantry, arousing the millions to their rights and eradicating the timidity and passivity which were the Taoist-Confucian legacy of centuries. Snow himself knew well that while famine and disease prevailed in the countryside, in the towns hoarders of rice and wheat, moneylenders, absentee landlords and profiteers of every kind were callously prospering. And what he observed in the Red territories was an effective mixed economy, balancing private capitalism, state capitalism and primitive socialism.

supported by the confiscation of the surplus produced by the exploiting classes. Out of this pioneering adventure grew his admiration for its guardians, the Red Army, He noticed at once that its commanders led rather than followed their men into battle – hence the high casualty rate among them. Not only did they eat and dress like the soldiers but, contrary to popular belief, they fought without the help of Soviet arms. In his *The Battle for Asia* (1941), Snow described in detail the re-organization of the Red Army and the strategy of guerrilla warfare. "By the summer of 1944," he later wrote, "it had thus become manifest that the tiny band of youths who raised the Red flag on the lonely mountain of Chingkangshan far back in 1928 had launched a demonstration which evolved into a crusade which finally rose to the stature of a national movement of such scope that no arbiters of China's destiny could much longer deny its claims to speak for vast multitudes of people."[5]

The Red Army also represented a noble crusade to another intrepid advocate of communist China in the 1930s, Agnes Smedley. Having worked for some years with the Hindu nationalists, she arrived in China in 1929 as correspondent for the *Frankfurter Zeitung*, thereafter collaborating with Madame Sun in the cause of civil liberties, workers' rights and communists' rights. She interviewed Mao himself a year after Snow did, having put the urban life of Shanghai behind her in order to make a pilgrimage into the Red areas. A woman of impressive courage and fortitude, she shared the itinerant life of the Red Army when it became the Eighth Route Army: "The strength of this army, and of the communists who lead it, has never been in military force, but chiefly in its intimate organic connection with the people."[6] She belonged, clearly, to a modern species of secular saints: "I eat the same food as they do and feel ashamed if I do not share mine with them. Does this mean that I am indulging in weak, middle-class sympathy?"[7] But a tough saint: when her horse slipped and fell on her, her spine was badly injured. No medical help was available. Half-crippled, she lived with the soldiers in caves, later describing the sweeping of the earth into the Yellow River by drenching rains, the floods, famines and incessant deaths. She lay on a stretcher in acute pain while her underfed but gallant bearers repeatedly collapsed from exhaustion as men and animals laboured through landslides of waist-deep mud. Only in the Red areas, she concluded, had public health measures been impressed upon the population; elsewhere China still wallowed in the Middle Ages. Horrified to see that even in the Red Army the cooks wiped their faces, the chopsticks and the eating bowls with the same filthy rags, she herself was continually pouring boiling water over her chopsticks, an action both protective and, she hoped, exemplary. She lay beside these soldiers at night, in the caves, wishing the pain in her back would ebb so that she could snatch a little sleep, and observing with interest that they never moved a muscle in their sleep but lay like corpses all night. In November 1937 she visited the headquarters of Lin Piao on the eve of a Japanese attack: "The iron Chinese people, destined to decide the fate of all Asia and, in countless ways, the destiny of mankind, stepped up out of the darkness, passed ... a great excitement filled me: I wanted to follow ... to be with these men of destiny."[8] Fellow-travelling words, certainly, but words typed out in appalling conditions and read eagerly in distant countries; neither Smedley nor Snow belonged to the tribe which, flitting from the Hotel Metropole to Bolchevo prison, proudly announced: "*veni, vidi*, I was conquered". But of course Smedley and Snow enjoyed one inestimable moral advantage: they praised not a regime but a resistance movement, not a state apparatus but a rebellion, at a time when the KMT State itself, with its squandering of American aid, its nepotism, corruption and inefficiency, its persistent preference for fighting Reds rather than fighting Japanese, was both easy and legitimate to despise. But after 1949 problems with which we are familiar must dominate our assessment of the fellow-travellers.

What, for example, of the post-Liberation purges? According to Chou En Lai, 830,000 "enemies of the people" had been "destroyed" during land confiscation, the mass trials and the round-up which ended in 1954. Writing after his 1960 visit, Snow reflected that the term "hsiao-mieh" does not necessarily mean *physically* destroyed – so we are immediately back in the sphere of question-begging. In any case, he said, this figure represents only fourteen per million, whereas the Civil War had cost millions of lives. Moreover the communist regime had to cope with hundreds of thousands of former KMT soldiers who turned bandit after 1949; a judge had assured him that the death sentence was imposed only when the culprit's actions had caused the death of a citizen. By 1960, he was told, executions were no more than eight to twelve a month. But there were no official statistics – usually, one feels, an ominous sign, except to fellow-travellers. Simone de Beauvoir, who spent six weeks in China in 1955, also exonerated the regime from charges of repression. Flying over Mongolia from Moscow, she recognized the figures, horses and steppes she had seen more than twenty years earlier in *Storm Over Asia*; then the Gobi desert. "And now my nose to the porthole glass, gazing down at this colourless and naked desert beneath this misty sky, I was coming around to convincing myself that pretty soon, I would be arriving in Peking.'"⁹ She soon came around to convincing herself that, contrary to the accusations levelled by Gérard Rosenthal and David Rousset, the critics of the *univers concentration-naire* with whom she and Sartre were locked in combat, Chinese citizens were liable to arrest only in cases of sabotage or when they had agitated in such a way as to endanger the State. And she was willing to trust the communists to interpret the phrase "endanger the State" fairly. She admitted that the figure provided to her of political prisoners sentenced – six hundred thousand – could not be checked, but she was sure the trials were conducted according to the rule of law. There was no equivalent to the administrative internment or arbitrary imprisonment earlier practised in the USSR: "no citizen in China is bothered on account of his opinions".[10] A bold assertion indeed.

Democracy in China? "Are not all the popular elections an irrelevant façade?" asked Snow in 1960. "The answer must be that they are not."[11] Because in the course of these elections vast numbers of people were brought to participate in and to become psychologically committed to the communist regime. By participating in the choice of local administrators, argued Snow, the peasant commits himself to the whole process of power delegated by proxies to the higher administration: very much what the Webbs had said of Russia. Felix Greene, who first visited China in 1957, also echoed the mood of the Webbs: "The idea that explanation, talk, discussion, will eventually convince, runs through Chinese society today."[12] The fact that Mao had proposed his own resignation as Chairman of the Republic in 1958, and that this proposal had been discussed for a full month at every level of society, seemed to him impressive (as did Mao's painful decision not to resign after all). Furthermore, said Greene, all boss-figures in the new China must serve one month a year in the ranks – a feature of life which later excited admirers of Castro's Cuba.

What of leader-worship: was it repeated a second time round? Worship is perhaps too strong a word. Of all the men she met at Taiyüan, Agnes Smedley was most impressed by the able, realistic, cultured, handsome Chou En Lai. Snow shared her feelings about Chou. As for Mao, he detected in him "a certain fire of destiny"; yes, "one felt that whatever there was extraordinary in this man grew out of the uncanny degree to which he synthesized and expressed the urgent demands of millions of Chinese and especially the peasantry".[13] The Red Army commander Lin Piao likewise fascinated Western observers who came into contact with him. When he returned to China in 1960, Snow was delighted to discover that for twenty-five years there had been no open split in the Party leadership; nor was the Politburo composed of Mao's creatures or yes-men; none of its members had been in the Party for less than thirty years. Certainly the cult of Mao had grown but Mao himself had never aspired to the absolute power popularly but mistakenly attributed to him. Unlike Stalin, Mao did not exterminate his colleagues, even though Chou and Liu Shao Ch'i had once been in opposition to him (Snow was writing before the Cultural Revolution and Liu's disgrace). But if Snow's comments here were in many respects justified (though he, like the pro-Soviet fellow-travellers, was prone to justify the cult of the leader in terms of a permanent national crisis brought on by foreign encirclement), the Dean of Canterbury, once he crossed the Gobi Desert, could be relied upon to exercise his customary gift for hagiography. Meeting Mao, he encountered another hero: "He had the beautiful head of the portraits ... as he spoke his whole expression lit up with warmth and radiance."[14] Greene agreed with Snow that the Chinese leadership had much to recommend it compared with the men who ruled in the Kremlin: no obsequiousness, no yes-men, no jockeying for power, no personal rivalries; when Mao visited a factory or farm the people were never nervous or flustered.

In fact a remarkable feature of pro-Chinese fellow-travelling was the conscious distinctions it drew between Chinese and Stalinist attitudes, combined with a naïvety of interpretation which often echoed to the letter that of the pro-Soviet intellectuals. Thus when Professor Joan Robinson visited China during the Cultural Revolution and caught sight of the ubiquitous portraits of Mao, the omnipresent quotations from Mao, the obligatory Little Red Book of Mao and the fanatical cult of Mao, she nevertheless concluded: "But nothing could be further than Mao's style from the vanity and paranoia of Stalin's last years. The prestige of Mao is a national asset and he is using it, very coolly, to preserve unity in the face of sharp conflict."[15] But, on the contrary, the cult of Mao was being exploited to exacerbate conflict. She also contrived to argue that Mao-worship was focused less on the man than on his "Holy Scriptures" – a distinction difficult to sustain particularly when Professor Robinson went on to quote a telegram from the Shanghai Red Guards to Mao, calling him "our great teacher, great leader, great supreme commander, and great helmsman, and the red sun that shines most brilliantly in our hearts".[16] Ultimately Snow himself fell into the trap of those who fail to recognize that the leaders of communist regimes, rather than history, are two hundred per cent responsible for the cult of their own personalities and, as such, are to be condemned for reducing national thought to the level of the nursery. Snow, of course, had to be careful; as the Western reporter with the most privileged access to the Chairman he must have realized that if he gave the slightest offence confidence would crumble and future visits would be in jeopardy. After talking with Mao in 1965 he had made an almost fatal mistake by reporting the Chairman's own admission that a cult of personality existed in China and that there was good cause for one; as a result ultra-left-wing officials blocked his return to China in 1967 and 1968. Then in 1971, in the course of yet another interview, Mao explained his earlier remarks: the Mao cult had at that time been a vital weapon for stimulating the masses to dismantle the anti-Mao Party bureaucracy (which again demonstrates the absurdity of Joan Robinson's hypothesis). On the face of it, Snow accepted this explanation, adding: "Of course the personality cult had been overdone. Today, things were different. It was hard, the Chairman said, for people to overcome the habits of 3,000 years of emperor-worshipping ... those epithets applied to Mao ... what a nuisance. They would all be eliminated sooner or later. Only the word 'teacher' would be retained – that is, simply schoolteacher."[17] Whereupon Snow offered Mao the kind of trusting naïvety which Stalin had expected (and exacted) from Feuchtwanger. " 'I often wonder,' I said, 'whether those who shout Mao the loudest and wave the most banners are not – as some say – waving the Red Flag in order to defeat the Red Flag.' " Stalin had suggested that Trotskyite wreckers were boosting the cult of his personality in order to discredit him; Mao's response to Snow's suggestion was slightly different. The Mao-shouters, he said, fell into three categories: the sincere people, the opportunists who drifted with the tide, and the hypocrites. What Mao did not mention was that to drift with the tide or, rather, gallop with the stampeding herd, had become the price of survival in the course of a Cultural Revolution which he had stage-managed from first to last.

Some fellow-travellers discharged pro-Soviet and pro-Chinese enthusiasms without discrimination. But others, like Snow and Joan Robinson, for whom an earlier god had failed, found the Chinese Revolution an immense improvement on its Soviet predecessor. Snow held Stalin responsible for the débâcle of Comintern policy in China in 1927; he noted how Stalin abolished the Comintern with the stroke of a pen in 1943; and when he worked in Russia as a correspondent during the war he apparently suffered from no illusions about the trials and purges. In December 1948 he suggested in the *Saturday Evening Post* that Tito's heresy marked the beginning of communist heterodoxy and foreshadowed a Sino-Soviet dispute in the future – prophetic enough for the Russians to refuse him a visa. He also described the communist states of Eastern Europe as "satellites", thus demolishing any suspicions that he might be a fellow-traveller in relation to the USSR.

But did not China, too, possess labour camps on the Soviet model? Well, said Simone de Beauvoir, there certainly existed centres of "re-habilitation" and "re-education" – which isn't properly speaking a labour camp. And Peking apparently contained its "Bolchevo": the fellow-travellers flocked to it, enthralled, as Simone de Beauvoir was, to find it located "in the depths of a kind of park ... no warders, no guards, only ... unarmed overseers ... a theatre where a movie is shown or a play presented once a week...." Visiting what was ap-parently the same prison in 1960, Snow was delighted to note the absence of sentries (except one), although the prison was said to contain 1,800 prisoners many of whom were classified as counter-revolutionary. Yes, they had their own band, opera and outdoor theatre; movies once a week; no window bars; clean white rooms with open doors; prisoners running their own barber shop, library and canteen. Would Sing Sing, he asked, remove armed guards for the benefit of foreign journalists? (But what evidence is there that this was the Chinese Sing Sing?) As for forced labour, he did not doubt that the detention system was integrated with the production system and that a ceaseless campaign was conducted to bend minds and wills to the regime, but he had seen men yoked to-gether like cattle in the old China and you never saw that now. Nor the concentration camps surrounded by barbed wire which he personally had discovered in the Soviet Union. Taiwan's claim of twenty-five million slave labourers inside communist China was patently absurd, and he even doubted the ILO's estimate of forced labour "on a vast scale". But who could tell?

Of course many of the things which visitors to the new China admired resembled those aspects of Soviet development which had seemed so attractive in the twenties: mass education, health services and women's rights. In 1936 peasants had told Snow how the Red Army had taught them to read and write, or how to use a radio, and after four years the Reds had achieved a higher literacy rate than had been reached in centuries. According to Simone de Beauvoir, during the seven years following the Liberation ten million adults had learned to read, write and calculate. But there were still fewer than 1,400,000 primary school teachers confronting 70,000,000 pupils. So the people taught itself by chain-action. Felix Greene noticed that children in the new China could do no wrong, they were the only truly privileged class – an impression which corresponded to those of visitors to Russia during the Civil War. Even so, Greene still carried traces of his Western scepticism: how, he asked a teacher to her considerable indignation, does one teach a child of four politics? As a feminist, Simone de Beauvoir naturally took a keen interest in the status of women in China, in the Marriage Act of 1950, the eradication of child marriage, arranged marriages and infanticide, and in the new, easier divorce provisions. She strenuously denounced the lie that China was killing either individualism or the family. For her this was a "stirring and reasonable revolution which had not only delivered peasants and workers from exploitation, but had rid an entire land of the foreigner".[18] True. And in Peking she noticed that "nobody is arrogant here, nobody is grabby, nobody feels himself above or below anybody else"[19] – roughly what Waldo Frank had felt in Leningrad in 1932 and what Simone de Beauvoir herself had felt in Yugoslavia. The prevailing order and decency was greatly to her tidy taste: no drunkards about, no litter, nothing but healthy, exuberant children frolicking. "I made a tour of a village. Not one speck of garbage, not a pool of stagnant water left; the air smelled clean – I had not thought that a village could be so neat."[20] A schoolmistress at heart, she laboured conscientiously over her homework, reading scores of books on China's history and absorbing vast quantities of statistics, determined, as she later told the Helsinki Peace Congress, to give the lie to Hong-Kong propaganda. "For the first time I touched the Far East ... for the first time I participated in that hard work: the construction of socialism."[21] The arguments of the anti-communists infuriated her: yes, everyone in China wore blue clothes: so what? Did they forget that under the old regime three-quarters of the population wore nothing (well, almost nothing). She worked herself almost to the point of illness writing *The Long March*, but later she felt vindicated when other non-communists like René Dumont, Josué de Castro and Tibor Mende confirmed her conclusions in essence.

The fetish of production statistics soon surfaced among China's fellow-travellers. As Simone de Beauvoir put it (and she might easily have been referring to Russia after 1928): "The heroic age was now over; the problem at present was to industrialize." Felix Greene, noticing the amazing speed with which offices, houses, hospitals, schools, hotels, stadiums and gymnasiums were springing up, plunged headlong into iron and steel statistics. "We employ fifty-one thousand workers today!" a factory manager told him. "Two years ago it was only twelve thousand." In a city commune containing 162,000 souls, he discovered that the amenities included 184 kindergartens, 356 public dining rooms, 433 nurseries and 18 large factories: "the figures make one's head reel". Quoting the calculations of Dr Bettelheim, Greene announced that in a single year after 1958 Chinese industrial growth went from a level lower than that of the USSR in 1932 to a level not reached by the Russians

industry from 1941 to 1945 had something to do with it, but really until thirteen or fourteen years later! Perhaps the devastation of Soviet such absurd claims are as much pie-in-the-sky as Greene's later bid to *treble* China's industrial production in the *three* years after the Great Leap Forward began in 1958. Even so, as he said, China's economic expansion did indeed compare favourably with India's continued stagnation.

Three phases of China's internal policy demand our special attention: the "Hundred Flowers" episode, the "Great Leap Forward" and the "Cultural Revolution". Each came under heavy criticism in the West, provoking in turn a predictable vindication by the friends of China.

It will be recalled that according to Simone de Beauvoir no citizen of China was bothered on account of his opinions. As soon as the Hundred Flowers began to bloom, however, she concluded that previously communist China had been crippled by hidebound orthodoxy and that fear of being accused of "idealism" had paralysed every independent thinker. The fellow-traveller almost invariably maintains that things are fine *now* – until the authorities announce they are not fine and that something must be done; whereupon things once again become fine. So: "The gag has been removed. . . . Never has a popular democracy carried liberalism so far."[22] Explaining that although both politics and culture reflect class tensions, culture does so in a more subtle form, she made herself the mouthpiece of the Party by insisting that the Hundred Flowers would enable materialism to overcome idealism in the cultural field by means of an open contest – as Lu Ting Yi, head of the propaganda section of the Central Committee, said in May 1956. Actually the gag soon came back and with a vengeance, so that Greene had to admit that some who had dared to criticize the regime under the proclaimed immunity had for their pains been sent to work among the peasants, which didn't seem to him fair play. Snow wrote a careful and critical analysis of the whole episode, showing how critics had challenged Party dogmatism, arrogance, sectarianism, abuse of power and the promotion of incompetents to skilled posts, how the lack of civil liberties had also come under fire, and how a cross-section of these attacks had been published for six weeks before the clamp-down was ordered. As a result liberals like Lo Lung Chi, vice-chairman of the China Democratic League, who had actually called for a legal parliamentary opposition, were publicly humiliated and forced to confess their errors. Admitting that group criticism, denunciation and recantation on the Chinese model was a real form of torture, Snow somehow contrived ultimately to explain it all away. And when Joseph Needham

372

(who had been scientific attaché to the British embassy in Chungking during the war) returned from a visit in 1958, he reported having encountered much less evidence of ideological pressure on non-communist scholars and scientists than he had expected.*

Even so there were aspects of the bland, prefabricated optimism officially inculcated which Simone de Beauvoir and other Western sympathizers found difficult to swallow, and she spoke of "this seamless China polished smooth by official optimism". It was intolerable to be told, when she asked what was done with lazy students – "there are none". She rebelled, also, when a certain Chou Yang directed that "the writer must describe heroes and in them omit the unheroic aspects": the idealized positive hero seemed to her the worst aspect of modern Chinese literature. But then she began to backtrack: was this not really pre-literature for the semi-literate masses? And perhaps, after all, the Chinese authorities had a good case when you considered our own "pseudo-liberalism" which implied "contempt for the great mass of the people it puts at the mercy of a certain number of profiteers specializing in the printed page".²³ But wait a minute! What of Editions Gallimard and their highly successful author, Madame de Beauvoir? Besides, who displays the greater contempt for the masses: the publishers of salacious detective stories or Mr Chou Yang, with his demand that all unheroic aspects be eliminated from heroes? A toss-up, no doubt, but at least France had no Mr Chou to dictate what everyone should write and read. And Felix Greene, much to his credit, felt the same way. Even Joan Robinson sadly admitted: "Political content is all, the only form to be seen derives from a debased socialist realism which was imported by the Russians before they were repudiated as revisionists."²⁴ Greene described the English-language edition of the official news agency's *Hsinhua* as "bombastic, boastful, repetitive and boorish. ..." The mania for patriotism and the correct political line, for conformity rather than originality, worried him if only because, like so many fellow-travellers, he was a good deal more sensitive to attacks on the liberties

---

* Needham is one of the leading experts on science and society in China. As a young man he was influenced by Karl Wittfogel's Marxist study, *Wirtschaft und Gesellschaft Chinas*, with its central concept of a stifling Asiatic bureaucratism derived from Marx, Engels and, partly, from the seventeenth-century scholar François Bernier. But the problem was this: why modern science had failed to develop in the Chinese and Indian civilizations even though China had been more successful than the West between the first and fifteenth centuries in applying natural knowledge to human needs. The solution proposed by Wittfogel and adopted by Needham was that when feudalism gave way to Asiatic bureaucratism, the dominant mandarin class of scholar-gentry prevented the rise to power of the entrepreneurial merchant class, which played so important a role in the Western leap forward at the time of the Renaissance. For one thousand years China had had a one-party state. Needham regarded the rule of the Communist Party as a historically valid sequel to the rule of the Confucian party.

of his fellow intellectuals, with whom he could empathize and identify, than to those on other sections of the population with their fatal anchorage in an intractable and foreign history. But Professor Yang explained to him: the majority in China wanted socialism. Greene was not satisfied: "Majorities can be wrong. All advance comes from a few who don't like things as they are. After all, *your* revolution was led by dissenters."[25] He also met Mr Han, a writer-bureaucrat who talked like a tape recorder, leaving Greene with the impression that life might be unpleasant if such a man were "arbiter of my destiny". But methodically the traveller squeezed the pus of bourgeois prejudice from his metabolism and soon the kind of incident which had surprised him on the train from Shenyang no longer disturbed him. On that occasion his peace was soon interrupted by the voice of a girl situated in a broadcasting booth in the middle of the train and trotting out a local brand of commercial: "Now with the start of the train our life of travel begins. . . . We are moving across the face of our beloved Motherland. . . . We all have different destinations but we all have one aim, to reconstruct our country quickly. . . ."[26]

Born in 1904, Greene had lived for many years as an English resident of the United States. Indeed, in coming to China his British passport proved invaluable. At one time a BBC official, a businessman and a freelance journalist, he first came to China in 1957 "taking with me all the assumptions and apprehensions prevalent in the United States. . . . I expected to see fear as I had seen it in Russia in the early thirties and later in Germany and Italy."[27] Three years later he made a return visit, became the first Westerner to interview Chou En Lai on TV, and subsequently wrote a book which enjoyed considerable success, *The Wall Has Two Sides*. What made him (after his rapid conversion) a typical fellow-traveller was the radical dualism of mind which led him to dismiss much of what he most admired in China as being totally irrelevant to the West. Defending China to the Americans, he also found himself defending America to the Chinese, assuring them that life in the US was more varied, complex and lively than they imagined and that the portrait of Britain and America inculcated in Chinese schoolchildren was eighty years out of date.

He made excellent documentary films not only about China but also on the theme of Vietnam's struggle for independence; he was engaged on lecture tours, he attended protest rallies. But during the 1960s great upheavals took place both in South East Asia and in the US which completely altered his outlook. Greene became one of the few fellow-travellers of the older generation to fall under the sway of the New

Left, of the "Movement". But this is not quite accurate: orderly, centralized Leninism appealed to him more than anarchism, and this was the revolutionary solution he now proposed for the US, casting off his pacifism and adopting the view that non-violence within a violent society amounts to a form of complicity. However, these thoughts were formulated neither with conspicuous originality nor sophistication: "The revolutionary uses violence only where there is no other way, and never to protect his own interests, his wealth, his status, his privileges or his sense of personal virtue."[28] (In which case one can only conclude that the sole authentic "revolutionaries" are those martyrs who fall in the heat of a battle not yet won.) He now called for a dictatorial, one-party state in America, to stamp out neo-imperialism, urban corruption, advertising, drug addiction, racism, capitalism and no doubt pollution as well. Sincere, yes, but not at that crucial level where thought and action are one; a maverick performance, over-heated and shallow in argument, but nevertheless a conversion almost without parallel in the history of fellow-travelling.

The Great Leap Forward (1958–62) was the occasion of the massive birth of China's rural communes. It will be recalled how according to some friendly commentators the Soviet collectivization drive began on a "voluntary" or "spontaneous" basis, with the Party hardly able to keep pace with the socialist enthusiasm of the peasant masses. Well, according to Greene, this was precisely how the Chinese communes started. The Government was utterly taken by surprise. And if mistakes occurred it was only because the zealous masses over-extended their activities and capacities. Alas, this was not a true version of events. Collectivization had begun in 1955–6 after a directive from the top; Mao ordered that by 1957 there were to be 1,300,000 agrarian co-operatives containing half the rural population. The next step, the communes, was also initiated from above. But here again the excessive apologies and claims of China's defenders were in part a response to the ludicrous accusations of her enemies. In November 1958 John Foster Dulles spoke of the communists "imposing mass slavery on 650 million people", while American newspapers ran headlines like "Chain Gang Empire", depicting the family destroyed and bestiality rampant in the ant-like communes. This was grotesque fabrication. On the other hand a serious famine did occur in 1960 and the communization process – as in the Ukraine in 1932 – had something to do with its exacerbation. In general the fellow-travellers were loth to admit as much. Snow ridiculed the reports of Joseph Alsop and other experts who had never set foot in China that the Chinese were starving on six hundred calories a day.

The truth was, he said, that although food was short to the point where instances of malnutrition were visible, there was no starvation, the Government had done much to alleviate the crisis and the majority of the population remained healthy. Equitable food rationing had prevented the kind of disaster known to previous generations. The weather – natural calamity – was the main cause of the failure of the harvest; too rapid communization was a secondary factor. Furthermore, did anything in China compare with the hunger and beggary permanently prevalent in Calcutta or the villages of Bengal? Yet it is interesting that, reconsidering the matter in 1968, he listed the causes of the near-famine in the following order: (a) dislocations caused by the Great Leap Forward; (b) the withdrawal of Soviet technicians and (c) natural calamities.

Snow's was a more sophisticated analysis than the one offered by Greene, who attributed the whole thing to natural disaster and even argued that the communes had initially expanded production rather than reduced it. The Dean of Canterbury, meanwhile, visited China in 1959, met Anna Louise Strong in her flat in the grounds of the Peace Committee, and came away declaring that, "But for the communes and communism, millions of people would have died. . . ."[29] In 1969 Joan Robinson wrote: "It is true that there was a tight period following the Great Leap Forward. The historical analogue of this is the Russian famine of 1921. . . . No doubt many elderly people died sooner than they would have done, but no one is able to find evidence of famine."[30] Except, perhaps, the "elderly people" who died.

And so to the Cultural Revolution. According to Greene, it was a national self-inquiry of a profound nature, necessary in order that the Chinese might throw off the false trappings of bourgeois conditioning. This was written after Greene had staged his own private cultural revolution. But the most ardent justification came from the pen of Joan Robinson* in a short book which combined gullibility with latent authoritarianism in doses which were virtually standard among fellow-travellers of a certain stamp: "Political argument for the broad masses of the population must necessarily be simplified. To sophisticated listeners it cannot but appear crude. . . . The Rightists were presented as evil men. . . ."[31] This said, a blatant contradiction (subservience to a myth) was not long in following: "The movement, however, was still bubbling up from below, with little control from above."[32] But when she explained the motivation behind this spontaneous bubbling, it hardly

* Born in 1903, she was Professor of Economics at Cambridge from 1949 to 1965, as well as the author of a number of neo-Marxist works such as *Essays in the Theory of Employment* (1933) and *Essay on Marxian Economics* (1942).

seemed compatible with popular thought or inspiration: "The people were to re-educate the Party and at the same time to learn that the Party was necessary to them."[33] Only an Orwellian Big Brother could have conceived so dialectical a programme. Apparently hoisted on her own contradictions, Professor Robinson resolved it thus: "In one sense it was led and instigated by Chairman Mao while in another sense it was spontaneous and unregulated."[34] Perhaps she meant that things got out of hand. Which is why, in a situation of near-anarchy, the manipulators speedily reversed the images, holding up Mao as a symbol of discipline and Party control, while the revisionist bureaucrat Liu Shao Ch'i re-emerged in the popular consciousness as a downright anarchist. But in Joan Robinson's pages even this was upheld as a vindication of the original aims of the Cultural Revolution. Though writing in a non-Leninist, non-Marxist vocabulary and style, she put to rout the "bourgeois" values of the USSR and the Chinese Right, and also accepted the testimonies of those "converted" in the course of the Cultural Revolution at face value. But surely any cool-headed observer of events such as those which recently passed in China would at least consider the role played by Mao's personal vendetta with the Soviet leaders, and by the fact that powerful elements within the Chinese Party were demanding a *rapprochement* with the CPSU. Certainly one would not gather from Professor Robinson's pages that life in China at this time was as Mao subsequently described it to Edgar Snow: "Later the conflict during the Cultural Revolution developed into a war between two factions – first with spears, then mortars. . . . When foreigners reported that China was in great chaos, they were not telling lies. It had been true."[35]

Finally, we should look briefly at certain aspects of China's foreign relations. Needless to say, the fellow-travellers with every justification resented America's paternalistic attitude towards China. In August 1946 Anna Louise Strong was granted an interview by Mao. Wishing merely to be his mouthpiece, she asked: "If the American people ask what the Communist party is fighting for what should I reply?" Mao told her: national independence and social justice. Snow had good cause to feel exasperated by Washington's relentless hostility towards Peking and her policy of propping up Chiang's bankrupt rump dictatorship on Formosa (though if the run of American journalists had been freely allowed into China during the past two decades, Snow's occasional, spectacular interviews with the enigmatic dragon Mao would not have been such valuable currency.) In the late 1950s he complained that it was Dulles, not Peking, who was preventing Eleanor Roosevelt, Harriman and

377

himself from visiting China. He believed that the American press was controlled by wealthy men with a vested interest in denigrating and distorting China's remarkable progress. And later he wrote: "durable peace between China and the US remains impossible while any part of Asia is subject to armed American intervention."[36] Appropriately enough, his most recent interview with Mao early in 1971 provided one of the first signals that a thaw was on the way, though Mao's friendly appraisal of American federalism had more to recommend it from a diplomatic than a historical standpoint: "China should learn from the way America developed, by decentralizing and spreading responsibility and wealth among the fifty states."[37]

No fellow-traveller doubted that China's eventual military intervention in Korea was a legitimate defensive measure, but the question of Tibet presented greater ambiguities. Simone de Beauvoir, who in fact went nowhere near Tibet, depicted the "roof of the world" as thriving amid new schools, generously redistributed farming land, interest-free loans and thrusting new highways. A few minor disturbances, yes, because the nomadic tribes "tried to revive their anarchic traditions" – an affront to Enlightenment schoolmistresses everywhere. She foresaw no serious future troubles but no sooner were her words written and published than the Tibetans became anarchic enough to stage a rebellion. However Felix Greene, writing after the event, explained that the insurrection had been confined to "twenty thousand" landlords and reactionaries who practised serfdom and the mutilation of slaves (as indeed they did). Anna Louise Strong, who had settled in Peking in 1958 at the age of seventy-two, promptly and gallantly set out for Tibet to see what it was all about. Tibet, she reported, had been a "living museum of the Middle Ages" but then became under Chinese sovereignty after 1951 a country "exploding into modern farms and primary schools".[38] As for the sovereignty question itself, she rightly pointed out that no other nation, not even Britain, had recognized Tibet's full independence. (But in fact Tibet had long enjoyed a substantial measure of regional autonomy, which was the crucial issue.) She referred to the 1951 agreement between China and the Dalai Lama as if the latter had entered into it voluntarily and not as the result of an invasion by superior forces he was incapable of repelling. Interviewing Tibetans who had been slaves, she made much of the ghastly existence they had endured at the hands of rapacious landlords and monasteries. Depicting the Chinese army of occupation as discreet, respectful and restrained, she unblushingly accepted the official statistics which put Chinese forces in Tibet no higher than fourteen thousand. Why the rebellion? The serf owners had grown desperate at the prospect of the forthcoming land reforms. Thus the repression of the rising was really a godsend for the majority of poor Tibetans who had immediately responded by forming peasant associations, ending serfdom and building more schools. "In the valleys the barley sprouts." Edgar Snow read her account. Though his style was less gushing than hers, he had to accept the Chinese point of view. A million and a half Tibetans had lived in fear of devils and hellfire; fugitives from serfdom met barbaric fates; the ruling class had finally rebelled in desperation when the whole lamaist system was about to topple. Mass literacy, moreover, had posed a severe threat to a religious ideology depending on such props as prayer wheels and sorcerers. In all this Snow was no doubt right; but he had the realism to admit – and that is all one really asks for – that many Tibetans who were not sorcerers or even lamas deeply resented the eradication of their own culture by one imposed from outside.

Anna Louise lived on in Peking, housed in a three-room apartment in the "Peace Compound" and provided with a car, a chauffeur, a cook, a maid (both shared) and a secretary. More than any other foreigner, resident or visiting, she was privy to the swimming and dining of Mao, and when her eightieth birthday came along he threw a gala party in her honour. She deserved it. Every month she sent out her four-page newsletter to China-Watchers and sympathizers all over the world, the world which she had helped to make a smaller but not a meaner place. The Chinese way of life was one she loved: "In China they respect old age!" she told a friend. To prove that youthfulness is all in the mind, she became an honorary Red Guard during the Cultural Revolution, which is about as far as a fellow-traveller can go. Several times she thought of returning to the States, but decided no. In 1970 she died of a heart-attack in Peking.

The Sino-Soviet conflict provides the last, culminating irony in our story. While the unity and monocentrism of the world communist movement disintegrated amid a barrage of invective and, on occasion, even gunfire, the fellow-travellers turned a blind eye to the rupture until it could no longer be ignored. Coming across a Soviet technician on a Chinese train in 1960, Greene concluded that talk of a mass exodus of Russian personnel from China was exaggerated. But it wasn't. The Soviet image was now tarnished; it was not so much Russia's ideological "revisionism" which disturbed the fellow-travellers as her combination of Great Power imperialism, "bourgeois" respectability, and an increasingly blatant accommodation with the United States in the era of the Vietnam war. Besides, Russia's anti-Chinese propaganda was worthy of the most hysterical sections of the capitalist press. As Joan Robinson asked: "How does it strike a Russian reader to hear that sending young people to the virgin lands is an atrocity, that spending national re-sources on defence is wanton waste, or that education is vitiated by political ideology?"[39] Greene and Anna Louise Strong remained loyal to China and to the purity which is born out of poverty, while the Dean of Canterbury flew hither and thither, smiling benignly and assuring Chou that the disagreements would soon be resolved – news which the Chinese Premier received with a polite but enigmatic silence. Snow for his part responded coolly and analytically, taking an expert's comfort in having predicted just such a confrontation as far back as 1948. Khrushchev, he wrote, had advocated peaceful coexistence, offered aid to India and disparaged the communes, while reacting sharply to Peking's threats to liberate Taiwan. When the Chinese had declined to buckle under, Khrushchev in the best imperialistic style had decided to teach them a lesson (just as de Gaulle, one recalls, had taught Guinea a lesson in 1958). In 1971 Mao remarked to Snow that the Russians looked down on the Chinese; they thought they only had to speak and all people would obey, including his "humble self", Mao. But they had miscalculated.

Now a Sino-American thaw of limited but significant dimensions appears to be taking place. Soon a flood of inquisitive Western tourists will burst into China, discharging the fraternity and goodwill which has for so long been dammed up. If the Soviet pattern repeats itself, it will not be long before China cares more about travellers than about fellow-travellers.

References

INTRODUCTION: The Future is There

1   ALEXANDER HERZEN, *Works*, vol. ix, St Petersburg, 1906, pp. 400–1

2   Quoted, MAX EASTMAN, *Love and Revolution*, New York, 1964, p. 103

3   LEON TROTSKY, *Literature and Revolution*, Ann Arbor, 1960, pp. 57–8

4   Quoted, ISAAC DEUTSCHER, *Trotsky: The Prophet Unarmed, 1921–9*, London, 1959, p. 184

5   KONNI ZILLIACUS, *I Choose Peace*, London, 1949, p. 415

6   Quoted, ISAAC DEUTSCHER, *Trotsky: The Prophet Outcast, 1929–40*, London, 1963, p. 434

7   ROCKWELL KENT, *This Is My Own*, New York, 1940, p. 371

8   *The Letters of Lincoln Steffens*, vol. 2, New York, 1938, p. 759

9   ELLA WINTER, *Red Virtue*, London, 1933, p. 48

10 ANNA LOUISE STRONG, *I Change Worlds*, London, 1935, p. 418

11 Quoted, CHARLES P. CURTIS, *The Oppenheimer Case. The Trial of a Security System*, New York, 1955, p. 47

12 RAYMOND ARON, *The Opium of the Intellectuals*, tr. by Terence Kilmartin, London, 1957, p. 108

13 *Labour Monthly*, January 1936, p. 14

14 *Problems of Soviet Literature. Reports and Speeches at the First Soviet Writers' Congress*, London, n.d., p. 103

15 LION FEUCHTWANGER, *Moscow 1937*, London, 1937, p. 9

16 Quoted, JÜRGEN RÜHLE, *Literatur und Revolution*, Berlin & Cologne, 1960, p. 174

17 *Letters of Theodore Dreiser. A Selection*, edited by Robert H. Elias, Philadelphia, 1959, p. 678

18 NADEZHDA MANDELSTAM, *Hope Against Hope*, tr. by Max Hayward, London, 1971, p. 363

1: THINKING OF RUSSIA

1 ARTHUR RANSOME, *Six Weeks in Russia in 1919*, London, 1919, pp. 1–2, 4
2 M. PHILIPS PRICE, "Witnesses of the Revolution", *Survey*, April 1962, p. 16
3 *The Communist*, London, 9 April 1921, p.4
4 See H. N. BRAILSFORD, *The Russian Workers' Republic*, London, 1923
5 SAMUEL HARPER, *The Russia I Believe In*, Chicago, 1945, p. 99
6 RANSOME, op. cit., p. 80
7 Ibid., p. viii
8 Quoted, CHRISTOPHER LASCH, *The American Liberals and the Russian Revolution*, New York, 1962, p. 134
9 ROBERT MORSS LOVETT, *All Our Years*, New York, 1948, p. 155
10 *The Autobiography of Lincoln Steffens*, vol. 2, London, 1931, pp. 745–6
11 *The Letters of Lincoln Steffens*, vol. 1, pp. 395–6
12 *The Autobiography of Lincoln Steffens*, vol. 2, p. 754
13 Ibid., p. 759
14 *The Letters of Lincoln Steffens*, vol. 1, p. 433
15 *The Autobiography of Lincoln Steffens*, vol. 1, p. 521
16 SEAN O'CASEY, *Mirror in My House. Autobiographies*, vol. 2, New York, 1956, p. 220
17 PAUL LANGEVIN, *La Pensée et l'Action*, Paris, 1950, p. 268
18 Quoted, CARTER JEFFERSON, *Anatole France: The Politics of Skepticism*, Rutgers, 1965, p. 12
19 JACOB AXELRAD, *Anatole France. A Life Without Illusions, 1844–1924*, New York, 1944, pp. 419 and 434
20 See GEORGES COGNIOT, *Les Intellectuels et la Renaissance Française*, Paris, 1945, p. 22, and *Humanité*, 12 October 1945
21 *Humanité*, 12 October 1954
22 Quoted, ANNETTE VIDAL, *Henri Barbusse, Soldat de la Paix*, Paris, 1953, p. 168
23 *Humanité*, 20 February 1922
24 Quoted, AXELRAD, op. cit., p. 423
25 *Le Temps*, Paris, 18 March 1922
26 Quoted, JEFFERSON, op. cit., p. 232
27 ARTHUR HOLITSCHER, *Drei Monate in Sowjet-Russland*, Berlin, 1921, p. 16
28 Quoted, EASTMAN, *Love and Revolution*, p. 347
29 RANSOME, op. cit., p. 82
30 ILYA EHRENBURG, *Memoirs. Volume 2: First Years of Revolution*,

1918–21, tr. by Anna Bostock in collab. with Yvonne Kapp, London, 1962, p. 9

31 Ibid., p. 13

32 Quoted, MAX EASTMAN, *Artists in Uniform,* New York, 1934, p. 58

33 Quoted, JAMES BURKHART GILBERT, *Writers and Partisans: A History of Literary Radicalism in America,* New York, 1968, p. 69

34 *Problems of Soviet Literature,* p. 236

35 Quoted, BERTRAM WOLFE, *The Bridge and the Abyss. The Troubled Friendship of Maxim Gorky and V. I. Lenin,* New York, 1967, p. 52

36 MAXIM GORKY, *Untimely Thoughts. Essays on Revolution, Culture and the Bolsheviks, 1917–18,* tr. by Herman Ermolaev, London, 1968, p. 14

37 Ibid., p. 74

38 Quoted, WOLFE, op. cit., p. 26

39 GORKY, op. cit., p. 89

40 Ibid., p. 95

41 Ibid., p. 114

42 Ibid., p. 165

43 Quoted, WOLFE, op. cit., p. 138

44 Quoted, ibid., p. 160

45 *Liber Amicorum Romain Rolland,* Zurich, 1926, p. 396

46 Quoted, WOLFE, op. cit., p. 31

47 Quoted, ibid., p. 32

48 Quoted, ibid., p. 143

49 See ROBERT CONQUEST, *The Great Terror. Stalin's Purge of the Thirties,* London, 1968, p. 84, and RICHARD HARE, *Maxim Gorky. Romantic Realist and Conservative Revolutionary,* London, 1962, p. 147

50 MAXIM GORKY, "The Responsibility of Soviet Intellectuals", in G. B. de Huszar (ed.), *The Intellectuals,* Glencoe, 1960, p. 235

51 GEORG LUKÁCS, *Studies in European Realism,* New York, 1964, pp. 207–235

52 ERNST TOLLER, *Which World: Which Way,* tr. by Hermon Ould, London, 1931, p. 80

53 ERNST TOLLER, *I Was a German. An Autobiography,* tr. by Edward Crankshaw, London, 1934, p. 142

54 Ibid., p. 169

55 ERNST TOLLER, *Masses and Man,* tr. by Vera Mandel, in E. TOLLER, *Seven Plays,* London, 1935, p. 151

56 TOLLER, *I Was a German,* p. 278

57 ILYA EHRENBURG, *Memoirs, 1921–41,* tr. by Tatiana Shebunina, New York, 1966, p. 195

58 *Das Wort,* 3 Jg (1938), Heft 10, Moscow, p. 123

59 Quoted, KLAUS MANN, *Der Wendepunkt*, Frankfurt am Main, 1953, p. 419

60 Ibid., p. 420

61 Quoted, MARTIN ESSLIN, *Brecht: The Man and His Work*, New York, 1961, p. 149

62 Quoted, JOHN WILLETT, *Brecht on Theatre*, London, 1964, p. 130

63 Quoted, ESSLIN, op. cit., p. 185

64 Quoted, GORDON A. CRAIG, "Engagement and Neutrality in Weimar Germany", *Journal of Contemporary History*, vol. 2, no. 3, Cambridge, 1967, p. 57

65 Quoted, PETER GAY, *Weimar Culture: The Outsider as Insider*, London, 1968, p. 57

66 HENRI BARBUSSE, *La Lueur dans l'Âbime*, Paris, 1920, p. 123

2: CONDUCTED TOURS

1 THEODORE DREISER, *Dreiser Looks at Russia*, London, 1928, p. 21

2 WALDO FRANK, *Dawn in Russia*, New York, 1932, p. 32

3 ANDRÉ GIDE, *Journals*, vol. 3, tr. by Justin O'Brien, New York, 1949, p. 245

4 BERNARD SHAW, *The Rationalization of Russia*, ed. by Harry M. Geduld, Bloomington, 1964

5 DREISER, op. cit., p. 258

6 *The Letters of Lincoln Steffens*, vol. 2, pp. 627–8

7 FRANK, op. cit., p. 7

8 CHARLES VILDRAC, *Russie Neuve*, Paris, 1937, p. 206

9 *Commune*, Paris, January 1936, p. 573

10 Quoted, HERBERT A. DEANE, *The Political Ideas of Harold J. Laski*, New York, 1955, p. 212

11 Quoted, GILBERT, *Writers and Partisans*, p. 101

12 O'CASEY, *Mirror in My House*, vol. 2, p. 222

13 HARRY F. WARD, *In Place of Profit*, New York, 1963, *passim*

14 JULIAN HUXLEY, *A Scientist Among the Soviets*, London, 1932, p. 89

15 ARON, *The Opium of the Intellectuals*, p. 174

16 FREDA UTLEY, *Lost Illusion*, London, 1949, p. 164

17 SIDNEY and BEATRICE WEBB, *Soviet Communism: A New Civilisation?*, vol. 1, London, 1936, p. 120

18 CORLISS LAMONT, *Soviet Civilization*, New York, 1952, pp. 198–9

19 BERNARD SHAW, *Platform and Pulpit*, ed. by Dan H. Laurence, London, 1962, p. 222

20 GIDE, op. cit., p. 359

21 LOUIS FISCHER, *Men and Politics*, New York, 1941, p. 189

22 SHAW, op. cit., p. 227
23 GIDE, op. cit., p. 232
24 Ibid. (23 April 1932), p. 225
25 LUDWIG MARCUSE, *Mein Zwanzigstes Jahrhundert*, Munich, 1960, p. 239
26 SIDNEY and BEATRICE WEBB, op. cit., vol. 2, p. 655
27 HEWLETT JOHNSON, *Soviet Success*, London, 1947, p. 75
28 SIDNEY and BEATRICE WEBB, op. cit., vol. 1, p. 170
29 Ibid., p. 188
30 Ibid., p. 199
31 ALEC NOVE, "Was Stalin Really Necessary?", *Encounter*, London, April 1962, p. 90
32 GIDE, op. cit., p. 279
33 *New Statesman and Nation*, London, 7 March 1936
34 FEUCHTWANGER, *Moscow, 1937*, p. 24
35 MANDELSTAM, *Hope Against Hope*, p. 97
36 STRONG, *I Change Worlds*, p. 152
37 EUGENE LYONS, *The Red Decade*, New York, 1941, p. 121
38 DREISER, *Dreiser Looks at Russia*, p. 12
39 *Letters of Theodore Dreiser*, p. 932
40 LAMONT, op. cit., p. 82
41 MAURICE HINDUS, *The Great Offensive*, London, 1933, p. 42
42 EDGAR SNOW, *Journey to the Beginning*, London, 1959, pp. 280 and 283
43 *New Statesman and Nation*, 17 November 1934, p. 709
44 Ibid.
45 SIDNEY and BEATRICE WEBB, op. cit., vol. 1, p. 7
46 Ibid., p. 30
47 Ibid., pp. 434 and 436
48 Ibid., p. 439
49 Ibid., p. 430
50 SIDNEY and BEATRICE WEBB, *The Decay of Capitalist Civilisation*, London, 1923, p. 166
51 Quoted, MARCEL LIEBMAN, "The Webbs and The New Civilisation", *Survey*, no. 41, April 1962, p. 66
52 *Beatrice Webb's Diaries, 1924-32*, ed. by Margaret Cole, London, 1956, p. 106
53 Ibid., p. 245
54 Ibid., p. 296
55 MANDELSTAM, op. cit., p. 51
56 STEPHEN SPENDER, *Forward From Liberalism*, London, 1937, p. 275

57 ANNA LOUISE STRONG, *The New Soviet Constitution*, New York, 1937, p. 47

58 *New Statesman and Nation*, London, 20 June 1936, p. 959

59 STRONG, op. cit., p. 90

60 Ibid., p. 111

61 FISCHER, op. cit., p. 335

62 BERNARD SHAW, *The Intelligent Woman's Guide to Socialism, Capitalism, Sovietism and Fascism*, London, 1937, p. 442

63 *The Plebs*, London, January 1925, pp. 238–41

64 TOLLER, *Which World: Which Way*, p. 164

65 Quoted, DEUTSCHER, *Trotsky: The Prophet Outcast*, pp. 29–30

66 *New Statesman and Nation*, London, 12 October 1935, p. 525

67 *The Letters of Lincoln Steffens*, vol. 2, p. 1001

68 STRONG, *I Change Worlds*, p. 290

69 *The Letters of Lincoln Steffens*, vol. 2, p. 1000

70 STRONG, op. cit., p. 348

71 FEUCHTWANGER, op. cit., p. 115

72 STRONG, op. cit., pp. 337 & 347

73 BERNARD PARES, *Russia and the Peace*, London, 1944, p. 11

74 HEWLETT JOHNSON, *Searching for Light*, London, 1968, pp. 228–9

75 *Sinn und Form, Beiträge zur Literatur.* "Sonderheft: Arnold Zweig", Berlin, 1952, p. 261

76 FEUCHTWANGER, op. cit., p. 93

77 DREISER, *Dreiser Looks at Russia*, p. 97

78 TOLLER, op. cit., p. 102

79 FRANK, op. cit., p. 180

80 SPENDER, op. cit., p. 199

81 SIDNEY and BEATRICE WEBB, *Soviet Communism*, vol. 2, pp. 1037–8

82 JOHNSON, *Soviet Success*, p. 116

83 SIDNEY and BEATRICE WEBB, op. cit., pp. 1026–7

84 FEUCHTWANGER, op. cit., p. 82

85 SPENDER, op. cit., p. 202

86 *The God That Failed*, ed. by Richard Crossman, New York, 1959, p. 165

87 GIDE, op cit., p. 225

88 Quoted, EHRENBURG, *Memoirs, 1921–41*, p. 301

89 ANDRÉ GIDE, *Retouches à mon Retour de l' URSS*, Paris, 1937, pp. 67–8

90 RAMON FERNANDEZ, "Littérature et Politique", *La Nouvelle Revue Française*, Paris, 1 February 1935, p. 286

91 *The God That Failed*, p. 165

92 See advertisement in *Fact*, London, May 1937, p. 7

93 Quoted in SIDNEY and BEATRICE WEBB, op. cit., vol. 2, p. 590

94 HAROLD LASKI, *Law and Justice in Soviet Russia*, London, 1935, p. 28

95 TOLLER, op. cit., p. 134

96 SIDNEY and BEATRICE WEBB, op. cit., vol. 2, p. 567

97 Letter in *New Statesman*, London, 11 October 1968

98 Letter in *New Statesman*, London, 13 October 1967

99 SIMONE DE BEAUVOIR, *La Force des Choses*, Paris, 1963, p. 190

100 JEAN-PAUL SARTRE, "Reply to Albert Camus", *Situations*, tr. by Benita Eisler, London, 1965, p. 85

101 DE BEAUVOIR, op. cit., p. 365

102 Introduction to Utley, op. cit., p. viii

103 O'CASEY, op. cit, vol. 2, p. 128

104 MANDELSTAM, op. cit., pp. 82, 88, 113, 297

105 FEUCHTWANGER, op. cit., pp. 26 and 16

106 MANDELSTAM, op. cit., p. 98

107 GEORGE ORWELL, *The Collected Essays, Journalism and Letters of George Orwell*, ed. by Sonia Orwell and Ian Angus, vol. 1, London, 1970, p. 370

108 Ibid., vol. 3, p. 273

109 HOLITSCHER, *Drei Monate in Sowjet-Russland*, p. 146

110 Quoted, JOSEPH FREEMAN, *An American Testament*, New York, 1936, p. 349

111 Letter of Toller's friend Dr Kurt Pinthus to W. Willibrand; see William Anthony Willibrand, *Ernst Toller and His Ideology*, Univ. of Iowa, 1945, p. 27

112 ALEXANDER WICKSTEED, *My Russian Neighbors*, New York, 1934, p. 14

113 JOHN DOS PASSOS, *In All Countries*, London, 1934, p. 22

114 DREISER, op. cit., p. 115

115 *Letters of Theodore Dreiser*, p. 629

116 *The God That Failed*, p. 243

117 HUXLEY, op. cit., pp. 31–2

118 *The Letters of Lincoln Steffens*, vol. 2, pp. 988 and 995

119 ARON, op. cit., p. 212

120 LASKI, op. cit., pp. 9, 17, 24

121 Ibid., p. 24

122 SHAW, *Platform and Pulpit*, p. 233

123 *Labour Monthly*, London, October 1921, p. 306

124 Quoted, EASTMAN, *Love and Revolution*, p. 161

125 *The Communist*, London, 22 October 1921, p. 5

126 SHAW, *The Intelligent Woman's Guide*, p. 454

127 Quoted, *Labour Monthly*, London, September 1931, p. 582

128 *The Anti-Stalin Campaign and International Communism: A Selection of Documents*, New York, 1956, pp. 40 and 14

129 JOSEPH DAVIES, *Mission to Moscow*, London, 1942, pp. 35, 38, 39, 175

130 THOMAS MANN – HEINRICH MANN, *Briefwechsel 1900–49*, Frankfurt, 1968, p. 212

131 Quoted, WALTER LAQUEUR, "Russia Through Western Eyes", *Survey*, no. 41, London, April 1962, p. 10

132 *Commune*, Paris, 1937, pp. 804–5

133 Quoted, *Left Review*, London, March 1937, p. 112

134 JEAN-RICHARD BLOCH, *L'Homme du Communisme. Portrait de Staline*, Paris, 1949, p. 19

135 HEINRICH MANN, *Ein Zeitalter Wird Besichtigt*, Berlin, 1947, p. 56

136 Quoted, LYONS, op. cit., p. 253

137 FEUCHTWANGER, op. cit., p. 135

138 Ibid., p. 132

139 ELIZABETH K. PORETSKY, *Our Own People. A Memoir of "Ignace Reiss" and his Friends*, London, 1969, p. 198

140 FISCHER, op. cit., p. 502

141 LOUIS FISCHER, *Stalin and Hitler*, London, 1940, p. 74

142 DEUTSCHER, op. cit., p. 368

143 FISCHER, *Men and Politics*, p. 530

144 MANN, op. cit., p. 121

145 UPTON SINCLAIR and EUGENE LYONS, *Terror in Russia?*, New York, 1938, p. 53

146 Letter to *New Statesman*, London, 13 October 1967

147 Quoted, JEAN PÉRUS, *Romain Rolland et Maxime Gorki*, Paris, 1968, p. 21

148 *Liber Amicorum Romain Rolland*, p. 9

149 Quoted, EASTMAN, op. cit., p. 175

150 ROMAIN ROLLAND, *Quinze Ans de Combat (1919–34)*, Paris, 1935, p. 36

151 Ibid., p. xlv

152 *Humanité*, Paris, 25 December 1937

153 M. BRUNELLE, "Le Vrai Romain Rolland". *La Pensée,* Paris, Jan.-Feb. 1952, p. 49. Rolland's friend, Mrs Fearn, gave a copy of the letter to Mme Brunelle.

3: THE POPULAR FRONT ERA

1 Quoted, DEUTSCHER, *The Prophet Outcast*, p. 434

2 ARTHUR KOESTLER, *The Invisible Writing*, Boston, 1955, p. 205

3   Quoted, GÜNTHER NOLLAU, *International Communism and World Revolution*, tr. by Victor Andersen, London, 1961, p. 345

4   Ibid., p. 345

5   *Tribune*, London, 15 January 1937, p. 7

6   *Commune*, Paris, May 1934, p. 867

7   W. DRABOVITCH, *Les Intellectuels Français et le Bolchévisme*, Paris, 1938, pp. 36–43

8   KENT, *This Is My Own*, p. 391

9   Ibid., p. 291

10   LYONS, *The Red Decade*, p. 265

11   Ibid., p. 197

12   GUSTAV REGLER, *The Owl of Minerva*, tr. by Norman Denny, London, 1959, pp. 232–3

13   *Das Wort*, 2 Jg, Heft 4–5, Moscow, April-May 1937, p. 174

14   LION FEUCHTWANGER, *Success*, tr. by Willa and Edwin Muir, London, 1930, p. 23

15   Quoted, KLAUS SCHRÖTER, *Heinrich Mann*, Hamburg, 1967, p. 136

16   Quoted, ibid., p. 137

17   *Neue Deutsche Blätter*, 1 Jahr, no. 1, Prague, 20 September 1933, pp. 1–2

18   *Das Wort*, Jg 1 Heft I, Moscow, 1936, p. 3

19   ANDRÉ CHAMSON, *Devenir ce qu'on est*, Paris, 1959, p. 59

20   Letter to the author, 1963

21   D. N. PRITT, *Autobiography*. Part I; London, 1965, p. 97

22   HAROLD LASKI, *Communism*, London, 1927, p. 168

23   Ibid., pp. 229–30

24   *Tribune*, London, 13 August 1937

25   *Labour Monthly*, London, November 1936, pp. 667–8

26   Ibid., March 1937, p. 141

27   Ibid., February 1936, p. 131

28   *Tribune*, 13 August 1937

29   See STUART SAMUELS, "The Left Book Club", *Journal of Contemporary History*, vol. 1, no. 22, Cambridge, 1966, and John Lewis, *The Left Book Club*, London, 1970

30   Letter to *New Statesman and Nation*, London, 4 September 1937, p. 334

31   Letter from G. B. NEAVILL, *TLS*, London, 6 November 1970

32   NEAL WOOD, *Communism and British Intellectuals*, London, 1959, p. 43

33   JOHN STRACHEY, *The Theory and Practice of Socialism*, London, 1936, p. 451

34 JOHN STRACHEY, *The Strangled Cry*, London, 1962 (*Encounter*, 1960), p. 188
35 STRACHEY, *The Theory and Practice of Socialism*, p. 49
36 STRACHEY, *The Strangled Cry*, p. 188
37 JOHN STRACHEY, *The Coming Struggle for Power*, London, 1934, pp. 357–8
38 Quoted, WALTER GOODMAN, *The Committee. The Extraordinary Career of the House Committee on Un-American Activities*, London, 1969, p. 57
39 Quoted, ibid., p. 58
40 GRANVILLE HICKS, *Where We Came Out*, London, 1954, p. 51
41 *The Autobiography of Lincoln Steffens*, vol. 2, p. 799
42 Ibid., p. 819
43 Ibid., p. 817
44 Ibid., p. 832
45 Ibid., p. 824
46 *The Letters of Lincoln Steffens*, vol. 2, p. 961
47 Ibid., p. 1006
48 EASTMAN, *Love and Revolution*, p. 474
49 CHAMSON, op. cit., p. 61
50 *Commune*, Paris, October 1936, p. 135
51 ORWELL, *The Collected Essays, Journalism and Letters of George Orwell*, vol. 1, p. 312
52 *Tribune*, London, 21 May 1937
53 JEAN-RICHARD BLOCH, "Anniversaire d'Octobre", *Europe*, Paris, 15 November 1935, p. 403
54 T. C. WORSLEY, *Fellow Travellers*, London, 1971, p. 108
55 *New York Review of Books*, New York, 25 September 1969
56 Quoted, JOHN MANDER, *The Writer and Commitment*, London, 1961, p. 25
57 Quoted, FREEMAN, *An American Testament*, p. 379
58 Quoted, GOODMAN, op. cit., p. 38n
59 Quoted, DANIEL AARON, *Writers on the Left*, New York, 1965, p. 463
60 Quoted, STANLEY WEINTRAUB, *The Last Great Cause. The Intellectuals and the Spanish Civil War*, London, 1968, p. 299
61 FISCHER, *Men and Politics*, p. 413
62 ANDRÉ MALRAUX, "L'Art est une Conquête", *Commune*, Paris, Sept-Oct. 1934, p. 69
63 Quoted, DEUTSCHER, *The Prophet Outcast*, p. 370

4: The Pact and the War

1   O'CASEY, *Mirror in My House*, vol. 2, p. 164
2   Quoted, GOODMAN, *The Committee*, p. 71
3   Quoted, HICKS, *Where We Came Out*, p. 78
4   KENT, *This Is My Own*, p. 384
5   HARPER, *The Russia I Believe In*, p. 269
6   PARES, *Russia and the Peace* p. 33
7   Quoted, A. ROSSI, *Les Communistes français pendant la Drôle de Guerre*, Paris, 1951, pp. 18 and 22
8   *New Statesman and Nation*, London, 26 January 1940
9   KENT, op. cit., p. 384
10 HARPER, op. cit., p. 272
11 *New Statesman and Nation*, London, 13 July 1940
12 Ibid., 16 December 1939
13 JOHNSON, *Searching for Light*, p. 159
14 FISCHER, *Stalin and Hitler*, p. 44
15 Quoted, JULIAN SYMONS, *The Thirties. A Dream Revolved*, London, 1960, p. 173
16 *Tribune*, London, 23 February 1940
17 COMM. EDGAR P. YOUNG, R.N., *A People's Peace*, London, 1941, p. 11
18 *The Letters of Theodore Dreiser*, p. 880
19 Ibid., p. 965
20 Ibid., p. 971
21 ORWELL, *The Collected Essays, Journalism and Letters*, vol. 2, p. 175
22 *Forward*, London, 1 November 1941

5: Revolution, Go East

1   Quoted, ISTVAN DEAK, *Weimar Germany's Left-Wing Intellectuals. A Political History of the* Weltbühne *and Its Circle*, Berkeley, 1968, p. 151
2   JEAN GUÉHENNO, *La Foi Difficile*, Paris, 1957, p. 59
3   Quoted, *Problems of Soviet Literature*, p. 93
4   *Beatrice Webb's Diaries, 1924-32*, p. 304
5   Quoted, DEUTSCHER, *The Prophet Outcast*, p. 21
6   EDGAR SNOW, *The Other Side of the River. Red China Today*, London, 1963, p. 12
7   HEWLETT JOHNSON, *The Socialist Sixth of the World*, London, 1941, p. 355
8   HEWLETT JOHNSON, *Soviet Strength: Its Source and Challenge*, London, 1942, p. 139

9   Quoted, DEANE, *The Political Ideas of Harold J. Laski*, p. 206
10 Quoted, AXELRAD, *Anatole France*, p. 423
11 *Left Review*, London, August 1936
12 FRANK, *Dawn in Russia*, p. 164
13 *The Letters of Lincoln Steffens*, vol. 2, p. 988
14 Quoted, KINGSLEY MARTIN, *Harold Laski (1893–1950)*, London, 1953, p. 88
15 SHAW, *The Rationalization of Russia*, p. 59
16 Ibid., p. 40
17 *Problems of Soviet Literature*, p. 105
18 STRONG, *I Change Worlds*, p. 154
19 SIDNEY and BEATRICE WEBB, *Soviet Communism*, vol. 2, p. 1115
20 SHAW, *Platform and Pulpit*, p. 226
21 LANGEVIN, *La Pensée et L'Action*, p. 301
22 DE BEAUVOIR, *La Force des Choses*, p. 58
23 WORSLEY, *Fellow Travellers*, p. 145
24 BEATRICE WEBB, op. cit., p. 47
25 STRONG, op. cit., p. 226
26 Ibid., p. 418
27 SNOW, *Journey to the Beginning*, p. 249
28 JOHN DOS PASSOS, *The Theme is Freedom*, New York, 1956, p. 101
29 ELMER RICE, *Minority Report: An Autobiography*, London, 1963, p. 327
30 *The Letters of Lincoln Steffens*, vol. 2, p. 921
31 Ibid., p. 934
32 Ibid., p. 949
33 Ibid., p. 983
34 Ibid., p. 988
35 Quoted, JOHN BERRYMAN, Afterword to *The Titan*, New York, 1965, p. 508
36 DOS PASSOS, op. cit., pp. 73–4
37 *The Letters of Theodore Dreiser*, p. 982
38 SNOW, op. cit., p. 247
39 *The Letters of Theodore Dreiser*, p. 928
40 Ibid., p. 984
41 *Labour Monthly*, London, July 1924, p. 431
42 YOUNG to Cripps, 13 August 1933, Papers of Comm. E. P. Young
43 Ibid., 10 November 1934
44 YOUNG to G. R. Shepherd, 31 October 1939, ibid

6: ALTERNATIVES TO MARX

1   LION FEUCHTWANGER, *Josephus*, London, 1932, p. 266

2   GIDE, Journals, vol. 3, pp. 276 and 308
3   FEUCHTWANGER, *Success*, p. 196
4   JULIEN BENDA, *The Treason of the Intellectuals*, tr. by Richard Aldington, New York, 1928, p. 37
5   JOSEPH NEEDHAM, *History is on Our Side*, London, 1946, p. 54
6   *New Statesman and Nation*, London, 16 February 1935, p. 218
7   *Left Review*, London, February 1935
8   HUXLEY, *A Scientist Among the Soviets*, p. 3
9   KENT, *This Is My Own*, p. 367
10 Quoted, DAVID KRAUSE, *Sean O'Casey. The Man and His Work*, London, 1967, p. 274
11 WICKSTEED, *My Russian Neighbors*, pp. 147–8
12 *Labour Monthly*, London, October 1921, p. 311
13 Quoted, ALAN CHAPPELOW, letter to *TLS*, London, 23 April 1971
14 Introduction to Pat Sloan, *Russia Without Illusions*, London, 1938, p. viii
15 SHAW, *Platform and Pulpit*, p. 219
16 SNOW, *Journey to the Beginning*, p. 138
17 ANDRÉ GIDE, *Littérature Engagée*, Paris, 1950, p. 58
18 Ibid., p. 64
19 *Fact*, London, July 1937, p. 29
20 TOLLER, *Masses and Man*, p. 111
21 Quoted, RÜHLE, *Literatur und Revolution*, p. 169
22 CECIL DAY LEWIS, *A Time to Dance, and Other Poems*, London, 1935, p. 55
23 *Left Review*, London, July 1935, p. 399
24 *The Sean O'Casey Reader*, ed. by Brooks Atkinson, London, 1968, p. 984
25 *Problems of Soviet Literature*, p. 79
26 LION FEUCHTWANGER, *The Jew of Rome. A Historical Romance*, tr. by Willa and Edwin Muir, London, n.d., postscript, p. 601
27 FEUCHTWANGER, *Josephus*, p. 348
28 Ibid., p. 504
29 Quoted, ALFRED KANTOROWICZ, *Deutsche Schicksale: Intellektuelle unter Hitler und Stalin*, Vienna, 1964, p. 151
30 HEINRICH MANN, *Essays*, Hamburg, 1960, p. 11
31 Quoted, SCHRÖTER, *Heinrich Mann*, p. 96
32 Quoted, ibid., p. 100
33 Quoted, ibid., p. 101
34 MANN, *Essays*, p. 389
35 Quoted, SCHRÖTER, op. cit., p. 100
36 Quoted, ibid., p. 100

37 Quoted, ibid., p. 136
38 MARCUSE, *Mein Zwanzigstes Jahrhundert*, p. 205
39 Quoted, GOODMAN, *The Committee*, p. 70
40 Quoted, LYONS, *The Red Decade*, p. 356
41 NEEDHAM, op. cit., p. 47
42 JOHNSON, *Searching for Light*, p. 368
43 Quoted, ZILLIACUS, *I Choose Peace*, p. 408
44 NEEDHAM, op. cit., p. 14n
45 Ibid., p. 17
46 JOHNSON, op. cit., pp. 393–4
47 Ibid., pp. 274–5
48 Ibid., p. 281

7: A Postscript to the Enlightenment

1 BRAILSFORD, *The Russian Workers' Republic*, p. 206
2 SNOW, *Journey to the Beginning*, p. 330
3 KENT, *This Is My Own*, p. 368
4 JOSEPH NEEDHAM, *The Grand Titration. Science and Society in East and West*, London, 1969, p. 144
5 GEORGES FRIEDMANN, "Forces Morales et Valeurs Permanentes", in *L'Heure du Choix*, Paris, 1947, p. 87
6 Quoted, RÜHLE, *Literatur und Revolution*, p. 174
7 MANN, *Ein Zeitalter Wird Besichtigt*, p. 56
8 FEUCHTWANGER, Moscow, 1937, p. 8
9 Quoted, RÜHLE, op. cit., p. 219
10 ROBERT OWEN, *Report to the County of Lanark*, and *A New View of Society*, ed. by V. A. C. Gatrell, London, 1969, p. 129
11 GORKY, *Untimely Thoughts*, p. 47
12 Quoted, ALAN MOOREHEAD, *The Traitors: The Double Life of Fuchs, Pontecorvo and Nunn May*, London, 1952, p. 73
13 J. G. CROWTHER, *Soviet Science*, London, 1936, p. 14
14 Quoted, ALFRED SHERMAN, "The Days of the Left Book Club", *Survey*, no. 41, London, April 1962, p. 77
15 C. H. WADDINGTON, *The Scientific Attitude*, London, 1948, p. 95
16 In JOSEPH NEEDHAM and JANE SYKES DAVIES (eds), *Science in Soviet Russia*, London, 1942, pp. 37 and 38
17 Quoted, SHERMAN, op. cit., p. 77
18 JULIAN HUXLEY, *If I Were Dictator*, London, 1934, p. 23
19 SIDNEY and BEATRICE WEBB, *Soviet Communism*, vol. 2, p. 602
20 Quoted, ibid., p. 981
21 GEORGE ORWELL, "Second Thoughts on James Burnham"

(1946), *The Orwell Reader*, introd. by Richard H. Rovere, New York, n.d., p. 340

22 Quoted, DANIEL AARON, "The Three Faces of Lenin", *Survey*, no. 41, April 1962, p. 52

23 Quoted, LIEBMAN, "The Webbs and the New Civilization", p. 68

24 SHAW, *The Rationalization of Russia*, p. 21

25 SHAW, *Platform and Pulpit*, p. 225

26 SIMONE DE BEAUVOIR, *The Long March*, tr. by Austryn Wainhouse, London, 1958, p. 315

27 SHAW, *The Rationalization of Russia*, p. 60

28 Ibid., pp. 80–1

29 WICKSTEED, *My Russian Neighbors*, p. 159

30 H. G. WELLS, *Experiment in Autobiography*, vol. 2, London, 1934, p. 735

31 DAVIES, *Mission to Moscow*, p. 89

32 ALEXANDER SOLZHENITSYN, *The First Circle*, tr. by Michael Guybon, London, 1968, pp. 343–4

33 CHARLOTTE HALDANE, *Truth Will Out*, London, 1949, p. 255

34 MANN, *Ein Zietalter Wird Besichtigt*, pp. 37 and 36

35 SIDNEY and BEATRICE WEBB, *Soviet Communism*, vol. 1, p. 211

8: THE COLD WAR

1 Quoted, DWIGHT MACDONALD, *Henry Wallace: The Man and the Myth*, New York, 1948, p. 93

2 Quoted, ibid., p. 148

3 I. F. STONE, *The Truman Era*, London, 1953, p. 67

4 Quoted, MACDONALD, op. cit., p. 100

5 Ibid., p. 147

6 DE BEAUVOIR, *La Force des Choses*, p. 43

7 ZILLIACUS, *I Choose Peace*, p. 104

8 Ibid., p. 112

9 Quoted, ibid., p. 154

10 EDGAR P. YOUNG, "East Germany Revisited", *Contemporary Review*, London, July 1955, pp. 21 and 23

11 Quoted, RÜHLE, *Literatur und Revolution*, p. 300

12 Quoted, K. BÖTTCHER and P. G. KROHN, *Lion Feuchtwanger: Schriftsteller der Gegenwart*, Berlin, 1960, p. 67

13 Quoted, SCHRÖTER, *Heinrich Mann*, p. 150

14 *Die Weltbühne*, Heft 46, Berlin, 11 November 1930, p. 707

15 ARNOLD ZWEIG, *Insulted and Exiled. The Truth about the German Jews*, tr. by Eden and Cedar Paul, London, 1937, pp. 130–1

16 Quoted, RÜHLE, op. cit., pp. 272–4
17 JOHNSON, *Searching For Light*, p. 289
18 Ibid., p. 257
19 Ibid., p. 294
20 *London Calling*, 13 March 1947
21 ZILLIACUS, op. cit., p. 218
22 LAMONT, *Soviet Civilization*, p. 327
23 *Lucknow Times*, Lucknow, 10 March 1948
24 *Daily Worker*, London, 1 March 1950
25 Ibid., 21 March 1953
26 ANDRÉ WURMSER, *Réponse à Jean Cassou*, Paris, 1950, p. 3
27 DE BEAUVOIR, op. cit., p. 152
28 CLAUDE AVELINE, "Réalisme et Vérité", in *La Voie Libre*, Paris, 1951, p. 31
29 Ibid., p. 40
30 FEUCHTWANGER, *Moscow 37*, p. 128
31 Quoted, EHRENBURG, *Memoirs, 1921–41*, p. 304
32 "Questions du Communisme", *Confluences*, 18–20, Paris, 1947, p. 48
33 EHRENBURG, op. cit., p. 190
34 MONICA FELTON, *That's Why I Went*, London, 1953, p. 13
35 Ibid., p. 26
36 EHRENBURG, *Memoirs: Vol. 2, 1918–21*, p. 32
37 Ibid., p. 80
38 EHRENBURG, *Memoirs, 1921–41*, p. 235
39 ILYA EHRENBURG, *Men, Years—Life. Vol. 6. Post-War Years, 1945–54*, tr. by Tatiana Shebunina in collab. with Yvonne Kapp, London, 1966, p. 112
40 Ibid., p. 332
41 Ibid., p. 323
42 Quoted, MAX HAYWARD and PATRICIA BLAKE (eds), *Dissonant Voices in Soviet Literature*, New York, 1962, p. xxxix
43 ILYA EHRENBURG, *The Thaw*, tr. by Manya Harari, London, 1961, p. 53
44 ALEXANDER WERTH, *Russia: Hopes and Fears*, London, 1969, pp. 199–200 and 204
45 Quoted, CHRISTOPHER LASCH, *The Agony of the American Left*, London, 1970, p. 108
46 Quoted, ibid., p. 103
47 Quoted, ibid., p. 106
48 D. N. PRITT, *Autobiography*, vol. 2, London, 1966, p. 295
49 FELTON, op. cit., p. 295

50 See WILFRID BURCHETT, *Passport. An Autobiography*, London, 1969

9: THE WITCH-HUNTS

1   WHITTAKER CHAMBERS, *Witness*, London, 1952, p. 30
2   Ibid., p. 301
3   Ibid., p. 275
4   Quoted, GOODMAN, *The Committee*, p. 303
5   *Nova*, London, July 1971, p 74
6   Ibid., p. 79
7   SIDNEY HOOK, *Common Sense and the Fifth Amendment*, New York 1957, p. 109
8   LOVETT, *All Our Years*, p. 332
9   Ibid., p. 290
10 Ibid., p. 346
11 Ibid., p. 342
12 LAMONT, *Soviet Civilization*, p. xi
13 Quoted, HENRY HATFIELD, "Thomas Mann and America", *Salmagundi*, nos. 10–11, Saratoga Springs, p. 180
14 Quoted, HAROLD W. HOROWITZ, "The Legal Aspects", in John Cogley, *Report on Blacklisting, vol. 1, Movies*, New York, 1956, p. 181
15 J. B. MATTHEWS, *Odyssey of a Fellow-Traveler*, New York, 1938, p. 280
16 Quoted, CAREY MCWILLIAMS, *Witchhunt – The Revival of Heresy*, Boston, 1950, pp. 215–17
17 Quoted, ibid., p. 230
18 Quoted, GOODMAN, op. cit., p. 329
19 Quoted, ibid., p. 335
20 Quoted, ibid., p. 390
21 Quoted, GILBERT, *Writers and Partisans*, p. 257
22 ISAAC DEUTSCHER, *Heretics and Renegades*, London, 1955, p. 14
23 Quoted, LASCH, *The Agony of the American Left*, p. 86
24 Quoted, ibid., p. 88
25 PETER VIERECK, extract from his "Shame And Glory of The Intellectuals" (1953), in Huszar (ed.), *The Intellectuals*, p. 504
26 HICKS, *Where We Came Out*, pp. 6 and 43
27 Quoted, HOOK, op. cit., p. 111
28 Quoted, JOHN WEXLEY, *The Judgement of Julius and Ethel Rosenberg*, London, 1956, pp. 591–2
29 Quoted, JONATHAN ROOT, *The Betrayers. The Rosenberg Case*, London, 1963, p. 219

30 Quoted, EARL LATHAM, *The Communist Controversy in Washington*, Cambridge (Mass.), 1966, pp. 301–2
31 OWEN LATTIMORE, *Ordeal by Slander*, London, 1952, p. 193
32 Ibid., p. 183
33 Ibid., p. 219
34 Ibid., p. 167
35 OWEN LATTIMORE, *The Situation in Asia*, Boston, 1949, p. 80
36 Ibid., p. 58
37 LATTIMORE, *Ordeal by Slander*, p. 151
38 LATHAM, op. cit., p. 302
39 CURTIS, *The Oppenheimer Case*, p. 54
40 HAAKON CHEVALIER, *Oppenheimer. The Story of a Friendship*, London, 1966, p. 108
41 Quoted, CURTIS, op. cit., p. 54
42 Quoted, HERBERT H. HYMAN, "England and America: Climates of Tolerance and Intolerance" (1962), in Daniel Bell (ed.), *The Radical Right*, New York, 1964, p. 281n
43 Quoted, S. MACCOBY, *English Radicalism, 1786–1832*, London, 1955, p. 43
44 Ibid., pp. 45–6
45 Ibid., p. 60
46 Ibid., p. 63

10: THE RECKONING

1 SIMONE DE BEAUVOIR, *La Force de l'Âge*, Paris, 1960, p. 34
2 JEAN-PAUL SARTRE, *What Is Literature?*, tr. by Bernard Frechtman, London, 1950, p. 189
3 ROGER GARAUDY, *Literature of the Graveyard*, tr. by Joseph M. Bernstein, New York, p. 61
4 JEAN-PAUL SARTRE, "Merleau-Ponty", *Situations*, tr. by Benita Eisler, London, 1965, p. 287
5 Ibid., p. 287
6 JEAN-PAUL SARTRE, "Les Communistes et la Paix", *Les Temps Modernes*, Paris, April 1954, p. 1779
7 Ibid., July 1952, p. 49
8 *Libération*, Paris, 22 June 1953
9 *L'Express*, Paris, 9 November 1956
10 SARTRE, *Situations* (1965), pp. 90 and 104
11 JEAN-PAUL SARTRE, *Le Diable et le Bon Dieu*, Paris, 1961, pp. 235 and 35
12 *New Statesman and Nation*, London, 3 December 1955

13 JEAN-PAUL SARTRE, *Sartre on Cuba*, New York, 1961, p. 134
14 DE BEAUVOIR, op. cit., p. 386
15 *Les Temps Modernes*, Paris, Oct.-Nov., 1960, p. 140, and *La Voie Communiste*, Paris, July 1962
16 JOHNSON, *Searching for Light*, p. 369
17 *Railway Review*, 9 November 1956
18 Ibid., 16 November 1956
19 O'CASEY, *Mirror in My House*, vol. 2, pp. 220–1
20 Ibid., p. 128
21 Quoted, ibid., p. 140
22 Ibid., p. 142
23 Ibid., pp. 137–8
24 Ibid., p. 134
25 *Tribune*, London, 26 July 1968
26 Ibid.
27 *The Journal* (Birmingham Trades Council), November 1968

11: INTO CHINA

1 BURCHETT, op. cit., p. 184
2 EDGAR SNOW, *Red Star Over China* (revised ed.), New York, 1968, p. 190
3 Ibid., p. 57
4 Ibid., pp. 198–9
5 Ibid., p. 418
6 AGNES SMEDLEY, *China Fights Back. An American Woman With The Eighth Route Army*, London, 1938, p. 31
7 Ibid., p. 32
8 Ibid., p. 141
9 DE BEAUVOIR, *The Long March*, pp. 9–10
10 Ibid., p. 378
11 SNOW, *The Other Side of the River*, p. 326
12 FELIX GREENE, *The Wall Has Two Sides. A Portrait of China Today*, London, 1962, p. 111
13 SNOW, *Red Star Over China*, p. 90
14 JOHNSON, op. cit., p. 316
15 JOAN ROBINSON, *The Cultural Revolution in China*, London, 1969, p. 29
16 Ibid., p. 106
17 *Sunday Times*, London, 2 May 1971
18 DE BEAUVOIR, op. cit., p. 10
19 Ibid., p. 54
20 Ibid., p. 108

21 DE BEAUVOIR, *La Force de l'Âge*, p. 355
22 DE BEAUVOIR, *The Long March*, p. 286
23 Ibid., p. 320
24 ROBINSON, op. cit., p. 39
25 GREENE, op. cit., p. 227
26 Ibid., p. 80
27 Ibid., p. 8
28 FELIX GREENE, *The Enemy. Notes on Imperialism and Revolution*, New York, 1971, p. 293
29 JOHNSON, op. cit., p. 389
30 Letter to *Tribune*, London, 24 January 1969
31 ROBINSON, op. cit., p. 16
32 Ibid., p. 19
33 Ibid., p. 20
34 Ibid., p. 26
35 *Sunday Times*, London, 2 May 1971
36 SNOW, preface to revised edition of *Red Star Over China*, p. 30
37 *Sunday Times*, London, 2 May 1971
38 ANNA LOUISE STRONG, *Tibetan Interviews*, Peking, 1959, p. 7
39 Letter to *Tribune*, London, 24 January 1969

Bibliography

The source material provided below does not include works already described in the References. I have not attempted to list the innumerable studies of the historical background to the period. Readers interested in Soviet history since 1917 are referred to the bibliographies in such works as: Merle Fainsod, *How Russia is Ruled,* Cambridge (Mass.), 1956; Leonard Schapiro, *The Communist Party of the Soviet Union,* London, 1960; Isaac Deutscher, *Stalin,* London, 1949; the three volumes of Isaac Deutscher's *Trotsky,* London, 1954, 1959, 1963; and the many volumes of E. H. Carr's *A History of Soviet Russia,* London, 1954–

Since a given work may have relevance to several fields of inquiry, the books and articles listed below are grouped on a national basis, and not in accordance with the chapter headings under which the References appear.

BRITAIN

COLE, MARGARET (ed.), *The Webbs and their Work,* London, 1949
  Beatrice Webb, London, 1945
CROWTHER, J. G., *Industry and Education in Soviet Russia,* London, 1932
DAY LEWIS, CECIL, *We're Not Going To Do Nothing,* London, 1936
  "English Writers and a People's Front", *Left Review,* October 1936
  "Labour and Fascism: The Writer's Task", *Left Review,* London, November 1936
DEWAR, HUGO, "How They Saw It: The Moscow Trials". *Survey,* London, no. 41, April 1962
DUTT, R. PALME, *Fascism and Social Revolution,* London, 1934
GOLLANCZ, VICTOR (ed.), *The Betrayal of The Left,* London, 1941
JOHNSON, HEWLETT, and Others, *Report of a Religious Delegation to Spain,* London, 1937
LASKI, HAROLD, "Labour and the Constitution", *New Statesman and Nation,* 10 September 1932

"The Limitations of the Expert" (1933), in Huszar (ed.), *The Intellectuals*, Glencoe, 1960.

Democracy in Crisis, London, 1933

Where Do We Go From Here?, London, 1940

LEHMANN, JOHN, "Should Writers Keep to Their Art?", *Left Review*, London, January 1937

"Letter from Tiflis", *Left Review*, February 1937

"Epic and the Future of Soviet Arts", *Left Review*, November 1937

The Whispering Gallery. Autobiography, vol. 1, London, 1955

I Am My Brother. Autobiography, vol. 2, London, 1960

MIRSKY, DMITRI, *The Intelligentsia of Great Britain*, tr. by Alec Brown, London, 1935

MITCHELL, SIR PETER CHALMERS, *My Fill of Days*, London, 1937

PRICE, M. PHILIPS, articles in *The Plebs*, London, October 1924, January 1925, February 1926, October 1926, July 1927

PRITT, D. N., *The Zinoviev Trial*, London, 1936

Autobiography, vol. 3, London, 1966

ROBINSON, JOAN, "Something to Live For". *New Statesman*, 7 May 1971

SHAW, BERNARD, controversy with H. G. Wells, *New Statesman and Nation*, 3, 10 November, 1, 8 December 1934

SPENDER, STEPHEN, *Trial of a Judge*, London, 1938

World Within World, London, 1952

STRACHEY, JOHN, letters to *New Statesman and Nation*, 28 September 1935, 19 October 1935

Introduction to R. Osborn, *Freud and Marx: A Dialectical Study*, London, 1937

Why You Should Be A Socialist, London, 1938

Hope in America, New York, 1938

WEBB, BEATRICE, review of W. H. Chamberlin's *Russia's Iron Age*, *New Statesman and Nation*, 9 March 1935

WELLS, H. G., *After Democracy*, London, 1932

YOUNG, EDGAR P., *That Second Front*, London, 1942

"Why Be Unjust to Bulgaria?", *Railway Review*, 18 April 1947

"Le Nouvel Ordre Roumain", *Démocratie Nouvelle*, Paris, no. 11, November 1947

"Socialist Revolution By Consent", *Journal of Central European Affairs*, vol. 8, no. 1, April 1948

FRANCE

AVELINE, CLAUDE, and JEAN CASSOU, ANDRÉ CHAMSON, GEORGES

FRIEDMANN, LOUIS MARTIN-CHAUFFIER, VERCORS, *L'Heure du Choix*, Paris, 1947

AVELINE, CLAUDE, and JEAN CASSOU, LOUIS MARTIN-CHAUFFIER, VERCORS, *La Voie Libre*, Paris, 1951

DE BEAUVOIR, SIMONE, *Les Mandarins*, Paris, 1954

BENDA, JULIEN, "À Un Jeune Communiste", *La Nouvelle Revue Française*, Paris, 1 July 1935

Précision (1930–37), Paris, 1937

"Anti-Communisme et Patriotisme", *La Nouvelle Revue Française*, 1 August 1938

BLOCH, JEAN-RICHARD, *Offrande à la Politique*, Paris, 1933

"Philosophie Soviétique du Travail", *Europe*, Paris, 15 January 1934

"Le 12 Février", *Europe*, 15 March 1934

"Paroles à un Congrès Soviétique", *Europe*, 15 September 1934

"D'URSS", *Europe*, 15 December 1934

"Témoignage", *La Pensée*, Paris, July-October 1947

CASSOU, JEAN, *La Mémoire Courte*, Paris, 1953

CHAMSON, ANDRÉ, *Retour d'Espagne*, Paris, 1937

Ecrit en 1940, Paris, 1944

COTTON, EUGÉNIE, "Irène Joliot-Curie", *La Pensée*, May-June 1956

BRACHFELD, GEORGES, *André Gide And The Communist Temptation*, Paris, 1959

DUBOURG, MAURICE, *Eugéne Dabit et André Gide*, Paris, 1953

DUHAMEL, GEORGES, *Les Espoirs et les Epreuves, 1919–28*, Paris, 1953

DURTAIN, LUC, "L'autre Europe: Moscou et sa Foi", *Europe*, October 1927, November 1927, December 1927, January 1928

FERNANDEZ, RAMON, "Lettre ouverte à André Gide". *La Nouvelle Revue Française*, 1 April 1934

FRIEDMANN, GEORGES, *De la Sainte Russie à l'URSS*, Paris, 1938

GIDE, ANDRÉ, "Le Communisme et le Problème de la Guerre", *La Nouvelle Revue Française*, 1 April 1933

Retour de l'URSS, Paris, 1936

Preface to Yvon, *L'URSS Telle Qu'elle Est*, Paris, 1938

MALRAUX, ANDRÉ, "L'Attitude de l'Artiste", *Commune*, Paris, November 1934

The Fascist Threat to Culture, Harvard. 1937

NAVILLE, CLAUDE, *André Gide et le Communisme*, Paris, 1936

ROLLAND, ROMAIN, *Par la Révolution la Paix*, Paris 1935

Pages Choisies, vol. 2, Paris, n.d.

"L'Art et l'Action", *Europe*, 15 January 1934

"L'URSS en a vu bien d'autres", *Humanité*, 18 January 1937

Lettres à un Combattant de la Résistance, Paris, 1947

SARTRE, JEAN-PAUL, *L'Affaire Henri Martin*, Paris, 1953
  Nekrassov, Paris, 1956
  "Le Réformisme et les Fétiches", *Les Temps Modernes*, Paris, February 1956
  "Réponse à Pierre Naville", *Les Temps Modernes*, March 1956
  "Le Fantôme de Staline", *Les Temps Modernes*, January 1957
SERGE, VICTOR, *Mémoires d'un Révolutionnaire, 1901–41*, Paris, 1951
VERCORS (JEAN BRULLER), *Le Silence de la Mer*, London, 1943
  "Une Paix Véritable", *Défense de la Paix*, Paris, August 1951
  For The Time Being, tr. by Jonathan Griffin, London, 1960

GERMANY

Der Deutsche Kommunismus: Dokumente, Herausgegeben und kommentiert von Hermann Weber, Cologne-Berlin, 1963
FEUCHTWANGER, LION, *Jew Süss*, tr. by Willa and Edwin Muir, London, 1926
  Unholdes Frankreich, Mexico, 1942
  "Der Ästhet in der Sowjetunion", *Das Wort*, Jg 2, Heft 2, Moscow, February 1937
  "An meine Sowjetleser", *Das Wort*, Jg 3, Heft 7, July 1937
GOLDSCHMIDT, ALFONS, *Moskau 1920*, Berlin, 1920
GROSZ, GEORGE, *A Little Yes and a Big No*, tr. by Lola Sachs, New York, 1946
GRUBER, HELMUT, "Willi Münzenberg: Propagandist For And Against The Comintern", *International Review of Social History*, vol. x, part 2, The Hague, 1965
  "Willi Münzenberg's German Communist Propaganda Empire, 1921–35", *Journal of Modern History*, vol. 38, no. 3, September 1966
MANN, HEINRICH, *Diktatur der Vernunft*, Berlin, 1923
MOSSE, GEORGE L., "The Heritage of Socialist Humanism", *Salmagundi*, nos. 10–11, Saratoga Springs, 1969–70
PACHTER, HENRY, "On Being an Exile", *Salmagundi*, ibid.
PAETEL, KARL O., "Oskar Maria Graf", *Monatshefte für Deutschen Unterricht*, Wisconsin, 1944
PISCATOR, ERWIN, *Das Politische Theater*, Berlin, 1929
WALTER, HANS-ALBERT, "Schwarzschild and Das Neue Tage-Buch", *Journal of Contemporary History*, vol. 1, no. 2, Cambridge, 1966
STERNFELDE, WILHELM, *Deutsche Exil-Literatur. Eine Bio-Bibliographie*, Heidelberg, 1962
WEGNER, MATTHIAS, *Exil und Literatur: Deutsche Schriftsteller in Ausland, 1933–45*, Frankfurt am Main, 1967

Das Wort, Jg 2, Heft 4–5, April-May 1937—see this issue for short biographies of many anti-fascist émigrés.

ZWEIG, ARNOLD, "Emigranten Literatur", *Das Wort*, Jg 2, Heft 4–5, April-May 1937

"Roman, Realismus und Form", *Das Wort*, Jg 3, Heft 10, October 1938

ZWEIG, STEFAN, *The World of Yesterday*, London, 1942

ZUCKMAYER, CARL, *Als wär's ein Stück von Mir*, Frankfurt, 1966

RUSSIA

LUNACHARSKY, ANATOLE, "Les Intellectuels et l'Internationale Communiste", *Clarté*, Paris, 19 November and 3 December 1921

"La Révolution et la Culture en Russie", *Clarté*, Paris, 1 February 1923

SERGE, VICTOR, "Les Ecrivains Russes et la Révolution", *Clarté*, 15 July 1922

"La Vie Intellectuelle en Russie des Soviets", *Clarté*, 15 November 1922

UNITED STATES

BARTH, ALAN, *The Loyalty of Free Men*, London, 1951

BENSON, FREDERICK R., *Writers in Arms. The Literary Impact of the Spanish Civil War*, London, 1967

BESSIE, ALVAH, *Inquisition in Eden*, Berlin (Seven Seas), 1967

COOK, FRED, *The Nightmare Decade. The Life and Times of Joe McCarthy*, New York, 1971

DAVIS, NUEL PHARR, *Lawrence and Oppenheimer*, New York, 1969

FISCHER, LOUIS, *The Soviets in World Affairs*, London, 1930

review of the Webbs' *Soviet Communism*, in the *New Statesman and Nation*, 7 December 1935

KEMPTON, MURRAY, *America Comes of Middle Age. Columns, 1950–62*, Boston, 1963

The Lamont Case. History of a Congressional Investigation, ed. by Philip Wittenberg, New York, 1957

LAMONT, CORLISS, *Freedom Is As Freedom Does*, New York, 1956

The Philosophy of Humanism, London, 1958

LASCH, CHRISTOPHER, *The New Radicalism in America, 1898–1963*, New York, 1965

MACDONALD, DWIGHT, *Memoirs of a Revolutionist*, New York, 1958

NIEBUHR, REINHOLD, *Moral Man and Immoral Society*, London, 1933

RIEFF, PHILIP, "The Case of Dr Oppenheimer", in *On Intellectuals*, ed. by P. Rieff, New York, 1969

ROGIN, PAUL, *The Intellectuals and McCarthy*, Cambridge (Mass.), 1967

ROVERE, RICHARD H., *Senator Joe McCarthy*, New York, 1959

SHILS, EDWARD, *The Torment of Secrecy*, London, 1956

STOUFFER, SAMUEL A., *Communism, Conformity and Civil Liberties*, New York, 1955

(STRONG, ANNA LOUISE): Mao Tse Tung, *Talk With The American Correspondent Anna Louise Strong*, Peking, 1961

WARREN, FRANK A., *Liberals and Communism*, Bloomington, 1966

WALLACE, HENRY A., *Soviet Asia Mission*, New York, 1946

WARD, HARRY, F., *Which Way Religion?*, New York, 1931

Index